PUBLISHING

Collection Directors and Authors : Dominique AUZIAS and Jean-Paul

Editorial manager : Eric VOILLEQU of Pascale LEFORT and Florence PE

Authors: Delphine TABARY, Cynthia BENZIAI Elsa MELENDEZ, Lætitia STEIMETZ, Noémie FAVRE-COQUERET, Isabelle Marie-Chantal BAYOL-SORET, Anne ARCHAMBAULT, Isabelle PARRY, Jea COLLET, Claire DELBARD, Cédric BLA Jérémy GAUTHIOT, Sophie THOZET, François AUBERT, Valérie ALAMO-BARBELIVIEN, Pascaline KROMICHEFF, Frédéric BRUN, Valérie MAYINGILA, Fabienne AUSSERRE, Jean-Paul LABOURDETTE, Dominique AUZIAS and alter

Publishing Director : Stéphan SZEREMETA

Publishing Team : François TOURNIE, Maurane CHEVALIER, Silvia FOLIGNO , Bénédicte PETIT, Patrick MARINGE, Caroline MICHELOT, Morgane VESLIN, Pierre-Yves SOUCHET, Talatah FAVREAU and Hector BARON

STUDIO

Studio Manager : Sophie LECHERTIER, assisted by Romain AUDREN

Layout : Julie BORDES, Élodie CLAVIER, Sandrine MECKING, Delphine PAGANO and Laurie PILLOIS

Pictures Management and Mapping : Audrey LALOY

WEB

Web Director : Louis GENEAU de LAMARLIERE

Technical Director : Lionel CAZAUMAYOU

Web Management and Development : Jean-Marc REYMUND, Cédric MAILLOUX and Florian FAZER

Community Manager : Cyprien de CANSON

PUBLICITY TEAM

Local Publicity Manager : Caroline CHOLLET

Local Publicity Responsible : Michel GRANSEIGNE

Customer Relationship Management : Vimla MEETTOO and Sandra RUFFIEUX

NATIONAL PUBLICITY TEAM

Advertising Managers : Caroline AUBRY, François BRIANCON-MARJOLLET, Perrine DE CARNE MARCEIN, Caroline GENTELET and Caroline PREAU

INTERNATIONAL PUBLICITY TEAM

Advertising Managers : Jean-Marc FARAGUET, Guillaume LABOUREUR assisted by Elisa MORLAND

CIRCULATION AND PROMOTION

Sales Promotion Director : Bénédicte MOULET assisted byAissatou DIOP and Alicia FILANKEMBO

Sales Manager : Jean-Pierre GHEZ, assisted by Nathalie GONCALVES

Press-Sponsors Partnership Management : Jean-MaryMARCHAL

ADMINISTRATION

Chairman : Jean-Paul LABOURDETTE

Administrative and financial director: Valérie DECOTTIGNIES

Human Resources Director : Dina BOURDEAU assisted by Sandra MORAIS and Vianney LAVERNE

Information Technology Manager : Pascal LE GOFF

Accounting : Jeannine DEMIRDJIAN, Christelle MANEBARD and Adrien PRIGENT

Collection : Fabien BONNAN assisted by Sandra BRIJLALL

Switchboard : Jehanne AOUMEUR

PETIT FUTE BEST OF BURGUNDY

Le Petit Futé was founded by Dominique Auzias.
It is published by Les Nouvelles Editions de l'Université
18, rue des Volontaires - 75015 Paris.
✆ 01 53 69 70 00 - Fax 01 42 73 15 24
Internet : www.petitfute.com
SAS with a capital of 1 000 000 € -
RC PARIS B 309 769 966
Cover : Cluny Abbey © VENTDUSUD - SHUTTERSTOCK.COM
Printed by : IMPRIMERIE CHIRAT - 42540 Saint-Just-la-Pendue
Completion date : 27/07/2016
ISBN : 9782746998049
To contact us by email, indicate the surname in tiny follow-up of @petitfute.com
For the letters to the editor: info@petitfute.com

MW01687951

Land of history, land of culture and heritage, land of gastronomy, land of passions... Burgundy is all of this at the same time ! From one place to another, our guide will make you discover the infinite richness of this region : concerned about their lifestyle, burgundians are proud of the diversity of their land, and either for its culture or its gastronomy with many culinary specialties, you will quickly be influenced by local traditions. The application of the *Climats de Bourgogne* in order to be classified as a Unesco World Heritage site has become everybody's business, opening new horizons on the transmission of knowledge, know-how and the preservation of the traditions rooted in burgundy from generations. Witnesses of the past abound, castles, churches, abbeys, medieval cities, monuments ... exceptional heritage sites where history is told and tamed down through the countless museums of the region. Do not miss paying a visit to the new Ceramics Museum in Nevers, or rediscovering the Musée des Beaux-Arts de Dijon, recently reopened after a phase of renovation. Want to relax in the heart of a generous nature ? Here you can escape, glide over the water on the canals of Burgundy and Nivernais, explore the area by bike along greenways and cycle routes, visit the hiking trails or try water activities on one of the great lakes of the Morvan. From Dijon to Châlon-sur-Saône, through Auxerre and Nevers, Burgundy can also vibrate : festivals and events punctuate the seasons and boost the smallest village in summer. You will obviously talk about the « Garçon la Note » which made followers throughout the region, or the Festival du Mot held each year on the side of La Charité-sur-Loire... So, whether you are a tourist, alone or with family, events are not lacking, and there is truly something for everyone ! During your stroll, flip through the pages of our guide, and let yourself be carried away by our favourites, our addresses and our smart tips, and succumb to the authentic charms of Burgundy !

PRINT IN FRANCE

Digital version FOR FREE

See page 107

SOMMAIRE

KNOWING MORE ABOUT BURGUNDY

CÔTE-D'OR

direct access to the beach
bar
laundry
air conditioning
nightclub
cash machine
drinking water
horse riding
smoking area
non-smoking
fitness
miniature golf
hard of hearing disability
visually impaired disability
mental handicap
motor disability
garden or park
games
washing machine / laundry
bicycle rental
grocery store
airport shuttle
fishing
indoor swimming pool
outdoor heated pool
outdoor pool
take away
room service
fitness room
playroom / tv
modern sanitary
water sports
tennis
archery
waterslide
fan
toilet drain
sailing

NIÈVRE

SAÔNE-ET-LOIRE

© PHB.CZ – FOTOLIA

Vergisson, at the foot of the Solutré rock.

YONNE

FIND THE BEST VISITS

★ INTERESTING ★★ EXCELLENT ★★★ UNMISSABLE ★★★★ UNFORGETTABLE

Burgundy

To Paris
To Fontainebleau
Villeneuve-la Guyard
D606
Yonne
A5
Thorigny-sur-Oreuse
To Troyes
To Troyes
Pont-sur-Yonne
Seine-et-Marne
Saint-Valérien
D81
Sens
Villeneuve-l'Archevêque
D660
To Paris
A19
D660
Cerisiers
Chailley
To Troyes
Villeneuve-sur-Yonne
Piffonds
To Orléans
Saint-Julien-du-Sault
Brienon-sur-Armançon
Saint-Florentin
Joigny
Flogny-la-Chapelle
A6
Migennes
N
O
E
S
Senan
D606
Pontigny
Charny
Seignelay
Ligny-le-Châtel
Armançon
Aillant-sur-Tholon
N77
Grandchamp
AUXERRE
Tonnerre
D965
Loiret
Yonne
Chablis
Yrouerre
Champignelles
Ouanne
D965
Serein
Toucy
Bléneau
Mézilles
Coulanges-la-Vineuse
A6
Noyers
Leugny
Vermenton
Nitry
Saint-Privé
Loing
To Paris
St-Fargeau
Saint-Sauveur-en-Puisaye
Mailly-le-Château
To Gien
Courson-les-Carrières
Cure
N151
Saint-Amand-en-Puisaye
D606
Neuvy-sur-Loire
A77
Loire
Entrains-sur-Nohain
Clamecy
Vézelay
Avallon
Dornecy
Cosne-Cours sur-Loire
Donzy
Menou
Varzy
Canal du Nivernais
Quarré-les-Tombes
Brinon-sur-Beuvron
Lormes
Pouilly-sur-Loire
Châteauneuf-Val-de-Bargis
Champlemy
N151
Corbigny
Vauclaix
N7
La Charité-sur-Loire
Prémery
Moussy
To Bourges
Loire
Saint-Saulge
Aron
Guérigny
A77
Nièvre
Château-Chinon
Pougues-les-Eaux
Châtillon-en-Bazois
Fourchambault
Cher
NEVERS
Saint-Benin-d'Azy
Moulins-Engilbert
Imphy-les-commes
Vandenesse
La Machine
Saint-Honoré-les-Bains
D981
Canal du Nivernais
Canal latéral à la Loire
Allier
To Bourges
Fours
N76
Decize
Luzy
Loire
Saint-Pierre-le-Moûtier
Charrin
La Nocle-Maulaix
N7
Cronat
Issy-l'Évêque
To Moulins
Bourbon-Lancy
Digoin
To Moulins
Allier
Loire
0
15 km
Reproduction interdite
Jean-Baptiste Nény
Avril 2011
Loire

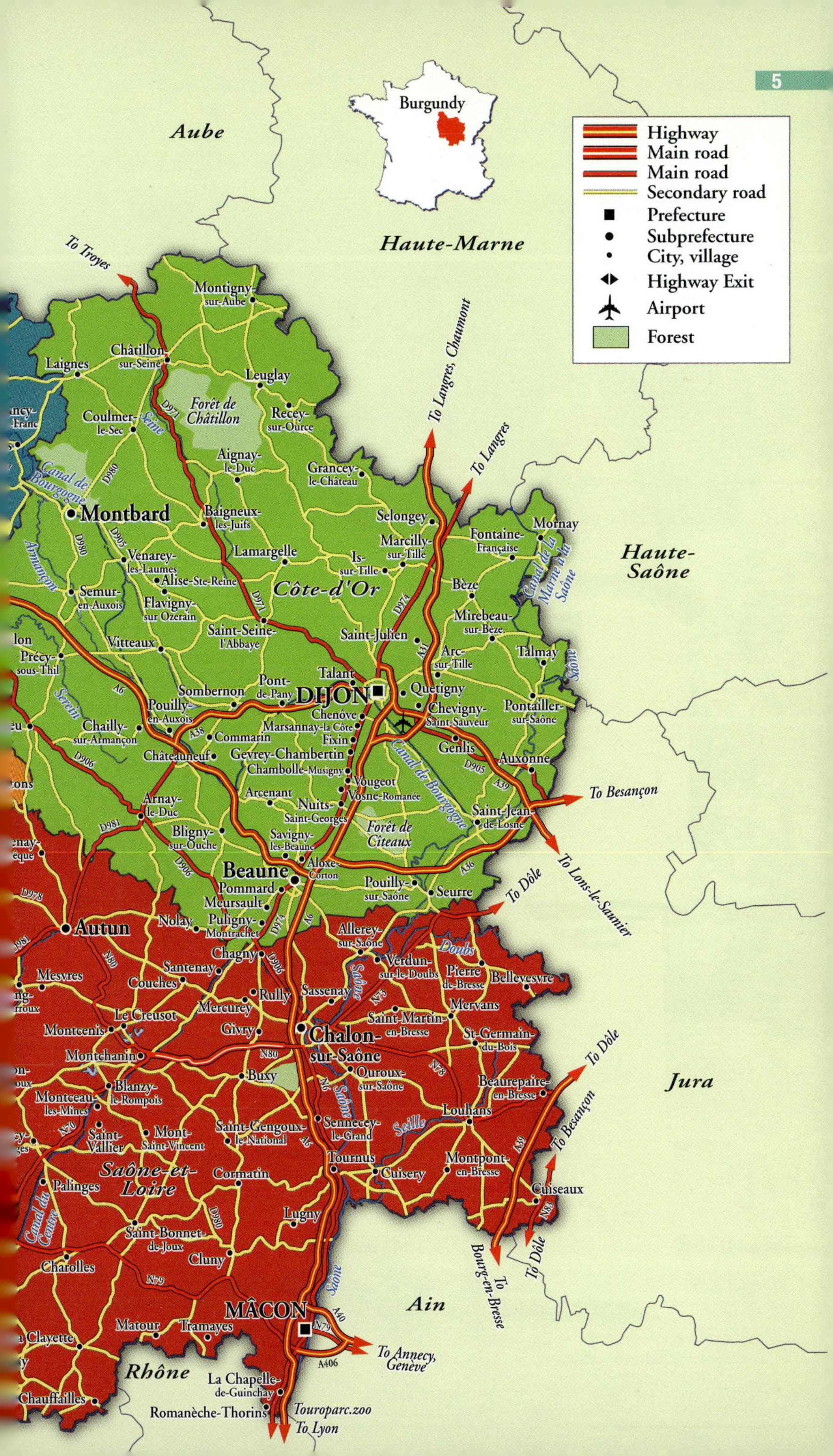
Burgundy
Highway
Main road
Main road
Secondary road
Prefecture
Subprefecture
City, village
Highway Exit
Airport
Forest
Aube
Haute-Marne
Haute-Saône
Jura
Ain
Rhône
Côte-d'Or
Saône-et-Loire
To Troyes
To Langres, Chaumont
To Langres
To Besançon
To Lons-le-Saunier
To Dôle
To Bourg-en-Bresse
To Annecy, Genève
To Lyon
Touroparc.zoo
Montigny-sur-Aube
Châtillon-sur-Seine
Laignes
Leuglay
Forêt de Châtillon
Coulmer-le-Sec
Recey-sur-Ource
Aignay-le-Duc
Grancey-le-Château
Canal de Bourgogne
Montbard
Baigneux-les-Juifs
Selongey
Marcilly-sur-Tille
Fontaine-Française
Mornay
Canal de la Marne à la Saône
Venarey-les-Laumes
Alise-Ste-Reine
Lamargelle
Is-sur-Tille
Bèze
Armançon
Semur-en-Auxois
Flavigny-sur Ozerain
Mirebeau-sur-Bèze
Saint-Seine-l'Abbaye
Saint-Julien
Vitteaux
Arc-sur-Tille
Talmay
Précy-sous-Thil
Talant
Sombernon
Pont-de-Pany
DIJON
Quetigny
Chevigny-Saint-Sauveur
Pontailler-sur-Saône
Serein
Pouilly-en-Auxois
Chenôve
Marsannay-la Côte
Chailly-sur-Armançon
Commarin
Fixin
Genlis
Châteauneuf
Gevrey-Chambertin
Chambolle-Musigny
Auxonne
Vougeot
Vosne-Romanée
Arcenant
Nuits-Saint-Georges
Saint-Jean-de-Losne
Arnay-le-Duc
Forêt de Cîteaux
Bligny-sur-Ouche
Savigny-les-Beaune
Aloxe-Corton
Beaune
Pommard
Pouilly-sur-Saône
Seurre
Meursault
Puligny-Montrachet
Nolay
Autun
Allerey-sur-Saône
Verdun-sur-le-Doubs
Doubs
Chagny
Santenay
Mesvres
Couches
Pierre-de-Bresse
Bellevesvre
Rully
Sassenay
Mercurey
Mervans
Le Creusot
Saint-Martin-en-Bresse
Montcenis
Givry
Chalon-sur-Saône
St-Germain-du-Bois
Montchanin
Buxy
Ouroux-sur-Saône
Blanzy-le-Rompois
Montceau-les-Mines
Beaurepaire-en-Bresse
Louhans
Saint-Vallier
Mont-Saint-Vincent
Saint-Gengoux-le-National
Sennecey-le-Grand
Seille
Tournus
Montpont-en-Bresse
Cuisery
Palinges
Cormatin
Cuiseaux
Canal du Centre
Lugny
Saint-Bonnet-de-Joux
Charolles
Cluny
Saône
MÂCON
Matour
Tramayes
La Clayette
La Chapelle-de-Guinchay
Chauffailles
Romanèche-Thorins
A6
A31
A36
A38
A39
A40
A406
D971
D980
D905
D906
D974
D981
D978
N80
N70
N79
N73
N78
N83

Château de la Clayette.

KNOWING MORE ABOUT BURGUNDY

In the streets of Beaune.

NOT TO BE MISSED

CÔTE-D'OR ★★★

Hospices De Beaune

■ **L'HÔTEL DIEU – LES HOSPICES DE BEAUNE** ★★★★
Rue de l'Hôtel-Dieu
BEAUNE
✆ +33 (0)3 80 24 45 00
www.hospices-de-beaune.com
hospices.beaune@ch-beaune.fr

Low season : open every day from 9am to 11.30am and from 2pm to 5.30pm. High season : every day from 9am to 6.30pm. Free for under 10-year-olds (and for the disabled guests). Adult : €7.50. Child (from 10 to 18 years old) : €3. Group (10 people) : €6.50 (school, 10-18 years : €2.50). Reduced rate : €5.50. Guided tour (€2.50). Shop. Activities.

Also known as Hôtel-Dieu, the Hospices de Beaune undoubtedly embodies the most famous image of the Côte-d'Or in the world. With its sharp spiers and glazed tiles, the building, immortalised by La Grande Vadrouille, remains one of the jewels of Burgundian medieval heritage. The story began in the fifteenth century, in a country ravaged by the Hundred Years' War and bloodthirsty armed gangs, the « Ecorcheurs ». In 1443, Nicolas Rolin, chancellor of the Duke of Burgundy, Philip le Bon, and his wife Guigone de Salins, decided to create a pious foundation and had a hospital built for the sick and the poor. The first patient was received in 1452. The last one would leave the hospices in 1971. Generations of Beaune were born here since the Hospices hosted the maternity of the city until the year 1970 ! A part of the place is still dedicated to health : it was occupied by a retirement home. The comments of audio-guides are very well made. The wine estate of the Hospices generates an important activity and the auction of its products, an unmissable annual event which attracts people of the entire world. If you must visit only one building in Beaune, we strongly recommend this one !

Castle Of Clos De Vougeot

■ **LE CHÂTEAU DU CLOS DE VOUGEOT** ★★★
Rue de la Montagne
VOUGEOT
✆ +33 (0)3 80 62 86 09
www.closdevougeot.fr
visites@closdevougeot.info

From April to October : open every day 9 : 00 at 6.30pm. Closed at 5pm Saturday. From November to March : open every day from 10am to 5pm. Adult : €7. Child (from 8 to 16 years old) : €2.50. Group (10 people) : €5. Pass-wall (yearly subscription for the frequent visitors) : €20 all year. Children welcome. Guided tour (free tour. Guided tour by reservation or at 11.30am and 2.30pm €2.50 (45 min of visit. English and German, Italian visit on request)).

A must-see. The castle of Clos de Vougeot, proudly built in the middle of the vineyard, is one of the icons of Burgundy. The visit of this building is enthralling, it leads you from the former fermenting room (storeroom) of the 17 th century to the Renaissance manor house, passing by the former kitchens and the fermenting room of the Middle Ages.

The course has been, since summer 2015, marked out by multilingual and tactile interactive terminals where you discover anecdotes, superb old photographs, videos... Ludic and very instructive ! Upstairs, where the dormitory of the monks was once installed, Do not miss the movie *Jamais en vain, toujours en vin* (motto of the brotherhood of the Knights of Tastevin). From the first stones laid by the monks of the abbey of Cîteaux in the 12 th century to the chapters of the Brotherhood, this film recalls the rich and tumultuous history of the castle which is managed since 1944 by the Brotherhood of the Knights of Tastevin. It is Pierre Arditi, member of this emblematic Brotherhood, who tells these 9 centuries of history. During the visit, in the small storeroom, do not miss a treasure acquired very recently by the castle : an exceptional painting of the famous painter of Montmartre, Maurice Utrillo. Gourmet friends, in the courtyard you can contemplate some of the menus of the dinners organized by the Brotherhood of the Knights of Tastevin. Did you know ? The Castle also accommodates school visits and banquets throughout the year, prepared by the chef resident, Olivier Walsh and his team. If you should make only one stop between Dijon and Beaune then do it in this magical place ! Note : nowadays the castle does not produce wine anymore and cannot offer tasting sessions.

Fontenay Abbey

ABBAYE DE FONTENAY ★★★★
D32
MONTBARD
✆ +33 (0)3 80 92 15 00
www.abbayedefontenay.com
info@abbayedefontenay.com
6 Km North-East of Montbard, via Marmagne.

Open all year. Low season : every day from 10am to 12pm and from 2pm to 5pm. High season : every day from 10am to 6pm. High season from March 26th to November 13th, 2016. Adult : €10 (€12.50 with guided tour). Child (up to 26 years) : €7 (€7.90 with guided tour). Group (15 people) : €8.80 (€5.70 -26 years in free tour. Package guide : €90 by reservation). Shop.

© GUILLAUME RAPITA

Roman legionaries of the muséoparc Alésia.

© CLAUDE NISSENS – FOTOLIA

Gardens of the abbey of Fontenay.

© ERIC LETELLIER – FOTOLIA

Clos de Vougeot.

© JEAN-JACQUES CORDIER – FOTOLIA

Hospices de Beaune.

This masterpiece of the Cistercians is part of the first French building classified as a Unesco World Heritage site since 1981. The visit of Abbaye de Fontenay and its superbly maintained gardens is unforgettable. By the way, it is the third consecutive time that the Ministry for Culture awards it the label « *Jardin remarquable* ». These gardens consist of 9 spaces on 2 hectares. You can find a bicentenary plane tree planted in 1780, which is also exceptional. The monks of Cîteaux settled here, away from the world and people, in 1118. The abbey church was consecrated by the Pope, thirty years later, and from the late 12th to the 16th century, the abbey experienced great prosperity. During the Revolution, it was sold and transformed into a paper mill, then bought in the 19 th century by the Montgolfier family. Every year, more than 100,000 people visit this place with bare architecture stripped of all ornament, beautifully restored at the beginning of the 20 th century by Edouard Aynard and perfectly preserved since then. The Cloister, the chapter house, the abbey church, the dormitory, the forge... Each stage takes us back to the daily life of the monks, in their existence of silence, prayer and work. The visit can be self-guided or guided, in several languages. Do not hesitate to complete it by a small round in the shop/bookshop, you will find exciting works and some craft products there. Abbaye de Fontenay is a sublime, imposing and soothing place that you will continue to admire when you leave. And the show is striking each season.

Musée Des Beaux-Arts De Dijon

MUSÉE DES BEAUX-ARTS DE DIJON ★★★★
Palais des Ducs et des États de Bourgogne
Place de la Libération
DIJON
✆ +33 (0)3 80 74 52 09
museedesbeauxarts@ville-dijon.fr

Closed on January 1st, May 1st, May 8th, July 14th, 1st and November 11th, December 25th. Low season : open Wednesday to Monday from 10am to 5pm. High season : Wednesday to Monday from 9.30am to 6pm. Closed of the donation Granville (modern art, €2 and €3 floor) of 11.30am at 13 : 45 . Free. Audioguide (FR, GB, ALL) : €4. Guided tour : €6, reduced : €3. Concert, show : €6. Workshop : €6. Guided tour. Catering facilities. Shop. Activities. The museum organizes workshops, conferences, guided tours, games, the night ones.

This museum is one of the most beautiful in France. It occupies a part of the former Palais des Ducs et des Etats de Bourgogne, built between the 14th and the 19 th century. A building full of history : first a residence of the dukes until the death of Téméraire, in 1477, it became the residence of the governors who represented the king in the province, then welcomed the assemblies of the States of Burgundy and the offices of elected representatives. The 80,000 works that are preserved there have an overview of the history of Western art. If the museum is especially known for the tombs of Burgundy's dukes and the incredible mourners that support them, they must not make us forget the other treasures it houses : funeral portraits of Fayoum (dating back to Roman Egypt), masterpieces of Flemish primitives, Swiss and Rhenish, of Titian, Philippe de Champaigne, Eugène Delacroix, Théodore Géricault, Edouard Manet, Claude Monet and Nicolas de Staël... And let us not forget Burgundian artists such as François Pompon ! The interest of the visit is also strolling in a former palace, ascending Tour de Bar, built by Philippe le Hardi around 1365 and discovering the old ducal kitchen built by Philippe le Bon around 1430. You will have understood : this museum should absolutely be visited ! Note that it has been under renovation since 2008. The first phase was completed last September. Since 2013, the course dedicated to the collections of the Middle Ages and the Renaissance has completely been renovated. The second and third portions of the works have just begun and concern the collections and the buildings of the 17th, 18th, 19th and 20th centuries. Tour de Bar will also be given a facelift. These works will finish in 2019. In the meantime, the museum remains open. To know the future exhibitions, visit www.mba.dijon.fr

NIÈVRE ★

La Charité-sur-Loire

A Major site of the burgundy Romanesque art, La Charité-sur-Loire, City of Art and History today and « eldest daughter of Cluny », once was an important step on the way to Saint-Jacques-de Compostela. Founded on March 9th, 1097 and dedicated in 1059, the priory of cluniac could accommodate 5,000 devotees. The tower St. Croix, now isolated, recalls, as well as Notre-Dame church in the twelfth century, one of the largest buildings of Christendom.

The choir and transept are marked by the elegance of the architecture of the eleventh and twelfth centuries and the richness of their sculpted decor largely contributed to the fame of the priory church. Saved from a certain destruction by Prosper Mérimée, then inspector of Historical Monuments, it was declared an UNESCO World Heritage in December 1998. The conventual buildings offer their architectural splendours during exhibitions and concerts in these sacred places, and cloisters, opened to the public after 10 long years of restoration, will be in the future a crossing point for the public but also a place of stage and show during the many festivals in the city. Like its church, the heart of the charitoise city is dotted with history : here at the bend of a narrow street, a passage or old stairs, you will discover the salt cellar where people had to pay of the salt tax, a shop of the fifteen th century, and further on the 84 steps of Chemin des Pèlerins which are still used today and this since the 12'h century. Stroll in the old town, raise your eyes in search of architectural detail that will attract your attention, the least quote engraved on the wall sections, and end your captivating stroll at the foot of the ramparts where you can admire the city and its priory, and beyond, the Loire, wild river so dear to Charitois.

SAÔNE-ET-LOIRE ★★

BIBRACTE, MUSÉE DE LA CIVILISATION CELTIQUE ★★
Mont-Beuvray
SAINT-LÉGER-SOUS-BEUVRAY
✆ +33 (0)3 85 86 52 35
www.bibracte.fr
info@bibracte.fr

The museum is open from March 12th to November 13th, 2016, from 10am to 6pm and until 7pm in July and August. Exceptional opening until 10pm Wednesdays in July and August. Possibility of opening all year for groups, by reservation. Free for under 12-year-olds (and for €3 the child of a family). Adult : €7.50 (reduced rate : €5.50). Rate Passport (visit of the site, the museum and the temporary exhibition) : 12€ for an adult; 10€ in reduced rate. Rate Gallic Day (visit of the site, the museum and the temporary exhibition + meal to the Cauldron) 27€ for an adult; 12,50€ in reduced rate. Tourism label & Disability. For the reception of disabled people, please contact the following address e-mail : p.plaza@bibracte.fr. Children welcome (stroller three wheels any ground and baby carriers lent free to the museum). Guided tour. Catering facilities (Le Chaudron restaurant, baby chair). Shop. Activities.

Located in the heart of Burgundy, Bibracte is an extraordinary natural and archaeological site, labelled Grand Site de France since 2007. This label was renewed in 2013 for a further 6 years period. Nestled in the stunning setting of the regional natural park of the Morvan, the Bibracte archaeological site invites you to discover the riches of the Celtic civilisation of the 2nd and 1st century before Christ. In fact, the antique city of Bibracte would have been built on Mont Beuvray by the Gallic people of Eduens. It is also in Bibracte that Vercingétorix held the first general uprising of the Gallic tribe against the Romans in 52 BC. Stretching over 200 hectares, this magnificent site offers a large number of activities to visitors where the pleasure to discover a majestic nature mingles with scientific and historical knowledge. The Bibrate site houses a rich museum on Gallic life, installed on the slopes of Mount Beuvray. The permanent exhibition allows you to discover the Celtic civilisation and to better understand the utility of the *oppida*, fortified towns that played the role of economic and political centres. These oppida are often coinsidered as the first towns of the north of the Alps. At Bibracte, you can find thrilling archeological pieces as well as replica and video. These cultural mediation processes allow visitors to place them into the history and to get themselves to the daily life of our ancestors. The site of the archeological excavation is visitble throughout the year. The nature is also worth a detour. Mont Beuvray is covered by a 1,000 ha forest of beech softwood. During the fine weather, you can even see the Mont Blanc. Bribracte is an exceptional natural and archeological site that offers you a historic stroll in an obiquitous and magnificent nature.

© SYLVAIN SONNET

Vaults of the Saint-Pierre-et-Saint-Paul Cluny abbey.

The Chantier Médiéval de Guédelon.

YONNE ★★★

Vézelay

A site listed on the UNESCO World Heritage site and admired every year by a million visitors. The « eternal hill » stands Vézelay. Founded in the nin th century, a monastery developed there and received in 1050 the relics of St. Mary Magdalene, the « repentant sinner. » The city grows as there is a mass flow of pilgrims. It became a famous starting point for the pilgrimage to Compostela. Saint Bernard of Clairvaux preached the Second Crusade in 1146, in the presence of King Louis VII. The sovereign Philippe Auguste and Richard Lion Heart gave an appointment there in 1190 to the start of the third Crusade. And in 1248, St. Louis went there several times on pilgrimage. It is also here that the Franciscans founded their first convent in France in the early thirteen th century. But that same disasterous century ! New « true » relics of Mary Magdalene were discovered in Provence, at Saint-Maximin. Quickly, the icaunais pilgrimage declined. The abbey was sacked by the Huguenots and secularized during the Revolution. A fire breakout destroyed the early nineteen th century. It was not until 1840 that Viollet-le-Duc saved it from a certain ruin. Today, the basilica has regained its splendor. Tourists and pilgrims still climb the long steep street leading to the esplanade. The Landrooted in the history of Catholicism, Vézelay nevertheless saw born in 1519 Theodore de Bèze, who participated in the Reformation with Calvin. The author Romain Rolland lived there at the end of his life. The natural beauty and the charm of the narrow streets of this village are inevitable, to get there, we are not asked !

Castle Of Ancy-le-Franc

■ CHÂTEAU D'ANCY-LE-FRANC ★★
18, place Clermont-Tonnerre
ANCY-LE-FRANC © +33 (0)3 86 75 14 63
www.chateau-ancy.com
information@chateau-ancy.com
Open from March 19th to November 13th, 2016. Open every day, except nonholiday Mondays. Free tour from 10.30am to 12.30pm, from 2pm to 5pm; and in July and August from 10.30am to 5pm. Free for under 6-year-olds. Adult : €10 (guided tour, reduced : €9; free tour, adult : €9, reduced : €8, child : €6). Child (from 6 to 15 years old) : €6. Group (20 people) : €8 (possibility of wine tasting, at an extra charge). Reduced rate : €9. Visit château+parc : €13 by adult, €8 by child, reduced : €11. Pass' Ancy Solo : €40, Pass' Ancy Duet : €65. Audioguide : €3. Guided tour (departure at 10.30am, 11.30am, 2pm, 3pm, 4pm (5pm from April to September). Audioguides available to the reception of the castle, for adult (5 languages) and child (4 languages). Musical entertainments all in summer). Shop. Visit for groups and the pupils all year by reservation. Premises hire (seminars, weddings, cocktails…).

© JULIA VALENTIN

The Château d'Ancy-le-Franc.

This Renaissance castle is undoubtedly one of the finest of Burgundy; it is some sort of Versailles miniature ! Built between 1542 and 1550 according to the plans of the Italian architect Sebastiano Serlio, it was meant for count Antoine de Clermont, the governor of Dauphine and grand master of Eaux et Forêts de France, husband of Diane de Poitiers, sister of the mistress of Henry II, the Diane of Poitiers. He greatly participated in the influence of the Italian Renaissance in France. Setup on a square plan with four corner pavilions, the building was originally surrounded by a moat, protected by drawbridges. The first Marquis of Louvois owned it for some time, and had to fill these pits. You will enjoy this trip another time, both for the richness of its scenery and the elegance of its 50-hectare park, opened to the public in the year 2012, where the lake and its island with its eighteen th century splurge makes it conducive for beautiful romantic walks. Many events are held throughout the year to further sublimate this monument.

Castle Of Maulnes

■ CHÂTEAU DE MAULNES ★
Hameau de Maulnes
CRUZY-LE-CHÂTEL
✆ +33 (0)3 86 72 92 10 / +33 (0)3 86 72 89 37
www.maulnes.com
maulnes@cg89.fr

Open from March 19th to November 1st, 2016. Low season : open at weekends and public holidays from 2.30pm to 5.30pm. High season : every day and public holidays from 2.30pm to 5.30pm. Free for under 18-year-olds. Adult : €4 (reduced €2). Group (10 people) : €2.

This Tonnerre castle is a real enigma of the Renaissance. In pentagonal architecture, organized around a central shaft and an impressive spiral staircase, this building, which is unique in France, fed many legends. Built in the sixteen th century around a subtle play of light and water, this maze is at same time the hunting lodge of the first Duke of Uzes, and one of the greatest utopian architecture that mark the imagination. Classified as a historical monument, acquired by the General Council of the Yonne in 1997 and now under study and restoration, here rendered to our common heritage, to the delight of all lovers of history and magical places. Not to be missed !

Castle Of Tanlay

■ CHÂTEAU DE TANLAY ★★
2, Grande-Rue-Basse
TANLAY
✆ +33 (0)3 86 75 70 61
www.chateaudetanlay.fr

Open from April 1st to November 2nd. Closed on Tuesday. Open Wednesday to Monday from 10am to 12.30pm and from 2.15pm to 6pm. Free tour : €3. Guided tour : €5 for the 8-18 years, €10 for the adults, €8 for groups (20 people). Guided tour (guided interior visit : approximately 50 minutes; departures at 10am, 11.30am, 2.15pm, 3.15pm, 4.15pm and 5.15pm).

This castle surrounded by moats and set in a beautiful park consists of several buildings. The small castle in Louis XIII style was built in the 17 'h century. The big castle built from the middle of the 16th on a former castle, is a superb Renaissance building. It frequently hosted Protestant chefs during the League. The interior has magnificent paintings as well as frescoes and remarkable furniture.

NATURE

GEOGRAPHY

Climate

Located in the middle of the land, Burgundy is a climatic crossroad. The reliefs and the western territory (mount Morvan) undergo an oceanic influence. The continental grip manifests itself in the plains and valleys. Some Mediterranean shifts, by rushing into the hallway of the Rhone valley, prolonged by the Saône, just occasionally disrupt the pattern.

This geography favors hot summers and cold winters ... (in addition of being long) ! Snow and frost are waiting for you, and has a tendency to be more in the heights of the Morvan. On contrary, summers are marked by a pronounced heat when compared to those of most other French regions.

The storms are not to be underestimated, nor mist in the offseason. Météo France provides an average (to be taken as such !) for temperatures from 1960 to 1990 : for the month of January, the minimum is less than 1 °C and the thermometer may have the audacity to go up to 4 °C ! For the month of July, we can assume that range from 14 ° C to 25 ° C is indicative. Whatever the temperature, Burgundy can boast his own share of sunshine hours : between 18 : 00 hours and 20 : 00 hours each year.

Which is, ultimately, the best season to visit the area ? Rest assured, facing the wintry weather, many hotels and restaurants make light up a fire place and offer food and shelter that are cozy and comforting.

And during hot weather, many lakes make us with refreshing ideas. Fall reserves superb decors to those who appreciate its colors, with the highlight beauty of the vineyard.

Relief

Characteristic Landscapes

▸ **Morvan : at the heart of the region.** Between the four departments of Burgundy, the old massive formed itself to the Paleozoic era, at the same time as the Vosges. Rocks from its heights, undermined, planed, suffered from a steady erosion, the slow and inevitable wear of wind and weather, the ravages of time. The little summits exceed 900 m. To the west of the massif slopes glides smoothly to the Loire.

▸ **Nivernais.** Nivernais is bordered to the east by the mountains of Morvan and to the west by the valleys of the Loire and Allier. The slopes of the vineyards of Pouilly-sur-Loire cereal plantations and meadows countryside follow one another, not to mention the 230 acres of woodlands and numerous rivers that still adorn the landscape Nivernais.

© AM STOCK NATURE

Landscape.

The Icaunaises countryside. Composed of Puisaye-Forterre, Sénonais and the Pays d'Othe. La Puisaye is the childhood country of the writer Colette, who knows how to describ it so well into words not always tender but revealing. It is difficult place to live. Many lords seem to have their castle nestled between forests and ponds to better survive the history.

The Forterre. The Forterre extends to Puisaye from the south and to l'Auxerrois from the southwest. Originally « Forterre » means a « High Land », a difficult land to work. Rather, the term seems to evoke the fortifications that pushed down since Celtic times. Deep campaigns, mysterious rivulets, fortifications, lakes and parks are a delight of tourists.

The Sénonais. An ancient center of Christianity, ruined by the Hundred Years of War, the region of Sens now depend on its relaxed lifestyle , especially to attract Parisians spree. The forms quietens the town – some speak of the flatness – and offer pastoral landscapes between rivers and walks in the valleys.

Pays d'Othe. This small area that extends to the borders of Burgundy and Champagne is very marked by rurality. Its forest is the thickest of the department. It has the distinction of having specialized particularly in the production of apples and there is an excellent cider.

Châtillonnais. In Côte d'Or. The thick lowland forest shares the spotlight with stone and water. The underground exposes a stone of exceptional quality found in large buildings such as the Louvre pyramid. The water is of course that of the Seine, which originates from the Dijon Mountain and crosses, calm and serene, Châtillon-sur-Seine. In the South Châtillonnais the Dijon conglomerate is outlined far off. The Chalonnais. Located in Saône-et-Loire, Chalonnais, falls between Chagny in the north and the Sennecy-le-Grand in the south, is characterized by the important position held by the vineyard. Vines, the wine growers' house that mark the landscape, but also Chalon-sur-Saône is a populated and dynamic city.

The Maconnais. In the south of Burgundy, it somehow makes the link between the wines of Burgundy and those of Beaujolais. These lands are also a Mecca of prehistory, with sites like the (famous !) Solutré rock, caves Aze or Blanot .

The Creusotine region. Between Chalon-sur-Saône and Mâcon, cross the coalfields region, marked by its rich industrial heritage : the metal in Le Creusot coal mine in Montceau-les-Mines (the most recent city Saône-et- Loire , born in 1856, in time master forges, large families such as Schneider, and paternalism business). The country oscillates between conservation and conversion, with leisure parks built on old sites.

Charolais and Bresse. To the west of the Saône-et-Loire, Charolais is the birthplace of the famous breed of cattle whose white colour sprinkles the green of the fatty Burgundy pastures. As for La Bress, it is a vast plain and bocage country. This is the paradise of white chicken with blue feet, the only poultry in the world to receive a designation of origin.

Morvan : At The Heart Of The Region

Between the four departments of Burgundy, the old massive raises itself to the primary era, at the same time as the Vosges. Rocks from its heights, undermined, planed, suffered from a steady erosion, the slow and inevitable wear of wind and weather, the ravages of time. The little summits exceed 900 m. To the west of the massif slopes glides smoothly to the Loire.

Nivernais

Nivernais is bordered to the east by the mountains of Morvan and to the west by the valleys of the Loire and Allier. The slopes of the vineyards of Pouilly-sur-Loire cereal plantations and meadows countryside follow one another, not to mention the 230 acres of woodlands and numerous rivers that still adorn the landscape Nivernais.

The Icaunaises Countryside

Composed of Puisaye-Forterre, Sénonais and the Pays d'Othe. La Puisaye is the childhood country of the writer Colette, who knows how to describ it so well into words not always tender but revealing. It is difficult place to live. Many lords seem to have their castle nestled between forests and ponds to better survive the history.

The Forterre. The Forterre extends to Puisaye from the south and to l'Auxerrois from the southwest. Originally « Forterre » means a « High Land », a difficult land to work. Rather, the term seems to evoke the fortifications that pushed down since Celtic times. Deep campaigns, mysterious rivulets, fortifications, lakes and parks are a delight of tourists.

The Sénonais. An ancient center of Christianity, ruined by the Hundred Years' War, the region of Sens now depends on its relaxed lifestyle, especially to attract Parisians spree. The forms quietens the town – some speak of the flatness – and offer pastoral landscapes between rivers and walks in the valleys.

Pays d'Othe. This small area that extends to the borders of Burgundy and Champagne is very marked by rurality. Its forest is the thickest of the department. It has the distinction of having specialized particularly in the production of apples and there is an excellent cider.

Châtillonnais

In Côte-d'Or. The thick lowland forest shares the spotlight with stone and water. The underground exposes a stone of exceptional quality that is found in large buildings such as the Louvre pyramid. Water is of course that of the Seine, which originates from the Dijon Mountain and crosses, calm and serene Châtillon-sur-Seine. In the South Châtillonnais is outlined far off the Dijon conglomerate.

Châlonnnais

Located in Saône-et-Loire, Chalonnais, falls between Chagny in the north and the Sennecy-le-Grand in the south, is characterized by the important position held

Burgundy vineyard.

PHBCZ - ISTOCKPHOTO

Semur-en-Auxois village.

by the vineyard. Vines, the wine growers' house that mark the landscape, but also Chalon-sur-Saône is a populated and dynamic city.

Mâconnais

In the south of Burgundy, it somehow makes the link between the wines of Burgundy and those of Beaujolais. These lands are also a Mecca of prehistory, with sites like the (famous !) Solutré rock, caves Aze or Blanot.

The Creusotine Region

Between Chalon-sur-Saône and Mâcon, cross the coalfields region, marked by its rich industrial heritage : the metal in Le Creusot coal mine in Montceau-les-Mines (the most recent city Saône-et- Loire, born in 1856, in time master forges, large families such as Schneider, and paternalism business). The country oscillates between conservation and conversion, with leisure parks built on old sites.

Charolais & Bresse

To the west of the Saône-et-Loire, Charolais is the birthplace of the famous breed of cattle whose white colour sprinkles the green of the fatty Burgundy pastures. La Bresse, for its part, is a vast plain and bocage country. This is the paradise of white chicken with blue feet, the only poultry in the world to receive a designation of origin.

Rivers & Valleys

The Loire. 1020 : is the number of kilometers that this river (the longest in France !) runs before emptying into the Atlantic Ocean. Among its tributaries in Burgundy, Bourbince , the Bremen, Arconce and Arroux, which crosses Autun and Gueugnon voisinnent with the mounts of Morvan; as forTernin enjoys the beautiful scenery of the Parc Naturel Régional du Morvan.

Saône. The river stretches in all on about 482 km, rises from Vioménil in the Vosges, and ends up joining the Lyon Rhône. It therefore crosses the Côte- d'Or and Saône-et-Loire. The Saône has seen for a long time passing on transit in the Vosges woods, grains, cast iron, sand, clay, cement. On the contrary, it is wines and spirits back that go back up as well as spices, slate ... It is also one of the richest fish rivers in Europe. With the development of green tourism and recreational boats, here are assets that the territories bordered by the river Saône can take advantage of.

The Yonne. Yonne experienced centuries of glory, depending on it and its moods. Frequented by the Gauls, who devoted themselves to the foster mother veritable cult, it is actually used by the Romans, who find in it a way to rally the Saône. Then it becomes a course used for economic purposes, as transport by inland water way develops to feed the region ofcourse, but also the capital region before competition of the Railway. Nowadays, its banks are places of popular promenade.

Le Bec d'Allier. « Grand Wild River », the Loire has a unique natural environment, a changing landscape, a fragile heritage that requires attention. From where the necessity of endowing the river of a zone protected from any development, a protected space, where it can spread at leisure. This notion of space or freedom of the river area or natural rambling was raised jointly by the Federation of natural spaces and associations known as WWF : it will be the Bec d'Allier, at the confluence of the Loire and Allier.

The first Ligurian islands are emerging. Here, the area of freedom encompasses 57 acres purchased by the department of Nièvre. These lands and banks see a whole fauna frolic again, on land and in the air, starting with swallows shores and kingfishers. In the acts of conservation combined actions of valorisation has as objectives opening with great conscious and sensitized public. Thus the path of Treader follows in perfect discretion the last kilometers before the confluence. Explanatory terminals come to mark the course, which leads to an observatory within walking distance to the Bec.

Forests & Woods

Burgundy became the fifth most forested region of France, with almost 970,000 hectares of forests identified. Local disparities are marked : Morvan sees its area covered by nearly 40 %. These forests are a major biological asset. They host the third natural areas of ecological fauna and flora, which anwsers to the good name of ZNIEFF. Listed as from 1982, are area sheltering rare species or features of the region. Besides deer, squirrels, hedgehogs and wild boars, the forests provide shelter to rare animals like the woodpecker which enjoys the company of oaks. Black stork, as for it, settled down since twentie th century only, in the woods of Châtillonnais.

Bertranges Forest. Located in the Nièvre, the forest became state owned during the Revolution. It covers nearly 10,000 hectares, mainly planted with oaks. Its straight fairways and many trails are perfect for hiking, they are done on foot, bike or horse, and deers that inhabit the places also attract curiousity, especially during the period of slab.

The Châtillonnais Forest. The forest extends from a single block of nearly 9,000 hectares and is the largest wooded area across the Côte-d'Or. The woods are full of varied animal population, deer, birds and small carnivores will find desired preys of the most common species in high demand of morels, while passing through the delicious chaterelles. In season, the Mycological Society ofChâtillonnais organizes guided tours. For more information, inquire at the tourist office.

A new national park ! Parc national des forêts de Champagne et Bourgogne

France will have in the years to come an 11th National Park located in northern Burgundy and southern Champagne-Ardenne ! It is a territory of 230,000 hectares made up of hardwood forests of over 50%. Another new feature, this National Park will have the largest reserve of France in Arc en Barrois where the forest will be left in free evolution. The area of the heart of the future park, located primarily on the forests of Châtillon-sur-Seine, Arc-en-Barrois, Châteauvillain and Auberive, will preserve the natural, cultural and landscape heritages. The objective of the National Park will also to develop all the richnesses of its territory on educational, scientific and tourism domains. Several themes will thus be explored : the forests which are majority in this territory, but also the sources, resurgences and rivers that feed the land, the presence of the man who left archaeological remains that are still sheltered by the forests and finally the industrial and religious past which left a unique architectural heritage. Information : www.forets-champagne-bourgogne.fr

FAUNA & FLORA

Parks & Nature Reserves

The Regional Natural Park of Morvan : nature dominates the bumpy landscape of reliefs covered with forests separated by wooded country side, rivers, lakes and picturesque villages. Since its creation, it is beyond the scope of departmental administrative boundaries. The Morvan Regional Park has an area of 240 000 ha of which 105 000 ha are agricultural land, 129,000 ha are forest, 1,600 are surface water and 7,000 ha a humid zone. On these lands, there are over 36,000 people living in the member municipalities and more than 32,000 souls who live on the outskirts of the park, in daily contact with it. If we count the marked trails networked, we arrive at – all types merged : hiking, horseback riding, mountain biking trails – nearly 3,600 available. A little less than 250 protected species represent the fauna and sixty the flora. Regarding the fauna, are just less than 250 species protected. For the flora, there are nearly sixty. Another advantage to assert : the Regional Natural Park Brand (www.parcdumorvan.org). It is a collective trademark with the INPI – National Institute of Industrial Property – by the Ministry of Town Planning and the Environment, who is the owner. In 2010, the park celebrated its forty years !

© BERND KRÖGER – FOTOLIA

Wild boar.

© ITZAK NEWMANN – ICONOTEC

Herd of cows.

The Natural Reserve of the Val de Loire : The site was listed in 1995 and covers the departments of Cher and Nièvre. The reserve stretches over nearly 1,500 hectares for 20 of Loire. It covers the municipalities of La Charité- sur-Loire, Mesves-sur-Loire, Pouilly -sur- Loire and Tracy-sur-Loire Nièvre; Couargues, Herry and La Chapelle-Montlinard for Cher. The river is home to thirty species of fishes such as lamprey, shad and salmon. The beaver has reappeared here and found his rights. About 500 species of plants and 190 species of birds have been recorded here.

The Nature Reserve of Truchère : It flourishes in the heart of the Bresse, in the department of Saône-et-Loire. Its ecosystem offers an astounding summary, gathering both vegetation having seaside characteristic with a landscape of dunes, moors or scenery worthy of the Nordic countries with their bogs. In the center of this reserve is a lake, pond Fouget, flourishing on nearly 16 hectares. Again, sand islets and swamps provide the ideal setting for rare and diverse fauna and flora. A nature trail has been set up to explore this amazing universe.

Wood Nature Reserve Park : An old warm sea extending at the foot of the limestone cliff on which is perched above the Village of Mailly-le-Chateau in Burgundy : a surprising nature reserve where a 45 ha receives you. Limestone is here from a gigantic fossilized coral reef, dating from the Jurassic, when the warm waters covered the site. Besides fossil corals, you will discover by climbing the staircase to the top of the cliff, dry grass and sub-Mediterranean flora, one of the most persistent in the north of France. A trail allows the public to walk through the forests and the grasslands of the high cliff.

The Swamp of Cônois Côte-d'Or : Acquired in 1991 by the Academy of Burgundians Natural Sites. The marsh extends over 7 hectares, and is among the most beautiful marais tuffeux du Châtillonnais. Fed by springs whose water is heavily charged with lime, the marsh has very interesting geological features : in contact with air and vegetation, the limestone present in water develops faster into a more or less friable rock, the tufa. In addition, due to the presence of a cold microclimate on Châtillonnais the swamp is home to a very specific flora including plants with mountain characteristics, such as gentianne and perennial swertie. A path allows the public to discover these riches.

The Natural Park of Boutissaint : Located in the west of the Yonne and extending over an area of about 400 hectares. The natural reserve park of Boutissaint has preserved the wildness of the oak woodland and coniferous forest, characteristics of Puisaye forests. Animals that inhabit this forest are in the wild, such as deer, roe deer and cervus deer, other fenced in, such as wild boar, deer or wild sheep that can be observed in a wide meadow near the castle pond, and also through regular towers installed along the different routes that walks through the park. It can also be explored on foot, by bike or on horseback.

HISTORY

Antiquity

The Celtic implantation. The Bronze Age (2 200-750 B.C.) and the Iron Age (from 750 BC.) were the properous periods for the region. The territory is now generally busy.

Early, trade with Greek traders, Phoenicians and Italians are established along the tin route, through Burgundy, linking northern Europe to the Mediterranean basin. It set up a new society in the region, politically and economically dominated by a warrior caste that provides control communication channels.

These treasures of Blanot and Rochepot are certainly beautiful testimonies, but the tomb of Vix, on a hilltop outside of Châtillon-sur-Seine, is undoubtedly one of the most important archaeological wonders ever discovered. These days mark the beginning of the Gallic civilization, and the region is honored by the presence of many Gallic tribes, the first of which are implanted into the second century : the Senones, Lingones Insurbes and then in the first century, Aedui, from Morvan. The latter base their capital Bibracte on Mount Beuvray.

Alesia and Gallo-Roman Burgundy : Faced with Helvetii threats, Eduens appealed to Caesar, who began, the Gallic campaign by 58 B.C. The Gallic tribes in the region have a policy in favor of the Romans and Burgundy becomes a food depot for the glorious Romans until the day, allying Arverni, led by Vercingetorix, the Aedui oppose Caesar.

We are then in 52 BC., the year of the famous Battle of Alesia, which Caesar comes out glorious. Gaul became a Roman. Autun (Augustodunum), city of Augustus, became the capital at the expense of Bibracte, former Gallic oppidum.

Then born on the territory are many Gallo-Roman cities, with comfortable houses, baths, temples and schools and the most famous are those of Autun. This Pax Romana time will be introduced in the territory of a new culture : that of the vine.

The end of the Roman period is marked by the formalization of the Christian religion, which brings to light the development of this religion and the worship for martyrs, as is the case in Dijon on the tomb of St. Benignus.

Middle Ages

Religious orders in Burgundy and the splendor of the Dukes :

It is in Burgundy that the two largest monastic reform movements of the Middle Ages were born : Cluny and Citeaux were, the tenth to the twelfth centuries, both spiritual and intellectual, artistic and political centers. Vézelay in Paray-le-Monial, Fontenay La Charite- sur-Loire, the Middle Ages Burgundy shines throughout Western Christendom.

Cluny and the Cluniac order : Cluny is at the heart of the Western medieval. Abbey will experience an unprecedented success in the history of Christianity and if they are twelve monks who settled initially at Cluny, the number of religious will reach more than 10,000 people gathered in the same physical and spiritual community : the Cluniac order. I must say that Cluny owes much to the personality of the first abbots to its influence. Besides the reigns of exceptional longevity, these men lead a major policy. Cluny monks are trained to go to regain control of religious institutions in trouble, and it soon identifies nearly 1,000 monasteries affiliated to Cluny. The community swarms throughout the West, maintaining close ties with its various « houses "like" a mother with her daughters. »

Citeaux and Cistercian monks : Initially, some dissident monks, supporters of a return to a strict observance of the monastic rule. After a journey that leads them to the Thunder land to those of the Saône, they decided to establish their community in these difficult places, in the midst of a hostile geography. At their head was Robert Molesme; we are in 1098, one hundred years after the founding of Cluny. But it is the year 1112 that ushers in a new era with the arrival of Cistercian Bernard, the youngest son of a noble of Fontaine-lès-Dijon who was later known by the name Bernard of Clairvaux, St. Bernard. He is at the head of thirty something companions and intends to permanently install as new Cistercian monastic model. Fairly quickly, the community founded four abbeys, from La Ferté from 1113, Pontigny in Yonne, Clairvaux and Morimond, which will in turn swarm in France and then abroad. Saint Bernard, the first Abbot of Clairvaux, gives life to the Abbey of Fontenay in Côte-d'Or. The Cistercian Abbey was radiating a monastic order, that of the Cistercians. Those who are also nicknamed « white monks « would establish their own rules of life, define their spiritual commandments, and also boost a current architectural and artistic, an economic operating system, technical progress, advances in environmental protection and in particular those of the culture of the vine ... Cistercians accumulate wealth over the centuries and hardware requirements gradually prevail over spiritual concerns, despite unsuccessful attempts to reform the sixteenth and seventeenth centuries. The Revolution seized lands and buildings, and community driven, is dissolved. The site will eventually serve as a template for a utopian community experience and will host a penal colony and a theater ... Since 1898 Cistercian shelters monks again. Its 900 years were celebrated in 1998.

The way of St. James (pilgrimage route) : It croses the region and offers splendid steps, rich in history and landscape. Saint-Jacques-de-Compostela was one of three great pilgrimages in the Christian Middle Ages with those of Rome and Jerusalem. Four official roads led to this high place where St. Jacques le Majeur rests, with Paris, Vezelay, Le Puy-en-Velay and Arles as assembly places for pilgrims from all over Europe. The path from Vézelay allowed pilgrims from Germany and Central Europe to rally Saint-Jacques-de-Compostela. This long path then crossed the Loire to La Charité and Nevers, as described, in 1140, in the Pilgrim's Guide .

Vezelay : the eternal hill : An unusual fate for an exceptional site, the first to be registered in the World Heritage Site by UNESCO, in 1979. In the middle of the nin th century, a certain Girart Roussillon, Count of Paris and his wife Bertha, decided to base monasteries on their land, including one at the foot of the hill of Vézelay, therefore placing these institutions under the direct protection of the Pope. Vézelay became independent of lay powers as ecclesiastical powers and responds only to the King of France. On the path that leads to the Council of Troyes, the Pope blessed the church of Vezelay in 878. In 887 In the Scandinavians sacked the abbey of Flavigny-sur-Ozerain and step at Vézelay. The Religious order decided to leave the lowlands to enjoy the natural heights of the hill. An enclosure was built and a new buildings, including the abbey church and its crypt. It will receive the relics of St. Mary Magdalene in the middle of the eleven th century.

The Golden Age and the dark hours : The remains of St. Mary Magdalene arouse the fervor of the pilgrims. Around the place of worship develops a village with fairs and markets for artisans, changers, stopover cottages ... Later in the twelf th century, Vézelay became one of four starting points of routes to reach Saint-Jacques-de-Compostela. Travelers then arrive from all over Europe. On their land, it is the Father himself who performs the duties of justice. Powers that affect the local population, a wealth that tempts the neighboring dictators such as the Count of Nevers, the abbot of Cluny and the Bishop of Autun. Vézelay also knows riots, violence, blood punishments and unexplained fires. To the nickname of eternal hill was added the name Mount of Scorpion : light and the dark side.

Decay and resurrection : In the nineteen th century, the walls crumbled when the young architect Viollet -le-Duc arrived on the site. The reasons for this neglect ? The long decline of the early thirteen th century until the Revolution. The state launched a restoration project on March 29th, 1840 which started under Louis-Philippe and completed under Napoleon III. The twentie th century, with advances in transportation and the advent of tourism, gives the necessary impetus to the hill to preserve and maintain its heritage. A renewed spiritual activity is accompanied by an intellectual breath. The hill attracts painters and men of letters. In July 1979, the site is listed in the World Heritage Site by UNESCO.

The splendor of the Dukes of Burgundy : After the heavy woolen robes of the monks are the rich fabrics and jewels of the Dukes of Burgundy. They played a major role in the prestige of the area and placed the name of Burgundy on the European scene.

The Capetian Dukes : it is at the end of the nin th century that Frankish Burgundy became Duchy. It has the cities of Langres, Troyes, Sens, Nevers and Macon. The first branch of the Dukes of Burgundy and the Capetians come on scene. It is they who, in 1+33 (0)31-1362, will layed the foundation of the duchy. The authority and the ducal function therefore remain in the hands of the same family. With strong personalities such as Richard I the Avenger or Henry the Great, Burgundy regained some prosperity. In 1+33 (0)31, the Duke Robert I made Dijon its capital. Under this dynasty the city really took shape : the planning of Suzon, population growth, new walls to encompass the suburbs and municipal charter. The main monuments are positioned : the Ducal Palace, Notre Dame church etc. The Hundred Years War, the Great Plague of 1348 and the effects of the massive earthquake of Basel in 1356, which undermine the monuments and walls of the city, began the end of the reign of the Capetians.

The Dukes of Valois : The duchy returned to the King of France, from the branch of Valois, who then set up his son, Philippe le Hardy in 1363. The young man left Paris to Dijon. He detached from the kingdom of France and led a senior diplomacy : the so called « Grand Dukes of the West » is across all of Europe. By getting married to Margaret de Flandre, Philippe le Hardy, Duke of Burgundy and son of Jean II le Bon, brought many Flemish artists to his courtyard. Desiring to ensure his family has a burial worthy of its name, he built the Chartreuse Champmol. On the death of Philippe le Hard, the duchy was ruined; this does not prevent his successor, Jean sans Peur, to start a merciless war against the Orleans, a war whose outcome is marked by a thundering conflict between Burgundians and Armagnacs, for the benefit of English people during the Hundred Years War. It was while seeking the favors of the future Roi Charles VII that Jean sans Peur was assassinated in 1419. Wishing to avenge his father, Philippe le Bon then joins the English until the Treaty of Arras, where the Duke revives with the king, enriching, while still in it, its Holland territory, Flanders, Hainault, Artois and Luxembourg. On the occasion of his marriage to Isabella of Portugal in 1429, Philippe le Bon founded an order that became famous, that of the Toison d'or. Dreaming of being the new Alexander, the last of the Valois, Charles le Téméraire, will do anything to enlarge its territory. Still at war, a fierce enemy of the King of France Louis XI, he died besieging Nancy XI in 1477. Louis XI annexes then Burgundy and links a part to the crown while the other returns to Maximilian de Habsburg, who married Marie de Bourgogne (daughter of Charles le Téméraire). Philip le Beau the son was born of their union , Charles Quint, resumed, facing François 1er, the fight against the house of France.

From The Renaissance To The Revolution

Burgundy is now attached to the crown, and history tends to get linked with that of the kingdom. With a few exceptions, however, as it will continue to lead independent lives after acquiring Bresse, Bugey and Valmorey. Among the many governors of Burgundy, Conde (until the French Revolution) will equip the region with a rich architectural heritage. Burgundy is a wise province applied to portray in his land, the splendor of the architecture in Paris and Versailles.

Dijon boasts of the presence of a parliament that takes possession of the old palace of the Dukes. Beaune, permanently relegated to second in the city of the region, see the first hatch of the wealthy wine trading companies.Nobility of the robe, Bourgeois elite : inner circle that passes control of the sumptuous mansions. The historic heart of Dijon is full of these constructions. Beaune, Auxerre and Nevers are more subtle, but nevertheless possess some remarkable buildings.

From the revolution to the 21st century

The nineteenth century and the industrial revolution. During the French Revolution in Burgundy, there were relatively riots and just a few heads fell, while several representatives of the active lawyer circles in the course of the agitation amounted to Paris where they succeeded financially. In 1790 the departments were created; it is now the new administrative districts. The Dijon Member of Parliament, André Arnoult, representing the third state, will cause the name of Côte-d'Or, led by the idea of assimilating « « vineyard produces to the most precious metal ». In Yonne, calmness prevailed and aided the economic reconstruction of the country. The proximity of Paris and freight on the river Yonne allow the department to be a sort of granary and wood reserve for the capital. This is the heyday of floaters. They are transported by the timber water way of Morvan, the Auxerrois wines, the Tonnerre, Chablis and Avallon, and also new crops such as sugar beet. The Yonne Canal was completed in 1832 and two years later, the Nivernais Canal was inaugurated, joining the Loire and the Yonne. Another great water way awaited, was the Burgundy Canal, whose construction began in 1775. Finally, it connected the Seine to the Saône in 1832. The first boats had hardly used the waterway when a new mode of transport erupted in France and in the region. This is the railway. In 1851 the Dijon train station was inaugurated with great pomp in the presence of Louis-Napoleon Bonaparte, Dijon is now connected to Paris. This transport revolution accompanied and supported the growth of the economy of this century.

It is the culmination of mines and factories in Saône-et-Loire, Le Creusot and Montceau-les Mines in mind. The discovery of a coal deposit at Creusot in 1502, marks the starting point of the metallurgical operation, which the Schneider family associated its name four centuries later. From the sixteenth to eighteenth centuries, coal mining was done as outcrops. It was not until 1769, when the concession granted by Louis XV to François de la Chaise, for a large scale rational exploitation to begin. In 1782, under the patronage of the king, the royal Fonderie was built in Le Creusot, supplied with fuel by coal. Requisitioned during the Revolution, the Royal Foundry is operated on behalf of the Nation. But after the signing of the peace in 1815, only coal mining continued. In 1833, an award puts Creusot factories in the hands of Schneider brothers. These would make major changes : the reputation of the plants became significant and coal production doubled. In the interest of constant performance, Schneider is the first to use a steam locomotive for bulky transportation. As from 1888, Schneider created large artillery workshops for export of war material, and installed electricity workshops in Creusot.

As the end of the century is approached, other companies were now talking about them and their reputation quickly goes beyond the borders of Burgundy in Dijon particularly, it must now rely on Terrot and Cie Company, which manufactures bicycles, motorcycles, and very soon automobiles. Yet it is a model of local competitors, Cottereau, who in 1900 broke the world record speed of 100, in one forty-four minutes. But the nineteen th century also includes periods of unrest. Besides the importance of the Franco- Prussian conflict, the second half of the century suffered the epidemic of phylloxera, which ravaged all the vineyards of France. Burgundy vines were gradually and inexorably affected. The plants could only be saved by grafting healthy plants from America. The landscape is heavily modified. Surfaces were significantly reduced : the wine lost in quantity to gain quality wine. The plants will no longer be held « in group », but in strictly aligned rows. Times were changing for Burgundy wine. The affected wineries were to be retrained and be found the opportunity to develop a culture that previously represented a booster emerging economy of crème de cassis.

The Terrot factories in Dijon. In seventy years of existence, the brand Dijon radiated in the world. The plant opened in 1887 and the mode of transport being by bicycling, Charles Terrot, a young entrepreneur, manufactured bikes ! Followed by other vehicles. After the turmoil of the First World War, productions restarted : Terrot was at this time a model plant, a symbol of power, quality and sporting success. The building lines show the ambitions and the politics of the factory : both modernism and rationalizing tasks.

Nowadays

The two wars have affected the region, which began a policy of reconstruction and development in the early fifties. Dijon definitely takes precedence over the other Burgundian cities.

In 1964, the four departments are grouped into a new entity, the HKSAR. The headquarters of the Burgundy region will be located in the former capital of the Dukes.

These twenty-five years, the region has developed logically, assuming its role as an economic and cultural hub. The transport network is adapted to the requirements of the time. Its location makes the region a hub of communication. She is well endowed in terms of road, motorway and rail network but with important differences depending on the country of Burgundy. The TGV crosses Burgundy for nearly 30 years (TGV Dijon in 1981). Air traffic is concentrated around the activity of the Dijon-Bourgogne Airport far ahead its competitors, airfields of Auxerre Branches, Nevers-Fourchambault and Chalon-Champforgueil. Dijon, the capital of Burgundy, has established a theater in exceptional acoustics, the Auditorium, inaugurated in 1998.

Several Burgundy politicians of origin or by adoption with François Mitterrand in mind, who ruled the country between 1981 and 1995, marked the destiny of France. Pierre Bérégovoy was mayor of Nevers and the Prime Minister; Robert Poujade Mayor for almost thirty years of Dijon; Jean-Pierre Soisson Auxerre; Dominique Perben in Chalon-sur-Saône and François Rebsamen in Dijon. For a longtime very discreet on the sporting spectrum, Burgundy is now talking about it, in particular thanks to the AJ Auxerre and to the FC Gueugnon.

A concerns research and training, the University of Burgundy is implanted in Dijon, but has several branches throughout the region. Today it offers nearly 400 degrees and increases its international openness. Among the big schools present in Burgundy, note among others, ENSBANA (National School of Applied Biology on Food and Nutrition), the ENESAD (National Institution of Higher Education in Agriculture at Dijon) or even the ISAT (National Institute of Transportation and Automobile). Burgundy therefore focused on the future, while retaining the legacy of its historical heritage, which actively supports the development of tourism in the region. Conservation areas, pedestrian streets, museums, open-air museums : the region has repeatedly played a pioneering role. To those who visit it to appreciate the wealth and diversity.

Cultural Heritage

Artists in Burgundy. If the animal sculptor Pompon appears in the lead, the new art did not fail to leave some traces here and there in Burgundy before settling there in modern and contemporary art. Burgundy, remember, and perhaps especially the Yonne, has become a mecca for artists who find both the space for the creative act, and the necessary calm for its emergence, and also the proximity of Paris and more affordable rents : one of the finest examples is probably the Bruyère farm at Parly, not far from Auxerre, where prints of Alechinsky, Soulages, Texier etc. among others, are made.

Contemporary art. The Consortium in Dijon radiates contemporary art throughout the Cote-d'Or, relying on partners who founded this association.
This flexibility in the structures allows it to follow better the diffuse paths taken by the artists of our time. By means of activism,
The Consortium has been able to build a collection of first order, which was invited in prestigious museums in large European cities : the Georges Pompidou center in Paris or Seville. Also in Cote-d'Or, and in the Ouche valley this time, take a stroll in the gardens of Barbirey-sur-Ouche among crops : vegetables, horticultural or contemporary art, dance and ephemeral installations ... in all, eight acres of gardens and greenery are dedicated to creation. The municipalities and gardens dates from the seventeenth and eighteenth centuries and the mansion rebuilt in the nineteen th century, introduce us to the work of contemporary artists.

Other centers of contemporary art of Côte-d'oriens. the Atheneum university cultural center in Dijon, Dijon Nü Koza (art gallery and art library), Factory in Dijon (former factory, alternative pole for concerts and exhibitions managed by the Consortium), the Espace autogéré de Tanneries à Dijon (former factory, squat artists) FRAC also in Dijon (Regional Fund for Contemporary Art), Art and Materials in Saulieu (artists' association) the Porcherie à Ménetreux-le-Pitois (venue for exposition and experimentation of contemporary art), Art'Planète in Nuits- Saint- Georges (contemporary art and raw art festival), Château de Chassagne- Montrachet in the Côte de Beaune (venue for exposition that for information which also makes wine !). And more on the website : www.dijonart.com.

The Art Centre for Schématism movement. Going to Yonne in the charming village of Walnut-sur-Serein. It is in a building of the fifteen th century at the de l'Hôtel de Ville square which paid tribute to this avant-garde movement born at the dawn of the sixties. Part of the technological and structuralist of his time, the schematic divert the laws of functional graphics and visual electronics. Thus, arrows, cartridges and executives entirely became objects of artistic language. It is better to go on site (or call ✆ +33 (0)3 86 67 65).

Dijon – Half-timbered houses on place François-Rude.

Architectural Heritage

The region, in addition to its hundred museums, has more than 2,000 monuments on its four departments, among which there are nearly 600 churches, 320 castles, 100 buildings, 200 old houses, 80 monastic establishments, 280 sites, 22 archaeological sites, 20 hotel-Dieu, 12 factories and many gardens. Three sites are listed as World Heritage by UNESCO, namely Fontenay Abbey, Basilica of Vézelay and the priory site of La Charité-sur-Loire. Beaune and Paray-le-Monial are classified as city of art; others have the title of City of Art and History : Autun, Auxerre, Chalon-sur-Saône, Cluny, Joigny, Nevers, Dijon and La Charité-sur-Loire. Finally, the site of Mount Beuvray is honored as qualifier country of art and history.

Towns & Villages

- **Prehistory :** Valuable evidence can be seen in the caves of Arcy-sur-Cure and Saint-Moré, in Yonne, on the site of Solutré and Chassey-le-Camp in Saône-et-Loire.

- **Antiquity :** For the Yonne, the principal concern remains the Fontaines Salées, near Saint-Père-sous-Vezelay, the archaeological site of Cora near Saint-Moré. The Gallo-Roman museum of Sens and Auxerre have the status of excavations in the department.

For the Côte-d'Or, the site of Alesia Alise-Sainte-Reine is of prime importance. Archaeological museums of Dijon and the Museum of Country chatillonnais have rare coins, including the famous Vix vase.Autun, Saône-et-Loire, is in itself a real in situ evidence of a Gallo-Roman villa with its Roman theater and Saint-André and Arroux doors are the remains of the temple of Janus and its lapidary museum. See the Gallic oppidum of Bibracte on Mont Beuvray and the site Compierre in the Nièvre.

Castles

- **The feudal architecture.** The Middle Ages saw the flowering of new forms of architecture, such as the feudal architecture. In Yonne, it illustrates the fortifications of Villeneuve-sur-Yonne, the Chastellux-sur-Cure castles, Châtel-Girard and Druyes-les-Belles-Fontaines are to be discovered. Côte-d'Or, there is a trace of feudal architecture in parts of the Ducal Palace in Dijon, and in the castles of Châteauneuf, Rochepot, Mont -Saint -Jean-la-Thoizy Berchère, Antigny- la-Ville and Montbard. But these fortifications of Semur -en- Auxois are undoubtedly the best example.

In Saône-et-Loire, they are probably fortifications of Berzé-le-Châtel that best illustrate this feudal architecture. The Gothic will also leave its mark on the Burgundian religious architecture. The Synodal Palace of Sens and the Hospital of Tonnerre are beautiful examples in Auxerre. In Côte -d'Or, the gothic civil architecture gave us the Hotel des Ducs de Bourgogne and Hotel-Dieu de Beaune (with the polyptych of the Last Judgment of Van der Weyden, a sign of the Flemish influence arts of the time).

- **The Renaissance.** With the Renaissance, religious architecture undergoes a number of changes, including those made by the flamboyant style then in vogue in northern Burgundy. However, it is civil architecture which then developed mainly with its wooden houses, hotels and some stone castles such as Ancy-le-Franc, which definitively breaks with the style of feudal architecture previously in effect. Among the jewels of the Renaissance art, Yonne can be proud of its churches of Sautour Neuvy-Saint-Florentin and Cravant, its archiepiscopal palace of Sens, its old houses of Joigny, Auxerre and Noyers and, finally, its Tanlay and Vallery castles (the famous castle of Condé) of Fleurigny. Côte-d'Or is not left out since you can admire the church of Saint-Michel in Dijon, the Pagny churches, the castle and the chapel Bouton in the heart of Notre- Dame church of Beaune, its Philandrier house in Chatillon-sur -Seine, the hotel de la Mare in Beaune, its courthouse in Dijon, its Flavigny-sur-Ozerain and Seurre old houses and finally the castles of Bussy-le-Grand, Jours and Epoisses. Finally, how can one talk about Renaissance without highlighting the Nièvre and the magnificent Ducal Palace of Nevers, the first Renaissance castle of the long list of castles of the Loire and its magnificent esplanade that runs all long before the palace, offering a wide panorama on the Loire River.

- **Classicism.** the Classical art, from Versailles, is not only expressed at Dijon in the development of the Royale (now the Liberation square) Square, but also in the construction of the palace of the States of Burgundy. It was at this time that many mansions appeared and are still visible in all major cities of the region. The castles are not so far neglected and among the buildings of the seventeenth and eighteenth centuries, it will not fail to mention the castle of Bussy-Rabutin or that of Menou. They will then often be adorned with works of renowned artists such as Bouchardon the sculptor or Greuze and Mignard the painters, originating from Champagne) and host concerts directed by the famous composer Jean-Philippe Rameau, from Dijon origine.

Religious Architecture

- **The Carolingian and pre-Romanesque Church architecture.** The crypt of Saint-Germain-d'Auxerre is among the masterpieces of Carolingian art best known worldwide. In the past, there are those of Sainte-Benign-de-Dijon, those of the abbey of Sainte-Reine in Flavigny-sur-Ozerain, those of the church of Tournus and Hagia Vorles Châtillon- sur-Seine.

- **The Romanesque art.** Regarding religious architecture, Romanesque buildings are recognizable by their large sanctuary preceded by a narthex decorated with big tops and a storied tympanum. The Churches of Sainte-Madeleine de Vezelay, Saint-Lazare d'Avallon and Auxerre St. Eusebius are among the finest examples of the architecture in the Yonne.

The Yonne certainly has a Cistercian building, and it is of extreme beauty : it is the Pontigny Abbey.

Côte-d'Or is also rich in Romanesque buildings. Among the best known are, Saint-Philibert de Dijon, Saint-Pierre and Saint-Nicolas de Châtillon-sur-Seine, Notre-Dame de Beaune and Saint Jean de Til-Châtel. Like Yonne, Côte-d'Or only lists one Cistercian building, classified as World Heritage by UNESCO : the Abbey of Fontenay.

Cote-Saône-et-Loire, lets first of all mention the cathedral of Autun (whose portal has been restored), and then the Abbey of the Cluny and Tournus churches, Paray-le-Monial and Anzy-le-Duke of Semur-en-Brionnais, Bourbon-Lancy, Bois-Sainte-Marie, of Champaize and Uchizy Brancion, Berzé-la-Ville, Montceaux, Iguerande and Chateauneuf. The Nièvre finally houses two jewels of the Romanesque art with the La Charité-sur-Loire and Saint-Etienne's church sites in Nevers. Do not miss to also evoke the beautiful small Cluniac churches that dot the surrounding region, such as the Béard, Rouy Garchizy or Saint-Saulge buildings.

The Gothic art : Among the finest Gothic icaunais buildings, we must mention the cathedrals Saint- Etienne (and treasure) of Auxerre and Sens, the Abbey of Saint-Germain of Auxerre, the churches of Saint-Pierre d'Auxerre, Notre Dame Thunder, those of Villeneuve-sur-Yonne, Chablis, Saint-Julien-du- Sault, Saint-Père-sous-Vezelay and Toucy, Appoigny and Saint-Bris-le-Winey (murals), Montreal and Chitry.
In Côte-d'Or, the finest specimens of this style are the St. Benign cathedrals of Dijon and Saint-Vincent de Chalons-sur-Saône, Chartreuse Champmol (the Well of Moses of Claude Sluter) of Dijon church, the Notre-Dame de Dijon (remarkable murals paints), Saint-Nicolas de Châtillon-sur-Seine, Saint-Genest Flavigny-sur-Ozerain, and those of Saint-Seine l'Abbaye Saint-Thibault and Semur-en-Auxois, Seurre and Auxonne, Rouvres-en-Plaine, Talant and Vitteaux.Similarly, in Saône-et-Loire, we can admire the Saint-Vincent Cathedral Chalon-sur-Saône and the churches of Cluny and Cuisery, not to mention the frescoes of Clayette and Paray-le-Monial. Nièvre is not left to offer tourists fine examples of Gothic art, like the Saint-Cyr-et-Sainte-Julitte cathedral which dominates Nevers and its old neighborhoods, like the collegiate church of Saint-Martin, a gothic jewel, anchored in the heart of old Clamecy.

Highway Structures

On the side architectural side, neoclassicism leaves its mark, especially that of Nicolas Ledoux, a visionary architect to whom we owe the salines of Arc-et-Senan and also the Church of St. Bartholomew in Cruzy-le-Châtel in Yonne. Industrial architecture then takes over; Burgundy is also the birthplace of Gustave Eiffel, to whom we owe the famous tower, built according to the principle of the lattice truss for the Universal Exhibition of 1889.

TRADITIONS & WAYS OF LIFE

Language

Language geography in France is complex and it doesn't overlap the boundaries of the various administrative divisions of the region or department.
Events, passageways, landscapes have contributed to the development of a common identity in the heart of the famous Duchy. The Burgundian dialect is born around Dijon and the Côte-d'Or countries.
There is evidence to the east of the territory of the Yonne as east of Nièvre. It is also found north of the Saône-et-Loire. Similarly, it crosses the borders to fade into the Haute-Marne, around the countryside of Langres, and in Franche-Comté.
Other influences come, like that of climate, to moderate the accents of the local dialect. The words of northern Yonne take the color of neighboring Champagne. Those of the Nivernais plain and the Puisaye have more to do with those in the center of France than Dijon.

The Burgundian accent... It will once again be necessary to draw from the heritage of Henri Vincenot to find the good description.
« The way to put rocks in the mouth and develop words. These bearings, these languor, coming straight out of the ground and drawing their roots as the vine stocks from the vineyard. »
In his book The Daily Life of Burgundian peasants at the time of Lamartine, Henry Vincenot traces the portrait of the little lame messenger, a door-to-door sales person who fought campaigns here and elsewhere at that time.
In his book The Daily Life of Burgundian peasants at the time of Lamartine, Henry Vincenot traces the portrait of the little lame messenger, a door-to-door sales person who fought campaigns here and elsewhere at that time.

Arts & Crafts

The Nevers Earthenware. The origin of Nevers earthenware is situated in the second half of the fifteen th century, thanks to the artistic patronage and the intervention of the Duke of Nevers who invited the Italian ceramists to settle in the city; not to mention the presence of raw materials on the Nivernais soil, the proximity to sources of energy for the furnaces (the Morvan wood) and inland waterways promoting the commercialization of production. Nowadays, the Art Potters Nevers perpetuate this artistic tradition, while providing for some, a more contemporary approach. By refusing industrialization, but allowing mass production, they chose the manual production of essentially artistic earthenware.

The stoneware from Puisaye. Land of woods and forests, the Puisaye is, by the nature of its subsoil, rich in clay and is a land of choice for pottery. For several centuries, the working of the sandstone has shaped the local life. This favorable environment and the importance of pottery tradition inspired some artists to settle in Puisaye at the end of the nineteen th century. Marked by Japonisme and Art Nouveau, they developed around their master Jean Carries (1855-1894) an active artistic movement for nearly seventy years, geared towards decorative and innovative creations.

The Pressure cooker. At the pantheon of departmental trademarks, add what is now a famous generic product : the pressure cooker ! It is at Selongey, a few kilometers north of Dijon, in 1953, that the Société d'Eboutissage de Bourgogne (the famous SEB, a French consortium that produces small appliances) launched on

© JULIA VALENTIN

The cabrette and the accordion are part of the Burgundian folklore.

the market, a new product that will literally revolutionize the lives of the household. The invention meets the favor of open markets context of the Trente-Glorieuses, came out with the first edition of the must-see publication of Françoise Bernard, Les Trois cents recettes spéciales Cocotte-minute (Three hundred pressure cooker special recipes)...

The vanished tiles, a present for the dukes of Burgundy. The roofs with their colorfu geometric patterns print a strong image in the memory of travelers who discover the Côte-d'Or. Yellow, green, red, black, brown and gold, terracotta glazed tiles also brighten many buildings along the route of the great wines of Meursault in Dijon, from Beaune to Rochepot, whether castles, religious buildings, mansions , civil hospices or even unpretentious homes. Among the roofs to which it is essential to look at, are Hotel-Dieu de Beaune, Hotel de Vogue and the St. Benign Cathedral in Dijon, the castle of Rochepot and the City Hall Meursault.

The Bresse furniture. On the left bank of the Saône, the Bresse style from the baroque inspiration, is characterized by the systematic use of two different types of wood in general, the elm associated with a fruit tree, the first being for the panels and the second for building.

This technique is highly reminiscent of the achievements of German cabinetmakers of the eighteen th century. The typical cabinet has doors to the inspired by « Louis XIV » strengthening its archaic appearance. Cabinet doors seem to be the latest and feet are often curved. The Bressan style has developed a taste for composed furniture such as cabinets and sideboard-clocks.The diverse and dynamic marks of furniture add bright colors, all forming an original baroque style.

The Sennecey style : In the words of the Old Comrades, the resemblance between the Sennecey furniture and those of Provence is quite normal; the Sennecey-le-Grand style was created by comrades from Midi while making their Tour de France. What about reality ? It is certain that it is less obvious. Called a « great Coulomb » brought back from Midi a sideboard with two ancient sides, and installed it in the cafe run by his wife. That's when Claude Petit, a companion set in Sennecey, was inspired to achieve, in 1834, the first Sennecey cabinet. Its rather dynamic and vigorous mark is tempered by the softness of a bright walnut tree and the sobriety of a richly ornamented decor. This style was a smash hit with the wealthy rural population in search of originality and character. Thousands of furniture were then produced of this model and that, until the late nineteen th century when the rural exodus and the arrival of manufactured goods contributed to the end of production.

Traditional Houses

The winegrower's house : Present where vines have been established : the Côte des Vins, Basse Bourgogne winery (Yonne) and even Auxois and the plain of the Saone. Composed of one place when the winemaker is poor, the house is built on an underground cellar or an accessible walk-in pantry. The house then serves as an attic. The house is accessed by a few degrees or a stone staircase, sometimes covered with a canopy or a gallery that can occupy the entire wall.

The farmer's house : It has an equally strong but more complex architecture. The home no longer consists of a single level, but a whole floor dedicated to the farmer or small notable staying in the house; the lower part of the house is for labor. Access to the first level is via a staircase attached to the facade, covered wholly or in part, and whose variations distinguish each building. It is often in stone and sometimes shelters a chicken poultry, a niche or an apprentice.

For the record, note that in the Charolais mainly, are found houses flanked by one or two turns to the use of dovecot, a sign of notability.

LOCAL FOOD & GOURMET PRODUCTS

Local Specialities

Truffles

Burgundy truffle became a popular gourmet product with the chain of its production organized, whether in the wild or in plantations. There are more and more restaurants offering menus with truffles.

Many actors working in Burgundy for the promotion of the truffles as one already made by the other regions of France. On can mention the Brotherhood of Burgundy Truffle Is-sur-Tille which has always been one of his favorite places of preference for truffle since as texts dating back to the fourteen th century describe it as one of the main sources of supply for the royal tables. Nothing else but that !

The Association La Truffe side-d'orienne, www.truffe-bourgogne.fr, which is the relay of the truffles Producers' Union of Côte d'Or, unites the organization of this sector in terms of its recognition by national and interregional bodies. Multiple research programs are ongoing to control its culture and optimize its growth (could be from 15 to 20 years 4 years !) And better still know its molecules. You should know that 80% of truffles come from the natural environment and the number of villages in the canton have places called Truffle attesting to their glorious past, they become current ! Certain private operators passionate about this black gold propose a commercial and very interesting discovery offers. L'Or des Valois or the Maison aux mille truffles et aux Champinions are perfect examples of Côte-de-Nuits.

Basket of fresh truffles.

There is still much to learn from this Uncinatum Tuber, how to grow, to find it with a caveur dog, recognize, prepare or enjoy it.

Burgundian snails

Also called *Helix pomatia*, it seems that this gastropod was valued since prehistoric times in the Burgundian land. Already in Roman times, officials farms provided enthusiasts.Archaeology helps us in gastronomy by providing irrefutable evidences : empty shells were found and dated from the third century. Monks and convents make breeding a specialty, but do not deign to taste their products. This local glory still has its most fervent followers who ensure that the Burgundy snail is not be confused with any other species encountered on the road after rainfall. The caliber of the Burgundy snail is unique and larger than most other species. The shell is yellow with dark bands. The best places to drive out the animals were still not long ago inbetween-row and slopes of vineyards. The use of fertilizers and herbicides did make them flee to the point of reaching a critical situation that led to a regulation of hunting schedules ! It is now most often served in its shell with herb butter, it is at least as its lovers would prefer. Other variations embellish the menu cards the ingenious restaurant owners and stalls of some craftsmen.

Meat, poultry & game

- **The Andouillette sausage of Clamecy and Chablis.** This stuffed hose with chopped intestines is a specialty in both Chablis and Macon, as well Clamecy, another stronghold of the sausage. Traditional made, the sausage is « pulled to the string » and the components scalded, cut into long strips, scraped and prepared. They are then « put in the oven » manually (not at the button) in the oven, the noblest part of the chaudin. Once completed, the sausage cooked in broth between three hours thirty minutes to five hours, according to the establishment. As for the famous letters contiguous « AAAAA » listed in the shelves and restaurant menus, they simply mean : Friendly Club of Lovers of Authentic Andouillette.

- **Charolais meat.** Burgundy is home to white color cow which provides undoubtedly the most famous meat in the world... The Bourguignon belief ! The animal has its cradle, in Saône-et-Loire where, since the eighteen th century, it walks its generous curves in the lush meadows. Livestock is also the mainstay of this country and many cattle fairs, including Saint-Christophe-en-Brionnais reflect the dynamism of this activity. The meat itself is characterized by its excellent slaughter provisions. Lean and slightly marbled, Charolais is sought after by butchers for its lack of fat cover.

Duck and its variations : Whether it is of the barbarism or mularde race, it seems that these animals have found a shelter in Burgundy. Of course, the foie gras have the honors. To realize this, simply go to the Morvan countryside, not far from Saulieu to Mairey in Pascal Laprée, the artisan of talent. Also in the Morvan are very fine products which attract the consumer's attention to choose from : terrines, smoked duck breast, confit, rillettes, and also the duck sausage.

Bresse chicken. Bresse poultry is one of the jewels of Saône-et-Loire. Be careful, all Bresse poultry are not Bresse chicken ! To authenticate, a ring must be affixed to its left leg with the name and address of the producer, a tricolor seal disposed at the base of his neck, not to mention the A.O.C label and seal of authentication for capons and pullets. A good period of rest and « mash » which is served to it will give the gallinacean a flesh with fondant and incomparable finesse. Since 1862, the end of the year is an opportunity to celebrate these fine birds during the Glorieuses competition, held successively in Bourg-en-Bresse, Montrevel Louhans and Pont-de-Vaux.

Fish

Trout and other river fish. There is only wealth in the rivers and lakes of the Yonne and Nièvre ! Trout, char and Arctic char, whitefish, pike and zander bring their flavor to delicious dishes such as the famous pochouse. Note that our beloved rivers see improved many crayfish often used in the local cuisine, like the frogs. Fishes to enjoy, on dish, on the plates of restaurants across or in some locals who offer cooked variations : fillets of smoked trout, fine mousse, rillettes and even poached trout !

Cheese & dairy products

The cîteaux. In 1930, the Cistercians opened a cheese factory to bring more money. The monks currently produce 55 tonnes per year. It is a great success for cheese that has nothing special, except the inimitable aroma of grazing nearby.

The Chavignol goat cheese. Since 1976 AOC, the only cheese made from raw goat milk has its origins in the Sancerre soil. Offering an infinite variety of flavors depending on its maturity, it goes very well with a Pouilly-Fumé or Coteau-du- Giennois from the same terroir.

The Cosne. Made exclusively in the Farm near Port-Aubry close to Cosne-sur-Loire in the Nièvre, this fine cheese from goat's milk has a homogeneous creamy and dense flesh.

The Nivernais : Typically Nivernais produce, the cheese made from unpasteurized cow's milk offers its marbled-like heavy cream, giving it an exceptional tender character.

Epoisses de Bourgogne. Cheese for the less tenacious. This is an AOC since 1991. Cheese from cow's milk is refined by marc de Bourgogne. Its color is orange, its fragrance, especially its consistency, is smooth and soft. It is the oldest and most famous cheeses of the region. The court of Louis XIV swore by it. Production returned back to more traditional methods in the 70s. The syndicate defending Epoisses of the Auxois country was founded in 1989. Its cousins are Chambertin and ami Chambertin. The Aisy Cendré is an époisses that is refined with wood ash.

Snails.

The nuits-saint-georges. Prepared with cow's milk. Its typicality and smoothness is surprising. It cannot be considered without being accompanied by a glass of wine : Local wine that is more than recommended !

The pierre-qui-vire : This cow's milk cheese from the department of Yonne is produced by the monks of the abbey of the same name. It is appreciated for its soft paste and for its washed rind refined in wet cellar after drying for about two months.

The soumaintrain. From Yonne origin, it is a whole milk, cheese in natural lactic fermentation, soft paste, washed-rind, which, after refining, takes a nice shade between honey yellow and orange-brown. It has a strong smell (especially in summer), but soft in the mouth. This already famous cheese played the role of currency exchange to pay rents or taxes in the middle Ages. The Groupement des producteurs de fromage soumaintrain was created in 1991 with three objectives : To safeguard production, definition of criteria for the production and promotion, obtaining an AOC. The soumaintrain now has a generic brand, « sousmaintrain terrior d'Armance » at the crossroads of several natural areas and departmental entities. Collection, production and refining areas were defined based on historical traces of production and the geology of the area.

The gougère. Spread throughout Burgundy, this is basically a choux pastry, to which is added before cooking, diced comté from the neighboring region of Franche-Comté. This detail highlights the rivalry between these two countries who both claim the kinship of the gougère. Small bacon or diced ham can complement this preparation. The gougère also serves as a base for starters such as profiteroles snails to noilly -prat. Another suggestion was that of a soup, broth, spices, herbs and garlic, sprinkled with herbs at the last moment, on which is deposited three small cheese puffs fresh from the oven.

Fruits & vegetables

Blackcurrant. It was not until the nineteen th century that the culture grows with the popularity of blackcurrant liqueur and its alter ego, white currant. Also add the effects of phylloxera that ruined many winemakers who have to seek other means of livelihood, including the culture of the bay. This is m. Joly, distiller of his state, who developed the recipe for black currant liqueur. The beginnings are difficult, but the character is smart and knows how to provide buyers a wide range of diversified products : double cassis and fine liqueur or superfine. In recent years, two Dijon houses came to compete with the famous houses of Lhéritier Guyot and Lejay – Lagoute . The culture of the bay was thriving at the beginning of the 1870s. Nearly a million feet in the department is counted. Five companies currently share the market and more than ten million liters come from of them about 80% of French production. Nuits- Saint- Georges and Dijon are the two capitals of the small fruit, both host respectively the Vedrenne and Lejay – Lagoute companies.

The Cherry marmot. A symbol of the Auxerrois. A fleshy and sweet cherry, a hybrid variety, a fruit of chance and mixture of two types of cherries. Sharing the same ground and the same slopes as grape vines, the cherry enjoy the same favorable conditions and have experience related to the development of the vine. Orchards began to increase in the mid- nineteen th century after the creation of a Laroche Auxerre railway, which greatly facilitated trade with Paris. The great era of cherry Yonne really began at the end of the nineteen th century. The establishment of new lines of railway and road improvements contributed to this growth, but the phylloxera crisis significantly reoriented the farms.

Onions of Val de Saône : Around the Pontailler-sur-Saône and Auxonne regions. The bulb is the subject of several culinary variations as the well-known summer soup and also activities like the onion parties, with of course, the peeling contest that attracts between 5000 and 6000 people each year.

Oils, spices & condiments

Mustard. A mixture of husked grain, milled, sieved and grape juice, and this condiment finds Côte-d'Or an enabling environment : land enriched with potash for the plant, vineyards and a sufficiently rich aristocracy to eat meat all days. At the table of the Dukes of Burgundy, it is appreciated for its taste and for its digestive and antiseptic virtue. The leaders of the duchy, aware of the success of this condiment, use it for diplomatic purposes. In addition to official giveaways during the time, Philippe le Hardi affix on the crest of Dijon the same inscription as on the stoneware pots « Moult me tarde ». Because of commercial success and already counterfeiting, manufacturing was then regulated from 1390. In the seventeen th century the vinegar and mustard Corporation of Dijon was created under the patronage of St. Vincent. Production goes to industrial production in the nineteen th century. About twenty mustard-makers shared the market. In 1867, their specialty is presented at the universal Fair. The seeds are no longer provided by the surrounding land for a long time now. Providers live in Bombay, India, Sicily, Calabria and Bari in Strasbourg. The production processes are permanently fixed by decree in 1937. The term does not refer to a terroir notion, but to a trademark, a mixture of vinegar, white wine and grape juice from green raisins watering the wisely sorted grains. There are now a variety of mustards. That of Dijon is the joy of experts who appreciate its strength.

Sweets

The Anise of Flavigny. It was not until the French Revolution that the productions of the Ursuline convent of Flavigny-sur-Ozerain, Côte-d'Or, had a stronger reputation. Despite the competition (including that of Verdun), the Grand Larousse dictionary then only recognizes one real and true anise : that of Flavigny. If techniques have evolved, ingredients, preparations remain the same. And it is always at the Abbey that they are made. Defects are blacklisted through a rigorous screening. One centimeter in diameter and five grams of weight ! If the final dominance is always the same, flavorings (natural) can vary, violet, mint, licorice, coffee, rose, orange blossom, jasmine, mandarin...

Biscuits from Chablis or Duchy biscuits. Rectangular, light and crunchy biscuits, these Yonne cookies have a vanilla sweetness. The neighboring Côte-d'Or region widely broadcast these sweets which accompany with delight champagne and mulled wine.

accès direct à la plage
bar
blanchisserie
climatisation
discothèque
distributeur d'argent
eau potable
équitation
espace fumeurs
établissement non-fumeurs
fitness
golf miniature
handicap malentendant
handicap malvoyant
handicap mental
handicap moteur
jardin ou parc
jeux
lave-linge / laverie
location de vélos
magasin d'alimentation
navette aéroport
pêche
piscine intérieure

The cassissine. It is a paste of black currant fruits with a liquid heart based liqueur, which can be obtained at Dijon.

The Nougatine and the Negus of Nevers. Invented by Jean-Louis Bourumeau in the nineteen th century, the nougatine was made famous by the Empress Eugénie, who on her returned from a trip to Nevers Napoleon III in 1862 was conquered by its delicate taste and placed a large order. As the Negus is the GRELIER House that we owe the creation in 1902 of the toffee chocolate encased in baked sugar in honor of the official visit to the ducal city, of the ruler of Ethiopia.

The Baratin and Chi dans iau of Clamecy. Emmanuel Portal continues the tradition of Baratin specialty composed of two almond meringues rested on a praline cream and created by Mr. Barat, pastry at Clamecy last century. As for Chi in iau, is an original creation composed of a sweet nougat , almonds, pistachios, candied oranges, all wrapped in a black sequined. The name is a tribute to floats of Clamecy, which has not commodities on rafts, floats above water to satisfy...

Gingerbread. It is primarily Reims which prides itself on providing « Boichets » and other « pain de Gaulderge » of a much better quality. It was not until the nineteen th century that Dijon took off. The Houses of Mulot Cergy Petitjean, Auger, Boucher, Bourgeois, Couturier, Loidreau, Rondot, Michelin, Guilleminot (honey bread) and that of Veuve Agron contribute to the success. The consecration was formalized in 1900 by the Grand Encyclopedia : « In France, the Gingerbread most famous for its finesse is that of Dijon. » The war of 1914-1918, destroying Reims industries, was leaving the field open to the Côte-d'Or. The rye or wheat flour, honey and spices, each major has its own recipe, and a lot of mystery...

Alcohol & Spirits

Alcohol, brandies & liquors

Kir. The aperitif par excellence in Côte- d'Or ! Used since the last century in the taverns where the blackcurrant was used to make any poor quality wine drinkable, it becomes the prerogative of local politicians who rise to the rank of official drinks of banquets and electoral campaigns.
This is the Canon Kir, who took over the recipe to his own account up to signing a contract with a manufacturing house. The « rinse pig » debuts , then the cocktail takes its current name, the kir , and even enters the dictionary of common names of Petit Larousse in 1976. For the Bourguignon kir, use a flat-bottomed glass. First pour the crème de cassis then the white wine (usually a white grape) in the following proportions : 1/3 and 2/3. However, there are other compositions inspired by this mixture. The Communards : same but with red wine and this time add blackcurrant.

The Pomace (Marc) and Ratafia. Marc is eau-de-vie produced with pressed grapes residues. With an Amber color it is consumed as a digestive. This alcohol has about 40 % alcohol by volume. It is not uncommon to find it on some vintage tables, after meals, with coffee, specimens without labels which you can easily add an additional 20 % conservative estimate ! Marc is made after the harvest or winter. It is allowed to age in oak barrels. Ratafia is a mixture of grape juice, Must and Pomace. Some call it the « riquiqui », perhaps because it is twice as strong as the eau-de-vie ... to be consumed with moderation.

Burgundian Wines

History of the Burgundian wine

Burgundian wine or the longest reign in history. Burgundy, Bordelais and Champagne carry worldwide the renowned prestigious wines of France. Since the earliest times, the history of Burgundy is linked to the land and particularly the vine. Here are a few lines a brief summary of the history of Burgundy wine, which is also the tens of generations attached to their land.

A history dating back to the first century of our era. « Burgundy wine ensures the longest reign in history, » says Raymond Dumay. If the origin of the vineyard in Burgundy is very old, the date of birth of the Burgundy vineyard remains unclear. However, Columella and Strabo speak of the existence of the Burgundy vineyard with certainty in the first century of our era. The oldest text which show the presence of the vine and wine in Burgundy dates back to 312.

Vignoble & Découvertes Label

Launched in 2009, the Vineyards and Discoveries label aims to promote tourism on the theme of wine and vine. It is awarded for a period of 3 years by the ministers responsible for tourism and agriculture, on the recommendation of the Superior Council of wine tourism at a destination for tourism and wine offering a range of multiple and complementary tourism products (accommodation, catering, winery visit and tasting, museum, event, ...) and allowing the client to facilitate the organization of your stay and guide on qualified services and quality.
For tourism professionals and wine, this label should improve the readability of their offer which remains difficult to access due to the multiplicity of products and designations; increase visitation and tourism consumption through this factor of attractiveness; and develop tourism market for the wine industry.
In Burgundy it was granted the Hill of Corton, the Hill of Montrachet, the axis of Dijon-Côte-de-Nuits and Chablis vineyards.

A vineyard of Côte-d'Or.

This is a tax advocacy for the emperor written by Eumenes, president of the University of Augustodunum (Autun), which forms the Gallo-Roman elite. This Autun citizen makes the description of Beaune vineyard. In the six th century, Gregory de Tours saw Dijon surrounded by vineyards. Wine replaces Celtic beer.

The predominant role of the monks. At the beginning of the second millennium, aristocrats and religious communities represent the majority of the owners of vineyards. It is the activity of the Benedictine and Cistercian monks that linked the real development of the quality of Burgundy wine. For the sake of perfection, the monks carefully studied everything that could contribute to improving quality : size, cuttings, and grafting and also winemaking methods. However, their greatest contribution was made by the development of the concept of « climate". By creating enclosed plots, the monks gave the wines of Burgundy their identity. By building cellars, abbeys have played a key role in the development of the vineyard.

This same wine served at the table of popes and kings quickly became synonymous with hospitality and prestige.

A fashionable drink in the court of the Dukes. At the end of the fourteen th century, we witnessed the marriage of Philip of Valois, the first Duke of Burgundy, with Marguerite de Flandre. The court of the Dukes particularly appreciate the wines of Burgundy, called at the time « vin de Beaune « and thus contributes to promote its renown that has spread to all countries of the world. Between the same century and the end of the following, Burgundy became a powerful, prosperous and fully independent state of the kingdom of France.

A dynamic trade in search of identity. In the eighteen th century, trading is organized by improving the road network that will greatly facilitate trade especially with Paris and also with the rest of the world through major European ports. This is followed by a dynamic evolution, firstly on wine maturation that occurs in new oak barrels, and secondly with the appearance of the bottle in 1750, which is accompanied by a production of wines with longer care.

This century is dedicated to science : seeking to understand the excellent wine of Burgundy. Is it the soil, sub – soil, climatic events, grape or human influence ? Father Claude Arnoux published in London in 1728 the first book devoted to Burgundy. He does not just describe the vineyards, he explains the best wines from every village already sold under the name of the designation of their country. The vocabulary of tasting appears. The color, the aromas, the taste became increasingly accurate.

How Burgundy supplanted the Champagne... deprived of river outlet carrier, the Burgundy winegrowers work quality by giving the wine a new less austere value and open to export, enabling a higher price for wine than that of transportation. Be calm, wine of the champagne is the only rival of Burgundy wine. Chosen as a physician to Louis XIV (1693), Fagon writes a prescription that prescribes his patient « old Burgundy wine" as dieting wine. Its effects are beneficial. At once the Court drinks burgundy... and abandons champagne. At the same time Claude Brosse, a winemaker in Macon, went to Versailles with his barrels : the pioneer of direct seales !

The first merchants – breeders. To the gourmets-Brokers of old who welcomed and guided the client succeeded at that time the first merchants-breeders present in the Rhin. The upper middle class, the noble got interested in the vineyard and gradually took more monasteries in decline. In 1760, Louis-François de Bourbon, Prince de Conti acquired an enclosed Abbey of Saint-Vivant in Vosne : the Romanée which he illustrates beautifully. Thomas Jefferson visited the vineyards of Burgundy in 1787. He gives the first description by a foreign pen.

Two centuries later, the hierarchy he established remained approved. The first bottles of Burgundy in the basement of the White House are owed to him.

Changes shortly after the Revolution. 1789 had the effect of a bombshell. The church property was confiscated as well as those of some of the nobles, becoming « national » and soon auctioned.
The very important redistribution of the property, especially in the most prominent vineyards, benefits from the Burgundy bourgeoisie or the Parisian speculators. A page is turned, a new one opens. Napoleon admits only Chambertin at his table while also following the advice of his doctors.

Progress and development of Burgundian wines. The nineteen th century is the symbol of progress and development thanks to the opening of the Canal de Bourgogne in 1832 and the creation of the railway track between Paris and Dijon in 1851 with free trade treaties of the Second Empire with Germany, Belgium, Holland and Britain. He also saw the Burgundy express an identity that colors her image : a red wine high in color, opulent, robust; a nobleman, a bon vivant. The first rankings appear (1827, 1831 and especially that of Dr. Lavalle in 1855) : offline, tête de cuvee, premiere cuvée, etc. . . . Each climate is well judged by its heritage and its abilities. The glory of the white wine of extreme Burgundian sensitivity culminated later. In addition, the public auction of the Hospices de Beaune, the first edition of which was held in 1851, contributed effectively to the promotion of the wines of Burgundy.

The dark ages. the merchant-Breeders provided almost all the marketing : it saw its golden age and highly developed export to Russia and America. But in the last quarter of the nineteen th century, the phylloxera (black evil) appeared and devastated everything in its path. We then practiced the transplant, mixing the American root-stock transplants and the old French vine. Far from giving up, the tenants organize, replant vines only on the best soils, and do away with the production of table wine. The phylloxera crisis puts order in the vine. Cooperatives are responsible also to respond to the economic slump of the dark years. Replanting is completed thirty years later, but the landscape has completely changed, all is now intelligently in order.

Direct sales : a response to economic hardship. In the aftermath of the First World War, families and heritage dispersed. Wine was poorly sold. Small wineries bought small parcels of vines. The « Ownership » was born and many important areas today were born during the twenties and thirties. At the end of thirties, and according to economic difficulties, direct selling was developed and it continued to increase its presence on the market by boosting production signed by the domain.

The AOC (appellations d'origine controlée). The most important event of the twentie the century is the official recognition of designations of origin from the thirties, which established rules that really protect the consumer and deeply moralize the market. In 1975, we saw the recognition of the AOC Crémant de Bourgogne that put the excitement in the land. Beaujolais took its autonomy in 1989. A prestigious part of Beaujolais (Moulin-à-vent, saint-amour) however lies in southern Burgundy (canton de la Chapelle-de-Guinchay).

Production of grapes

Soil and climate : The Burgundy vineyard is compared to a huge mosaic made up of many small parcels of vines sometimes enclosed by stone walls. The complex composition of the soil of each area can differ much in the space of just a few meters : its depth, altitude, exposure gives the wine its character with aromatic nuances and special flavors. Burgundy benefits from a continental climate with cold and dry winters and hot, sunny summers, conducive for good pinot grape and chardonnay ripening that are perfectly adapted. When the appellations of origin were instituted during the thirties, each French vineyard chose a point of contact : The Property and the land entity in Bordeaux; the Champagne brand; the varietal grape in Alsace; the Burgundy terroir. What is called the climate in Burgundy is a strictly defined piece of land, recognized for its unique wine properties, applied by the meter, bearing its name for centuries and having one or more localities. Each climate produces its own wine appellation, sometimes in monopoly but often shared by multiple domains. That is the idea of terroir, the most direct and sincere link between the vine and the wine.

Not To Be Missed

SAINT-VINCENT TOURNANTE 2017 À MERCUREY
MERCUREY
www.mercurey2017.fr
From January 28th to January 29th, 2017.
On the initiative of the Confrérie des Chevaliers du Tastevin, a village of the Burgundy wine-growing region has hosted since 1938 the festival of Saint-Vincent Tournante and accommodates the gathering of all the brotherhoods or mutual aid associations of the region. On 28th and 29th January 2017, the city of Mercurey will accommodate Saint-Vincent Tournante. The 80 statues of the Saint Vincent companies will cross the climates and the streets at the time of the processions. Small reminder : on 22nd January, the Saint-Vincent's day, is generally a period of transition between the state of hibernation of the vine and that of the return of the vegetation. By the way, formerly people used to say : « During Saint-Vincent's day, the winter goes away or starts again ». Is that for this reason that the vine growers made Vincent their patron saint ? Is that because in Vincent there is « wine » ? Mystery... On its side, the village of Mercurey is primarily known for its full-bodied and elegant red wines. Produced in small quantity, its white wines are as delicious as these latter. You can taste them on 28th and 29th January 2017 at the two communes of Mercurey and Saint-Martin-sous-Montaigu.

© AM STOCK NATURE

Pinot Noir – Grapes.

This explains the high number of Burgundy AOC, since they express true and strong personalities. Fans know it. They take pleasure in knowing and them, recognizing them. The soil (terroir) unites many climatic factors such as : exposure to the sun and the wind, frost susceptibility, and the effects of the conduct of the vine, etc. . . . The soil and subsoil are the bedrock. It owes much to the geology, but also phenomena such as erosion.

The varietal grape If, since the phylloxera, the indigenous grape uses the strength and roots of an American varietal grape, rootstock, to protect and feed itself, it has not changed and remains similar to what it was before. The term varietal is not a strict botanical unit, but groups of individuals (strains) with a number of common external characters (even the same leaf morphology). The four main Burgundian grape varieties are Pinot Noir, Gamay, Chardonnay and Aligoté.

Pinot Noir. Pinot Noir has been famous for its red wines since the creation of the Burgundy vineyards. It produces compact clusters of purplish-black grapes with small tight grains containing colorless and sweet abundant juice.

Please note : the juice of the pinot noir is colorless; therefore it is vinified differently; the same juice from the same grape is also used for some champagne. In Burgundy, it is at the time of maceration and fermentation in the dye that coloring, contained in the skin of grape berries, gives the wine its lovely red color.

The Gamay. Gamay has borrowed its name from a hamlet of Saint-Aubin, near Puligny-Montrachet. It is mentioned in several texts of the fourteen th century. This is a fairly fertile plant whose grapes are more or less tight depending on the variety. The one that interests us here is the Gamay Noir with white juice which, the granite hills of Beaujolais, produces fine red wines, and pleasant bouquet , while in the clay-limestone soils of the Côte-d'Or it only gives more boorish wines. But this is the plant that red wines of Mâcon and Beaujolais owe their reputation to.

Chardonnay. The Chardonnay is also, for centuries now, a Burgundian plant. We owe it the reputation of great white wines of Côte de Beaune, Côte Chalonnaise, Maconnais and Chablis where it is commonly called Beaune. It produces beautiful golden grapes that are smaller than those of pinot, but more elongated and less tight in clusters. Its grains are small, but rich in white deliciously sweet juice.

Aligoté. Aligoté is an ancient mid-size plant in Burgundy. A strong enough white varietal grape that have larger and more numerous grapes than those of chardonnay and, consequently, its performance is superior. This varietal grape has spread around the land that is not suitable for pinot and chardonnay, but still remained an excellent vineyard land.

The wine it produces is not named after the village where it is grown (one exception : Bouzeron !), but it is legally called Burgundy Aligoté. It may also enter into the composition of Crémant de Bourgogne. Some other varietals of lesser importance are also found in the Auxerrois vineyard, including sauvignon and Caesar. The first produces a white light and fruity wine called Saint-Bris and the second, associated with pinot noir, gives strength and some longevity to the red wine of Irancy appellation.

Sauvignon. This variety acquired its letters of nobility in the early twentie th century following the reconstitution of vineyards after the phylloxera. Boasting of the ocean climate specific to Val-de-Loire, specifically the region of Pouilly-sur-Loire, this variety blooms there in the best conditions, and using the clay-limestone soils to determine the delicate aroma of the Pouilly-Fumé wines.

The Know-how. But it is not enough to choose a good variety to obtain quality wines, it must also know how to perform the right size and that fits the soil and know especially how to plant it where it is likely to grow in the best conditions. It is here that all the expertise and talent of the winemaker begins. In cultivating the vineyard, by converting grapes to wine, by raising the wine, the artisan directs, controls the manual labor of the birth and maturation of wine. With patience, discernment and engineering, each has its own style. As many growers and traders are all different so are wines marked with the seal of the winemaker and the breeder. Burgundy wines are characterized by their aroma, born from the subtle combination of soils, climate, grapes and work of the vineyard. They know to be highly complex and evolve to defy time. All vintages are not equal, but the richness of Burgundy, it is also the variety of vintages.

Different appellations of the Burgundian vineyard

Understanding Burgundy The vineyard of Burgundy does not exactly cover the administrative Burgundy and is an unparalleled geological and human puzzle. However, in this maze of various common and traditional uses, a clear hierarchy of some 100 designations of origin would help us navigate. The Burgundy vineyard extends from the north to the south of Joigny in Burgundy in Mâcon in Saône-et-Loire, on nearly 300 km of land. It is divided into five major regions of production, plus the vineyards of Pouilly-sur-Loire and Pouilly-Fumé, which will be presented in a moment. To understand the appellations of Burgundy wines, the rules are simple. A coherent hierarchy allows us to understand Burgundy at a glance :

Grand cru (Great growth) appellations. They are 33 in number (32 Côte-d'Or and one in Chablis with 7 climates) and represent 2 % of the production with 57 % of red wines.

They are accessed with, the highest honor at the most prestigious terroirs of Burgundy, wines whose unique character and excellence is most remarkable. Even if most villages have climates (characteristic geographical area) classified in Premiers Crus, only a few have the privilege to claim the Grand Cru appellation. In the case of this grand cru, the name of the climate, because of his fame, prevails only on the name of the municipality or municipalities in which it extends.

The premier cru (First growth) appellation. There are 561 Premiers Crus climates. They represent 11 % of production with 53% of white wines. There are plots or characteristic geographical areas that, within each village are the subject of special recognition for their own characteristics and their consistent quality. The majority of villages have several first growths of very different personality. The names of these geographic areas or the most reputable climate are generally attached to the name of the village.

Communal appellations. There are 41 in number and represent 34 % of production with 66% of white wines. Also known as village appellations, they designate wines which legally took the name of the town on the territory of which they are produced.

Regional appellations. They are 22 in number and represent 53 % of production with 54% of white wines. This category comprise of names which may be harvested throughout the wine country of Burgundy bounded on their specific production areas. The sign of appearance in this category is the word "Burgundy" which appears in most names of these appellations. We distiguish several regional naming among which the characteristics, the differences and the names are attached either to the grape vine (for example Burgundy Aligoté) or in the preparation method (e.g. Crémant de Bourgogne) or a production area (example : Bourgogne Hautes-Côtes de Beaune, Bourgogne Côte Chalonnaise, Burgundy Côtes d'Auxerre, Macon), and finally either a production municipality (e.g. Chitry Burgundy, Burgundy Epineuil, Bourgogne Coulanges).

The Regions of Production

The Coast of wines. The Coast of wines is a band covered almost continuously all along with vines between Dijon (Chenôve to be precise) and Santenay. Only towns like Beaune and, to a lesser extent, Nuits-Saint-Georges emerge from this sea vegetation. Its layout is a general north-south gradient. A grande dame (50km from head to toe) with an hour glass figure (sometimes measuring less than 300m from one point to another in the direction of the width). The horizon widens while in Beaune. The vines may extend up to 3000 m. What are the secrets of her charms and fame ? A remarkable climatic situation, exceptional geological conditions, an ideal slope and, above all, the know-how of the winemakers which was refined over several centuries. In all, there are 2,200 homes that grow more than 9000 ha. Obviously, compared to its rival Bordeaux is just fifteen times less exactly to the area. But here, all the land is in controlled appellation of origin. The annual production is between 350 000 and 460 000 hectoliters with three-quarters in red.

Grapes were already cultivated in the first century AD. The Church, monasteries and nobles of the duchy gave the necessary impetus to the full development of production. The bourgeoisie and the first great traders of the eighteen th century ensured the success of these wines : business success, first big houses and big fortunes debut ! Besides the multitude of terroir, the wines coast is divided into three parts.

Côte de Nuits. About 35 km apart Chenôve « Porte de Côte de Nuits » Corgoloin border village with the Côte de Beaune. The 2,500 hectares here provide 15 million bottles of which 90 % are red. On either side of its capital, Nuits-Saint-Georges, Côte de Nuits is home to almost all wines.

Oenology Courses

Logically, the offer on the subject is vast. Not to mention the Burgundy wine school, here are some places where you can get practical information.

The Middle Jurassic limestone terrain, soil and stones, slope gradient, microclimate, sunshine, everything contributes to the development of these masterpieces. But we never stop saying that these qualities are not much without the expertise of those who worked the land and watched over the vines and winemaking. In this succession of villages : Fixin, Gevrey -Chambertin, Morey-Saint-Denis, Chambolle-Musigny, Flagey-Echezaux, Vougeot (with its enclosure and its castle), Vosne-Romanée and Nuits-Saint-Georges.

The Côte de Beaune. It extends from the town of Ladoix-Serrigny in the north to the south slopes of Maranges. These, moreover, does not belong to the Gold Coast but the neighboring department of Saône-et-Loire. The surface is more important than for the Nuits. The 4,800 hectares of vineyards offer the market more than 25 million bottles. The vine stretches and eases. This part of the coast is what Jean-François Bazin called "Champs Elysées of Burgundy".

In majesty, the city of Beaune offers each year thousands of visitors, a trip to the heart of the historical heritage of the region, culminating in the visit of the famous Hospices. The grounds are younger : marly limestone, marl Middle and Upper Jurassic. As one goes south, the landscape stretches. The white wine is better represented than at the neighbors. It is present in 30% of the volume of vinified grapes and offers the most prestigious wines. The big names of the soils parade following : Chassagne-Montrachet, Meursault, Pommard, Aloxe-Corton, Santenay...

Hautes-Côtes. Here it is above all a question of altitude ... As their name suggests, these land overlooking the famous coast have about forty kilometers long with a width of 10 km. The altitudes vary between 300 m and 640 m. The cropland combines both vines and cereals and fruits, such as blackcurrants. Two names are ongoing haute-Côtes-de-nuit and haute-Côtes-de-Beaune, obtained in 1961. They make up 550 and 650 hectares respectively for 1/8 and 1/7 of the total area of the route of Vins. Magny-les-Villers serves as the border between the two denominations.

Auxois Wines. The Auxois has for centuries provided the cellars, and not the least, especially those of Versailles. It was then found « more bouquet than wines from the coast. » The nineteenth and early twentie th century is detrimental to production, and almost all of the 700 hectares disappeared. A Villaines-les-provosts and Viserny, we do not hear it that way !

A happy experience pushes us to think seriously. The local administration, regional, personalities from the world of vine unite their knowledge. The study results in 1991 and three varietal grapes are selected : Chardonnay, Auxerrois, and Pinot Noir. INRA (National Institute for Agronomic Research) offers a technology adapted to auxois soils : trellising with lyre, which increases the sunny surface with a wider spacing. Five varieties share their space : Pinot Noir, Chardonnay, Auxerrois, Pinot Gris and Aligoté . The first harvest took place in 1997. Efforts rewarded by the appellation wine of the country hills of Auxois changed in 2012 to a IGP (PGI : Protected Geographical Indication) for the three auxois producers, based at Villaines les – Prévote, Flavigny sur Ozerain and Thorey in Charny .

The Châtillonnais Wines. Once widely extended, the vines here shared the landscape with the forest. And the crater of Vix, 2500 years old is already used as a receptacle for the divine drink ! At the end of the nineteen th century, the phylloxera crisis, followed by increased competition from other wine regions of France and colonies and ended up having a series of disastrous harvests in this vineyard. The culture is not abandoned but so far it is limited to the bare minimum. Some plots got the name Burgundy in 1937. For the past thirty years now, some fierce ones bustle to provide a second life for local production. And vines fumble again in this Châtillonnais area. Obtaining the AOC appellation in 1975, official awards last since twenty years ago, the signs were encouraging. About sixty something winegrowers spread over twenty something municipalities are currently involved. So welcome to the land of bubbles because it is the sparkling which now plays the stars !

The wines of Saône-et-Loire : the department located further south of Burgundy is one that is the largest producer in the region, with no less than 13 000 hectares of vineyards AOC. Further evidence that the burgundy is not limited to the coast wine, which itself pierces the border between Côte d'Or and Saône-et-Loire.

In terms of global production, advantageous to white wines which represent an annual production of 424,000 hectoliters against 317,000 hectoliters of red wine.

Maranges region. It is still part of the Côte de Beaune. Its red wines bear the name of one of its three towns : Sampigny-les-Maranges, Dezize-les-Maranges, Cheilly-les-Maranges or the Côte de Beaune Villages.

Local wines of Couchois : They stretch between the towns of Couches, Dracy-les-Couches, Saint-Sernin-du-Plain, Saint-Jean-de-Trezy and Saint-Pierre-de-Varennes. It includes the four noble grape varieties : Pinot Noir, Gamay white, Aligoté and Chardonnay.

The vineyard produces mostly red wines of the regional appellation (red burgundy and Passetoutgrain burgundy) and some white regional appellations (Bourgogne Aligoté, white and (sparkling) Cremant burgundy).

Côte Chalonnaise. It has four main designations which are : rully, especially with white wines, and mercurey and givry, with mainly red wines, and montagny with exclusively white wines.

The Maconnais. Here mainly white wines produced. The most extensive area in the north of the small Grosne is the area of Macon-Villages and senior Macon, the most popular are those Lugny and Vire.

The south of the small Grosne is the sphere of four white wines : Pouilly-Fuissé, Pouilly-vinzelles, Pouilly-loché and the Holy Véran.

The South of Arlois. Three of the ten great wines of Beaujolais encroach on the Saône-et-Loire : the holy love, Moulin-à -vent and chenas.

The wines of the Nièvre. Pouilly-sur-Loire stretches along the banks of the Loire, along the RN7 (2 hours from Paris). Approximately 1,050 hectares are exploited, including 50 varietal Chasselas (AOC Pouilly-sur-Loire) and the rest in sauvignon variety (AOC Pouilly-Fumé). The average production is 55,000 hectoliters. The appellation area covers the territory of Pouilly -sur- Loire and the municipalities of Saint -Andelain, Tracy -sur- Loire, Saint-Laurent and Saint -Martin- sur- Nohain. The clay-limestone soils, kimmérid – gian marl, clay with flint and Portlandian limestone allow a wide variety of wines. Pouilly -Fumé is a dry white wine with very characteristic smoky aromas. Its flinty taste acquired respectability here by expressing itself in greater complexity. Its pale golden color with green hues, its aromatic variety with floral, fruity or more mineral, is worthy of Pouilly-Fumé to be present in the best French and foreign tables. Il accompanies shellfish, fish, white meat and goat cheese.

The wines of the Yonne. Engulfed in 25,000 hectares of the total area of the Burgundy vineyard, the vineyard of the Yonne is still too little known by the general public; which will, again, find a few bottles at a good price. The highlight, all the same, Chablis is most famous White wine in the world. Yonne was there not so long ago, one of the largest wine producers in France. The vineyard then covered an area of 40,000. Proximity to major waterways such as the Yonne and the Canal du Nivernais allow effective marketing, especially to Paris. This abundance was the result of at least twelve centuries of attention paid to the vine. The prosperity of the Yonne vineyards experienced a crash in the late nineteen th century, phylloxera. Today, the Yonne vineyards cover more than 5,500 hectares (over 4000 nothing but Chablis) with a production of 300 000 hectoliters.

The Auxerrois wines. This vineyard that produced the wine of kings and had been ravaged by the phylloxera, remains to Auxerre as the Clos de la Chainette.
Surrounding villages have taken over. Chitry and Saint-Bris-le-Vineux produce on 500 acres of excellent white wines (Chardonnay, Aligoté , Sauvignon de Saint-Bris or Sacy ...), but the red has become the flagship of Auxerre wines. Especially since obtaining the communal appellation at Irancy (see Irancy). Burgundies of Irancy (120 ha) or Coulanges-la-Vineuse (70 ha), produced from Pinot Noir, are highly valued for their beautiful red color and bright red fruit flavors. Their tannic support is also makes excellent wines.

Chablis wines. Another famous name on the white wine side is : Chablis. This young wine brings together probably all suffrage, even though prices have become, for some, unaffordable : Chablis is divided into seven grands crus (Preuses , Bougros , Vaudésir , Valmur frogs Blanchot and Clos), and also first growth, such as Montmain, Vaillons Vaucoupain, etc., not forgetting the plus Petit Chablis which is very nice too.

The wines of the Saint-Jacques coast. A tiny plot on the large map of Burgundy wines, the cote-saint- Jacques deserves no less our attention. High on the hills of Joigny, the cote Saint-Jacques is the result of hard work of a few wineries attached to their history and their heritage. The secret cote Saint-Jacques : pinot gris , which makes it a unique wine in the entire region.

Wines from Vézelien. Vézelay is a vineyard in full resurrection. At the foot of the basilica many vines bloom again like melons, a very old varietal is one of the jewels.

Wines of Tonnerre. Known and recognized early on the table of the kings of France, the tonnerrois now experiencing a second wind thanks to the dynamism of young winemakers eager to give Tonnerre what Tonnerre deserves. The Tonnerre has always indeed established itself as one of the flagship wine of Burgundy, and if for some time it seemed striped off maps, it is ended today because it has resuscitated . Among the treasures of Tonnerre, the Epineuil is arguably the most coveted !

Crémant de Bourgogne in Yonne. A Bailly and Saint-Bris-le-Winey. Designed around the department, Crémant de Bourgogne is an ideal companion for any holiday meal. Worked according to the Champagne method, Crémant de Bourgogne is now recognized and appears on menus of many renowned restaurateurs.

The wine routes. Combine pleasure of the palate and pleasure of the eyes, that's what you offer these wine routes. Burgundy is a region of art and enjoyment of life. It is known for its world famous wines but also for its sense of hospitality, fine restaurants, its hilly landscapes, rivers and canals.

The routes of grand crus : of Dijon, where Marcs d'or still shows the history of the wine capital of Burgundy, to Santenay, a prestigious wine village overlooking the Canal du Centre, the route of grands crus is the tourist thread through the cote de Nuits and of Beaune and Hautes Côtes.
Not less than 33 localities, villages and small towns dotted along this route of 80 km that combines countless opportunities for tasting and discover priceless treasures of art and history. The famous Hotel Dieu de Beaune and the Château du Clos de Vougeot, an emblematic places of Burgundy, its wines and its history, are only the most famous landmarks. A well-marked route takes you from one place to another, and you can discover these prestigious vineyards by taking the pedestrian and bike path running through them. Sites : www.route-des-grands-crus-de-bourgogne.com and www.bourgogne-tourisme.com

The road to Crémant du chatillonnais : More than 70 panels mark 120 km from the Châtillon vineyard so you can follow its heritage and vaults. The route traverses the 23 classified municipalities and towns of Canton. www.chatillonnais.fr

National Stud Of Burgundy In Cluny

The Cluny stud is the Centre of horses in France and is one of the 23 representatives of the National Stud. Supervised by the Ministry of Agriculture, its jurisdiction extends from production to marketing, the use of horses, and the development of regional equestrian activity. Fifty equestrian events take place each year (April to October), the most famous being the National Horse Show Ascension. Free tours are available throughout the year as well as guided tours for groups.

Outdoor Activities

Cycling, cycle touring & mountain biking

The region has many advantages regarding the two-wheeled vehicles, both for the road and the paths of mountain biking. Just for the latter, over 3000 km of slopes were listed, including 2476 km, located in the heart of the Parc Naturel Régional du Morvan, which has altogether nearly 137 tours from 4 km to 50 km, and whose colourful marking varies depending on the level of difficulty.

In Saône-et-Loire, 400 km of course on 25 marked tours have been setup. In Nièvre, around the site of Saint-Saulge, 16 tours namely 550km of marked paths that wind from this site for tourism. Space mountain bike FC of Parc du Morvan offers, meanwhile, 2 476 km of marked tours for 137 routes varied difficulties. More information :

SIMONOTS LEISURE CENTRE
SAXI-BOURDON
✆ +33 (0)3 86 58 26 81/+33 (0)6 31 13 79 57
www.centreloisirs-simonots.com

REGIONAL NATURE PARK OF THE MORVAN
Park house
SAINT-BRISSON ✆ +33 (0)3 86 78 79 00

The city and cycling. The practice of cycling also showcases the city centre. Cycling is developing. In Auxerre, in parallel with the discovery tour of the city, the Tourist Office is renting mountain biking and electric bike to roam at your own pace the streets of the city. The city of Macon meanwhile, designed the towpath along the Saône on 15 km, offering biking from the marina in the direction of Fleurville. The extension of this Blue Way towards north provides a connection with the Voie Verte, for more substantial loops in mi !

In Dijon, several axes were privileged. To what already existed to link the city to the lake Kir, by the greenway, are added central ways, that connect the four cardinal points . You can also take bikes at city self to roam central Dijon freely. Information :

VELODI
✆ 08 00 20 +33 (0)3 05
www.velodi.net

River tourism

VNF Actions (Navigable Waterways of France)

Supervised by ministry of Ecology, VNF, a public institution, exploits, modernizes and develops the network of the whole French waterways, made up of 6700 km of developed canals and rivers, to which the banks of rivers

Nivernais canal.

Véloroutes

As a mean of ecological and trendy transport cycling can also be a way of visiting the area. Along the Burgundy canal, from Ouges to Rougemont in Côte-d'Or, then until Migennes in Yonne, the véloroute offes secure course and many points of interest. The layout of the véloroutes is within the ambitious project development in Burgundy on the initiative of the State, the Regional Council and the four General Advice of Côte-d'Or, Saône-et-Loire, Nievre and Yonne. 800 km of véloroutes and greenways will allow you to drive around Burgundy and admire the main attractions, using the towpaths, the disused railways, the small country roads or paths of the vineyard. Bicycle rentals are available, and for the transport of the luggage, you can rent a taxis. Some rental of bicycles and shelterers also offer this service. For information, it is best to speak to the various Tourist Offices, or check the website of the tower of Bougogne cycling.

Information : www.le-tour-de-bourgogne-a-velo.com

are added, namely, an area of 80 m 000 acres, listed on the public domain. In addition to the river tourism, VNF focuses its action on the offer of the river transport, a doubtless solution to pollution and the nuisance of heavy takes on the road, and motorway paths.
More information on www.vnf.fr

Boat hire

It's an activity that is already well developed at our neighbours across the rhine and across the channel. Year after year, French families are a little more interested in yatching. From then on, we witness an important traffic of these tourist boats, barge-hotels for freshwater cruise boats, andt also of coastal traffic, of all sizes, independent, which most of the time are driving without license.

In Côte-d'Or

THE BOAT
Port de Plaisance – Rue de La Gare-d'Eau – SAINT-USAGE
✆ +33 (0)3 80 27 +33 (0)3 50

H2OLIDAYS
Port de Plaisance
21170 Saint-Jean-de-Losne (France)
✆ +33 (0)3 80 29 13 81
www.vacancesfluviales.com
hello@h2olidays.fr

In Nièvre

AQUA FLUVIAL – BASE DE BAYE
Port des Pougeats – BAZOLLES – BAYE ✆ +33 (0)3 86 38 90 70
www.aquafluvial.fr

LOCABOAT HOLIDAY
Port de la Vauvelle – CORBIGNY ✆ +33 (0)3 86 20 07 29
www.locaboat.com

In Saône-et-Loire

PAVILLON SAONE
Chardonnay – TOURNUS
✆ +33 (0)3 85 40 55 50 – www.house-boat.net

In Yonne

AQUARELLE
Port de Plaisance
Quai Saint-Martin AUXERRE ✆ +33 (0)3 86 46 96 77
www.aquarelle-france.fr

Navigable water ways

The Yonne : departure for the capital. From Auxerre with Montereau, where Napoleon delivered one of his last battles, this river crosses Lower Burgundy and Ile-de-France by sprinkling many cities : Auxerre and its surprising urban landscape, the medieval Joigny, Sens.

The Seille : ecological reserve. Tributary of Sona, the Seille offers, from Tournus to Louhans, 39 km of a green course, where only four locks come to stop the ride through the Bresse.

The Sona : river which has the majesty of a river. Considered as one of the most beautiful French rivers, its upper has long been a border between the kingdom of France and the empire of Austria. It waters many fortified towns, including Auxonne and Saint-Jean-de-Losne. In the lower part, chalon in Tournus, then Macon and finally Lyon, it also waters wine hills of Chalonnais, mâconnais and Beaujolais.

The canal Burgundy-Champagne : the Marne in the Sona. In the southern part in Côte-d'Or, this canal follows the Vingeanne valley, lined with elegant castles such as Talmay and Beaumont-sur-Vingeanne.

The Briare canal : royal ancestor. Work of Sully, this canal was built between 1604 and 1612. It is both the ancestor and the archetype of all the French canals. With the canal of Loing, these two ways still allow the cereal barges to cross Gâtinais. Among the wealth of these canals, there are the Briare acqueduc and the seven locks of Rogny-en-Puisaye, classified as a Historical Monument.

The Burgundy canal : influence of architecture. Linking the Yonne valley to that of the Sona, this canal follows the valley of Armançon, then arrives at Pouilly-en-Auxois via a long underground of 3 m. This winding course, dotted with locks crosses several tourist regions, including Tonnerrois, Auxois with a Cistercian past, the Hautes-Côtes and finally Dijon, before reaching the plain of the Sona.

The canal de Roanne in Digoin : novel. It extends to the south, the beautiful canal du centre and the canal latéral à la Loire. Crossing the Brionnais with its beautiful romanesque churches, this canal therefore takes care of warm colour of its stones and the exceptional quality of its landscapes, both soft and hilly.

The canal du centre : the memory of the « canalous ». Of all the canals of Burgundy, it is undoubtedly the one which commercial activity remains the most important, especially on the Sona slope, between Montceau-les-Mines and Chalon-sur-Saône, where the locks are mainly automated to the detriment of these houses lockkeepers, formerly full of life and now abandoned. But that does not takes anything to the charm of its course between Chagny and Santenay, and Le Creusot. Below, through the plains of the Charolais towards Paray-le-Monial and Digoin.

The canal du nivernais : nature in all its splendour. From Auxerre to Clamecy and Corbigny, the canal faithfully follows the Yonne valley on a very wild course. And then, by the beautiful flight of Sardy locks and « vaults » of La Collancelle, it reaches the ponds of vaux and Baye, which are the highest points of its course. The canal goes down, then to the Loire Valley, through Bazois via Châtillon and Cercy-la-Tour. Opened in 1843, after 60 years of work, the canal du nivernais connects the Seine to the Loire with the collusive help of Yonne. This canal, designed to supply the capital of wood, is one of the most beautiful in Europe. The wild Yonne valley and green meadows of Bazois move the crews on the banks of happiness. From Auxerre, the boats leave in their wake, the Saint-Etienne cathedral, to cross the land of vineyards, with the villages of Saint-Bris, Irancy Cravant, and Vermenton. So the Saussois rocks appear, and then the canal is swinging then in sync with Yonne up to Châtel-Censoir. The course covers its most beautiful attire, with green surroundings at steep cliffs and villages favourites. It will not leave them anymore until the arrival to Decize. Coulanges-sur-Yonne indicates the entrance to Nievre and the pearl of Vaux d'Yonne : Clamecy. The rest of the trip is spent then in Nièvre, a sector cherished by its wild nature and its bucolic landscapes.

The Burgundy Fishermen's Federation

The Federation for Fishermen and Aquatic Environment and Protection is designed to protect streams and the management of piscicultural park. Several brochures are available as well as valuable annual guides informing as well on sites that are on good places, accessibility and modes of accommodation.

Côte-d'Or : 25, rue Courtépée – DIJON. ✆ 03 80 57 11 15 – www.fedepeche21.com

Nièvre : 7, quai de Mantua – NEVERS. ✆ 03 86 61 18 98 - www.federationpeche.fr/58

Saône-et-Loire : 123 rue Barbentane-Sennee – MACON. ✆ 03 85 23 83 00 – www.peche-Saone-et-loire.fr

Yonne : 26, avenue Pierre de Courtenay – AUXERRE. ✆ 03 86 51 03 44 – www.federationpeche.fr/89

The canal latéral à la Loire : seasons rythm. Built on the left bank of the River which crosses in Digoin by a Navigable acqueduct, this peaceful river with the limited number of locks, allows you to enjoy the rural and some unmissable stops, including Decize, Nevers, La Charité-sur-Loire and, of course, the sancerrois vineyard.

Hunting, Fishing & Nature

Fishing

Côte-d'Or : The presence of the Saône, ponds and rivers of Morvan and also the streams of Châtillonnais just the rising Seine invites to the early morning stroke. A rich and varied fauna will delight the expert fisherman, like that of Sunday ! The center of big game fishing in Macon : As big as it is, the catfish is not the monster you thought. All is out of danger, so you will poke the animal in an epic battle, the Saone River is a particularly full of fish. The center provides all the equipment and supervision required for sport fishing.

Information : www.peche-au-silure.com

NièvreThis green department is proud of the presence of the longest river in France, the Loire and its tributaries, of which the Allier is sometimes tempestuous. It should be noted that throughout the summer, fishing activities take place among young people staying in the campsites of the department located near a fishing spot.

Lake Panneciere : this site recognized as the largest Morvan lakes, and also the wildest, is a paradise for fishermen. The 520 hectares of the water have all the advantages related to « worship » the pike, and also the carp. Sectors of night fishing were also organized.

Saône-et-Loire : From fries to the big catfish, the richness of aquatic population here is not a legend. The department can count on 4,500 rivers and canals, and 1,500 acres of water. The Saone and the Doubs Seille are water bodies being sought after by fishermen. The Morvan Rivers also make their happiness like the Arroux which is rich in salmonids (with trout records of 3 kg !).

Yonne : The River with the same name is full of varied species. It is not uncommon to meet specialists who tackle trout over 2 kg ! A grayling population was reintroduced some years ago.

The Fly fishing reservoir in Griottier-Blanc : Not far from Avallon, near the village of Morvan Quarré-les-Graves is this 7 hectacres reservoir nestled in a sumptuous setting. Only 4 hectares are open to fishing. If it is the fly that is preferred, other techniques also have their place.

The « Fishing Points » : These points spread over several villages of the four departments states the activity in the country with several maps and brochures. The staff (mostly in tourist office) was formed to best meet the needs of all kinds of fishermen. Some places involved in the operation are :

For Côte-d'Or : Arnay-le-Duc, Is-sur-Tille, Pouillly-en-Auxois, Pontailler-sur-Saône, Saulieu, Semur-en-Auxois, Seurre...

Is-sur-Tille.

- **For the Nièvre :** Montsauche-les-Settons Clamecy, La Charité- sur-Loire, Decize...
- **For the Saône-et-Loire :** Bourbon-Lancy, Etang-sur-Arroux Louhans, Verdun-sur-le-Doubs...
- **For the Yonne :** Avallon, Vézelay and Migennes.

Health & Fitness

Thermal Bath

- **Bourbon-Lancy :** Located on the right bank of the Loire, Bourbon-Lancy is the only spa at Saône- et-Loire. In the Middle Ages and in modern times, cures are gaining notoriety with distinguished guests visit such as Catherine de Medicis in the mid-sixteen th century and later that of her daughter-in-law, Louise de Lorraine, wife of Henry II. These royal tours offer one of the sources the name of « source de la Reine ». The characteristics and qualities of the water of Bourbon-Lancy are due to the rate of sodium chloride, low minerality and touch of bicarbonate. It manifests itself in four hot sources of 400 m^3 per day. The original temperature is between 56° C and 60° C, it must be cooled in order to be used for cures. *More information on www.thermes-bourbon-lancy.com*
- **Saint-Honoré-les-Bains :** this spa located South of the Morvan Natural Park is the only one present on the Nivernais territory. Particularly recommended for respiratory diseases, these sulfidic hot springs were discovered by the Roman army of Julius Caesar during their passage in the Morvan. The first thermal baths were, therefore, born with the Roman troops, and work until the four th century. It was not until the discovery of Roman settlements in 1839 and the creation of a spa in 1855 that the sources and their use were declared a public utility in 1860. Consequently, the city and the spa knew a constant growth. These thermal waters, currently collected at three sources, are from rainwater infiltrated on the summits of Morvan. Penetrating to a depth of 2500 m to 3 000 m, and undergoing a maximum temperature of 105° C, they emerge at a temperature of 24° C to 30° C at the spa level.
Information on www.st-honors-les-bains.com.
- **Santenay :** In Santenay, wine and water are excellent. Here, thermal waters, considered the most Lithined in Europe, have been known since antiquity. At the end of the nineteen th century, there were four main sites : the salted fountain, the Santana source, the Carnot source and the Lithium source. It's Sadi Carnot, the President of the region's Republic, which rose Santenay to the rank of spa town. The local water is bottled and stamped Apollo. The guests stayed at the Hotel des Bains. Due to this status of thermal town, casinos are emerging. Out of the three that were built here, only one, from 1885, is still experiencing an activity boosted by the introduction of slot machines in 1991. Since 2010, a prefectoral order has been authorizing the town of Santenay to exploit its natural mineral waters for therapeutic purposes. In other words, in 2016 – no later than 2017 – Santenay will become a true spa town again, that's for sure ! A spa town but also a leisure one since a large public space will allow having access to exceptional baths and spas. More information on www.ville-de-santenay.fr

CÔTE-D'OR

Dijon.

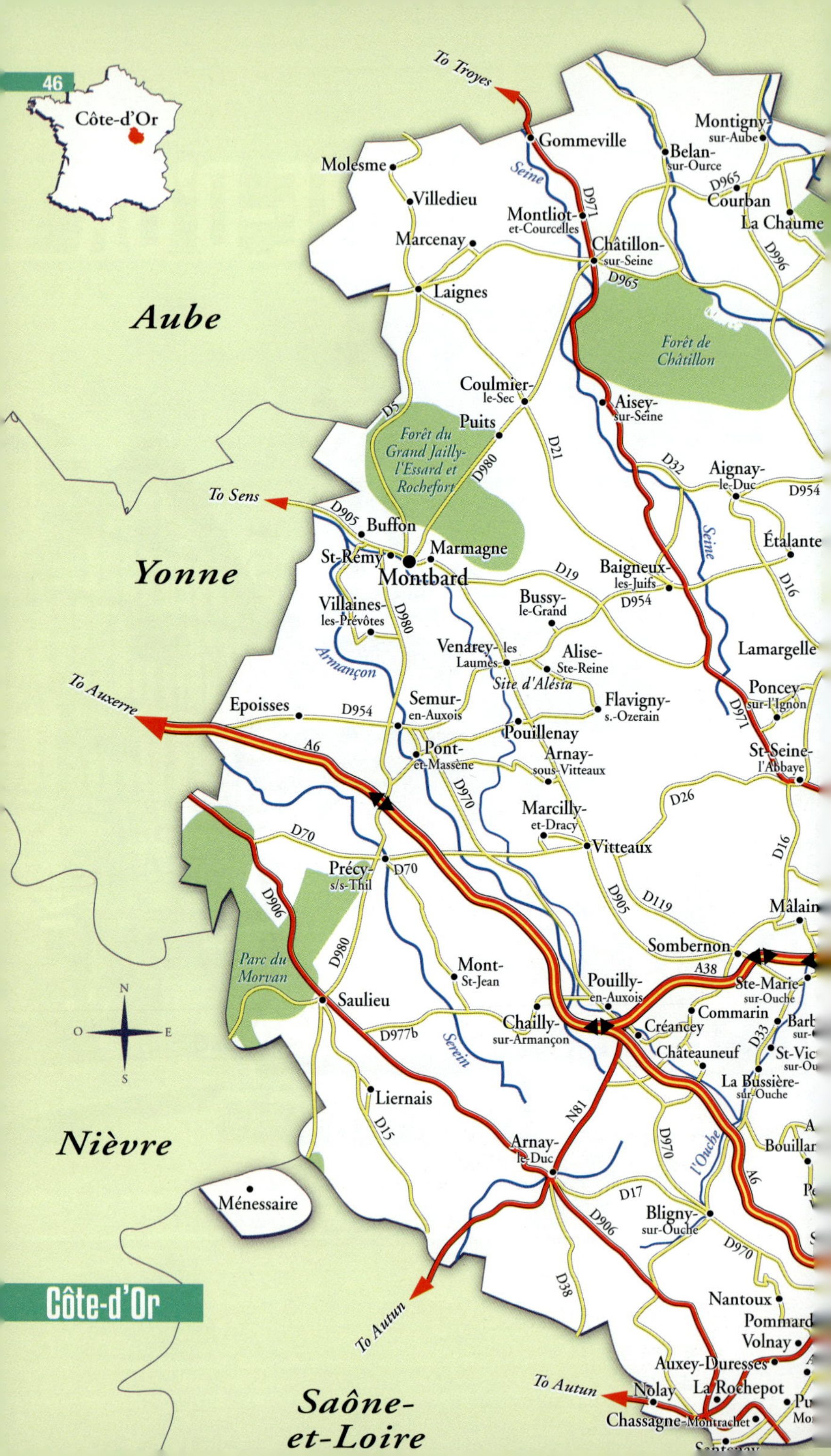
Côte-d'Or
Aube
Yonne
Nièvre
Saône-et-Loire
To Troyes
To Sens
To Auxerre
To Autun
To Autun
Gommeville
Molesme
Villedieu
Marcenay
Laignes
Montliot-et-Courcelles
Châtillon-sur-Seine
Montigny-sur-Aube
Belan-sur-Ource
Courban
La Chaume
Forêt de Châtillon
Coulmier-le-Sec
Puits
Aisey-sur-Seine
Forêt du Grand Jailly-l'Essard et Rochefort
Aignay-le-Duc
Étalante
Buffon
St-Rémy
Montbard
Marmagne
Baigneux-les-Juifs
Villaines-les-Prévôtes
Bussy-le-Grand
Venarey-les Laumes
Alise-Ste-Reine
Site d'Alésia
Lamargelle
Epoisses
Semur-en-Auxois
Flavigny-s.-Ozerain
Poncey-sur-l'Ignon
Pouillenay
Pont-et-Massène
Arnay-sous-Vitteaux
St-Seine-l'Abbaye
Marcilly-et-Dracy
Vitteaux
Précy-s/s-Thil
Mâlain
Sombernon
Parc du Morvan
Mont-St-Jean
Pouilly-en-Auxois
Ste-Marie-sur-Ouche
Saulieu
Chailly-sur-Armançon
Commarin
Créancey
Châteauneuf
La Bussière-sur-Ouche
Liernais
Arnay-le-Duc
Bligny-sur-Ouche
Ménessaire
Nantoux
Pommard
Volnay
Auxey-Duresses
Nolay
La Rochepot
Chassagne-Montrachet
Seine
Armançon
Serein
l'Ouche
A6
A38
N81
D971
D965
D996
D5
D980
D21
D32
D954
D905
D19
D16
D970
D26
D70
D906
D119
D977b
D33
D15
D17
D38
N
E
S
O

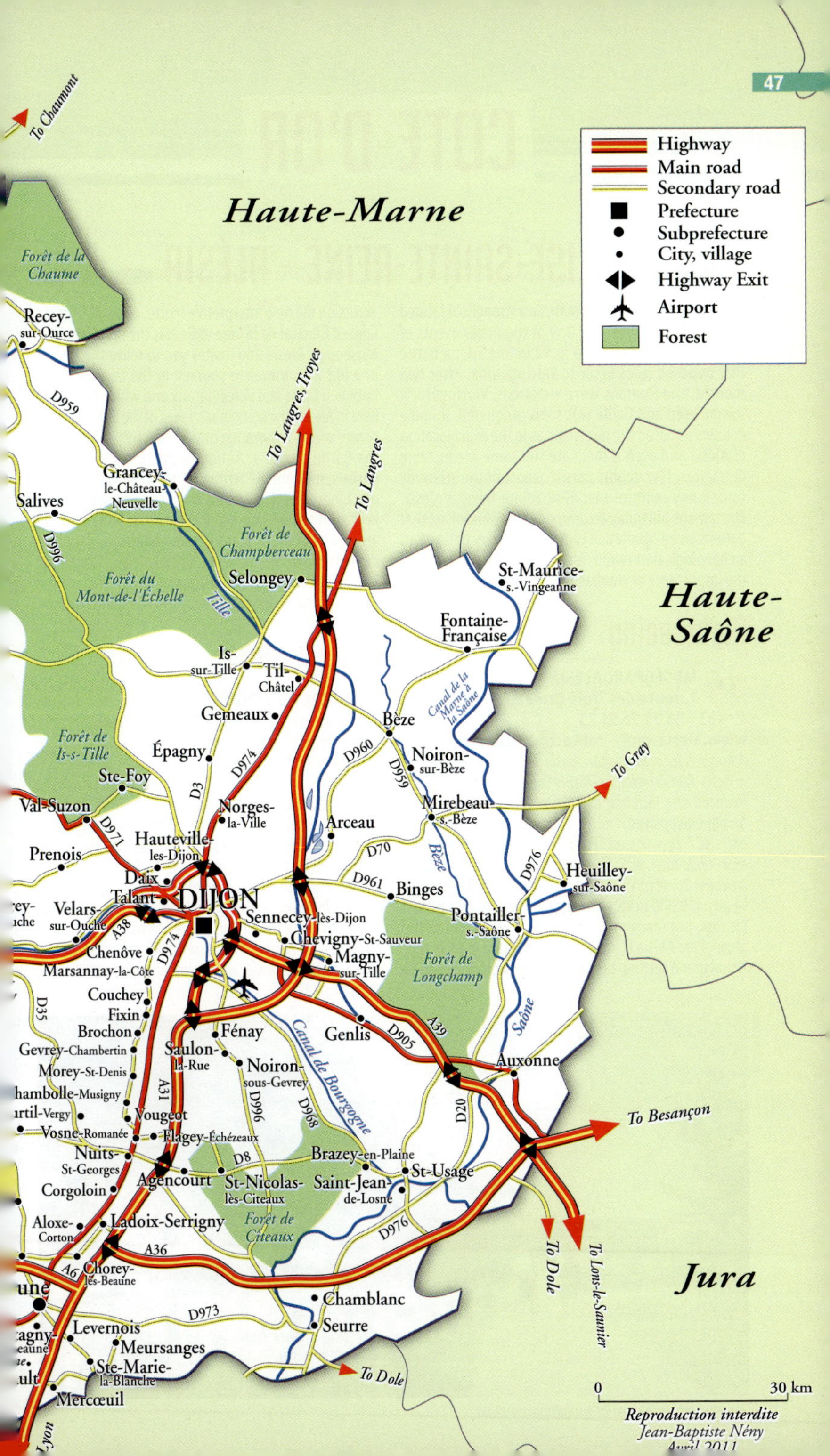
Highway
Main road
Secondary road
Prefecture
Subprefecture
City, village
Highway Exit
Airport
Forest
To Chaumont
Haute-Marne
Haute-Saône
Jura
Forêt de la Chaume
Recey-sur-Ource
D959
Grancey-le-Château-Neuvelle
Salives
D996
Forêt de Champberceau
Forêt du Mont-de-l'Échelle
Tille
Selongey
To Langres, Troyes
To Langres
St-Maurice-s.-Vingeanne
Fontaine-Française
Is-sur-Tille
Til-Châtel
Canal de la Marne à la Saône
Gemeaux
Bèze
Forêt de Is-s-Tille
Épagny
D974
D960
Noiron-sur-Bèze
D959
To Gray
Ste-Foy
D3
Norges-la-Ville
Mirebeau-s.-Bèze
Val-Suzon
D971
Arceau
Hauteville-lès-Dijon
Prenois
D70
Bèze
D976
Heuilley-sur-Saône
Daix
D961
Binges
Talant
DIJON
Velars-sur-Ouche
A38
Sennecey-lès-Dijon
Pontailler-s.-Saône
Chenôve
D974
Chevigny-St-Sauveur
Magny-sur-Tille
Forêt de Longchamp
Marsannay-la-Côte
Couchey
D35
Fixin
Brochon
Fénay
Canal de Bourgogne
Genlis
D905
A39
Saône
Gevrey-Chambertin
Saulon-la-Rue
Morey-St-Denis
Noiron-sous-Gevrey
Auxonne
A31
D996
D968
Chambolle-Musigny
D20
Vougeot
To Besançon
Vosne-Romanée
Flagey-Échézeaux
Nuits-St-Georges
D8
Brazey-en-Plaine
St-Usage
Agencourt
St-Nicolas-lès-Cîteaux
Saint-Jean-de-Losne
Corgoloin
Forêt de Cîteaux
Aloxe-Corton
Ladoix-Serrigny
D976
To Dole
To Lons-le-Saunier
A36
A6
Chorey-lès-Beaune
Chamblanc
D973
Seurre
Levernois
Meursanges
Ste-Marie-la-Blanche
To Dole
Mercœuil
0
30 km
Reproduction interdite
Jean-Baptiste Nény

ALISE-SAINTE-REINE - ALÉSIA

Alésia is located on an *oppidum*, i.e a stronghold located on a high place of 97 ha. One of the major events of our History was held here in 52 before J-C : a battle that opposed Jules César to Vercingétorix. After two months, the Romans were victorious, Vercingétorix surrendered and Gaule was soon conquered. If many debates opposed the historians as to the exact location of Alésia and even if there are still some irreductable detractors, few doubts persist : most of the scientific community confirms that Alise-Sainte-Reine is Alésia. The famous hill today accommodates a MuséoParc that gathers an interpretation center, a discovery trail and an archaeological museum. A crucial place to understand the importance of this battle in our History !

Sightseeing

MUSÉOPARC ALESIA ★★
1, route des Trois-Ormeaux
✆ +33 (0)3 80 96 96 23
www.alesia.com – contact@alesia.com
Admission fee in Museoparc Alesia (Center of interpretation + Gallo-Roman remains) Haute Saison : Full price : €12 - Reduced rate (Student of – 26 years, apprentice, large family, unemployed) : €10 - Child rate (from 7 to 16 years old) : €7. Low season : Full price : €10 - Reduced rate : €9 - Child rate : €6. Tourism label & Disability. Children welcome (toy library). Catering facilities. Shop. Free parking.
Nearly 419,000 tickets since its opening, 100% satisfied visitors, popular entertainment... the success of the MuséoParc Alésia is indisputable. Located in an exceptional green setting, take the time to explore during an excursion the new interpretive centre, equipment of the Conseil Général de la Côte-d'Or. It is the first link of the Museoparc Alésia and invites you to relive the History in a big way. Immerse yourself in the famous battle between César and Vercingétorix and which took place here in Alésia. The scenography area of the interpretation centre offers a dynamic and interactive discovery of the Battle of Alesia. Antique objects, diorama, films, models, multimedia terminals, reconstructions of war machines, life-size Roman fortifications give you the keys to understand the history of the site. Many activities are also offered all year long for children and adults : demonstration of legionaries battles, demonstrations of ancient know-how... The restaurant on the site : various formulas and recipe inspired by the Antiquity period.

Knife & Fork

AUBERGE DU CHEVAL BLANC
9, rue du Miroir ✆ +33 (0)3 80 96 01 55
www.regis-bolatre.com
regis.bolatre@free.fr
Restaurateurs de France. « Maître Restaurateur » label. Closed from December 26th to February 10th. And first week of September. Open Wednesday to Sunday. closed Sunday for dinner and Mondays and Tuesday. Menu from €35 to €52. Children's menu : €10.50. Lunch menu : €19 (starter and main course). Caterer.
Settled for more than ten years in Alise-Sainte-Reine, headquarters of the famous Battle of Alesia, Regis Bolâtre has given his house a real Burgundian style : Burgundy stone, solid oak tables and white tablecloths that make

Interpretation centre of muséoparc Alésia.

General view of Pouillenay.

up the memories of yesteryear. Comfort is not forgotten : the air conditioning cools hot summers while the fireplace brings warmth and friendliness in the harsh continental winter. The recognised expertise of Regis Bolâtre does the rest and we gladly let ourselves linger in the heart of Burgundy gastronomic tradition : snails of Burgundy in shells, duck foie gras terrine in gingerbread crumbs, Charolais beef fillet with mustard of tarragon, roasted Bresse pigeon and its spiced broth, roasted beef steak and its sauce with red wine, free range chicken pot-au-feu with truffle oil... Gourmet dishes jostle and after leaving the place, we can assure you, you will not be hungry anymore ! Carte and menus vary according to the seasons and the chef's creativity, guided only by the will of « eating well ». Since 2010, Regis Bolâtre has opened Le Bistrot de Louise in Venarey, a second address that is simpler, more economical but with very high quality !

In the surroundings

Bussy-le-Grand

CHÂTEAU DE BUSSY-RABUTIN ★★
5, rue du Château
Bussy-le-Château ✆ +33 (0)3 80 96 00 03
Low season : open every day and public holidays from 9.15am to 12pm and from 2pm to 5pm. High season : every day and public holidays from 9.15am to 1pm and from 2pm to 6pm. Low season from mid-September to mid-May. High season from mid-May to mid-September. Free for under 18-year-olds. Adult : €7.50. Reduced rate : €6. Group rate : €6. Label House of famous and Gardens Remarkable. Permanent exhibitions and temporary. Guided tour. Shop.
Count Roger de Rabutin caused a lot of ink to flow : his own, first of all, in his works and the correspondence he exchanged with his famous cousin, Madame de Sévigné. But also other people's ink, thanks to the comments inspired by the life of this courtier who was expulsed from Louis XIV's court. His castle is one of the most beautiful in Burgundy. It has more than 500 portraits of personalities of the time.The entrance to the castle is by the Currencies hall, on the ground floor. Continue the visit on the first floor, in the lounge of the Grands Hommes de guerre, where you can find the paintings of seventy-five outstanding personalities... Including the count represented as a Roman emperor ! It's hard to miss his many conquests : almost all have been represented. The park and the gardens were designed by the owner and were inspired by those of Versailles. A garden of thirty four hectares surrounds the castle in a very beautiful way and the French-style garden is listed as a « jardin remarquable ». Note that the possibility of visiting the apartments furnished in the nineteenth century by the Sarkus family, on reservation, by reserving it one month earlier.

ALOXE-CORTON

Known for its wines, Aloxe-Corton nevertheless retains a rich architectural heritage, including three castles : the Corton Grancey who was inhabited as from the mid eighteenth century, and the wine sections (cellars and winery of the 1830s), that of « Corton André », of the nineteenth century, and the one called « Corton » which are old buildings belonging to the Vergnette de la Motte family, and which was transformed in the late nineteenth century.

Aloxe-Corton, with Ladoix-Serrigny and Pernand Vergelesses, are among the most picturesque towns of the region. They are located at the foot of the hill of Corton, in front of which lie the famous vineyards that produce to only Red Grand Cru of Côte de Beaune : the Corton and the unique white Grand Crus : the Corton-Charlemagne.
Charlemagne would have had vineyards on a hill... hence the name of Corton-Charlemagne.

© PHOVOIR

General view of Aloxe-Corton.

Knife & Fork

HÔTEL LES PAULANDS / RESTAURANT LA CARTE DU SOMMELIER
RN74
Route de Beaune
✆ +33 (0)3 80 26 41 05
www.lespaulands.com
contact@lespaulands.fr

Open all year. Annual closing between Christmas and New year. Thursday to Tuesday from 12pm to 1.30pm and from 7pm to 9.30pm; Monday for lunch; Wednesday for dinner. Booking advised. Menu from €28 to €39. À la carte : Around €17. Children's menu : €9. Lunch menu : €15 (starter, main course or main course, dessert. €20 starter, main course and dessert). Wine by the glass. Reception hall. Groups welcome. Terrace. Shop.

Christophe Fasquel has been in charge of Paulands for 20 years. Always anxious to accommodate his guests in the greatest comfort and peace, he does his best to satisfy us. Whether we are guest of the hotel or not, the restaurant is opened to us. In the kitchen, the chef Patrick Bayen and all his team work in a space of 100 m² dedicated to the preparation of gourmet dishes. According to the seasons, the recipes and the combinations evolve. However the meticulousness is constant. À la carte, we make our choice among authentic suggestions which emphasize local products. As starter, what about discovering the ham with parsley and its shallots confit with blackcurrant, a casserole of snails with red wine butter, meurette eggs in Burgundian way ? As for the dishes, meats and fish are honoured. We appreciate the Charolais beef estouffade and its potato with the juice, a success, without any doubt ! The regional cheeses come to end our meal, as well as the numerous desserts that the gourmet ones will adore. Our recommendation on this subject is without any hesitation the crusty drinking cup with the white chocolate cream and its black chocolate crumble. With regards to the wine, trust Christophe Fasquel, the brilliant owner and sommelier of the house who proposes you grand crus at privileged prices.

Sleeping

HÔTEL LES PAULANDS / RESTAURANT LA CARTE DU SOMMELIER
RN74
Route de Beaune
✆ +33 (0)3 03 80 26 41 05
www.lespaulands.com
contact@lespaulands.fr

Castles & Hôtels Collection. Annual closing between Christmas and New year. Reception until 11pm (or later, on prior request. Catch of the rooms between 2pm and 6pm, later on request. departure at 11am). 20 rooms. Double room from €90 to €95; studio/apartment €120. Double rooms Twin (two beds 1 person €95. Half-board (from €70 to €155). Breakfast : €13. Extra bed : €7. Stop-over with special rates for reps at €92. Pets allowed (€3). Seminars. Free Wifi. Catering facilities (set menu at €15 and €20. Menu at €28, €34 and €39). Sale (sale and wine tasting of Burgundy).

Les Paulands accommodates you in Aloxe-Corton, between Beaune and Dijon, deep in the heart of the Burgundian vineyards. The atmosphere is cordial in this house of the 18th century, entirely built with stones of Burgundy. You will soon see by the exterior the flowers and the vineyards taking part to provide it a rustic and soft ambience. The outdoor pool adds a touch of relaxation. As for the rooms, they sublimate the stay. They are 20, all decorated in a rather modern way with soft and soothing colours : some touches of gray, lime green and red in particular. Many configurations are possible; simple or superior double room, twin, duplex apartment that can accommodate up to 4 people. Very practical, a free and enclosed car park is at the disposal of the clientele. The professionals are also accommodated properly for their seminars and their business meetings. A cosy bar and a lounge is an invitation to quiet discretion. Without forgetting the restaurant and the storeroom to discover the local cuisine and its very high-quality wines.

Shopping

■ DOMAINE CHAPUIS
3, rue Boulmeau
✆ +33 (0)3 03 80 26 40 99
www.domainechapuis.com
info@domainechapuis.com
Visit and tasting by appointment from Monday to Sunday morning.
Le Domaine Chapuis, located in the heart of the Climates of Burgundy is a family estate where the winemaking job is transmitted for 7 generations. Anne-marie and Maurice Chapuis, now assisted by their son Pierre, exploit 11.5 hectares of vineyards by practising the sustainable culture on plots located on Aloxe-Corton, Savigny-les-Beaune and Chorey-lès-Beaune. Maurice Chapuis produces here the jewel of the region, one of the most famous Grands Crus of Burgundy, the Corton-Charlemagne. More than a treat, it is undoubtedly one of the best white wines of the world. The catalogue includes two other Grands Crus, in red this time, Corton-Languettes and Corton-Perrières. The Aloxe Corton red 1er Cru which constitutes the heart of range allured for its price and its light style. For fifteen years, the estate has completed its production by the trade of some appellations in Côte de Beaune and Côte de Nuits. While Maurice works in his vineyards or in cellar, it is Anne Marie who welcomes you. It is always with outstanding kindness that she presents you the estate in the beautiful cellars of the 14th century which run under the house. Tasting will allow you to appreciate the quality of the superb wines, and as is often the case, you will probably be tempted to come back every year for new vintages. Besides, Maurice Chapuis confirmed us that among the faithful guests of the house, there is often the... Senate which places order !

■ HÔTEL LES PAULANDS / RESTAURANT LA CARTE DU SOMMELIER
RN74
Route de Beaune
✆ +33 (0)3 03 80 26 41 05
www.lespaulands.com
contact@lespaulands.fr
Open every day from 8am to 6pm. Free visit and tasting. Annual closing of Christmas in mid-January.
The cellars of Les Paulands are a true gold mine. Christophe Fasquel, sommelier and manager of the establishment is an authentic passionate. Already at 19 years old, he obtained the title of third better young person sommelier of France. He is thus at your disposal to make you discover his selection of best raw of Côte de Beaune and Côte de Nuits. Its wines are aged in barrels then bottled. More than 50,000 bottles a year are sold and dispatched in the world. Of course, you can benefit from exceptional tastings of the white, red, AOC wine, premier and grand crus. On the programme of Pernand Vergelesses, Aloxe Corton, Pommard, Gevrey Chambertin, Meusault etc. « Oenophilic meetings » are also organized to satisfy your thirst for knowledge. For more information, browse the website of Les Paulands.

ARNAY-LE-DUC ★

■ OFFICE DE TOURISME DU PAYS D'ARNAY
Maison Bourgogne
Place Bonaventure des Périers
✆ +33 (0)3 03 80 90 07 55
www.arnay-le-duc.com
ot.arnayleduc@gmail.com
Shop. Exhibitions.
The Tourist Office of Arnay-le-Duc is located in Maison Bourgogne, a fine building of the late 15th century of which you can admire the watch tower and the spiral staircase. Between 1860 and 1930, this residence sheltered the Burgundy confectioner then Burgundy biscuit factory of the famous pastry chef Monsieur Noblat. You will obtain here all the information useful for your stay. You can also buy local produces from local producers there. Two labels are thus represented : *Morvan Terroirs* and *Auxois Naturallement*. Themed exhibitions are organized throughout the year within the Tourist Office. If you cannot benefit from the guided tour of the city, inquire information at the reception. You can make a self-guided visit of the main monuments of the city with a brochure. The little plus ? A very professional reception and a lot of information on the Facebook page of the Tourist Office.

Sightseeing

MAISON REGIONALE DES ARTS DE LA TABLE

15, rue Saint-Jacques
✆ +33 (0)3 80 90 11 59
musee-artsdelatable.fr
arts.de.la.table@wanadoo.fr
Coming from Paris via the A6 motorway : go out at Pouilly-en-Auxois, Direction Arnay-le-Duc by N81.

Open April beginning at November 11th. Every day from 10am to 12pm and from 2pm to 6pm. Free for under 8-year-olds. Adult : €6. Child (from 8 to 14 years old) : €5. Group (10 people) : €5. Private and guided visits possible. Catering facilities (tea room, tastings). Shop.

La Maison Régionale des Arts de la Table can charm the gourmet ones as much as history enthusiast ! Installed in the old Saint-Pierre hospices, a splendid building of the 17th century, surrounded by splendid gardens populated with roses, this unique museum in France receives more than 10,000 visitors every year. Each year, a gourmet exhibition related to the Tableware is organized. Many events are also implemented throughout the year around subjects such as food or gastronomy. In autumn, cucurbitaceous are honoured before leaving room to the traditional Christmas market. In 2016, the exhibition is devoted to tobacco and alcohol ! Nothing inciting, rest assured. It is a matter of putting forward beautiful objects such as shaped bottles, splendid decorative bottles which should charm the lovers of glassmaking. This exhibition is also interested in stoppers and corkscrews because even the smallest objects can surprise you by their originality. Old tobacco pots come to enrich this unique exhibition.

Knife & Fork

BRASSERIE-RÔTISSERIE LE TERMINUS

2, rue de l'Arquebuse
✆ +33 (0)3 80 64 16 29
www.brasserie-leterminus.com
leterminuscharolais@gmail.com

Open all year. Closed Monday for dinner, open 7 days a week for lunch. Menu from €15 to €22.50. Children's menu : €8. Daily special : €13 (starter, main course, dessert and coffee). Wine by the glass. Fixed rate formula take-away daily special at €7.50. Holiday voucher, Chèque Restaurant. Groups welcome (evening birthday, the meal is offered to that which celebrates this day with his/her friends his birthday). Terrace.

Since May 2015, Franck and Karen accommodate you in Le Terminus brasserie-grill after having repurchased it from Joy-Astrid Poinsot. If the painting of the room were remade in more modern colours, Franck and Karen still propose us a simple and tasty cuisine which allows you to taste the Charolais bull of local breeding prepared in all ways possible. Primarily from local breeding, the meat is of an exceptional quality. You find very authentic local main courses like traditional terrine as starter, ham with parsley, bourguignon beef and homemade desserts with seasonal fruits. To summarize : a nice address, a simple cooking but especially efficient and inventive and benevolent owners ! If you wish to prolong your stay, know that a hotel part can accommodate you.

CAFÉ DU NORD

12, place Bonaventure-des-Périers
✆ +33 (0)3 80 64 10 50 / +33 (0)6 43 76 59 48
www.cafedunord.eu
contact@cafedunord.eu

Low season : open From thursday to Tuesday noon; Friday and saturday evening. High season : daily lunch and dinner. Opening from 8:00. High season in July and August. Lunch menu : £ 16.80 (daily special + cheese or dessert). Wine by the glass. Terrace. Entertainment. Exhibitions. Theater. Concerts : € 7, with meal : € 27.50. Evening-movies Tuesday per month : € 17 with supper. € 5 for the film alone.

Located in a house dating back to 1650, Le Café du Nord managed to cross the time while keeping an authenticity which makes its charm. There is something unusual and pleasant in the establishment : a decoration of the 30s, high profiled ceilings, scrubbed chandeliers and eleven huge mirrors with the copper frame that the Germans left during the war. Here, a homemade cooking is offered, simple but gourmet : homemade terrine, calf's head with gribiche sauce or stuffed cabbage. In addition to the regional wines, you will find local fruit juices and Morvan beers. The dishes are seasonal, the French fries are « homemade » and organic, the Bourguignon beef revisited.... This café also became a cultural place that hosts concerts, theatre plays but also exhibitions in a spacious adjoining room. On Sunday, you can bring your favourite games to have a good time between friends. Le Café du Nord is even converted into cinema every Tuesday of the month... All programs are available on the website or the Facebook page. Since 2016, the establishment works on offering a delicatessen service. In a wild cherry tree wardrobe, you can find jams, caramels with the salted butter or snail terrine : only local produces !

CHEZ CAMILLE

1, place Edouard-Herriot
✆ +33 (0)3 80 90 01 38
www.chez-camille.fr - chez-camille@orange.fr

Open all year. Daily for lunch from 12pm to 2pm and for dinner from 7pm to 9.45pm. Menu from €25 to €105. Children's menu : €12. Wine by the glass. American Express, Holiday voucher, Chèque Restaurant. Groups welcome (up to 60 seats). Caterer. Organization of receptions. Boxes gifts.

Installed in a house of the 16th century, the Chez Camille restaurant offers a setting full of charm, comfortable and cordial. The room was arranged in an old courtyard and resembles a conservatory. Chez Camille, the rules of hospitality are followed to the letter and the old-fashioned service is in itself a real show : the dresses of the room personnel are typical of Morvan, the dishes are presented in an artistic and neat way, the quantities are always copious. This establishment has an excellent reputation primarily thanks to the cuisine of its chef, Armand Poinsot, who is both charismatic and charming, and his second, Pascal Gaudillot. The team offers you authentic Burgundian cuisine, prepared with regional produce. This restaurant that offers beautiful culinary surprises like the « Nationale 6 » menu which offers the same dishes as in the 1950's. On the menu : chicken vol-au-vent, ham with parsley, calf's head with gribiche sauce or Bourguignon beef... But the restaurant has also managed to evolve and show that, despite the passing years, it remains contemporary. An address nestled in the heart of the Burgundian countryside to absolutely discover... Note : the premises of the Chez Camille restaurant are also available for the organization of your banquets. You can also buy there gingerbread with honey and walnut wine of the estate.

Sleeping

■ CHEZ CAMILLE
1, place Edouard-Herriot
✆ +33 (0)3 80 90 01 38
www.chez-camille.fr
chez-camille@orange.fr

Hotel and restaurant. Open 7 days a week. Reception 24/24. 24 rooms. Double room €50. Half-board : €185 (for 2 people with gourmet menu). Breakfast : €12. Open parking included. Stop-over with special rates €93. Holiday voucher. Pets allowed. Seminars. Free Wifi. Catering facilities.

Do not hesitate to discover the region in the exceptional setting of a warm and authentic charming hotel. Nestled in the heart of the Burgundy countryside, the Chez Camille establishment welcomes you in a bourgeois house of the 16th century and makes every effort to provide you with an appropriate welcome. The elegant rooms all have a bathroom with separate toilet, a telephone, television and wi-fi... the wooden beams give character to the spacious rooms that are offered to you. The owners also own the 2-star hotel Le Clair de Lune, adjacent to Chez Camille. No matter what hotel you choose, you can dine at the restaurant of the establishment. The team of Armand Poinsot is famous in the region and their cuisine is as warm as their reception. Inspired by the culinary traditions of the French regions, the chef seduces by the tasty and authentic expression of his gastronomy.

Campsites

■ CAMPING DE FOUCHÉ
Etang de Fouché
Rue du 8-Mai-1945 ✆ +33 (0)4 37 64 22 34
www.campingfouche.com
info@camping-indigo.com

Open from April 14th to October 10th, 2016. Booking advised. Reception until 8pm. 209 campsites (including 20 mobile home + village of 19 chalets). Exposure : mid--shaded. Ground : grassy. Possibility of activities for the children the morning. Parking except campsites. Campsite + vehicle + 2 people from €15 to €25. Mobile home for 4-8 people from €227 to €805 per week; chalets for 4-6 people from €227 to €714. Chalets (from 4 to 6 people) : from €54 to €104 per night. Mobile home : from €66 to €117 per night. Possible campsite. Day rates. Rental barbecue : €6 per day. Refrigrerator : €6 per day. Holiday voucher. Saitaires. Pets allowed (€3). Area for camper van. Free Wifi. Catering facilities (fast food vis-a-vis the swimming pool).

Located a few metres from the nautical base, the Etang de Fouché campsite is an ideal place to enjoy swimming and leisure. With 209 locations for caravans and tents, 20 mobile homes and a village of about twenty wooden chalets, this space has the necessary comfort. You can stay there as of April to the autumn. In October 2015, the site was taken over by the Huttopia company. Renovations are planned for 2017 as well as the Toile&Bois tent rental for 4 to 5 people. These large tents are designed to optimise the space and to offer a comfortable and practical living place. The campsite also has a superb heated swimming pool with water games, a grocery store, a bar restaurant and playground for children... Throughout the summer, shows and entertainment are organised... An ideal campsite for holidays in the greeny, certainly far from the sea, but in nature, at the edge of the Morvan park, near the town of Arnay (accessible on foot) and many touristic attractions of Burgundy.

Shopping

■ LE CAVEAU
12, rue Saint-Honoré
✆ +33 (0)3 80 90 28 57
www.lecaveau-arnay.com
lecaveau.sthonore@gmail.com

Open from Tuesday to Saturday from 9am to 12.30pm and from 2.30pm to 7pm; on public holidays from 10am to noon. Open on Sunday (on holiday weekends in May, July and August).

For lovers of local food, there is Le Caveau in the heart of Arnay-le-Duc. A shop where you find inescapable products but also treasures that Emmanuel Bretin unearths in a network extremely well made up. Remember that he worked at Bernard Loiseau in Saulieu, hence his taste for the quality ingredients and the sense of welcoming. Special mention for the conviviality of the place, because Le Caveau is also a wine bar. Each season, there are tastings accompanied by a small dish of cheese or charcuterie. As for the wines, the Côte de Nuits and Côte de Beaune are very well represented and always with attractive prices. Emmanuel also sells cellar articles, an even richer range of glass and carafes in 2016. As for artisanal beers, cremants, champagnes or strong alcohols (whisky Couvreur, rum, marc...) there is enough to please you. As for local produce, also good : sausages, terrines, honey of the apiaries of Morvan, fruit juice and syrups Raoul Gey, Ratatruffe, Prunelle de Bourgogne... Since the end of 2015, the Caviar arrived at Le Caveau, it is Marque de Neuvic that Emmanuel chose, a producer located in the heart of Dordogne. To consume with a Crémant de Bourgogne, that is really classy ! An address where you find good produce to offer, but finally also for yourself because the advices are competent.

In the surroundings

Jouey

LE DOMAINE DES PRÉS VERTS-SPA

Hameau de Pochey
10, impasse des Pres Verts ✆ +33 (03 45 44 05 60
www.domainedespresverts.fr
info@domainedespresverts.com

Open all year round. Hôtels & Préférence label. La Cabane for 2 people : €180. La Réserve spa for 2-3 people : from €280. Le Refuge spa for 2 people from €220. Le Logis gîte for 6 people €240 per night for 2 nights minimum. Chambres d'Hôtes au Logis between €140 and €220 per night. Le Petit Logis spa for 2-3 people from July 2016. Bio et Terroir breakfast in room : €16. Treatment room open to outsiders from 2pm to 5pm. Massage between €40 and €75. Le Cube spa and Vinésime treatments from July 2016. Rent of 2CV : €90 per day. Rent of Solex : €45 per day. Car park. Holiday Vouchers. wi-fi. Catering service (the Ardoise Bio et Terroir : €45 for two people (assortment of cheeses and charcuteries from the region, salad and dessert + wine lists). Shop (Prés Verts shop. Local products and « eco-design » objects). Excursions.

Domaine des Prés Verts is a refined and chic place to stay in a relaxing atmosphere as it is located at the countryside but yet near the most beautiful places of Côte-d'Or. You have your stay at the gate of Morvan, halfway between Beaune and Saulieu, in a single place which joined in 2015 the network Hôtels et Préférence. Lucie Onno and Jérémie Leleu do not cease perfecting their concept, with the rooms and cottages offering of the breathtaking view of the Auxois landscapes, ultra neat landscaped area with the many fountains and pools and where the facilities give access to the pleasures of the spas and the personalized treatments. The living places are intimate, are mainly decorated with wood natural and stones where digital technology allows having customizable musical atmospheres among other things, inside and outside as well. The organic products, that it is in decoration, the breakfast or the blackboard meal. Superb 2 CV and solex are available for guest's use for memorable stroll on the roads of Morvan ! What is striking is the fact of finding such a luxury hotel codes in such calm and resting place. Offer yourself some souvenirs at Boutique des Prés Verts : organic and stylish objects, high-quality local produce. The magical moment is the tasting of an organic wine of Coteaux de l'Auxois on your terrace overlooking the panoramic landscape which gave birth to Les Prés Verts.

Le Fête

LE RELAIS DES TROIS PONEYS

5, rue des Chouettes ✆ +33 (0)3 80 90 17 61
www.lerelaisdestroisponeys.fr
chantal.bonhomme@nordnet.fr

Closed from 2 January to 27 March. The relay of summer (from 28 March to 27 September) : open from Thursday to Monday, midday and evening. The relay of winter (from October 02 to 20 December) : open from Friday to Sunday, midday and evening. Booking recommended. À la carte menu + single menu at €24.50. Wine by the glass. Main courses from 14,90€. Cheese dish : €5.10. Desserts starting from €4.90. Sunday corkage charge : €12. Groups are welcome (on booking). Garden. Terrace.

Set up in an old rural priory, Relais des Trois Poneys offers you a gourmet break in the small village of Le Fête, between Auxois and Morvan. During 37 years, the house used to be an equestrian center that hosted children for pony course. In 2014, Chantal Bonhomme decided to change trade and opened a nice restaurant in the family house. The winter invites you to laze around the fireplace in a room with authentic Burgundian charm. In the summer, the shaded terrace overlooks a pleasant Morvand landscape. The chef is just the hostess who devotes to change her menu every 2 months in order to produce only dishes with seasonal products and 100% homemade. Chopped poultry meat, velvet sauce with foig gras would be the classics of the year. You can also enjoy the trout fillet accompanied with pike quenelle or a cassolette of snail with petit-chablis. The organic vegetables come from the garden of Lanneau in the neighboring district. The cheeses are from Cîteaux, Epoisses, Bresse or Franche-Comté. As for the desserts, they are subtle and delicate whether it is a chocolate fondant and its vanilla and caramel ice-cream or a creme brulee with green anise and Flavigny. Anyway, you will spend a pleasant moment.

Longecourt-lès-Culêtre

CRÊPERIE CHEZ LA CONSTANCE

15, rue des Tourelles
✆ +33 (0)3 80 64 04 98
✆ +33 (0)6 40 73 80 79
michel.charles24@wanadoo.fr

Open on Friday and Saturday from 7pm to 10pm; on Sunday from noon to 8pm. Continuous service on Sunday afternoon; Pets allowed, games for children; wi-fi. À la carte for galettes and crepes – personal composition available as an option. Children's menu : €7.50. Wine by the glass. Terrace. Activities. Private car park. Concerts or film screenings every last Sunday of the month.

In the vicinity of Arnay-le-Duc, when you want to eat crepes or pancakes, you go to « Chez la Constance » without an ounce of hesitation. Breton in the soul, Jocelyne and Michel refitted a former barn to transform it into a lovely dining room with Breton and marine spirit. Teak floor, walls covered of collections of sailor nodes or models of boats, paintings, buoys... You would almost see the sand dunes beaten by the wind or the cliffs which throws into the ocean. After several formations with Breton pancake chefs, Jocelyne Briel-Charles became a true specialist. To crown it all, know that most products are organic (flour, garnishing, cider, wine) and that the local producers provide eggs, milk or vegetables. If however, the combinations suggested do not satisfy you, you can compose your own pancake starting from a list of ingredients. Our advice, try the pancakes menu. You will find some with Camembert or Epoisses accompanied by salted butter caramel and toasted almonds or with sardine and candied lemon. The winter, choose a galettiflette with Reblochon, potatoes, Morteau and Raclette. You are not the end of the story, in particular about the prices, very reasonable.

AUXONNE ★

Old frontier town, a stronghold since the Middle Ages, Auxonne has a prestigious military history : Louis XI built a castle, Vauban reworked the strongholds, created an artillery arsenal in 1689 and a century later, Napoleon Bonaparte, then a young lieutenant, was a student at the School of artillery. Capital of Val de Saône, it enjoys a privileged geographical location, allows many activities on the water, and has a brand new harbour. The city centre is a large architectural unit : there are many houses dating back to the late middle Ages. They enable visitors to walk in a picturesque setting and discover authentic architectural details : a wooden staircase turning balusters, studs with covered porch (on the Place d'Armes), a beautiful Renaissance facade with pieta (Bourg Street). And even if the castle is being fully renovated, it is possible to walk around. It therefore delights lovers of history, of nature and boaters.

OFFICE DE TOURISME D'AUXONNE

11, rue de Berbis
✆ +33 (0)3 80 37 34 46
www.auxonne-tourisme.fr
tourisme.auxonne@wanadoo.fr

High season : open Monday to Friday from 9am to 12pm and from 2pm to 6pm. Low season : Tourist Office closed on Saturday from 1pm. From mid-June to mid-September : open every day including Sundays and public holidays. The river stopover is open from May 15th to June 15th Monday to Friday from 9am to 12pm and from 2pm to 6pm and from June 15th to September 15th, every day from 9am to 12pm and from 2pm to 6pm.

This tourist office is located in the heart of the city, next to Armes square. You find plenty of information about Auxonne and its surroundings, but also about the Burgundy and neighbouring Franche-Comté there. One room is devoted to temporary exhibitions featuring the works of local artists : painters, sculptors, potters. The office has set up original circuits to discover the city. Circuits thus allow you to follow in the footsteps of Bonaparte, to learn the history of the downtown, to meet the great men who marked the history of Auxonne or to combine historical and natural wealth by visiting the facilities related to water such as the marina, the bridges and the dams. But the must-visit is the Louis XI fortified castle of the 16th century. Since 2013, major rehabilitation work has been carried out in some building. On this occasion, a historic tour has been arranged in the castle. The center of interpretation is opened right now to the public during the second phase of the construction site. The tourist Office offers guided tours of about 1 hour and a half, available all year round upon reservation. You can also stroll along the marina. Auxonne offers the possibility of all water sports : sailing, canoe-kayaking, rowing, water skiing, mononautisme... You cannot get bored !

Sightseeing

ÉGLISE NOTRE-DAME

Place d'Armes
✆ +33 (0)3 80 37 34 46

Open all year. Every day and public holidays from 8am to 12pm and from 2pm to 6pm. Guided tour on request to the Tourist Office. Free.

Feel free to join the church Notre-Dame, located in the center of the Place d'Armes : it hides some treasures. The entrance is through the south gate, the statues that adorned it originally, disappeared during the Revolution. They were replaced in the 19th century with copies of the prophets of the Well of Moses of the Champmol. The south tower is the oldest part of the building : it dates back to the late 12th century or early 13th century. The church was restored in the 19th century : the roof of the nave was then covered with slates and the tower was raised. The side chapels date back to the 14th and 15th centuries. They are now undergoing restoration works. The military chapel has already been renovated : new paint, lighting, cleaning of stonework, rehabilitation of the furniture and floor. It regained its former splendour. The left one, at the entrance of the church, is being restored and will soon be finished. Don't miss the statue of St. Anthony and the Christ of Mercy, also called « *Christ aux liens* » in the first chapel on the left; a mural depicting St. Hubert, the patron saint of hunters, the fifth pillar of the nave, near the entrance; a lectern in bronze, and finally in the right apse chapel, two statues of the Virgin dating from the 15th century which is *Vierge au raisin*. The recent repairs and cleaning facades of the church give all its splendour.

FORTIFICATIONS ★

Open all year. Free.

As a former border city and former military stronghold, Auxonne remains the only Burgundian witness of classic fortifications. Although completely redesigned in the 17th century following the first system of Vauban, they remain ingeniously amazing. Today, you can still see two-thirds of the bastions and curtain walls, as well as two monumental gates : the so-called « from Comté », built in 1503 and the Royal gate built in 1677. In 2015, as the entire site, fortifications and ramparts are renovated. New viewpoints are thus accessible !

Knife & Fork

HÔTEL RESTAURANT DU CORBEAU

Place de l'Eglise
1, rue de Berbis
✆ +33 (0)3 80 40 06 15
www.hotel-auxonne.com
hotelducorbeau@orange.fr

Open all year. Open Monday to Saturday for lunch and dinner. Open Sundays of festivals and for groups by reservation. Booking advised. Menu from €26 to €36. Children's menu : €10 (up to 12 years). Lunch menu : €14 (2 main courses, €18 3 main courses). Wine by the glass. Holiday voucher, Chèque Restaurant. Groups welcome (up to 40 people (by reservation)). Baby chairs. Terrace. Hotel 9 rooms from €60 to €80.

Ideally located at the centre of Auxonne just near the covered markets, Le Cordeau offers a spacious dining room nicely decorated in a modern and elegant style. If the shades of the restaurant are simple and resting, some touches of bright colors come to wake up our senses and to whet our appetite. Pascal Ramel offers a creative menu with tempting dishes, Burgundian flavours and seasonal ingredients worked with the current taste. Burgundy snails, cream spotted and soft-boiled egg, Duck breast with raspberry reduction, Creme brûlée with Macvin : all the main courses are of a remarkable quality ! From May to September, the terrace allows to enjoy the fine days for the meals. The service is attentive and jovial for an enjoyable culinary moment. Everything here is homemade with fresh and local ingredients. This creative cuisine of the terroir offers dishes that will charm the most delicate palates. An address which reserves beautiful surprises and which is part of the best tables of the surrounding area.

Leisure

PORT ROYAL

Port de plaisance
✆ +33 (0)3 80 39 23 00 / +33 (0)3 80 39 08 08 / +33 (0)3 80 39 08 08
www.portroyal.fr
max@h2ofrance.com

Port Royal is the marina of the town of Auxonne since October 2010. Located at the foot of the ramparts built by Vauban, Port Royal was designed in a sumptuous 6-hectare setting. Established and managed by the company H20, the 150 locations of the harbour are made for boats up to 15 metres long and can also accommodate larger boats up to 40 metres. H20 will have maintenance buildings in Auxonne and at the moment the harbour office welcomes sailors with all the H20 professionalism, toilets, showers and relaxation room, wi-fi and webcam to supervise their remote boat. For the technical part, the headquarter of the company is in Saint-Jean-de-Losne, at 15 minutes by car to deliver the services of the company. For your information, expansion project of the harbour are being planned for increasing its capacity up to 300 boats.

In the surroundings

LES TEMPS MODERNES NEW

2, avenue Jean-Jaurés
GENLIS
✆ +33 (0)3 80 55 31 77
www.les-temps-modernes.com
infos@les-temps-modernes.com

Open all year. Tuesday to Saturday for lunch and dinner; Sunday for lunch. Booking advised. Menu from €26 to €52. À la carte : Around €20. Children's menu : €10.50 (fish or meat). Lunch menu : €16.20 (2 main courses). €18.50 : starter, main course and gourmet coffee. Wine by the glass. Chèque Restaurant. Groups welcome (up to 20 people). Baby chairs.

This restaurant is a small jewel for the eyes and tastebuds and it also offers a « catering » service for our greatest pleasure. At the origin of this project : Séverine Jacques and his/her husband Jean-Bernard, passionate and the graduated at the graphic arts school. Leader of an agency of advertising creation of furniture entitled Gringos Production and which celebrates its 20 years in 2016, Jean-Bernard Jacques wanted to create a restaurant that appeals to all the sense. A successful bet for Les Temps Modernes ! The decoration of the establishment is a nod to modern times. The industrial and mechanical universe is omnipresent with references of the universe of the welding, car and motorbike. Your napkin rings thus have the shape of gears made with wood while the rails of a mini train passes around the room. The atmosphere is soft with orange lightings, cordial exposed stones and touches of red in furniture. On the wall, the ads of Terrot pay homage to the manufacturing company of mechanical machines founded in 1887 by Charles Terrot in Dijon. As for cuisine, the excellent chef Laurent Klisz is in charge. He has done several interships with recognized restaurants. Laurent Klisz was interested in the pastry at Lenôtre, in fish at Thuriès but also in game, sugar and in the decors. This impassioned chef is continuously learning new things and reinventing his cuisine, in an innovating and boastful manner, so as to surprise you at each of your visit. His love for drawing can be felt in the presentation of the dishes that is always neat. This restaurant with gourmet trend promises friendly and subtle meals. Think of booking and taking your time because the dishes are prepared on order, which guarantees a nice quality.

Fortifications of Auxonne.

Collegiate church of Notre-Dame de Beaune.

BEAUNE ★★★

Beaune was a very rich and powerful city during the Middle Ages, particularly thanks to the act of grace of the Dukes of Burgundy. It preserved a remarkable heritage that can be admired throughout its cobbled streets. The small town formerly accommodated sumptuous banquets and several royal entrances : the Dukes of Burgundy, the most important character of the kingdom, Louis XIV, Anne of Austria and even Christine de Suède had a stay there. But, if a character marked the city for eternity, it is the chancellor Rolin. Very near to Philippe le Bon and Jean sans Peur, he founded in 1443 Hospices de Beaune, universally known, where it is hold each third weekend of November, the most famous sale of the wines of the world. Also visit, collegial Notre-Dame, one of the first large Romanesque churches of the region. You will also discover the coloured roofs and one of the most beautiful vineyards of France. Beaune is the second town of Côte-d'Or after Dijon, but also the capital of the Burgundy wines. The climates of Burgundy are now classifiedas a Unesco World Heritage site. It is also one of the most important motorway crossroads of Europe. You can reach it by A6 (from Paris or Lyon), A31 (of the Northern France) and A36 (if you come from the east or Switzerland), N74 (of Langres and Dijon). Welcome in the capital of the wines, cultural city with its cinema and jazz festivals, in full bloom !

■ OFFICE DE TOURISME INTERCOMMUNAL DE BEAUNE ET DU PAYS BEAUNOIS

Porte Marie de Bourgogne
6, boulevard Perpreuil
✆ +33 (0)3 80 26 21 30 – www.beaune-tourisme.fr
contacts@beaune-tourisme.fr

From the 02/01 to the 24/03 and the 01/11 to the 31/12 : Monday to Saturday from 9am to 12.30pm and from 1.30pm to 6pm and Sunday and public holidays from 10am to 12.30pm and from 1.30pm to 5pm. From the 25/03 to the 31/05 and the 01/10 to the 31/10 : Monday to Saturday from 9am to 6.30pm and Sunday and public holidays from 9am to 6pm. From the 01/06 to the 30/09 : Monday to Saturday from 9am to 7pm and Sunday and public holidays from 9am to 6pm. 18.19 and 20/11 from 9am to 6pm. Closed the 01/01 and 25/12. Online store.

The intercommunal Tourist Office of the Beaune country makes every effort to organize a perfect stay for you. You have two reception centre in Beaune but also in Chagny, Meursault, Nolay, Santenay and Savigny-Les-Beaune. By the way, the whole reception center underwent a modernisation which started in Nolay, Savigny or Meursault. If can't go to the place, the new website is an ideal alternative. Esthetics, ergonomic, fast and effective, it indicates what it is necessary to discover, see, visit, taste and even where to stay. All the addresses are referred with guided tours at advantageous price in cellars, castles, estates, vineyards as well as the local heritage sites. The leisures are not forgotten with a large suggestion of horse, bicycle and even in helicopter ride ! The activities around the wine are numerous and varied and among others there are : the visit of Musée du Vin de Bourgogne, Cave de Pommard, the village of Meursault, initiation wine course at École des Vins de Bourgogne, etc. The Tourist Office offers a wide range of services, including a online reservation, your hotel and your outings with the tourist office ticketing for about forty activities with the Pass Pays Beaunois that allows you to benefit from discounts on a selection of the most beautiful visits and activities in Burgundy ! On the spot, the team of the Tourist Office of Beaune is very accessible and multilingual. An essential stopover to prepare well your stay ! And if you do not go there, you could come across delivery tricycle of the Office Beaunois you should profit. Also good to know : the Facebook page Beaune Tourisme informs you in real time.

■ LA MOUTARDERIE FALLOT ★

31, faubourg Bretonnière
✆ +33 (0)3 80 22 10 10
www.fallot.com – moutarde@fallot.com

Open from Monday to Saturday from 9.30am to 1pm and from 2pm to 6pm. And some Sunday mornings in high season. Free for under 10-year-olds. Adult : €10. Child (from 10 to 18 year-olds) : €18. Discovery and tasting space in free access. Visits organized at set times throughout the year. Additional visits in summer. Get more information at the Tourist Office of Beaune.

La Moutarderie Fallot, producer of mustard in Beaune since 1840 offers a museographic site dedicated to the kingdom of old-fashioned mustard, that of the mustard seeds ground with the grindstone, a handmade process preserved in an industrial universe. La Moutarderie Fallot produces more than 200,000 tons of mustard per year in Beaune, including 50% are exported to the United-States, Canada, Japan or Germany. The other part of the production is sold to delicatessens, and in the two shops Fallot of Beaune and Dijon. You can discover its manufacturing process which goes back to the Antiquity throughout the visit.

The tour *Découvertes* (Discovery) is really interactive and interesting for children. The latter takes place in the old Napoleonic style buildings that housed the mustard-maker in its origin. During the visit, you will discover the secrets of the mustard production that you prepare yourself before enjoying some sweet petits fours with mustard. The second proposal is the tour *Sensation* (thrills) that is only for groups visiting the production site. A revolutionary staging, visual, aural and sensory allow you to follow all the transformation stages of mustard seeds to the packaging of the finished product. After the tours you will have free access to place « Enjoy Fallot, » an ultramodern boutique that allows you to enjoy unprecedented mustards in Bar à Mustardes and buy some products of the mustard-maker. You will find this same concept in the boutique of the rue de la Chouette in Dijon.

La Moutarderie Fallot is commited to the history and the heritage of the mustard, what explains its programming. The mustard became the prime condiment to innovative and daring recipe : Pinot Noir, Espelette pepper, Madras curry, honey, figs, Marc de Bourgogne... As a wine cellar, visits and tasting are a must !

Beaune

A
B
C
D
E
2
3
4
5
6
7
8
9
Avenue de l'Aigue
Che. des Amandiers
Av. de Bensheim
Rue des Roles
Lycée Technique du Clos Maire
Berthet
Rue des Grands Jardins
Clair Matin
Pothier
L'Aigue
Gymnase Omnisport M. Bon
Stade
Ruelle
Rue du Clair Matin
Rue du Clos Pothier
Promenade des Buttes
Lycée du Sacré Cœur
Allée du Docteur Bouley
Rue du Faubourg St-Martin
R. des Capucines
Faubourg St-Martin
Sylvestre Chauvelot
Boulevard Maréchal Foch
Tour des Filles
Oratoire
Rue du Collège
École de Musique
R. M. Emmanuel
Théâtre Bambou
Rue Paul Bouchard
Rue H. Michaud
Avenue du Parc
Bastion St-Martin
Square des Lions
R. du Rempart des Lions
Rue Sainte-Marguerite
R. Gandelot
École Bx-Arts
Pl. J Marey
Rue J. Marey
R. J.B. Étienne
Cours des Chartreux
R. Labet
Bibliothèque
Lycée Agricole
Rue des Villas Fondet
Bd Georges Clemenceau
Avenue de la République
Dames
École J. d'Arc
Maizières
Laneyrie
R. N. Dame
Beffroi
Place Monge
Pl. au Beurre
Pl. du Gal Leclerc
Cathédrale St-Vincent
Imp. N. Dame
Musée du Vin
Paradis
Carnot
Avenue Charles Jaffelin
Square J. Petasse
R. J. Petasse
Rue Ch. Cloutier
Sous-Préfecture
École
R. Vivant Gardin
R. Frayssé
R. d'Enfer
Hôtel des Ducs
Ruelle Galiéni
Rue Monge
R. Ziem
R. Vergnette de Lamotte
Rempart
Place Fleury
Pl. de la Halle
R. Pasumot
Pl. Carnot
Rue Maufoux
Rue Louis Very
Hôtel Dieu
Hospices
Rue de l'Hôtel-Dieu
R. N. Rollin
R. V. Millot
Passage Ste-Hélène
Rue Poterne
Rue des Verottes
Ruelle Morlot
Rue des Noisetiers
Rue des Levées
Rue des Prévoles
I. Corzal
Rempart de l'Hôtel-Dieu
Bd Bretonnière
Rue du Faubourg Bretonnière
Rond-Point de l'Europe
Bd St-Jacques
R. des Tanneries
R. du Moulin St-Jacques
CPAM
Poste
Rue de la Colombière
Molay
R. des Papillons Blancs
Square de Cluny
Dunant
Avenue du Général de Gaulle
Place St-Jacques
Rue du Faubourg St-Jacques
École Notre-Dame
Rue Bourgelat
Rue Henri Dunant
Avenue de la Résistance
Imp. E. Darviot
Pl. Xavier Fornerat
Rue Xavier-Fornerat
R. Colette
R. L. Braille
Rue J. des Vignes Rouges
R. Gaston Roupnel
Hôtel de Police
Faubourg St-Jacques
Impôts
P

F
G
H
I
J
1
2
3
4
5
6
7
8
9
RUE DU FBG ST-NICOLAS
RUE DE REON
RUE DES CASTORS
RUE DES LILAS
RUE PASTEUR
CHOREY
RUE DE BEAUSÉJOUR
FAUBOURG ST-NICOLAS
P. DE LA SORCIÈRE
Porte St-Nicolas
ST-NICOLAS
Gendarmerie
RUE DU 16E CHASSEURS
IMP. M. H. DASTÉ
Théâtre
BOULEVARD MARÉCHAL JOFFRE
Bastion Notre-Dame
REMPART
RUE OUDOT
Hôtel de Ville
PL. MORIMONT
RUE DE LA COMÉDIE
Stade Nautique
BOULEVARD JACQUES COPEAU
R. DE L'ARQUEBUSE
R. DU COLONEL GRANCEY
RUE PASTEUR
RUE COLBERT
LES COUTURIÈRES
RUE DE VIGNOLLES
RUE RICHARD
RUE J. BELIN
FAVARD
R. MORIMONT
RUE E. SPULLER
RUE DU GRENIER À SEL
RUE DU TRAVAIL
R. BELLE CROIX
RUE FAVARD
RUE ROUSSEAU DESLANDES
RUE DES TONNELIERS
PL. DR JORROT
R. THIERS
RUE JEAN
RUE DU CHÂTEAU
Château
Bastion St-Jean
RUE CHAUMERGY
RUE GÉNÉRAL VOILLOT
R. J. VINCENT
AVENUE DU 8 SEPTEMBRE
GARE SNCF
PLACE DE LA GARE
Chapelle St-Étienne
RUE DU TRIBUNAL
Tribunal
S. LEGAY
RUE A. GOUFFÉ
SAINT
BD JULES FERRY
GOUSSERY
Collège Jules Ferry
RUE DU FAUBOURG SAINT-JEAN
Temple
R. DES CHIENS
Bastion Ste-Anne
RUE D'ALSACE
RUE E.
RUE DES NAIGEONS
RUE JOIGNEAUX
AV. DES LYONNAIS
RUE DE CHEVIGNEROT
R. DU FAUBOURG MADELEINE
RUELLE MADELEINE
RUE PIERRE
RUE POISSONNERIE
RUE CELER
PERPREUIL
R. DU FAUBOURG MADELEINE
PLACE MADELEINE
RUE
RUE DE BELLEVUE
RUE CHAFFOTTE
N
O
E
S
RUE DE SEURRE
IMP. DE L'ÉCOLE
RUE E. MARTIN
ROUTE DE CHALLANGES
LA COLOMBIÈRE
RUE PIERRE GUIDOT
RUE DU SENTIER PERPREUIL
RUE DE LA CHARTREUSE
RUE DU FAUBOURG PERPREUIL
RUE DU LIEUTENANT DUPUIS
RUE PHILIPPE TRINQUET
LES ECHALIERS
P. TRINQUET
0 100 m
Reproduction interdite
Jean-Baptiste Nény
Mars 2012

Street index of Beaune

■ **JOSEPH DROUHIN**
1, cour du Parlement ✆ +33 (0)3 80 24 84 05
www.drouhin-oenotheque.com/fr
oenotheque@drouhin.com
Low season : open from Monday to Saturday from 9.30 am to 6 pm. High season: from Monday to Saturday from 9.30 am to 6.30 pm. Visits in French and English upon appointment. Visit and tasting: €38, wine shop. Visits at 10.00 am, 2 pm and 4 pm. Themed visits and tastings, wine pairing dinners, concerts and vineyard tours, tailor-made programs. Wine shipping possible within France, to the USA, Australia, Japan, Hong Kong and Singapore.
In 2016 the Oenothèque Joseph Drouhin has new experiences to offer. After offering tours of the historical cellars belonging to the Drouhin family in the centre of Beaune, and themed wine tastings and dinners, the pleasure is now extended into the vineyards. As well as the visit of the cellars, it is possible to visit some of their parcels of vines. Transport is arranged in an air-conditioned minibus. What do you say to tasting a glass of the famous "Clos des Mouches", accompanied by some typical Burgundy gougeres, in the parcel of Clos des Mouches, with explanations about the parcel and the method of viticulture? Excursions will also be organized to a beautiful 18th century water mill, the Moulin de Vaudon in Chablis, or to discover the fascinating Hospices de Belleville in the Beaujolais. These excursions both include lunch and a selection of emblematic wines. Rendez vous on the website to discover these new themed visits. Private events can also be arranged upon request. Welcome to the new wine tourism experience at Joseph Drouhin.

Sightseeing

LES CLIMATS DU VIGNOBLE DE BOURGOGNE INSCRITS AU PATRIMOINE MONDIAL DE L'UNESCO NEW
12, boulevard Bretonnière
✆ +33 (0)3 80 20 10 40 / +33 (0)6 08 11 34 95
www.climats-bourgogne.com
info@climats-bourgogne.com
More than 60,000 supports ! The project of classification of the *Climats du Vignoble de Bourgogne* as UNESCO World Heritage has a genuine popular plebiscite ! Since this project was officially validated by France, the association that brings the project has continued its efforts to make it known.

- **By publishing educational booklets** to young people and the application form for Éditions Glénat.
- **By participating in the Week of sustainable-development** and in the Agricultural Show.
- **By organising the Week of Climats** (a big conference at Collège de Bernardins in Paris in February 2015 but also many actions and awareness events, especially at the moment of Heritage Day.
- **By internationally developing the cooperation.**

A remarkable work and a constant mobilisation that remains strong in the heart of Burgundians.

■ **DALINEUM**
26, Place Monge ✆ +33 (0)3 80 22 63 13
www.dalineum.com – info@dalineum.com
Closed in December and January, except the Christmas week. Open every day from 11am to 6.30pm. Low season : every day from 2pm to 6pm. Free for up to 12-year-olds. Adult : €7. Group rates. Reduced rate : €5. Ticket sales on line on the website of the Tourist Office of Beaune. Guided tour (€10 per person by reservation). Shop.
Dalineum is a rather exceptional and unexpected art museum. Set up in a mansion of the 18th century, an old building of Banque de France, the gallery devoted to the work of Salvador Dalí extends on 350 square meters. The passionate artist Jean Amiot is behind the creation of this impressive place. As a art merchant and collector, he puts at your disposal works of his personal collection and not the least ones ! You will discover there the bronzes, drawings, prints, watercolours, photographs and other unusual objects, in total more than 200 works. A permanent quality and very original exhibition, even comical sometimes. In fact, Dalí has always intrigued and challenged with its quirky works, it is thus the opportunity to understand him a little better while entering in his universe. You can admire particularly *La Vénus de Milo aux tiroirs* who makes the reputation of the place. New works come out regularly and others make at tour to the European museums some time. The shop is very interesting with very beautiful reproductions, books, postcards, canvases, bronzes... Souvenirs and decorative pieces caters for all the budgets and all the tastes. Thanks to an excellent immersion museography, you leave Dalineum happy to have discovered or have found Dalí, here, in Beaune. To visit absolutely !

GALERIE MICHEL PERNÈS
19, rue Monge
✆ +33 (0)3 80 24 92 67
www.pernes.com
michel-pernes@orange.fr
Open Tuesday to Saturday from 10.30am to 12pm and from 2.30pm to 7pm. On appointment except opening. Closed in January and February. Open on Sunday on appointment. Exhibitions, sales, expeditions.
If you love art and painting, do not miss the Gallerie Michel Pernès which is located opposite the Hospices de Beaune. You cannot miss it because the works exposed in the shop window are always eye-catching. Michel Pernès, who has been painting since 1961, found his own style, that of a painting carried out with great finesse, with oil, on canvas and always with palette knife on formats often large. His unceasingly renewed collection makes you travel, in Beaune and in many charming towns of the region. You will even go to India, in the United States, in Qatar or Venice. His canvases express the moments of life of landscape with a disconcerting reality with moderate sets of light transparencies nuanced with transparencyies and shadow, specific to the artist. The melancholy point of the work of Michel Pernès is the joyful colors he uses. He always has on him his notebook on which he crunches the landscapes that inspire him according to his travels. It is in its workshop, opened on nature and conducive to

creation, that his drafts come to life and are metamorphosed in bright paintings in a contemporary figurative style that is appreciated and is seducing. Michel Pernès exhibits in France but also in Switzerland, in Belgium, in Germany and in the United States. You are cordially accommodated at the gallery by Mrs Jocelyne Pernès who presents you creations of her husband. If you wish to add Pernès to your collection, note that your painting can be sent everywhere in the world. Enjoy the quality of the framings !

■ L'HÔTEL DIEU – LES HOSPICES DE BEAUNE ★★★★
Rue de l'Hôtel-Dieu
✆ +33 (0)3 80 24 45 00
See page 9.

■ TEMPERA ART GALLERY
5, rue Édouard-Fraysse
✆ 03 80 22 86 52
www.artgallerytempera.com
info@artgallerytempera.com
Low season : open on Tuesdays and Saturdays from 10.30 a.m. to 1.00 p.m. and from 2.00 p.m. and 7.00 p.m. High season : from Tuesday to Sunday from 10.30 a.m. to 1.00 p.m. and from 2.00 p.m. to 7.00 p.m. Small artworks prices as from 350 Euros.
Chantal Elshout has set her gallery in Beaune in March 2013 after spending more than twenty years in Belgium. Art lovers as well as casual visitors will enjoy it. First of all, Tempera Gallery which owes its name to a painting technique used during the Middle Ages is very beautiful. Its French ceiling and its lighting ideally enhance the works exposed. The paintings and sculptures there invite you to dream; one can find one's own meaning in them. There is an imaginary atmosphere which awakens different feelings in everyone. You can lose yourself in the works of one of the main artists of the gallery : Paul Delmee. This Belgian who settled in Bourgogne offers paintings which blend architecture and mythology. You will also discover the work of Frederic Brigaud – who makes bronzes with stunning assemblages at times -, of Berit or; Emmanuel De Reggi. All the works exposed are for sale. Chantal Elshout will show you all the secrets behind the production and the inspiration of recognised artists by international clients present in Beaune.

Knife & Fork

■ LE BACCHUS
6, rue du Faubourg-Madeleine
✆ +33 (0)3 80 24 07 78 – lebacchus21@orange.fr
Open Tuesday to Saturday for lunch and dinner. Booking advised. Menu from €29 to €31. Lunch menu : €14 (2 main courses, €16.50 for 3 main courses). Air-conditioned.
Le Bacchus is a small charming restaurant of Beaune for the quality of its cuisine and for its hospitality. Olivier Baduel brilliantly showcases his talent and offers a modern and fine cuisine of revisited classics elaborated with subtlety and know-how.

Of course, 95% of the dishes bears the precious mention « homemade », an additional guarrantee of undeniable quality. Anna-Sophie Adao, Olivier's wife guarantees the service with communicative happiness. You will appreciate the contemporary and sober decor in the air-conditioned room. At noon, during the week and on Saturdays, the chef offers his Market Menu with two or three choices of dishes at a very reasonable price. An outstanding quality top formula ! The menu Burgundy makes you discover the essential dishes of the terroir : snails with parsley butter, poached eggs in meurette sauce, cheek of Burgundy beef and the famous Charolais Burger. Let's stop at this higly prized choice of the visitors and the reason is that : 280 gr of Charolais beef : colossal ! And with galette of potatoes and époisses, it is the reference Burgundy burger. As far as the dessert : the toasted brioche, it's THE sweet delight of the house. Remember to book for a place in this little paradise : it is not unusual that the address do not allow client to enter.

LE BÉLÉNA

1, place Madeleine
✆ +33 (0)3 80 22 12 25
www.lebelena-beaune.fr

Open every day and on public holidays for lunch and dinner. Possibility of themed or birthday meals. Menus from €17.90 to €35. Children's menu : €10. Lunch menu : €12 (for 2 main courses. €14 for 3 main courses). Wine by the glass. Groups welcome (100 seats in the dining room. 60 in terrace). 2 closed terraces that are heated in winter.

Le Belena is the reference Beaune brasserie where people come to seek a warm and friendly atmosphere. It is even more obvious since the beginning of 2016 because Le Belena is refurbished, the brasserie was completely redecorated and rearranged. It even more cosy, « trendy » also with white walls and black wood panelling, white tablecloths, benches, chairs or armchairs black velvet. Floor in bolon felt sound environment. It is very elegant. Le Belena daily accommodates hundreds of guests at any time of day, the service is continuous in high season. Two terraces completely covered and heated in winter are also at your disposal throughout the year. The chef Florent Imbault elaborates varied menus which that suits every taste. You are in Burgundy, thus you find a Burgundian Menu which makes you discover what is the best in the terroir : parsley seasoned ham, poached eggs, snails with chopped parsley, Charolais rumpsteak, beef cheek, cheese from the house Hess à Beaune amongst others. You will have a great pleasure with the menu *Wine Route* by its with gourmet side. The original *Diet Menu* prepared at the request of a female clientele but which also found its accustomed among the man. It's evident as dietetics does not mean tasteless, quite the contrary. As for the à la carte menu, you will have an important choice ! In Le Belena, all is made house as everyone know. You found an reliable address where you eat well and it is known also. Then mind, reservation is recommended at midday !

BIEN ET BON

22, rue Carnot
✆ +33 (0)3 80 21 78 99
www.facebook.com/bienetbon

Open from Monday to Saturday from 8am to 7pm; on Sunday from 10am to 7pm. Children's menu : €7.90. Breakfast formulas : €2.30 and €5.90. Main course formulas from €7.90 to €11.90. Suggestion of the day : €8.90. Terrace.

Brigitte Bayle and Marie-Hélène Coulon are two friends who know the world of catering and trade well. Attracted by a very personal adventure, they have embarked on the creation of a brand new Béaune address of gourmet catering. Certainly, here we can eat quickly and on the go, at any time and even for breakfast, but without neglecting the quality. Everything is homemade with 100% fresh products ! The choice is very wide : sandwiches, quiches, pies, pancakes, soups, salads, toasted sandwiches, and a daily special, omelets and a dessert of the day. The small pot of homemade food is omnipresent on the slates. When we went there, the moussaka of the day was a success ! The products are simple and good. Bien et Bon obviously pays attention to detail. We enjoyed a Raclette sandwich and raw ham as well as a piece of pie with chocolate and pecans... a delight ! Like all other skillfully prepared desserts. Wines by the glass, wide choice of coffees, teas and even hot chocolate, this one with chamallow is remarkable for its delicacy. Do not hesitate to sit inside, in a modern bistro decor with tables and high-bar tables. Bien et Bon bears well its name !

LE BISTROT BOURGUIGNON

8, rue Monge
✆ +33 (0)3 80 22 23 24
le.bistrot.bourguignon@orange.fr

Open from Tuesday to Saturday for lunch and dinner. Lunch formula : €14.90 (from Tuesday to Friday only). Wine by the glass. Terrace.

The Bistrot Bourguignon which was one of the first wine bars in Burgundy, has been enjoying a great success since its opening in 1985. Jean-Jacques and Agnès Hegner have set up a cellar of over 300 references twenty of which available by the glass. Here, even if Burgundy is very well represented, there is no regional sectarianism : the wines of our region come alongside those of Rhône or Loire wines. To accompany them, the Bistrot Bourguignon offers a simple but homemade and quality cuisine, in a warm, friendly and genuine atmosphere. Many objects, winks to the wines and arts of life, richly decorate the room; it is typical and you immediately feel comfortable there. People like to come to this friendly place to taste the unmissable Burgundian specialties : poached eggs, snails, salad with toast of Cîteaux, hamburger of Epoisse charolais.... at very attractive prices. Wine side, let Jean-Jacques advise you. He regularly updates his selection while leaving a place for the new generation of winemakers. The Jazzy musical background reminds us that Jean-Jacques Hegner was the creator of Jazz festival in Beaune which takes place during harvest time !

■ BRASSERIE LE CARNOT

18, rue Carnot ✆ +33 (0)3 80 22 32 93
brasserie.lecarnot@orange.fr

Open every day from 7am and until 11pm. Service from 11 : 30am to 11pm. Menus from €25.90 to €29.70. Children's menu : €10.50. Daily special : €8.90 (lunch menu main course dessert coffee : €15.50). Carte, pizzas and suggestions of the moment. Reception of groups. Terrace.

Ideally located in the centre of a pedestrian shopping street of Beaune, few steps from the famous hospices, the brasserie Carnot is open from the morning until late in the evening. Welcome to a real brasserie with its 1900 bistro decor and the atmosphere : small wooden tables, benches, slates, collection of Byrrh ads on the walls, retro lighting. Regulars and tourists who eat out, have a snack, a drink, a café, chat, philosophize, work here from 7 : 00 at 23 : 00... They love enjoying quality cuisine where all dishes are homemade as the famous parsley seasoned ham. Therefore, there are Burgundian specialties on the menu but also of the omelettes, pizzas, steaks or beef fillet, hamburgers, onion soup, andouillette... The list of main dishes (and desserts !) is long; the choice is difficult but the pleasure is guaranteed. Note that the Brasserie changed management, it is now Frédéric Laleure who runs the address. This former winemaker is also a connoisseur of the restoration. We do not for one second doubt of the success that he will have ! Especially with a menu at 100% accessible prices. It is more than an extremely friendly place whose terrace is never emptied, Carnot is a real institution !

■ LE CAVEAU DES ARCHES

10, boulevard de Perpreuil ✆ +33 (0)3 80 22 10 37
www.caveau-des-arches.com
info@caveau-des-arches.com

Open all year. Tuesday to Saturday. Booking advised. Menu from €25 to €54. À la carte : Around €30. À la carte. Groups welcome.

Caveau des Arches is one of the address of Beaune that the experts love, as much for the exceptionally friendly setting of the vault of the 17th century, as for the table. As for the cuisine, the chef works with fresh and tasty ingredients elaborated with finesse and intelligence. Here, tradition is respected while allowing a slight change... Thus the Burgundian specialities are enhanced by some little extras like snails with garlic and hazelnuts or bourguignon beef with mushrooms, bacon and small onions. These are wonders for the palate. As for the meats, you have fine pieces, of the Charolais steak of 450g to supreme of farm poultry via the nice veal, you will have a treat. The fish are also honoured : trout with almonds and cod loins. The suggestion of the desserts is as great. The delights are worthy of the reputation of the house which, it should be noted, is made by Michel Simon, well-know in the region, and who is also at the helm of the Athanor hotel... An overview ? The cup of black and white grape, granita and Marc de Bourgogne aged 10 years. The plus : the long wine list that keeps the best for you and the bar with the soft atmosphere of the top (club chairs...).

CARLINE HOTEL-RESTAURANT

12, rue Yves-Bertrand-Burgalat
✆ +33 (0)3 80 22 79 58
www.carline-beaune.com
contact@carline-beaune.com

Logis (2 cocottes). « Maître Restaurateur » label. Restaurateurs de France. Open Monday to Saturday for lunch and dinner. Menu from €25 to €35 (+ à la carte). Children's menu : €10.50 (up to 12 years). Lunch menu : €11.90 (2 main courses). Terrace. Hotel 3-stars 2 cheminées Logis.

Le Carline is a restaurant of Beaune set up in a three-star comfortable and accessible hotel. The chef, Sylvain Brugnot, chef but also pastry chef loves his job. As a Master restaurateur, you can trust him as he offers an authentic cuisine made up with the fresh and seasonal ingredients and through which you can find real specialties. In particular the fondue vigneronne with fillet of beef. For those who wish to discover the Burgundian delights, you have the poached eggs with the Burgundy wine or the époisses, the spotted ham, the gourmet époisses, cheek's walnuts of Bourguignon beef... The à la carte menu changes according to the seasons, but the suggestions are always inventive around the classics of the terroir, like the beef fillet and its morels sauce and foie gras or the beaun'burger with a rumsteack of Charolais beef, a mayonnaise with Fallot mustard, refined époisses and gingerbread. We like the beautiful presentation of the dishes. Admire also the comfort of the room with the « modern chic » trendy deco, but not that much. Innovations will be brought to the bar, in particular with a new decoration made up around the theme of wine. To discover soon at in January 2016...

LES CHEVALIERS

3, petite Place Carnot
✆ +33 (0)3 80 22 32 26
restaurant-chevaliers-beaune.fr
les-chevaliers0817@orange.fr

Annual closing 3 weeks in February. Low season : open from Wednesday to Monday. High season : every day. Service from 11.30am to 6.45pm. Menus from €19.80 to €32.80. Children's menu : €10. Daily special : €13.80. Wine by the glass. Groups welcome. Terrace. Vault.

This restaurant is undoubtedly one of the best in Beaune. Patrice Barré who was the friend of Bernard Loiseau settle his property on the small Place Carnot, more than 26 years ago ! The place is very pleasant, in the downtown centre, without continuous passage of car and in a typical setting. You can choose to stay in the dining room, in a rustic vault or outside, on a large terrace, open from March to November. It is well exposed and can accommodate up to 70 people. As for the cuisine, it is authentic. We enjoyed the Charolais rumpsteak with epoisses accompanied by fries... A delight ! A simple dish but simply delicious. Everything is homemade and you can immediately notice that. The meat is carefully chosen from the origin. The beef is exclusively Charolais and the others, like the chicken are fresh, from France and are home-cooked. On the menu, you have the choice among the Burgundian traditional dishes : poached eggs in red wine, parsleyed ham, onion soup, snails, duck breast of cassis sauce, beef bourguignon... and many others. The Burgundian farandole deserves a « very good » rating, a big plate with small Burgundian classic, in Beaune « tapas » way, ideal for the aperitif or for the main course. Two menus are entirely dedicated to Burgundy ! Special mention for service's schedule, the service is impeccable, smiling and welcoming, a real pleasure.

LE GRAND BLEU

12, place au Beurre
✆ +33 (0)3 80 24 70 70
www.restlegrandbleu-beaune.com
legrandbleu9@orange.fr

Closed in January. Closed 1st half of January. Open Tuesday to Sunday for lunch and dinner. Possible reservation on the website. Menu from €26 to €48. Lunch menu : €15 (2 main courses, €19 3 main courses). Wine by the glass. Seafood platter from €48 to €72 per person. À la carte. Terrace.*

As you can guess, the specialties of Grand Bleu are seafood and other fish dishes. The decoration of the room *Marine* does is not misleading with its large dominant blue with wood panelling and ropes all along the walls. However, surprises await you as the

direct access to the beach	visually impaired disability	take away
bar	mental handicap	room service
laundry	motor disability	fitness room
air conditioning	garden or park	playroom / tv
nightclub	games	modern sanitary
cash machine	washing machine / laundry	water sports
drinking water	bicycle rental	tennis
horse riding	grocery store	archery
smoking area	airport shuttle	waterslide
non-smoking	fishing	fan
fitness	indoor swimming pool	toilet drain
miniature golf	outdoor heated pool	sailing
hard of hearing disability	outdoor pool	

vault built in authentic stones which reminds you that the restaurant also offers local dishes. All the seafood come directly from Brittany with guaranteed freshness. To enjoy them, we recommend the menu Grand Bleu. On the programme : salmon, prawns, turbot, sea-bass, cooked with great precision and accuracy. On the à la carte menu, you may also notice the pike-perch, scallops and even a soup of the fisherman that you can enjoy as on the seafront. As for the land, the Burgundian menu will delight the fans with the parsley seasoned ham, snails, Bourguignon beef, cooked with époisses and blackcurrent. The rib steak and the herb butter will make you come back for more. A restaurant that combines many different dishes but does not skimp on quality, freshness and the presentation.

■ LE JARDIN DES REMPARTS

10, rue de l'Hôtel-Dieu
✆ +33(0)3 80 24 79 41
www.le-jardin-des-remparts.com
info@le-jardin-des-remparts.com

1 Michelin star. Closed a few days in December (between the 20 and 30) and a month between the beginning of January and the beginning of February. Open Tuesday to Saturday for lunch and dinner. Open on Monday in July and August. Booking advised. Menu from €71 to €91. Children's menu : €16. Lunch menu : €30 (starter + main course + dessert, €34 with cheese). Wine by the glass. American Express. Groups welcome. Garden. Terrace. Private parking. 1 star in Michelin.

Christophe Bocquillon who runs Jardin des Remparts managed to preserve the always so emblematic image of this gastronomic restaurant of Beaune. You will appreciate the places, this great establishment organized in several rooms, furnished with taste and neatly decorated. Classic and modern styles mingle brilliantly. Christophe Bocquillon likes revisiting with subtlety the Burgundian dishes by mixing original flavours or working with the noble products of other regions like these roasted Bay of Morlaix's scallops served with fondant and soufflé, watercress. As for dishes, you should not miss the roasted sweetbread and cushion of veal mixed with organic celery with the coffee and citrus fruits. These are exquisite flavours that will lead you to the desserts, called poetically « *les gourmandises du Jardin* » (delicacies of the Garden). Do you wish to go somewhere or to enjoy freshness ? The crunchy smoked chocolate mousse and sweet pepper accompanied by its ice-cream with cottage cheese will totally satisfy you. What a softness in the flavours combinations ! The wine list that Christophe Bocquillon and his wife Audrey offers makes you discover the treasures of the cellar of the Garden of the Ramparts. Note the very wide choice of Puligny-Montrachet and Meursault. La Côte de Nuits is not forgotten with of raw Nuits-Saint-Georges or Morey Saint-Denis 1er cru. You will like the plush atmosphere of the rooms, the quality of the service and the calm and shaded beautiful terrace in summer. It is a very beautiful gastronomy full of poetry and starred since 2014.

CÔTE-D'OR

■ **LA FERME AUX VINS**
9, rue Yves-Bertrand Burgalat
✆ +33 (0)3 80 22 46 75
www.lafermeauxvins.com
h0971-gr@accor.com
Qualité Tourisme label. Open all year round. Every day from 12pm to 2pm and from 7pm to 10pm. Menu from €28 to €39 (the menu of €28 goes to €37 with 2 glasses of wine. Fondue at €26). Menu for children : €13. Lunch menu : €15.90 (2 main courses and 3 main courses for €20.90). Wine by the glass. 3-star Hôtel Ibis of 103 rooms. Groups welcome. Garden. Terrace. Vignobles & Découvert label.
There's a lot of innovations at La Ferme aux Vins. After having renovated the restaurant room in a very modern tones, it's the turn of the function rooms to undergo a complete refurbishment. From now on, a pretty laminated coating covers the floor with purple and gray colors. In short, more modernity and an soothing atmosphere for your evenings, cocktails, seminars or any other private event you wish to organize here. As for the restaurant, the chef Xavier Bitarelle has always the same requirements : a homemade cuisine with fresh and choice ingredients. There is always touches of the terroir and originality in your dish. The menu is renewed each season. This autumn, the frogs' leg in chopped parsley came out but also the duck breast with blackcurrant bays or the heart of rumsteak and its époisses sauce... a delight ! Let us also note the vegetarian suggestion of the chef : lasagnas of vegetables with basil and its tomato sauce with herbs. The daily special in the form of cold and warm buffet that allows you serve yourself is always successful. The novelty is the breakfast « as at the market » opened to all the guests, whether they are resident or not in the hotel. The terrace is the ideal place to enjoy it. Do not miss the wine list with more than 200 references of best vintage, often from the region but there's more. Note that the wine farmhouse is also a reputable caterer for your banquets !

■ **KOKI FOOD AND SHOP**
10, place Ziem
✆ +33 (0)3 80 24 06 61
www.kokifoodshop.com
beaune@kokifoodshop.fr
♿
Open all year. Thursday to Monday for lunch from 12pm to 3pm and for dinner from 7pm to 10pm. À la carte : Around €20. Children's menu : €10 (less than 10 years). Wine by the glass. Fixed rate formula at will. For lunch : €16. For dinner (week) : €21.80. For dinner (weekend) : €24.80. Groups welcome. Terrace. Take-away. Shop.
Kaishu and his wife are the owners of this fashionable and modern sushi bar namely so thanks to the bar in the middle of which the chef cooks : Julien Maréchal. Here, the chef revisits the Japanese cuisine with Chinese, Vietnamese but also French touches. A blending that results in a contemporary and inventive cuisine with multiple flavours. You will appreciate the all-you-can-eat formula « Kokienne » in which we always discover new specialties. As for the suggestions, many originalities like the snail rolls, a bourguignon beef, varied raviolis, tempura vegetables, maki, nigiri, yakitori of chicken... As for the refreshments, you will appreciate the discovery of the Japanese lemonade as well as Japanese whisky, Nikka. Without forgetting the delicatessen and the cooking classes on the spot for reproducing superb recipes at home. Special mention for the cosy terrace and charming welcome.

■ **LOISEAU DES VIGNES**
31, rue Maufoux
✆ +33 (0)3 80 24 12 06
www.bernard-loiseau.com
loiseaudesvignes@bernard-loiseau.com
♿
1 Michelin star. Closed in February. Open from Tuesday to Saturday for lunch and dinner. Menus from €59 to €95 (+ À la carte). Lunch formula : €23 (starter, main course or main course, dessert. €29 : starter, main course and dessert). Wine by the glass. Wine by the glass from €5 to €45. Wines for accompaniment packages from €45 to €75 for 5 wines. Oenological evening : €99. Groups welcome. Terrace.
Loiseau des Vignes is a must-go gourmet appointment located in the idyllic setting of Le Cep Hotel at Beaune. This restaurant of the group Loiseau found its niche in the middle of the wine capital of Burgundy. Appreciate the refined style with the gilded and red tones of the room of the yesteryear with stylish furniture. The attentive reception and service of Maison Bernard Loiseau awaits you soon at the entrance. In cuisine, the starred chef

Mourad Haddouche shows audacity and subtlety while deeply respecting the spirit of the Master. What a talent! The lunch menu during the weekday (very affordable) seduces the hurried gourmets. The à la carte menu announces fair promisess that combines flavours local and Mediterranean flavours at the same time. They are excellent combinations, precisely proportioned to make tastebuds of the visitors travel. Candied duck foie gras with the Melegueta pepper accompanied by date molasse and lemon, and marsh mallow with Granada... But where does he find such good ideas ? It is the only place where you can taste homemade quenelles of sea bass in coral sauce with the coconut milk and a crunchy black rice and cauliflower with Madras curry. The dessert is a feast both for the eyes and the mouth with an apple pie with pistachio slivers and glace de Turkish ice-cream with rose of Vence. A simply exceptional meal. The other wonders of Loiseau des Vignes is its wine bar, with more than 70 references wine under nitrogen. In summer, enjoy this exquisite cuisine in an inner courtyard of the 16th century.

■ MERCURE BEAUNE-CENTRE
7, Avenue Charles-de-Gaulle
✆ +33 (0)3 80 22 22 00
www.mercure-beaune-centre.com
h1217@accor.com

Open all year round. Every evening. As from March 2016, open for lunch and dinner. Seasonal menu, homemade cuisine. Wine by the glass. Market menu : 22 Euros (starter, main dish or main dish, dessert); 27 Euros (starter, main dish, dessert). 4-star hotel with 107 rooms. Groups welcomed (six lounges for seminaries. Adaptable restaurant menus) Terrace. Tesla supercharger- standard recharge station

Le M7, the restaurant of the hotel Mercury of Beaune is back on the top on the catering services offer. From March 2016, Le M7 will be opened the every day at midday and in the evening, which is a good news when you know the professionalism of this 4-star hotel. The large room overlooking a lovely terrace and the pool is an invitation to a quality gourmet break. The team in the kitchen was reconstituted around a new chef who will work within the code of the traditional and local cuisine, just revisited to be aesthetic and tasty. 100% homemade, snails in shell, beef bourguignon with dishes which are inspired by the seasons. The whole, obviously accompanied by a pretty Burgundian wine list. In the room, the subdued atmosphere of contemporary setting with gray and fuchsia hues and with very modern furniture will your meal. In spring, the terrace will offer a new comfort with its new installations and its renewed furniture. The hotel Mercury Beaune-Center also has 300 m^2 spaces for the seminars, distributed on 6 lounges. The names of the room evoke the most beautiful Climates of Burgundy : *Chambertin, Meursault, Pommard, Puligny, Savigny...* Rooms in which you can be restored with your colleagues, up to 80 people. Many catering facilities formulas are offered for groups. Le M7 meet all the clientele's demand. For a snack at any hour, the appetite of the small hungers offers a pretty choice of fast, salted or sweetened dishes concocted by your chef.

LE M7 RESTAURANT

Mercure Beaune Centre
7, Avenue Charles-de-Gaulle
✆ +33 (0)3 80 22 22 00
www.mercure-beaune-centre.com
h1217@accor.com

Open all year round. Every evening. As from March 2016, open for lunch and dinner. Seasonal menu, homemade cuisine. Wine by the glass. Market menu : 22 Euros (starter, main course or main course, dessert). 27 Euros (starter, main course, dessert). 4-star hotel with 107 rooms. Groups welcome (six lounges for seminaries, adaptable catering formula). Terrace.

The M7, the restaurant of Mercure de Beaune Hotel is back in force among Beaune's restaurants. As from March 2016, M7 will be open every day for lunch and dinner, a good news when you know the professionalism of this 4-star hotel. The large room opening on a magnificent terrace and the swimming pool invites you to a quality gourmet pause. The kitchen's team has been reconstituted around a new chef who will work according to traditional terroir cuisine codes revisited for the presentation and taste. It is all homemade : snails in shell, beef bourguignon with its seasonal dishes. The whole thing is of course accompanied by a nice Bourgogne wine list. The subdued atmosphere in the contemporary setting -grey and fuchsia tones and very modern furniture – will surely make your meal more dynamic. As from spring, the terrace will offer you new comfortable arrangements and furniture. Mercure Beaune-Centre Hotel also has 300 m^2 of space for seminaries, divided in 6 rooms. The names remind of the most beautiful Climates of Burgundy : Chambertin, Meursault, Pommard, Puligny, Savigny... You can also have meals with your colleagues in these rooms accommodating up to 80 persons. Numerous catering formulas are offered to groups. The M7 aligns to the clients requirements. The Carte des petites faims offers a nice choice of quick meals prepared by your chef, for snacks at any time, whether salty or sweet.

LA PART DES ANGES

24 bis, rue d'Alsace ✆ +33 (0)3 80 22 07 68
restaurant.la.part.des.anges@orange.fr

Open from Tuesday to Saturday from 11am to 3pm and from 7pm to 10.30pm. Set menu at €39 (+ à la carte). Lunch menu : €18 (main course and dessert), €21 (starter and main course), €26 (starter + main course + dessert). Wine by the glass. À la carte. Terrace.

La Part des Anges remains a must in Beaune, a stylish and friendly restaurant where you can come at any hour to chat between friends around a café or a glass of wine, but especially to enjoy the specialties of Julien Nicolas at lunch and dinner. The concept of La Part des Anges is 10 years

Beaune vineyard.

old soon, it did not take a wrinkle, 100% homemade cuisine, selections of finest ingredients (the list of the suppliers is indicated on the à la carte menu) and a large amount of good mood. Whether they are cooked at low temperature, made crusty, in fricassées, roasted or in Tartar minute, fish, shellfish and the meats receive the best treatments according to the chef's inspirations ! A festival of colours and flavours are offered to you. You can choose the bar to eat on the go some snails or the tapas called here « *salaison ibérique* » (Iberian salting) by tasting the wines selected by the fine and merry team. You can also opt for the room under the inner, bright veranda in the daytime, it offers a very cosy atmosphere in the evening when the white tablecloths are lit by their respective spotlight. On Saturdays of summer, the small terrace stretches on the pedestrian street. You can show up at La Part des Anges !

LE MONGE NEW

7, place Monge
✆ +33 (0)3 80 22 30 68
www.brasserie-lemonge.com
brasserie.lemonge@orange.fr

Open every day for lunch and dinner. Menus from €23.80 to €36.50 (carte – pizzas). Children's menu : €9.50. Lunch menu : €15 (2 pentree, main course, dessert. €15.50 with the coffee). Terrace.

The former Comptoir de Gaspard left room to a new restaurant : Le Monge, whose name always honours the famous mathematician Gaspard Monge, born in Beaune and whose statue decorates the place of the restaurant. The new owner, Éric Cremmens, after having developed Le Lamartine with Mason, come back to Beaune. Its restaurant was fully renovated. It can noticed by the remarkable exterior architecture of blinds and door frames in anthracite. Everything was also redecorated inside, a brasserie style enough classical to make you feel immediately well. You will appreciate the quality of the reception, which is very cordial and followed by a faultless service. The chef, Christophe Chartenay, who has got experiences in many cuisines, in particular in Dijon, offers a menu filled only with homemade cuisine. The daily specials are perfect, fillet mignon of pork in puff pastry and its rizotto, vol-au-vent of the sea... only exquisite dishes. On the à la carte menu, you can falll for for the Burgundian classics : andouillette with mustard, supreme of poultry in Gaston Gérard's way, bourguignon beef, duck breast with blackcurrant bays... The à la carte menu also offers a pretty choice of pasta, grilled meats, fish or pizzas and even of authentic dishes of brasserie : omelette, croque-monsieur and burgers. The menu caters for everyone. The terrace will have much success this summer with its white tablecloths, its brand new sun blind and all the rest !

LE SUSHIKAI

50, faubourg Saint-Nicolas
✆ +33 (0)3 80 24 02 87
www.restaurant-sushikai.fr
sushi.kai@orange.fr

Open all year. Wednesday to Sunday for lunch from 12pm to 2pm and for dinner from 7pm to 10pm. Booking advised. Menu from €36 to €54. Lunch menu : €19 (2 main courses, €25 for 3 main courses). Wine by the glass. Menu from €36 for dinner. À la carte from €25. Garden. Terrace. Take-away. Takeouts from €12. Home delivery on Beaune and its neighbourhoods.

For a delicious and soothing meal. Located a little away from the centre of Beaune, this Japanese restaurant is worth a stop there. The Asian decoration and the serene atmosphere that reigns there soothe the senses. The chef blends flavours with textures for dishes marked by fineness. The presentation is always sublime, even impressive sometimes ! Dishes decorated with real orchids, dishes under the bell, smoke that flies away with grace and lightness... Besides being superb, the dishes are delicious. Three menus are available on the à la carte and perfectly adapted to your desires. The first, « *Au fur et à mesure de nos désires* » blends Japanese and French culture with the truffles and mushroom soup but also the beef fillet in thin slices with coddled eggs sauce. There is also a Japanese menu in which you can find a poached cod piece accompanied with bacon and soup with miso but also a farm chicken yakitori. Even the Charolais beef is revisited in an exceptional way. Finally, the menu « *Vite et simplement* » is nice surprise when we are in a hurry and when we want to eat well. The terrace behind is a small haven of peace surrounded by bamboos. Do you wish to enjoy fresh and healthy Asian products ? This place, run by Mr. Zhao and his team, will delight you ! Moreover, a service of take-away dishes and home delivery is possible. A place where the dishes change very regularly but where quality and Zen spirit prevails.

LA TAVOLA CALDA
20, rue Poterne - Passage Sainte-Hélène
✆ +33 (0)3 80 24 24 57
www.latavolacalda.fr - bertrand-jw@orange.fr

Open from Tuesday to Saturday for lunch from noon to 2.30pm and for dinner from 7pm to 10.30pm. Reservations recommended. Charcuteries or cheeses on the slates – Italian salads – Pizzas, pasta, meats and fish on the à la carte. Lunch formula : €17 (main course or pizza of the day + dessert + coffee. Main course or pizza of the day €11.50). Wine by the glass. All the ingredients of the dishes are on sale. Terrace. Shop.

La Tavola Calda is a small restaurant serving italian cuisine where it is good practice to book your restaurant, because people rush there within a walking distance from the Place of Carnot, passage Sainte-Hélène. When a chef like Jérôme Bertrand puts his talents of local cuisine at the service of an Italian cuisine, the result seduces ! The fresh pastas are served with sautéed fresh tuna or razor clams with parsley; the risotto is dressed with truffles or seafood. The salads and pizzas are garnished with the best cheeses, Italian delicatessen meats and others balsamic vinegars ! The choice of pizzas is important, we recommend the Tavola Calda with truffle cream, fresh mushrooms, bressola, rocket and parmesan chips, with the gourmet assembly. You can also make it yourself. Otherwise, choose the antipastis, a board of delicatessen meat or cheese to accompany one of the selections of Italian wines. Alongside Burgundian wines, you will also appreciate the presence of Beaujolais and Languedoc wines. Finally, note that you can order key blades during the end-of-year celebrations.

Sleeping

HOSTELLERIE LE CÈDRE / RESTAURANT LE CLOS DU CÈDRE
10-12, boulevard Maréchal-Foch
✆ +33 (0)3 80 24 01 01
www.lecedre-beaune.com

Qualité Tourisme label. Open all year. Reception 24/24. 40 rooms (including 4 junior suites and 2 duplex family). From €195 to €355. Half-board (between €165 and €250 per person). Buffet breakfast or in room : €20. Extra bed : €30 (depending on availabilities). Garage : €16. American Express. Label Vineyards and discovered. Babysitting. Pets allowed (supplement €20). Seminars. Receptions and weddings. Internet corner. Free Wifi. Catering facilities (restaurant Clos du Cèdre). Satellite TV.

Raphaël Meyer runs this exceptional residence hostellerie the Cedar in a very professional way. The least we can say is that it is a little corner of paradise within walking distance from the historic center of Beaune. Soon after your arrival, you will find a pretty green area in the courtyard. In the lobby, with its soft lighting, the wood panelling and the armchairs are an invitation to relaxation for the travellers. After a warm welcome, choose your room among the 40 à la carte suggestions : comfort room, superior, privilege, deluxe, junior suite... The configuration,

decoration and room furnishing are perfect. The Deluxe rooms are particularly ideal for their wide space, between 32 and 35 m^2, as well as for their desk and lounge corner that allows you to have a stay in a great comfort for a long time. Each atmosphere was thoroughly studied for your greater pleasure. Relax by the fireplace in the lounge bar where a piano, a library and a selection of wines and cocktails are at your disposal. Of course, an underground garage is at your disposal to facilitate your parking during the time of your stay. Several proposals for tailored stays are offered : Beaune Getaway, discovery and relaxation, Burgundy and spa, getaway by bike, wine colors or flavours and traditions. Note that at the time you book your room, you can take an option « romantic reception » and rose petals will await you on the bed ! Do not miss to taste the great cuisine of the chef, Christophe Ledru, who has arrived very recently. The restaurant Clos du Cèdre will satisfy all your expectations. Hostellerie du Cèdre is undoubtedly one of the excellent Burgundian addresses.

HOTEL LE CEP - SPA MARIE DE BOURGOGNE
NEW

25-33, rue Maufoux
✆ +33 (0)3 80 22 35 48
www.hotel-cep-beaune.com

Open all year round. SLH – Small Luxury Hotels. Reception 24 hours a day. 65 rooms (including 29 suites). style or in room : €20.50 (served in cellar, living room, terrace or room). Extra bed : €30. Car park : €19. Pets allowed (€19). Seminars. Free Wifi. Catering facilities (Loiseau des Vignes restaurant 1 Michelin star). Satellite TV. Complete care offering at Spa Marie de Bourgogne.

Located in the historic heart of Beaune, within a walking distance from the Hospices, the Hôtel Le Cep exudes an exquisite charm that delights all demanding travellers passing through the wine capital of Burgundy. Le Cep is housed in two mansions built between the 14th and the 18th century, connected by two classified courtyards of the 16th. Welcome to a world where elegance blends with comfort and History ! The few contemporary touches at the reception or the plant wall of the inner courtyards adds a contemporary and refreshing touch with sublime old stones. The lighting beautifully enhance the heritage of the address which has all the facilities you would expect in this category of hotel : concierge, massage room, mini gym, bar with an impressive wine cellar, room service... Among the 65 rooms, 29 are suites, some newly created, they are richly furnished and decorated. Some, such as Meloisey, seem to come straight out of a castle of a fairy tale ! Others, the work of a contemporary interior decorator. The service and the reception are always perfect thanks to a discreet available and attentive staff. And we recommend that you have lunch or dinner at the Michelin-starred restaurant of the hotel : Loiseau des Vignes, one of the best gourmet restaurants in the region. Le Cep is a must to relax and explore Beaune under wonderful way !

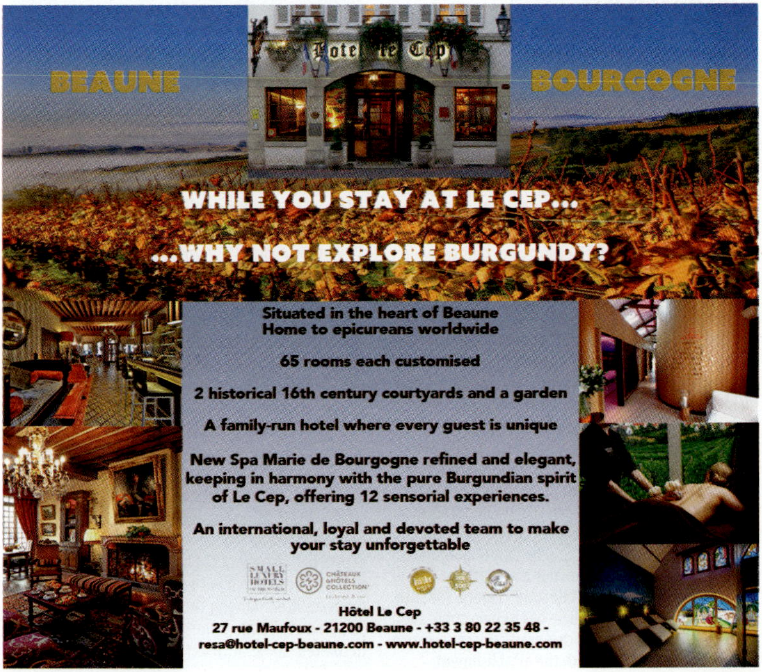

HOTEL GRILLON

21, route de Seurre ✆ +33 (0)3 80 22 44 25
www.hotel-grillon.fr joel.grillon@wanadoo.fr

Logis (3 cheminées). Annual closure : the whole month of February. 20 rooms (including 6 junior suites and a Disabled room); from €80 to €135. Breakfast : €11 (€7 for less than 12 years). Extra bed : €20 (free for child). Closed car park. Holiday voucher. Pets allowed (€7). Satellite TV.

Charming, calm, comfort and discretion are the watchwords of this Beaune's hotel. Located in a residential area, in the heart of a small park, just minutes from downtown and less than 1 km from Hospices De Beaune, the beautiful bourgeois building from the 19th century that is run by Martine and Joël Grillon offers quality catering services. Assisted by their son Rémi, they maintain their establishment with taste and care. All rooms are air-conditioned with classic, refined and contemporary decor. They have a new bedding of 160 or 2 x 90 cm. If you choose one of the suites at the outbuilding, you can enjoy a very spacious accommodation as well an ultra-design bathroom. On sunny days, take time to have a very pleasant relaxation in the swimming pool. Under the veranda, the very elegant breakfast room offers a peaceful view of a Japanese garden. Yes, that's the main feature of Hôtel Grillon, its great peace ! In addition to this beautiful painting, the host's care and professionalism ensure a perfect stay. And the first restaurants are within walking distance !

HOSTELLERIE DE BRETONNIERE

43, rue du Faubourg-Bretonnière
✆ +33 (0)3 80 22 15 77
www.hotelbretonniere.com
infos@hotelbretonniere.com

Reception until 11pm. 32 rooms. Buffet breakfast : €11. Closed parking. Possible one-night stopover with special rates. Single, Double and Family rooms from €75 to €140. Pets allowed (€8). Seminars. Free wi-fi. Satellite TV.

Hostellerie de Bretonnière is a hotel of Beaune that lives with its time. Perfectly maintained and renovated, it offers a comfort that is largely worthy of a 3-star, it has a large car park in its interior courtyard, thus you won't have any problem for the access. The reason is that you are in the downtown and at five minutes walk only from the cobbled streets of the heart of Beaune. This former coaching inn of 18th kept a certain charm with an inner courtyard flowered in summer, a true bubble of greenery. You have the choice among the 24 very comfortable rooms, the standard model upstairs, via the family one. Each of them has a modern decor with a view of the garden or the courtyard. In addition, 8 duplex suites, more luxurious, with private terrace are also offered. The generous, tasty breakfast and carefully prepared is served in the room, in the garden or in the bright veranda. The bar and two lounges enable you to dawdle around a drink. By the way, note the selection of Burgundian estates on the wine list. For your dinner, the staff will guide you towards the best Beaune's eatery. The little plus, Hostellerie de Bretonnière has its own application available on Apple Store, which is practical for reservation and the communication with the establishment.

HÔTEL ATHANOR BEAUNE CENTRE

9-11, avenue de la République
✆ +33 (0)3 80 24 09 20 – www.hotel-athanor.com
hotel.athanor@wanadoo.fr

Open all year. Reception until 11pm. 34 rooms (including 4 suites). Single room €99; suite €160. Buffet breakfast : €12. Pets allowed (free). Free Wifi. Satellite TV.

This hotel, ideally located is run with expert hands by Michel Simon. Most places to discover in the city are just a few minutes : the collegiate church of Notre-Dame, Hospices, ramparts... This property offers neat surroundings in the heart of the city. All the charm and authenticity of this former convent of the are still visible despite the arrival of modern comfort. Spiral staircases of stone, authentic beams on the ceiling, beautiful tiles on the floor, a fireplace in the main room... Everything has been preserved to offer a memorable stay. However, the modern furniture is perfectly integrated into the environment. Comfort and aesthetics above all ! Choose your offer standard room, with a shower and a bath after Junior who stands himself by a lounge area, with wood-panelled walls... You will find necessarily what suits you. Le Wifi is provided and all rooms are of course equipped with tvs. A bar and a pool are available. As for breakfast, it awaits you in the form of a buffet of delights in a beautiful old room. And even the most demanding guests will agree with it : the staff, including Caroline the manager, is really caring !

HOTEL LE CEP - SPA MARIE DE BOURGOGNE

NEW

25-33, rue Maufoux
✆ +33 (0)3 80 22 35 48
www.hotel-cep-beaune.com
resa@hotel-cep-beaune.com

Open all year round. SLH – Small Luxury Hotels. Reception 24 hours a day. 65 rooms (including 29 suites). style or in room : €20.50 (served in cellar, living room, terrace or room). Extra bed : €30. Car park : €19. Pets allowed (€19). Seminars. Free Wifi. Catering facilities (Loiseau des Vignes restaurant 1 Michelin star). Satellite TV. Complete care offering at Spa Marie de Bourgogne.

Located in the historic heart of Beaune, within a walking distance from the Hospices, the Hôtel Le Cep exudes an exquisite charm that delights all demanding travellers passing through the wine capital of Burgundy. Le Cep is housed in two mansions built between the 14th and the 18th century, connected by two classified courtyards of the 16th. Welcome to a world where elegance blends with comfort and History ! The few contemporary touches at the reception or the plant wall of the inner courtyards adds a contemporary and refreshing touch with sublime old stones. The lighting beautifully enhance the heritage of the address which has all the facilities you would expect in this category of hotel : concierge, massage room, mini gym, bar with an impressive wine cellar, room service... Among the 65 rooms, 29 are suites, some newly created, they are richly furnished and decorated. Some, such as Meloisey, seem to come straight out of a castle of a fairy tale ! Others, the work of a contemporary interior decorator. The service and the reception are always perfect thanks to a discreet available and attentive staff. And we recommend that you have lunch or dinner at the Michelin-starred restaurant of the hotel : Loiseau des Vignes, one of the best gourmet restaurants in the region. Le Cep is a must to relax and explore Beaune under wonderful way !

■ HOTEL IBIS BEAUNE SUD
La Ferme aux vins
9, rue Yves-Bertrand-Burgalat
✆ +33 (0)3 80 22 46 75
www.hotel-ibis-beaune.com
H0971@accor.com

Open all year round. Dynamic rates. Round the clock reception. 103 rooms. Double room from €74, the night. Stopover with special rates. Buffet breakfast : €9.90 (served from 4am to 12pm). Extra bed : €12. Closed park car included. Pets allowed (€10). Seminars. Free wi-fi. Catering facilities (restaurant Ferme aux Vins. At midday from €15.90 to €20.90. Menu from €28 to €39). Web Corner with international sockets. Canal+.
Hôtel Ibis Beaune Sud and La Ferme aux Vins offer a package of comfort and quality service above the average ! Located at a few minutes of the downtown and the exit of A6 highway, it also offers the convenience of access. The particularity of this hotel is the fact that it belongs to a very demanding Hotel group on the quality. The rooms respect the Ibis line, *Coquelicot*, contemporary with the warm colors and harmonious. They are perfectly maintained and renovated with a bedding changed between 2012 and in 2014. The entrance hall and the restaurant are both redecorated in more welcoming way with wooden surfaces that contrasts with colours. The restaurant La Ferme aux Vins features also a new atmosphere with the soft colors, anise, orange and taupe and its discreetly contemporary furniture. We love. Xavier Bitarelle, the chef, offers a refined regional cuisine, accompanied by a selection of more than 120 wine references of the region. We appreciate the shaded terrace at the edge of the pool, the bar and the flowered lovely park ! The novelty of the beginning of 2016, the function rooms underwent a complete refurbishment that brings more modernity and a cosy atmosphere for your evenings, cocktails, seminars or any other private event you wish to organize here.

■ MERCURE BEAUNE-CENTRE
7, Avenue Charles-de Gaulle
✆ +33 (0)3 80 22 22 00
www.mercure-beaune-centre.com
h1217@accor.com

Open all year round. 107 rooms (among which 13 junior suites). Double room from 115 Euros to 220 Euros. Breakfast : 16.90 Euros. Closed car park included (Tesla superchargers – standard charging station). Promotional packages depending on date and booking period. Animals admitted (8 Euros) Seminaries. Wi Fi.

Restaurant (M7 restaurant open 7 days a week for lunch and dinner as from March 2016. 6 lounges devoted to seminaries). So chic, so practical ! The hotel Mecure Beaune, which is a few minutes walk from the hyper-centre of the city offers you to stay in completely renovate rooms. Médéric Fauchille, the new manager of the address reminds that all the works ended on March 2016. Then you will stay in modern rooms, the flooring with soft colour atmosphere. You will like the giant photos in headboard that reproduce the glazed tiles, symbole of Beaune. The others are greenish watercourse's photo. They will delight nature lovers. As for comfort, you are undoubtedly in a 4-star address : ultra design bathrooms, curtains with bright colours matching the duvet cover, flat-screen TV, ambient lighting, office chair... To crown it all, some rooms overlook the park, others on Beaune. A stunning view for an establishment that perfectly meets the needs of a demanding clientele. Note that 4 rooms can accommodate disabled people. The restaurant M7 will be open at midday and in the evening on March with a new team, offering a stylish and warm universe. Enjoy the swimming pool during the sunny days. As for the catering services, you can count on the professionalism of the staff, paying attention to the quality charter of Mercure. From the spring 2016, the completely renovated terrace will be a must for relaxation.

Guesthouses

■ LE CLOS DE LA CHALLANGETTE

Hameau de Challanges
225, rue de la Bretenet ✆ +33 (0)6 19 48 01 93
www.clos-challangette.fr
reservation@clos-challangette.fr

Gîte de France (4 épis). Open all year. Label Vineyards and Discovered. 5 rooms (including 2 caravans + 3 cottages). Breakfast included (for the rooms). Closed parking included (in interior courtyard). Room 2 people €120, room 4 people €220, caravans from €100 to €120. 3 Cottages from 2 to 6 people. Seminars. Free Internet access. Catering facilities (table d'hôte on reservation €45 to €48 without the wines – kitchen of chef). Sale (wines and products of region). Sauna. Massages by reservation. Organization of sightseeings and professionals with themes.

Located at Hameau de Challanges in Beaune, Clos de la Challangette offers a rather surprising place to stay. Indeed, if you are in an adventurous mood, you should get to this place. You have the chance remain in one of the two... gypsy caravans ! They were decorated on the romanticism theme, the one was named « *Valentine et Cupid* » while the other is named « *la roulotte des Amourettes* »(caravan of fancy). In both cases, you will spend an unusual moment. The estate is comfortable with heated outdoor swimming pool within a huge green private courtyard. In a more classical way, you can also choose the guest houses and the cottages. Even if there are different universes, the style remains refined and of good taste. Bright colours are present, as well as a contemporary and old furniture at the same time. Jackie David, your host, accommodates you with professionalism by offering a whole panel of services : table d'hôte concocted by the chefs in Beaune, sauna, massages. Tastings, even themed weekends can be organized. For the most studious, a huge lounge can be used as conference room equipped with overhead projectors and other modern tools. In the evening, the terrace and its soft lighting rejoice the night birds.

Leisure

■ ECOLE DES VINS DE BOURGOGNE

6, rue du 16e-Chasseurs ✆ +33 (0)3 80 26 35 10
www.ecoledesvins-bourgogne.com
ecoledesvins@bivb.com

Open all year. Discovered and initiation with oenology : 2 : 00 and tasting of 3 wines : €39. ½ day with tasting of 6 wines : €75 (option lunch : €50). Day with lunching : €199. Fixed rate formulas sets of themes will be proposed in 2016 : programs and rates in the course of programming.

École des Vins de Bourgogne, created in 1973 by the Bureau Interprofessionnel des Vins de Bourgogne, proposes fun but studious training courses for wine lovers. Each year, some 2500 people attend the school ! During the stay in Burgundy, this training brings a real asset to your œnotouristic stay. Completely adapted to all, the range of training courses is wide and varied : stroll between vineyards and wines for 2 hours for a careful discovery, training between 3h to one day for the most curious. There are even customized formulas, for individual or group registrations. A thematic program is also offered. L'École des Vins takes part in many events around wine each year, and seizes this opportunity to make everyone discover its famous « Cave aux Arômes ». 12 oak barrels, topped with a large balloon glass, each representing one of the aromatic families of the Burgundy wines. To breathe without moderation ! Thus do not hesitate to reserve a training in this school unlike any other. A gift to give to someone or to offer yourself !

Relaxation & Fitness

NEW

■ HÔTEL LE CEP - SPA MARIE DE BOURGOGNE

25-33, rue Maufoux
✆ +33 (0)03 80 22 35 48
www.hotel-cep-beaune.com
www.spasdefrance.fr
resa@hotel-cep-beaune.com

Le Cep hotel, which has four stars, is a luxurious and comfortable establishment that you would wish to attend only the time of a temporary stay. Good news, it is possible! Indeed, the brand new Spa Marie de Bourgogne welcomes you, without being necessarily guest of the hotel, it brings you the best of relaxation and body wellness with advanced services: cryotherapy, waterbike, balneotherapy, pressure therapy, massages, body and face care, body wrap, steam room, sauna, heating beds, sensory showers etc. It is a flood of exceptional services in a single place of more than 300m^2 in the presence of a qualified team. Perfumes, lights and sounds adapt to each space. The atmosphere is zen and relaxing with expensive woodworks at Le Cep, some recalling the wrath, these giant barrels. The rest room, as for it, is installed facing beautiful stained-glass windows. Go through the tearoom and its shop signed Vinésime. Without forgetting the fitness room which is open every day at any time of day or night. The Spa Marie Bourgogne is a pole of relaxation that makes Le Cep hotel one of its kind.

Two-Wheeled Vehicle Rental

■ BEAUNE À SOLEX

48, faubourg Saint-Martin
✆ +33 (0)6 69 08 76 62 – beauneasolex@orange.fr

Rental of a park of 10 solex from April to October. By reservation on weekdays. €24 2am, €40 4am, €75 per day, provided helmets and waistcoats fluo. Stroll supplemented by a tasting with the estate Baptist Guyot.

If you are in search of an unusual way to go for a spin between friends around Beaune, don't do like everyone else, ride a Solex ! Baptiste Guyot suggests it. Tjhe Solex of Baptiste, cousin of the Vespa and ancestor of the mob, allows you to discover the wine capital and its surroundings by riding in « tranquility » in the open air and without any danger. About ten genuine Solex in perfect operating condition are available for about 2h tour per day, with retro, bell, bags, helmets and fluorescent jackets included ! For groups of more than 10 people, you can also rent an electric Twizi to accompany your group. The most of a pleasant trip on the greenways in the local area, uphill and climbs eased by the valiant engine of 49 cm^3 consuming only one liter for every 70 km. The ideal journey ? The véloroute Beaune/Santenay, 22km in the heart of vineyards. Back at the estate, do not miss the friendship drink around a bottle of the estate. Remember to reserve your Solex in advance. But beware, you must all the same be at least 21 years old !

■ BEAUNE VÉLO TOUR

4, impasse du Pigeou ✆ +33 (0)6 23 31 15 93
www.beaunevelotour.fr – guydelepau@sfr.fr

Labels : Vignobles et Découverte + Accueil Vélo. Open all year round. High season from April to October ffrom Monday to Saturday from 9am to 7pm. Low season by appointment. VTC : €18 per day, VAE : €25 per day. Mountain bike course : €30 per half-day. Rental of accessories. Cheaper rates depending on the duration. Guided and commented bike rides. Formula with wine tasting : €29/person in VAE. A la carte formula.

To visit the region of Beaune by bicycle, no need to clutter your car up. Beaune Vélo Tour rents hybrid bicycle and electric bicycle which will perfectly make your day. Guy Delepau practices mountain biking for over 20 years, he is graduated with three sports instructor's certificates : physical activity for everyone, mountain-bike option cycling and scuba diving; he is moreover a member of the Moniteurs Cyclistes Français and is a first-aid trainer. At Beaune Vélo Tour, there is only guarantee of reliability. He offers for rent a comprehensive park of bicycles, more than twenty hybrid bicycle, four for children, about ten Electric bicycles. Useful to visit comfortably the Hautes Côtes ! Bicycles can be delivered in your departure place or in your hotel. There are several options : stroll in full freedom with itinerary recommended by Guy but we recommend you the one where you are assisted on courses from 20 to 30 km with excursion in the heart of the vineyards by electric bicycle, commentaries, photo posing and tastings at remarkably selected winemakers. A good way to combine sport, relaxation and wine tourism. Note : the menus also range around Nuits-Saint-Georges and Guy also offers mountain-bike training. Beaune Vélo Tour actively contributes to the development of bicycle touring in Côte-d'Or. Think that the TER of the region can embark your bicycles allowing you a forward or backward trip without pedalling.

Shopping

■ LA CAVE DES SAINTS-PÈRES

16, place Fleury
✆ +33 (0)6 11 49 41 46
www.lessaintsperes.com
lacave@lessaintperes.com

Open from Tuesday to Saturday from 10am to noon and from 2pm to 7.30pm. Closed at 9pm on Friday. The prices go from €8 to €500. A beautiful range of wines is sold between €20 and €80.

Welcome to « guard cellar », as we like to say in Béaune. Indeed, the Cave des Saints-Pères is mostly open on public holidays and Friday evenings until 9pm. If an aperitif is improvised at the last moment with your friends, do not panic, Adrien Dumay is there. It is located in a very nice place to find a good wine, a good champagne but especially some good advice. The shop located just a few steps of the hospices is attractive, it is rather chic, just the way you need it. Terracotta-tile floor, walls of mirrors endlessly responding to each other, lounge with a hushed atmosphere and with dark and thick carpet in the background. Adrien has chosen for guests over 250 references. There are often novelties, one more reason to go there regularly. For Burgundy, he retained fifty producers and his offer takes you to other regions : Loire, Rhône or Provence or but also in Italy or Switzerland. You will also find a collection of ten champagnes. You can trust him : he has tasted everything, his recommendations are based on his experience of great wine connoisseur and he does not sell a label to you, but the assurance of drinking a fine wine, in an optimum pleasure/price ratio. Adrien offers exclusively the Caviar de Neuvic of Aquitaine, ideal with an Aligoté Bouzeron, you see, you can be simple regarding wine.

■ CHANSON PÈRE & FILS

Bastion de l'Oratoire, 10, rue du Collège
✆ +33 (0)3 80 25 97 97
www.vins-chanson.com
chanson@domaine-chanson.com

Open Monday to Saturday from 9.30am to 12.30pm and from 2pm to 6pm. Visits of the Bastion and tastings by appointment.

Located in the historic site of the Bastion de l'Oratoire, one of the old defense towers of the city of Beaune, former military buildings built in the 17th century, Maison Chanson has existed since the middle of the 18th century.

In 1999, Chanson Père & Fils joined the family group of Bollinger champagnes. Maison Chanson produces more than one million bottles of wine per year on more than 100 appellations, distributed between the Beaujolais and Chablis. The wines from the estate are produced from the 45 hectares of vineyards owned by the group in Côte de Beaune, with a majority of Premiers and Grands Crus. The vineyards that use reasoned culture ensure 50% of the supplies, the other grapes come from purchases from carefully selected growers. Since 2002, Jean-Pierre Confuron brings his skills in winemaking and oenologist to the vinification quality. Maison Chanson renewed its image, after the new charter of graphic labels which become more rewarding with blue and taupe colors, it is now the turn of the new website to seduce us. There, Aesthetics is successful again. Discover the vineyards, visit the Bastion, access the large wine list of the cellar to finish at the virtual tasting cellar. You should visit it in real to appreciate the historic setting and the wine quality.

CAVEAU DÉLICAVE

24 bis, rue des Tonneliers
✆ +33 (0)3 80 22 45 10
www.delicave.over-blog.com
caveau@delicave.com

♿

Open from Monday to Friday from 9am to 12pm and from 2pm to 6pm. Open on Saturday by appointment for groups. Open on Saturday of the Sale of Wines from 9.30am to 12pm and from 2pm to 6.30pm. Admission fee during weekend of the sale of wines : €25 per person. €2 is transferred to an association helping families in difficulty.

Délicave is a place of wine purchase in Beaune which is distinguished under several aspects. The first is that it is held by a subsidiary company whose first trade is that of selecting the best cru of Burgundy and other regions of France and the world since more than thirty-five years. This is what you must retain, because here you do not yield to any fashion, the selections are rigorous and it is a choice of more than 500 references which is proposed to you. Go down in this splendid cellar where the « descents » of white, red and even grand cru will make you dream. Délicave is located within walking distance of the centre of Beaune, rue des Tonneliers, near Place Gaspard Monge. Let yourself be attracted by the coloured stained-glass windows of the cellar. The suggestion is renewed with the season of the selections of the year. After quality, the prices are excellent and make of Délicave an address of choice. Each year at the time of the sale of wines of Hospices de Beaune, the tasting formula of about ten fine wines is at €25. Délicave, which engages in actions of solidarity, transfers part of the price to charity associations. To combine wine and generosity is a principle which is completely anchored in the ethics of the Délicave cellar.

DOMAINE DU LYCÉE VITICOLE

Beaune-Viti-Agro-Campus
16, avenue Charles-Jaffelin ✆ +33 (0)3 80 26 35 80
www.domaine.lavitibeaune.com
marie-jeanne.jouquet@educagri.fr

Open Monday to Friday from 9am to 12pm and from 2pm to 5pm; Saturday from 9am to 12pm. Saturdays on appointment in January and February. Reception vault. Œnotouristic fixed rate formulas and group tours on appointment. Course « Stock in Verre », duration 2am, starting from 8 people, €10/person. Tour discovered, free, in the middle of the Climates of the Estate.

Domaine du Lycée Viticole is a Beaune's estate which offers a double interest. That of being the most important grape grower of the city, and of being a training place and a center of experimentation of wine and viticultural techniques, platform of competences with the agriculture room and the professional organizations of the wine as partners « la Viti », as it is presented in this high school in the region. Its 23 ha of vineyards, almost with Beaune appellations, ideally south facing, southeast that give birth to fine wines, produced with the last techniques on which the high school invests regularly, 2 ha of vineyards are in organic culture in order to teach this kind of culture. A new fermenting room will be set up in 2017. More than 100,000 bottles with 40% Premier Crus are produced, half of the production is sold to individuals. The vault for reception and tasting is arranged perfectly for this purpose. In addition to tastings and the visit of the cellars, several formulas are proposed, including a course to discover the Climates of the estate with English or French comments. This visit allows to join 6 plots with the different typical features with panoramic views and illustrated panels to understand their characteristics. By the way, Le Millésime 2015 is made with high-quality grapes that emphasize perfectly their climate as the production director of the estate pointed out to us. Domaine du Lycée Viticole takes part in many salons, you can discover its wines with the presence of motivated and promising school student. In 2016 the wesite online sales will enable you to buy your choices from your home.

DOMAINE LOÏS DUFOULEUR

8, boulevard Bretonnière
✆ +33 (0)3 80 22 04 62
www.domaineloisdufouleur.com
contact@domaineloisdufouleur.com

Open every day. Sale tasting on appointment – Guestrooms and furnished with tourism of charm : Les Jardins de Lois.

Domaine Loïs Dufouleur is a small beaunois area located a few steps from Hospices de Beaune. The happy owners, Anne-Marie and Philippe Dufouleur, exploit five hectares of vineyards, mainly on Beaune but also in Savigny-les-Beaune which gives rise to 14 names. Eight of them are in red, that is to say 85% of a total volume of 30,000 bottles approximately each year. Passed the porch, you discover with happiness an area whose fermenting room and cellars are next to five chambres d'hôtes and an absolutely refine furnished apartment : « Les Jardins de Loïs ». The work of the vineyard in reasoned farming is ensured by Anne-Marie Dufouleur. Philippe Dufouleur ensures the work of vinification respecting the typical feature of each one of his locals, of each climate. Appreciate the jewels of the house which are Beaune 1er Cru rouge, Clos des Perrières, Clos du Roi and Cent-Vignes. To remain on the 1st raw ones, the white Champs Pimonts could also attract you. Very favorite for the quality of the reception of this area, Philippe and Anne Marie Dufouleur are happy to make you taste their wines in their cellar, by appointment, unless you are resident of the chambres d'hôtes, in which case you are their guest.

■ ENJOY FALLOT – LA MOUTARDERIE

31, faubourg Bretonnière ✆ +33 (0)3 80 22 10 10
www.enjoyfallot.com – accueil@fallot.com

Open Monday to Saturday from 9.30am to 6pm. Open certain Sunday morning in high season. Closed from 1pm to 2pm November 15th at March 15th. Possible courses of visits. Course Discovered (interactive and ludic space museographic) or Strong Feelings (visit of the current production). Online booking or near the Tourist Office of Beaune.

Enjoy Fallot is the beaunoise shop of La Moutarderie Fallot. A shop with very modern architecture to discover absolutely. La Moutarde, which became a premium seasoning with innovating recipes, is the star of the place. Imagine ! You have a bar with mustard accessible to all in order to taste the most popular mustards. On request all the range is « dégustable ». A funny distributor of mini-pots for 1 euro gives you the impression of dealing with confectioneries. Tasting is essential to make your choice because there are many recipes of which you need to know the exact taste. Some are very soft, others very strong or a little sweet ! The subtle flavours come from the use of curry, rosemary, Pinot Noir, truffles, Espelette pepper, gingerbread, honey, marc of Burgundy... Some are signed Bernard Loiseau, fines and exquisite. For the classical ones, of Dijon, Burgundy, in grain or with gingerbread, the bulk distributors allow you to eat from the famous stoneware jars. If you still have time, you can choose the discovery tour, immersion in the history of the house in order to become unbeatable on the manufacturing of mustard with ground mustard seeds with the stone grinder. Another shop of Moutarderie Fallot is installed in Dijon, rue de la Chouette. Little reminder Moutarderie Fallot produces more than 200 000 tons of mustard a year in Beaune, 50% of the production is exported, the rest is sold in delicatessen and in its 2 côte-d'oriennes shops.

GALERIE MICHEL PERNÈS

19, rue Monge ✆ +33 (0)3 80 24 92 67
www.pernes.com – michel-pernes@orange.fr

Open from Tuesday to Saturday from 10.30 a.m. to 12.30 p.m. and from 2.30 p.m. to 7.30 p.m. Closed in January and February. Open on Sundays on appointment. Exhibitions, sales, expeditions.

If you are an art and painting lover, you should not miss the Michel Pernès galerie opposite to Hospices de Beaune. You can't miss it because the works displayed on the shop window always attract attention. Michel Pernès, painter since 1961, found his own characteristic style, a painting carried out with great finesse, with oil on canvas and always with the palette knife on often large formats. Its collection that is unceasingly renewed makes you travel, in Beaune and in many charming towns of the region. You travel to India, the United States, Qatar or Venice. Its paintings show the moments of life of a landscape with a disconcerting reality by moderate set of lights of transparencies and shades, specific to the artist. The melancholy point of the work of Michel Pernès is that he uses merry colors. He always has on him his notebook on which he crunches the landscapes that inspired him throughout his travels. It is in its workshop, opened on nature and conducive to creation, that its drafts are born and are changed in bright paintings in a contemporary figurative style that seduces and that everyone likes. Michel Pernès displays his works in France but also in Switzerland, in Belgium, in Germany and in the United States. You are warmly accommodated in the gallery by Mrs Jocelyne Pernès who shows you the her husband's creations. If you wish to add Pernès to your collection, note that your painting can be sent everywhere in the world. You will appreciate the quality of the framings !

■ MAISON LOUIS JADOT

62, route de Savigny ✆ +33 (0)3 80 26 31 98
www.louisjadot.com – visit@louisjadot.com

Open Monday to Friday from 3pm to 7pm; Saturday from 11am to 5.30pm. By reservation visit of the fermenting room and the cellars followed by a tasting : €20. Tasting only €10. Shop of sale.

The first vines of the Maison Jadot were planted in 1826, three generations of this family succeeded there. In 1984, Jadot became an American property but retained its Burgundian soul. Today, Maison Louis Jadot controls 220 hectares in Burgundy, including 80 in Beaujolais. Since the spring 2013, Maison Louis Jadot has been open to individuals. Its shop is installed in the north of Beaune, in the heart fermenting rooms. The architecture of the fermenting room of Rouges is impressive; it is reminiscent of a cathedral. That of the white, equally large, is more contemporary and contrasting sharply with the previous one. The long raising cave of a hundred metres, houses nearly 4,000 references. The tasting that closes this memorable visit allows you to discover the Louis Jadot wines. The tours are only in small groups; the shop is accessible without the visit.

■ JOSEPH DROUHIN
1, cour du Parlement
✆ +33 (0)3 80 24 84 05
www.drouhin-oenotheque.com/fr
oenotheque@drouhin.com

Low season : open from Monday to Saturday from 9.30 am to 6 pm. High season : from Monday to Saturday from 9.30 am to 6.30 pm. Visits in French and English upon appointment. Visit and tasting : 38 €, wine shop. Visits at 10.00 am, 2 pm and 4 pm. Themed visits and tastings, wine pairing dinners, concerts and vineyard tours, tailor-made programs. Wine shipping possible within France, to the USA, Australia, Japan, Hong Kong and Singapore.

The Oenotheque of the Maison Joseph Drouhin is situated in the heart of Beaune in the former Burgundy Parliament, just in front of the collegiate church of Notre-Dame, and is a unique architectural and historical building. It is the showcase of the wines of the domaine that have acquired worldwide renown. Founded in 1880, the Domaine is now under the management of the 4th generation of the Drouhin family. Veronique, Frédéric, Laurent and Philippe take charge of the wine-making, management, export and viticulture respectively. The Oenotheque is a fabulous boutique where a selection of more than 90 appellations can be found, including some of the old vintages coming directly from the family's' reserve cellar. Not to be missed is the visit of the cellars including parts of the former Roman Castrum, and including the beautiful vaults of the 13th century church cellars. This historical and cultural journey is followed by the tasting of a selection of 6 wines. The Oenotheque regularly offers different themed dinners and tastings, surprise tastings, old vintages and Chablis tastings…. Always upon reservation and for groups limited to 30 people. Reservations are possible by clicking on the event on the website. Tailor-made wine events are also available upon request. In 2016 vineyard visits will also be arranged in order to discover more far flung parcels belonging to the family. There is no shortage of things to see, if we remember that the family are the owners of 73 hectares of vines from Chablis, the Côte de Nuits, Côte de Beaune and Côte Chalonnaise; all bio-dynamically farmed, and not forgetting 160 hectares in Oregon.

■ MARCHÉ AUX VINS
7, rue de l'Hôtel-Dieu
✆ +33 (0)3 80 25 08 20
www.marcheauxvins.com
e-boutique@marcheauxvins.com

Low season : open every day from 10am to 12pm and from 2pm to 5.30pm. High season : every day from 10am to 6.30pm. Low-season from November to March. The weekend of the sale of the wines of Hospices de Beaune, open from 9.30am to 6pm. Closed the 24 and December 25th, on January 1st. Delivery (free on Beaune). Cocktails and receptions. Dinners for groups from €85 to €105 by reservation. Tastings of 7 (€11/pers.) with 12 wines (€25/pers.). More fixed rate formula Prestige at €45. Tastevin or drink offered depending on the fixed rate formula. Group rate (sea-green 20) : tasting of 3 or 5 wines from €6.50 or €8/pers.

Marché aux Vins of Beaune is set in the former Cordeliers church. Owned by the Halley family, just like château de Meursault and château de Marsannay, this emblematic place full of history was redesigned last year. It is beautiful ! The rue de l'Hôtel Dieu window allows you to see the interior of the former church founded at the end of the 14th or at the beginning of the 15th century. Once inside, you will cross the beautiful cellars lined with oak barrels, while tasting different appellations of Burgundy, with very evocative names. The candle light gives a unique atmosphere to the place. You can continue the visit by discovering the lateral chapels, the history of wine in Beaune, the presentation of the famous climates and finish the tour at the foot of the only white grape vines of the city. Amazing ! The Franciscans cultivated it in the 13th century to make their sacramental wine. Enjoy the new, modern and air-conditioned shop, of this market like no other, where all the productions of the châteaux de Marsannay and Meursault are offered and where you can also buy mustard, fruit nectars or other snails. Finally, Marché aux Vins offers many tasting formulas up to dinner, or receptions. An ideal place to buy and taste delicious drinks. Quality welcome and guaranteed feast for the eyes !

■ MILLÉSIMES À LA CARTE
1, rue du Moulin Noize
✆ +33 (0)3 80 20 68 68
www.millesimesalacarte.com

Open from Tuesday to Saturday from 10am to noon and from 2.30pm to 7pm; on Sunday from 10am to noon. Possible delivery (on line store). Easy parking. Tastings. Tasting à la carte menu from €5. Wine by the glass price from €0.70 to €15. Tasting workshops(between €15 and €40 per person). Sale at local prices. Old vintages.

Millésimes à la Carte is a specialised universe to discover, taste and buy wines. Thierry Prat, who worked in great estate house of the Côte, chose to share his passion with us throughout formula offers that meets the expectation of tourists who are curious on understanding the climate of Burgundy. Located in a hotel zone and easily accessible, you are welcomed is very bright 200 m² store where you can find at least selected 500 references in the region, « the best of the best » according to Thierry Prat. You can especially taste 40 wines via automated wine bars. The principle is simple : you buy a prepaid card and you enjoy freely the offered wines. The rates are indicated and deducted from your credit, the offer is regularly renewed : Chablis, Côte-de-Nuits, Côte-de-Beaune, Côte-Chalonnaise and Mâconnais, wines that are prestigious or produced by new talent and always one or two old vintages. If you require some further explanations, the team is at your disposal. Several themed workshops are offered to groups. La Pyramide des Crus allows you to have a good understanding of the difference between the appellations and especially for a better reading of the labels. Otherwise, tastings are free, fun, educational; they make you discover the flavours of our terroir. The other asset of the address is that it offers a choice of 1,000 old vintages, aged from 10 to 98 years. You should not miss to visit this cellar during your passage in Beaune.

■ NUITON-BEAUNOY – LA CAVE DES HAUTES-CÔTES

93-95, route de Pommard ✆ +33 (0)3 80 25 01 03
www.nuiton-beaunoy.com
lecaveau@nuiton-beaunoy.fr
Motorway exit Beaune-Center No. 24.1

From January to March : open from Monday to Saturday from 10am to noon and from 2pm to 6pm. From April to June and from October to November : every day from 10am to 12.30pm and from 2pm to 7pm. From July to September : every day from 9am to 7pm. December : Every day from 10am to noon and from 2pm to 6pm. Large car park and children's corner. Groups welcome between 10 and 35 people and personalized tasting on request (€6 per person). Space gifts for wine lovers. Reception of seminars. Free entry. Elevator.

88 winegrowers form the Nuiton-Beaunoy today, all of them are associates at Côtes et Hautes-Côtes. Therefore, this large collaboration covers 520 hectares of vineyards, i.e a production of 25,000 hectolitres of wine per year. A carefully controlled culture and reasonable cultivation, while maintaining the health of the land and the vineyard, carried out with passion. The associate winemakers under the Nuiton-Beaunoy images represent the Côtes et Hautes-Côtes de Nuits, the Côtes et Hautes-Côtes de Beaune. Thus they represent all the diversity of Burgundy with grand crus, village appellation (with premier crus), regional appellation, Bourgogne Hautes-Côtes de Beaune and Hautes-Côtes de Nuits. Therefore, you will find AOC, white, red, crémant de Bourgogne of all the territory : Pommard, Volnay, Pernand-Vergelesses, Santenay, Gevrey-Chambertin, Marsannay, Aloxe-Corton and so many others. The tasting cellar, enjoying panoramic views of the vineyards, is located close to Beaune. Cindy and his team invite you to discover a prestigious range. Gourmet tastings, exhibitions and events are held throughout the year and especially the third weekend of November, during the sale of wines, or in April during open days of the vault. The exhibition "*Terre de Bourgogne*" organised by Jean-François Caillot, has taken place at the vault since 9 January. Think also of Nuiton-Beaunoy for your meetings : fully equipped, the room of Grand crus can accommodate up to 35 people.

■ PASSION MILLOT – PATISSIER – CHOCOLATIER

1, place Monge ✆ +33 (0)3 80 22 10 35
www.passionmillot.com
passionmillot@gmail.com

Open from Tuesday to Friday from 9am to 12.30pm and from 2pm to 7pm; on Saturday from 8am to 7pm; on Sunday from 8am to 1pm and from 3pm to 6.30. Tearoom with terrace. Breakfasts.

Pascal Millot and his wife Virginie, who took over in 2011 the famous Maison Bouché, have now anchored their own brand, Passion Millot, signature of quality and inventiveness of refined products. Pascal Millot implements on the spot, with a team of twelve people, pastries, chocolates, ice creams, macaroons as well as many confectioneries. Everything is homemade with much technicality, precision and talent. The choice of a pastry is not simple. If you like entremets, choose the Marion or the Mathieu, two creations of Pascal Millot which allow you to discover the taste of the yuzu and the combava, two rather powerful citrus fruits which will not leave you indifferent. The classic of the house is the Concorde, heritage of Maison Bouché, composed of a chocolate meringue combined to a chocolate mousse, a simplicity which delights the gourmet ones. The chocolates are manufactured with a selection of cocoa beans from the four corners of the world available in about forty candies and not less than eighteen references in tablets. There is great originality in flavours. The chef regularly offers innovations, transitory cakes which exist only for one to two weekends, depending on the market and good mood. Take advantage of the tea room where you can warm yourself around a rare tea, black or green, an infusion, a hot chocolate or a coffee, but especially accompanied by a unique delicacy. Do not miss the splendid window displays of the moment. In the summer, there is the terrace for the sweet snack.

PATRIARCHE PÈRE ET FILS
5-7, rue du Collège
✆ +33 (0)3 80 24 53 87
✆ +33 (0)3 80 24 53 78
www.patriarche.com
crichard@patriarche.com

Open every day from 9.30am to 11.30am and from 2pm to 5.30pm. Closed at 5pm on Saturday and Sunday from October 1st to March 31st. Closed on December 24th, 25th, 31st and January 1st. Reception in English, German, Italian, Dutch, Spanish, Russian, Chinese and Japanese. Shop. By reservation, visit-tasting formulas from €20, visit diner tasting formulas, tastings and initiations to tasting open to individuals and groups. Possible delivery. Free tour and tasting of 13 wines : €17 tastevin offered. By reservation (20 people minimum) : audio-guided tour and tasting of 8 wines : €12 tastevin offered.

Since 2015, Patriarche renews its offer and confirms its position of privileged actor for the discovery of the Burgundian climats listed in the UNESCO World Heritage site. Visit the largest cellars of Burgundy, property of the group Castel, worldwide number 1 of French wines. Built between the 13th and 18th century, they shelter 3 million bottles, their visit leads you to the heart of 5 km corridors with magical lighting marked by interactive terminals and tasting stopover. You will discover a history that began in 1796 when Jean-Baptiste Patriarche bought the former convent of the Visitandines and creates his trading company. In 1940, André Boisseaux took over the address and becoming one of the leading traders-breeders-owners-collectors in the region, company sold to the Groupe Castel in 2011. Access a range of more than 300 wine references, Regional appellations, 1er Cru, Grands Crus, Crémant… During the visit, you can fill your basket or go directly to the new completely refurbished shop where all Patriarche wines are developed alongside produce and arts of wine tasting. The visit's formula is also renewed, whether recurrent or specific, from small budget to upscale formulas, they go with gourmet dinner and with a sommelier. Remember to book.

THE COOK'S ATELIER
43, rue de Lorraine
✆ +33 ()03 80 24 61 80 / +33 (0)6 84 83 16 18
www.thecooksatelier.com

Open Tuesday to Saturday from 10am to 7pm. Gourmet wines, products and tablewares. Cookery classes personalized €250 per person.

The Cook's Atelier is not just a place where cooking classes are taken, it is also the address of a wine merchant, AP Wine, managed by Kendall and Laurent Franchini. Marjorie Taylor, former Chef, teaches the art of local cuisine, her daughter and her son-in-law manage the wine shop. AP Wine offers fine selections, Kendall, sommelier ensures the selling. Burgundy, Alsace, the Loire, Champagne, Bordeaux, all regions of France are represented. Small productions, original and exclusive suggestions in the region. The shop is integrated into The Cook's Atelier, you can also buy delicatessen products including some kitchenware, those used in the Atelier, Williams Sonoma or Mauviel 1830 copper pans… AP Wine is also an online store, practical. But the must is to go to the shop where this entire small world is set in a beautifully furnished place that has a lot of charm. A loft spread over three levels at rue de Lorraine.

In the surroundings

Chorey-lès-Beaune

ERMITAGE DE CORTON
Route de Dijon ✆ +33 (0)3 80 22 05 28
www.ermitagecorton.com
contact@ermitagecorton.com

Châteaux & Hôtels Collection – Vignobles et découvertes label. Open every day for lunch and dinner. Menus from €37 to €77. Children's menu : €15 (2 main courses, €18 3 main courses. Up to 10 years-old). Lunch formula : €29 (menu of the market 3 main courses – starter €8 - main course €16 - dessert €6). Wine by the glass. Hotel 4 stars with 12 rooms. American Express. Garden. Terrace.

L'Ermitage de Corton, installed in an idyllic setting on the wine roads, is a high-quality hotel and a restaurant. At the helm of the kitchens : Vincent Chirat, who already officiated in starred establishments, but who has also perfectly found his niche here. He carries out an authentic cuisine, entirely homemade, working his products and his suggestions with care and talent. The served dishes are as aesthetic as tasty ! Appreciate the comfort of the restaurant room, white topping and the impeccable service. Also enjoy the unique view on the mountain of Corton. It is also that, the charm of L'Ermitage. For lunch in week and until Saturday, the menu of the market constitutes an excellent choice. It is the daily surprise of the chef. With the à la carte or the menus, offer yourself the gourmet excellence of L'Ermitage. Lasagnas of snails, line-caught bar in scales with truffle of Burgundy, Breton lobster with mustard, royal wild hare of the Ardennes... Everything is beautiful, delicious and subtly prepared. The surprise is the vegetarian suggestion whose flavours are worked carefully : carrots fondant with candied lemon, walnut nougatine or risotto with ceps. The travellers who visit Burgundy will appreciate the menu of the climates of Burgundy inspired by the regional grounds. L'Ermitage is an establishment which maintains a unique atmosphere, the key of its success.

La Rochepot

LE CLOS DES 4 SAISONS

Hameau Les Lourchardes
✆ +33 (0)3 80 21 37 73 / +33 (0)6 89 77 45 42
www.leclosdes4saisons.com
contact@leclosdes4saisons.com
3 km from La Rochepot, at the exit to Louchardes, turn into a small road to the left; it is here at 300 m.

Open all year round. 5 rooms. Double room from €88. Breakfast included. Extra bed : €25. Closed parking (convenient, vast and well lighted). Holiday vouchers. Pets allowed (puppies only). wi-fi. Catering facilities (aperitif and full meal without wines : €30).

The guest house of Sylviane Zapla has everything to allure. Like her, who left her native country Switzerland for Nolay, you will fall in love with this place. The five rooms are installed in an outbuilding of the house. Vast and very comfortable, an absolute tranquillity reigns there and they are equipped with many highlights like a memory form bedding. They all have a direct access to the garden by a lovely terrace and a stunning view on the mounts and valleys of the south of Nolay. The name of the first four rooms recalls the seasons. The last one is called « La Cinquième Saison », that of the love which lasts forever ! After the comfort of her house, Sylviane Zapla invites you to share her table d'hôte. Her dinners are gourmet, She attends cooking classes regularly, by passion and desire to please. Aperitif is offered, starter « En passant par la Bourgogne » with some snails, parsley and an egg in meurette way. Then, a Gaston Gérard chicken or a cockerel with Chardonnay... Regional cheeses and gourmet dishes with several migniardises. All are homemade. You are cherished in summer like in winter, on the sumptuous terrace or in the spacious dining room with refined decor. The mission of Sylviane would not be complete without her advice to visit the region. She can organize you tastings at local vine growers. By the green lane, by bicycle, you can go to Santenay which is 8.5 km away. You are located well to enjoy the best of Burgundy.

Levernois

HOSTELLERIE DE LEVERNOIS

Rue du Golf ✆ +33 (0)3 80 24 73 58
www.levernois.com/restaurant
levernois@relaischateaux.com

Closed from end of January to beginning of March. Low season : open Thursday to Monday and public holidays for dinner. High season : every day and public holidays for dinner. High season from April 1st to October 30th. Booking advised. Menu from €70 to €105. Wine by the glass. À la carte. American Express. Groups welcome. Terrace. Valet. Activities.

Hostellerie de Levernois shelters a renowned gastronomic restaurant, whose Michelin star chef, Philippe Augé, is undoubtedly one of best in the region. He elaborates exceptional dishes in an idyllic place, in the middle of a green nature. Throughout the season, the chef shows an incredible creativity to highlight the products he works with, the vegetables is at the bottom of the park of the Hostellerie. Foie gras, frogs, snails, lobster, bar, veal, are tickled pink... The nobility of the à la carte menu is impressive but what is better is the manner he sublimates these products. As with charolais beef with marrow accompanied by shallot leaves with Pinot Noir, pomme soufflé and endive or turbot with algae crusts, its Zita pasta and shellfishes with marinara sauce. The royale hare, pumpkin tatin, beets and apples with velvet sauce are delicious ! As for the desserts, they are presented on a whole à la carte menu and we quickly understand why. They are stunning like the whole chocolate with pecan and the ivory ice cream and delicacies with caramel, with broad Tonka bean and bourbon vanilla... Miam. Without talking about the elaborate ambitious menus according to the themes : garden, gourmet, gourmand, surprise... A table that combines refinement, passion and impeccable service. And note that you can prolong the pleasure by spending one night at Hostellerie.

BEST WESTERN GOLF HÔTEL COLVERT

23, rue du Golf
✆ +33 (0)3 80 24 78 20
www.golf-hotel-beaune.com
hotelcolvert@wanadoo.fr

24 rooms. Double room from €95 to €155. Buffet breakfast : €14. Extra bed : €20. Garage : €8. Family rooms (communicating) : from €195 to €270. Suite for 3 and 4 people €330. Pets allowed (€8). Seminars. Free Wifi. Catering facilities (tray meal on request : €22 main course, cheese and dessert excluding drinks. Simple main course : €15). Satellite TV. Excursions (fixed rate formulas visits estate + catering facilities + hospices of Beaune – bike rental).

Golf Hôtel Colvert is a charming hotel located in the greenery, outside the city with a choice of several restaurants, including one starred, nearby. You will enjoy the pretty light that bathes this establishment with large bay windows. Living spaces and the rooms upstairs, accessible by lift, have a pleasant and green view, without any opposite. In 2016, all rooms will have been completely renovated, bathrooms, furniture, decor, flooring, everything has been reviewed. The designer chose to colour the rooms, none is identical, they retain a contemporary style. They are always spacious : at least 25 m² and each have a balcony with little garden furniture. The heated pool completes the assets of the hotel. Agnès Debeaux, the owner of the hotel, knows the numerous touristic sites of Beaune and its surroundings well. She is happy to help you ! The « séjour œnotouristique » formula offers the best of the region. It includes one night with breakfast, a glass of sparkling wine offered on arrival, a dinner at the restaurant, a visit and a tasting in a vineyard and finally a short trip in a tourist site of Beaune.

■ HOSTELLERIE DE LEVERNOIS

Rue du Golf
✆ +33 (0)3 80 24 73 58
www.levernois.com/restaurant
levernois@relaischateaux.com

Relais & Châteaux. Closed from February to mid-March. Reception 24h a day (reception, night porter and concierge). 22 rooms (and 4 suites); from €150 to €500. Half-board (from €354 to €704). Buffet breakfast : €22 (€11 for children). Extra bed : €45 (free cot). Parking included (valet). Pets allowed. Seminars. Receptions and weddings. Free Wifi. Catering facilities (gourmet restaurant menu from €70; Bistro Au bord de l'Eau : menu from €30). Satellite TV.

Hostellerie de Levernois is a 5-star establishment and has been a part of Relais & Châteaux since 1991, where luxury blends blissfully with nature. A great deal of works has been undertaken (still 12 rooms renovated this year) since the repurchase of this establishment by the Bottigliero spouses 12 years ago ! With 20 rooms, two of them are accessible to disabled person, and 4 suites and 2 bright and very modern junior suites, a starred gourmet restaurant with an exceptional cellar and a bistro, the setting is magnificent. The rooms are scattered in three places : the main building, the pavillion and the Meix des Glycines, all of them are havens of peace. This modern holiday resort attracts exceptional travellers for whom everything has been designed to make their stay unforgettable. The charm of Burgundy are within walking distance : cultural (Beaune is less than 10 minutes) or gourmet thanks to Philippe Augé and where you can enjoy the cuisine at « Bistrot au Bord de l'Eau », or opting for the classic, must-go and unforgettable « gourmet restaurant ». La Boutik (regional produces, kitchen accessories, decoration...) offers you a warm welcome and souvenir gift idea to offer or to take home. Note also that you can organise tasting of quality in the cellar for a small number of insiders or lovers... The sommelier awaits you on Thursday and Saturday at 6.30pm for the tasting of 4 wines from the same village (€20 per person). All the commercial offers of different establishments of the Bottigliero spouses are gathered on the website : www.bourgogne-experience.com. Do you feel like going to an exceptional setting ? This is the ideal place !

Sainte-Marie-la-Blanche

■ CAVE SAINTE-MARIE-LA-BLANCHE

15, route de Verdun ✆ +33 (0)3 80 26 60 60
contact@cavesaintemarie.fr

Open from Monday to Saturday from 9am to noon and from 2pm to 6pm. Wine tasting cellar. Sale of wine in bottles and in bulk.

Located a few kilometres from Beaune, Cave Sainte-Marie has a wide range of wines at very affordable prices. The ceiling with exposed beams gives charm to the bright and spacious room that serves as a retail point. You will find a wide variety of names illustrating the shades of terroir of Burgundy on beautiful wooden shelves such as passe-tout-grain, aligoté, appellation village, premier cru... without forgetting the pretty shelves of crémants and liqueurs (Fine Bourgogne, cream of cassis, of vine peach, of cherry, etc). Meursaults, Monthélie, Volnay, Pommard and Beaune are well represented, as well as Gevrey-Chambertin and Nuits-Saint-Georges. Aline, Catherine and Ghislaine give advice on successful food and wine pairings. Cave Sainte-Marie-La-Blanche also offers wines in bulk or in BIB (Bag In Box). As for tasting : the sessions are open to everyone, rich in information and friendly. Do not miss the fair with the wines organised by the house in October. Open for nearly 60 years, the cellar Sainte-Marie has loyalty cards today offering nice discounts. We strongly recommend this address that has the advantages of providing a staff attentive to your desire and at the same time reasonable prices !

Savigny-lès-Beaune ★★

■ R... DE FAMILLE

5, place Fournier
✆ +33 (0)3 80 21 50 00 – www.rdefamille.fr
restaurant@rdefamille.fr

Open all year. Low season : Tuesday to Sunday for lunch; Thursday to Sunday for dinner. High season : Tuesday to Sunday for lunch and dinner. Low season from November to March. Children's menu : €9.50. Lunch menu : €13.50 (3 main courses, €15 4 main courses except in July and August). Wine by the glass. Menu at €28 : starter, main course, cheese or dessert. Menu at €31 : starter, main course, cheese and dessert. Pizzas from €9. Groups welcome. Terrace. Take-away pizzas. Theme parties except summer period.

R... de Famille maintains its capital conviviality and sympathy. Sandrine and her brother Olivier keep on renovating their establishment. Regulars will have noticed the completely mobile new facade that seems to expand the terrace inside, once it is open in summer. Le Château de Savigny and the beautiful place Fournier are always the good neighbours of the restaurant. It is hard to find better.

The menu changes according to the days of the week and the seasons. In summer, you can enjoy salads, parsleyed homemade Ham or the famous snails. In October, you will find with pleasure the winter's dishes : poached eggs, frog legs with parsley, marrowbone or Burgundy beef in grandmother's way. Everything is accompanied by a glass of Savigny ! And do not forget the pizza ! Soon at the end of the summer, R... Family organises themed evenings, *Tête de Veau, Cassoulet Toulousain, Œufs Meurette*... In low season, the menu is perfect, cheese and dessert for €15. Suffice to say that the prices are fine. We love the atmosphere and the efficient service.

LE HAMEAU DE BARBORON

Lieu-dit Barboron ✆ +33 (0)3 80 21 58 35
www.hameau-barboron.com
lehameaudebarboron@wanadoo.fr

14 rooms. Double room from €99 to €145; suite from €165 to €210. Breakfast : €15. Seminars. Receptions and weddings. Catering facilities (to dine : €39.50 by reservation for the residents of the hotel. Festive meals starting from 15 people up to 80 people in the storerooms and up to 400 people under structure frame wood from April to October). Satellite TV.

Le Hameau de Barboron is a hotel with timeless style in a green setting at just a few minutes from Beaune, amidst nature, between wood and valleys. This perfectly restored farmhouse offers a genuine and absolutely unique charm. The area is secluded from the hustle and bustle and is a convenient place to enjoy the peace of the countryside. In the rooms, wood and rustic furniture offers a great confort. They are real cocoon of impeccable sweetness and each of them is personalised. If you don't want to move away from the place, which will probably happen, you will be served a Burgundian meal (upon reservation) in a charming dining room. You can find « everything » on the spot, in fact in the paved courtyard, the small shop offers local products : jams, gingerbreads, mustards with multiple flavours, organic infusions... and a wide range of wines from the estate ! The address develops business tourism with à la carte services offering several work areas. Banquets are possible for small groups in the storerooms and up to 400 people in the « Prairie » space, a beautiful structure with wood frame. Le Hameau de Barboron maintain marvelously its capital comfort which is, at risk of repeating, unique in the region.

CHÂTEAU DE SAVIGNY-LÈS-BEAUNE

Rue Vauchey-Véry
✆ +33 (0)3 80 21 55 03
www.chateau-savigny.com
contact@chateau-savigny.com

Low season : open every day from 9am to 12pm and from 2pm to 5.30pm. High season : every day from 9am to 6.30pm. Last entrances 1.30am before closing. Closed the first 3 weeks of January. Adult : €10. From 9 to 15 years old children : €5. Free for child up to 9 years. Tastings with sale of wine by the glass. Fixed rate formulas reception with meal caterer starting from 20 people by reservation.

The Château de Savigny-lès-Beaune is an unusual estate. 12 hectares of greenery surround this castle which dates back to the 14th century. It is primarily a wine estate of about twenty hectares run by Christophe Pont. The vineyards and appellations spread over Savigny-lès-Beaune, where four acres of vineyards produce the Cuvée du Château Monopole, on Beaune, Meursault, Pommard, Volnay, Auxey-Duresses, Monthélie... Adults will appreciate the visit of « Petit Château ». This building, built in the 17th century, was used as stables and outbuildings ! It is arranged today for tasting and take-away sales of grands crus bottled in the beautiful cellars of the castle. Children and adults will undoubtedly be impressed by the visit of museums. The first contains nearly 250 motorbikes that date back to 1902 until 1960, multiple nationalities. In the museum of racing car, you will discover an exceptional collection of 30 « Abarth » prototypes some of which are unique. But that is not all ! 80 fighter planes are exhibited in the park. And do not forget the many models of planes, the fire trucks, the thirty straddle tractors and the wine equipment. Fascinating ! Note that you can also enjoy the wines of the castle during a candlelight dinner arranged upon reservation for groups. A place that makes children and adults dream !

DOMAINE JEAN-JACQUES GIRARD

16, rue de Cîteaux
✆ +33 (0)3 80 21 56 15
www.domaine-girard.com
contact@domaine-girard.com

Open Monday to Saturday from 8am to 12pm and from 2pm to 7pm; Sunday from 8am to 12pm. Visits on appointment.

The history of this estate of Savigny which belongs to one of the oldest families of Savigny-les-Beaune wine growers dates back to 1529. Since 1977, Jean-Jacques and Agnès Girard have been in charge of the estate whereas Vincent, one of the children starts to put his mark on the vinifications which while respecting their climates evolve subtly. The estate exploits 18 ha of vineyards mainly in Savigny but also in Pernand-Vergelesses, Aloxe-Corton, Volnay, Pommard and Beaune. Reasoned culture and tradition go together very well. The estate offers wines whose prices are very reasonable for their quality. Nearly twenty names including the Grand Cru Corton Charlemagne and red Corton Grand Cru « En Charlemagne ». It is through the small rue de Cîteaux, where the monks formerly lived, which we can reach the historic residence of the estate. Passed the porch, you discover a beautiful square courtyard surrounded by various buildings housing the winery and the home cellar. It is at the cellar that tastings take place ! Discover the wealth of these beautiful samples of the Climats de Bourgogne, red or white, Villages, 1ers Crus and Grands Crus, in a place with a great charm.

HENRI DE VILLAMONT

2, rue du Docteur-Guyot
✆ +33 (0)3 80 21 52 13 / +33 (0)3 80 21 50 59
www.hdv.fr
contact@hdv.fr

Open from Tuesday to Friday from 10am to 12.30pm and from 1.30pm to 6pm. By appointment on Monday, Tuesday and Saturday. Closed on Sunday. Many fixed rate formulas of tastings and visits.

Domaine Henri de Villamont located at the foot of slopes of Savigny at 5 minutes from Beaune is undoubtedly a crucial stopover for the connoisseurs of wine and history. Its building, which were built by Léonce Bocquet in 1880, have a remarkable architecture. Once you park your car in the large courtyard, you are in the quiet in front of the vineyards and the park of the estate, it is very beautiful. As owner and breeder, he has more than 10 hectares of vineyards including 6.5 hectares in Savigny-the-Beaune, under your eyes, and 4 hectares in Côte de Nuits. Henri de Villamont completes his productions in grape trade to produce a very full range moreover 70 names of which 50% are white ! They go from Chassagne-Montrachet, in Côte de Beaune, in Fixin, in Côte de Nuits, Meursault, Pommard, Gevrey-Chambertin.... The wine bar is installed in the old cooperage transformed into a shop. It is also the starting point of a really spectacular visit that takes you in the fermenting room and the impressive cellars whose vaults go up to 6 meters in height ! Pierre Jhean, the director of the estate, managed to impose his brand on the vinifications by skilfully balancing modernity and tradition. The vineyards cultivated in a reasoned culture and the investments in fermenting room make it possible to produce quality wines in the perfect respect of their climates. In 2016, Henri de Villamont markets his first vintage produced from his new vineyards : Les Savigny Beaune Chardonnay « 1er cru Clos des Guettes » and « Le Village » whose first harvests took place in 2014.

■ PAVILLON DES VIGNERONS
13, rue Vauchey-Very
✆ +33 (0)3 80 22 19 86 / +33 (0)3 80 21 50 46
alimentation-mhbize@orange.fr
♿

Open from 10am to 12.30pm and from 2.30pm to 7pm. High season, closed on Monday morning. Low season, closed on Sunday afternoon and Monday. Wines and sparkling wines from the Savigny-les-Beaune areas : from €5.50 to €65. Local products.

Le Pavillon des Vignerons is the ideal and practical place to reach all the estates of Savigny-lès-Beaune. Marie-Hélène and Michel Bize, natives of the village and born traders since they are managers of the Au Panier Sympa grocery, near the pavilion, created « the » window display of the climats of Savigny-lès-Beaune. It is in all simplicity, but with a great pleasure that they propose us wines and 25 Cremants of the town's estates. Each estate is represented by several wines, which gives access to a full pallet of the regional offer. Indeed, the estates have all the plots distributed on the Côte de Beaune and even to the Côtes de Nuits. In addition to the Savigny names, you find in villages and Premiers crus of Beaune, Pernand-Vergelesses, Aloxe-Corton, Chorey-lès-Beaune, Pommard, Meursault, Saint-Romain, Rully and thus also Chambolle-Musigny or Nuits-Saint-Georges. Among the Grand Crus you can find Corton Charlemagne, Corton Les Perrières and Corton Le Rognet. To complete your basket, offer yourself inescapable local products : Fallot mustard, fruit nectars of Emmanuelle Baillard, gingerbreads of Mulot and Petit Jean, without forgetting the Paul Cholet and Parigot Crémants. The marked prices are the same as in the estates which are not always worth visiting. The house also offers printed clothing and linen in an iconography reminiscent of Burgundy which, once at home, will remind you of your visit to this beautiful area...

BÈZE ★

Bèze is one of the (700) most lovely villages of France, nestled at the bottom of a green and shaded valley. Bèze takes its name from the Celtic Bezw and means « river at its source » or « fountain with still waters ». The Dukes of Burgundy, Amalgaire, received all the grounds located east of Dijon from the king Dagobert. He lets his horse drink from the source and he is so charmed by the places that he decides to found there an abbey. We are in 630. Favoured by the history, the village is as beautiful with the nature that he built splendid caves there. Little place of paradise where the stone and water blend perfectly : as you stroll there, you discover a source from the Vaucluse, underground lakes, sheltered sculptures in the cave, but also many medieval remains. A place full of history(s) where was born the name Côte-d'Or at this department, in 1790 : the deputy Arnoult.

The canon Kir was the priest of the parish between 1910 and 1924. And the monks of the abbey transplanted, in the 13th century, the vines of the village to the land of Gevrey. Le Clos-de-Bèze is now the oldest vineyards of Burgundy.

Beza is a nice tourist destination in Côte d'or. The rehabilitation project of the *Cure de Bèze* augurs a new beautification of the village. On this occasion, a new bridge will span the river to pass directly from the Caves to the park and garden of the address whose building will be renovated, allowing visitors to easily reach the centre and Abbey. Between restaurants, hotels, cottages, shops, arts and crafts, cultural and natural heritage, there are numerous reasons to have a stay in Bèze.

■ OFFICE DE TOURISME DU MIREBELLOIS / ANTENNE DE BÈZE
Chalet des Grottes
chemin des Grottes
✆ +33 (0)3 80 36 76 17
www.tourisme-mirebeau.fr
contact@tourisme-mirebeau.fr

Open in April Saturday and Sunday from 2pm to 5.30pm. In May, June and September Wednesday to Sunday from 2pm to 5.30pm. In July and August from 2pm to 6pm. For detailed schedule, consult the www.tourisme-mirebeau.fr site.

The tourist office of Mirebellois opens an office in Chalet des Grottes de Bèze during the summer season. Practical, it offers many documents on the village, the caves, the abbey and other fun walks in the commune streets. Outside the opening period, contact the tourist office of Mirebellois in Mirebeau-sur-Bèze.

■ GROTTES DE BÈZE

Chemin des grottes
✆ +33 (0)3 80 75 31 33
www.beze.fr/grottes-de-beze

April and October, weekends and public holidays, 10 : 30 - 12/14-17h30, school holidays, 2pm-5.30pm, May-June-September every day except Monday (except public holiday or bridge) 10am-12pm/2pm-5.45pm, August July, 10am-12pm/2pm-6pm. It is preferable to telephone before the visit. Free for under 4-year-olds. Adult : €5.20 (more than 13 years). Child (from 4 to 12 years old) : €2.70 (€4.20 for the 13-18 years). Group (10 people) : €4.20. Guided tour (attention, is not appropriate to the people in wheel chair). Drinks – Souvenir shop.

Grottes de Bèze is a must-go address whose visit will make children and adults live a unique experience ! The caves were built in the years 1970, a very subtle lighting bewitches the caves, showcasing their size, it attracts more than 20,000 visitors each year. The caves are filled with many little treasures such as fossilised fragments of mammoths and rhinoceros. The visit of theses latter is on foot and by boat on about 300 metres of an underground lake. Departures are programmed every fifteen minutes during busy days. You will sail on an underground lake while admiring the beauty of the galleries. A 40-minute tour that is both fun and educational. The guide will teach you the stages and the characteristics of the discovery of the place. Remember to take a jumper because the temperature in the caves does not exceed 13 °C ! A brochure about visiting the caves of Bèze is available at the tourist reception of the town hall of Beza. Reservation of the visit is required. Before or after underground strolls, take the trail that leads to the belvedere above the caves for a stunning view on the village.

Sightseeing

■ ABBAYE DE BÈZE ★

Rue de l'Encloître ✆ +33 (0)6 17 64 24 41
abbayedebeze.blogspot.fr
3ab.beze@free.fr

♿

Open in July and August Wednesday to Sunday from 3pm to 6.30pm. Open at the time of the event. Appointment with the gardens 3.4 and June 5th, 2016. To visit during the Heritage Days the 10 and September 11th, 2016. Free for under 12-year-olds. Adult : €4. Child (from 12 to 18 years old) : €2. Guided tours by appointment starting from 15 people. Guide of visit available in French, English, German and Dutch.

Founded in 630, the Abbey of Bèze was the fourth of the Merovingian abbeys of the Langres diocese. What remains of this Benedictine abbey was classified on the supplementary historic monument list in 2010. Closed for a long time to the public, this site is now open to visitors, especially during Heritage days. Seven times destroyed and seven times rebuilt between the 7th and the 10th centuries, it experienced a strong revival in the 11th century and reached its peak in the 12th century under the Abbot of Etienne de Joinville. Important figures passed there : such as this Piémont religious Guillaule de Volpiano who was transferred to the Abbey of Bèze to restore respect for the rule of Saint-Benoit after being appointed priest and abbot of Saint-Bénigne in Dijon in 990. The abbey also hosted Pope Paschall II on 1107. Fortified in 1423 by the abbot Simon de Torcenay, it lost its beauty from the 16th century before being revived for the last time with the Saint-Maur congregation in mid-17th century. Bought at the Revolution as national property by an entrepreneur from Langres who destroyed the church and most of the building, then it became at the end of the 19th century the property of a Dijon industrialist, Philippe Breuil, whose descendants are the current owners. Today, five generations later, the family heir takes care of the domain with passion, whether in maintaining the garden or by giving explanations to the public. In the park, you discover a sequoia, a red beech and centuries-old trees. In the English garden, more than 200 antique roses are to discover during the « Rendez-vous aux jardins » event in early June. In July and August, meet the owners for personalized and rich tour information. And if the hot summer weather is a problem for you, know that the abbey park will give you more freshness thanks to the trees and the Bèze river.

■ LA SOURCE ★

Allée de la Source
✆ +33 (0)3 80 75 30 84

Located below the cave, Source Vaucluse is the second largest in France and it has an average flow of 15 000 to 18 000 litters or about 17 m^3 per second. In winter, they are real bubbling water jets out of the ground and from there a river begins : the Beza, along which you can enjoy a stroll while admiring the beauty of the surroundings and clarity of the water. Beautiful shaded promenade and picnic tables are available.

Knife & Fork

■ LE BOURGUIGNON

Rue de la Porte-de-Bessey
✆ +33 (0)3 80 75 34 51
www.lebourguignon.com
hotel-le-bourguignon@wanadoo.fr

Restaurateurs de France. Logis (2 cocottes). 7 days a week. Annual closing from October 20th to November 17th, 2016. Open every day from 12pm to 2pm and from 7.30pm to 9pm. Booking advised. Menu from €24.50 to €47. Lunch menu : €13.70 (Monday to Friday). Wine by the glass. À la carte. Hotel. Holiday voucher, Chèque Restaurant. Groups welcome (by reservation). Garden. Terrace. Banquets, receptions, meetings of family, business meal, seminars.

Nicole and Jacques Bourgeois have been welcoming guests in a warm and in a very professional way for years now. In addition to be a very high-quality hotel, the establishment is also a remarkable restaurant that offers dishes made up of fresh ingredients and season. If you choose the à la carte menu, compose yourself your menu by choosing your dishes. The choice will be difficult because everything is enticing : salad with piccatas of monkfish, fillets of red mullets and panfried scallops on bed of freshness and gravlax of salmon, flaky pastry with Burgundy snails with soft garlic, crust with morels and yellow wine or duck breast with blackcurrant bays... Nothing will deceive you. And for those who wish to discover the flavours of the region, there is the *Menu bèzois*, to honor the village, the *Menu of the terroir*, which makes you taste the Burgundy region (snails, steak of Charolais bull, cheeseboard...) and a daily menu which reserves many surprises according to the mood of the chef. As a native of Franche-Comté, to see these two region joined together is a happiness to Jacques and he will be delighted make you discover the gastronomy of Burgundy-Franche-Comté. The Burgundy wines are the icing on the cake suggested by the chef, the vintage of the local wine growers that goes perfectly with the dishes. For the family meals and other events, Jacques and his team prepare you « tailor-made » meal. The menu that favours the Burgundy specialties and change in the course of the years... This is a precious address, with exemplary regularity to spend a pleasant gourmet moment at the gates of Dijon.

Sleeping

■ LE BOURGUIGNON
Rue de la Porte-de-Bessey
✆ +33 (0)3 80 75 34 51
www.lebourguignon.com
hotel-le-bourguignon@wanadoo.fr

Qualité Tourisme label. Logis (2 cheminées). Open all year. 7 days a week. Annual closing from October 20th to November 17th, 2016. 25 rooms. Single room €58; double room from €73 to €78; triple room €92. Full-board (from €94 per person). Half-board (from €77 to €85 per person). Buffet breakfast : €9.50 (€6.50 for the children). Garage : €8 (and free secured parking space). Family rooms from 4 to 6 people : from €113 to €126. Stop-over with special rates for reps : €77. Pets allowed (€5 at an extra charge). Seminars. Free Wifi. Canal+.

Le Bourguignon is aptly named. This hotel has been set in a traditional building of the region. Admirably run by Jacques and Nicole Bourgeois, the place is friendly, charming and very comfortable. 25 rooms are awaiting you and is suitable to every possible configurations. From the single room to the family one through the double, the twin and the triple, you can stay here between friends, in couple or with your entire family. The rooms with modern decoration are cosy, maintained and well organised. The prices are very soft, it is the ideal location to visit Bèze, its medieval historic centre and even the vineyards of Burgundy.

Shopping

■ ATELIER L'ARGILE AU BOUT DES DOIGTS
12, chemin Combottes ✆ +33 (0)3 80 75 85 47
www.argileauboutdesdoigts.fr
argileauboutdesdoigts@orange.fr

Open from Tuesday till Friday from 10h till 12h and from 14h30 till 18h; Saturday from 14h30 till 18h. Open all year long. Open on Sundays by appointment. Groups are accepted. Shop, exhibitions. Training courses during the small school holidays and in July. Wednesday during school periods for children 7 - 12 years old at 14h to 16h, teenagers from 16h to 18h. Adults from September till June on Tuesdays of 10h to 12 h. Rate for 10 sessions, children 115 €, adults 319 € all inclusive.

L'Atelier L'Argile Au Bout de Doigts is a must-go address founded by Danièle Serravalle when you pass to Bèze. Graduated of Applied Arts Montreal, she created her workshop after 10 years spent at Musée des Arts Décoratifs in Quebec. It is in Beza that she settled in 2000, where she shares her passion for ceramic art in her shop, you can enjoy her productions there or during courses for children and adults. Danièle welcomes you enthusiastically with her Canadian accent to make you discover her favourite art : the earthenware. Her creations are really beautiful, she uses many transformation, decoration and enamelling techniques. The results are striking, reliefs, gilding, pencil wax, enamels, pole, coloured paste effect... Classic or contemporary, each unique creation can become an object of desire because of its artistic, decorative or practical aspect. Our favourite is the vases made with printed burnishing with white matt enamel of the most beautiful effect. The painted and object, gilded with fine gold are very beautiful ! It's impossible to resist to the charm of this workshop where the curious and the most addicted attend courses to learn modelling of clay.

Tourist Info Point

The Arcelot Castle has a Tourism Information centre during its opening hours.

In the surroundings

Arceau

CHÂTEAU D'ARCELOT
1, rue du Colombier
✆ +33 (0)3 80 37 00 73 – www.arcelot.fr
chateaudarcelot@orange.fr

Open from July 1st to September 6th, 2016 from 10am to 12pm and from 2pm to 6pm every day except Mondays and Tuesday (and Sundays mornings). Free for under 10-year-olds. Adult : €6. Group (20 people) : €5. Visit of the park using a documentation : 3€. Possible rental of the vault (up to 100 people).

Built in the 18th century, the Arcelot castle is a former house of the members of Parliament. This neoclassical architectural jewel has preserved its beautiful stucco and polychrome marble decoration. The large lounge realised by a group of Bavarian and Italian artists is entirely decorated with exceptional stucco. Created in 1805 by the landscape gardener Jean-Marie Morel, the 45-hectare park is an outstanding achievement. By breaking the 12th century French garden tradition, Morel created the first landscaped English park. In this haven of peace, pond, path with trees and flower, gentle slopes and forests mix together. There is even an orange grove with heady fragrance in season. The park has received the « Jardin Remarquable" label. The owners organize, once or twice a year, large banquets with costumes, music and menu of time. Do you dream of eating at the table of princes ? You can find the future dates on the castle's website. An idyllic setting !

MAISON TOUSSAINT
Zone artisanale d'Arcelot
Allée du Gourmerault ✆ +33 (0)3 80 65 03 80
www.boutiquemaisontoussaint.com
maisontoussaint@orange.fr

Gluten friendly. Open from Monday to Friday from 10am to 1pm and from 2pm to 6pm; on Saturday from 2pm to 6pm. A tea or a coffee offered for any purchase. Online order.

Corinne Toussaint and her team work with passion to offer you the best of her creations, which are always presented with great subtlety and elegance ! This excellent house is set in the recent buildings in Arcelot within walking distance from the castle. You will discover there the cake with Toussaint spices sweetened with honey that you enjoy natural that you can enjoy as much as you want as well as gingerbreads flavoured with candied oranges, with AOC nut of Grenoble with soft citrus fruit, gianduja chocolate molten cake. Also discover the special gingerbread and foie gras that will perfectly accompany the festive tables or a range of Good Shortbread which has 5 varieties now : nature, rosemary and parmesan, dark chocolate, caramel and speculoos. The *Demoiselles* (gluten-free cookies with rice flour) with lemon or orange are true marvels. Corinne's personal creations are Arcelottes, fine meringues with gingerbread or with chocolate whose name is related to Arcelot. Also find the « EFTI coffee », without gluten, delicacies with hazelnut on a coffee meringue. Between two bites, run and discover the showroom and visit the production shop. In the store, your can also buy these small delicate sweets with violet, cassissines, many jams that are 100% natural or organic and all kinds of fruity and stuffed delicacies ! In this shop, linger in the coffee-tasting space and do not forget to buy here the BEST spread with hazelnut of Dijon, 100% natural and contains 50% of hazelnuts. You can also buy coffee that can be ground on request. For those who can not go to the address, consider the online order that allows you to buy at Christmas the small biscuits with cinnamon and candied orange. From January to August, we advise you to test the Bouchons de Bourgogne, small mouthfuls of spiced cakes filled pulp of fruit with raspberry or apricot : a sheer delight !

Fontaine Française

SYNDICAT D'INTIATIVE DE FONTAINE FRANÇAISE – VAL DE VINGEANNE
2, rue Honorine-de-Monaco
✆ +33 (0)3 80 75 92 71
fontaine.francaise.free.fr
si.fontainefrancaise@gmail.com

From June 14th to August 30th open Wednesday to Sunday from 2.30pm to 6pm. From August 31st to September 20th open Saturday Sunday from 2.30pm to 6pm. Wednesday to Saturday from 10am to 12pm and from 2pm to 6pm. Sunday from 2.30pm to 6pm.

In summer, Fontaine-Française has a tourist information centre with a dynamic team at the helm. Tourists can acquire information on the canton's wealth. Several marked hiking routes are offered. Their names are pastoral : circuit of the Deer, Fountain, Canal... These are additional to the paths of curiosity concocted by the castle of Fontaine-Française allowing you to enjoy the heritage and the pretty views of the town. Namely the site of the tourist office is very complete and there will be an entertainment agenda.

CHÂTEAU DE FONTAINE-FRANÇAISE ★
Rue Honorine-de-Monaco ✆ +33 (0)3 80 75 80 40
www.chateau-fontainefrancaise.fr
contact@chateau-fontainefrancaise.fr

Open in July and August Wednesday to Sunday from 10am to 12pm and from 2pm to 6pm. Open in September Saturday and Sunday from 10am to 12pm and from 2pm to 6pm. Free for under 12-year-olds. Adult : €6. Child (from 12 to 18 years old) : €4. Group (15 people) : €4. Labeled Remarkable Garden.

The Château de Fontaine-Française is listed as a Historical monument. It was built in 1754 on the site of the old fortress which had witnessed in June 1595 the famous victory of King Henry IV over the the Spaniards. At the beginning of the nineteenth century Madame de Saint-

Jullien held at the castle a flourishing literary salon, frequented by Voltaire and madame de Staël. Mr and Madame de Saint-Jullien bequeathed their castle to their grand-nephew, René de La Tour du Pin de La Charce and, so far, the castle has remained in the hands of his descendants. The architecture is classic, typical of large French residences of the Enlightenment. It consists of a central main building flanked by two wings and faces a beautiful pond. Its gardens have nearly 400 lindens pruned into yew porch and cut into balls, this enabled him to be labelled Jardin remarquable in early 2015.

■ L'ENTRE-POT

58, rue de la Maladière
✆ +33 (0)3 80 85 54 16

Open all year. Monday to Saturday for lunch; Friday and Saturday for dinner. Thursday for dinner from June 15th to August 30th. Menu from €14.50 to €19.50 (for dinner for 2 to 3 main courses – daily special €11). Lunch menu : €14.50 (for 3 main courses, €12.50 for 2 main courses, €9.60 daily special). Wine by the glass. + À la carte. Calf's head 1st Thursday of the month. Holiday voucher, Chèque Restaurant. Terrace. Service of sale of bottles of gas 7 days a week.

The restaurant L'Entre-Pot is comfortably set up in a former warehouse, everything here is new, beautiful and pleasantly decorated for pleasant gastronomic moments between friends or family ! Cédric Bonvalot can accomodate up to 40 guests. With his 20 years of experience at the service of very important restaurants in Beaune and Dijon, Cédric Bonvalot rapidly imposed his cuisine as a real local reference. We love his traditional « homemade » dishes prepared with local and fresh products : fricassee of calf sweetbread and snail, fillets of quail with gingerbread, beef chunk with époisses... As far as the menu is concerned, the slate offers three choices per dishes at lunchtime and at dinner time, including the farm omelette or a premium beef steak. The dessert changes according to the season with delicious fruit pie or the black chocolate mousse or inovative île flottante with Carambar... It is delicious and the prices are very affordable, just like the wine list that is full of wines mainly from Burgundy.

Mirebeau-sur-Bèze

■ TOURIST OFFICE OF MIREBELLOIS

1 bis, rue du Moulin
✆ +33 (0)3 80 36 76 17
www.tourisme-mirebeau.fr
contact@tourisme-mirebeau.fr

From September to April : open Wednesdays and Saturday from 10am to 12pm and from 2pm to 5pm and Tuesday and Friday from 2pm to 5pm. From May to end of August : open Tuesday to Saturday from 9am to 12pm and from 2pm to 6pm.

The tourist office invites you to discover the beautiful landscapes of Mirebellois. From Mirebeau-sur-Bèze to Bèze via Beire-le-Châtel, Beaumont-sur-Vingeanne or Arch, the territory of Mirebellois matches to the contours of the old canton. In addition to the information that the tourist office provides you, many leaflets giving all the informaion on all that you can do in the Vingeanne – Val de Saône. A guidebook offers many suggestions of hikings and bicycles are available for rent. Many tours are proposed to visit the churches of the canton (with music concerts inside) or to discover Mirebeau-sur-Bèze. In fact, the Mirabel cat course is a playful tour which invites you to follow the paw prints of the cat while this last takes you in front of the remarkable monuments of the town. If you liked the visit, know that you can buy a bronze plate representing the chat Mirabel as a souvenir of the tour. The buildings of the Tourist Office also houses a souvenir and local produce shop which emphasizes the know-how of the craftsmen of Mirebellois. The welcome is warm for a territory rich in heritage and outings.

■ LA VENELLE

1, rue du Rempart
✆ +33 (0)3 80 39 22 34
www.lavenelle.fr
lavenelle@orange.fr

Closed the first 3 weeks of August. Open Thursday to Tuesday for lunch; Thursday to Saturday for dinner. Booking advised. Set menu at €24.50 (+ À la carte). Children's menu : €9.90. Daily special : €9.50. Evenings frogs Thursday for dinner by reservation from mid-May to September. Chèque Restaurant. Groups welcome (up to 35 people). Terrace. Catering.

Patrick Cannet, who has been at the helm of Auberge de l'Aiguillon in Binges for 16 years, offers a gourmet cuisine, adapted to suit each season. Prepared with fresh ingredients, the dishes are renewed every two months. The dining room was recently renovated and displays the beautiful green and white tones. The dishes are appetizing and are carefully prepared. You will also appreciate the small appetizers, offered before your meal. As a starter, we strongly recommend you the poached eggs with chips of foie gras. Then continue with nice pork confit with the thyme of Mirebeau, a fillet of beef with époisse sauce or a goose breast with Morello cherries. As for the desserts, everything is delicious and homemade, of the île flottante with the pear Charlotte cake. In summer, enjoy the terrace that is located in the quiet area, in the small inner courtyard of the restaurant. New chairs and plants make it a pleasant and welcoming space. In winter, Savoyard fondues with three cheeses warm the hearts and from the summer 2016, Patrick Cannet organizes barbecue party with grilled meats you can take as much as you want.

BLIGNY-SUR-OUCHE & OUCHE VALLEY

Bligny-sur-Ouche and its canton are located at the crossroads between the valley of Ouche, Auxois and Hautes-Côtes. The landscapes are surely among the most beautiful of Côte-d'Or. It is nicknamed « Burgundy Swiss » area. The hills are covered with woods which dominate green meadows that border the river. Ouche takes its source upstream in Lusigny, it still stammers and try to find way because this low altitude imposes meandering path start.
Good walks are required, unless you prefer the sloshing of the steam train. The latter follows the line established at the beginning of the railroad in the 19th century. The municipality is proud of benefiting from the third line of France ! This latter linked Epinac to Pont-d'Ouche. The municipality was also specialised in the hemp treatment once. Five inhabitants continued this activity at the beginning ot the century. Along Ouche, there are twelve mills and the oldest dates from the 13th century. As for its emblem, they bear proudly the Bligny symbols : fortress and towers as the crown, whisp of wheat as necklace – the two biggest production of the town - red crest enhanced with a bow and arrow, symbols of the local confraternety of Saint-Sébastien, archer company that was guardian of Bligny wall in the 18th century. The website of the community of communes : www.cc-cantondeblignysurouche.fr

OFFICE DE TOURISME DE BLIGNY-SUR-OUCHE

21, place de l'Hôtel-de-Ville
✆ +33 (0-3 80 20 16 51
www.ot-cantondeblignysurouche.fr
ot.blignysurouche@wanadoo.fr

April and October : open Tuesday to Saturday from 9.30am to 12.30pm and from 2pm to 6pm. From May 1st to September 30th : open on Monday from 9am to 1pm, Tuesday to Saturday from 9.30am to 12.30pm and from 2pm to 6pm, Sunday and public holidays from 9am to 1pm. Closed from November to March.

Located on the main square of Bligny, this Tourist Office is easily accessible. The decoration, made by a local craftsman, highlights the wood recalling the « nature and green tourism » of Bligny and its surroundings. The office has a space dedicated to exhibitions and a playground for children. A shop selling local produce delight the curious and gourmets : honey, candies, anise of Flavigny, blackcurrant juice, terrines, mustard, truffles... You will also find original and artisanal souvenir. The bookstore provides you invaluable information concerning the territory : books of local authors, historic books and even hiking roads. Among them there is one that the families will appreciate particularly : the « Vach' d'enquête ». During an educational and fun hiking of 7 km, find clues to discover the identity of a little veal. An original idea to learn the different characteristics of the Charolais cow while enjoying the beautiful landscapes ! The Tourist office, in partnership with Chemin de Fer de la Vallée de l'Ouche, organises parties in train making a gastronomic stopover in Thorey-sur-Ouche, with tasting of regional products. You will also find a brochure describing all municipalities in the canton and the activities proposed there.

CFVO-CHEMIN DE FER TOURISTIQUE DE LA VALLEE DE L'OUCHE

Gare Route d'Arnay
✆ +33 (0)3 80 20 17 92 / +33 (0)6 30 01 48 29 / +33 (0)3 80 20 16 51
info.cfvo@gmail.com

Open from May 1st to late September. May, June and September : departures only on Sundays and public holidays at 2.45pm and 4.30pm. July and August : departures every day at 3.30pm. Diesel from Monday to Saturday and Vapeur on Sundays and public holidays at 2.45pm and 4.30pm. Free for up to 3-year-olds. Adult : €8 (round trip). Children (from 3 to 10 years old) : €2.50. Adult : €5 (one-way), children : €2 (one-way), disabled people : €5 (round trip). Specific installation of 2 coaches for the disabled people.

Touristic train of Ouche Valley.

Small museum of the train at the station visible before or after the ride. From April to late September : possibility of booking a special train for an event. Possibility of get on or off the train at Pont d'Ouche.

The Tourist train of Bligny-sur-Ouche has become an institution since the members of the Association CFVO revamped and sustained this old line, one of the first in France. The way that the train follows dates back to 1830 and linked Epinac to Pont-d'Ouche. The machine that crossed the countryside allowed the transportation of iron ore and coal to the canal. The diesel or steam engines used today are small jewelry pampered by a group of enthusiasts. The train accommodates up to 260 people and some wagons are specially adapted for the disabled. A coach is designed for the transportation of bikes. It is available on request for groups. Whatever your age, you are delighted by the charm of the trip and the noise of the engine. During the stroll, you have the impression to change century. You only have to open your eyes, follow the driver dressed in period costume and listen to the history of this old railway. Be sure to have 1 hour and a half in front of you for the roundtrip. Since 2015, a parking located at the terminal of Pont-d'Ouche allows buses and cars to wait for the passengers who take a one-way.

■ EXPOSITION CFVO- LE FERROVIAIRE DE LA GRANDE GUERRE
Gare – Route d'Arnay
✆ +33 (0)3 80 20 17 92 / +33 (0)6 30 01 48 29 / +33 (0)3 80 20 16 51
chemindefervalleedelouche.blogspot.fr
info.cfvo@gmail.com

Station open of May 1st to at the end of September. May, June and September : departures Sunday and public holidays at 2.45pm and at 4.30pm. July and August : departures every day at 3.30pm. Diesel Monday to Saturday and vapor Sunday and public holidays at 2.45pm and at 4.30pm. Specific installation of 2 coaches for the disabled guests. Small museum of the train at the visible station before or after the walk. From April to end of September : possibility of reserving a special train for an event.

Organized by the CFVO (Chemin de Fer de la Vallée de l'Ouche), this exhibition commemorates the centenary of the First World War and will be visible until 2018 at the station of Bligny-sur-Ouche as much outside than inside. You can discover there railway equipment having been used by the allies, of the documents, the medals as well as reproductions minatures of scenes of war. Certain exposed objects come from the members of the combination while others are lent by inhabitants of the region. To finish, you can supplement this visit by a walk in the train of time in the valley of Ouche. A travel in time and space !

In the surroundings

Crugey

■ LE CARYMEJOR NEW
13 bis, route de Thorey
✆ +33 (0)3 80 43 46 07
www.le-carymejor.fr
billancarole21@gmail.com

Open all year round. From Tuesday to Sunday for lunch; from Tuesday to Saturday for dinner. Menus from €19.95 to €32 (middle menu at €26). À la carte : around €18. Children's menu : €10 (up to 10 years (main course and dessert of the day)). Daily special : €14 (served only for lunch from Monday to Friday). Supplement cheese in menus. Dishes filled with vegetables or French fries. Groups welcome. Terrace.

Since July 1st, 2015, the restaurant of Crugey has been back in service and it is a great pleasure that we find Carole and Yves Billan again, that we had known in Bareuzai of Chorey-lès-Beaune, as well as their children. Located on the village square facing the Burgundy canal, this establishment is an obligatory stop to eat in a pleasant place that exudes the joy of living. The dining room is full of charm, rustic and warm. To build the menu, Carymejor chose to take inspiration from Renoir painting *Le déjeuner des Canotiers*. If children logically opt for moussaillon menu, you can choose between mariner menu, Burgundian menu or business menu. Among the dishes : duck breast with myrthes, salmon steak or frogs' legs sautéed with parsley according to supplies. Homemade skewers are also offered at this property that works as well meat as fish. It is the dreamed place for those who love enjoying a tasty local cuisine accompanied by a good bottle. In the image of Renoir painting, the restaurant exudes shared good mood. To discover !

Thorey-sur-Ouche

Knife and Fork

■ **AUBERGE DU PONT D'OUCHE**
Pont d'Ouche
Départementale 33 – route de Thorey
✆ **+33 (0)3 80 43 21 10**
aubergedupontdouche@orange.fr
Open all year round. Every day for lunch; on Tuesday and from Thursday to Saturday for dinner. Possibility of opening on Sunday evening by reservation. In high season : open from Monday to Sunday for lunch. Booking advised. Menus from €12.50 to €25 (Cycliste menu at €12.50 with fresh pasta and drink). Children's menu : €8. Fixed rate formula : €13.50 (starter, main course and cheese or dessert). Wine by the glass. Barbecue formulas in summer. Prepayment by phone. American Express, Holiday vouchers, Cheque Restaurant. Groups welcome (up to 150 people). Garden. Terrace. Private parking under surveillance. Automatic cash dispenser nearby. Motorbiker relay.
In this old Irish pub that looks like a real inn, your hosts offer you to enjoy homemade cuisine that adapts to the seasons. Karinne Alluin is from the North and grand-daughter of mariner. As for Jean-Claude Chazay, he is from Savoy. He is chocolate maker, pastry chef, confectioner and glacier... what to make your mouth water. The exposed stone work, beams, barrels, garlic braids and huge fireplace make the room a warm and relaxing space. In addition to the fondue bourguignonne in the heart of rump steak, Auberge du Pont d'Ouche will make you appreciate the Savoyard cuisine. Croziflette, tartiflette, Raclette : a whole range of dishes that will let you get warm around a meal with friends. The chef's specialty, the calf sweetbreads flambéed with cognac or Armagnac. As for vegetables, they are untreated and Karinne plants them directly in the vegetable garden of the restaurant. There are no more local ! Squash, tomatoes, beans, cabbage, radishes and aromatic herbs... When an ingredient is missing, Jean-Claude and Karinne favour local producers. And to add to the quality of the cuisine and the excellent service, the inn regularly organizes themed evenings. Each August 15th, the feast is accompanied by an orchestra for a festive and dancing evening.

Sleeping

■ **AUBERGE DU PONT D'OUCHE**
Pont d'Ouche
Départementale 33 – route de Thorey
✆ **+33 (0)3 80 43 21 10**
aubergedupontdouche@orange.fr
€
Open all year round. Reception 24 hours a week. 5 rooms (including a family room). From €60 to €120. Full-board. Half-board (€18 for dinner. €15 for lunch). Breakfast : €7 (or €10 for a full breakfast). Open parking included. Pets allowed. Free wi-fi.
Auberge du Pont d'Ouche has 5 rooms including a family suite composed of 2 rooms and can accommodate up to 5 people. The simple and classic decor promises a relaxing stay in a friendly and relaxed atmosphere. They overlook the harbor or the garden, each room is spacious and equipped with a desk, a walk-in shower (a bathtub in the family suite) open to the bedroom as well as new and quality bedding. In this authentic place, Karinne Alluin and Jean Claude Chazay surround you with respect. They also offer a half-board or full board formula at attractive prices. A special welcome is planned for bikers who can store their vehicles in the barn, pitch a tent on the ground adjoining the inn and enjoy a special menu at the restaurant. Auberge du Pont d'Ouche is the ideal place if you want to enjoy the peace of a rural village while visiting Beaune, Dijon or Pouilly-en-Auxois. You can also walk along the canal and board the tourist train of Bligny-sur-Ouche.

Shopping

■ **GALERIE MYSRAËL**
Rue de Pont-d'Ouche
✆ **+33 (0)6 12 17 20 46 – www.mysrael.com**
myriam.israelmeyer@gmail.com
Visit of the gallery by appointment.
Myriam Israël (Mysraël, his artist's name) opens the doors of her private gallery in Thorey-sur-Ouche on appointment. Nestled in the middle of Burgundy, her workshop is an invitation to creation, just as its garden with the coloured flowerpots. After a passage at the school of the Beaux-Art of Besançon, this adopted Thorésienne continues her career in the contemporary art. She is

specialized in nude painting and the set of themes of the Jewish mystic, she also offers abstract canvases and more original creations like her paintings painted at the bottom of the drawer, easy to expose and already framed! Admiring the works of Mysraël is immersing yourself in the movement and listen to the music of a dynamic and cheerful painting. The painter appreciates the dance scenes and her painting displays a festive atmosphere. When you look at her landscapes of Eastern Europe, for example, the klezmer music is not far. The works of Mysraël were already exposed to London, Geneva, Paris, Strasbourg but also with Biennial of Florence in 2003.

CHAMBOLLE-MUSIGNY

Knife & Fork

LE MILLÉSIME
1, rue Traversière
✆ +33 (0)3 80 62 80 37
www.restaurant-le-millesime.com
info@restaurant-le-millesime.com

Closed from January 1st to January 15th and from August 1st to August 15th. Open from Tuesday to Saturday from noon to 2pm and from 7pm to 9.30pm. Booking advised. Menus from €32 to €49.90 (+ à la carte). Lunch formula : €19.90 (market menu. Starter, Main course and Dessert). Wine by the glass. Groups welcome (private lounge).

Le Millésime, Mathieu Maoyer's restaurant is always highly prized at Petit Futé. We love its chic and a sober decoration, its wals with clear and soothing tones, its window blinds. But what will undoubtedly convince you that you have made a good choice is the cellar standing behind the bar. Hundreds of bottles displayed in huge windows at 12 degrees. Now, let us go to the menu ! Always imaginative and talented, Matthieu Mazoyer blends flavours from the whole world with the finest produce of our terroir. The preparation of desserts is delegated to his pastrycook chef who prepares sublime creations. Each dish is a surprise for the eyes, the presentations are studied and the flavours explode in the mouth. Very beautiful gastronomy. You will remember your meal for a long time ! And if you want to buy wines, Le Millésime has also a wine merchant : the Caveau des Musignys.

In the surroundings

CASTEL DE TRÈS-GIRARD
7, rue de Très-Girard
MOREY-SAINT-DENIS ✆ +33 (0)3 80 34 33 09
www.castel-tres-girard.com
info@castel-tres-girard.com

Restaurateurs de France. Open every day and public holidays for lunch and dinner. Booking advised. Menu from €40 to €60 (without the wines, from €70 to €95 with the wines). Children's menu : €15. Lunch menu : €19 (2 main courses. €25 for 3 main courses). Wine by the glass. Groups welcome. Terrace.

In Morey-Saint-Denis, perched in the vineyards, the Castel de Très-Girard is an imposing building. Its dashing figure says a lot about the services that it will offer you... Old wine press of the XVIIth century, this residence with typically Burgundian architecture houses a charming hotel restaurant. The chef Chern Hweit Gan, of Malaysian origin, offers a cuisine sometimes traditional, sometimes creative but always well inspired. Here, freshness and quality are guaranteed. The menu is simple and is reinvented daily ! You have the choice between the eternal Burgundian Menu, consisting of poached eggs or snails followed by a beef bourguignon, and the Set Menu that changes every day. During our stay, it was egg, pumpkin and truffle of Burgundy, pan-fried foie gras and figs, haddock and red onions, beef whiting, beetroot and parmesan, and finally Belle Hélène pear. You choose 4 or 6 dishes. A delight ! To accompany them, if you hesitate among the 1,000 wines available, let yourself then be transported by the sommelier's selections at the Agreements Dishes & Wines formulas. You can fully trust in them. A superb hotel.

CHÂTEAUNEUF-EN-AUXOIS

It is a crucial stopover for whoever visits Burgundy ! From the top of its rock, Châteauneuf-en-Auxois dominates its surrounding area and offers one of the most beautiful view points of the region. The village is located around its castle. Path, narrow streets and venerable flowered buildings : the place is listed among the most lovely villages of France. In opposition to noise of the weekends of the summer, you have the calms the rest of the year : a pure breath of fresh air and a getaway to the country of Henri Vincenot. One of its ancestors was a farrier here. The few 500m ascending dedicated to the site with defensive function and this from the Gallic time. The fortifications and later, the castle is oriented to the three directions : La Côte Des Vins, the forest of the Dijon's mountain and Auxois's wheat fields. Thus it was natural that the town becomes a center of well-attended fairs. We could count four place of this type in the 14th century and six at the late 19th century. The trade brings a relative prosperity to the place. However, the 19th century is favorable for him. During that time, the inhabitants of the region – farmers for the majority – were leaving for survival elsewhere. The site is extremely highly prize today and the places are rare for those who want to become owner of a house in this little place of paradise.

The Château de Châteauneuf-en-Auxois.

Sightseeing

CHÂTEAU ET SITE DE CHÂTEAUNEUF-EN-AUXOIS

✆ +33 (0)3 80 49 21 89 – www.chateauneuf.net
chateau.chateauneuf@cr-bourgogne.fr

Closed on January 1st, on May 1st, on November 1st, on November 11th and on December 25th. Low season : open Tuesday to Sunday from 10am to 12.30pm and from 2pm to 5.45pm. High season : Tuesday to Sunday from 9am to 12.30pm and from 2pm to 6.45pm. Low season : from January 3rd to May 14th and from September 16th to December 31st; high season from May 15th to September 15th. Free for under 12-year-olds. Adult : €5. Child (from 12 to 17 years old) : €3.50. Supplement for the visit of the roofs, €1.50. Free for all first Sundays of the month, from October to April. Guided tour (for groups, by reservation : German or English visit, visit in French language of the signs, visits roofs). Activities.

The original castle of this town was built in the second half of the 12th century, just as the square tower. But the main contractor was Philippe Pot, Knight of the order of the Golden Fleece, who gave it its current appearance. Having received the bastion by the decision of Philippe le Bon, he opted for a wall of five sides. The towers, the wall and the fortified entrance date from the 13th and 14th centuries. The interior chapel reveals painting with the watercolour of the 15th century. The tomb of Philippe Pot is in the Louvre. The one visible here is a replica. Today, it is the region that ensures the management, maintenance and operation. Period furniture arranged in the rooms allows visitors to better imagine life at the castle. Châteauneuf-en-Auxois, is also a special atmosphere, which perhaps reigned in the courtyard of the dukes of Burgundy or at the time of Louis XVI. Be sure to add to this visit those of the medieval garden, the village of Châteauneuf and the interpretation center located in the Logis des Hôtes. It is the opportunity to discover the history of the castle with a fresh look. On the programme : video projection, touch screens, original archiveson audio support... A real abundance of information and culture.

LE POINT DE VUE DE LA CROIX DE MISSION

Open all year.

A little place of paradise, almost magic, which offers a 180 degrees view on the landscapes of Auxois. Sit peacefully on the stone overhung by a crucifix, surrounded by secular trees, and admire the horizon, the hills, the surrounding villages, the local vegetation... While continuing in the direction of the wood, several marked out hiking trails are offered. Generally affordable distances and difficulties for the entire family. Some examples : the walk of Chaume (estimated duration : 5 min), the walk of the Notre-Dame-du-Chêne chapel (15 min), the walk of the Saint-Julien hermitage (25 min), the walk of the point of view (35 min), and the walk of the mountain of Solle (1h).

Knife & Fork

L'ORÉE DU BOIS – RESTAURANT CRÊPERIE SALON DE THÉ

Grande-Rue
✆ +33 (0)3 80 49 25 32
www.ldb-chateauneuf.com
loreebois@orange.fr

Closed from December to January. Open the weekends of February and March. Open every day from April to November. (closed on Tuesday, except in July-August). Non-stop service from noon to 9.30pm. Dishes between €13.90 and €16.50/Crepes from €9.30. Children's menu : €9.50 (up to 10 years). Assiette de l'Auxois and coffee €14.50 (selection of cheeses and pork-butcheries of the region). Holiday voucher, Chèque Restaurant. Terrace. Tea room.

The L'Orée du Bois restaurant is easy to find, it is found almost at the highest point of the Chateauneuf village and it is located in the unique half-timbered house of the village dating from the fifteenth century. In summer, we prefer the small quiet and shady terrace, in winter, we bask near the large central fireplace of the room. You will appreciate the local atmosphere and « the small accent » by Stéphen Houchin, who has gourmet flair. L'Orée du Bois is at the same time, a restaurant, a creperie, a grill and a tea room at its hours where you can satisfy all your needs. We come to L'Orée du Bois for its sweet and salty pancakes, but we come back for its two specialties : the Auxois dish, composed of cold meats and cheeses from the region and the l'Orée du Bois sausage, a sausage prepared by the best local butcher according to a recipe of Stephen (a little lemon, sage, onion comfit...). The farmhouse pâté or the duck potted meat are « homemade » and when the winter comes, Stéphen Houchin prepares delicious seasonal dishes. The selection of wines is entrusted to Lionel Leconte, best wine waiter of France in 1992. The prices remain reasonable, as it is always the case here !

CHÂTILLON-SUR-SEINE ★

Châtillon-sur-Seine suffered from quite a few wars and conflicts. The name of the town, inspired by the fortress that made its reputation soon from the 9th century. Advanced bastion of the dukes faced to the counts of Champagne or the kings of France, town of negotiations between Napoleon, Austria, Russia, England and Prussia, headquarters of the marshal Joffre during the First World War : a heavy warrior heritage marks the city. At the confluence of a wide valley, the city offers, from its heights, an important field of vision and a defensive shelter. The Gaullic enjoyed already from this advantage. From the top of mount Lassois, the vision is amazing on the region. The famous *vase de Vix* was discovered on this hill in 1953, imposing treasure from the tomb of a Celtic princess. These discoveries is found now in the Musée du Pays Châtillonnais. Located in the heart of a region rich in archaeology, the city is crossed by the Seine river and has had the label of Ville fleurie and the most beautiful detours in France. On 15 June 1940, the city was besieged by German aviation. The bombings and fire destroyed a good part of the city, but Châtillon-sur-Seine remains a city with many tourist sights. The St. Nicholas church and the Saint-Vorles church are worth a visit, as well as the maison Philandrier where is the Tourist Office now. The walker who are not afraid to go on the steep streets with evocative names, can discover mansions, convents, mansions and wander at the antique shops.

COMMUNAUTE DE COMMUNES DU PAYS CHATILLONNAIS
9-11, rue de la Libération ✆ +33 (0)3 80 81 57 57
www.pays-chatillonnais.fr
pays@cc-chatillonnais.fr
Open Monday to Thursday from 8.30am to 12pm and from 1.30pm to 5.30pm; Friday from 8.30am to 12pm.
Communauté de Communes du Pays Châtillonnais gathers 107 municipalities from 6 cantons : Aignay-le-Duc, Baigneux-les-Juifs, Châtillon-sur-Seine, Laignes, Montigny-sur-Aube and Recey-sur-Ource. This community of communes extends on a territory of 1,900 km^2 and has over 20,000 inhabitants. On this land rich in history, many archaeological discoveries bear witness to an important activity since the Antiquity. It is the case with the Trésore de Vix. In the medieval era, the religious orders boost the region : Benedictines in Molesme, Cistercian in Clairvaux, Templar knights in Bure... The economic growth reached its peak in the 19th century with metallurgical industry. Then comes the time for rural exodus. Bordered by motorways and major railways, Châtillonnais has many advantages and assets : the forest (which covers 45% of Pays Châtillonnais), the stone that is exported worldwide, agriculture, unspoilt countryside, dynamic arts and crafts and Economic Activity Zones. Within its expertise, the Community of towns ensures the economic, touristic and environmental activity of this territory, in order to offer a favourable life quality to all actors : inhabitants, businesses and tourists. A successful bet !

City Center.

■ **MAIRIE DE CHÂTILLON SUR SEINE**
Place de l'Hôtel-de-Ville ✆ +33 (0)3 80 91 50 50
www.mairie-chatillon-sur-seine.fr
contact@mairie-chatillon-sur-seine.fr
Open Monday to Friday from 9am to 12pm and from 1.30pm to 5.30pm; Saturday from 9am to 12pm.
Châtillon-sur-Seine belongs to Communauté de Communes du Pays Châtillonnais which includes 107 towns ! Real crossroads between Troyes, Dijon, Auxerre, Chaumont and Langres, carrier of a certain brand image around the art of living, local produce and richness of the heritage. Châtillon-sur-Seine can boast about having on its town Musée du Pays Châtillonnais and its famous Trésor de Vix, as well as Théatre Gaston Bernard whose programming is worthy of a theatre of big city ! You should not miss the ruins of the castle of the dukes of Burgundy listed as a historical monument and the entombment of the Saint-Vorles church. As for shopping, the city has more than 280 with small craftsmen who work in old way. The green areas are not forgotten with nearly 27 acres of relaxation and walks in nature. Do not miss the municipal greenhouses that produce 60,000 plants each year. Whether you stroll, walk up the stairs of the library, whether you swim at the source of Douix or admire the Saint-Vorles church, Châtillon-sur-Seine is a town where it feels good to live.

■ **OFFICE DE TOURISME DU PAYS CHÂTILLONNAIS**
1, rue du Bourg ✆ +33 (0)3 80 91 13 19
www.chatillonnais-tourisme.fr
contact@tourisme-chatillonnais.fr
Open Monday to Saturday from 9am to 12pm and from 2pm to 6pm. In July and August : open Monday to Saturday from 9am to 7pm and Sunday from 10am to 1pm. The detailed schedule of activities, visits and other events is available on the website.
The Tourist Office of Pays Châtillonnais is located at Maison Philandier, rue du Bourg. You will find all the necessary information for a successful stay here : accommodation, restaurants, sites to discover, road of Crémant, nature maps with many ideas of hiking and mountain biking. All along the year, the tourist office offers guided tours of the city for groups, but also the Mont-Lassois where the Vix krater was discovered. In summer, it sets up a wonderful programme of visit, entertainments and discovery of Châtillon and its surrounding : « Balad'z' en Châtillon », « Balad'archéo », « Balad'âne » tour. You can thus discover the city, its history, all its charm and its surrounding on foot, in carriage or even with a donkey ! A must ! From 21 July to 25 August, don't miss also the « mardi-découvertes » for discovering the know-how of the local craftsmen and hidden heritage of this beautiful region, specially open for the occasion... A boutique offers a wide choice of local products, souvenirs and notebooks telling the Châtillonais' history. And as bonus, a SNCF boutique is installed in its premises. It is open from 9 : 30 am to 11 : 30 am and 2 : 30 pm to 5 : 30 pm. Practical !

Sightseeing

■ **ÉGLISE SAINT-VORLES** ★
Rue Saint-Vorles
Closed from October 1st to April 15th. From June 21st to August 31st : open every day. April, May and September : the afternoon only. Guided tour (duration : one hour, by appointment; reservation at the Tourist Office to the +33 (0)3 80 91 13 19).
Saint-Vorles is the most beautiful Romanesque jewel of Châtillon-sur-Seine. Attributed to the Bishop of Langres, Brun de Roucy, the construction of this church began in the 10th century. It honours saint Vorles, whose relics were moved from Marcenay to Châtillon in 868. Its external facade is decorated with bands characteristic of Lombard art. The four bays nave is covered with a high semicircular cradle. A span extended by the semi-circular apse was the only remaining of the original choir. After a series of renovations, the Saint-Vorles church finally found its splendour of yesteryear. Recent works were skillfully carried out and inscriptions from the two world wars give this church a moving character. Outside, on the porch, remnants of polychrome murals still exist, revealing hands, legs and past faces. The lactation miracle might have been performed in this church. Bernard de Clairvaux who enrolled in the monk's school of Châtillon is said to have received three drops of milk from the breast of the statue of the Virgin in front of which he prayed. Each year, the festival of Saint-Vorles leads to a gathering during which the life of the priest of Marcenay in the presence of the Brotherhood of Saint-Vorles is evoked. Formerly, a certain number of children of Châtillon-sur-Seine were called Vorles or Vorlette.

Discover the future National Park in the forests of Burgundy & Champagne

Park being created for 2017. Since the announcement in July 2009 of the creation of a National Park stemming from the Grenelle Environment Forum and dedicated to the plain hardwood forests, we have come a long way ! In 2010, the Public interest grouping of the future National Park of the forests in Champagne and Burgundy was born. The GIP pilots the creation of the National Park by gathering together the various stakeholders of the project : representatives of the State and its services, local communities and the actors of the territory. Thus, more than 200 structures work in the construction of this unique project for the territory. If this structure already employs ten people in Leuglay, ultimately, it will be about forty people who will be hired by the National Park, especially on the tourism section. The project runs its course : local institutional consultation launched in late 2014 reported 76% of favourable opinions on the project that will be finalised in 2017. Good news, in the meantime, we can already enjoy it ! If all these riches are not yet developped, they are already definitely there, within our reach. Information : www.forets-champagne-bourgogne.fr

The Pays Châtillonnais
in Burgundy
We are happy to welcome you
to the Pays Châtilllonnais
in the heart of the future national park called
« Parc des forêts de Champagne et Bourgogne » !
Crédits photographiques : © Jacques Blanchard ; William Fautré
fice de Tourisme
Pays Châtillonnais
ue du Bourg
400 Châtillon-sur-Seine
. : 33 (0) 3 80 91 13 19
ntact@tourisme-chatillonnais.fr
vw.tourisme-chatillonnais.fr

LA FORÊT CHATILLONNAISE ★

Open all year.

Do you dream to see a doe on the wood corner, chanterelles under a bed of leaves or climb to the top of the trees ? Welcome to La Forêt Châtillonnaise ! This forest stretches from one block on nearly 9,000 acres, and it is the largest wooded mountains of all Côte-d'Or. Part of this forest of broad-leaved trees will become a National Park, as well as Vanoise or the Cévennes, in 2017. The project that straddles between Champagne and Burgundy, is being elaborated (see the website : www.forets-champagne-bourgogne.fr). These woods are rich in a varied animal population and rare plants, including the lady's slippers or the Siberian ligulaire, renowned for their beauty. 21 tours marked on Châtillonnais are offered to walkers, with very different landscapes from one tour to another : circus of the shell, caves, monuments, vineyards, castles, abbeys... Every Thursday, from September 15th to March 31st, hunting with hounds will take place. It is possible to attend as a spectator. Information at the abbey of Val des Choues on 03 80 81 01 09.

MUSEE DU PAYS CHATILLONNAIS – TRESOR DE VIX ★

14, rue de la Libération
✆ +33 (0)3 80 91 24 67
www.musee-vix.fr
accueil@musee-chatillonnais.fr

Open all year. Closed on January 1st, May 1st, November 11th, 25 and December 31st. Low season : Wednesday to Monday from 9am to 12pm and from 2pm to 6pm. High season : every day from 10am to 7pm. Free for under 7-year-olds. Adult : €7. Child (from 7 to 18 years old) : €3.50. Group (10 people) : €3.50. Tourism label & Disability. Guided tour. Shop. Audioguides available in 4 languages : French, English, German and Dutch. Application for smartphone related to the audioguides.

Almost 2,000m^2 large, the museum of Châtillonnais contains one of the most representative collections of Celtic and Gallo-Roman times in France. The centerpiece of this collection is of course the *Trésor de Vix* ! In 1953, at the foot of Mont Lassois, the funerary chamber of a Celtic princess was discovered. Among the furnitures found : two attic ceramic bowls, a golden torque, a silver phiale with golden umbilicus, a wine jug, three bronze pools and... a huge crater with Laconian volutes that is also bronze, the largest vase known so far. 1.64 m high, with a diameter of 1.27 m and a 1.2 mm thick, it can contain up to 1,100 liters. Its weight is also impressive : 208 kg ! The elements found in the tomb of the beginning of the 5th century tell us about the exchanges between the region of Vix and the Mediterranean. If *Trésor de Vix* makes the reputation of the museum, it is far from being the only wealth of Pays châtillonnais. The collections cover the Gallo-Roman period until the 19th century. Temporary exhibitions embellish the collections regularly. Some novelties for 2016 : audio guides are available in 4 languages and an application for smartphone to prepare or complete the visit.

LA ROUTE DU CRÉMANT

Office de Tourisme du Pays châtillonnais
1, rue du Bourg
✆ +33 (0)3 80 91 13 19
www.chatillonnais-tourisme.fr

The Crémant road supplements the two other prestigious wine roads which criss-cross Burgundy, the Vignobles de l'Yonne road and the Grand Crus road. It enables you to leave on a tour of the Châtillonnais vineyard, of its grape varieties and its singular history. Crémant is a wine with bubbles and which constitutes one of the best kept secrets of Burgundy. The itinerary, marked out of 74 panels, covers the 120 km of the Châtillonnais vineyard and offers incursions into the valleys of the Seine, Laigne or Ource. Around Châtillon-sur-Seine, Laignes and Montigny-sur-Aube, several tours propose you to discover the wealth of the heritage of the region. You criss-cross the sunny slopes, admire the splendid valley of Ource, cross valleys, villages of dry stones and beautiful preserved forests, discovering various AOC of Crémants from Burgundy. Do not hesitate to make some stopovers because it is always with great pleasure that the vine growers open you the doors of their cellar for a tasting. In March, do not miss the festival of Crémants and the Tape-Cauldrons, in Châtillon-sur-Seine where nearly 5,000 visitors go each year to honour Crémants and the return of spring ! For those who are thirsty for discovery, all information is available on the website : www.routeducremant.fr. Enough to arouse your senses !

SOURCE DE LA DOUIX ★

Rue de la Douix

Open all year.

Source of Douix is a really charming site ! At the foot of a rock of more than 30 metres high surrounded by greenery, a clear water springs, slightly swept by the branches of an old willow tree. La Douix is a resurgence of an important flow that flows into the Seine in Châtillon. This resurgence, located in a picturesque setting is associated with magic and religious practices since Antiquity. It is, in addition, an enigma for all speleologists since Douix has a driveable neck up to 180 m before the progress is blocked by a large blocks of stone. From every indications, it could communicate with a huge underground network on the other side. The source has already delivered some beautiful archeological treasures, including the statuettes, pottery and jewels dating back over 700 years BC. It was actually a sanctuary and many offerings were carried out there. The Gallic divinity associated with groundwaters was called Divona. Today, in the summertime days, the children still bathe in the clear and fresh water of Douix.

VESTIGES DU CHÂTEAU

Rue Saint-Vorles

Open all year. Free.

Built between the 12th and the 14th century by the dukes of Burgundy as an advanced stronghold facing the nearby Champagne county and the royal domain, the castle then provides the town a martial appearance and this warrior atmosphere strongly displeased the inhabitants. It must be said that the soldiers are not always refined and restful guests. To the great satisfaction of the inhabitants, the building was destroyed in 1598 by orders of King Henry IV. Now, the remains of the wall, the tower of Gissey, which offers a panoramic view of the city, and its crenellations watch over the cemetery of the city. This cemetery has a number of interesting tombs, including that of Marmont Marshal, Louis Cailletet (physicist-chemist), or the clergy members : a funerary heritage to discover.

Knife & Fork

L'HOPLITE – LE RESTAURANT DU POTIER
Place de la Ville-du-Puy
✆ +33 (0)3 80 91 43 62
www.le-bistrot-du-potier.fr
pascal@lebistrotdupotier.fr

Low season : open Monday to Saturday for lunch; Friday and Saturday for dinner. High season : Monday to Saturday for lunch and dinner. Open with groups for dinner on weekdays by reservation in low season. Set menu at €19.50 (vegetarian menu €16). Children's menu : €9.50. Lunch menu : €14.50. Wine by the glass. Daily specials : 9,80€, €12.50 or €13.50. À la carte and slate. Large salads. Possibility of visiting the workshop of the tortoise in high season. Groups welcome.

Pascal Pierre, owner of Bistrot du Potier, opened a restaurant baptized « L'Hoplite », in tribute to infantrymen who decorate the famous vase of Vix. Exposed stones, large fireplace, beautiful sconce, rattan chairs : the room is charming. The tons are warm and bright. In a family atmosphere, L'Hoplite offers you a 100% homemade traditional cuisine accompanied by excellent regional wines. The chef's speciality is the bourguignon beef but we also advise you to taste its delicious andouillette of Troyes with two cheeses. For dessert, you may choose a tart. They are always exquisite whether they are with rhubarb or pear. In high season, let yourself be tempted by the complete formula with meal, visit of the pottery workshop and discount on the products of arts and crafts sold at the shop La Poterie de la Tortue. You find there works of Pascal but also some works of his son Reynald, sculptor and stonecutter. Before leaving, do not forget to have a look at the statue representing a hoplite of 2,50 m high carried out by Pascal Pierre. It is under a covered exhibition courtyard, within walking distance of the restaurant.

HÔTEL – RESTAURANT LA CÔTE-D'OR
2, rue Charles-Ronot ✆ +33 (0)3 80 91 13 29
www.hotel-delacotedor.fr
remillet.gerard@club-internet.fr

Logis (2 cocottes). Qualité Tourisme label. Hotel closed from January 1st to February 15th. Open Wednesday to Sunday and public holidays for lunch and dinner. Menu from €22 to €65. Hotel 3 stars. Logis 1 cheminées label of 9 rooms from €70 to €110. Garden. Terrace.

Gérard Remillet is a restaurateur who has only one will : honour his guests. The restaurant of Côte d'Or takes good care of its image, people come from afar to taste his specialties and enjoy the charming setting of the former coaching inn. This hotel has a very pleasant terrace in summer. The large half-classic half-contemporary dining room of the restaurant is in harmony with the cuisine of the chef. The latter indeed prepares recipes with authentic and creative features and changes with the seasons. Since all worked produce arrived on the very day and cooked fish are noble (monkfish, turbo, sole, trout...), the poultry comes from Bresse and meat from local producers, as well as vegetables or cheese, we would highly recommend this first choice restaurant.

O CHAPO RON
21, rue de la Libération
✆ +33 (0)3 80 81 85 43
ochaporon@gmail.com

Closed from December 23rd to January 2nd. Open daily for lunch and dinner. À la carte salads, grilled meats, galettes and crepes. Children's menu : €6.50. Wine by the glass. Holiday vouchers, Cheque Restaurant. Terrace.

The restaurant O Chapo Ron is easily identifiable at the northern entrance of Châtillon-sur-Seine and is rather proud-looking, you can park easily and its proximity to the city centre makes it an ideal tourist stopover since it is also within walking distance of Musée du Pays Châtillonnais. The revival brought by David Innocent in 2013 confirmed its status of good address for those who want meat grilled over a wood fire or a tasteful savoury or sweet pancake. O Chapo Ron suits every season. In winter or rainy days of summer everything happens in the room from forty cover, as soon as the weather is fine, it is the huge shaded terrace that is open, similar, with forty seats. Each space is equipped with a grill. A salad specialty O Chapo Ron, the pancake made up of tomatoes one, ham, mushrooms, eggs, cream and Gruyère is perfect. The gourmet pancake Chapo is garnished with cream, chestnut ice-cream, hot chocolate. David Innocent favours 100% homemade sauces, main courses and desserts. The wines and Crémants are served by the glass or by the bottle. Nothing to say for the service, it is efficient and very attractive from Valérie.

Sleeping

CAMPING MUNICIPAL LOUIS RIGOLY
Esplanade Saint-Vorles
✆ +33 (0)3 80 91 03 05
camping-chatillon-sur-seine@orange.fr

Open from April to end of September. Booking advised. Reception until 8pm. 54 campsites. Exposure : shaded. Campsite + vehicle + 2 people from €16.50. Rental of mobile home from €240 to €350 per week for 1-4 people. Holiday voucher. Games for children. Pets allowed (if up to date vaccinations). Area for camper van. Wifi. Public swimming pool with 50 Mr.

A convivial campsite within few steps from the city center. The 50 location is peacefully located between the public swimming pool and the Saint-Vorles church. Peace is guaranteed in this part of the city, which is within walking distance of the city centre. You just need to take the steep shortcuts down the cliff to the sources of Douix. If you want to relax, the swimming pool of Châtillon-sur-Seine is at close proximity where the campers enjoy a preferential rate.

Shopping

PÂTISSERIE-SALON DE THÉ SERGE BARBIER
27, rue Maréchal-Leclerc
✆ +33 (0)3 80 91 13 22

Open Tuesday to Saturday from 7am to 7.30pm; Sunday from 7am to 1pm; public holidays from 7am to 1pm.

Famous in Châtillon-sur-Seine and in the surrounding area, the bakery Serge Barbier is a pleasure for the eyes as much as for the tastebuds. Moreover, the shop is victim of its success and is full all day long whether it is in the tea room or in front of the cake windows. The chocolates of the chef are excellent just as his charlottes with raspberry, but what we prefer are the chiffonnades with caramel. This pastry is a real treat in which flavours and textures blend perfectly ! If you prefer the salty, you will not be disappointed since a catering service is also available. You will find in the menu : meat pie, terrines, quiches, cakes, salads, meats or gratins. Whether you choose a cold main course or a hot main course, you can be sure that it will be tasty and well presented. During the Easter holiday, the window is worth a look : Serge Barbier makes chocolate eggs worthy of a stage set. Lastly, as soon as the fine days is back, the Barbier house prepares its delicious homemade ice-creams. This pastry shop keeps all its promises and the number of its guests proves the quality of the products that are sold there. If you visit Châtillon-sur-Seine, a gourmet detour is must. Once you enter the shop : it's impossible to resist.

LES VIGNERONS DE HAUTE BOURGOGNE
26, rue Maréchal-De-Lattre-de-Tassigny
✆ +33 (0)3 80 91 46 63

Open Tuesday to Saturday from 9.30am to 12pm and from 2.30pm to 7pm. Tastings.

Since May 2015, SICA "Les Vignerons de Bourgogne Haute" has been part of Caves Bailly Lapierre located near Auxerre on the town of Saint-Bris-le-Vineux. Les Caves allows today 430 wine growers of Côte-d'or and Yonne to vinify and to bottle their crémants of Burgundy. Despite of being part of the entity Bailly Lapierre, the shop of the city center of Châtillon-sur-Seine continues to sell part of its products and offer free tastings. You will find cremants of course, always sold under the brand "*Les vignerons de Haute Bourgogne*" but also white and red wines, local produces (terrines, honey, gingerbread...) or accessories related to the wine (carafes, boxes sommelier, corkscrews...). The visit is recommended !

In the surroundings

Chaumont-le-Bois

DOMAINE SYLVAIN BOUHÉLIER
Place Saint-Martin
✆ +33 (0)3 80 81 95 97 / +33 0)6 48 12 32 00
www.bouhelier.com - contact@bouhelier.com
Less than 10 km north of Châtillon-sur-Seine. To get there, take D971 towards Troyes on 7.5 km and turn right and drive on D102 during 2 km.

From September to June : saturdays of 15 : 00 to 18 : 00. From July 1st to August 25th : Monday to Saturday of 15 : 00 to 18 : 00. On booking other days. Annual closing : last week of August. Possible delivery (site of online sales. Free tasting for the individual ones. Reception of groups on reservation. Booklet-games for the children). Creaming : between 7,20€ and 12,60€ the bottle (75cl). Burgundy : between 6€ and 6,60€ the bottle (75cl). Ratafia liqueur : 8€ the bottle (50cl). Marc de Bourgogne : 14€ the bottle (50cl).

Chaumont-le-Bois is a charming village of high Côte-d'Or which is among the stopovers of the Road of Crémant. In the 14th century, they already lived almost exclusively on the vineyard. Anne and Sylvain Bouhélier perpetuate this tradition and are committed to transmit their passion for Crémant. They even built a Museum of the vintner, true mine of information on the history of Crémants in Châtillonnais. The tools are particularly emphasized and a slide show explains you the various stages of the manufacturing of the barrels. In summer (and upon appointment the rest of the year), Sylvain takes you for a stroll in his vineyards for a discovery of the slopes, the grape varieties, the work of the vine grower. He cultivates today 6 hectares of vineyard in sustainable farming. Free tastings are offered in the vaulted cellar of the 17th century. The Estate is adherent to the Quality charter « *De Vignes en Cave* » of the Bureau interprofessionnel des vins de Bourgogne (BIVB). Sylvain Bouhélier also has a traditional still for a soft distillation and the production of marc or ratafia. He has finally a workshop-wine press to produce upon request a pasteurized fruit juice. The workshop is opened to all, upon registration and starting from 25kg of fruit.

Courban

CHÂTEAU DE COURBAN HÔTEL RESTAURANT & SPA
7, rue du Lavoir ✆ +33 (0)3 80 93 78 69
www.chateaudecourban.com
contact@chateaudecourban.com

Closed 24 and on December 25th. Reception until 11pm. 24 rooms. Double room from €99 to €260; suite from €180 to €360. Buffet breakfast : €18. Extra bed : €30. Open parking. Room Pigeon : between €200 and €400 per night. American Express, Holiday voucher. Possible boxes gifts (for meal, stay, spa). All inclusive fixed rate formula (1 night, breakfast, gourmet meal, spa) from €590 for 2. Pets allowed (€12). Seminars. Receptions and weddings. Free Wifi. Catering facilities (menu from €45 to €89). Spa, jacuzzi, sauna, hammam, body care. €30 per person for 1 a.m.

Located in the,Burgundian countryside, surrounded by greenery, forests and vineyards, Château de Courban is a heavenly place. Full of charm, it is an invitation to serenity and escape. Every room and suite of this characterful old building have a unique atmosphere. The decor is refined, elegant and warm. The rooms in the main building are in a classic style, those located in the new dependent parts are larger and modern. For a romantic stay, offer yourself the most original room built within the former dovecote. The hotel provides you numerous services : infinity pool, terraces, Nuxe spa (with hammam, sauna, whirlpool, hydrojets, massages and body care), bicycles, garden... There is everything you need to make your stay unforgettable. The gourmet restaurant that is located in the former orangery of the castle is an extra advantage. You can taste a subtle cuisine prepared by the new chef, Takashi Kinoshita. His experience in renowned establishments (Le Pré aux clercs, Les cuisines du palais de l'Elysée...) allows you to enjoy inventive meals on a wonderfully presented table. Take also advantage of the reliable advice of the sommelier. A visit is a must in this family castle with cosy decor.

Grancey-sur-Ource

DOMAINE ROLAND VAN HECKE

5, Rue de l'Eglise
✆ +33 (0)3 80 93 79 07 / +33 (0)6 88 04 70 63
www.rolandvanhecke.com
roland.van-hecke@wanadoo.fr

Open on Monday, Wednesday and Saturday from 9am to 12.30pm and from 2pm to 7pm; Sunday from 9am to 12.30pm. Opening by appointment other days of the week. Possible delivery (for the orders except Metropolitan France, please contact the estate). Respect of the charter of reception « Vineyards in Caves ». Reception of the group up to 50 people and possibility of initiation to tasting. Price of the wines : between €6.50 and €11.70. Mail order selling 7 days a week. Direct sales with the estate.

Located at the top of Côte-d'Or, in the charming valley of Ource, the estate of Roland and Christelle has a superb reception premise, a small house located next to the fermenting room, at the foot of the statue of the virgin of Beauregard, the « protector » of the village of Grancey-Sur-Ource. More than 20 years ago, Roland Van Hecke who is also farmer chose to diversify his activity while opening himself up to viticulture. He has vinified and handled his Crémants since 2003 for our greatest pleasure. The 5-hectare vineyards of the estate are located in the town of Gomméville. Among the range of Crémant, you can find the Cuvée Rosé, the Cuvée Demi-sec, the Virtuose Brut (80% pinot) or the Cuvée 100% Chardonnay which obtained in 2015 the silver medal at the Concours des Féminalise in Beaune and silver medal at the World Competition of Brussels. You can also taste the vintage of prestige « Beauregard », flagship of the estate resulting from an assembly of 60% of Chardonnay and 40% of Pinot Noir. Vinified in oak barrel, this vintage gained the gold medal at the national competition of Crémants in 2015. A range of Burgundy wines comes to supplement this offer, as well as the production of Ratafia. Recently, the website of the estate enables you to buy your wines directly on line. If you prefer to pass to the estate, know that Christelle and Roland welcome you for tasting sessions. You will appreciate their quality work, always respectful of the nature and rich in ancient know-how.

Marcenay

L'ÉGLISE ET LE HAUT-FOURNEAU

Open all year. Free.

The church of Marcenay is presented as the place where were discovered and preserved the remains of Saint Vorles, a priest who lived at the end of the 6th century. They were then transferred to the church of Chatillon-sur-Seine. It has in its chancel the tomb of Saint Vorles. The blast furnace is the result of the will of the prince of Condé, who dictated the operations of the construction in 1742, near lake. The blast furnace is doubled by a market coal which houses the exhibitors of Maison du Terroir from April to October. Everything is next to the lake. The furnace has operated for over 120 years now. If it still seems too alert, it is due to the assistance provided to Forges de Buffon during its renovation.

LE CAMPING LES GREBES DU LAC DE MARCENAY

5, route du Lac
✆ +33 (0)3 80 81 61 72
www.campingmarcenaylac.com
info@campingmarcenaylac.com

Open from April to October. Booking advised. Reception 24/24 (hotline from 9am to 9pm). Ground of 3 ha. 90 campsites. Exposure : mid--shaded. Campsite from €5.50 to €7.50. 2 people from €9 to €11. Mobile home from €250 to €400 per week. €45 per night for 2 people. Games for children. Pets allowed (if tattooed and vaccinated). Free Wifi. Activities. Billiards, table footballs, canoe and boat free.

It is a warm and friendly campsite that is offered to you. The 90 well-defined locations is spread over no less than 3 ha. Dirk and Séverine welcome you with great sympathy and offer varied and free activities : swimming pool, games and paddling pool for children, billiards, table football, petanque, canoeing, sailing... They can even lend a sailboat to the expert ones ! A large lobby allows to shelter in rainy weather and cook on site. If you have a little cold, do not hesitate to warm up around the fireplace. It is because of these small attentions that Camping de Marcenay drives camper loyalty. Every morning, fresh bread and croissants await you. Music lovers are particularly popular and a range of instruments is available to them for musical sessions. On Wednesday and Saturday, drums, guitar, piano and bass thus resound in the large music room, open to all. Crepe and galette evenings are also organized. Grèbes are successful, and we understand why ! The beach of Lake Marcenay is accessible directly : holidays on the waterfront, a natural setting, beautiful walks in perspective, on foot, by bike, motorcycle or on horseback. This family campsite, well attended and carefully maintained, is worth your visit. A nice destination between vineyards, fields and forest.

Find the index at the end of this guide book

■ DOMAINE GUILLEMAN
28, rue Principale ✆ +33 (0)3 80 81 40 03
www.domaineguilleman.fr
domaine.guilleman@orange.fr
Reception every day at the vault. Groups up to 50 people allowed. Website for online purchase. Possible delivery.
The vineyards of the Guilleman estate now covers 4.25 hectares facing south-south-east. Trained at the Viti in Beaune, Fabien Guilleman is now the head of this estate well equipped with working tools. Behind the facade of the family house, there is a farmyard where the winery and the vault are located optimally. Crémant and still wines are squeezed, vinified and handled at the estate in a vault that can accommodate 50 people. One site are held tastings, presentation of the history of the area and some indications of the town of Marcenay where the story of Saint Vorles begins. Currently 8,000 bottles are sold in the domain while the remaining grapes are purchased by traders on the spot. The range of Crémants is complete : Tradition 60% of Pinot, Blanc de blanc, Blanc de noir, Tradition (aged in oak barrels) and Elégance, a blend of 50/50 Pinot/Chardonnay. As for the country wine, the estate now offers a Pinot gray. Great news for lovers of aromatic white wines !

Massingy

■ OENOCENTRE AMPÉLOPSIS
L'Univers de la Vigne au Vin – Domaine Brigand
Rue derrière l'Église
✆ +33 (0)3 80 91 15 12 / +33 (0)6 87 07 30 50
www.oenocentreampelopsis.magix.net
Opened from April 1st to December 31st. Friday, Saturday and Sunday in free tour : opened 9 : 30 at 12 : 30 and 14 : 30 at 18 : 30. Other days on booking starting from 8 people. Open at weekends and holidays of 9 : 30 to 12 : 30 and 14 : 30 to 18 : 30. Opened the every day in August. Free for under 5-year-olds. Adult : €8.50. Child (from 5 to 17 years old) : €4.50 (and students). Rates understand the visit, 3 tastings and a drink ampélopsis in remembering. The shop is open the every day of the year except on December 25th. Tourism label & Disability. Guided tour. Shop. Entertainments. Label « High environmental value » allotted to the estate in 2015.
Located in Châtillonnais, at the doors of Champagne, Oenocentre Ampélopsis accommodates you for an initiatory journey into the universe of the vineyard. Ghislain Brigand, inventive young person and a welcoming wine grower, developed a space dedicated to the vineyard, its culture and its history right in the middle of his estate. Go on a tour of Burgundian traditions, for a cultural, ludic and sensory travel throughout the world of the wine. Models, videos, entertainments : you will know all about the vineyard, various grape varieties, the wine tools via the vinification or the manufacturing of the barrels... Several courses are available. Workshops are also offered as well as an à la carte day on reservation. The visit of the permanent course does not require a reservation and lasts approximately 2 hours. The 2016 novelties ? A space, The « *Cirque Vigne en Bubble* » outside, dedicated to Crémant de Bourgogne. Oenocentre Ampélopsis is a unique, ludic and instructive museum in Châtillonnais. An sparkling initiative and full with passion !

■ DOMAINE BRIGAND
3, rue derrière l'Église
✆ +33 (0)3 80 91 15 12 / +33 (0)6 87 07 30 50
www.domainebrigand.com
6 Km North-East of Châtillon.
Open every day from 9 : 00 am to 12 : 00 pm and 14 : 00 pm to 19 : 00 pm. Closed on 25th December. Free tasting.
The Chatillonnais is affirming itself as the excellent land of the Crémant de Bourgogne and Ghuslain Brigand wishes to transmit his passion and his curiosity about the wine. His estate has existed since 1902 and its particularly reknown. It stretches over 10 hectares, exhibited in the southern slopes, the development of sparkling wine is on 8 hectares. Karine, the wine of Ghyslain, joined the exploitation in 2007. As a real cook, she is interested in gastronomy and will be of good advice for preparing dishes based on crémant. The estate has obtained the certification « *Haute Valeur Environnementale* » which is a reward for the effort made to protect the environment. There are about seven different crémants. Special wines are also available : Vieux Milléssimes, ancestral vintage, semi-dry... You can also buy wines (red, white or rosé) at very reasonable price. A little plus : in the shop, the glass engraving workshop allows you to personalize drinks and bottles. Ghyslain Brigand welcomes you and makes you share his passion for the vineyards. He is also the creator of the Ampélopsis museum on the production of wine and the growth of the vines. You should not miss it !

■ DOMAINE HENRI MUTIN
La Grange aux Clercs ✆ +33 (0)3 80 91 06 05
✆ 06 07 17 55 11 – www.henri-mutin.com
Open every day and on public holidays from 8am to noon and from 2pm to 6pm. Tastings, visit and purchases by appointment. Mail-order selling. Open door on March 20th the day after the Crémant de Chatillon festival with about fifty exhibitors. Belongs to the Bienvenue à la Ferme network.
Domaine Henri Mutin is set up in a farmhouse built before 1600 and whose origins go back to the bishops of Langres. With Henri Mutin, your knowledge about the crémant will be improved. Since he started to cultivate the vineyard in 1995, Henri Mutin has always been a passionate of the vinemaking profession, he is today one of the most enthusiastic promoters of Crémant du Châtillonnais. He started elaborating his own wines in 2003. Since then, he has gathered many medals. In 2016, his vineyards stretch over 4 ha, all in conversion to Organic. In 2016, Crémant Tradition will be the first vintage with the famous label. Henri Mutin offers many other vintages : *Prestige, Tête de Cuvée, Rosé, M pour la milléssimée, Brut, Demi-Sec*... The *Cuvée Brut Nature* that is renewed in 2016, 100% sugar-free Pinot Noir is a balanced vintage, conducive to this daring formula wich will please some. As 2015 the harvest is of high quality, the estate will produce still wines, Bourgogne Pinot Noir and Bourgogne Chardonnay 100% Massingy. In fact, apart from the grapes, the barrels reserved for their breeding are also from village. They were made with oak cask-wood of Massingy and especially carried out with the estate by a young person Meilleur Ouvrier de France during the open day of June 2015. Henri Mutin thus confirms his talents and his total passion for the Crémants.

petit futé
BEST OF
BURGUNDY
FREE
WWW.PETITFUTE.COM

© ERIC VOILLEQUIN

A hillside in the Chatillonnais.

Montigny-sur-Aube

LE CHÂTEAU DE MONTIGNY-SUR-AUBE & SES VERGERS-POTAGERS CONSERVATOIRES

© +33 (0)3 80 93 55 23 / +33 (0)6 08 90 75 10
www.chateaudemontigny.com
info@chateaudemontigny.com
Take the A5 motorway exit 23 towards Montigny sur Aube(17 km).

From January 1st to April 29th and from November 15th to December 31st, 2016 : open Monday to Friday from 10am to 12pm and from 2pm to 4.30pm (except public holidays); from April 30th to November 13th, 2016 : open Tuesday to Sunday and public holidays from 2pm to 6pm. From June 2016, by reservation : visit of the interiors of the castle for groups of 15 people minimum (associations, companies...) with visit of the productive kitchen garden by the chief cook, tasting of products and possibility of lunching. Free for under 6-year-olds. Adult : €8 (with audioguide). Group (10 people) : €7.50 (with audioguide). Are accessible the chapel, the park, the orangery, the temporary exhibitions and the orchard-kitchen gardens academies.

Fortress built at the 12th century, this castle was embellished seriously in the Renaissance. From this time, there remains only the « red tower », the moats, the chapel and the southernmost wing of the original castle, the rest having been destroyed with the Revolution and during a fire in 1817. In front of the castle, a vast picturesque park from the first part of 19th extends, it is also classified in the title of Historical monuments since 1961. The chapel of the castle is worth a glance and is the copy of a chapel of the cathedral of Langres. Before he becomes president of the United States, Harry Truman stayed several months in the castle whereas he was a student at the artillery school of Montigny-sur-Aube. A true renaissance of the two places has been led for a dozen years and this sublime castle is now opened for the public. The orchard-gardens academies alone gather some 250 old fruit varieties in a vast closed space of 5,600 m^2. A honey garden surrounding a superb apiary allows the pollination of all this space. The discovery of these places is done using an audioguide and initiates you to the world of the insects present in the gardens. Starting from June 2016, it will be possible to taste the products of the exploitation organized by a chef who ensures the supervision of the production. Le Chateau de Montigny-sur-Aube constitutes a getaway not to miss.

Mosson

DOMAINE GHEERAERT

EARL des Vignes de Jours
1, rue Haute
© +33 (0)3 80 93 71 67
www.cremant-gheeraert.fr
claude.gheeraert@nordnet.fr
In Châtillon-sur-Seine, go towards Chaumont, the village is just a few kilometres away.

Open from Monday to Saturday from 10am to noon and from 2pm to 6pm. By appointment on other days of the week. Tasting and sale cellar. Possible delivery. Gîte for 2 people : from €150 to €295 per week depending on the season.

Vine grower since 1991, Claude Gheeraert chose at that time to leave the breeding of cattle to devote to his agricultural domain and his vineyards. It is today more than 6 hectares of Chardonnay and Pinot Noir which are exploited on the Slopes of Mosson. The last planted plots will produce their first Chardonnay in 2016, an increase in production which answers the growing request of the Crémants Gheeraert ! Le Domaine proposes Crémants but also still wines, Bourgogne Chardonnay, Pinot Noir and rosée 100% Pinot Noir of pretty pink currant. The flagship of the house is Crémant Tradition Brut, an assembly of 70% Pinot Noir and Chardonnay which regularly earned it rewards like that of being selected in the Hachette guide of the wines 2016 or being distinguished by a silver medal to the Concours Mondial des Vins Féminalise 2015. The Crémant is also Rosé, pure Chardonnay or pure Pinot Noir. Claude Gheeraert vinifies and handles his wines in the property, in compliance with the tradition, having a fermenting room perfectly equipped for automatic moving. Appreciate the charm of the family farmhouse where a small vault is arranged for the tasting of Crémant refreshed just right. It is possible to receive groups up to 20 people and a visit of the estate can be organized upon appointment. Christine Gheeraert proposes you to personalize your bottles by adding a photograph, a date and a name on them. Claude Gheeraert is also interested in truffle of Burgundy, he maintains truffle-field which will enable him soon to make you also discover the famous *Tuber Uncinatum Chatin*. Do not miss this beautiful stopover of the Route du Crémant !

Veuxhaulles-sur-Aube

■ PISCICULTURE LES TRUITES DE L'AUBE

9, rue du Mont Remin
✆ +33 (0)3 80 93 52 58
www.truites-laube.fr
truites-de-laube21@wanadoo.fr

Low season : open Wednesday to Monday from 9am to 12pm and from 2pm to 5pm. High season : Wednesday to Monday from 8am to 12pm and from 1pm to 6.30pm. Low season October, November, February, March. High season from April 1st to September 30th. Open every day in July and August. By appointment only in December and January. Free admission and loan of free equipment. Fished fish sold with the kilo and shop of processed products. Products available in delicatessen and with the future farm Drive Welcomme to the farm of Dijon. Label Welcomme to the farm.

Lovers of nature and fishing, you will like it. This breeding of trout and salmons is a fascinating place to discover. To understand the interest of the fish farm which is done respecting the well-being of fish and their growth rate, but also, to enjoy fishing ! This fish farming indeed offers, to all, children and adults, experts or not, to fish trout in a green and relaxing setting. Preparation of equipment, launch of line and waiting... Once the trout takes the bait, it is a touch. You have then to set a barbed hook on the fish's jaw and take it out of the water and put it delicately in a bucket, well in the shade. There is even a wild course which is offered to the most reckless ones. For those who would not fish, there is the pleasure of the observation of the place where a multitude of plants, insects and fish live together. As of the summer 2016, an educational trail will be implemented to precisely explain this biodiversity. With a little luck, you will see a grey heron or a kingfisher ! Admission is free, the loan of the equipment is free, you pay for... what you fish per kilo ! The shop sells its processed products : terrines and rillettes of fish, smoked trout, trout sausages that comes in several sauces... Enough to feast, but especially to spend a beautiful moment at the edge of water (be).

CHENÔVE

An old peaceful village, a centre fuelled by cultural diversity, a great attractive economic centre, the second of the Dijon area... These are the many facets of the town where the living-together is not a dark concept but a moving reality ! The 15,000 inhabitants benefits therefore from the dynamic of many association, various sports facilities, a quality public service. And, for a few years, the city has been in total reconstruction : implementation of the tramway, renovation of many areas, construction of a cultural centre with futuristic appearance... « Chenôve in Burgundy, an energizing city », that is the motto of the town and it is saying something ! Ideally located at the Southern entrance of the Dijon, Chenôve is a undeniably charming, at the forefront of modernity, respectful of the environment... and with ancient heritage ! The pressure of the Dukes of Burgundy, the vineyards trees, the narrow streets of the old village make it the first crucial stopover of the prestigious route des grands Crus. The plateau of 240 hectares offers very sought-after landscapes and an environmental quality. Labelled « Ville de Paix », open and convivial, it also hosts many events and events : a large market every Sunday, the Fête de la Pressée in September, a documentary film festival in November, a Christmas market in December, a carnival in spring... Its heart beats with energy and enthusiasm, throughout the year !

Chenôve.

Sightseeing

PARC URBAIN DU MAIL

Since October 2014, nature makes a major comeback in the city, in the heart of the city itself : on place Coluche and cours Général-de-Gaulle. Plane trees, hedges, lawns, plantations, fountains and stream of water... The Parc Urbain of Mail combines water and greenery. Children can enjoy the playgrounds and adults, play petanque. The new green lung of the city !

Knife & Fork

L'AUBERGE DU CLOS DU ROY

2, place Anne-Laprévôte ✆ +33 (0)3 80 27 17 39
www.aubergeduclosduroy.com
aubergeduclosduroy@orange.fr

Open from Monday to Saturday for lunch from 12pm to 2.30pm; Friday and Saturday for dinner from 7pm to 11pm. Reservations recommended. À la carte : around €15. Lunch formula : €16.50 (2 dishes). Wine by glass. Terrace.

This authentic address, which is nestled in a charming stone house, is worth a visit. Not only it is a beautiful place located in the old Chenôve but it is also an excellent regional restaurant. Inside, decoration is modern, the red walls recalls the vineyards, just like the old tools that we can see. In the kitchen, a talented chef, Philippe Poillot, who evolves his à la carte menu according to the season with very tempting specialties. A friendly and charming service of Karine and a remarkable value for money for this restaurant. Here, the strong points are cumulated ! What we like particularly is this cuisine inspired by the old generation but revisited by the chef like the pork loin candied with cider, the endives with turkey and with bechamel sauce cooked au gratin with the melted morbier, the fillet of whiting with walnuts and capers... There are many tasty suggestions that is accurately and generously cooked. The wine list presents a beautiful panel of what is done in Marsannay and Gevrey... at very reasonable prices. Think of booking, especially the summer : we rush towards the beautiful terrace which overlooks a pretty place. An crucial stopover at few minutes of Dijon to discover what Côte des Vins have to offer us the best in regards to beverages and gastronomy. Possibility of catering service with available quotation if needed.

LE CLOS DU ROY

Quartier des Grands Crus
35, avenue du 14-Juillet ✆ +33 (0)3 80 51 33 66
www.restaurant-closduroy.com
clos.du.roy@wanadoo.fr

Open all year. By reservation, only for groups starting from 10 people, for meals at the restaurant or outside (catering). Monday to Thursday from 12pm to 2.30pm; Friday and Saturday from 12pm to 2.30pm and from 7pm to 11pm. Booking is essential. Menu from €36 to €72 (many choices of possible main courses. Quotation free Caterer and without commitment). Children's menu : €16. Groups welcome.

As a native of Marsannay, Philippe Poillot was trained at « Gourmets », then at « L'Espérance » of Marc Meneau and at Lenôtre in Paris. He is at the helm of Auberge du Clos du Roy (in the old Chenôve) and this restaurant, Clos du Roy. Since last year, he decided to devote it to banquets and group meals. You can reserve the places for 8 people up to 170 people divided in three different rooms : the spacious dining room, the smallest and the private lounge. There are two available possibilities for your business meals, tourist, discovery, cocktails, seminars, wedding, etc : contacting its catering service or reserving on the spot. The staff is charming and the chef, as you can well imagine, is talented. Five different menus for delicious and more than complete meals. They change according to the season and the desires of the chef. Naturally, Philippe Poillot gets supplied at the market and works only with fresh ingredients. The main courses are top-of-the-range and honour the foie gras, crayfish, chestnut, snails, prawns, gingerbread, lobster... In short, you will find only good and well-seasoned dishes ! For proof, its fine turnip broth with matcha tea, mashed fingerling potatoes with Espelette pepper, the mashed garlic soup with flat-leaf parsley, the gingerbread breadcrumbs... You will not be disappointed and the desserts are also extremely well elaborated decorated with broad beans of Tonka scattered here and there. The chef's speciality ? The extraordinary desserts decorated with puffed sugar that he uses as a glass-blower. The wines are obviously from Burgundy : Marsannay, Fixin, Savigny... Note that the restaurant is open to everyone during certain festivals... with special menus at reasonable rates. An address that we particularly love.

LA MAISONNETTE

1, rue Pasteur
✆ +33 (0)3 80 54 33 81

Open all year. Monday to Saturday for lunch; Wednesday to Saturday for dinner. Possible opening Sunday for lunch for groups of more than 20 people. Wine by the glass. Dish alone : 8.50 or €10. Starter, main course or main course, dessert : 10.50 or €13.90. Starter, main course, dessert : 13.40 or €16.80. Groups welcome. Terrace. Activities.

The name of this establishment refers to the warm atmosphere and the authentic cuisine that you find here. Indeed, La Maisonnette is an authentic restaurant whose ambition is to cook dishes with sauces and offals. The room is pleasant, the shades are bright, the straw-bottomed chairs give it a small rustic side, not unpleasant. Here, everything is homemade and the whole à la carte menu changes every week. As starter : a well furnished buffet. The dishes are traditional : pig liver with chopped parsley, andouillette with tomato sauce, truffade of tomme with bacon, sliced beef with Munster sauce, beef tongue with gherkins... You appreciate the choice in the accompaniment which can be special : mashed squash, gratin of cauliflowers, leek crumble and zucchini flan are some examples. Of course, there is always a regional specialty like the Gaston Gérard chicken. Sweetened flavours (apple roasted with honey and almonds, caramelized pineapple and chocolate mousse, French toast) remain in the same spirit : simple and homemade. Sure values. The wine list, at reasonable prices, is well-stocked. It is a practical stopover for a lunch before going for a visit of the road of the Grand Crus !

Burgundy & Tourism

The competence of the regional council regarding transport and economic development are known, but less often evokes its work in favor of tourism, which however is one of the engines of the regional economy. The regional council coordinates both public and private initiatives in the tourism sector. As part of this broad mission, it plans and defines the medium-term objectives of tourism development in the region. That is why it elaborates the Regional Tourism Development Scheme (TDRS), which sets the terms and conditions of implementation of guidelines for tourism development, particularly in financial terms. After two years of consultation which brought together nearly 500 participants, the Burgundian TDRS was adopted in late 2005 for 10 years and therefore runs until 2015. This regional plan identified four priority areas to develop tourism in the region :

- **The development of the brand « Burgundy ».**
- **Opening to the public who rarely come to our region :** disabled persons and low-income public
- **Improving the accessibility and readability of the tourist offer :** information, transportation, development of new routes of discovery (vine roads or river tourism, especially along the canals).
- **Developing innovative stays.**
- **Contact :** 17, boulevard de la Trémouille. © +33 (08 00 88 81 11 (free). www.cr-bourgogne.fr

DIJON ★★★★

Dijon, splendid ancient city of the Dukes of Burgundy, is the administrative capital of Côte-d'Or but also, since January 1st, 2016, the capital of the region Bourgogne-Franche-Comté. With more than 150,000 inhabitants, the city is located in Paris and Lyon. It is the heiress of an exceptional historic past that you can visit by following the Parcours de la Chouette (symbol of the city). It is at the same time a tourist, gourmet (a small visit at the starred restaurants of the city is a must !), commercial town, with an eco-friendly and sporting tradition (big club of tennis and football, the JDA and the DFCO). Moreover the newspaper l'Equipe classified Dijon in the top 10 of the most sporting cities of France and Arte classified it like the most cultural city of France.

The major asset of the city is especially its region with its climates, its terroir, its vineyards and its wines. Now, the climates of Burgundy is listed as a Unesco World Heritage site, just like the city of Dijon and its preserved area.

www.bouger-nature-en-bourgogne.com

The General Council and Côte-d'Or Tourism decided in 2009 to combine their skills to create a website dedicated to natural recreation for tourists and côte-d'oriens. Oriented at first on walking, cycling and swimming, this site now has the authority to integrate other natural leisure activities and also offers a schedule of the different sporting events in the territory throughout the year. A comprehensive site redesign done in spring 2013 now offers a new, more graphic and more ergonomic version allowing the internet user to prepare his special travel diary « nature and leisure activities » in a simple, playful and fast way.

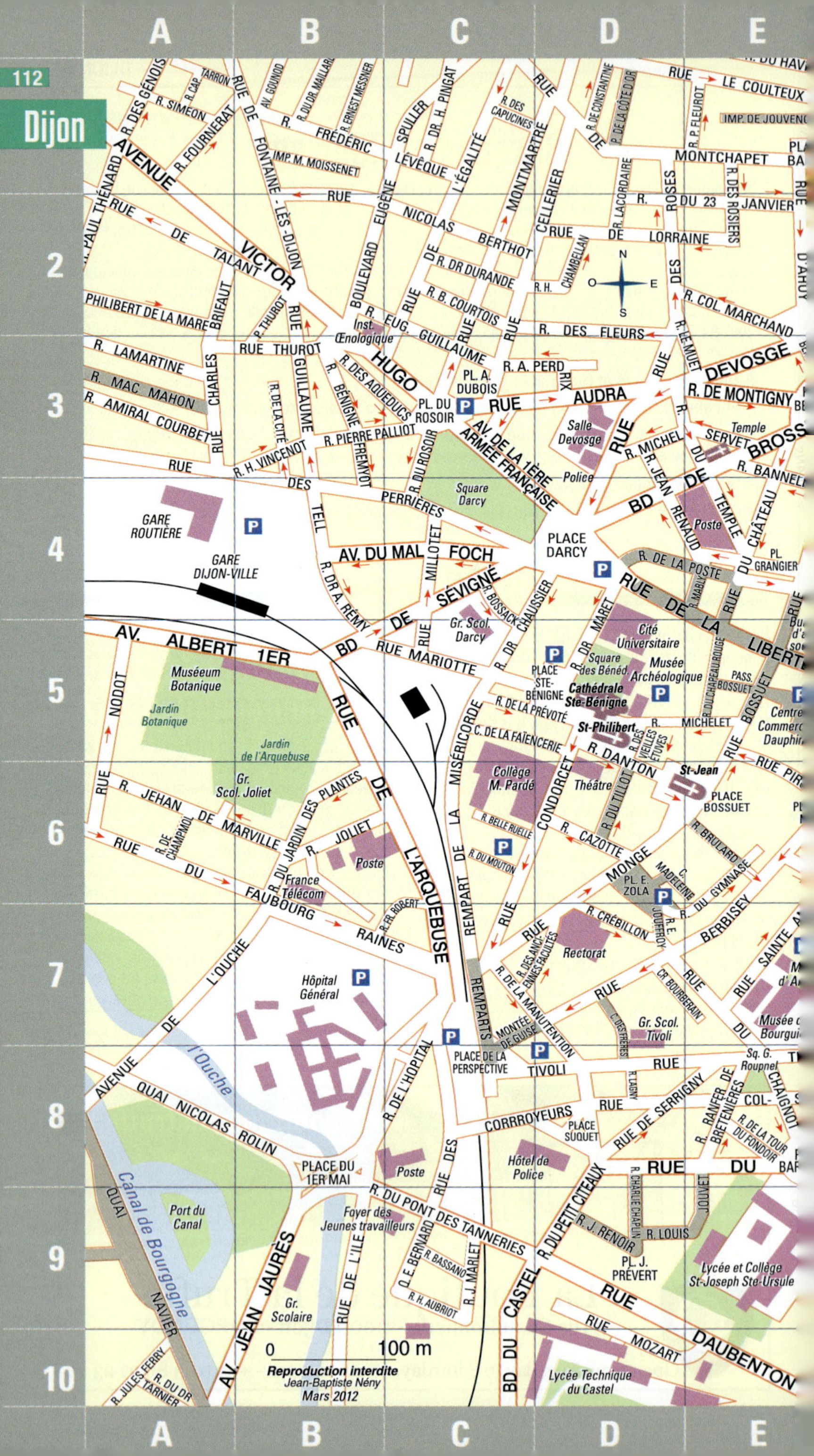
A
B
C
D
E
2
3
4
5
6
7
8
9
10
AVENUE VICTOR HUGO
R. DES GÉNOIS
R. SIMEON
R. CAP. TARRON
R. FOURNERAT
RUE DE FONTAINE - LÈS-DIJON
AV. GOUNOD
R. DU DR MAILLARD
R. ERNEST MESSNER
R. FRÉDÉRIC
IMP. M. MOISSENET
SPULLER
R. DR H. PINGAT
LÉVÊQUE
L'ÉGALITÉ
R. DES CAPUCINES
RUE MONTMARTRE
R. DE CONSTANTINE
P. DE LA CÔTE D'OR
RUE LE COULTEUX
IMP. DE JOUVENCE
R. P. FLEUROT
MONTCHAPET
R. DES ROSIERS
RUE DU 23 JANVIER
R. LACORDAIRE
R. ROSES
RUE DE LORRAINE
CELLERIER
RUE NICOLAS BERTHOT
BOULEVARD EUGÈNE
RUE
R. DR DURANDE
R. B. COURTOIS
R. CHAMBELLAN
R. H.
RUE DES FLEURS
R. COL. MARCHAND
D'AHUY
PAUL THÉNARD
RUE DE TALANT
PHILIBERT DE LA MARE
BRIFAUT
P. THUROT
RUE THUROT
R. EUG. GUILLAUME
Inst. Œnologique
R. LAMARTINE
R. MAC MAHON
R. AMIRAL COURBET
CHARLES
RUE
R. DE LA CITÉ
GUILLAUME
R. DES AQUEDUCS
BÉNIGNE FREMYOT
PL. A. DUBOIS
PL. DU ROSOIR
R. A. PERDRIX
RUE AUDRA
R. DE MONTIGNY
DEVOSGE
R. LE MUET
Temple
R. PIERRE PALLIOT
R. H. VINCENOT
R. DU ROSOIR
AV. DE LA 1ÈRE ARMÉE FRANÇAISE
Salle Devosge
RUE
R. MICHELET
SERVET
BROSSES
RUE DES PERRIÈRES
TELL
Square Darcy
Police
R. JEAN RENAUD
BD DE
R. BANNELIER
TEMPLE
CHÂTEAU
GARE ROUTIÈRE
GARE DIJON-VILLE
AV. DU MAL FOCH
MILLOTET
PLACE DARCY
Poste
PL. GRANGIER
R. DE LA POSTE
R. DR A. RÉMY
SÉVIGNÉ
R. BOSSACK
CHAUSSIER
RUE DE LA LIBERTÉ
R. MABLY
RUE
AV. ALBERT 1ER
BD DE
Gr. Scol. Darcy
R. DR MARET
Cité Universitaire
RUE MARIOTTE
Muséum Botanique
Jardin Botanique
RUE DE L'ARQUEBUSE
Jardin de l'Arquebuse
Gr. Scol. Joliet
NODOT
PLACE STE-BÉNIGNE
Square des Bénéd.
Musée Archéologique
Cathédrale Ste-Bénigne
R. DE LA PRÉVOTÉ
R. DU CHAPEAU ROUGE
PASS. BOSSUET
BOSSUET
Centre Commercial Dauphine
R. MICHELET
St-Philibert
R. DES VIEILLES ÉTUVES
R. DE LA FAÏENCERIE
R. DANTON
St-Jean
RUE PIRON
PLACE BOSSUET
Collège M. Pardé
Théâtre
R. DU TILLOT
CONDORCET
REMPART DE LA MISÉRICORDE
RUE R. JEHAN DE MARVILLE
R. DE CHAMPMOL
RUE DU FAUBOURG RAINES
RUE DU JARDIN DES PLANTES
R. JOLIET
Poste
France Télécom
R. BELLE RUELLE
R. DU MOUTON
R. CAZOTTE
MONGE
PL. E. ZOLA
C. MADELEINE
R. BRULARD
R. DU GYMNASE
R. FR. ROBERT
R. CRÉBILLON
R. E. JOUFFROY
BERBISEY
RUE SAINTE-ANNE
RUE
R. DES ANCIENNES FACULTÉS
Rectorat
RUE
CR BOURBERAIN
RUE
Musée
AVENUE DE L'OUCHE
Hôpital Général
R. DE LA MANUTENTION
REMPARTS
MONTÉE DE GUISE
C. DES FRÈRES
Gr. Scol. Tivoli
Musée de la Vie Bourguignonne
DU
l'Ouche
PLACE DE LA PERSPECTIVE
TIVOLI
RUE
R. LAGNY
Sq. G. Roupnel
CHAIGNOT
R. DE L'HÔPITAL
RUE CORROYEURS
PLACE SUQUET
RUE DE SERRIGNY
R. RANFER DE BRETENIÈRES
COL-
R. DE LA TOUR DU FONDOIR
QUAI NICOLAS ROLIN
PLACE DU 1ER MAI
Poste
RUE DES
Hôtel de Police
RUE DU BAR
R. CHARLIE CHAPLIN
JOUVET
R. DU PONT DES TANNERIES
R. DU PETIT CÎTEAUX
QUAI
Canal de Bourgogne
Port du Canal
Foyer des Jeunes travailleurs
R. J. RENOIR
R. LOUIS
NAVIER
Q. E. BERNARD
R. BASSANO
R. J. MARLET
PL. J. PRÉVERT
Lycée et Collège St-Joseph Ste-Ursule
AV. JEAN JAURÈS
RUE DE L'ÎLE
R. H. AUBRIOT
BD DU CASTEL
RUE DAUBENTON
Gr. Scolaire
RUE MOZART
0
100 m
Reproduction interdite
Jean-Baptiste Nény
Mars 2012
R. JULES FERRY
R. DU DR TARNIER
Lycée Technique du Castel

F
G
H
I
J
1
2
3
4
5
6
7
8
9
10
Crèche
IMP. DE LA SABLIÈRE
IMP. GAGNEREAUX
RUE GAGNEREAUX
R. CH. DE VERGENNES
PL. GAL ESTIENNE
RUE AUGUSTE FREMIET
Caserne Vaillant
AV. GARIBALDI
SAMBIN
COURS FLEURY
PTER DE POUILLY
MARCEAU
BD DE LA MARNE
Palais des Expositions
PLACE JEAN BOUHEY
Auditorium
RUE L. BLANC
PARMENTIER
R. FR. MAURIAC
Cité Judiciaire
R. PH. PAPILLON
BD G. CLÉMENCEAU
Poste
R. FERD. DE LESSEPS
École sup. de Commerce
I.N.F.O.P. LE MADRIGAL
COURTÉPÉE
PRUDHON
COURS
RUE DEVOSGE
R. CLAUS SLUTER
R. GAB. PEIGNOT
Cité Judiciaire
RUE
ALL. CAL DE GIVRY
Parc Clémenceau
École
RUE ANDRÉ MALRAUX
PLACE DE LA RÉPUBLIQUE
URSSAF CAF
R. JEAN DE CIREY
R. DE COLMAR
ROLLIN
PIERRE
Conseil Général
R. J. TISSOT
BD DE LA TRÉMOUILLE
PRÉFECTURE
R. DU NORD
RUE DE MULHOUSE
R. LALLEMAND
CRS DU MOUTON
CR AUX LIONS
CRS DU CHEVAL BLANC
RUE DIETSCH
BOULEVARD THIERS
LEDRU
R. HEUDELET
Conseil Régional
R. DEMONTRY
R. DE SUZON
RUELLE DE SUZON
R. MÈRE JAVOUHEY
R. DU CARON
Préfecture
Clinique
ROUSSEAU
CR STE MARIE
CR ST NICOLAS
VANNERIE
RUE
R. FÉLIX TRUTAT
Banque de France
R. DE SOISSONS
PL. DE LA BANQUE
PETITE RUE DE SUZON
RUE BANNELIER
RUE DE LA
R. DU CHAMP DE MARS
RUE D'ASSAS
ODEBERT
QUENTIN
Halles Centrales
R. C. RAMEY
Police
VERRERIE
P.R. POUFFIER
COMTE
J. J.
R. PROUDHON
R. DES HALLES
Serv. départ.
Lycée Carnot
DIDEROT
R. GALOCHE
Gendarmerie
RUE DE METZ
MUSETTE
Hôtel Voguë
RUE CHAUDRONNERIE
PL. NOTRE DAME
Notre-Dame
R. DE LA CHOUETTE
R.A.
RUE
RUE DU LYCÉE
R. COL DE GRANCEY
PLACE DU 30 OCTOBRE ET DE LA LÉGION D'HONNEUR
RUE DES FORGES
R. DES FORGES
R. RABOT
PL. DES DUCS DE BOURGOGNE
PL. DE LA STE CHAPELLE
R. LAMONNOYE
R. MORIVEAU
R. LONGEPIERRE
RUE JEANNIN
PAUL CABET
R. ST LIÉGEARD
R. P. AUX LIONS
Hôtel de Ville
Musée des Beaux-Arts
R. RAMEAU
Théâtre
PL. ST MICHEL
St-Michel
R. VAILLANT
P. RUE DE LA MONNAIE
RUE
R. PELL DE CHAMBURE
Lycée tech. S. Weil
BOURG
MERCIER
PLACE DE LA LIBÉRATION
R. DES BONS ENFANTS
PL. DU THÉÂTRE
St-Étienne
R. DUBOIS
SAUMAISE
École Berlier
R. NEUVE DAUPHINE
R. DU
PL. ST FIACRE
VAUBAN
R. BOUHIER
R. P. FOT
R. DU PALAIS
Ch. des Métiers
CR H. CHABEUF
Sq. Carrelet de Loisy
BUFFON
R. DU VIEUX COLLÈGE
Éc. St-Michel
R. VERCINGÉTORIX
R. D'ALISE
R. H. BAUDOT
R. FR. BAUDOT
BERLIER
CARNOT
R. M. CHAUMES
R. J.B. LIÉGEARD
Palais de Justice
RUE CHABOT CHARNY
R. LEGOUZ GERLAND
RUE
BAUDIN
RUE DE L'AMIRAL ROUSSIN
R. CHARRUE
R. DE L'ÉCOLE DE DROIT
RUE CH. DE L'HÔPITAL
Bibliothèque
Cité administrative Dampierre
RUE DE MIRANDE
VOLTAIRE
PLACE DES CORDELIERS
R. HERNOUX
RUE DU PETIT POTET
Fac. de Lettres
R. PRIEUR DE LA CÔTE-D'OR
RUE
TURGOT
PETITE RUE DU PRIEURÉ
Sr. scol. Dampierre
RUE
R. JACOTOT
BOULEVARD
BAPTISTE
PASTEUR
R. DU REMPART
Synagogue
R. DE LA SYNAGOGUE
Lycée technique H. Fontaine
RUE
R. FRANKLIN
TIVOLI
R. SISLEY
R. CLAUDE BASIRE
JEAN
Éc. É. de la Trinité
R. ANDRÉ COLOMBAN
R. TABOUROT DES ACCORDS
R. VIVANT-CARION
R. GASTON PARIS
R. ALFR. DE MUSSET
R. PIERRE CURIE
R. FREVET
PLACE DU PRÉSIDENT WILSON
RUE
BOULEVARD
Pompiers
St-Pierre
TRANSVAAL
R. C. DE LONGVIC
RUE
RUE ALPHONSE MAIREY
DUMONT
IMP. ST-PIERRE
COURS DU GAL DE GAULLE
RUE DE LONGVIC
IMP. POULETTY
R. DE VENISE
Crèche
BORDOT
CHARLES
École St-Pierre
Faubourg St-Pierre
D'AUXONNE
École Voltaire
Mosquée
ALL. DE MA RIE-NOËL
R. RENÉ FLEUTELOT
RUE
RUE LENÔTRE
R. VIOLLET LE DUC
R. DES PRINCES DE CONDÉ
Clinique
R. M. THIBERT
R. DOCTEUR LAVALLE
R. MAGENTA
PLACE EMMANUEL ADLER
Sq. Ed. Debeaumarché
R. DES PETITES ROCHES
R. DES BONS AMIS

Index des rues de Dijon

M

N

O-P

Q-R

S

T

V

W

Z

University city, a town that hosts many foreign students, Dijon is also an economic center and business, with moving and diversifying infrastructures : eco-neighborhoods, renovations of the municipal buildings, an economic pole (the Valmy neighborhood)... Dijon is developing and owns an urban community of 22 communes with more than 250,000 inhabitants and a pool of more than 320,000 jobs. Within less than 2 hours in TGV from Paris, Dijon has its Velodi, its tram, its olympic pool and redevelops the activities of its airport. A younger population, even if the city takes a good care of its seniors, makes the regional capital a place that is attractive for everyone ! It is a metropolis where it is good to live, on a human scale and pleasant for inhabitants, tourists and companies. Culturally, it caters for everyone ! Rock music at La Vapeur, celebrities at Zenith, operas at the Auditorium, all kinds of playhouses at the TDB, contemporary art at the Consortium... In the image of the place de la Libération that is refurbished during the recent years and the fully renovated Beaux-Arts museum, Dijon awoke ! Who said that it was beautiful sleeping city ? On the contrary, there is on its walls a wind of freshness and revival !

MAIRIE DE DIJON
Hôtel de Ville
Place de la Libération, Cour de Flore
✆ +33 (0)3 80 74 51 51 – www.dijon.fr

With the reception of the town hall, located at the ground floor of the city hall, you will find many information of a practical nature for better living Dijon with the daily newspaper : useful sports, culture, accommodations, addresses, etc For the young people, the students, the seniors and the tourists, the municipality publishes informative booklets also regularly. In short, there is always documentation useful to glean when you pass by there. Moreover, of the town halls of neighborhood are there for services near the inhabitants. More in connection with the activities of the city, of the construction sites to come, the cultural events and the projects in all kinds, do not fail to divide into sheets *Dijon Mag*. He will enable you to know the main actions of the city.

Getting There

MOBIGO – ALL INFORMATION TO TRAVEL IN BURGUNDY
17, boulevard de la Trémouille
✆ +33 (0)3 80 11 29 29
www.mobigo-bourgogne.com

♿

Power station of call open Monday to Saturday from 7am to 8pm. Available in French and English. Since February 1st, 2016, this service is also accessible to the deaf and deaf people thanks to the Acceo service. More information on the www.acce-o.fr/client/mobigo site. Open Monday to Friday from 9am to 12.30pm and from 1.30pm to 5.30pm.

The central office of Mobigo was created by the regional council of Burgundy in partnership with the departments of Burgundy and a certain number of urban areas (Grand Dijon, Grand Chalon, urban areas of Nevers, Creusot-Montceau, Côte de Beaune and Beaune Sud, the Auxerre and the Communities de Commune of Sénonais

Pass Dijon – Côte De Nuits

This year, thanks to Pass Dijon – Côte de Nuits, you will have access to the main sites and monuments of these two destinations without constraint and at your own pace ! Pass Dijon – Côte de Nuits gives travellers access to 11 services on Dijon and the Côte de Nuits.

Dijon

- **Guided Tour** : Discover Dijon. Door to William Street Owl, through the old mansions, discover the rich heritage of the former capital of the Dukes of Burgundy and its secrets.
- **Ascent to the Philippe le Bon Tower** : 46 m high, the majestic tower of the fifteenth century offers you a magnificent view over the city of Dijon and its surroundings.
- **Golf Owl Course.** Let yourself be guided by the owl ! With your book, follow the arrows and discover Dijon otherwise : in 22 steps to learn the essential and 3 new trail to go beyond...
- **The Well of Moses :** Come and admire this masterpiece of medieval sculpture, with beautiful sculptures impressive of realism, and take the opportunity to discover the ancient Certosa Champmol.

Côte de Nuits

- **Château de Marsannay in Marsannay-la -Côte.** Winery located in the Golden Gate of the Côte de Nuits, the Château de Marsannay opens its cellars and its best wines (tasting of 7 wines field Marsannay Rosé, Red and White, Fixin, Gevrey-Chambertin...)
- **Domaine du Clos Saint Louis in Gevrey-Chambertin/Fixin.** A traditional and family winery, located in Fixin. Guided tours of the vineyards, the fermenting room and the cellar. Tasting and sitting in a wine cellar. Fromagerie Gaugry – 21220 Gevrey-Chambertin/Brochon. Through a specially designed area, you can freely watch the production of the famous Burgundy cheeses such as Epoisses PDO or Ami du Chambertin. Tasting of 5 cheeses and a glass of wine.

and Autunois). The purpose of the website and the call center of Mobigo is to prepare your travels in the region. Whether you travel by train, bus, tram, bus or by bike, whether you are a lover of the carpooling or carsharing, you cannot ignore the existence of Mobigo ! An ergonomic, simple of use, reliable and relevant website that gives you all the information you need. Updates are made in real time, and even on event of disruption. It is simple : you just indicate your departure point like your arrival point and several schedule is proposed, mixing hiking route, bus and TER connections. Ultra practical ! You can easily find all the schedule that you need and you can even buy your tickets and tickets on line. Mobigo also makes it possible to discover the other existing means of transport : car-pooling, bicycle and carsharing or a system of car rental for one hour, one day, one weekend. 16 cars are available in self-service in the 7 stations from the urban area of Dijon. Find also on this site all the plans and necessary map for your getaway. Mobigo is the crucial website to profit from an economic mobility and without concern ! Beware : within the fusion of the regions, this device may continue to evolve.

Burgundy Cycling !

What could be better, by a beautiful sunny day, than visiting Burgundy pedaling ?
It is time to enjoy it, because our green area offers many cycle routes and greenways for tourists. But what is a bikeway ? A bikeway is a long-distance cycle route which is particularly adapted for cyclists. Do not worry about a bikeway there are no steep climbs. On the other hand it is nice, you will share your bikeway with the rollers, pedestrians and disabled persons. Do not forget to dress your bike with a small bell, it is always useful ! You can choose the greenways formula : we are in fact in one of the regions of France to have the greatest number of it ! The greenways are open up for all non-motorised circulations and designed by pretty green panels... ! No more time to loose, all in saddle ! But beware leave covered : helmet and jacket are highly recommended !
For all information go to www.le-tour-de-bourgogne-a-velo.com

Sightseeing

Museums

■ MUSÉUM D'HISTOIRE NATURELLE

1, avenue Albert-Ier
✆ +33 (0)3 80 48 82 00
www.dijon.fr – museum@ville-dijon.fr
Open on Monday and Wednesday to Friday from 9am to 12.30pm and from 2pm to 6pm; the weekend from 2pm to 6pm. Free.
Muséum de Dijon is fully integrated in the Jardin des Sciences de l'Arquebuse. So, when you go to the museum, you are on a complete site that includes a historic and exceptional botanical garden but also the Pavillon du Raines (and its planetarium) which organizes scientific and playful exhibitions regularly and the Natural History Museum. A museum that has been completely renovated and redesigned a few years ago. It invites you in the heart of the history of life and biodiversity. With more than 100,000 visitors a year, it is very popular with people of Dijon, adults and children and visitors of the city. The collections are surprising, between the skeletons of dinosaurs and many windows which present scenes of animals in nature... You will not be bored. You will learn a lot about the birds, fish and jungle animals like gorillas, elephants, giraffes, lions, the tiger... A little part is even reserved for animals found in the region. A museum that is simply fascinating.

© DOIN OAKENHELM / SHUTTERSTOCK.COM

City center of Dijon.

CÔTE-D'OR

To discover Burgundy On The Water

Burgundy has 1,000 km of navigable waterways, what makes it the most important network of waterways in France. In order to explore this beautiful area with the current, a very large tourist offer is set out.For those who feel the marine away : it is possible to rent livable boats for a week or a weekend. These boats are easy to control. The proof... you will not need license. The speed is limited to 5 mph, what strongly produces boarding or collision risks. The boats are fully equipped; some even have bicycles allowing you, during your stopovers, to discover Burgundy as you pedal away ! If you prefer more Zen holidays, the barge-hotels will seduce you ! it is one of the most luxurious ways to discover the region. The interior and the exterior of the barges were completely renovated, and are now magnificent floating hotels. These barges offer every comfort : comfortable cabins, dining room, lounge, bar, excellent food, etc. the little more of barges : excursions organized to put the foot on the land and visit an abbey, a castle or a cellar.Cruises are also possible on the canals. The cruise boats are real river cruise ship, which can take 100 to 180 passengers on board in a comfort that does not have much to envy maritime than their counterparts. Two shipping companies operate in Burgundy, just of the Saône, within the framework of cruises to Lyon, the Rhone valley and Provence. Three Burgundian towns (Chalon-sur-Saône, Tournus, Mason) are concerned, either as a starting point, or stopovers, for excursions are organized to burgundy first rate sites, among others, Beaune to Cluny, château de Cormatin or the picturesque medieval village of Brancion.Finally by a beautiful sunny afternoon, you can enjoy a simple boat trip whether on the canals, rivers or on the lakes of the National Park of Morvan.

For any information (reservation and rates, etc.) you should contact tourist organizations.

Walks & Strolls

LA CITÉ INTERNATIONALE DE LA GASTRONOMIE DE DIJON
3, rue du Faubourg-Raines
www.citedelagastronomie-dijon.fr

French gastronomy has been officially listed as Unesco World Heritage since 2010. To embody, preserve and showcase this exceptional know-how, a unifying tool was set up : the network of the cities of gastronomy. Four cities were chosen : Lyon, Paris-Rungis, Tours and... Dijon ! Our city has thus the important and nice responsibility of representing the French gastronomy, and more precisely of developping and promoting the culture and traditions of the vine and wine. And the project presented by Dijon is up to this, with an entire investment estimated at about 200 million euros ! Cité internationale de la Gastronomie will take seat within walking distance of the downtown, at the zero kilometer from the road of the Grand crus, on the site of the former general hospital. This city of 21,365 m² (15,000 of which is historic buildings), on a site of 6.5 hectares, will be organised around four major poles. First of all, a Culture and Training pole, provided by a house of the gastronomy – giving access to wide databases on the wine and the gastronomy – a pavilion of wines on 1 000 m², where are honoured the Climates of Burgundy as well as the wines of the world. But also a training centre and research and development, which will offer workshops, seminars, courses, a laboratory of taste, a conference center with an auditorium of 400 seats, three restaurants, a shop, as well as a multiplexes with 10 rooms. The commercial pole will gather shops, restaurants, wine bar, bookstore and stands on 3 220 m². The hotel pole – a 4-star hotel with 90 rooms and a tourist residence – will guarantee a top-of-the-range reception. Lastly, a logistic pole will manage and coordinate the whole. Cité internationale de la Gastronomie won't be used only by visitors and tourists. It will enter into an eco-neighbourhood of 3.5 hectares, which will have 640 accommodations and a student residence. Eiffage, one of the leaders of the French urban development, eventually won the call for interest launched by the City. A big project whose work is due to begin at the end of 2016 aiming at completion by the end of 2018. Finally, it will benefit from its ranking in historic centre zone, since July 2015, in the UNESCO World Heritage site, with the Climates of Burgundy and the historic center of Beaune. Dijon will thus become the reference pole in the field of valorisation and the development of culture, gastronomy and the vine and wine.

Knife & Fork

AMERICAN WAY
44, avenue Françoise-Giroud
Parc Valmy
✆ +33 (0)3 80 70 11 37
www.american-way-dijon.fr

Open Monday for lunch from 11.30am to 2.30pm; Tuesday to Saturday from 11.30am to 2.30pm and from 6.30pm to 11pm. Booking advised. À la carte : Around €25. Children's menu : €8.50 (less than 10 years). Groups welcome. Shop. Activities.

Definitely, American Way does not cease developing and multiplying novelties. We announced the arrival of a new restaurant last year, it is now open in Chenôve, in a simply stunning decor. You will discover a semi-buried Statue of Liberty, a small reproduction of road 66, a plane on the roof ! On a wider scale, American Way has also a new mascot : Ted, which curiously resembles to Elvis Presley. Is that happening by chance ? We do not think so. It will notably appear in the small quarterly newspaper that you will find in each restaurant to keep you abreast of the current news (in particular the launching of a limousine service !). In fact, it is necessary since American Way took over the franchise and a new project should come out in Chalon-sur-Saône in September 2016. In all the restaurants, the quality of the dishes and flavours made in the USA are always present, just like the dynamic reception and always smiling of all the team and Romuald, the owner. A contagious good mood ! It is undoubtedly the restaurant you should frequent. Lots of people used to eat there, especially during the weekend... You need to book to be sure you get a table. And if there is no place, do not panic, you can opt for the take-away meal ! You can eat while leaning against the bar as in Texas or you can take a small table. Good to know, the burger and buns bread are handmade. You can choose from a wide range of specialities : salads, tacos with crispy wheat tortillas, tapas, grilled fish, bagels, hamburgers, tartars, fajitas, grilled meats and a wide range of homemade specialties inspired by the tex mex culture with chili con carne or roast pork ribs to soak in the barbecue sauce and many others. According to your choice, each dish is accompanied by fries 100% homemade, salad, coleslaw, green beans, rice or potatoes. Regarding the desserts, you will not resist the delicious homemade brownie or a New York cheesecake and ice-creams. And, if you want to start with the suggestions of the day, you can get some at a reasonable price. The plus is also the marketing of the homemade beer : « furious beer », we just loved it ! Moreover, have a look at the website that reserved you derived products including t-shirt, towel holder, mugs. A real burger... the quality... undoubtedly the best in the region !

■ BRASSERIE B9

9, place de la Libération
✆ +33 (0)3 80 38 32 02
www.brasserie-b9.com
contact@brasserie-b9.com

Open Tuesday to Saturday for lunch and dinner; Sunday for lunch. À la carte : Around €18. Daily special : €13. Wine by the glass. Chèque Restaurant. Groups welcome. Terrace.

The advantage of B9 is that you feel like in a simple brasserie in. The atmosphere cordial and relaxed, we have a magnificent view of place de la Libération, a terrace heated in winter and often very animated by many guests. But don't get it wrong, the owners are Jean-Pierre Billoux, who is just the chef in Pré aux Clercs, and his sons Alexis. Thus, Aas for the catering, you can eat with your eyes closed. When we came, we started to quench our thirst with a delicious and artisanal strawberry juice made by Alain Milliat. As main course, we chose the 250 g steak à la plancha, a real treat ! Medium-rare cooked, just as we asked and accompanied by fresh French fries. To finish, a cheesecake with nutella, its vanilla ice-cream and roasted hazelnuts... It should be said, that does not resemble a cheesecake but the taste is there and the presentation is pretty. The final touch is very correct ! The fox recommends this good address where we are always served with a smile.

Place Darcy.

2015-2019 : musées des Beaux-Arts resumes its work

Since its reopening on March 30th, 2013, visitors to the museum were able to discover the new floor in the courtyard of Bar, foreshadowing the renovated museum, and during the Nuit Des Musées, on May 18th, visitors will exceptionally access the new rooms (still empty). You will have to wait until September 7th to discover the new course through 14 rooms dedicated to the Middle Ages and the Renaissance. This first course will introduce you to reciprocity between the works of the Burgundian medieval art and those of Renaissance art, and the place. The entrance by the Bar courtyard, connected to the renovated square of the Ducs, with two areas reserved for the reception, a cultural café and a bookshop, under the arches of the Bellegarde gallery. The latter will regain its original beauty with red tiled roof and panelled oak vault. Works from the Italian Renaissance will be showcased here. The tour begins with the tombs of the dukes, accessible by stairs and a panoramic elevator hidden by the contemporary rooftop that you can see from the Bar courtyard.
Festivities will coupled this inauguration : theme shows, concerts and street procession which will also cheer the return of Mourners at the museum.

LE CENTRAL PLACE

3, place Grangier
Rue du Château
✆ +33 (0)3 80 30 44 00

Open Monday to Saturday from 11am to 11pm. The restaurant is open from 12pm to 2pm and from 7pm to 11pm. Lunch menu : €18.50 (starter, main course and dessert. Starter and main course : €14.50). Wine by the glass. Chèque Restaurant. Terrace.

Le Central Place is a bar-restaurant that offers bistro cuisine highlighting the gastronomy of the terroir. The prices are rather low here and the products are of quality. Dishes that everyone appreciated because they are both simple but tasty. Thus you can enjoy the snails of Burgundy, époisses, foie gras, poached eggs in red wine sauce, parsley seasoned ham... Those who want to discover Burgundy will be pampered with grilled Charolais fillet with refined Berthault's époisses, a grilled andouillette of Troye served with a mustard of Dijon sauce and a beautiful plate of cheese. You can also try the *bourgui-burger* (salad, tomato, onion, beef, époisse and fries) and you have the authentic club sandwich if you wish to have a quick lunch. We also like the drinks that accompany the dishes. As for the wines, there are good selection of wine, white, red and rosé. The regional aperitifs are also showed off with a crémant de Bourgogne or a royal kir. Finally, sitting on the terrace is a real pleasure, in the city centre and feeling like in a cocoon. Bon appétit !

LA DAME D'AQUITAINE

23, place Bossuet
✆ +33 (0)3 80 30 45 65
www.ladamedaquitaine.fr
dame.aquitaine@wanadoo.fr

Open Monday for dinner; Tuesday to Saturday for lunch and dinner. Closed on Sunday and Monday for lunch (except feastdays). Booking advised. Wine by the glass. Package of reception €29 + choice à la carte (price understood between €3 and €14). Groups welcome. Air-conditioned room. Catering. Receptions, banquets.

La Dame d'Aquitaine has all the necessary arguments to make you give in to the temptation of having a lunch there. First of all, the place. The room where you sit down is located in the basement of the private mansion Perreney de Balleure, built for Antoine de Bretagne in 1618. And surprisingly, in this basement, a crypt of the 13th century remains, the only vestige of an abbey church. Laurent Perriguey, the chef and his wife Sabine, are happy to share with you this buried culture. You will be pleased to be part of that for a while and around a cuisine that is up to the history. Moreover, you will be surprised to see all the low prices on the menu, result of new concept launched by the house. Indeed, for good prices and to allow guests to understand what they pay, Sabine Perriguey and her sister had the good idea to set a package of « welcome ». This package is the operating costs of the establishment, everything is transparent. Then, you choose on the menu where all the prices are low and all the product are from a short distribution channels, they are only quality products. At the cost of a « sandwich with butter ham », you will be served a roasted saddle of rabbit stuffed with its kidneys in the Dijon way, a magnificent monkfish, a sole, a half squab... The Burgundian menu will also cost the price of a formula in a bakery and yet you will enjoy poached eggs in red wine sauce, a beef bourguignon and cromesquis of epoisses. Excellent initiative ! To complete your visit, visit the tasting cellar... Parties by the Atelier au Caveau de la Dame are regularly organised ! The catering service is available on request.

HIPPOPOTAMUS CENTRE COMMERCIAL TOISON D'OR

Centre commercial Toison d'or
✆ +33 (0)3 80 41 27 29
www.hippopotamus.fr
hippopotamus21@orange.fr

♿

Open all year. Opening 7 days a week Shopping arcade opens from 10am. Every day from 9am to 11pm. Menus from €11.90 to €29.90. Children's menu : €7.50. Wine by the glass. Hippopotamus à la carte with discount. Groups welcome. Baby chairs. Garden. Terrace. Activities.

Saint-Michel church, Dijon.

Hippopotamus, at the shopping center of Toison d'Or, is first of all an ideal place where you can have a break between two shopping sessions. With its appearances of French bistro, the atmosphere that reigns there is cordial. A large bar, at the entrance invites you to sip a cold or warm drink. The tables are placed all along the bay window so as to get a maximum of luminosity during your meal. And the weather is good, you can settle down in terrace. Families will appreciate the « corner of the kids » at the bottom of the restaurant where the children can play while you finish your meal quietly. The owner, Thierry Rouprich, has designed everything for your comfort. Here, you will enjoy a copious meal, Thierry does not hesitate to work with products sorted by him and presents also a fine wine list, partly regional... You can choose for example the menu duo that consists either with a starter and a main course or a main course and a dessert (or three) for a mini price. Choose the main course and the dessert is the guilty pleasure of the almost everyone. In a few minutes, you will be served a surprise as 180 grams beef (meat of special breed) on which you can add the garnishing of your choice. There are five of them on the whole : rice, French fries, potatoes, green beans, salad. There are two in the menu but you can add some to your own way with extra. You can also choose a double fillet of marinated chicken or a cod fillet... And to round off your meal, an ice-cream with two balls or a chocolate mousse XXL ! In short, a very nice and very pleasant address in addition to be effective !

HOSTELLERIE DU CHAPEAU ROUGE
5, rue Michelet
✆ +33 (0)3 80 50 88 88
www.chapeau-rouge.fr
contact@chapeau-rouge.fr

♿

Closed the first 3 weeks of janiver and from August 1st to August 15th. Open Tuesday to Saturday from 12pm to 1.30pm and from 7.30pm to 9.30pm. Menu from €50 to €145. Lunch menu : €50 (3 main courses, Tuesday to Friday). Wine by the glass. Two Michelin stars. American Express. Groups welcome. Valet.

William Frachot is in love with the Burgundian terroir. He makes all his creativity and his know-how in a rich cuisine that mingles the best of the regional produces with more unexpected horizons. It should be said that he has the knack for improbable and happy alliances. Who else would mix a wild boar shoulder with a cranberry juice accompanied by a pressed Celery and Pear ? His audacity is always rewarded by the delighted smile of the guests. You will enjoy his dishes in a bright dining room with contemporary decor and soft atmosphere. To facilitate your choice between all these tasty dishes, the menus are at your disposal : the menu *Affaire* is made up of three main courses, the menu *découverte* elaborate elaborated in advance, and the menu *Au fil de la Bourgogne* that condenses the best local cuisine, the William Frachot menu that is prepared according to the chef's inspirations and the *Signature* menu elaborated with seasonal ingredients ! For the adventurers and discoverers of flavours, we obviously recommend the à la carte menu. Between completely revisited local Burgundian dishes and creations, it is a true culinary travel. A quite particular poached eggs in red wine sauce, an sweetbread in brioche crust accompanied by roast apples, Jerusalem artichokes and truffles, an Iberian rack of pork with organic vegetables... The master cheese-maker offers a selection that changes according to the seasons. The desserts are divine ! Excellence in the explosion of flavours, the pleasure at each mouthful, an incredible meal served by a very attentive staff ! As for the wine, the list is beautifully oriented towards the local grand crus but gives a good place the other regions. William Frachot is rightly rewarded by the Michelin Guide with 2 stars. Having a lunch or dining at his table is offering yourself an unforgettable moment.

LE JACQUEMART
6, rue Musette ✆ +33 (0)3 80 30 34 40
www.brasserie-lejacquemart.com

Open all year. Tuesday to Sunday. From 8am to 11pm. Catering facilities for lunch only. For dinner : boards of pork-butchery or cheeses. À la carte : Around €13. Daily special : €8.90. Wine by the glass. Menu : €11.50 (main course, dessert, coffee). €13.50 with drink. Groups welcome. Terrace.

A very nice brasserie located at Rue Musette and attracts a clientele of regulars and tourists. It is difficult to be better located : in a pedestrian street, between the market, the Notre-Dame church and Palais des Ducs. The young owner, Yoann Correia, is overflowing with energy, attentiveness and efficiency. Here, you are always welcomed with a smile ! The prices are stable, very affordable and the products are of good quality. We recommend the lunch menu, valid even on Saturdays, which has beautiful surprises for a very decent price. On market days, the products freshly come from Halles. The day when we passed, we treated ourselves with an Italian dish consisting of a salad, a half melon garnished with tomato tapenade and raw ham. Fresh and well made, a real treat especially in summer. For dessert, a hardly seized homemade tiramisu which proves that it was made in the morning, in the kitchen. Throughout the year, you have the choice (among other things) between beef flank steak, Dijon andouillette or tartare cut with a knife. As for the wine list, the prices are unbeatable and it is very well supplied, especially with bourgognes : about fifteen of red and white ones from Marsannay to Givry. Special mention for hautes-côtes-de-nuits. You can also order beautiful platters of cheeses or cold meats. A place as we like them to be with an excellent value for money and very friendly welcome. Well done !

LES JARDINS BY LA CLOCHE

Hôtel de la Cloche
14, place Darcy
✆ +33 (0)3 80 30 12 32
www.hotel-lacloche.fr/le-restaurant
H1202@accor.com

Opened all the year. The every day of 12 : 00 to 14 : 00 and 19 : 00 to 22 : 00. In winter, closing at 21 : 00. Booking advised. Menu from €36.50 to €54. With the à la carte : 17€ the entrance, 27€ the main course and 12€ the dessert. Lunch menu : €28.50 (main course, dessert, café. Served as the Monday to Friday with the lunch). Wine by the glass. Brunch Sunday of 11 : 30 to 15 : 00 : €38. American Express. Groups welcome (on booking). Garden. Terrace. Valet.

Entirely renovated, the restaurant of the big hotel of La Cloche accommodates you in blue and black hues. A soft atmosphere reigns in the room whose splendid glass wall opens onto the garden. In summer, let yourself be tempted by the terrace where you can find fountain and pools. Recently, you can also admire there *L'ours marchant*, a creation of the sculptor Richard Orlinski. In a green setting, the statue is a nod to the famous White Bear that is visible in the garden Darcy. Within the restaurant, the table is impeccably laid : candles, fresh flowers and refined tableware come to perfect the majestic decor. The service is discrete and effective. The chef Aurélien Mauny offers a exquisite à la carte menu that highlights the flavours of Burgundy. At lunchtime, you can choose the Menu *Affaire* and its appetizing trout fillet with the soft almond cream, accompanied by a caramelized onion and celery risotto. The Menu *Jardins* changes according to the season : duo of mousse and conserve of duck with toasted slice of bread, pork cooked at low temperature with reduced red wine sauce and a finish in beauty with a crunching biscuit with litchi mousse, its rose foam and a sorbet raspberry. On the à la carte menu, you can try a Black Angus burger made with black bread or a snacked scallops with the cream of sea urchin. The restaurant *Les Jardins By La Cloche* offers you an exceptional cellar (150 crus and Grands Crus de la Bourgogne) for a table whose reputation is firmly established ! Every Sunday at lunchtime, the address offers a brunch with a range of dishes including drinks, hot pastries as much as you want, pancakes, crudities, main courses and dessert buffet. An enchanted stopover in a prestigious setting !

LOISEAU DES DUCS

3, rue Vauban
✆ +33 (0)3 80 30 28 09
www.bernard-loiseau.com
loiseaudesducs@bernard-loiseau.com

1 Michelin star. Open from Tuesday to Saturday from noon to 1.30pm and from 7.30pm to 10pm. Closed from August 21st to August 29th, 2016. Booking advised. Menus from €51 to €95. Lunch formula : €23 (main course and dessert or starter and main course, €29 starter, main course and dessert). Découverte Wine Packages, 4 wines by the glass €45, 5 wines €55, Prestige 5 wines €75. American Express. Groups welcome (by reservation a room can accommodate from 8 to 20 people). Terrace.

Dijon inhabitants has had the opportunity to enjoy the delights of the house Bernard Loiseau thanks to Loiseau des Ducs since July 2013. It is Louis-Philippe Vigilant who was chosen to be the chef of the 5th restaurant of the Group. He works on fresh ingredients with passion and audacity, just like the pastry-chef, Lucile Darosey. Both of them have been at Relais Bernard Loiseau for 4 years. The establishment is located near the place de la Libération, in the vaulted dining room of a mansion of the 16th century, listed as Historic monuments. It is chic, intimate, comfortable and... welcoming ! In 1975, the young chef Bernard Loiseau arrived in Côte-d'or... Between 1975 and 2015, forty years elapsed with an irrevocable success. This great adventure continues in 2016 with the same desire of surprising guests and mixing tradition and modernity. As a starter, choose artichoke in all its forms before enjoying a pike-perch with crispy skin in Bernard Loiseau's way. Meat lovers will hesitate between roasted hazelnuts of deer with tamarin and sweetbreads fried golden on a high-sided frying pan. As for the desserts, let yourself be tempted by one of the creations of Lucile Darosey. Her quince confit with Szechuan pepper and grapefruit is a real delight. As it has been always the case at Bernard Loiseau Group, the welcome is warm, and the service discreet and attentive. The wine bar offers 30 wines by the glass, from Burgundy and the world, that change according to the selections of the sommelier. In the Salon Auxois-Morvan can accommodate your seminars or family meals up to 20 people. The business guests will enjoy the equipment at their disposal, from the video projector to the notepad via the laptops on rental. To satisfy your culinary desires, do not hesitate to go to at La Part des Anges, an authentic wine bar adjacent to the property with a beautiful vault of the 16th century. The team of Loiseau des Ducs offers a fine selection of charcuterie, cheeses and sweet/savoury appetisers there.

Dijon.

LA MAISON DES CARIATIDES*

28, rue Chaudronnerie ✆ +33 (0)3 80 45 59 25
www.lamaisondescariatides.fr
lamaisondescariatides@orange.fr

1 Michelin star. Open Tuesday to Saturday for lunch and dinner. Booking advised. Wine by the glass. For lunch, Menu of the Market : €21 (main course and dessert), €22 (starter and main course), €27 (starter, main course and dessert). Tasting menu (7 main courses) : €58. Groups welcome (by reservation). Terrace.

La Maison des Cariatides is the symbol of a dazzling ascent : that of Jean Pouffier, simple commercial iron-monger who has became an alderman at the beginning of the 17th century. Today, this fine Dijon's residence brings luck to its occupants since the establishment was rewarded a Michelin star. For a few years, Thomas Collomb has offered to its guests a refined cuisine, prepared with fresh and quality ingredients. At the end of 2014, the chef settles in La Rôtisserie du Chambertin with Gevrey and decides to pass the reins to his second Angelo Ferrigno. Particularly well trained by Thomas Collomb, this 23 year-old young chef does brilliantly his job until he gets the precious sesame. In 2016, he is the youngest chef to get reward ! He likes to highlight products thanks to a cuisine full of finesse but without fuss. When you pass at la Maison des Cariatides, you will undoubtedly appreciate the decor : old floor, exposed stones and ultra-trendy lamps come to embellish the dining room where you will see the kitchen. In summer, the terrace is set up in one of the most beautiful inner courtyards of Dijon. As the restaurant fights against food waste, it offers a set menu that changes according to the market, the season and the inspiration. On the menu : thigh of guinea fowl, Brussels sprouts with bacon and oyster mushrooms or fatty froie mid-cooked with the lemon pasta, horseradish and vinaigrette with the ginger. The very affordable price of the lunch menu enables you to enjoy delicate dishes without breaking the bank. As for your first passage to La Maison des Cariatides, you will learn to trust the chef and to discover flavours you are not accustomed to. A recommended establishment !

MAISON PHILIPPE LE BON-BAR RESTAURANT LA CLOSERIE

18, rue Sainte-Anne ✆ +33 (0)3 80 30 73 52
contact@hotelphilippelebon.com

Restaurateurs de France. Open all year. Monday to Friday from 12pm to 2pm and from 6.30pm to 9.30pm; the weekend from 6.30pm to 10.30pm. Booking advised. Menu from €31 to €76. Lunch menu : €14.50 (starter, main course or main course, dessert. Starter, main course, dessert : €18). Wine by the glass. Groups welcome (seminars, receptions, weddings, baptisms). Garden. Terrace.

Great change in Maison Philippe Le Bon. No Les Œnophiles and Autre Entrée anymore, welcome to Closerie, côté Jardin and côté Cour. For the occasion, the room côté Jardin was entirely redesigned and it is splendid. Large revisited portraits of Philippe Le Bon are displayed on the walls, the fireplace heats the atmosphere, the large banquettes invite you to have a sit comfortably, and the stone walls provides an additional the charm to the room. Of course, in the fine days, you can choose the terrace installed in a superb Gothic courtyard. The à la carte menu has also undergone much change at the time of fusion between the two tables of Maison Philippe le Bon. Each lunchtime, the house offers the daily special. We enjoyed, as starter, a fine goat cheese pie with crunchy vegetables, then a pork filet mignon seasoned with Epoisses. A real treat whose presentation is extremely neat in the dish. For dessert, tiramisu-style entremet with a light and sweetened ice-cream. As much to say that the value for money is excellent. Moreover, three menus (Bourguignon, La Closerie or Menu des Climats). You can find on the à la carte menu fine pieces of meat, some « brasserie » main courses and the fish fillets prepared under the eyes of the guests. Do not miss revisited parsley seasoned ham as starter, served with a whipped cream with old mustard. In main course, we fall for the vegetarian burger or beef fillet served with homemade fries. Some beautiful suggestions of local cheeses. The menu of the desserts will delight the most gourmet who will have a feast with a homemade religieuse with caramel and with salted butter. Without forgetting the sea dishes, ultra fresh, suggested each day by the oyster seller of the house. The prices are as enticing as the oysters, lobsters, langoustines, shrimps, mussels etc. And of course, the house proposes a sublime wine list. A place, in full metamorphosis, that we loves. Here a « new » and exiting address, to discover without any delay.

MASAMI

79, rue Jeannin ✆ +33 (0)3 80 65 21 80
www.restaurantmasami.com
contact@restaurantmasami.com

Open Monday to Saturday from 12pm to 2pm and from 7pm to 10pm. Booking advised. Menu from €22 to €48. Wine by the glass. Menus for lunch from €14.50 to €24. Take-away.

Here is an authentic Japanese restaurant (they are only two in Dijon), which gained its reputation in a few years only thanks to Masami Akaogi, the owner and chef. As a true Master in the art of the Japanese cuisine, he studied in Japan, he makes you discover a cuisine that you do not know so far. The presentation itself is already impressive. The dishes are bigger, colors, mix textures... From the starter to the dessert, what you see will captivate you and tantalize you each time. What could be better than a main course with beautiful aesthetic and in addition more tasty ? That's what you will find here, perfection on all levels. The products are fresh and prepared on the spot. You have the choice among several dishes, all of them delicious one as the other. Do not miss the Yakitori menu and its chawanmushis with scallops and monkfish cheek as well as the farm chicken skewer, yakitori, and rice. Our favorite goes undoubtedly to the Masami menu that brings Burgundy closer to Japan with a subtle blend of the two culinary cultures illustrated by this suggestion of sashimis followed by a fillet of Charolais beef with foie gras and soft-boiled egg sauce, a speciality of the chef. Sometimes you can also find truffles in the main courses... An excellent address to attend absolutely and especially with a true Japanese chef !

Darcy place.

Darcy garden.

LE PALAIS DIT VIN NEW
74, rue monge
✆ +33 (0)3 80 66 88 03 / +33 (0)6 48 88 95 71
www.palaisditvin.fr
lpdvdijon@gmail.com
Ouvert du mardi au vendredi de 11h30 à 14h et de 19h à 21h30; le samedi de 11h30 à 14h30 et de 19h à 22h. Réservation recommandée. Carte : 20 € environ. Formule du midi : 12,50 € (entrée+plat ou plat+dessert). Accueil des groupes. Terrasse.
À la tête de ce nouveau restaurant traditionnel où tout est fait maison, où tout est frais, en privilégiant des produits issus de la filière courte : Meriem et Eddy. Un duo à la vie comme en affaires qui fait très bon ménage. Meriem est chef en cuisine et Eddy reçoit en salle. L'accueil est irréprochable, souriant, sympathique et très agréable. Du côté de l'assiette, c'est tout simplement un délice. La chef apporte parfois ses plats elle-même et elle a raison, car il n'y a pas de quoi rougir. Nous avons dégusté, en entrée, un œuf poché et chips de jambon cru accompagnés d'une salade très bien assaisonnée. Une mise en bouche idéale, bien réalisée et légère. En plat, un dos de Lieu Noir fondant, saisi à la perfection, sous lequel se cache une polenta. En dessert, des fraises, chantilly et coulis de cassis. En bouche, les textures et les saveurs sont décuplées. On sent, sans aucun doute, le « fait maison » avec amour. La carte des vins est travaillée et change régulièrement. Un restaurant à visiter absolument pour un moment gastronomique unique.

■ LE PRÉ AUX CLERCS
13, place de la Libération
✆ +33 (0)3 80 38 05 05
www.alexisbilloux.com
contact@alexisbilloux.fr
♿
« Maître Restaurateur » label. Open all year. Closed one week in August and a week in February. Tuesday to Saturday for lunch and dinner. Booking advised. Menu from €59 to €105. Lunch menu : €32 (except Sunday and public holidays). Wine by the glass. Groups welcome. Terrace. Pets allowed.
If you are looking for a large restaurant, stop off at Place de la Libération. A real Dijon institution, Le Pré aux Clercs welcomes you in an intimate and elegant decor where wooden beams and French ceiling harmoniously blend with stone walls. Ironed tablecloths with silver cutlery, everything is done so that your visit to the restaurant leaves you an unforgettable memory. Today, it is Alexis Billoux, the son of Jean-Pierre Billoux who gradually took over the reins of the restaurant under the watchful eye of his father. Among the specialties of this talented chef : Bresse chicken roasted in its juice and its truffle mashed potatoes or prawn mat with sherry vinegar. If he particularly enjoys cooking game, all the dishes of Alexis Billoux exude creativity and audacity. His duck foie gras is then accompanied by bittersweet aubergines with rosemary and a red-beetroot compote. During weekday, let yourself be tempted by the lunch menu that is both economical and generous. To make your choice in the wine list, ask Patrice Gillard, sacred best sommelier of the year 2015 in Trophées de la Gastronomie and wines of Côte-d'Or. Just steps away, Brasserie B9 welcomes you for lunch and dinner for a simple, modern but always inventive cuisine. You can also enjoy the 5 rooms of the establishment for a stay in the heart of Cité des Ducs. A must in Dijon.

RESTAURANT LE CHÂTEAU BOURGOGNE
22, boulevard de la Marne
✆ +33 (0)3 80 72 31 13 – h1227@accor.com
Open every day from 12pm to 2pm and from 7pm to 10pm. Bar Le Chanoine open every day until midnight. Catering. Booking advised. Menu from €30 to €69. À la carte : Around €45. Children's menu : €9. Lunch menu : €30 ("Around a main course" : put in mouth, starter and main course or put in mouth, main course, cheese platter or carriage of the desserts). Wine by the glass. Menu of the market at €40 (Put in mouth, starter, main course, cheese platter and carriage of desserts). Holiday voucher, Chèque Restaurant. Groups welcome. Garden. Terrace.

CÔTE-D'OR

This gastronomic rendezvous is a must for lovers of real cuisine. At Château Bourgogne, all the dishes are homemade, elaborated on the spot with raw products. The talented Gonzalo Pineiro varies his à la carte menu in the course of the season and succeeds in making us enjoy them. You should prepare to be satisfied from to the dessert. On the programme, you will always find the regional and traditional main courses with an original touch that of which only the chef knows the secret. Last winter, there was, for instance, a terrine of « Landes » duck foie gras mid-cooked with a delicious seasonal fruits chutney with four spices. The restaurant offers obviously Burgundy snails cooked with the Chablis and poached eggs in Chardonnay and the Pinot Noir sauce. The « Angus » Beef steak is succulent, just as the medallion of Monkfish raised in Tandoori and the cream with the yellow wine. With the à la carte menu, you have a wide choice of delicious dishes. You can also choose the menu « *Autour d'un plat* »(around a dish), for the « Menu of the market » or the gourmet menu « *Château Bourgogne* ». The best way to enjoy them is to settle down in terrace, in a friendly *lounge* atmosphere, from where you can see the chef cooking under your eyes. Do not miss the impressive wine list with 300 Burgundy names and France for the rest. In this establishment, the setting is as pleasant as the service. An excellent address !

■ RESTAURANT STÉPHANE DERBORD

10, place Wilson ✆ +33 (0)3 80 67 74 64
www.restaurantstephanederbord.fr
contact@restaurantstephanederbord.fr
♿

« Maîtres Cuisiniers » label. Open Tuesday to Saturday for lunch from 12pm to 1.45pm and for dinner from 7.30pm to 9.30pm. Booking advised. Menu from €53 to €102. Children's menu : €19. Lunch menu : €28 (except the weekend). Wine by the glass. Tasting of desserts €22. Good gift adapted to the guest. American Express. Groups welcome (up to 60 people). A Michelin star.

Renowned chef, Stéphane Derbord perfectly combines local flavours and creativity. Its starred restaurant offers you refined cuisine where Burgundian products have their place. In a hushed atmosphere, let yourself be tempted by the surprise lunch served every lunchtime or on weekdays. For less than €30, you will get an overview of the culinary talents of the house. If the room seduces with its simplicity and its warm colours, the dishes will delight you with their audacious originality. Fillet of hare to cocoa powder and quince caramel, tender and tasty meat of charolais beef Label Rouge matured for 70 days, melting beefchuck in its own juice with Genièvre de Bourgogne... all the inventions of the chef are an invitation to delicacy. To accompany the whole thing, a superb wine list awaits you. For dessert, elegance reigns with a tube with mango mousse foam and candied oranges accompanied with caramel with bergamot thyme and an exotic sorbet. Everything is done to make you spend a moment out of time, away from noise and speed. Upon your arrival, Isabelle Derbord welcomes you with extreme kindness. If you have to wait until a table is clear, no worries : a contemporary and cosy lounge is available at the entrance. Note : Stéphane Derbord also hosts your receptions or your family meals. For Christmas and New Year's Day, special menus are specially designed for you. This starred restaurant is open to all budgets and can meet the most diverse expectations with delicacy and know-how. Unmissable !

■ RÔTISSERIE LE CENTRAL GRILL

3, place Grangier
✆ +33 (0)3 80 30 44 00 – H0654@accor.com
♿

Open Monday to Saturday from 12pm to 2pm and from 7pm to 11pm. Beyond 11pm : only by reservation. Booking advised. Menu from €24 to €29. Wine by the glass. American Express, Chèque Restaurant. Groups welcome (by reservation).

Le Central (labeled Vignobles et Découvertes) is ideally located on place Grangier. This gastronomic restaurant makes you want to discover the most prestigious and the beautiful of Burgundy ! Some morsel are offered to you to immerse in the mood Burgundian local. On the programme, classical poached eggs in red wine sauce, the famous parsley seasoned ham and the Burgundy snails. You can continue with a grilled rumpsteak of Charolais bull in wine sauce or an Andouillette 5A with a mustard sauce. The meats and fish served are of a remarkable quality. As for the sea dishes, the sole meunière of the chef is worth the detour : it is very melting. For the lovers of good meat, the Charolais bull is with the honor : you have the choice between steak, prime rib or tournedos. All these meats can be accompanied by a morel and mushroom sauce. The wine list honors first of all the Burgundy. White and red, you can choose your wine by the glass or by the bottle. And regarding the bottles, the choice is wide : very affordable but very good Pinot Noir to the remarkable Richebourd of the Domaine Romanée Conti... Of course, there will be something for all tastes. A refined cheese board awaits you at the end of your meal. For dessert, the most gourmet can opt for the trolley of pastries. On the à la carte menu, Le Central offers a Delight iced with the griottines, a mousse iced with green Charterhouse or a delicious creme brulee with Bourbon Vanilla. There is many reasons to run to Rotisserie to spend a pleasant moment !

■ VILLA VAUBAN
15, rue Vauban ✆ +33 (0)3 45 83 07 76
Open Tuesday to Saturday for lunch and dinner. Menu from €28 to €36. Children's menu : €10. Wine by the glass. Daily special, coffee : €14. Starter, main course or main course, dessert : €19.90 (€25 with glass of wine and coffee). Starter, main course and dessert : €25 (€30 with glass of wine and coffee). Groups welcome. Terrace.
Villa Vauban ensures you a very pleasant moment in an original and stylish place. Indeed, it is rather unusual to lunch or dine inside, at the foot of very large silver palms beams planted in majestic pots. Some pieces of the Baroque furniture blend perfectly with the round tables and contemporary semi-circle benches. The restaurant also offers you its pleasant and quiet terrace in a pedestrian street in fine weather. Xavier Pernot offers 100 % homemade cuisine with fresh ingredients. The suggestions of the menu are simple and consist of two or three dish, the choice is up to you. The menu changes with the season. During our passage, we appreciated the diversity of the dishes and their original seasoning : Court-bouillon of monkfish withe fresh ginger or tarragon, thigh of Mulard's duck confit, juice with cocoa beans, pan-fried foie gras, chunk of Montbéliard beef fillet with pistachio crumble, vanilla mousse with hazelnuts roasted on a guianduja feuilletine... In short, these are dishes worthy of a gourmet restaurant. The other suggestion of the address is the privatization of the vault for the organization of business of family events. The restaurant takes in charge of all catering services, with an impeccable presentation and aesthetics. Villa Vauban is more and more excellent as years pass by.

Sleeping

■ CASTEL BURGOND
RN71, 3, route de Troyes
Daix ✆ +33 (0)3 80 56 59 72
cb2104@inter-hotel.com

Reception from 6.30am to 11pm. Night watchman. 46 rooms. Single room €72; double room €78; triple room €88. Buffet breakfast : €9.50. Parking included. Family rooms for 4 : €139, for 5 : €149, for 6 : €159. American Express. Pets allowed (€5). Seminars. Free Internet access. Free Wifi. Catering facilities (in partnership with the Three Duc). Satellite TV.
With a proud and imposing appearance of modern house, the Castel Burgond offers many services. Located near the car racing circuit of Dijon-Prenois, the equestrian centre of Bonvaux and three kilometres from the city centre of Dijon, the three-star hotel set on the calm, the comfort and the care given to its 46 rooms that can accommodate from 1 to 6 people, are equipped with TV and Wifi access. Forty of them are air-conditioned. The decoration is modern with a particular care given to the bedding. Common rooms are available so that you can relax in peace : small bar, room with bicycles... For the studious stays, conference rooms and seminars are at your disposal. Good point : a closed and free parking, contiguous to the hotel. At the reception, you can also buy regional products to take a souvenir home. Note : the adjacent restaurant Les Trois Ducs delights the finest gourmets.

■ DIJON LA BELLE ADRESSE
21, rue Monge
✆ +33 (0)6 67 54 99 91
www.dijonlabelleadresse.com
From €145/night.
Dijon La Belle Adresse offers short stays (for a weekend escape for example) in warm and design apartments hotels. All located on rue Monge, in the heart of downtown, in the same building, each apartment with its floor and its theme. On the first floor, Pain d'épices offers an unrivalled comfort with soothing colors, brown and orange, every detail has been carefully studied, you can even sleep under a splendid photo of the Hôtel de Ville at night. On the 2nd floor, Cassis, in purple tones, combines modernity, with very design furnishings, and rusticity, especially with wooden beams on the ceiling. Finally on the 3rd floor, Moutarde is certainly the most beautiful. You will fall under the spell of wooden furniture, of this sweet yellow color that reminds you the Burgundian delight. As for the fourth and last floor, it is the most audacious with, very rare in Dijon, a terrace on the roofs in the city center and bathrooms hidden in wine barrels integrated into the decor... we are fans ! Last noverlties, the vault of La Belle Adresse which was arranged to make it a private place where you can discover the best wines of the region. The VIP service also was created for all your needs : baby-sitter, pressing, discovery of the vineyards, booking of shows, delivery of shopping before your arrival... A service that is simply perfect for an must-go address.

■ GRAND HÔTEL LA CLOCHE
14, place Darcy
✆ +33 (0)3 80 30 12 32
www.hotel-lacloche.fr
H1202@accor.com

Open all year. Reception 24/24. 88 rooms. Buffet breakfast : €22. Closed parking. Room from €165, suite from €500. American Express. Pets allowed (€30 extra). Seminars. Receptions and weddings. Free Wifi. Catering facilities (the Gardens by La Cloche). Hammam, whirlpool, sauna, massages (Le Spa by La Cloche). Valet.

Grand Hôtel La Cloche, a real piece of heritage, is a must-go address in Dijon.
This institution of luxury accommodation is refurbished to get an ambitious and refined result. Labelled by the Accor Hôtels group, Grand Hôtel La Cloche belongs to the MGallery collection, which gathers the memorable hotels with a supplement of soul linked to their history. The hotel has always been receiving since its creation personalities in search of comfort, originality and prestige. The history, embodied by exceptional men and women (Albert 1er, Bourvil, Louis de Funès, Grace de Monaco...), crossed the walls of the hotel. Its five stars are justified by many assets : a landscaped garden, beautiful meeting rooms, private car park, valet service, room service, spa room with hammam, whirlpool bath, sauna and massage service... Everything is there and even more thanks to expansion and renovation works to offer more comfort and space to guests. The hotel is extended to 1,800 m^2. 88 rooms are now available (instead of 68 formerly) with an exceptional suites of 100 m^2. A projection room is built, just like a smoking room, a counter-current indoor swimming pool, a beautiful well-being and relaxation space... Grand Hôtel La Cloche is a real rebirth and it is now a reference of exceptional hotel. To appraise the collection of Musée des Beaux-Arts of Dijon, the address chose to decorate the wall of the rooms and the corridor with large-scale work reproduction. Thanks to discreetly placed flashcodes, guests can know everything on the masterpieces. The bar was completely rearranged in Napoleon III's lounge style, open onto Place Darcy. At Restaurant Les Jardins by La Cloche, the chef, Aurélien Mauny, always makes you discover subtle and refined dishes, superbly accompanied by one of the 150 Burgundy wines from the cellar. Perfect reception, extraordinary comfort, historic place... All the ingredients are gathered for a magical stay in the heart of the Cité des Ducs.

HOSTELLERIE DU CHAPEAU ROUGE

5, rue Michelet ✆ +33 (0)3 80 50 88 88
www.chapeau-rouge.fr
contact@chapeau-rouge.fr

Open all year. Reception 24/24. 28 rooms (including 3 suites). Double room from €100 to €295; suite from €274 to €295. Buffet breakfast or in room : €18. Parking : €15 (from 7.15am to 11.30pm with valet service). Free for children under 12 years old in the parents' room. American Express. Seminars. Receptions and weddings. Free Wifi. Catering facilities (gourmet restaurant open Tuesday to Saturday). Satellite TV, Canal+. Hammam, whirlpool, sauna.

An exceptional place located within walking distance of the cathedral of Dijon, theater of the place Saint-Jean and rue de la Liberté. In full heart of the city, Hostellerie du Chapeau Rouge is set up in a former coaching inn of the 19th century. It's impossible to miss its superb façade that was awarded the prize Label Ville 2015, designated by the Town of Dijon. Inside, the authentic luxury addresses modernity. The 28 rooms (of which 3 have just been entirely renovated) lay out of an top-of-the-range equipment, with minibar, safe, air-conditioning, latest bathroom and large bathtub... In each one of them, you can find a nod to the cuisine of William Frachot, the Michelin star chef who is the Master of the places : some of his dishes are displayed at the top of bed. The suites can accommodate four people comfortably. In the spa area, you can enjoy with the pleasures a sauna, a massage, a jacuzzi or a hydro-massage shower... At the restaurant of the hotel, William Frachot, with 2 stars, offers an inventive and subtl cuisine that enchants the gourmets. It is unquestionably one of the best tables of Dijon. An exquisite stay in sight !

HÔTEL B&B DIJON CENTRE

Place Grangier
5, rue du Château ✆ +33 (0)8 92 70 75 06
www.hotel-bb.com – bb_4706@hotelbb.com

Open all year. Reception 24/24 (2 family rooms). 60 rooms (from €57 in reception). Buffet breakfast : €6.15 (child breakfast : €3 up to 10 years). American Express, Holiday voucher. Pets allowed (€4). Free Wifi. Satellite TV.

Hôtel B&B Dijon Centre is a nice surprise. Behind the splendid glass doors, there are 60 rooms with modern and trendy decor. During your stay, you can benefit from a good sound-proofing, last generation flat-screen TV and even the air-conditioning. The bedding is very comfortable and ensures you a peaceful sleep. Recently, the hotel has also two brandnew family rooms. Designed for 4 people, they are modernly equipped. If you wish to stroll in the city and to look for emblematic places of Dijon, it is the perfect place to stay. The hotel is located in the city center and easily accessible from the station, within walking distance from the terraces that are highly prized by the Dijon inhabitants. You can work peacefully in the desk corner in the quiet room and the free wi-fi access. To top it all, a microwave oven is accessible in self-service, a hairdryer and an iron are available on request and you can obtain a hot drink at any time of day or night. What we particularly like is the closet of the room and the many sockets. You do not anymore have to choose which could be charged, the computer or the telephone. At breakfast, you can choose between sweet and salted or just not to make a choice : here, you have an all-you-can-eat buffet ! A good quality/price ratio. The fox recommends without hesitation.

HÔTEL CAMPANILE DIJON CONGRÈS CLEMENCEAU

16, avenue Raymond Poincaré
✆ +33 (0)3 80 71 10 56
www.campanile-dijon-clemenceau.com
contact@campanile-dijon-clemenceau.com

Restaurant in the vicinity. Multilingual reception : English, Spanish, German, Italian. Service snacking 24/24 – Lounge Bar. Reception 24/24. 90 rooms. Double room from €65 to €120. Buffet breakfast : €9.90. Closed parking : €10. American Express, Holiday voucher. Pets allowed (€5). Seminars. Free Wifi. Satellite TV.

Hôtel Campanile Dijon Congrès Clémenceau is located in the heart of the Dijon business district : close to the congress centre, the Auditorium and the sports palace. To ensure that you enjoy a comfortable stay, a private and enclosed car park awaits you. Another positive point : the tram passes in front of the establishment and takes you within a few minutes to the town centre. Practical ! The building has been recently renovated with state-of-the-art materials and a very modern architectural rendering. The 90 new generation rooms of this 3-star hotel are spacious and functional. Obviously, all of them are soundproofed, air-conditioned and perfectly equipped... Flat-screen TV, private bathroom with shower room, welcome tray : there is nothing missing ! The hotel offers a family and communicating room as well as rooms for disabled person. A lounge area has been arranged for relaxation. A sweet and savoury menu is available at any time of the day... The address is open 24 hours a day. You can have your breakfast served in a buffet style or directly in your bedroom. Do you want to bring a small delicacy before walking around ? A sweet dispenser has just been set in the lobby. Ideal for food lovers ! A smart piece of advice ? Ask for a bedroom on the sixth floor : the view of Dijon is breathtaking there.

■ L'HÔTEL DU PRÉ AUX CLERCS

3, rue du Palais ✆ +33 (0)3 80 38 05 05
www.alexisbilloux.com
contact@alexisbilloux.com

Castles & Hôtels Collection. Open all year. 5 rooms. Double room €130; suite €250. Two twin bed rooms from €170 to €200. Private parking. Pets allowed. Wifi.

This « hotel residence » is none other than the continuation of the gourmet restaurant Le Pré aux Clercs. Proudly run by Jean-Pierre and Alexis Billoux, it has five luxurious, modern and quiet rooms. The contemporary decoration has an excellent taste : we owe it to the same designer, Hugo Viguier. Each room has a special spirit. The « Contemporaine » (26m^2), design and simple decoration, was designed for people with reduced mobility. The « Naturelle » (36m^2) is placing a great emphasis on wood and panelling, with its private terrace, this is our favourite ! The « loft » reminds of an American spirit with more urban decoration in an industrial style (chrome steel, brushed or black) enhanced with some wood panelling (notably the beamed ceilings). The « Suite » (50 m^2) is more elegant and quiet even if it is in the city centre. Also more traditional, it offers the charm of the traditional style. And finally, the « Culinaire » (26m^2) is filled with nods to the parent-company and the gastronomy. The house has also introduced gift boxes combining a meal at the restaurant and a night at the Residence. We can do nothing but recommend these these beautiful rooms for a night long or during a weekend. It's a beautiful concept that is developed in the city centre to meet the demands of many guests of the restaurant.

■ HÔTEL IBIS CENTRE-CLEMENCEAU

2, avenue Marbotte ✆ +33 (0)3 80 74 67 30
www.hotel-ibisclemenceau-dijon.com
H5640@accor.com

Open all year. Rooms between €79 and €109 depending on the period. Reception 24/24. 102 rooms. Buffet breakfast : €9.90 (€5.50 for the early risers or late riser. €4.95 for children under 12 years old). Extra bed : €12. Parking : €6.90 (pass midnight). American Express, Holiday voucher. Pets allowed (€6). Seminars. Internet corner. Free Wifi. Catering facilities (service snack 24/24, and on the inch). Canal+.

Very close to the downtown, within walking distance from the Auditorium, the Chamber of Commerce, the Congress Center, the Sports Center and a tram station, Hôtel Ibis Centre-Clémenceau enjoys an ideal location ! Whether you came to Dijon for a professional stay or to visit the city, do not hesitate to make a stopover in this dynamic establishment do its utmost to satisfy its guests. If you are driving, an underground car park is accessible right in front of the hotel. You will find also a Vélodi station for your stroll in the open air. There are ongoing works to modernize rooms and corridors and to make your stay more comfortable. Soon at the entrance, you arrive near the relaxation area and the bar which will fill your aperitif desires while offering you a snack service. The 102 rooms are accessible by lift and some are even completely adapted to the disableds. They are perfectly soundproofed and highly modern with all the necessary amenities. wi-fi, TV, alarm clock, adjustable luminosity, air-conditioning... everything is thought out to make your stay as pleasant as possible. In order to remain fashionable, the rooms are rearranged and the news Sweet Room by IBIS offers an improved bedding, noble materials, modern relaxing colours for a very stylish setting. The high standard is now accessible at economic price and we are happy with that. Conference rooms are also available to accommodate your business meetings. The team of Hôtel Ibis Centre-Clémenceau is attentive and very professional. Thanks to them, you will undoubtedly live a stay that meets your expectation.

HOTEL HOLIDAY INN DIJON CENTRE-TOISON D'OR
1, place Marie-de-Bourgogne
✆ +33 (0)3 80 60 46 01 – www.holidayinn.com
dijon.reservation@wanadoo.fr

Open all year. Reception 24/24. 141 rooms (including 4 suites). Buffet breakfast : €17. Rooms from €99. Games for children. Pets allowed (supplement €20). Seminars. Free Wifi. Catering facilities (Gallery 412 restaurant, brasserie, bar). Hammam, sauna. More than 500 m² of shows and seminar rooms.

This high standing hotel with 141 rooms and 4 suites is located in Toison d'Or, opposite a 4-hectare park, steps from the shopping center, close to the Zenith and 10 minutes by tram from the city centre. With its contemporary style and its very trendy decor, it combines luxury, comfort and quality services, very cosy bedding, nice restaurant, cosy bar, fitness room, relaxation area, beauty, spa as well as an outdoor pool. The hall of the hotel already makes its effect with the bright colours and its stylish furniture and minimalist curves. The address also offers turnkey stays. An excellent gift idea for a charming and lovely stay.

HÔTEL IBIS DIJON GARE
15 A, avenue Albert-Ier ✆ +33 (0)3 80 43 01 12
www.hotel-ibisgare-dijon.fr
H1380@accor.com

Open all year. Reception 24/24. 128 rooms. Double room from €60. Buffet breakfast : €9.90. Parking included. 5 meeting rooms from 10 to 150 people. Business corner. American Express, Holiday voucher. Pets allowed (€6 of supplement). Seminars. Free Wifi. Catering facilities (Klub. Menu at €15 (two dishes), at €20 (three dishes). For lunch and dinner). Satellite TV. Excursions (stay Art and gastronomy).

Located in the heart of Dijon and within walking distance from the train station, this 3 -star hotel features 128 air-conditioned and soundproofed rooms. During your stay, you will enjoy an attentive service and every possible comfort. The wi-fi access is free unlimited and the bedding is cosy for soft nights. Business travelers appreciate the 300 m² air adaptable lounges with state-of-the-art technology. It is the perfect place to organise a seminar or a congress since the hotel can accommodate up to 100 participants. Its restaurant "Le Klub" highiligths the Burgundy specialties and some local wines rigorously selected. The dishes change with the seasons. In addition to all these assets, there is also a free private car park and a welcoming and flowered terrace. Now, you understand why we recommend this address year after year.

HOTEL IBIS STYLES DIJON CENTRAL
3, place Grangier ✆ +33 (0)3 80 30 44 00
www.hotel-ibiscentral-dijon.fr
H0654@accor.com

Reception 24/24 (7 days a week). 90 rooms. Single room from €76 to €126; double room from €96 to €136; triple room from €106 to €146; suite from €166 to €176. Half-board : €16 (at an extra charge). Breakfast included. Pets allowed (€10). Seminars. Free Wifi. Catering facilities (2 restaurants : Grill room Le Central and Brasserie Central Place. Catering). Satellite TV, Canal+.

It's hard to find better ! The hotel Ibis Styles Central is strategically located in the heart of Dijon : place de Grangier. You are at place Darcy within two minutes walk, at rue de la Liberté in one minute, and you are at place de la Libération in less than five ! With its 90 spacious, comfortable and air-conditioned rooms, its flat-screen TV and wi-fi internet access, this address deserves its three stars. The hotel is modern and accessible to everyone, some rooms are specially arranged for the disabled guests. During your business trip, you have all the necessary tools for your work : two fully equipped and extremely pleasant rooms can in fact accommodate up to 35 people. There are private lounges for business meals. Whether you are here for business or pleasure, we recommend you to enjoy the two restaurants : the rotisserie « Le Central Grill » and the brasserie « Le Central Place ». The first, very famous, allows you to discover the culinary treasures of Burgundy. The second serves simple meals and copious in a sympathetic atmosphere. Many assets for a hotel of quality, ideally located !

HÔTEL MERCURE DIJON CLEMENCEAU****
22, boulevard de la Marne
✆ +33 (0)3 80 72 31 13
www.hotel-mercure-dijon.fr
h1227@accor.com

Open all year. Reception 24/24. 123 rooms. Buffet breakfast or in room : €19 (been useful from 6.30am to 10am). Closed parking. Superior room from €99, privilege room from €115, Junior Suite from €135. Holiday voucher. Pets allowed (supplement : 15€). Seminars. Receptions and weddings. Free Wifi. Catering facilities (restaurant Château Bourgogne open 7 days a week; catering).

The four stars of the hotel Mercure are a true guarantee of quality : the decoration is at the same time simple and contemporary, the reception is professional and friendly, the restaurant is highly prized by the inhabitants of Dijon and the staff proves each day that his hotel deserves its place among the best establishments of Dijon ! Of course, the bedding is top-of-the-range, the TV enjoys a multiple choice of channel, the wi-fi is free and there's a minibar and a safe. They offer various room categories to you, among the 123 available : superior rooms, Privileges and the Suites Privileges. Their decoration is contemporary and refined, the colors are soothing and cordial for a maximum of harmony and wellness. In 2016, work of decoration will be carried out to modernize the lobby and offer more current colors to the visitors. Some changes are likely to occur on the side of the restaurant and the bar. Hôtel Mercure Dijon Clémenceau works permanently to offer its guests comfortable, cordial and smart spaces. We appreciate this discrete luxury borrowed from a modern simplicity where nuances and materials are selected with an aim of creating an intimate and relaxing atmosphere. Adjacent in Palais des Congrès et with the Auditorium, with its secure parking and free, this hotel is the perfect place for your travels of business. Since last year, you can also benefit from a *lounge* terrace at the edge of the heated outdoor swimming pool, offering a plancha service during the fine days. For your meals, you can trust the restaurant « Château Bourgogne », with the delicate cuisine of Gonzalo Pineiro and the very beautiful desserts trolley of the chef pastry chef Gérard Ledoux.

■ HÖTEL WILSON

1, rue de Longvic
✆ +33 (0)3 80 66 82 50
www.wilson-hotel.com
hotelwilson@wanadoo.fr

Castles & Hôtels Collection. Open all year. Reception 24/24 (night watchman). 27 rooms. Double room from €89 to €134; triple room from €135 to €160. Buffet breakfast : €13.50. Garage : €10 (closed). Family room (4 beddings) from €179. American Express, Holiday voucher. Pets allowed (€10). Seminars. Free Wifi. Catering facilities (the spangled restaurant Stephan Derbord is next to the hotel). Romantic stay in Dijon : from €145 per person. Stay Wellness and delicacy : from €185 per person. Stop-over with special rates : between 115 and 125€.

Hôtel Wilson is ideally located in the middle of the historic center of Dijon. This very charming establishment is a former coaching inn of the 17th century. In a well maintained courtyard, it raises a beautiful façade with half-timbering typical of the region. The beams and the exposed stones make it a cordial place where authenticity reigns. For a comfortable stay, you can leave your car in the private car park and visit on foot all curiosities of the City of the Duc. Practical ! The 27 rooms of this family-run hotel wonderfully associate charms, tradition and modernity with antique furniture, a top-of-the-range bedding, semi-sparkling colors (red and orange) or more resting (beige)... The outhouses are as pleasant as the rooms. The large lounge has a superb stone fireplace that is an invitation to relaxation after a nice sightseeing day and the bar accommodates you the every day until 23 : 30. A splendid exposed stone vault serves as conference room today. Entirely renovated, it can accommodate up to 20 people for a service that includes screens, video projector, paper board and wi-fi. The working conditions is great for successful professional seminars. The hotel also offers themed stays : « Wellness and delicacy » or « Romantic ». Lastly, a good news for 2016 : a construction of a Relaxation area is ongoing to allow the guests of the hotel to benefit from face treatment and massages. What more could you ask for ? Located on majestic Place Wilson, this establishment mixes elegance with comfort for a quality stay !

■ MAISON PHILIPPE LE BON-HÔTEL

18, rue Sainte-Anne
✆ +33 (0)3 80 30 73 52
www.maisonphilippelebon.com
contact@maisonphilippelebon.com

Castles & Hôtels Collection. Open all year. Open 7 days a week. Reception 24/24. 41 rooms. Single room from €99 to €195; double room from €119 to €195; suite from €165 to €255. Half-board (from €48). Buffet breakfast or in room : €15. Extra bed : €20. Stop-over with special rates : from €148. American Express. Seminars. Free Wifi. Catering facilities. Satellite TV.

Do you dream of a luxurious stay, in an authentic Burgundian building of the 15th, 16th and 17th centuries, listed as a Historic Monument ? Here is one of our favourites ! Located in the heart of Vieux Dijon, Hôtel Philippe le Bon offers comfort and high-quality services. The decoration of the place is beautiful. Noble materials, neat wallpapers, pretty carpets, exposed stonework, large fireplaces... You can choose a very bright room with large windows or an attic room with original beams, for a more intimate atmosphere. The decoration is personalised, in an elegant and classy style, in harmonious and relaxant tones. Obviously, the rooms are equipped with king-size beds, walk-in shower, a minibar, air conditioning and a safe. We particularly recommend you the Junior Suites that offer a truly exceptional setting. You can stroll in the inner courtyard of the hôtel, haven of peace in the city centre. A terrace has been set up for reading, drinking or eating. One of the numerous assets of this house is there : it houses one of the best restaurants in Dijon. Formerly known as Œnophiles, the *lounge* restaurant has been renamed La Closerie, an establishment whose memories remain engraved long in your mind... If you are lucky enough to stay there, do not hesitate !

■ **HOLIDAY INN EXPRESS*****
Rue de la Glacière - SAINT-APOLLINAIRE
✆ +33 (0)3 80 46 70 30
www.holiday-inn-express-dijon.fr
reservation@hiexdijon.fr

Open all year. Reception 24/24. 84 rooms. Double room from €79 to €119. Breakfast offered. Extra bed : €25. Parking included. American Express, Holiday voucher. Hotel not smoker. Free Wifi. Run by Christophe Delbecque,it has been two tears now that this 3-star hotel opened. Its location makes it an ideal holiday place for families but also for business trips. Located near the CHU, the University, the Exhibition Park and also the Gaston-Gerard stadium, this hotel is very easy to access and has a closed and free car park accessible for coaches and buses. The other positive point of this building is that it is certified BBC (low-consumption building) and labelled Tourisme Handicap. Business travellers will be delighted thanks to an entirely equipped business space : service of printing, mail, photocopy, Internet access, fax... For the night, 84 rooms are comfortable and cosy, soundproofed and equipped with all necessary comfort. Conceived like true living areas, they also have the advantage of owning very design walk-in showers. Some are obviously equipped to accommodate the disabled, others are communicating : practical for families ! Strong points ? The offered breakfast, the outdoor pool of 12 meters long (out of 6 meters wide) and free parking. You appreciate the excellent value for money of this establishment which offers 3-star services with attractive rates.

Going Out

■ **LE BAR BY LA CLOCHE**
14, place Darcy ✆ +33 (0)3 80 30 12 32
www.hotel-lacloche.fr - H1202@accor.com
Open from 9am to midnight on weekdays and from 10am to midnight the weekend. Wifi. Smoking-room.
Grand Hôtel La Cloche has been refurbished... its bar too ! Named Le Bar by La Cloche, it is now settled in the sublime Napoleon III lounge and thus enjoys an unobstructed view on place Darcy. A place that you should absolutely discover if you do not know it yet. Located in the most beautiful hotel of Dijon, it is open to everyone, even with those who do not have a stay at the establishment. In an elegant stylish and contemporary decor, you can benefit from a beautiful wine list or choose the cocktail « La Cloche » which is made of blackcurrant liqueur, white martini and crémant. Snacks are also offered to the guests, from the club sandwich to salad via dishes to share such as a board of Iberian charcuterie or a cream cheese fondue or époisse. A smoking-room is integrated into the space so as to offer you an absolute comfort at the time of your visit. On Fridays and every Saturday evening, entertainments are organized at the aperitif time. You can also profit from your passage to discover the new relaxation and wellness area of the establishment : Le Spa by La Cloche. A unique place, luxurious, elegant and making you experience a change scenery : in the image of the hotel !

■ **VILLA MESSNER**
5, rue Parmentier ✆ +33 (0)6 58 16 04 48
www.villamessner.fr - contact@villamessner.fr
Open on Tuesday and Wednesday from 7pm to 2am; Thursday to Saturday from 7pm to 5am. The entrance is prohibited to the minors and to the people of less than 25 years not accompanied by a member. From 11pm, only consumption with the bottle is authorized with the tables. Outfit extremely correct and good education required. Access forbidden with the « groups of the same individuals sexe ». Terrace. Activities. Concerts.
This very special building was originally the residence of Ernest Messner, an MP then senator but also wine-grower and brewer, now restored and which appears to be a very « select » address, the proof is that you must be a member to be able to enter. The investors (including Mario, a former member of the Star Academy) wanted to strike hard. To become a member, do not panic, you just need to fill out some lines on the website... nothing very complicated then ! And you will finally have the privilege to belong to the club very private that is the Villa. The bar, the lounge club, the cigar and whisky room, the swimming pool and lunches on the terrace, are yours. But be informed : if you lose the membership card, you will be charged €50, from 11pm the only way drink consumption allowed is by bottle at the tables (it's like encouraging alcohol consumption...), you must come dressed correctly, do not come in groups of people of the same sex, it is considered a gang and gangs are forbidden... For more information, just read the internal rules that are largely debatable on the website. In short, you are not entitled to blunder because the management reserves the right to throw out anyone who doesn't comply with the very strict rules of the house. The villa is also available to organise an event on request.

© SERGEY DZYUBA - SHUTTERSTOCK.COM
Liberation place of Dijon.

Shopping

■ LA BURGONDE NEW

6, Place des Ducs
✆ +33 (0)6 21 56 24 06 – www.la-burgonde.com
contact@la-burgonde.com
Manufacturer, wholesaler, distributor. Souvenir products of Burgundy in specialized shops. Brand presents on the great regional events. Made in Burgundy.
Keep Calm and visit La Burgonde ! Here is an advice of Petit Futé if you seek for a souvenir of Burgundy or a gift idea 100% original. The brand « La Burgonde » created by Nathalie Jacquey who is already well-known proposes materialization of his love for the region with a new product and of regional manufacturing. The facility of Burgonde place of the Duc makes it possible to discover the innovations of an already rich catalogue : Tee-shirt, magnets, printed sheets, engraved aprons, drinks or enamelled plates. All the products are personalized with new messages, expressing with humour and good taste the custom of the region. Burgundian round of applause, advices to remain calm... Must : enamelled plates superbly worked with the drawings of Battistini and manufactured at Is-sur-Tille. It should be noted that the productions of Burgonde are carried out in small numbered series. A conservator, an estate of wine, a town can make very well there produce a series of Tee-shirts or plates with his effigy to become a professional gift or guest. You can find also La Burgonde in the nice shops of gifts. Nathalie Jacquey presents his productions at the time of the Burgundian great events like Saint-Vincent, the sales of wines or other fairs artisanal. At the time of the opening of its Shop come to discover the new collection dedicated to our capital, « Dijon it is Nice », truly beautiful !

Gourmet Basket

■ BOULANGERIE PÂTISSERIE COLLARDOT

22, rue de Jouvence
✆ +33 (0)3 80 35 55 46
Open on Monday, Tuesday, Thursday and Friday from 7am to 12.30pm and from 3.30pm to 7.30pm; Saturday from 7am to 7.30pm; Sunday from 7am to 1pm. Also open public holidays.
When you are in Bretigny and Dijon, do not hesitate to make a detour at this bakery that will not disappoint you. Not only the bread of Mr Collardot is made in a traditional way, but in addition you will have a wide choice of special breads. You will find a whole range of traditional breads including the classical baguette (though made with a Red flour Label) but also the Festival, which has a slight hazelnut taste, and also the small individual bread at low prices. Always concerning the breads, you will find special breads with cereals and others, breads enhanced with fruits or walnuts as well as an organic bread list like the organic bread with cereals, with the German wheat (ideal for certain allergies) or complete. The novelty of this year : the organic French baguette, simply. Lightly flavoured and crunchy, you can consume it on a daily basis. As for the sweet, find all delicacies you are wild about and that caters for every taste. As for the entremets, you will have the choice among the classic opera, Paris-Brest, Black Forest but also among creations of the house like the Caramélia with the slight taste of croasted hazelnut or the Nirvana (the name is very quite selected !) composed of a biscuit brownie, of creme brulee, vanilla and chocolate mousse. Those who prefer the fruits will also find a whole creative range, without forgetting the frozen desserts and the macaroons (whose flavors change with the seasons). Note also that Arnaud Collardot concocts you chocolates he creates himself. The asset of this bakery is the catering servie which absolutely prepares all that you will need for a banquet in 48 hours after the order and whatever it is. Special mention for the impressive wedding cakes with small pastry puffs. They can take the shape of a guitar, a castle of princess, a pirate boat, a teddy or a drums (musical instrument). They are as splendid as delicious ! Have a good visit in a well-known specialist.

■ BOUTIQUE DE LA TRUFFE NEW

5, rue Chaudronnerie
✆ +33 (0)3 80 37 23 70 / +33 (0)6 23 13 09 46
www.boutiquedelatruffe.fr
info@boutiquedelatruffe.fr
Open every day from 10 am to 7 pm.
Dijon, the capital of Burgundy, can now claim to be the capital of truffle in Burgundy. La Boutique de la Truffe, open since 1 August 2015, is a new and an unique address in its kind. It is Thierry Bezeux who is at the helm, another site of the Or des Valois, which already exists at the castle of Entre-Deux-Mounts close to Nuits-Saint-Georges. La Boutique de la Truffe sells fresh truffles coming from France or Italy all year : *tuber aestivum*, white truffle of summer from May to September, *tuber uncinatum* (black golf of Burgundy) from September to January, *tuber melanosporum* from November to March, *tuber magnatum*, white Alba truffle available from September to December. Individuals and restaurateurs can easily purchase these products from there. Thierry Bezeux, truffle grower and marketer, passionate, offers his knowledge, his selections and his preparations. La Boutique de la Truffe abounds in products processed for some by local artisans as Ratatruffe (ratafia with truffle !), marbled ham with truffle or mustard with truffle as well as a multitude of preparations from France or Italy. Installed in Maison aux 3 Pignons, a historic house in Dijon, the Boutique has vaults that can be privatized for tasting session around truffle. An absolute novelty where the smell of truffle immediately awakens your taste buds and invites you to enjoy a truffle-based cuisine.

■ L'ÉPICERIE DE LA GARE LA LOCO

5, avenue Foch
✆ +33 (0)3 80 41 15 86
Open every day from 9.00am to 12.00pm. Open on Sundays. Regional products.
La Loco is a last-minute grocery shop, not far from the station and offers a little more than you would think. Indeed, it is not a small night grocery shop but an additional general and regional grocery shop with a great range of products.

Youcan buy here everything that you do not have : there is an impressive choice ! You can also find everything that you need for a last-minute meal like dried and frozen products. A large part of Burgundian products which make up the gourmet reputation of the region are represented : regional mustards (wide range of flavours), Flavigny aniseed, Mulot & PetitJean sweets, a great collection of quality red, white wines and champagne. They always welcome you warmly. We do not hesitate to go there when we are in the area looking for a particular product. The huge advantage is that it is open every day until midnight even on Sundays and there is a real welcome for locals and tourists ! This family-run business is really successful !

■ FABRICE GILLOTTE

21, rue du Bourg ✆ +33 (0)3 80 30 38 88
www.fabrice-gillotte.fr

Open on Monday from 2pm to 7pm; Tuesday to Friday from 9.15am to 12pm and from 2pm to 7pm; Saturday from 9am to 12.30pm and from 2pm to 7pm. Annual closing from July 28th to August 28th. Online sales on the website.

To be the pionneer in international chocolate creation : it is the ambition of Fabrice Gillotte, talented creator with a well-established reputation. Since he was awarded the title Meilleur Ouvrier de France in 1991, Fabrice Gillotte has been awarded many times. If the Guide of the chocolate cruncher list it among the must-go in 2015, the Dijon's inhabitant enjoy his know-how since the opening of his shop in 1985. In Japan, people also love his original creations and graphic elegance of the creation sold in the 4 shops of the country. Chocolate mix conquer the experts and charm the lovers. From the orange blossom to the jasmine, dried fruits to the spices via the flavoured touches of Earl Grey, Fabrice Gillotte blends all flavours with the same passion. In summer, the ice-cream of the house is very successful. In autumn, we advise for the lovely mushrooms filled with chocolate and caramel and praline almond-hazelnut. For Christmas, dare the advent calendar filled with culinary surprises. In the shop window cleverly decorated by Catherine Gillotte, fir trees in almond paste, truffles, macaroons and the orangettes. Finally on Easter, imposing sculptures sit prominently in the shop alongside cheerful characters in chocolate. We also love the collection of Burgundy Colours and its ganache and jelly made with fruits of the region. What is better than the perfection is the taste of the harmony found in the chocolates of Fabrice Gillotte.

■ FRANCK POURRIER

22, rue d'Auxonne ✆ +33 (0)3 80 66 49 50
www.franck-pourrier.com
contact@franck-pourrier.com

Gluten-free friendly. Open Tuesday to Saturday from 7.30am to 12.30pm and from 3pm to 7pm; Sunday from 8am to 12.30pm.

The talents of a pastry chef, chocolate maker and ice-cream maker of Franck Pourrier have been well proven. He pampers you and plays with your tastebuds... The shop, very renovated, is refined, aired that we could spend hours there. White interior with touches of purple, gray and black, an ultra chic new decoration that is up to the quality of the delicious pastries and the succulent chocolates that the chef Franck Pourrier elaborates with talent. If you hesitate between all the pastries, Julie his wife will be able to advise you ! We recommend you to taste the latest innovations, in particular the Garance, a soft and light cake created for the fine days : mousse with lime, raspberry compote and biscuit madeleine with thyme, all of that without gluten. A real treat that you will not leave a crumb. Do not miss either the new verrine piña colada with the coconut mousse, pineapple compote and Punch des îles that you will have pleasure to serve to your guests. As for chocolate, you have two new tablets : Biskélia with the melting milk chocolate and with biscuit as well as Madagascar with black chocolate that underwent a double fermentation. And then of course, there are all the other must-eat among the entremets, chocolates, cakes, macaroons, petit fours, candy, ice-creams, sorbets, verrines and even of the individual that are the very neat small entremets for the individual gourmet and always best king cake of all Dijon (we assume it) ! This splendid shop located within walking distance of the place Wilson is the paradise of all the gourmet people ! Some creations are without gluten or lactose and there are even some egg-free ones... for the pleasure of the greatest number ! One of the best addresses of Dijon, a perfect staff, achievements with worked esthetics ! Always charming reception.

■ GRAIN DE CASSIS

14, rue Rameau ✆ +33 (0)9 80 75 05 62
graindecassis@gmail.com

♿

Open Tuesday to Saturday from 10am to 7.30pm; Sunday from 11am to 6pm.

Stacie and Katia are the captains of this gourmet delicatessen that has been continuously surprised us for almost two years. They always have a good idea, an originality to enhance your meals with your family or with our friend. As for the visitors, who were passing in Dijon, they will inevitably find something typical of the region to taste or make youru surrounding discover : anise of Flavigny, little, Dijon mustard of all kinds... You can even affirm that certain products of the corner are only at them. We recommend to you to taste the blackcurrant liqueur of Mickael Antolin, entirely natural and made in the corner. A delight in the mouth and an essential product in the Burgundian culture. For those who would prefer beer, you find here the beer Dijonese Elixkir. Elaborated, brewed, labelled, bottled in Burgundy, in Couternon, it is a pure local produce. Moreover, do not miss the curiosities like the seasoned insects to taste at the aperitif, the artisanal marsh mallows, the pots of semi-sparkling sugar, the cocktail-mixing boxes or the spreads guaranteed without palm oil... A unique place ! Novelty : you can from now order on the website : www.graindecassis.com.

■ LA MOUTARDERIE FALLOT

16, rue de la Chouette
www.fallot.com – accueil@fallot.com

Open every day from 10am to 7pm.

You will find the second shop Moutarderie Fallot in the heart of historic Dijon, a mustard factory since 1840 in Beaune. Enjoy Fallot, the other shops, is located in Beaune's Moutarderie. As the identity of Dijon is closely associated with mustard, Moutarderie Fallot finds its niche perfectly with. The very modern shops, like that of Beaune, respects the rustic character of the half-timbered building, its walls are decorated with multicoloured pots of mustard subtly lit. All the recipes of the house Fallot are present : simple Dijon mustard, as grains, with white wine, with green pepper, walnuts, herbs, tarragon, cassis of Dijon, honey, basil, balsamic vinegar, etc. Go to the mustard bar, 8 are available in free tasting. Grainy mustard, with green pepper or Bourgogne labelled AOC, are self-service. A small mill ensures the small local productions, the unique productions of Dijon mustard ! This allows you to understand the manufacturing techniques of mustard in the old-fashioned way, they are in grains and made within original recipes, with Meursault or Pinot Noir for example. In the evening light shows animate the shop. Here, you watch, learn, touch, savour, let yourself be elated by this unique flavour that you know since your childhood. And above all, brew the presented mustard seeds, it brings luck ! Before or after the owl !

■ MULOT & PETITJEAN

13, place Bossuet ✆ +33 (0)3 80 30 07 10
www.mulotpetitjean.fr
mulotpetitjean@mulotpetitjean.fr

Open on Monday from 2pm to 7pm; from Tuesday to Saturday from 9am to noon and from 2pm to 7pm. Online sales.

Founded in 1796, the house Mulot & Petitjean keeps on astonishing its guests. Real institution in Dijon, the inescapable shop of place Bossuet knew how to preserve its pride and its chandelier of yesteryear with its half-timbering and its old-style windows display. She proposes especially a rich panel of typically Dijonese and Burgundian delicacies nicely presented. Once you cross the threshold, here you are plunged in another era. The tables and the displays give you the furious desire for tasting all that you see... And temptations are numerous : nonnettes, anise of Flavigny, blackcurrant liqueur without forgetting the gingerbread. If you like it natural, know that it is also declined with salted butter caramel, with honey of Burgundy, candied orange, fig and many other flavours ! To accompany your aperitifs, original recipes were also created like that with black olives and tomatoes. The shape of this emblematic product also varies with the special gingerbread toast, ideal for the foie gras. The respect of the tradition which ensures the notoriety of this family small company does not prevent therefore innovation. The latest innovation : mini-nonnettes with chocolate, a pure delight ! If you cannot go neither in the shop of Beaune nor in those of Dijon, do not hesitate to use the site of online sales. In 2016, to celebrate its two hundred and twenty years of existence, the house reserves a new box collector and redesigned packaging to you. Labelled « entreprise du patrimoine vivant » in 2012, Mulot & Petitjean proves us with each bite that tradition can be used to serve the future.

■ LE PÉTRIN TOUSSAINT

58, avenue du Drapeau ✆ +33 (0)3 80 72 11 11
toussaint.petrin@wanadoo.fr

Open from Monday to Friday from 7.00 a.m. to 1.30 p.m. and from 3.00 p.m. to 7.45 p.m.; during the weekend from 7.00 a.m. to 7.45 p.m. Closed on Tuesdays.

Le Pétrin Toussaint is still successful and it is for our greatest pleasure because not only are the products delicious, but moreover, the creators are from the country. Pascal Toussaint has successfully gained the loyalty of guests and expanded an artissan, family and friendly bakery. The adventure started with a first sign in Chenôve. There are now 5 shops in Côte-d'Or and one in the Jura... You can have fun while enjoying the classics of the bakery : from the simple baguette, found elsewhere in other forms in hedgehog and in crown, to the wholemeal bread whose recipe is homemade with biology flour Lemaire. You will also find the bread with spelt, the brioche sandwich loaf ideal for sandwiches, the bread with 7 cereals, the individual buns for snacks, etc. Obviously, do not miss the well-known gougères of Le Pétrin Toussaint which are extremely successful, we are not yet tired of them ! As for sweets, you cannot miss the great achievement of the house that is the cake with spices to enjoy natural, with candied oranges or with roasted nuts, or cakes with fruits (apples, candied fruit, with grapes and nature) that are exquisite. There is a wide choice of homemade pastries that also change with the seasons. This summer, the classic raspberry tart, apricot tart, pear-chocolate tart and Norman tart make the sunny days of the house. Note that you can also taste hot sandwiches that are entirely homemade and savoury pancakes in the shop of Avenue Victor Hugo. A service that is strictly attentive to guests and of constant innovation.

LA ROSE DE VERGY
1, rue de la Chouette
✆ +33 (0)3 80 61 42 22
www.rosedevergy.com
contact@rosedevergy.com

Open Tuesday to Friday from 10am to 12.30pm and from 2pm to 7pm; Saturday from 10am to 7pm. Visits from 10am the morning and 2pm the afternoon "On a tour of gingerbread", for groups booking compulsory, €3.50/pers (minimum package from €40). Online order.

In the middle of the neighborhood of the antique dealers, in the middle downtown, Rose de Vergy settled in 2005 in one of the more attractive half-timbered restaurants of Dijon. Gingerbread factory, confectionery, biscuit factory but also tea room, La Rose de Vergy offers constantly quality ingredients to its guests. Before the sun rise, in the laboratory installed in the basement of the house, Eric, Sophie and Marie already prepares biscuits or candies whose scents fill the whole shop. On the spot, try the croquets of Dijon with raw almonds, small crunchy rounds with anise seeds or a sachet of Wolf's Teeth that you let melt in the mouth by drinking a tea. That they are with anises, bergamot or blackcurrant, the candies are prepared with old and contain only natural flavours. As for the gingerbread, it is available in biscuits (frozen thin, orangines), in fingers of bread and even out of French baguettes, ideal for the lovers of foie gras. At the entrance of the shop, a seating area is an invitation to relaxation around a spiced hot juice of apple or a fruit juice of the local production. Do not forget have a look to the spice range and the homemade jams. For 2016, some innovations are eagerly expected : homemade chocolate, shortbreads and gingerbread with clementine, the shortbreads coated with chocolate and for the summer the sliced French baguettes with olives or mustard seed : perfect for toasts ! La Rose de Vergy is a sweet paradise where subtlety blends with good taste.

In the surroundings

Arc-sur-Tille

LA TABLE D'ARC
58, rue des Chézeaux
Galerie Super U
✆ +33 (0)3 80 37 08 34
www.restaurant-latabledarc.com

Open Monday to Saturday for lunch and dinner. And from 7am to 2am of the morning. Set menu at €35 (2 choices on starters, main courses, desserts. À la carte). Children's menu : €10. Lunch menu : €13 (distance across flats or main dish and dessert – €9 for a main course of the day). Take-away pizzas Monday to Saturday – L'Hôtel d'Arc in the vicinity, one 3 stars nine of 15 rooms. Terrace. Very easy parking.

La Table d'Arc has become inevitable since the disappearance of the massifs of trees that hid it until now. In 2016, La Table d'Arc confirms its status of inescapable gourmet stopover for those who want to have a good meal in a friendly atmosphere of brasserie. Christelle and Fernand put a know-how over nearly 30 years at the service of your culinary needs. The menu offers us a constantly homemade cuisine, fresh and quality products. Note that the single menu has become €35, just to offer some upscale dishes to us with as starter snails or scallops, a good quality meat or fish with cheese and gourmet dish for dessert. On a daily basis, we can enjoy traditional pizza and dishes that we begin to get used to. More than fifteen recipes of pizza, including that of the week, original and well garnished at €12. They are all take-away. For the main course, the choice of meats is extra large with among others, Tartar cut with a knife, beef steak with Epoisses, homemade burger, roasted knuckle of pork... The fish is well represented as well, prawn skewers, mussels, lobster stew... And always available, the plate of tapas for aperitif. From early morning until late evening, you can take your coffee, a drink even end the evening with a glass of champagne. Do not forget the presence within a hundred metres of L'Hôtel d'Arc, a beautiful 3-star establishment !

L'HÔTEL D'ARC
13, Route Nationale
✆ +33 (0)3 73 27 05 76
www.hoteldarc.com
contact@hoteldarc.com

Logis (3 chimneys). Open all year round. 7 days a week. Reception until 11pm (high season from May 1st to October 31st, 2014). 15 rooms (including rooms for 3 and 4 people). Low season : single room €84; double room €89. High season : single room €89; double room €96. Half-board (one-night stopover with special rates €85). Breakfast : €10.80 (in low season, €11.80 in high season). Extra bed : €10 (in low season, €15 in high season). Closed parking included (depending on available places). Room 3 people from €104 to €116, 4 people from €119 to €136. Seminars. Free wi-fi. Catering facilities (restaurants nearby including the Table d'Arc of the same owner).

Hotel d'Arc located near the beltway around Dijon is a very recent hotel built in 2013 in a characterful building of the village. Christelle and Fernand Dematos are also at the helm of La Table d'Arc, a new restaurant located near their hotel, which is furnished with the latest standard equipment, it is a success and crowned with 3 stars. The 15 rooms are very modern, bathrooms are made with top quality materials. The decor is contemporary, upscale materials, giant headboards, large screen TV, walk-in showers, washbasins original and air-conditioning. You will feel very well in no time. The reserved areas at the times of relaxation are numerous, lounge in the garden or on the covered terrace, cosy bar, where you find it difficult to leave once you have started the aperitif. L'hôtel d'Arc is indeed there, it is also furnished with high-standard equipments to host seminars. You will find an upmarket brasserie catering at Table d'Arc not very far from the address.

■ LES MARRONNIERS D'ARC

16, rue de Dijon
✆ +33 (0)3 80 37 09 62
les.marronniers.arc@wanadoo.fr

Logis (2 cheminées). Open all year. 19 rooms. From €75 to €90. Half-board (stop-over with special rates €85). Breakfast : €10. Extra bed : €15. 1 room with hammam. Pets allowed (€8). Catering(3 cocottes – « Maître Restaurateur » label – menu from €19 to €70 - 2 terraces – 2 seminar rooms).

Les Marronniers d'Arc-sur-Tille is a hotel restaurant ideally located 10 km east of Dijon and near the motorway exit. The residence of recent construction offers a rich choice of 19 rooms that were entirely renovated in 2013, some on the ground floor for people with reduced mobility or with independent access; other upstairs are attic and some family for 6-7 people. The atmosphere that prevails here is also family; a classic and coloured decoration, comfortable rooms and well-equipped bathrooms. Add to that the quiet old quarter of the city and the restaurant, famous for its fish and seafood specialties, among others, and especially its terraces for lunch or leisurely dinner. A huge parking lot is available to safely park your car. With all this, it is of course a great deal to have a stopover in Arc-sur-Tille.

Chevigny-Saint-Sauveur

■ ACRO'MANIA

Chemin des Grands-Pâquiers
✆ +33 (0)6 30 29 92 80
www.acromania.fr – contact@acromania.fr

Open from April to November. Wednesday, Saturday and Sunday from 2pm to 6pm for the individuals. Easter holidays and of All Saints : every day from 2pm to 6pm. Summer holidays : every day from 2pm to 7pm. Possible reservation in morning for groups. Adults : €17. Students and young people (11-17 years) : €15. Children (6-10 years) : €12. Kids (3-5 years) : €6. Reduced rates for groups and the families.

An unmissable place of leisure of the Dijon region, set in the centenarian trees of the forest of Chevigny-Saint-Sauveur. Parcours Aventure en Hauteur are for all, from 3 years old and, for the most intrepid, there is no age limit ! Of course you must come with sportswear with suitable shoes and cycling gloves. If you have long or half long hair, think of keeping them well ! On the seven courses of different levels, Fly weight to Black Belt, the security is omnipresent and the thrills guaranteed.

■ PISCINE DE CHEVIGNY-SAINT-SAUVEUR

Place Pierre-de-Coubertin ✆ +33 (0)3 80 43 60 41
www.service-sports-chevigny.com

Closed from April 26th to May 4th. The new external pool is open since July 13th, 2013. Low season : school periods – High season holidays July and August. During holidays except summer : Monday to Friday from 2pm to 7pm and Sunday from 9am to 12pm. Low season : open on Monday, Thursday and Friday from 5pm to 7pm; Wednesday from 2pm to 7pm; Sunday from 9am to 12pm. High season : Monday from 2pm to 8pm; Tuesday to Saturday from 12pm to 8pm; Sunday from 10am to 7pm. In June : Monday 5pm-8pm – Tuesday 12pm-2pm – Wednesday 12pm-8pm – Thursday and Friday 12pm-2pm and 5pm-8pm – Saturday 12pm-8pm – Sunday 10am-7pm – Aquagym, Relaxation area, School of Swim. Admission : €3.55 (€3.05 in winter). Child : €1.80. €1.55 in winter – free for under 6-year-olds. Summer card 12 entrances €35.50, €18 for the children.

The pool of Chevigny-Saint-Sauveur is a bathing site you should know for the qualities of its services. Completely renovated in 2013, it became a very pleasant place thanks to its modern architecture and its cutting edge equipment, solariums, relaxation area with an aquagym, spas and hammam, accessible after the work hours, some days during the lunch break and every Sunday morning. The covered part of 1,200 m^2 shelters the small pool of 12.50 x 12.50 m and a paddling pool for the kids. The 25 m outdoor pool is conforming with the competitions federation standards. Its renovation was carried out by the facility of a stainless pool, which makes the color of water very beautiful. The pool owns wide grassed open spaces for the sunbathing with a volleyball court. All the accesses and the solariums were reconsidered, renovated and enlarged. Many entertainments are proposed during the year, evenings carnival, zumba, games for the children in or out of water... Myriam, Francis and Eric, Master-swimmers are the favourite of the regulars, small and adults as well. The plus of this pool, it is its external pool, less attended at certain hours, ideal to swim a few lengths !

Daix

RESTAURANT LES 3 DUCS

5, route de Troyes ✆ +3 (0)3 80 56 59 75
www.les3ducs-restaurant.com
les3ducs@gmail.com

Restaurateurs de France. Open Tuesday to Friday for lunch from 12pm to 2pm and for dinner from 7.30pm to 9.30pm. Other days only for the receptions or meal. Menu from €36.50 to €55. (menu at €20 (main course + coffee or mineral water), Menu at €22.50 (starter and main course or main course and dessert), at €26.50 (starter + main course + dessert)). Wine by the glass. Catering and of reception. Groups welcome. Terrace.

Eric Briones, chef of the restaurant Les 3 Ducs is also the president of Restaurateurs de France and the Burgundy region. In his table, the products are obviously fresh, his dishes elaborated with passion and know-how and the irreproachable service. The à la carte changes regularly, in the course of the years and of the chef's inspirations. The entrées suffice to proof the inventiveness of the house as its raw-cooked fresh summer vegetables accompanied by a vinaigrette Soy sauce-Yuzu, cromesquis of a béarnaise with coriander. Slightly exotic flavours, just what is needed. As for the dish, the choice is intentionally restricted to ensure an exemplary quality. For example, the sparerib of pork are cooked during 7 hours, marinated with the thyme juice, and accompanied by a traditional black blood sausage, chanterelles and chips of Iberian ham. If you prefer the seafoods, the fillet of Salmon-basse of the Ajaccio Bay, cooked meunière and its candied vegetables and black olives, is for you. You will also like the gourmet desserts with regional flavours like the Tout K6 : éclair on a cracker of blackcurrant marmalade as well as its blackcurrant juice to drink with a straw and its little fruit spread and blackcurrant sorbet. In 2016, many innovations come out gradually. From now on, Les 3 Ducs have a second laboratory of over 200 m^2 to still develop the activities of banquet and caterer. On this subject, from March, the restaurant will have a space in Clos Champagnac with a splendid reception venue. A place that is perfect to fittingly celebrate the 20 years of the chef at the helm of the restaurant !

Fauverney

LE FAUVERNEY LODGE

3, rue de Chassagne
✆ +33 (0)3 80 55 60 62 / +33 (0)6 63 59 18 57
www.lefauverneylodge.com
contact@lefauverneylodge.com

Open daily for lunch and dinner. Menu from €19.90 to €36 (à la carte of Sri Lankian and Burgundian main courses). Children's menu : €8.50. Daily special : €8.90 (starter and main course or main course and dessert : €11, €13.50 three). Garden. Terrace. Theme parties, guestrooms and cottages, seminar room, conferences, cocktail bar, spa, yoga class.

That is not noticeable at first glance, but Fauverney Lodge is a restaurant of Indian and world gastronomy which enhance the value of french and Burgundy cookery. Welcome to both unusual and comfortable universe where it is fun to enjoy fine dining that takes you on a culinary and beneficent cultural journey .. The key words that come to your mind are : quality, zenitude and pleasure. Chantal and Kannan created in their farmhouse a place with multiple facets where you can relax during a meal, one festive evening, even for a night. In the kitchen, the chef is also Sri Lankan, say raita, samosas, rolls, curries and other exotic dishes are prepared in the rules of art, with flavours from India, ayurvedic cookery, it was even a health vertue before being a gastronomic menu. In Fauverney Lodge, the sauces that accompany your meat and basmati rice are delicious, original and 100% homemade. Remember that Kannan is an expert in cocktails, his experiences in the most beautiful bars of India or Paris allow him to prepare simple recipes with fresh products, wines and spicy liquors housemade. An experience to renew, the choices are multiple and tempting.

Fénay

LE RELAIS DE LA SANS-FOND

33, route de Dijon
Hameau de Chevigny ✆ +33 (0)3 80 36 61 35
www.lerelais-delasansfond.com

Closed in Christmas and the New year. Open Monday to Saturday from 12pm to 2pm and from 7pm to 9pm; Sunday from 12pm to 2pm. Closed Sunday for dinner. Menu from €29.90 to €50. Children's menu : €10. Wine by the glass. À la carte. Garden. Terrace. Heated swimming pool. Receptions. Banquets. Fixed rate formulas business.

In the small village of Fenay, a few kilometres from Dijon, this address is frequented for the cuisine of the chef Eric Chauve and the reception of Marie his wife. The must-eat of the Burgundian cuisine with the dishes duly preapared with seasonal ingredients, delicious cuisine is awaiting for passing guests. The menu of the house is renewed every trimester, with the rhythm of seasons, and some works were recently done, the rooms are splendid, with new tables and new chairs... We could note that the menu of the summer is always affordable and delicious with an Andalusian gazpacho, followed by a provençale tart of red mullet fillet and a duckling fillet with the amarena cherries, we could also have taken the homemade frying... as starter. Special mention for the Paris-Brest. Coming to these places is a real pleasure, for the retro charm of the room, the mild terrace in summer and of course the quality and the finesse of the dishes. It should be noted that you can prolong pleasure by taking a room. Le Relais de la Sans-Fond has 17. So profit from the quiet park and the pleasant swimming pool !

Magny-sur-Tille

LAC DE LA TILLE

Route Départementale 109
✆ +33 (0)3 80 31 56 39 – www.lacdelatille.net
contact@lacdelatille.net

Open from June to August. Open every day and public holidays from 10am to 8pm. Admission beach : adults €4.10, children (from 4 to 12 years old) €3.30. Free for under 4-year-olds. Subscription : €41 (for 12 adult admissions, €33 for the children). Admission mini-park with 2 tokens moreover : from 2 to 4 years old children €3, from 4 to 12 years old children €5.60. Reduced rates for groups. Boats from €3.60 per half hour. Fishing : €7/day. Possible campsite : €5 for a campsite, €2.60 per person. No pets allowed. Supervised beach, water slides, snack bar, mini-park. Rental of pedal boats, canoes, boats, kayaplanches.

Lac de la Tille is a place of bathing and pleasure that is ideal for a family outing, between friend, and the children are delighted to the adults experience a real change of scenery. Set up in a former sand pit, its water is very clean because it regenerates naturally, its temperature can vary from 20 to 30 °C. The friends of nature and water are welcome ! Located at 20 minutes from Dijon, this lake is easily accessible, it has a huge parking lot. In addition to swimming and sunbathing on the beach, the activities offered by Gérard Chauvin for adults and children. Some boaters are devoted to table tennis, beach volleyball or petanque, others embark on pedal boats, canoes, kayaplanches. On the shallower part of the water : an inflatable swing buoy makes you have a good time, it is for the one who will stay the longest time on it ! Water slides are still that exhilarating. Children can have access to the mini park : inflatable structures, car-moto tour, trampolines, small roundabout and playground. Please note that a part of the lake is reserved to the fishermen and it is possible to camp on the spot on request, with your tent, your caravan or your camper van. Lac de la Tille offers you a moment of holidays full with colors and joys.

Prenois

CIRCUIT DIJON-PRENOIS

✆ +33 (0)3 80 35 32 22

www.circuit-dijon-prenois.com

Calendar of the events on the website of the tour.

The Dijon-Prenois circuit created in 1972 is continuously adapting to the requirements of the automobile sport. Spectacular, ondulating, it is appreciated pilots and spectators as well. In 2016 its track of 3.8 km reaches an optimum of renovation and security enabling you to organize all types of events. 2016 marks also a new stage, that of the renovations of the infrastructures of reception that will be carried out over several years. Dijon-Prenois serves as setting of many events that are part of the history of the automobile sport, he accommodates nearly 250,000 visitors every year during a dozen of public events. The tour is also rented throughout the year by car, motorbike, French and Europeans clubs. This circuit is recognized by the pilots like one of most beautiful of Europe, a « number one » track. The diary 2016 is rich in superb races. Coupe de France des Circuits where prototype trucks, single-seaters race. Stage of Tour Car. Trophy of Burgundy. The fabulous Coupes Moto Légendes that became the greatest demonstration of historic motorbikes in Europe. Impassioned and collectors attend many races where more than 1,000 sportsmen are registered. Machine shops, exhibitions of French motorbikes and even races of Café Racer will take place lately. The Coupe 03Z offers modern races of motorbikes in supersport and hypersport where about 80 pilots are respectively registered. Between endurance and speed races, ambiance and show are guaranteed. The GPAO, Grand Prix de l'Age d'Or, is « a competition of the future » with more than 300 vehicles in competition of the cars of Grand Prix of the 70s to the 90s, the Classic Endurance Racing offers the most beautiful shows of Ford GT40, Porsche 910 or Ferrari 512. In 2016 races Group C will take place for the first time with prototypes of the 70s to the 90, cars taking part in the 24 hours of Mans… . Each year in October is organized the Rêves d'Enfants Malades day whose collected funds are intended for research on orphan diseases in the child. Le Dijon Motors Cup will close the season with a ultra-fast event of various categories of historic cars.

GRAND PRIX DE L'ÂGE D'OR – DIJON PRENOIS CIRCUIT

Circuit Automobile ✆ +33 (0)3 80 35 32 22

www.circuit-dijon-prenois.com

From June 3rd to June 5th, 2016. Admission : €15 (the day, €25 the weekend).

The GPAO, Grand Prix de l'Âge d'Or 2016 will gather 450 pilots from all over Europe on board of more than 300 vehicles. Cars of Grand Prize of the years 1950, the years 1960, Lotus, Brabham, Cooper, Formule 1 of the years 1970-1980, Mc Laren, Tyrrel, Williams, Ferrari. Sport scars of the years 1950 (Jaguar, Aston Martin…), prototypes of the years 1970, WP of the years 1960, Cobra, Jaguar Type E… For the first time in 2016, the races Group C will take place allowing you to admire prototypes that having took part in the 24 hours of Mans between 1970 and 1990. There will be also single-seat plates and junior formulas as well as cars of the years 1920 1930. Parades, demonstrations on the track, first run to win and many stands for the passionate where books are found, accessories, posters, miniatures… There is enough to have a treat and take a maximum of pictures and spend one formidable day in a dream ambience.

KARTING DIJON-PRENOIS

Circuit automobile

✆ +33 (0)3 80 35 36 50 / +33 (0)3 80 35 32 22

www.circuit-dijon-prenois.com

Open every day from 10am to 8pm. Gift Packs and Member card. Rates according to the power of karts. Mini-kart 4Times from 7 to 14 years from €13 for 10 min. + 15 years from €25 for 10 min karting 4 times; + 17 years from €45 for 10 min karting 2 times elite. Fixed rate formulas Courses personnalisées for the bachelor funerals birthdays, outings between friends. Conference room for incentive. Fixed rate formula caterer on reservation.

Open to all, from 7 years old, this ultra-modern track category 1, approved by FFSA, is 1.1 km long and is equipped with a stopwatch of F1 type. Beginners and advanced can safely discover the pleasures of driving and speed. After a short briefing, you put on your driving suit, your helmet and all safety equipment. You sit at the wheel of a racing car of 15 cv (for beginners) or 23 cv (for experienced pilots). Children from 7 to 14 years old roll on beautiful mini-karts of 4 cv. Strong sensations are yours ! Unique in Burgundy, the track is even accessible to disabled people. Two karts are indeed equipped with an accelerator and a brake at the wheel. The circuit can be reserved from 15 people to celebrate a bachelor party, a birthday or any other event. Bachelors can come with their personal kart. Every year, many challenges are organised there. Also enjoy the clubhouse overlooking the circuit. Strong sensations guaranteed !

Ruffey-lès-Echirey

■ ÂME DE LA TERRE

2, rue de Dijon ✆ +33 (0)3 80 47 81 45
www.chambresdijon.com
info@chambresdijon.com

Open Monday to Saturday from 11am to 7pm; Sunday from 9am to 1pm. Possible delivery (on the Dijonese region). Entertainment with presence of a wine grower all 1st Sundays of the month, except in July and August.

Welcome to Ruffey-les-Echirey at Philippe Meyroux, Master Sommelier. Âme de la Terre, which is a guest house, is also a wine merchant place. After being in the upscale catering servce, Philippe Meyroux is now 100% devoted to his guesthouse and his shop. The selections of wines are precise with a catalogue of more than 250 Burgundian references but also from other regions of France. Check on the website of the shop. You will notice that the prices are reassuring. The beers section is typical, only German beer, a good forty references that are renewed. Lovers will find to their happiness whether by units, with cases of 20 bottles of 50cl or or in 6 litres. Your basket can be completed with spirits and some local products. The shop Âme de la Terre is located in the heart of a charming village and easily accessible.

Sennecey-lès-Dijon

■ HOTEL-RESTAURANT LA FLAMBÉE

Route de Chevigny ✆ +33 (0)3 80 47 35 35
www.laflambee.fr
hotelrestaurantlaflambee@wanadoo.fr

Logis (2 cocottes). Open Monday to Friday for lunch and dinner; Saturday for dinner; Sunday for lunch. Menu from €27 to €32. À la carte : Around €30. Children's menu : €9.50. Wine by the glass. Groups welcome. Garden. Terrace. Receptions, fixed rate formulas business, seminars. Traditional cuisine, Burgundian and grill room.

Welcome at La Flambée, a hotel and restaurant managed by Christian Flamand and his nephew Jean-David, located in a green setting just a few kilometers of Dijon. The chef Sébastien Petite offers a regional and seasonal cuisine and a grill room. Within the setting, you have a large fireplace at the bottom of the restaurant room. Meats and fish are roasted there for the pleasure of the guests who are comfortably seated. A pretty decor ! A dynamic and very attentive service. The team makes every effort so that you spend a very pleasant moment, cozy in the winter at the corner of the fire, or under the shade in summer, on the terrace with a view of a lovely outdoor swimming pool (only for clients of the hotel). The meat lovers will be happy to enjoy an *Assiette du Grillardin* (beef, lamb, pork and chicken) or a *Grande Brochette du Boucher* (rib eye steak, fillet of beef). We chose a ham seasoned with parsley and its chantilly with mustard, followed by a tasty roasted whole bar and we finished the meal with Berthaud's époisses refined with the Marc of Burgundy. Done as we like them to be ! With juicy and perfectly browned meats, hearty dishes and an impeccable service, it is advisable to book because the establishment has already a very good reputation ! Whatever the season, change of scenery and pleasure is guaranteed !

FIXIN ★

Sightseeing

■ MUSÉE NOISOT ★★

Rue de la Perrière
www.mairiedefixin.fr/musee-noisot

Museum closed until June 2016 for reorganization of the course.

From Wagram to Dresden via Spain, Russia but also Waterloo... Who could have predicted the incredible destiny of Claude Noisot, grown up in a modest family in Auxonne ? As a loyal and fervent admirer of the emperor, he belongs to those who accompany him on Elba island. Retired now, the officer of the imperial Guard continues to honour the memory of the emperor by naming his wine « Clos Napoléon ». Now as a premier cru, it still exists today. By the way, its label represents « The awakening of Napoléon to immortality », a work that Noisot ordered to François Rude, famous Burgundian sculptor. The two men met in 1840, during the burial of Napoleon at Les Invalides. The museum of the former captain of the Imperial Guard of Napoleon presents the memories of the imperial campaigns, it puts on sale a DVD on the museum, the Noisot park and Clos Napoléon.

Note : Claude Noisot wanted to be buried standing, opposite the statue of the emperor to watch it forever but the rock was too hard... The bronze bust we owe the bronze bust adorning his tomb to the sculptor Paul Cabet, student of Rude.

Knife & Fork

■ AU CLOS NAPOLEON

4, rue de la Perrière ✆ +33 (0)3 80 52 45 63
www.clos-napoleon.com
contact@clos-napoleon.com

Restaurateurs de France. Quality Tourism. Open Monday to Saturday for lunch and dinner; Sunday for lunch. Bookings recommended. Menus from 20 € to 48 €. Carte : 30 € approximately. Children's menu : € 10. Lunchtime : 16 € (starter, main course, dessert of the day € 13.90 2 courses.). Wine by the glass. Vineyards and Discoveries Label. Groups are welcomed. Terrace. Takeaway. Shop. Seminars. Wine Bar. A la carte wine-tasting vault in the Cave of Clos. Charging-station for electric vehicles. Vehicle with driver for hotels of the surroundings.

And why not offering yourself an outing to « Au Clos », Au Clos Napoléon means this restaurant on the height of Fixin which offers a privileged setting. In 2016 the metamorphosis of the establishment still operates, its decoration smoothly evolves, without rupture compared to its Burgundian authentic style, tinted with contemporary touches. The colors of wood and the stone dominate thus making the place cordial and always so pleasant. A team of 6 people prepares the cuisine of Le Clos, it is 100% homemade and elaborated with produces that follow the seasons, traditional yet fundamental dishes will salivate you : eggs poached with the Epoisses cream sprinkled with parsley, flaky pastry with small chablis of the cheese factory Gaugry. Meats and fish are made in various and delicious recipes, sometimes confit, roasted or even steam cooked. The desserts are classical but very gourmet. As for the wines, Le Clos is a specialist with La Cave du Clos open every day, with a choice of more than 200 names, mainly Burgundian ones. The terrace at the bottom of vineyards is a unique place to have a drink accompanied by tasty charcuteries... We love the atmosphere of Clos Napoléon and its friendly cuisine... and we will come back there for its creativity and its quality ! The professionals also appreciate the place with its conference room, for 20 people equipped with the latest technology, video projector, screen, amplifier, wi-fi and splendid decoration. Le Clos Napoléon became a must-go institution !

■ **CHEZ JEANNETTE**
7, rue Noisot
✆ +33 (0)3 80 52 45 49
chezjeannette@orange.fr

Logis (3 pots). Open from Monday to Saturday for lunch and dinner; on Sunday for lunch. Menus from €20 to €74 (+ à la carte). Fixed rate formula : €14 (Burgundian plate). Wine by the glass. Hotel 8 rooms, 2 chimneys Logis. Garden. Terrace.

The *Chez Jeannette* restaurant in Fixin is classical of its kind, we mean by that a rather gourmet table preserving service traditions like the cloche for the hot dishes. The atmosphere is very Burgundian, cosy : room with exposed beams, white tablecloths, tables finely drawn up, present and discrete service, reliable advice for the wines. Regulars as well as the tourists of passage are always agreeably surprised. Reynald Hourlier maintains a quality à la carte which is renewed each season. Dishes often inspired by the Burgundian local produce where the snail, never in its shell, declines in multiple recipes. The snail and pig's trotter roll became a classic. There are always the incredible menu at €20 with appetizer, cheese trolley and dessert and the cloche. The tasting menu proposes its best shot with 6 main courses and a Burgundian trou. It can be declined in Gargantuan menu, for the whole table with 5 glasses of wine each. To finish, the invaluable coffee selection menu served with mignardises. Reynald Hourlier regularly enriches his cellar with new references, it has some more than 300 of which some are served by the glass of 18 Cl ! For those who are in a hurry, the Burgundian dish is ideal. Yield to the charm of a dessert, you will not regret it.

© PHOVOIR

View of Fixin.

Shopping

LA CAVE DU CLOS

6, rue de La Perrière
✆ +33 (0)3 80 52 45 63
www.lacaveduclos.com
contact@clos-napoleon.com

Open from Monday to Saturday from 10am to 6.30pm; on Sunday from 10am to 2pm. Commented tastings €10 for 3 wines. Theme evening parties from €25 per person by reservation. Cave du Clos is that of the restaurant Au Clos Napoléon.

Regulars of the restaurant Au Clos Napoléon know Cave du Clos well that is twinned with the property. The shop where you can buy wines of the restaurant. To access it, go up to Fixin towards the Noisot park, you cannot miss the elegant building of Cave du Clos, which is, moreover, facing Clos Napoléon, the first Wines of Fixin. It is Laetitia who welcomes you there, trained in wine tourism and passionate about the subjects of wine, she will be your guide to make the choices meet your needs. It is about sixty estates that are represented, more than 200 references, some of which are available in half bottles. Give yourself a tasting because the choice of wines by the glass will extend to thirty references. Everything you need to feel the differences between the Climates of Burgundy. The tasting can, moreover, be done on the beautiful terrace facing the vineyards of Fixin. A unique place for magic moments on beautiful days of summer. José Gonzalez and Gérald Ulmann has done it very well because La Cave du Clos is also a site of online sales. Enjoy the quality of the selections and the offered prices. What you need to quickly fill your basket and ask for a quick delivery, extremely well packaged.

FLAVIGNY-SUR-OZERAIN ★

The city of Flavigny is located at 421 meter of height, on an encircled rocky promontory surrounded by three rivers : the Ozerain, the Recluse and Verpant. Near the antique Alésia and classified among the « most lovely villages of France », the city owes its name to a general of César named Flavinius. It is this Romain who would have brought back anise seeds green from one of his travels. A few centuries later, in 719, a Burgundian lord founded the Saint-Pierre de Flavigny abbey, occupied by Benedictine monks. With the protection of Carolingian kings, it develops quickly and became more and more important. Today, the remains of the monastic buildings became the manufacturing place of the anises of Flavigny. This « good and tasty candy » makes the village famous in the world. More than 30 employees work in the coating workshops : they respect the same recipe since 1591 ! When we just arrive at the village, the delicious odor of anise follows us everywhere, whether we go along the ramparts, or we admire the facade of the houses or the charming cobbled streets. Among the jewels of

Flavigny-sur-Ozerain, you can find the Carolingian crypt of Sainte-Reine, in free tour with the Abbey. Built at the 13th century, the Saint-Genès church is also part of the stages not to miss just like the splendid facade of Maison au Donataire. Still today, Flavigny remains a spiritual ground as proven by the Saint-Joseph de Clairval abbey ste in old diocesan Petit Séminaire. In October, do not miss the fair of Saint-Simon. The rest of the year, try to wander through the narrow streets and enter the shops of the local craftsmen. You will not be disappointed.

■ POINT INFORMATION – MAISON AU DONATAIRE

Rue de l'Église
✆ +33 (0)3 80 96 25 34
maisondonataire@gmail.com

Open from April to October. Open Tuesday to Sunday from 11am to 1pm and from 2pm to 6pm. Free for under 12-year-olds. Guided tour (duration : 1.30am. All year by reservation). Shop. €5 per person. €4 for groups of more than 20. Reception and visits : French or English. Booklets : French, English or German.

Maison au Donataire takes its name from the character represented at the bottom of the statue of the Madonna with Child, today visible inside the building. Built in the Renaissance, the house belongs to the Société des Amis de la Cité de Flavigny (SACF) and serves as a tourist information point in high season. In 2016, Maison au Donataire celebrates its 25 years of opening to the public and the 60 years of existence of the SACF ! Real local relay of the Tourist Office of Venarey-les-Laumes, Maison au Donataire offers explanations on the village as well as information on accommodation and catering possibilities. You can also make an appointment for guided tours. Volunteers from the association are happy to present you the architecture and heritage of Flavigny. Behind the beautiful façade of Maison au Donataire, you will find free maps and books on the region, objects of local artists or postcards. Every year, the SACF organizes exhibitions within the building. "Flavigny, vu par..." is interested by the view that the artists have on the village, whether they are photographers, painters or cartoonists.

Knife & Fork

■ RESTAURANT DE L'ABBAYE

Rue de l'Abbaye
✆ +33 (0)3 80 96 27 77
www.restaurant-de-labbaye.fr
info@restaurantdelabbaye.fr

Closed in January. Low season : open Thursday to Tuesday for lunch; Thursday to Monday for dinner. High season : daily for lunch and dinner. High season of Easter to All Saints. À la carte : Around €35. Children's menu : €10 (less than 12 years). Lunch menu : €15 (2 main courses). €18 (3 main courses), €20 (3 main courses with cheese). Groups welcome. Catering. 2 terraces.

Run by Natacha and Philippe Guillier, the restaurant of the abbey offers you a cuisine centered on tradition and Burgundian local produce. Located on one of the gates of the village, at the bottom of the abbey which shelters the factory of anises, this establishment is simple and accessible. The terraces are comfortable, one of them offers a stunning view on the entrance of the village, the other which is in the courtyard is always very flowered in summer. Guaranteed shade. When you taste the steak and its sauce with Epoisses, you will understand why the classical ones are good, the meat is deliciously tender and the accompaniment is generous just in the right way. Only one regret : the choice of the wines by the glass is limited. As for desserts, the creme brulee with anises of Flavigny is inescapable and above all a specialty of the Guiller house. The building of the restaurant is the former post office of the village. A building of character with sober but contemporary decor ! Book your table at your arrival to enjoy the site quietly.

General view of Flavigny-Ozerain.

Shopping

LES ANIS DE FLAVIGNY

✆ +33 (0)3 80 96 20 88
www.anis-flavigny.com
contact@anisdeflavigny.com

Free tour of the workshop of coating every day from 9am to 11am except the weekends, public holidays and during Christmas holidays. Shop on the premises open all year. Museum and coffee.

The factory of Anise is set up in a former benedictine abbey. Founded in 719 by a important Burgundian seigneur, the abbey is parcelled in private estates during the French Revolution. There is nothing left of the abbey church that underwent many destructions and reconstructions and whose stones were finally used to build many houses in the village. Today, the oldest part of the building is the Carolingian crypt which can visited freely. The rest of monastic constructions was transformed into factory to produce this good good candy with the green anise : Les Anis De Flavigny. In 1923, Jean Troubat took over the company, followed by its sons Nicolas from 1965 and his daughter Catherine who has developped the company since 1990. Today, there are 10 different flavors but also organic anises and small anises not larger than grain of rice, to crunch or let melt. Whether they are large or small, in a metal box or in a case made of cardboard, Les Anis de Flavigny are sold in the four corners of the world. Their preparation is the result of a delicate and patient work of a a team of about thirty employees. Did you know that it took 15 days to manufacture anises ? And the recipe has not changed since 1591 ! In addition to be a coating workshop, you can now travel in time in the museum of anises, taste quality ingredients at the café of anises and scan or buy the books of the bookstore of the anises. And do not forget to pass by the shop for a tasting : there is something for every taste.

VIGNOBLE DE FLAVIGNY-ALÉSIA

Pont Laizan ✆ +33 (0)3 80 96 25 63
www.vignoble-flavigny.com
vignoble-de-flavigny@wanadoo.fr

Low season : open Friday to Monday and public holidays from 10am to 6pm. High season : every day and public holidays from 10am to 7pm. Shop gallery – Visits and tastings for individual and groups. Reception hall for 110 people – seminars, weddings, buffets. In low season : open only by reservation Tuesday to Thursday. Possible delivery. Member in the networks Welcomme to the farm, Auxois Naturally and France Passion.

Located in the valley of Ozerain, this beautiful estate of 14 hectares owns vineyards exposed south-east, planted in slopes and in lyre size to adapt it as well as possible to the climate of Auxois. It is installed in a former monastic farmhouse which depended on the abbey of Flavigny. Among white grape varieties, you find the Aligoté, the Chardonnay and... that of Auxerre. Not very widespread in Burgundy. As for the black grape varieties, you find Pinot Noir, of course, and César. As for the rosé, it is produced from the Pinot Beurot, formerly very much used in the region. Under the impulse of Cyril Raveau, the oenologist of the estate, the range of the wines of the estate evolves. The signature becomes « Flavigny – Alésia », « FA », an IGP which one day will end up in AOC ! The 100% Chardonnay, Pinot Noir and Aligoté crus are henceforth conditioned in classical bottles with the Burgundian identity. Besides, a distinction was made between two plots of Pinot Noir : on one side the Oppidum, on the other the Castellum, two names which point out the positioning of the vineyard, between Alésia and the former camp of César. The bottles in the shape of amphora henceforth condition the grape varieties that are not authorized in the Burgundy AOP. Medals 2015 were numerous, gold and bronze at the competitions of Féminalises and the independent vine growers. The shop emphasizes the wines of the estate and some local produce. Tasting courses enable you to finish, why not, with a stroll in the vineyards from where the view on the valley is simply unforgettable !

GEVREY-CHAMBERTIN ★

Gevrey-Chambertin is one of the most renowned places in the field of wine activity in Burgundy. Its climates are true symphonies ! Famous Grand Crus, pride of the Burgundian vineyard, are established on these stony and sunny slopes. The monks of Bèze, soon in the 7th century, are at the origin of the development of the vineyards in Gevrey-Chambertin. They received these grounds as allowance, originally wooded. After having cleared them, they import vine stock in the adjacent part of their abbey. Many years later, the intendant of the king Jobert repurchases the vineyard and works for the fame of this vintage. In the 17th century, this wine won a great fame. Did you know that this village produces 9 of the 33 Burgundian Grand Crus and 27 Premier Cru ? Here, nature is generous everywhere. At an extent that that a natural reserve protected this exceptional heritage in 2004. The combe Lavaux-Jean Roland indeed shelters unique and endemic species in the European level. Gevrey-Chambertin can be tasted, visited during the guided tours and listened with during the Music festival in Chambertin, every year in September !

OFFICE DE TOURISME DE GEVREY-CHAMBERTIN

1, rue Gaston-Roupnel
✆ +33 (0)3 80 34 38 40
www.ot-gevreychambertin.fr
gevrey.info@wanadoo.fr

Low season : open Monday to Friday from 9.30am to 12.30pm and from 1.30pm to 5.30pm; Saturday from 9.30am to 12.30pm and from 1.30pm to 5pm. High season : Monday to Friday from 9.30am to 12.30pm and from 1.30pm to 6pm; Saturday from 9.30am to 12.30pm and from 1.30pm to 5.30pm; Sunday from 10am to 12.30pm and from 1.30pm to 4pm. High season from May to September included – Closed on Sunday in low season. Free Wifi access on the premises. Billetery the SNCF.

Located in the heart of the village, the Tourist Office of the Gevrey canton offers cultural and artistic events throughout the year. It also organises guided tours and invites you to discover the historical and wine heritage of this famous village. A vine and wine workshop allows you to know the type of soil and climates of the vineyards of Gevrey-Chambertin, to understand everything on the Burgundy wines and to introduce you to their tasting (on reservation, for a minimum of 4 people, at €20 per person). With the visit « The vineyard through the seasons », go and have a walk in the vineyards with a winemaker ! You will know everything about the works carried out there in the course of the year. You then visit the cellar, the fermenting room, to understand the principle of vinification and the breeding of wines. To finish, a tasting is offered to you ! Heritage side, the Tourist Office invites you to visit some craft shops like a pottery, a cheese factory, a farmhouse... But also of the must-see sites like the Stephen Liegeard de Brochon castle, the Château de Gevrey-Chambertin and the Noisot museum in Fixin devoted to the memories of a former military of Napoleon. To discover the countries of Grevrey, several tours are offered : the Côte, the Hautes Côtes and the Plaine. Natural sites are not forgotten either Gevrey-Chambertin is not limited to its wines; also discover the atmosphere, the beauty of its slopes and gastronomy !

Knife & Fork

LE CLOS LENOIR 1623

61, route de Beaune ✆ +33 (0)3 80 27 37 14 / +33 (0)6 63 91 97 99 / +33 (0)6 81 31 37 69
charlotte_remond@orange.fr

Open from Tuesday to Sunday for lunch. Open for dinner by reservation from 15 people. Menus from €16.50 to €18.50 (à la carte). Daily special : €13 (starter main course or main course and dessert €16.50, starter main course and dessert €18.50). Wine by the glass. Garden. Terrace. Wifi.

Le Clos Lenoir 1623, a new restaurant of Gevrey-Chambertin, possesses every quality to seduce. You cannot miss it when entering to Gevrey from Beaune, the stone building completely renovated attracts the eye. It is an ancient hen house that housed a grain mill in 1623 that has been transformed into a charming place. The enclosed courtyard is isolated from the road, it overlooks the vineyards, the terrace is huge and room is typical of Burgundy with fireplace, beams and stonework. You will find the decor that is so important for Sandrine and Charlotte and that we already recommended in their little restaurant in the centre of Gevrey with works by Patrick Hardel that gets inspiration from the wine's items. As for gastronomy, Sandrine and her chef Virginie prepare beautiful well-made dishes, daily specials, grills, parsley seasoned ham, plancha of pigs or cheeses but also large salads, they cater for everyone. The dishes are always nicely prepared often with the soup of the day. Here sauces are also innovated such as the creation of Porto-Chestnut sauce. Above all, you have offer a real moment of conviviality, it is the strength of the house. As for wines, you could not have better as far as to the winemakers partners.

LA JEANNETTE

1, rue du Gaizot
✆ +33 (0)3 80 33 41 95
www.facebook.com/eurl.lajeannette
maccarine@hotmail.com

Open on Monday, Tuesday and Thursday to Saturday from 10am to 7pm; Sunday from 10am to 3pm. Closed at 5pm Sunday in summer. Fixed rate formula : €14.50 (starter, main course, dessert + à la carte. Breakfast at €6.80). Wine by the glass. Terrace. Shop. New in 2016 : Bike rental.

If you are in search of conviviality, quality and originality, the small gourmet break at La Jeannette in the middle of Gevrey Chambertin is for you. Small for its small room, gourmet because Carine Veysset decorates his à la carte menu with pretty products and finally very friendly. At La Jeannette, you can have a meal, a tea, a coffee but also to do your shopping. Offering yourself a small present, a souvenir, an original product, having a drink or eating or adorning yourself or decorating. Carine Veysset maintains La Jeannette in her image, merry and passionate of the Sixties where the American vintage is omnipresent. It's simple, you simply live a complete change of scenery by the completely original deco, especially on the side of the restaurant. Formica furniture, posters of cinema, Maggi ads, images of Pin-up, roadsters and always a musical background produced by one of its vinyls. Carine offers snacks, in 2016 the parsley seaosoned ham arrives straight from the « splendid » Rôtisserie du Chambertin, the snails, well sorted, are famous, charcuteries and cheeses, Bourguignon beef and as desserts, pancakes, gingerbread or homemade crumble. They are famous and so « nice ». A little wine list, beers and hot drink to accompany all that. We love to come here for all these good reasons. During the fine days, the small terrace is set up on the pavement. Some evenings, the street becomes a concert venue in collaboration with the close establishments transforming the rue du Gaizot into festive street. Unique !

Gevrey-Chambertin.

PIZZA VOSTRA

6, rue Richebourg
✆ +33 (0)3 80 40 40 10
www.pizza-vostra.fr
contact@pizzavostra.fr

Open on Tuesday from 18h till 22h; from Wednesday till Friday from 11h30 till 14h and from 18h till 22h; the weekend from 18h till 22h. Menu : approximately 15 €.

Pizza Vostra is a modern pizzeria in the heart of Gevrey. It is the possibility of eating on site but also ordering online and having your pizza delivered. The house uses only fresh and quality products to find the taste of the real Italian pizzas. If you do not feel inspired, choose one of the classic pizzas : Margherita, Prosciutto, Calzone, four cheeses or Regina... Daring people can make their pizza themselves with two different formulas : 3 ingredients at choice or 5 ingredients at choice plus a drink. Add, as you like, onions, cherry tomatoes, mushrooms, arugula, dry smoked ham, coppa, anchovy, bleu d'auvergne, Epoisses, seafood... Enough to prepare a real feast, but be careful they are quickly very rich ! And for dessert, do not deprive yourself of Italian ice cream... And if we tell you that it is Clos Napoléon, restaurant of Fixin which is behind it, you know it all ! Small terrace since summer 2015.

LA TABLE DE PIERRE BOUREE

40, route de Beaune
✆ +33 (0)3 80 34 13 97
www.pierre-bouree-fils.com
latabledepierrebouree@orange.fr

On booking. Open from Monday to Saturday from 11.30 a.m. to 4.00 p.m. From the third weekend of March to the third weekend of September. Menus from 30 euros to 100 Euros (with 5, 7, 9 wines or 5 vintage wines for tasting, menu without wine at 18 Euros, wine by the glass). Kids menu : 11 Euros. Choice of main course without wine 10 Euros. Cheese platter 6 Euros. Drinks list among which wine by the glass and wine bottles. Domaine du Caveau wine sales. Toilets equipped for persons with reduced mobility.

It was since 2008 that La Table de Pierre Bourée provides a wine tourism offer that is not finally as developed as that : tasting the wines of the estate around a good Burgundian meal. Open from the weekend of the sale of the Hospices-de-Nuits to the sale of Hospices De Beaune, Jean-Christophe and Bernard Vallet welcome you every lunchtime from Monday to Saturday. The atmosphere is friendly around a unique Burgundian menu, gougères, parsley ham, typical dish and dish of four cheeses from Gaugry. These dishes are chosen to fit in with the wines that you can enjoy as a group of five, seven or nine according to the menus from €30 to €50. For €100, the Sensations menu with five Grands Crus, Corton Charlemagne, Corton, Clos de Vougeot, Charmes and Mazis-Chambertin allows you to mix with the excellence. Domaine Pierre Bourée produces some forty appellations in Côte-de-Beaune and Côte-de-Nuits, white and red Bourgognes, Villages appellations, as well as Premiers and Grands Crus. Everything is commented by the kind hosts. A real tasting lesson during a meal and the opportunity to share experiences and passions. At the end of this pleasant moment, you can go down to the cellar, often in order to onfirm your favourite by a purchasing some bottles.

Sleeping

HÔTEL LES GRANDS CRUS

Rue de Lavaux
✆ +33 (0)3 80 34 34 15
www.hoteldesgrandscrus.com
contact@hoteldesgrandscrus.com

Logis (2 chimneys). Closed from December to February. Labels : Vignobles et Découvertes + Qualité Tourisme. 24 rooms. Double room from €89 to €99. Buffet breakfast : €13 (€6 for children from 6 to 10 years old). Extra bed : €20. Closed parking included. American Express, Holiday vouchers. Pets allowed (extra price €12). Seminars. Internet access. wi-fi. Satellite TV. Terrace.

Aptly named, Hotel Les Grands Crus is located opposite the most beautiful vineyards of Gevrey-Chambertin, in the heart of Burgundy's Climats. It is set up in a building full of character with an enclosed courtyard within walking distance from the centre of the village. Marie-Paule Farnier and her son Louis welcome you with an outstanding professionalism. The establishment offers 24 well-equipped and comfortable rooms which feature a classic, personalized, cosy, colourful and elegant decor. You can choose the very elegant comfortable rooms, installed at the ground floor and the first floor, with view on the Burgundian village or the slope of the Climat of the Premier Cru Cazetiers. You can also set your sight on a mansard-roofed room, prettier and preserving the view on the vineyards. Breakfast is a pleasant time since you enjoy a flowery terrace in summer, in the winter the dining room inside is enjoyable. Grands Crus is an ideal starting point for the visit of the region, Marie-Paule and Louis advise you to make the best choice of food and wine tastings nearby the hotel. You can book it for seminar, with large and bright equipped working room of 45 m². Let us add that very reasonable prices are added to the aspects of comfort and quality.

Shopping

DOMAINE PIERRE BOURÉE FILS

11-13, route de Beaune
✆ +33 (0)3 80 34 30 25
www.pierre-bouree-fils.com
contact@pierre-bouree-fils.com

Welcome only go. Also at the opening hours of the Table de Pierre Bourée of the third weekend of March to the third weekend of November.

Domaine Pierre Bourée Fils, owner and merchant-breeder, owns a vineyards of 8.5 hectares. The latest acquisitions and the fact that he is trader enable him to offer a catalog of over 40 appellations on a total of 20 hectares and twenty vintages from 1976 to 2014. The prices range from €9 to around €100, from Burgundy wine to the best Grands Crus. The address owes its success to the respect of tradition, the perfectly maintained and developped know-how. Carefully controlled culture, ploughed vines, sorting table, whole pressed bunches, long vinification in wooden wine vats in the winery and 100% of wines aged in oak barrels with about 15% of white. At the late 2017 and the early 2017, the new winery located at Gevrey on the land of the estate will be in service with cellar of 400 m² and winery of 400 m². The guarrantee of seeing the quality of the wine in steady progression but especially to discover the address. Domaine Pierre Bourée Fils has had its tasting table since 2008 at 40 route de Beaune, a place where you can quietly sit and discover the wines during a lunch with formulas including 5, 7 and 9 wines. All the tastings are accompanied by a Burgundian meal very Burgundy... Bernard and Jean-Christophe Vallet are waiting for you to share their passion there.

■ **DOMAINE QUIVY**
7, rue Gaston-Roupnel
✆ +33 (0)3 80 34 31 02
✆ +33 (0)6 07 32 93 73
www.gerardquivy.0rg.fr
gerard.quivy@wanadoo.fr

Open every day. Listed as historical monuments. Free visits and tastings.

In the heart of the old village of Gevrey-Chambertin, Domaine Quivy is located in a charming private mansion of the 18th century with cellars, fermenting room, tasting cellar and outbuildings. Built in 1710 by the Counsellor of Accounts Chifflot, the set of these remarkably preserved wine buildings is worth a visit. Their characteristic determined its inscription on the Historical monuments list in September 2015 as being representative of the wine and leisure estates built in 18th by the Dijonese members of Parliament and having preserved a permanent activity. In addition to its historic and artistic interest, the building is equipped with lush vegetation and it still shelters the cellars of the family estate. The room of tasting is also preserved in an authentic Burgundian style, it comprises the originality to have a wide glass slab overhanging the cellar that you can also visit. The 7-hectare vineyard of the property are cultivated in reasoned viticulture, the production of the estate is just like the place : refined, precise and constant. You will find several beautiful names, registered in the Climats de Bourgogne such as the Chapelle-Chambertin and Charmes-Chambertin in Grand crus, Gevrey-Chambertin 1er Cru the Corbeaux. Domaine Quivy also distinguishes itself on the village appellations obtained on beautiful named places located in edge of 1ers crus like « Les Evocelles » and « En Fields ». Gérard Quivy offers a tasting and sale which can accommodate up to 15 people on appointment. Domaine Quivy also achieved an international to China and the United States.

PHILIPPE LECLERC
Rue des Halles ✆ +33 (0)3 80 34 30 72
www.philippe-leclerc.com
philippe.leclerc60@wanadoo.fr

Open every day from 9.30am. Free tastings and visit of a museum of ancestral objects of the wine and viticultural world. Burgundian snack and tasting of wines from the Domaine by reservation for groups from 8 people.

Philippe Leclerc is a passionate, fascinating, authentic and generous character. As a man of the vineyard ground, he is also man of the stone because once the wines in cellar, he lives his passion for architecture, the art and the history of the trades of yesteryear by transforming gradually his cellars into true museum. The medieval touch of the place can sometimes turn to fantastic. It's astonishing ! Philippe Leclerc is owner of the 7.5-hectare old vineyards with Burgundy appellation, Chambolle-Musigny and Gevrey-Chambertin. The visit of the vault is always an enchantment, for the wines but for many others too ! On the list, 4 Gevrey-Chambertin 1er Cru, Les Champeaux, Les Cazetiers, La Combe aux Moines and Les Champonnets. Before tasting them, you are already going to rave on the qualities of Gevrey Village *En Champ*. Philippe Leclerc produces wines marked by distinctive climates. Each vintage has its typicality. In 2016, you can buy the 2011 and 2012. For old vintage 2015, you will have to wait a little while, even though they are already pleasant in barrel. Philippe Leclerc confides us that the year 2015 reminds him year 1985 which is is still good to drink after being kept for 30 years. You can also get old vintage, 2003, 2005, 2007... On reservation, it is possible for the groups to enjoy a Burgundian snack menu around a beautiful monastery table, charcuterie and cheeses plates, accompanied by the wines of the Estate.

In the surroundings

Brochon

FROMAGERIE GAUGRY
Route nationale 74
✆ +33 (0)3 80 34 00 00 / +33 (0)3 80 34 00 05
www.gaugryfromager.com
contact@gaugryfromager.com

Open Monday to Saturday from 9am to 12.30pm and from 2pm to 6.30pm. Free tours during the opening hours of the shop. Guided tours and tasting for groups or the individual ones, by appointment (Tel. 03 80 34 00 05).

The Gaugry cheese factory has been offering his know-how in cheese selection since 3 generations. It is a crucial stop between Dijon and Nuits-Saint-Georges ! Facing the vineyards of Gevrey-Chambertin, this temple of Burgundian traditional cheese is an invitation to taste the Epoisses AOP, Ami du Chambertin, Soumaintrain, Chaource, Brillat Savarin or Palet de Bourgogne. Also, treat yourself with the last novelty : the Pleasure with Crémant de Bourgogne that comes to complete the Pleasure with chablis and other delights with raw milk. It is possible to discover all the trade secrets thanks to visit of the state-of-the-art factory that makes these traditional cheeses. To prolong the enjoyment, a tasting accompanied by bread and wine is organised before you pass to the shop. On request, you can even leave with a vacuum-package in order to keep your cheeses during your return trip... and without smell ! The shop offers a selection of regional quality products that accompanies cheeses perfectly : cassis, gingerbreads, Dijon mustard... Do not miss the Petit Gaugry made with the same process as the soft cheese category and rind brushed with *Marc de Bourgogne*. With raw milk or pasteurized milk, it suits every palate... It is even more delicious with bread with linseeds that you can buy on site on Thursday ! The dairy offers also a beautiful sample of the best regional produce (jam, organic products, cassis, anise of Flavigny...). Upon reservation, the house offers the preparation of your cheeseboards for meals. All that remains to do is to enjoy them with your guests. You can also get supplied with Raclette cheese or fondue cheese for more quality. Still interesting, meals cheese served with mâchon, this Lyon speciality made with charcuteries, regional cheeses and wines... An excellent address to discover without any delay.

Saulon-la-Rue

CHÂTEAU DE SAULON
67, rue de Dijon
✆ +33 (0)3 80 79 25 25
www.chateau-saulon.com
info@chateau-saulon.com

♿

« Maître Restaurateur » label. Closed the first three weeks of March. Open daily for lunch from 12pm to 1.30pm and for dinner from 7.30pm to 9pm. Closed Sunday for dinner between November and April. Booking advised. Menu from €33 to €59. Lunch menu : €19 (2 main courses, €23 for 3 main courses). Groups welcome. Baby chairs. Garden. Terrace.

The gastronomic restaurant of Château de Saulon is a stopover of choice. The young chef Olivier Perreaut, only 34 years-old, is at its helm. Talented is certainly the word which defines him best. He develops authentic dishes, while not hesitating to take some chances, while making his guests discover the unexpected seasonings. Here are some perfect examples of his à la carte : snackéed Scallops with bacon of Colonnata and its flavours of Arabica, Black Angus Beef with the flavor of elderberry or Saddle of lamb roasted with violet olives of Kalamata... And they are only some of the suggestions of the chef ! Obviously those change according to the seasons, all is homemade and a good part of the products used comes from the local producers. You taste these dishes in a superb setting : vaults made of stone, tables with tablecloth, design chairs with compass feet... And on the terrace, a stunning view on the gardens and the historic facade of the castle. Your group meals are also welcome with dedicated dishes suggestions (starting from 15 people at least).

Philippe Leclerc
Gevrey-Chambertin
Estate owner Winemaker
w.philippe-leclerc.com
lippe.leclerc60@wanadoo.fr
Rue des Halles
21220 Gevrey-Chambertin
+ 33 (0)3 80 34 30 72
Visits of cellars and museum – Tasting at the vault – Burgundian snack

IS-SUR-TILLE ★

Town of 4,365 inhabitants located at 20 km north of Dijon, Is-sur-Tille is located at the confluence of two geographical entities : on one side the plateau of Langres in the west, with an average altitude of 400m and on the other side the agricultural argillaceous plain of the Saône in the east. The Tille river is present at the limit of the territory of the town and the Ignon, a tributary of the Saône and the Rhone, crosses the downtown. This river gives this picturesque aspect to the city, with a complex network of beams and millstream that many footbridges get across. The commune managed to keep an alive and animated center by a diversified and dynamic local shop including a weekly market of local produce. The small town also shelters a hundred of association including the Confrérie de la Truffe de Bourgogne. In fact, lovers of truffle of Burgundy know that these grounds are favourable with their growth ! Water is a significant element of the city and contributed to its development thoughout the centuries. It is likely that the name « Is » comes from a Celtic word indicating water or the river. From a cultural point of view, the inhabitants are not left behind since a festival of crossword is held each year in May, which is the opportunity to recall the preferred definition of the crossword enthusiasts of the corner : « In two letters on the Tille ». There is also a modern music festival as well as a drums festival. Lastly, since 1 January 2002, Is-sur-Tille is part of the COVATI (*Communauté de communes des Vallées de la Tille et de l'Ignon*) that gathers 23 communes.

■ **OFFICE DE TOURISME DES VALLEES DE LA TILLE ET DE L'IGNON**
Place de la République
✆ +33 (0)3 80 95 24 03
✆ +33 (0)3 80 95 58 25
www.covati-tourisme.fr
covati.tourisme@covati.fr
♿
From November to February : open Tuesday to Saturday from 10am to 12pm and from 2pm to 4pm. From March to October : open Tuesday to Saturday from 9.30am to 12.30pm and from 2pm to 6pm. In July and August : also open Sundays and public holidays from 9am to 1pm. Many programs of visits and free activities suggested. Advance reservation.
Located under the former covered market of Is-sur-Tille, the Tourist Office suggests you discover the wealth of its territory through its 23 towns : Avelanges, Chaignay, Courtivron, Crécey-sur-Tille, Diénay, Échevannes, Épagny, Gemini, Is-sur-Tille, Lux, Marcilly-sur-Tille, Marey-sur-Tille, Marsannay-the-wood, Moloy, Pichanges, Poiseul-les-Saulx, Saulx-le-Duc, Spoy, Tarsul, Til-Châtel, Vernot, Villecomte and Villey-sur-Tille. Booklets are at your disposal to make you discover the history, the cultural and natural heritage as well as the local handicraft. Numerous activities are proposed to you : guided tours in season, public swimming pool, equestrian centres, visit of a snail breeding, visit of artisanal workshops... The tourist mini train of Lavières accommodates you on Sunday and on holidays from 3pm to 7pm, with a departure every 20 minutes for a small tour in forest. Offer yourself a maiden flight or an initiation to piloting thanks to the flying-club of the community of towns. You can also discover the ninepins every Wednesday afternoon in July and August in Quiller d'Is-sur-Tille or admire the works which are exposed each month in the premises of the Tourist Office. The town of Is-sur-Tille also proposes you a market of the local products every Sunday morning.

■ **TRAIN TOURISTIQUE DES LAVIÈRES**
Rue des Pins
✆ +33 (0)3 80 24 60 21
✆ +33 (0)3 80 95 36 36
cfti.e-monsite.com
traindeslavieres@laposte.net
Open mid-June until the Heritage Days. Open Sundays from 3pm to 7pm. Open for groups starting from 20 people by reservation from April to October. Free for under 4-year-olds. Adult : €2. Child (from 4 to 15 years old) : €1.50.
A Plymouth locomotive dating back to 1945 takes you along for a stroll in the forest. It leaves the station of Lavières every 20 minutes for a tour of 1.4 km in a pine forest. Train passionates, who created the CFTI association (Chemin de Fer Touristique Issois) in 1977, are at the origin of this tourist project. Every month, about ten volunteers take one Saturday to upkeep the railways and to make necessary repairs. Their reward is the satisfaction of nearly 3,000 visitors who board it each year. Less expensive than a merry-go-round, the tourist train of Lavières is the ideal leisure to have a good time in family. The trainspotters will take advantage of the opportunity to ask all their questions. Among the treasures preserved in the building : a diesel power trolley manufactured in 1931 in the Dijon's factory Pétolat. Classified historical monument, the Pétolat locomotive is the last to be in operating condition in France. Playgrounds, picnic area and bocce ball field allow you to spend an excellent moment. In 2016, a great railway festival is scheduled on the last Sunday of August. So if you are a train passionate, join the CFTI without delay.

Sightseeing

■ **DÉCOUVERTE DE L'ARCHITECTURE ET DU PATRIMOINE D'IS SUR TILLE**
Place de la République
✆ +33 (0)3 80 95 24 03
www.covati-tourisme.fr
ot.tille-et-ignon@covati.fr
Open all year. Reception Tuesday to Saturday. Schedule : of November 1st at the end of February from 10am to 12pm and from 2pm to 4pm. From March to October from 9.30am to 12.30pm and from 2pm to 6pm. Exceptional opening in July and August Sundays and public holidays

from 9am to 1pm. Card of the course of the city available to the English and French Tourist Office. Guided tours in July and August only by reservation.

If you love history and culture, Is-sur-Tille will get your attention... Highly prized for a long time by the Dukes of Burgundy who devoted themselves to their favourite occupation, hunting, the commune has kept some memories of this precious heritage. The historic heart of the city is protected by a perimeter that includes the castle, the Charbonnel asylum, the Saint-Léger church and some private mansions with interesting facades. Le Compasseur de Courtivron hotel, located rue du Docteur Brulet is listed Historical Monument. The city is marked by bridges and footbridges, washing places and also has a pergola and a rose garden. You can enjoy the pleasant promenade of Capucins along the Courtines or strolling along the rivers. The Tourist Office of the valleys of Tille and Ignon also invites you to discover the history of the stone of Is-sur-Tille. Used in the region of Tilles as in Dijon for the construction of several buildings, this limestone is known for its resistance to water and frost. It was used in particular for wells curbstones, to build the monolithic baptismal tank of the Romanesque church of Til-Châtel in the 12th century, but also in various ways for the Saint-Léger church of Is-sur-Tille.

Knife & Fork

AUBERGE CÔTÉ RIVIÈRE

3, rue des Capucins
✆ +33 (0)3 80 95 65 40
www.auberge-cote-riviere.com
cote.riviere@wanadoo.fr

Closed one week in August. Open Tuesday to Saturday from 12pm to 1.30pm and from 7.30pm to 9pm; Sunday from 12pm to 1.30pm. Closed Sunday for dinner and Monday. Menu from €26 to €65. Menu of the market 2 main courses : €17; 3 main courses : €20. Menu of the week : €26. Menu At the edge of Ignon (for dinner and Sunday for lunch) : €26, €32 or €41. Menu around truffle of Burgundy 2 main courses : €52; 3 main courses : €65. Holiday voucher. Groups welcome (receptions. Fixed rate formulas business. Seminars). Garden. Terrace.

Aurberge Côté Rivière is undoubtedly one of the best restaurants in Pays des Trois Rivières. This former farmhouse, nestled in the heart of one hectare of greenery along Ignon, offers you a very pleasant gourmet stop, by the fireplace in winter or on the waterfront in summer. The large dining room is the place of all the culinary delights : the chef François Lagrue favours fresh, seasonal produces and his menu changes every month, offering gourmet dishes with multiple and constantly renewed flavours. He stringently selects the wines exclusively from Burgundian wine estates (Côte de Beaune and Côte de Nuits). Here, it's sure you'll enjoy a cuisine made on the spot thanks to the label Maître Restaurateur delivered in 2007. Various menus await you as well as a short but regularly renewed and delicious. You have : grilled flank steak, potatoes gratin with époisses, mushroom with red wine sauce, cod fillet with truffle and a pan-fried vegetable before ending with the caramelized pear or a delicious apple pie. What we especially appreciate is the children's menu which is not composed of the usual steak and chips but of a real menu of the chef that will perhaps awaken young people's tastebuds. A beautiful experience and a very nice terrace.

In the surroundings

Courtivron

LES LODGES DU GRAND CERF BLANC

6, chemin de la Charme
✆ +33 (0)3 80 75 10 73
www.leslodgesdugrandcerfblanc.com
contact@leslodgesdugrandcerfblanc.com

Breakfast included. 12 Lodges. 9 lodges from 1 to 3 people €189 + 2 familly lodges for 4-5 people €199 + 1 lodge for 1 disabled guest. Heating and air conditioning. 2 guestrooms, €70 for 2 and €90 for 4.

Les Lodges du Grand Cerf Blanc is a park of holiday chalets installed on one of the slopes of the valley of Ignon, above the village, in nature and at the edge of a park of 600 hectares reserved for the breeding of big game. These small chalets add to their unusual side the optimization of practical comfort, air-conditioning, bathroom with shower and toilets, table and stools and terrace with stunning view. It is not very large, but amusing and friendly. Your base camp thus established you reach the many sites of visit of the region. Near Is-sur-Tille or Dijon, you have many range of catering facilities. The breakfast is served in the early morning. The estate proposes also 4 guest rooms, great comfort in a splendid building close to the lodges.

Salives

LE PRÉ SAINT-GEORGES

Hameau de Larçon
✆ +33 (0)3 80 75 66 49
www.bruley-traiteur.fr/accueil.html
benoit.bruley@nordnet.fr

Open Monday to Friday for lunch. From €7.50 to €13.50. Cold buffet at will, daily special, cheeses, dessert, wine, coffee. Depending on slate.

This gourmet stopover is just an extra creation of Benoit Bruley. In addition to be a caterer and to charm his clientel (we would say almost his own guests) since years, he started in the adventure of the catering service. You can only go there at midday and during the week day but you will not be disappointed. What's the purpose ? To let yourself be carried by inventivenesses of the chef. Three very complete formulas are at your disposal, from the shortest to longest and in each an all-you-can-eat cold buffet as starter and a daily special surprise, according to slate menu. Let the talents of the chef guide you, you can only be delighted.

Selongey

HÔTEL-RESTAURANT LE NATURAL

11, rue du Moulin
✆ +33 (0)3 80 95 13 92
www.hotel-restaurant-lenatural.com
marie-turlot@orange.fr

Open from Tuesday to Sunday for lunch and dinner. Menus from €18.90 to €38.40. Children's menu : €9.50 (under 12 years old). Lunch formula : €13 (and €15.90 for dinner – starter, main course, dessert of the day with 1/4 of wine or cocktail of the house). Hotel of 8 rooms; single room €52; double room €54; triple room €78; one-night stopover with special rates €68. Holiday vouchers, Cheque Restaurant. Groups welcome. Garden. Terrace.

Le Natural welcomes you in a forestry setting, refreshing in summer when it is above all the sounds of nature that will rock you. Located along the Venelle in an old renovated sawmill, the hotel-restaurant of Marie Turlot has all the features of haven of peace with simple and warm reception. Marie, the chef, prepares us homemade cuisine with her traditional dishes and her desserts that are often regional but still successful, made with fresh and seasonal ingredients. The starters always remind the beautiful Burgundy including eggs meurettes with a very neat white wine or the unmissable snails of Burgundy... On the menu, we recommend that you choose the meat. On the program, a beautiful steak, a skewer of beef flank and a duck breast. You will not be disappointed. Marie regularly organizes thematic evenings : tartiflette, couscous... Her room is large, it can easily welcome groups. At Le Natural, we like the excellent quality price ratio but especially the kindness of the reception and the authenticity of the place far from the fuss of the city.

Til-Châtel

AÉROCLUB DU VAL D'IS

Aérodrome du Val d'Is
RD974
✆ +33 (0)3 80 95 17 87
www.acvi.org – acvaldis@orange.fr

Preliminary touch desired by telephone. Approximately 25 min. Maiden flight by appointment – 3 passengers on an aircraft : €30 per person; 2 passengers : €35 per person; 1 passenger : €50. € 5 discount for children under 12 years old. Initiation with piloting : €50.

L'Aéroclub du Val d'Is, formerly known as L'Aéroclub de Til-Châtel was founded in 1964. This combination law 1901 counts 150 voluntary members today and manages a park of 7 devices with more than 2,000 hours of flight recorded each year. Since 2006, the aerodrome of Til-Châtel is the property of Covati. The club proposes in particular flights above landscapes of Is-sur-Tille. Whether it is for you or a close relation, maiden flight is a formidable gift to take a little height and to discover the view in another manner. For the most enthusiast ones, an introductory course to piloting is also proposed. Accompanied by an instructor and after a briefing on the ground, take control of a plane or a ULM 3 axes for a flight of 25 minutes. The strong feelings are guaranteed ! Think of calling the club to reserve your maiden flight or your initiation to piloting.

LADOIX-SERRIGNY

Sightseeing

ÉGLISE SAINT-MARCEL

The choir and the transept date back to 13th century, the bell tower and the charpent from the 18th century. This church has the distinction of having an *oculus*, a Eucharistic eye that made it possible to contemplate the Blessed-Sacrament after a closed church and especially to give the Eucharist to the lepers without being contaminated. This rare and original piece dates from the 15th century. It is visible near the main door on the porch.

Knife & Fork

LA GREMELLE

Route de Dijon
✆ +33 (0)3 80 26 40 56
www.lagremelle.com
info@lagremelle.com

« Maître Restaurateur » label. Open Tuesday to Saturday for dinner; Tuesday to Sunday and public holidays for lunch. Menu from €25 to €58. À la carte : Around €25. Children's menu : €10. Lunch menu : €18 (starter and main course or main course and dessert. Starter, main course, dessert : €22). Wine by the glass. Hotel of 20 rooms with swimming pool. Catering facilities of groups to 30 even 70 people. Garden. Terrace.

The La Gremelle hotel restaurant changed owner in March 2014. Maryse Parigot is surrounded by a young dynamic team. The new room decoration is fashionable : unbleached tablecloths, large wooden chairs, exposed wooden beams, old fireplace and large windows that overlook the slopes of Ladoix and the swimming pool. A lovely setting ! In the kitchen, Quentin, the young chef, is full of ideas and talent. In 2015, he also received the title of Maître Restaurateur. The products are fresh, the dishes are homemade and beautifully presented. Gremelle gets off to a good start ! Real marbled ham from Burgundy with its light cream with mustard « Fallot », snails with garlic butter, eggs in red wine sauce, fillet of Charolais beef ...The Burgundy specialties are well represented ! Some dishes are quite unique including ballottine of foie gras with candied chestnuts or delicious scallops nuts snakées with quinua. To accompany these beautiful dishes, the wine list honors Ladoix and the prices are very reasonable !

Shopping

■ DOMAINE GASTON ET PIERRE RAVAUT

16, Grande Rue de Buisson ✆ +33 (0)3 80 26 41 94
www.gaston-pierre-ravaut.fr
gaston-ravaut@wanadoo.fr

Open Monday to Saturday. Tastings by appointment. Group 10 to 20 people by reservation. The range of price is from €6.50 to €50 the bottle.

Located in Ladoix-Serrigny in the small hamlet of Buisson, the Gaston and Pierre Ravaut estate is a family farm where 6 generations have followed one another. Today it is more than 19 hectares of vineyards that are exploited by Gaston Ravaut and his sons, Pierre and Vincent who have inscribed the estate in a very advanced procedure of reasoned culture, friendly to the terroirs. The catalogue of the estate offers 17 appellations, including 4 in white : Bourgogne Aligoté, Chardonnay, but also Ladoix and Corton-Charlemagne Grand Crus, without forgetting the superb red ones : Ladoix 1er Cru, Aloxe-Corton 1er Cru and Corton Grand Cru... The Ravaut property favours direct sales. Well, you are welcomed in the heart of superb cellars to taste and discover the treasures of the house. Vincent Ravaut, who created his trading-breeder company on grapes of Côte-de-Nuits generates a beautiful complement in the range of the family estate.

■ DOMAINE JEAN PIERRE-MALDANT

30, route de Beaune ✆ +33 (0)3 80 26 44 50
www.domainemaldant.com
jean.pierre.maldant@wanadoo.fr

Reception on appointment. Vault can accommodate groups up to 20 people.

Founded in 1895, this family estate bears the name of Jean-Pierre Maldant but now it is Pierre-François, his son, who took over the destiny of this exploitation of more than 8 hectares. Always been passionate by viticulture and his estate, Pierre François Maldant has signed vinifications of outstanding quality, with a sustainable farming : no herbicides, ploughings in the traditional way, manual harvest... The vineyards are located in the towns of Ladoix, Savigny-lès-Beaune, Chorey-les-Beaune and Aloxe-Corton. In 2012, the house purchased two plots of Ladoix on the climate « Les Buis ». These plots are located in the middle of the slope of the Premier Crus of the village. Thus in 2014, they are planted to get a Pinot Noir Village and Bourgogned Chardonnay. The estate produces a beautiful wine selection of Burgundy. In white : Bourgogne, Chorey-lès-Beaune, Ladoix and Corton Charlemagne. In red : Bourgogne, Ladoix, Chorey-lès-Beaune, Savigny-lès-Beaune in village and Premier Cru, Aloxe-Corton en Village and Premier Cru, including two exceptional Grand Crus : Corton Maréchaudes and Les Grandes Lolières. Domaine Jean-Pierre Maldant enjoys an ideal location on the road of Beaune. The estate has a beautiful tasting cellar located on the bank of Lauve, the small river crossing Ladoix. The place is particularly charming. The welcome is simple and very kind. You will be seduced by the very affordable price of the wines.

■ RÉSERVE DE BACCHUS

4, route de Dijon ✆ +33 (0)3 80 20 00 01
www.reservedebacchus.fr
reservedebacchus@gmail.com

Open Tuesday to Friday from 9am to 12pm and from 2pm to 7pm; Saturday from 9am to 12pm and from 3pm to 7pm. High season : Sunday from 10am to 1pm. Activities tastings with theme once a month. At the time of strolls gourmet in July, the Reserve of Bacchus sells the tasted wines at price estates. Open on Sunday of strolls + Monday.

Created by Saadia Chamali and Sébastien Cattoni, sales person for many estates, La Réserve de Bacchus is not only a wine merchant but also a well-stocked deli. Located at the northern entrance of Ladoix on the road to Beaune, the shop is easily accessible. A completely dedicated building renovated and air-conditioned. The wine selection, made by Sébastien Cattoni, is thorough and full of treasures ! Several poles are offered to you. Of course, the pole « vignerons de Ladoix » offers wines from the twelve areas of the township. That of the rosé invites you to discover the wines from Burgundy, Provence, Languedoc, Alsace, Argentina, Hungary, New Zealand, Chile. The beer's range started with the Belenium; it is going to develop. There is always the « wine at less than 10 euros » which has been tested. You can trust Sébastien and Saadia, great professionals to welcome you with a smile and advise you on wines, but also on crémant, champagnes, , whiskeys, rums, cognac and vodkas. La Réserve is also a deli (mustards Fallot, gingerbreads Mulot and Petitjean, fruit juices Alain Milliat produced next to Lyon...) and sells some items of tableware. La Réserve de Bacchus has a remarkable, qualitative and rich offer for the neophytes, the amateurs and the connoisseurs.

MARSANNAY-LA-CÔTE

Marsannay-la-Côte connects the capital of the dukes to the vineyards of the coast. The vine has been cultivated in these places since the seventh century, perhaps even earlier. The geographical location of Marsannay-la-Côte and the taste of its production naturally made it a supplier of the duchy. Described as « Golden Gate of the Côte de Nuits », this label has, since 1987, the unique privilege of producing the three colours of wine : red, white, rosé. This title which is now recognized covers the land bordering Chenôve Couchey, from north to south, which also relies on this reputation. Marsannay provides specific and authentic wines. It is said that Charlemagne has rested in Marsannay-la-Côte, near a tree. From then the site was venerated and has served as outdoor-court. At the foot of this tree the most important tournament of chivalry in the history of the Duchy of Burgundy was organized, the « weapons step of Marsannay » in 1443. Jousts, banquets, celebrations succeeded for 6 weeks. Some pretty vestiges of the past are still visible when walking in the streets of the town : the Church of the Assumption, a former dovecote, the Priory, the House of Corporations...

OFFICE DE TOURISME DE MARSANNAY-LA-CÔTE
41, rue de Mazy ✆ +33 (0)3 80 52 27 73
www.ot-marsannay.com
ot-marsannay@wanadoo.fr
Open Monday to Saturday from 9am to 12pm and from 2pm to 6pm. Open all year. Open public holidays from May to August. Closed on Sunday. Pass Dijon-Coasts of Nights : €16 (€8 for the 12-18 years, free for under 12-year-olds).
Set on the first floor of the former priory that is located in front of the town hall, in the heart of the village, the tourist office of Marsannay-la-Côte aims to promote sites, activities and the products of the municipality. It organises tours like the geo-wine one that we highly recommend to you and various events (gourmet days in March, a photo contest in autumn. . .). You will find all the necessary tourism documents and it is here that you can purchase the Pass Dijon-Côte de Nuits which facilitates tourist access to the offered services in Dijon and in the vineyards of Côte. It is also on sale in the tourist offices of Dijon, Gevrey-Chambertin and Nuits-Saint-Georges. This Pass is valid for 1 year from the date of issue and you can enjoy 11 services that match the chosen theme : Heritage, Tasting or Discovery. Note : the ground floor of the building is an old cellar, used for receptions and communal and private tastings. Do not hesitate to contact the Town Hall if you want to rent it...

Knife & Fork

LES GOURMETS
8, rue du Puits-de-Têt ✆ +33 (0)3 80 52 16 32
www.les-gourmets.com
detot-lesgourmets@orange.fr
Open Wednesday to Sunday for lunch from 12pm to 1.30pm and for dinner from 7.30pm to 9.30pm. Other days by group booking. Menus from €31 to €51 (+ carte. Tasting menu at €90/pers for the whole table). Children's menu : €15. Lunch menu : €20 (main course, cheese or dessert, ½ mineral water and coffee). All 1st Thursdays of each month, 1 menu offered for 1 menu bought for lunch and dinner on all the menus. Groups welcome (plus seminar room of 20 people). Terrace.
If you do not yet know Les Gourmets, hurry up and book your table there. This restaurant offers an impeccable service, a warm and relaxed reception and top quality soon at the first menus. Romain Detot offers an absolutely gourmet cuisine with constant and renewed quality with creativity. It is typically the restaurant to be because in addition to the treat you offer for yourself, you would also willingly choose those of your guests. The dishes are tempting, even their names attract you like Seduction menu which offers you salmon quenelle with langoustine bisque and cod fillet with herb and vichy carrots, which is very light. The Bourguignon menu will please people from the region and visitors. The meal opens with traditional poached egg in wine sauce, the small pot of snails and crayfish, the duckling with blackcurrant, the nonette with epoisses and finally a cubic gingerbread and pear in red wine with anise sorbet... How can you resist ? And that is not all, the *séduction-business* menu at low prices but with delicious flavours will surely gain customers. The must is the menu *tentation*. But for those who still prefer to make their choice themselves, there is the menu well stuffed with delights. You will enjoy the covered terrace in summer and the dining room with its delicate plum tone and its discreet atmosphere in the rest of the year. You can admire the chef's cuisines through a glass door.

LA TABLE DU ROCHER
85, route de Beaune ✆ +33 (0)3 80 52 20 75
www.latabledurocher.fr
rocher@orange.fr
Open all year. Tuesday and Wednesday for lunch; Thursday to Saturday for lunch and dinner. Exceptional opening first Sunday of each month, for lunch. Menu from €22 to €35 (for lunch and dinner). À la carte : Around €20. Children's menu : €10. Lunch menus : Starter and main course or main course and dessert : €13.30. Starter + main course + dessert : €17.40. Only on weekdays, except public holidays. Holiday voucher, Chèque Restaurant. Terrace. Take-away.
Founded at the early 19th century, Table du Rocher is one of the oldest café-restaurants of France that has preserved its original decor ! The frescoes made in 1830, by the creator of the establishment, a former soldier of Napoleon, are indeed admirably preserved. A decor and a history that provide a particular atmosphere to this restaurant. Michel Philippon and the chef Christophe Dumay repurchased it in 2011 and has offered since then, a quality traditional cuisine, homemade and only prepared with seasonal ingredients. The products of the terroir are well represented on the menu. From the starter to the dessert, the Burgundy makes a parade in your dish : farm eggs of Ferme de Pontot in red wine sauce with crémant de Bourgogne accompanied by small onions and bacon. We must say that Table du Rocher is doing things big. A first impression of the main courses ? We will quote you fillet of 180 grams Charolais beef with the green pepper, snackéed scallops seasoned with gray truffle oil accompanied by pumpkin and the cheek of braised pork of Burgundy. A beautiful overview of the delights of the house. The cheeses are obviously from the local producers. As for the desserts, simple recipes but enhance with little surprises : pie with shortbread with the black chocolate and orange sorbet, toasted gingerbread and pear cream with hydromel, acidulous lemon foams and pistachio biscuit... An address with an excellent quality/price ratio, not to miss for its timeless decor, its creative cuisine and its fine wine list : Marsannay (the choice is wide and the prices are competitive, Domaine Pataille, Huguenot...), Gevrey, Fixin, Morey Saint-Denis... Welcome to the road of the Grand crus !

Sleeping

HÔTEL BALLADINS SUPÉRIEUR – RESTAURANT L'ORMICHAL
84, route de Beaune ✆ +33 (0)3 80 51 10 00
www.burg-hotel-dijon.com
dijon.marsannay@balladins.com
Open all year. Reception until 11pm (10pm Sunday). 47 rooms. from €72. Room for 4 from €90. Buffet breakfast : €8.50 (€5.80 for the children). Extra bed :

€15. Closed parking included. Stop-over with special rates for reps from €80. American Express. Pets allowed (€6.50). Seminars. Free Wifi. Catering facilities (restaurant in the evening menu at €16.90 and €18.90). Satellite TV, Canal+.

Hôtel Balladins de Marsannay la Côte became an extremely recommended hotel since Florence Courtalin became the owner in 2010. The 47 rooms of this hotel are held rigourously by the landlady who already run 2 other hotels : perfecly clean with impeccable service. All the rooms are pleasant, air-conditioned and regularly renovated, with exclusive furniture and a neat decor. Little details are planned including the welcome tray offered in superior room. Rated 3 star, the property has an excellent soundproofing, particularly on side of the National road 74. The swimming pool, heated from May 1st to September 30th, decorates the landscape, but your stay especially. Once in your room, you forget the neighbouring city, because the hotel turns to the vineyard, a green and relaxing setting. Definitely an exclusive address, with the door of the vineyards of the Côte de Nuits with a restaurant that is only open in the evening.

Shopping

■ DOMAINE FOUGERAY DE BEAUCLAIR

44, rue de Mazy ✆ +33 (0)3 80 52 21 12
www.fougeraydebeauclair.fr
fougeraydebeauclair@wanadoo.fr

Open from 9am to 11.30am and from 2pm to 5pm. Weekend open by appointment. Closed from December 23rd to January 2nd and from August 10th to August 20th.

The estate Fougeray de Beauclair is a family business, now run by the Ollivier spouses... At the end of the 70's, Jean-louis Fougeray (the father of Laurence Ollivier's) created this estate stretching on nearly 20 hectares and produces 90 000 bottles per year. There's something for every budget : bottles range from €9 to €110. Marsannay in white, red and rosé, of course, Burgundy white and red, Cotes de Nuits, and also Vosne-Romanée « Les Damodes » « white and red Fixin « Clos Marion » Savigny-lès-Beaune red and white « Les Golardes ». Renowened and prestigious wines ! Note : a new name Côte de Beaune Puligny-Montrachet is on sale since last year. Know that you can also find Languedoc wines like Picpoul de Pinet black that goes well with seafood or the croix de Soupié in red, which is not everywhere, with cassis scent and the cinnamon. The quality of their wines are highly recommended and a warm welcome from Laurence Ollivier. The house organizes tastings sessions that last one to two hours depending on the chosen formula to discover wines from June to October : welcome to vault, presentation area, wines, vineyards and initiation to oenology. An accessible, valuable & precious address, perfect to discover the wines of the region, just a few minutes from Dijon or Beaune...

■ CHATEAU DE MARSANNAY

Route des Grands-Crus ✆ +33 (0)3 80 51 71 11
www.chateau-marsannay.com
tourisme@chateau-marsannay.com

Low season : open every day from 10am to 12pm and from 2pm to 6.30pm. High season : every day from 10am to 6.30pm. Low season from October to April. Closed in January, during the year's end celebrations and Sundays of mid-November at Easter. Receptions, business dinners, cocktails... Visit of the cellars and tasting of the wines of the estate €12 to €22. For groups of more than 20 people €9.50 per person. Fixed rate formulas déjeunatoires, Weddings, Day of business, Cocktails, Receptions...

Château de Marsannay is an important stopover to discover the Climates of Burgundy, a 39 ha vineyards property, of which 28 ha are on the commune of Marsannay. Plots that is in the course of being Marsannay 1er Cru by the National institute of the Origin and Quality (Inao). In Côte de Nuits, the Castle owns vines of the most famous names. Three Grand crus : Clos de Vougeot, Ruchottes-Chambertin, Chambertin and Premiers Crus : Vosne-Romanée, Gevrey- Chambertin Bel-Air, Gevrey-Chambertin Champeaux form the jewels of its vineyard. The family Halley who is henceforth the owner of this estate also bought Château de Meursault and the Marché aux vins de Beaune.

CÔTE-D'OR

Three sites that are commit to the research of the excellence of their wines. As with Meursault, Château de Marsannay benefits from many investments as well for the vinification as for the reception of the visitors. The visit of Château de Marsannay starts with its breeding cellars that shelters more than 350 barrels. The atmosphere is conducive to a guided tour that details the history but especially the news of the estate. This expressed quality upgrading can felt at the end of the visit by a tasting in the new shop where the crus of the Castle are superbly highlighted. Admire the photographs of the Estate that are true works art. A function room of 400 m^2 with the Cistercian vaults allows you to organize banquets of prestige, wedding, cocktails, gala dinners... up to 350 people under the best possible conditions.

■ FESTINS DE BOURGOGNE
23, route de Beaune ✆ +33 (0)3 80 54 39 39
www.festins-traiteur.fr
boutique.marsannay@festins.fr
Open Tuesday to Saturday from 8.30am to 7.30pm. Without interruption. Possible delivery Monday. Tray meals. Receptions. Cocktails. Buffets.
Festins de Bourgogne has met the Burgundian gustatory expectation since 1992 by sharing the beautiful French culinary heritage. All the dishes are ready to take home and to taste. Go to the shop to discover how wide is the choice and how big is the chances. You can choose a classical meal or a much more lavish offer : buffet with or without service, business meal, meal of galas, wedding, baptisms... This caterer can serve meal for one to... 4,000 people, since Didier and Evelyne Chapuis is at the helm of 240 employees... You will find in the sumptuous vivid red shop, a rich and varied à la carte menu that changes at each season and entirely prepared with fresh ingredients. The new 2016 à la carte menu showcases all types of meal, from the breakfast to the dinner with a very a wide choice of flavours. Some must-eat of the French gastronomy are honoured : the duck foie gras, the salmon of Bellevue, the scallops, the casserole dishes like the cockerel with the Burgundy wine, the beef stew, the cassoulet... And it is only a light overview. Without forgetting the cheese boards and the sweet delight to enjoy without restreint ! The dishes charm the eyes before delighting palates : the aesthetic, graphic is refined, studied... You can feel perfectly the completed work according the rules and know-how. Do not hesitate to call upon this « Caterer of France », the only one in Burgundy, the very attentive to the requests of the guests. In the shop, you will have the choice between many regional and high-quality produces to organize your banquet yourself. A wide refreshment space where you can choose to buy by the glass as retail, without forgetting some good cru that will make their effect at table. Do not hesitate to ask for advice on the spot, the team is very available to answer you. You can order your tray meals on the website. Practical ! A very good address with a very attentive staff and very affordable prices !

MEURSAULT ★

A holy ground for white wine amateurs. Even more since the Climats du Vignoble de Bourgogne are listed as World Heritage by Unesco. The so particular features of this vineyard provoked comments around the world. 62 hectares produce the so unique heady and full bodied Meursault (white wine). Their taste is consistent in the mouth and makes the meal they accompany even more tasteful. For many movie amateurs, Meursault remains, just like Hospices de Beaune, one of the symboles of Gérard Oury's movie, La Grande Vadrouille, with Bourvil and Louis de Funès. It is also an opportunity to discover the historic buildings like the church of Saint-Nicolas, the former leper colony that was restored, the castle of the Velle and many others. Get more information at the Tourist Office. The Town Hall of Meursault, the emblem of this masterpiece, has been rehabilitated in 2014 with the development of a new place which allows it to keep its role as a *starlette* with photographers all over the world ! The municipality is also known for the famous Paulée, which takes place on the Monday following the third Sunday of November, at the famous Château de Meursault. Welcome to one of the most beautiful towns of Burgundy !

© OLIVIER PONCELET – FOTOLIA

General view of Meursault.

OFFICE DE TOURISME INTERCOMMUNAL DE MEURSAULT
Place de l'Hôtel-de-Ville
✆ +33 (0)3 80 21 25 90
www.ot-meursault.fr – info@ot-meursault.fr
Low season : open Monday to Saturday from 9.30am to 12.30pm and from 2pm to 5.30pm. High season : Monday to Saturday from 9.30am to 12.30pm and from 2pm to 6.30pm. Mid-season : open from 9.30am to 12.30pm and from 2pm to 6pm.
The inter-communal Tourist Office of Meursault offers a varied agenda of events during the season and organises guided tours-getaways. It is the opportunity to discover the local heritage and the surroundings : the church Saint-Nicolas, the City Hall, Château de Cîteaux, Château de Meursault, the Leprosarium, etc. The visit ends with tasting in the cellar of the City Hall. They are held every Thursday from 10 to noon, from 1st June to 30th September, for the individuals. On reservation (minimum 10 people) at any other period of the year. You should also note that a visit is organised for the Heritage Days in September. And for those who prefer the sport outing, you can discover the vineyard by the bike path Beaune-Santenay whose brochure is available on the spot.

Knife & Fork

LE BOUCHON
1, place de l'Hôtel-de-Ville
✆ +33 (0)3 80 21 29 56
www.restaurant-le-bouchon.com
aubouchon@orange.fr
Open all year. Closed from December 20th to January 20th. Tuesday to Sunday for lunch; Tuesday to Saturday for dinner. Booking advised. Menu from €25 to €37. Children's menu : €8.50 (for children under 12 years old). Lunch menu : €13.50 (appetizers buffet, daily special and dessert of the day On weekdays only). Wine by the glass. Express formula at €11 : appetizers buffet or daily special + dessert. Menu at €12 : appetizers buffet + daily special. Menu at €10 : appetizers buffet or daily special. Chèque Restaurant. Groups welcome (up to 45 people). Terrace. Take-away. Family or professional receptions.
Set up on the mythical Meursault square and immortalized by *La Grande Vadrouille*, this restaurant whose interior has just been beautifully restored (clearly, chic and simple) offers a Burgundian gastronomy and many revisited regional dishes. The local produces is highlighted with quality traditional cuisine. Welcome to the friendliest eatery of the region with Mireille Bernard at the helm and accompanied by her chef and a very talented pizzaiolo... We appreciate the warmth of the reception and the relaxed atmosphere of this restaurant, the local inhabitants frequent the place very regularly ! The cuisine honours local and seasonal produces to fascinate the guests with homemade dishes. You can start your meal with typically Burgundian starter : genuine parsley seasoned ham of Burgundy, eggs poached with white and red wine or pan-fried snail. Do not hesitate to continue with bourguignon beef, a *fondue vigneronne* or a delicious sweetbread with the marc de Bourgogne or even a revisited pizza. And what would be a Burgundian meal without these cheeses and these typical regional wines ? Mireille will be very pleased to make you discover her extraordinary wine list. As for dessert, try the nicely revisited lemon pie. The restaurant has offered even take-away hand-made pizzas to you or to enjoy in the spot since one year, they are divine. An address that we recommend for the quality of its service and his good light 100% homemade meals. An address that you should frequent urgently !

LE CHEVREUIL
Place de la République
✆ +33 (0)3 80 21 23 25
www.lechevreuil.fr
reception@lechevreuil.fr
Open on Monday, Tuesday and from Thursday to Saturday for lunch and dinner. Menus from €25 to €60. Children's menu : €13. Lunch formula : €21 (market menu starter, main course, dessert). À la carte. Hotel of 10 rooms. Groups welcome. Terrace.
Taken over by Tiago Araujo and his wife Eléonore since 2011, the hotel Le Chevreuil offers a relaxing stopover and its restaurant seduces. Tiago, a Brazilian chef, challenges himself regularly to offer us a delicious, creative and graphic cuisine. He prepares his dishes with local produces including some forgotten vegetables, he blends with talent the classic gourmet dishes by adding sometimes Latin America touches. To illustrate this : the two-cooked Bresse chicken is roasted with oyster and mushrooms in coxinha way. A brilliant blend of Burgundy and Brazilian flavours !

Classic : The terrine of Mother Augier has been on the menu for 100 years. An extra countryside starter, served hot with a delicious marinade. In season, crust hazelnut of venison with turnip and butternut and its strong juice with pepper is a success. We find the same originality during the dessert : homemade Paris-Brest and sorbet with passion fruit or samossa with pineapple and caipirinha. The stone walls are decorated with a nice collection of deer. The restaurant has a beautiful terrace, quiet, overlooking Château de Cîteaux. Eléonore, which grew up in the world of wine, was a wine list, Meursaults as favourite, at least 20 Villages and First 20 Wines. A very nice restaurant that is brilliantly distinctive.

Sleeping

■ LA CUEILLETTE****
Château de Cîteaux
18, rue de Cîteaux
✆ +33 (0)3 80 20 62 80
www.lacueillette.com
contact@lacueillette.com

Castles & Hôtels Collection. Open all year. Spa de France. Reception until 22 : 19 rooms. Single room from €150 to €180; double room from €190 to €240; suite from €290 to €320. Breakfast : €19 (buffet or continental in room at €15 by people). Extra bed : €35 (up to 12 years). Closed parking. Rooms with large terrace : 260 at €360. Offers stays wellness from 2 to 4 nights. Holiday voucher. Pets allowed (€22). Catering facilities (La Cueillette restaurant open every evening). Spa de Fruitithérapie. Excursions (bike loans).

Château de Cîteaux, built in the 19th century on cellars of the 12th century and dug by the Cistercian monks, has became a unique resort hotel in Burgundy since 2012. Located in the heart of one of the most famous vineyards in the world, with stunning views of the village of Meursault, the hotel has 19 rooms. Beautifully decorated, they are very comfortable and well equipped, some have even a private terrace ! Château de Cîteaux has an indoor pool, hammam, sauna, whirlpool and many rooms for individual treatments. The particularity of this establishment that brilliantly blends chic and well-being ? The fruititherapy ! Here, fruits take care of you and your body. A unique place in Côte-d'Or, created by Jean Garnier, specialist in beauty and well-being with tea room, relaxation room, fitness room... And to complete this idyllic picture, a gourmet restaurant, several private rooms for business meetings and Cistercian cellars for exclusive tastings are available. The ideal place for an unforgettable stay.

Leisure

■ LA CUEILLETTE – SPA DE FRUITITHÉRAPIE
Château de Cîteaux
18, rue de Cîteaux ✆ +33 (0)3 80 20 62 80
www.lacueillette.com – spa@lacueillette.com

Spa de France label. For residents : open every day from 7.30am to 10pm. For visitors : from 7.30am to 8pm. Schedule of treatments : from Monday to Thursday from 9am to 6pm; on Friday from 10am to 7pm; on Saturday from 9am to 7pm; on Sunday from 10am to 4pm, Access to heated swimming pool, sundeck, whirlpool, hammam, sauna, relaxation room, tisanery and hot soft drinks. Treatments from €47. Fruitithérapie Cosmetics sale online.

In La Cueillette, the concept goes even further than Winetherapy, since it is from all the red fruits of Burgundy (blackcurrant, blackberry, grape, cherry, strawberry, raspberry), known for their powerful antioxidant properties that the treatment and the cosmetic product line are developed. This centre of Fruitherapy of 500 m^2 was created by Jean and Corinne Garnier, specialists in beauty and well-being. The establishment has the best facilities : rooms are well equipped, indoor swimming pool, hammam, sauna, whirlpool. A team of masseuses and beauticians welcome you to give you face and body treatments. Here we go for moments of extreme well-being ! Masks of fruits pulp, exfoliation to granita sweetness with raspberry and cassis, massage in the oil of grape seeds under a fine rain, modeling with tonic lotion and draining with cassis and red vineyard... The choice is wide ! The palace and its gourmet restaurant complete with refinement these programs of treatments. You can also order by Internet as cosmetic peeling mask with pink clay, red vine, black currant and cherry or hand cream with vine flower. Unrivalled fitness center and quality products to discover.

Shopping

■ CHÂTEAU DE MEURSAULT
Rue du Moulin-Foulot
✆ +33 (0)3 80 26 22 75
www.chateau-meursault.com
tourisme@chateau-meursault.com

Low season : open every day from 10am to 12pm and from 2pm to 6.30pm. High season : every day from 10am to 6.30pm. Low season from October to April. Closed in January and during the year's end celebrations. In February, shop open on weekdays – visit Saturday in day and Sunday until 1pm. Parking in the courtyard of the castle. Visit of cellars and tasting of the wines of the estate de19 € at €35, for groups €16. Organization of events : cocktail, dinner of gala, fixed rate formula déjeunatoire, day of business, general meeting. . . .

Château de Meursault and its origins date back to the 11th century. The successive owners were numerous. The latest is Olivier Halley who bought the operating company of the castle in 2012. The vineyard of 60 hectares whose 23 hectares in Grand and Premier Cru produces approximately 500,000 bottles each year ! With more than 20,000 visitors per year, Château de Meursault is always more popular among the wine connoisseurs. The tourist offer was reorganized in the summer 2015. The guided tours leave every 30 minutes in high season and every hour in low season. Comments and explanations are in French and English if needs to be. The experts can have more technical comments according to the request. The course starts with the historic cellars of the Castle. You can discover thousands of bottles and barrels of oak trees there. The visit ends with a tasting in the art gallery, favourable to a wine tour. Good to know, the Halley family also bought Château de Marsannay and the Marché aux Vins in Beaune. On the whole, these three sites focus on the research of excellence of their wines. Moreover, many investments are implemented in the fermenting rooms, optical sorting of the barks, use of oak barrels over 3 years maximum... As for the grape harvest, it remains manual in the frame of a reasoned culture. Know that Château de Meursault is also the place where to organize seminars, diner cocktails, dinners and lunch of groups. A room of 350 m^2 is at your disposal. It is simply an exceptional site.

In the surroundings

Auxey-Duresses

LA CRÉMAILLÈRE
Route de Beaune © +33 (0)3 80 21 64 48
sarlphbs.lacremaillere@sfr.fr
Closed 15 days in February. Open Thursday to Tuesday for lunch; Thursday to Monday for dinner. Menu from €22 to €44.50 (+ à la carte). Children's menu : €10. Lunch menu : €13.50 (3 main courses). Groups welcome. Terrace.
La Crémaillère, located in the middle of Auxey, continues its metamorphosis. After the large window bays of the facade and a more modern decoration of the tables, this year, it is the entrance which was revamped. Thus, we are accommodated in a clearer and refreshed space. The house remains in a very authentic spirit with ceilings made of exposed beams and its stone walls. Philippe Santailler, manager and chef is attentive to work out a cuisine of good quality, he ensures to use mainly local, raw and fresh products in order to compose the homemade recipes. In La Crémaillière, you taste a local cuisine, influenced by Burgundian culture : eggs in meurette way, snails, ham with parsley, homemade terrine, toasts of époisses... A reasonable and delicious choice of fish dishes and meats : prawns, fillet of monkfish, Bourguignon beef 100% Charolais, cockerel sauce with aligoté... As for the wines, the chef recommends us the best wines of Auxey, enough to make interesting discoveries ! Easy to locate, La Crémaillère is in the main street and to park your car, do not panic, you find places in the adjacent streets. Special mention for the very pleasant terrace in summer and the inescapable stroll to make in the village.

Merceuil

EMMANUELLE BAILLARD – NECTARS DE BOURGOGNE
Hameau de Cissey
1, impasse des Gillées © +33 (0)3 80 21 42 56
www.nectars-bourgogne.com
e.baillard@nectars-bourgogne.com
Products sold in delicatessens and on the online store.
Do you want to enjoy a fruit flavour ? Think of the products of Emmanuelle Baillard ! Coulis, fruit juice, jams and jellies, syrups... Blackcurrant, raspberry, mango, vine peach, mirabelle, guava, tomatoes... Whether they are from here or elsewhere, they are from France, Emmanuelle selects them himself; he does not hesitate to travel to the other side of the world. Three fruit nectars come from organic agriculture : the blackcurrant nectar, the apricot and the mirabelle one. He made two exquisite products for the Bernard Loiseau group : the nectar of Morello cherry and blackcurrant buds, the nectar of Lorraine mirabelle and grapefruit. This year, the range has extended with a salted butter caramel and blackcurrant of Burgundy. In sweets or spreads... A delight. In salted side dish, find vinegars with fruit pulp, confits, spices like the pepper with cassis, made from blackcurrant buds harvested in February. A noble product, with vegetable and fruity flavour. Our favourite ? The confit with mango of Reunion and the shallot of Brittany. An exeptional . Guess who won the innovation coup de cœur prize at the 2014 MIAM competition ? Emmanuelle Baillard with its 10 Cassis, a Sparkling of natural Blackcurrant of Burgundy, without additive nor preservatives and alcohol-free.

Saint-Romain

DOMAINE HENRI ET GILLES BUISSON
Impasse du Clou © +33 (0)3 80 21 22 22
www.domaine-buisson.com
contact@domaine-buisson.com
Open Monday to Saturday from 9am to 12pm and from 2pm to 5pm. Preferably, telephone before coming. Tasting and sale. Reception of groups on reservation up to 40 people.
Eight generations have already followed one another in this estate which, since 1947, began to bottle its wine and opened its cellar to tasting and direct sales. Today, the Domaine Henri et Gilles Buisson culvates 19.5 acres of vineyards spread in Meursault, Pommard, Corton, Volnay and Saint-Romain. Since it was taken over by Franck and Frédérick, the estate received label AB (Organic farming) from the Millésime 2012. The heritage of the house's tradition, the benefit of the values of respect for nature combined with their new skills in international trade and oenology produce good-quality results ! The welcome at the cellar of the estate is very comfortable. You will discover there appellations like Village, Premiers Crus and Grands Crus, in white and red. Special mention for their Corton grand cru, « Les Renardes ». The Saint-Romain, in red or white, are sold at unbeatable quality/price ratios. The white « Sous la Velle » with a buttered effect is really pleasant. New, the Saint Romain « Absolu », that can be described as natural, because after the organic farming, they are vinified without added sulphur. Profit from your visit to stroll around the village, a change of scenery guaranteed !

Buffon

Georges-Louis Leclerc, count of Buffon, is a major figure of the scientific thought of the Enlightenment. Born on September 7th, 1707 in Montbard, he shared his time between his hometown and Paris, and his presence still marks Montbard, also often known as the « city of Buffon. » He was a naturalist, a member of the Academy of Sciences and the French Academy, Intendant of the King's Garden for nearly 50 years, large landowner and ironmaster, architect and builder ... He greatly expanded what would become the Jardin des Plantes in Paris, and enriched the collections of the Royal Collection, which give rise to the Museum of Natural History. He is also the closer collaborator montbardois, Daubenton, who took over the management in 1793. Leading to front all these activities, Buffon has traveled extensively and deployed talent and extraordinary energy. He had an ambitious project to paint the entire nature and explain both the birth of the Earth and life which developed there. He is famous for his major work, General Natural History, and particularly with the description of the Cabinet du Roy, in 36 volumes, published from 1749 to 1789. Often opposed to the general ideas of his time, Buffon was an agitator of ideas who raised fundamental issues and open new paths in many scientific disciplines. He died in Paris on April 16th, 1788.

MONTBARD ★★

OFFICE DE TOURISME DE MONTBARD ET DU MONTBARDOIS
Place Henri-Vincenot
✆ +33 (0)3 80 92 53 81 – www.ot-montbard.fr
contact@ot-montbard.fr

♿

Low season : open Monday to Saturday from 9am to 1pm and from 2pm to 5.30pm. High season : Monday to Saturday from 9am to 1pm and from 2pm to 6.30pm. Low season : from November to March. July-August, also open Sunday and public holidays from 10am to 1pm and from 2pm to 5.30pm. Wifi. Tourism label & Disability.

Opposite the station, the Tourist Office makes every effort to make your trip easier on the territory. Take the véloroute and marked 800 kilometres road in Burgundy, the team offers an efficient and professional system bike rental for a day or more, especially with the service Bike'n'Drop that allows you to rent a bicycle, to go for a ride along the Burgundy Canal, and to return it at another Tourist Office, partner of the service. More information on www.velibourgogne.fr. Do not miss the shop space where regional produce is sold. The access to the wi-fi makes it possible to download the mobile application « Montbard sur les pas de Buffon » realized jointly by the town of Montbard, the museums, Côte d'Or Tourism and the Tourist Office of Montbardois. This application transforms your smartphone into audioguide and leads you through the city in a ludic way.

Sightseeing

ABBAYE DE FONTENAY ★★★★
D32 ✆ +33 (0)3 80 92 15 00

See page 9.

ÉGLISE SAINT-URSE ET CAVEAU DE LA FAMILLE BUFFON
Parc Buffon
Rue du Parc Buffon
✆ +33 (0)3 80 92 50 42 / +33 (0)3 80 92 50 57
musee-site-buffon@montbard.com

On guided tour only from April to September (guided tours with schedule fixes the week or by reservation). Reception Tour Saint-Louis. Free admission.

The church is located in the first wall of the castle and has preserved an architectural traces of the 11th century. It became a parish church at the beginning of the 13th century. Several paintings are classified Historical Monuments : An *Adoration of the Shepherds* of Ménassier's painting (1599), *a Presentation of the Blessed Mary Virgin* at the temple of the Charton brothers (1642); an altarpiece of the 18th century, an organ of the 19th century or contemporary fresco of the artist Montbardois Ernest Boguet are to discover. In the adjoining chapel, visitors can admire the vault of the family Buffon. Georges-Louis Leclerc, count of Buffon was buried here on 20th April 1788, joining his wife and his first daughter.

© TOM PEPEIRA – ICONOTEC

Abbey of Fontenay- Marmagne.

© ITZAK NEWMANN – ICONOTEC

Abbey of Fontenay- Marmagne.

© CLAUDE NISSENS – FOTOLIA

View of the Abbey of Fontenay.

HÔTEL DE VILLE

Place Jacques-Garcia
✆ +33 (0)3 80 92 01 34
www.montbard.com

Opened Monday of 8 : 30 to 12 : 00; Tuesday, Wednesday and Friday of 8 : 30 to 12 : 00 and 14 : 00 to 17 : 00; Thursday of 8 : 30 to 12 : 00 and 14 : 00 to 18 : 00; saturdays of 9 : 00 to 12 : 00.

The town of Montbard has automated systems of a great rarity called « Jacquemard » in the campanile of the town hall. Built with wood in the 18th century, Jacquemard and Jacquette were joined by a third character, Jacquot, in the middle of the 19th century whose origin is presented in the Salon d'honneur of the town hall.

MUSÉE-SITE BUFFON ★

Rue du Parc-Buffon
✆ +33 (0)3 80 92 50 42
✆ +33 (0)3 80 92 50 57
www.montbard.com
musee-site-buffon@montbard.com

Annual closing included from December 21st to January 1st. Admissions and free guided tours on the whole of the Site.Buffon museum : open from October 1st to December 21st, Wednesday to Friday from 2pm to 5pm, Saturday and Sunday from 10am to 12pm and from 2pm to 6pm.Buffon park and its monuments : guided tours of the monuments (Tour Saint-Louis, Tour of Aubespin, Study, Saint-Urse Church) and of Parc Buffon : Wednesday to Sunday at 11am, 2.30pm, 3.30pm and 4.30pm. Departure of the guided tours in front of the Tower Saint-Louis.

Musée Buffon. Labeled Musée de France and « Maison des Illustres », the Buffon museum presents a collection thoroughly selected to evoke the evolution of the scientific thought of the 17th to the 19th century, cabinets of curiosities at the Museum of Natural History. Microscopes, armillary spheres, herbaria... blends with more intimate objects (portraits, first editions) of two personalities who influenced sciences at the 18th century : Georges-Louis Leclerc, Count of Buffon (1707-1788) and Louis Jean-Marie Daubenton (1716-1800), both natives of the town of Montbard. Their name is linked to the editorial adventure of *L'Histoire Naturelle générale et particulière* in 36 volumes. Two rooms of temporary exhibitions offer, in conjunction with the museum's collections, a discovery of the artistic and scientific heritage of the two famous naturalists and introduce the visit of Parc Buffon. Many events, conferences, visits or workshops are scheduled throughout the year between art and science. Inescapable.

Parc Buffon. Designed by Buffon as of 1734 on the site of a former castle of the Dukes of Burgundy, this garden classified as a historical monument in 1947 and its fourteen terraces offer a remarkable view of Montbard and the Brenne valley. You will find the Saint-Louis and Aubespin towers, the study of Buffon, the Saint-Urse church.

Chapelle des Ursulines and museum of Fine arts. Located in the neo-Gothic former chapel of the Institution des Ursulines (1870), the fine arts museum offers temporary exhibitions in connection with the history of Montbard and its artistic life.

TOUR DE L'AUBESPIN ET TOUR SAINT-LOUIS

Parc Buffon ✆ +33 (0)3 80 92 50 42 / +33 (0)3 80 92 50 57
musee-site-buffon@montbard.com

On guided tour only from April to September (guided tours with schedule fixes the week or by reservation). Reception Tour Saint-Louis. Free admission.

The tower of Aubespin is the most important vestige of the dukes of Burgundy castle preserved by Buffon during the arrangement of his park in the 18th century. It is located at the northern tip of the site overlooking an area of about 40 metres away. If you find this appellation « tour de l'Aubespin » in an archive document by 1354, its construction is probably carried out around 1300 during the reconstruction of the whole fortress by the dukes of Burgundy. The tower of Aubespin was both an important element in the fortress defence system and an element of prestige for the dukes of Burgundy. Restored by the architect Viollet-le-Duc at the end of the 19th century, it is one of the first protected monuments in France (1862). The Saint-Louis tower, probably revamped by Buffon in the 18th century, used as summer study and library to the naturalist. It is nowadays the place of reception and starting point of the guided tours of the site.

Knife & Fork

LE CALYPSO

2, place Aline-Gibez ✆ +33 (0)3 80 92 05 30
www.calypso-montbard.fr

Closed the week of Christmas. Open from Tuesday to Saturday for lunch and dinner. Children's menu : €7.90 (+ à la carte). Take-away pizzas. Baby chairs. Terrace.

Chrystelle and Anthony Maratray are the happy owners of this successful pizzeria. A reputation that is obtained thanks to the house's likeability and the quality of the dish. The great 2016 novelty is the installation of a splendid veranda on the main terrace. This new space brings a total revival to Calypso. Viewed from outside, the architecture becomes remarkable and unmissable. The veranda with anthracite door frames is very successful. Inside this room, hot tons of brown camaieux, high and low wood tables, velvet armchairs and benches, design chandeliers, to the old-fashioned glasses. Awesome ! ! We like this cosy atmosphere which makes you want to extend the moment. The à la carte menu quickly makes us salivate with about thirty pizzas cooked on wood fire. There are always other suggestions like salads, fish and grilled meats, always seasonal and homemade. The dishes are well furnished and full with flavours. We never regret to pass here. Le Calypso is appropriate for families, business meals, buddies... Here, everyone smiles and they always accommodate you in a pleasant way. Note that a parking, which is just next to the house, allows you to park easily.

Sleeping

HÔTEL DE L'ÉCU

7, rue Auguste-Carré ✆ +33 (0)3 80 92 11 66
www.hotelecu-montbard.fr
Snc.Coupat@wanadoo.fr

♿

Logis (2 fireplaces). Open all year round. 29 rooms. From € 80 to € 115. Half-board (from € 85 to € 105). Breakfast : € 12.50. Stopover : € 89. Free wi-fi. Catering (3 cocottes; menus from € 24).

The Hotel-Restaurant L'Écu, a former relay inn of the 17th century, is a genuine traditional family house that blends the charm of hospitality with gastronomy. The Coupat family has run it since 1952, Gérard and Isabelle are the fourth generation and warmly welcome you in these recently refurbished rooms. Antique furniture mingled with a modern style, new tapestries, a comfortable bedding, armchairs and sofas... Everything is implemented to allow you to be installed comfortably. The double-glazed window ensures you a peaceful a stay. A free wi-fi access and flat screen TV come to complete the comfort of the hotel. For the bikers, it is one of the ideal departure points to discover Burgundy. In the kitchen, Gérard concocts tasty dishes.

Shopping

TENTATION

13, rue Edmé-Piot ✆ +33 (0)3 80 92 23 72
marieclaude.seraphin@free.fr

Open Tuesday to Saturday 9.15am at 12 : 20 and of 2.45pm at 19 : 20.

Tentation, a temptation of delicacy, is a confectionary and delicacy shop that you absolutely need to know. Marie-Claude Séraphin maintains with passion a gourmet and colourful fairyland that changes according the festive calendar. The magic operates as soon as you are in front of the shop window, like a child, animated by the Advent, Christmas and Easter or the Christening season. Once inside, there is a good scent of calisson and chocolate. Marie-Claude Seraphin, who has over 45 years of experience in the bakery and confectionery, renews her shop of sweet treats, chocolates, candies and often unrivalled sweet with a boundless passion. Above all, let yourself be guided by her advice, she only knows the history and secrets surrounding its endless number of delights. She selects them from the best artisans and offers chocolates that combine tradition and quality. For tea lovers, Tentation offers a choice of 210 varieties of teas and herbal teas, regulars would notice the new tone of the tea box colour ! You are always received with warm, after the dream, the choice; there is something for all tastes and prices, to be tempted and to offer as beautiful gifts.

Markets

MARCHÉ

Place Gambetta
www.hallesdemontbard.fr

from 8 : 00 to 12 : 30 (from April 1st to October 15th). from 8 : 30 to 12 : 30 (from October to March 31st).

Halles de Montbard were completely renovated in 2015. The food market, which is held every Friday mornings of the year, is now in a very bright new atmosphere. About 80 exhibitors are awaiting you. Cheeses, seasonal fruits and vegetables, organic products, charcuterie, special bread, meat and poultry in the area. The products are fresh and local. It is an ideal place to fill your basket with the flavours of the terroir, to meet the producers and farmers in the area and especially to come in the centre of Montbard !

NUITS-SAINT-GEORGES ★★

Nuits-Saint-Georges is the wine capital of Côte de Nuits. Located 21 km south of Dijon, accessible by the highway, by the RN74 or by the Route des Grands Crus, this oeno-touristic stopover is a must. It is said that the railway Company Paris-Lyon-Marseille wanted to rename the small town Nuits-sous-Beaune. It goes without saying that the population as a whole rejected this proposal and would prefer in 1892, to add the word « Saint-Georges » to Nuits, the name of the most famous cru of the surrounding. This reputation, Nuits also owes it to a certain Mister Fagon, Louis XIV's physician, who imposed the famous wine at the royal table. So, this was how all the court began to drink the wines of the region... a great bargain ! Nuits-Saint-Georges also has its Hospices, where an annual charity auction is organized and more...

OFFICE DE TOURISME DU PAYS DE NUITS-SAINT-GEORGES

3, rue Sonoys
✆ +33 (0)3 80 62 11 17
www.ot-nuits-st-georges.fr
info@ot-nuits-st-georges.fr

Low season : opened Monday to Saturday of 9 : 30 to 12 : 30 and 14 : 30 to 17 : 30. High season : Monday to Saturday of 9 : 30 to 12 : 30 and 14 : 30 to 18 : 30; Sunday of 10 : 30 to 13 : 00. Electric rates mountain bike rental : 1 : 10 € in rate discovered of the Monday to Saturday; 1/2 day €15, day €25, Weekend €45. On booking.

Located in city center, Office du Tourisme du Pays de Nuits-Saint-Georges is easily accessible with its many car park nearby. If you wish to initiate yourselves with the tasting of the wines, the Office welcomes you at the vault of the downtown where professional oenologist initiates you with the Burgundian terroir and the work of the vineyard before you spend the afternoon on the estate of a wine grower. Office de Tourisme de Nuits-Saint Georges can organize tourist tour and stay on request. The pass Dijon-Côte de Nuits enables you to discover the local treasures with the season of your desires. You can also rent electric mountain bike of an autonomy ranging from 60 to 120 km to discover the local heritage differently ! For an overview of what the territory has to offer to you, go on the digital application « *Vacances en Pays de Nuits-Saint-Georges* » available on smartphones and shelves. The application *Bourgogne rando vigne* enables you to discover the Burgundian vineyard Climate from the hiking trails. In summer, discover *« Dégust' ivales »*, a programme of the open cellars which is awaiting you each day with a privileged welcome. And for those who do not want to leave empty-handed, the shop of the Tourist Office offers a wide choice of articles about the territory : books, wine articles, « regional » beauty products or gastronomy...

Sightseeing

LE CASSISSIUM ★★

8, Montgolfier passage
✆ +33 (0)3 80 62 49 70 – www.cassissium.com
cassissium@cassissium.com

Open all year. Low season : Tuesday to Friday from 10.30am to 1pm and from 2.30pm to 5.30pm (last visit at 3.45pm); Saturday from 10.30am to 1pm and from 2.30pm to 6pm (last visit at 4.15pm). High season : every day from 10am to 1pm and from 2pm to 7pm (last visit at 5.15pm). High season from April 1st to November 16th. In low season, closing at 6pm during school holidays. Free for under 12-year-olds. Adult : €8.50. Group (10 people) : €7.50. Pupils and students : €6.50. Raised College/High school/ Student : €6. Primary education : €5. Tourism label & Disability. Guided tour (the last departure of visit 1.45am before closing. Tasting offered). Shop. Audioguide available in 6 languages.

A playful and friendly opportunity to discover the universe of blackcurrant while having fun. This museum reveals you its secrets and multiple possible uses, in the kitchen, pharmacy or perfumery. New tactile, visual, olfactory activities and obviously tasting come to complement your visit. You will discover the stages of production of the Védrenne blackcurrant liquor. When tasting, you will also tickle your taste buds with fruit creams made here, liquors and of course syrups. New flavors come out every year. You can find on the website and social networks nice topics, « fitness and health » secrets, recipes... This is one of the most beautiful touristic places in the region, that you can pleasantly visit with your friends or recommend to tourists. It is a discovery that will delight all generations !

L'IMAGINARIUM ★★

Avenue du Jura ✆ +33 (0)3 80 62 61 40
www.imaginarium-bourgogne.com
info@imaginarium-bourgogne.com

Open all year. Closed on December 25th and on January 1st. Monday from 2pm to 7pm (last visit at 5pm); Tuesday to Sunday and public holidays from 10am to 7pm (last visit at 5pm). Free for under 12-year-olds. Adult : €9 (€17 for tasting Prestige). Child (from 12 to 17 years old) : €6. Group (10 people) : €8. Students : €6. Tourism label & Disability. Guided tour. Shop.

L'imaginarium provides an entertaining wine stage and we prove them right for that. This modern and well-thought site invites you to understand the mysteries of the vineyards and to discover the secret of a thousand-year-old know-how. Adults as children will find their happiness thanks to an original visit designed for the individual as for the groups. The visit begins with a sounds-and-light show, *Sacrée Vigne*, which tells the story of the vine cultivation through the centuries. Voices with Burgundian accent, screens and tools come forward to explain the work of the vine growers, the vinification, cooperage... Surprises are awaiting for you in each room ! An interactive and ludic course, *La Magie des bulles*, which takes you along in the universe of the sparkling wines including the famous Crémant de Bourgogne. You will know everything about the various methods of development and the origin of the bubbles... Do not miss the wall by the flavours and the workshop of moving ! Very realistic scale models also enable you to retrace the various stages of manufacturing of the wine. The visit ends with a wine and Crémant de Bourgogne tasting (or fruit juice for the children). If you choose tasting *Prestige*, you can make your choice between the first 12 Grand Crus (4 white and 8 red). Before leaving, it is indispensable to pass to the Wine bar : the shop offers a wide selection of fine wine as well as many accessories and gift ideas. Note that L'Imaginarium accommodates the groups with custom-tailored services and rates. Do not hesitate to find out more information !

Knife & Fork

CAVEAU SAINT-UGUZON

3, rue du Grenier à Sel ✆ +33 (0)3 80 61 39 87
www.restaurant-saintuguzon.com
caveausaintuguzon@wanadoo.fr

Open all year. In winter : open Friday for dinner and Saturday for dinner like daily for lunch except Monday. In summer : open every day except Sunday for dinner and Monday. Booking advised. Menu from €15.40 to €25.90. À la carte : Around €15. Children's menu : €10 (with drink). Lunch menu : €13 (daily special + plate 3 cheeses or dessert of the day + coffee). Wine by the glass. Uguzon fixed rate formula : €15. Fixed rate formula Grill : €20.10. American Express, Chèque Restaurant. Groups welcome (up to 50 people). Terrace. Take-away. Activities.

A funny name for a restaurant that is nestled in the heart of Nuits-Saint-Georges... Do you know who Uguzon was ? An Italian shepherd who was killed by his master because he was used to distributing cheese to the poor... He is celebrated as a martyr each year in Lombardy and is the patron saint of the cheese. Cheeses are then kings at the Saint-Uguzon Vault ! The owner Frédéric Vanot placed his suitcases in Nuits-Saint-Georges in 2002, after an exciting career : Hostellerie du Chapeau Rouge in Dijon, Château du Clos-Vougeot, but also Monaco, Saint-Tropez and Courchevel... He serves local cuisine, prepared with fresh ingredients, at very attractive prices. The decor, with hints of flea market, is nice and authentic. Poached eggs in red wine, snails, beef bourguignon or grilled meat, Saint-Uguzon salad (cheeses that we love : epoisses, cîteaux, blue...). The menu is simple and the dishes are very good. If you come here for lunch and, like us, you are a cheese fan, we advise you to take the Uguzon formula : for less than 15 euros, you are entitled to a cheese salad, a croustade with fleur de Nuits (a bread with local cheese), a dessert and a coffee. To make the pleasure lasts, regional products, organic and from local production, are on sale in the restaurant. To accompany your culinary discoveries, Frederic selected the best wines of surrounding estates that you can also take away. A friendly address, reasonable prices, a lovely welcome. A gourmet, Burgundy and cheese visit, just the way we like them !

In the heart of Nuits-Saint-Georges.

LA GENTILHOMMIERE – LE CHEF COQ
13, vallée de la Serrée ✆ +33 (0)3 80 61 12 06
www.lagentilhommiere.fr
contact@lagentilhommiere.fr

« Maître Restaurateur » label. Closed from December 23rd to January 25th. Open every day except Tuesday for dinner and Saturday for lunch. Menu from €31 to €59. À la carte : Around €65. Children's menu : €17. Lunch menu : €24.90 (5 starters and choice of main dishes and 3 desserts; on weekdays only). Hotel of 31 rooms with swimming pool. Groups welcome. Terrace.

La Gentilhommière is a long story in Nuits-Saint-Georges. René Pianetti, a passionate Master restaurateur, runs this fine residence located in the bottom of a valley and bordered by local river that will charm its guests. Chef Coq, is a popular address for lunch, more romantic in dinner. The cuisine is tasty, there are choices to enjoy near the swimming pool in summer, and in the winter in the hushed atmosphere of the room to the « contemporary terroir » decor. The menus « *Village* », « *Premier Cru* » and « *Grand Cru* » combine land and sea flavours, Burgundy and remote countries ones… Imagine. As starter an organic Irish salmon mid-cooked then grilled with a crunchy white cabbage. Then a chicken vigolette of Burgundy with trumpets and its tart with roasted artichokes and cream of Foie gras. The desserts are very elaborate, judge by yourself by indulging yourself with original Breton galette with its apple ribbon confit with cider embellished with toffee apple. The wine list is rich and varied, for the sake of the neighbouring Côte De Nuits ! The additional good idea ? The children's area on the first floor enabling parents to have lunch peacefully !

Sleeping

LA GENTILHOMMIERE – LE CHEF COQ
13, vallée de la Serrée ✆ +33 (0)3 80 61 12 06
www.lagentilhommiere.fr
contact@lagentilhommiere.fr

Closed from December 22nd to January 31st. 31 rooms (including 11 air-conditioned suites). Double room €115; suite from €200 to €250. Breakfast : €15 (€18 in room). Cot : €16. Stop-over with special rates on request. Fixed rate formulas stays and boxes gifts and possiility to rent an old car. Pets allowed (€10). Seminars. Receptions and weddings. Catering facilities (open every day except Tuesday evening and Saturday lunchtime. Menu from €31 to €59. Card. Children's menu : €17. Lunch menu, even public holidays : €24.90). Excursions (proposal for Oenopass fixed rate formulas).

In this renowned three star hotel of the nuitonne coast, you are staying in an exceptional setting. Located outside the city in nature in the small valley of Meuzin, Gentilhommière is a charming hotel and restaurant with 31 rooms where you can profit from a 13-hectare park, a swimming pool and a tennis court. All rooms are on the ground floor. There are, 11 suites each offering a thematic and original decoration (Indian, pop, Zen…) and also have a terrace. The other 20 rooms renovated between 2010 and 2012, offer a more sober and trendy decor with very cozy comfort, immersed in tranquility and in a greenery setting. A good point, the site is entirely accessible for disabled people. The address is also a gourmet restaurant, René Pianetti offers original cuisine, sometimes local and sometimes more exotic. The wine list is rich with wines of the Côte de Nuits and an Oenopass formula is proposed to discover and visit several key areas of the Coast. Lovers of Nature, comfort and wine tourism, you will leave there fully satisfied !

HOSTELLERIE SAINT-VINCENT – RESTAURANT L'ALAMBIC
23, rue du Général-De-Gaulle
✆ +33 (0)3 80 61 14 91 – www.lalambic.com
info@hostellerie-st-vincent.com

Logis (3 cheminées). Qualité Tourisme label. Closed from December 18th to December 26th. Closed on Sunday evening in low season of November 15th until April. Reception until 10pm. 23 rooms (3 cheminées home). Single room from €90 to €125; double room from €97 to €140; triple room from €122 to €153; suite from €134 to €163. Half-board (as from 3 nights). Buffet breakfast : €11 (€8 for children under 12 years old). Open parking. Stop-over with special rates from €95. Regular promotional offers. Holiday voucher. 2 rooms are arranged for the disabled guests. Pets allowed (€11). Seminars. Wifi. Catering facilities (L'Alambic restaurant. Gourmet menu at €58. Fixed rate formulas of 17€ with 23,50€ at lunchtime). Sale (wines and local produce). Canal+.

L'Hostellerie Saint-Vincent is continueing to move upmarket, living up to its reputation of comfort. The hostelry passed to higher level. The atmosphere of the reception changed and displays now a beautiful contrast between the dark walls decorated of the shapes of bottles and light wood panelling or red and vanilla furniture. Today, all the rooms are renovated and own new bathrooms. The new rooms are very contemporary and are equipped with a minibar, a safe and a TV LCD. They are not standardized and that's good ! All have a particular charm that will seduce you. The selected colors are soft and the quality materials provide the hotel a top-of-the-range, simple and cordial atmosphere at the same time. The rooms are oriented towards the calmest side of the building for a stay in complete peace. These changes are accompanied by a new graphic charter. The logos in Raspberry and gray tons translates the dynamism of the establishment, just as the new website that proposes beautiful photographs of the hotel and which offers the possibility of booking online ! Do not leave the places without making a gourmet getaway at the restaurant of the hotel, L'Alambic, which promises you delicious moments of gastronomy in its splendid vault.

Cottages

GÎTES DU BEFFROI
1, rue du Grenier-à-Sel ✆ +33 (0)6 13 52 50 97
gitesdubeffroi@orange.fr

Gîte de France. From €400 to €500 per week depending on season. 4 cottages for 4 people – provided linen, cleaning included. Wifi. Dishwasher. Satellite TV.

Les Gîtes du Beffroi has four apartments ideally located in the downtown of Nuits-Saint-Georges. They are recently accommodated in in a historic residence opposite the famous belfry. Each gite can accommodate comfortably four people. Everything is new, you have a kitchen equipped with a dishwasher and a high-quality bedding. The surface area that ranges from 30 to 45 m^2 offers an other advantage and it must be said that it make you feel at ease, the largest one have an independent room. The simple and modern decoration is enhanced with Nuits-Saint-Georges photographs and the essential Côte de Nuits card that is practical to check the programmed itineraries of the stay. The access to the rooms is from a small inner courtyard and a very fine stone staircase. As soos as your base camp is established, you are halfway between Dijon and Beaune, in the middle of most beautiful names of the Climates of Burgundy and at the bottom of Hautes Côtes. You can reach numerous restaurants of Nuitons without the need to take your car. The rooms bear the soft names of 1st cru of Nuits-Saint-Georges, Clos des Corvées Paget, Les Cailles or Les Vaucrains... Good omens for the success of your stay which will be very likely œnotouristic !

Shopping

L'OR DES VALOIS – TRUFFES DE BOURGOGNE

Château d'Entre-Deux-Monts
Hameau de Concoeur et Corboin
✆ +33 (0)3 80 33 38 21
✆ +33 (0)6 23 13 09 46
www.truffedebourgogne.fr
info@truffedebourgogne.fr

High season : open from Thursday to Tuesday from 10am to 6pm. From February to March and from November to December : every day except Tuesdays and Wednesdays from 10am to 5pm. From April to May and from September to October : open every day except Tuesdays and Wednesdays from 10am to 6pm. Closed in January and February – High season from June to August. Discovery of digging for truffles from €10 per person, tasting of products stuffed with truffles from €12 per person, lunch "Tout Truffe" from €35 per person by reservation. Vignobles & Découvertes label – Member of the association Vives La Bourgogne.

L'Or des Valois is the black gold of Burgundy, the truffle of Burgundy called Tuber Uncinatum. Thierry Bezeux created in 2008 in the outbuildings of Château d'Entre-deux-Monts, his grower-merchant activity of truffles of Burgundy. His shop is full of truffle products, mostly prepared by local craftsmen. For example, there is the Ratatruffe (Ratafia with truffles !), the mustard and truffle, developed in partnership with Moutarderie Fallot (last traditional mustard factory of Burgundy), or even the Truffillé (a ham of Burgundy in Truffe de Bourgogne way). You can visit the truffle farm with digging demonstration but especially taste the truffle-based products. It is also possible to reserve a truffle meal for up to 20 people. On the menu : aperitif, charcuterie, meat and its sauce, fresh truffle cheese and finally ice-cream with truffle and coffee. The store also allows you to buy beautiful truffle-based products. Enjoy the stroll to admire the beauty of the Hautes Côtes de Nuits' landscapes. And if you pass through Dijon, discover Boutique de la Truffe, the second site that Thierry Bezeux devoted to Or des Valois.

LA MAISON DES VIGNERONS DE L'APPELLATION NUITS-SAINT-GEORGES

ZA Les Prés de Nuits
Rue Charles Arnault
✆ +33 (0)3 80 62 18 77
www.nuitsaugrandjour.com
contact@nuitsaugrandjour.com
♿

Open Monday to Friday from 9am to 12pm and from 2pm to 6pm. "Les Nuits au Grand Jour" Saturday 19 and Sunday March 20th, 2016, from 10am to 5.30pm : entrance €12 (with a drink).

The concept of Maison des Vignerons de Nuits-Saint-Georges is simple : to bring together in one place the best wine growers of the commune of Nuits and Prémeaux-Prissey. The wines that are available here are of quality and they are at unbeatable prices since they are the same as the ones of the growers ! 38 owners are brought together in that day and we wish them a resounding success ! Visit their website to discover the estates concerned, it would be too long to name them and we would not like to show favouritism ! The wine trade union also developed a line of clothing flocked with its effigy like a range of glassmaking. It takes part every year in the sale of the wines and tasting organized under the food markets of Nuits-Saint-Georges : « Les Nuits au Grand Jour ». Les Nuits au Grand Jour 2016 (8th edition) will be hold on the 19th Saturday and 20th Sunday of March, 2016, from 10 : 00 to 17 : 30. Naturally, he will also be the organizer of « Chemin Gourmand de Nuits-Saint-Georges » : a stroll of 7 km that will take place on Sunday 12 June 2016. Novelty : a shipping service was launched after the strong demand of the guests (the cost of success !). For your orders, you can contact Maison des Vignerons whether by e-mail : s.v.nuits-premeaux@wanadoo.fr or Tel/Fax or by postal dispatch (on the above-mentionned address).

SAVEURS DE BOURGOGNE

Rue Lavoisier
www.saveursdebourgogne.fr

Saveurs de Bourgogne is a shop of modern times, you will not find it in downtown but on the Internet. However, the quality and originality are there. You will find typically Burgundian products, of excellent and authentic quality because the site's team gets their supplies directly from the producers. A good idea which reduces the number of intermediaries, and therefore the final cost of the product. It is an opportunity to taste natural and local products for a reasonable price and exceptional quality. Meat, biscuits, candies, jams, honey, spices, mustard, oils, condiments, snails, flours, juices, alcohol... In short, you will find everything ! The smartest are fond of the dry ham of Morvan and Edmond Fallot mustard. But it is just a detail among all the choice you can have on the website.

In the surroundings

Argilly

LA MAISON DU PARC
31, Voie Romaine
✆ +33 (0)3 80 23 22 93 / +33 (0)6 82 84 84 95
lamaisonduparc21@gmail.com

Gîte de France (3 épis). 150 m², 4 rooms. From €945 to €1,500 per week depending on season. From 8 to 11 people. €500 2 nights. €650 3 nights. €800 4 nights. Catering facilities (barbecue. Table d'hôte on reservation : €25/person, €15/child from 6 to 12 years old). Sauna. Games for the children. Terrace. Outdoor lounges.

Julie and Philippe welcome you in the old outbuildings of an 18th century of the house arranged in guesthouses and lodge. The rooms are spacious and comfortable with shower or bathtub. The decor is contemporary, semi-Baroque, semi-contemporary and the exposed stones were preserved. The equipment that are awaiting you here is very comfortable : sauna, heated pool, games for children, large terrace and 2-hectare wooded park including an orchard ! A very peaceful setting for a very pretty decor ! Upon reservation, Julie (and Philippe !) prepare a Burgundian meal with gougère, rosé cremant, poached eggs and bourguignon beef. You can also choose to prepare your meals in well-appointed kitchen.

Curtil-Vergy

HÔTEL LE MANASSES
Rue Guillaume-de-Tavanes
✆ +33 (0)3 80 61 43 81 – www.hotelmanasses.com
yves.chaley@aliceadsl.fr

12 rooms. From €83 to €108. Breakfast : €14. Extra bed : €8. Closed parking. Tastings and visits offered. Wifi.

Welcome to the Hôtel le Manasses located in the heart of Hautes Côtes de Nuits. The owners, Yves, Francoise and Cécile Chaley are also owners of the vineyard of Domaine du Val de Vergy, a family estate since 4 generations. The hotel is located on the hillside and offers an exceptional view of the Meuzin valley and the domain forest of Mantuan which are more than 500 hectares. The hotel has 12 air-conditioned bedrooms, each with its own character in a classic style with marble bathroom. The Chaley family, with a sense of welcome, invites you to share its passion for wine grower. Yves Chaley tells the story of his village and his abbey in restoration. He also invites you to discover his wines, red and white Bourgogne Hautes Côtes de Nuits, Chardonnay grape varieties, Pinot Gris and Pinot Black around a table in the museum of the field. The tasting is always accompanied by a specialty mâchon, parsley ham, homemade terrine and cheese of the region. You can also discover the observatory of the family property of Forges, a path of 2.3 km crossing a grove of old fruit trees. You may also enjoy a stroll in « jalopy « aboard a Citroen B2 of 1923 .

Marey-les-Fussey

MAISON AUX MILLE TRUFFES ET CHAMPIGNONS ★
Route de Villers
✆ +33 (0)3 80 30 08 91
www.mille-truffes-champignons.com
contact@mille-truffes-champignons.com

Low season : open Monday to Friday from 1pm to 6pm; the weekend from 10am to 6pm. High season : every day from 10am to 7pm. High season from mid-April to mid-October. Free for under 7-year-olds. Adult : €8. Child (from 7 to 18 years old) : €5. Group (8 people) : €7. Pupils : €4 - fresh Shop produced truffle and truffles in season. Guided tour. Activities. France Passion reception.

Maison de Mille Truffes et Champignons is the ideal place for a leisurely family discovery. This is a unique place dedicated to lovers of nature and gastronomy located in the heart of the Hautes Cotes de Nuits. The Visit is both educational and fun through the house (with wood frame), the showroom before the opening onto the wooded park of 1.5 ha which traces the mushrooms season. On the educational path, adults find many well-documented panels delivering the secrets of mycology while humanized elves and trees watch over carved mushrooms on a x10 scale. Children must solve a puzzle in this magical, fun and educational space, meanwhile parents, must answer a quiz. You also go through a maze explaining the 5 modes of planting truffle species. During the truffle season, there are demonstrations of cavage (search for truffles with dogs) and tasting of truffle products. During the off season, you can find morels, mushrooms, chanterelles, porcini or trumpets available in our store that sells many truffle products.

Saint-Nicolas-les-Cîteaux

ABBAYE DE CÎTEAUX ★★
D 996 ✆ +33 (0)3 80 61 32 58
www.citeaux-abbaye.com
visites@citeaux-abbaye.com

Closed from November 3rd to April 27th. Such shop 03 80 61 64 28. High season : open Tuesday to Saturday from 9.45am to 6.30pm; Sunday from 12pm to 6.30pm. Low season, closed on Monday and Tuesday. Such Hotel : 03 80 61 35 34 for stays from 2 to 7 days – Guided tours course + film. Adult : €8.50. Child : €6 (and also students, people with unemployment, monk). Group rate : €7.50. Tourism label & Disability. Shop of products of the Abbeys of France.

The Abbaye de Cîteaux was founded in 1098 by a monk group of the Abbaye de Molesmes, under the leadership of st. Robert with a desire to seek after God in a greater loneliness and poverty. In the early thirteenth century the Abbaye de Cîteaux was at the head of an order which had nearly 500 houses. In 1789 it had 20,000 hectares of farmland, including the famous vineyards of the coast. Today, the abbey remains the headquarters of a hundred abbeys throughout the world gathering around 2,500 monks and 1,800 nuns. Each abbey lives by his work. At Cîteaux, the farm possesses 75 dairy cows. 100% of the 540,000 litres of milk produced per year, are transformed into cheese of Cîteaux consisting of a smooth pasta, with typical flavour almost like a reblochon. Since about fifteen years, the abbey is open to visitors, it receive each year 60,000 visitors, a guided tour allowing you to explore some of the places in the abbey with an overview of the monastic life, silence, reading in the library, listening, exhibitions and slide show. If you are interested in the meeting of the monastic tradition, you can stay at the abbey for 2 to 8 days.

Villars-Fontaine

■ **L'AUBERGE DU CÔTEAU**
Route de Côte-de-Nuits
✆ +33 (0)3 80 61 10 50
Open Wednesday to Sunday for lunch and dinner. Menu from €22 to €29 (meat fondue €41 for 2 people. Prime rib 1.2 kg €42 for 2 people). Lunch menu : €13.50 (starter, main course, dessert of the day, coffee and 1/4 of wine). Terrace.

Located in the Hautes Côtes de Nuits, l'Auberge du Coteau is an address of the most recommended one. It bears well its name with its rustic style, the good atmosphere of its spacious dining room always almost full and its cuisine. At lunchtime on weekdays, that is known, it is necessary to book because the daily menu is very attractive. Dishes are generous and carefully prepared by a team that comes straight from Millésime of Chambolle, it is indeed henceforth the same house. In Villars-Fontaine no great gastronomy, but just the essence of the Burgundian dishes, authentic, simple and good. There is no need to specify the « homemade », that is common sense and moreover, it is obvious. Fancy a good fondue bourguignonne, a braised prime rib ? It is possible. The homemade terrine is served on the table without any fuss. The salmon is candied, the homemade foie gras, the bœuf bourguignon served in a casserole, the grilled meats are accompanied by perfect tartare sauces or Epoisses... It is delicious like all, even the desserts. A place attended by a very diversified clientele who understood his interest !

POMMARD ★

Located in the middle of the Côte de Beaune, Pommard vineyard produces a wine known for its power. The Red ones are the most famous : village appellations and premiers crus appelations – 28 in total – or 335 ha in total. They are particularly recommended to be kept. Wait at least five years before opening and possibility to wait more than twenty years.

Shopping

■ **APPELLATION CHOCOLAT**
5, place de l'Europe
✆ +33 (0)3 45 63 85 89
www.appellation-chocolat.fr
contact@appellation-chocolat.fr
Open from Tuesday to Saturday from 9.30am to 7pm. Open some festive Sundays.

After being at the helm of a small pastry shop in Givry for about twenty years, Béatrice and Michel Dessolins chose Pommard to specialise fully in their passion : the chocolate. Appellation Chocolat become immediately a must-go place for fine chocolate lovers. The shop located in the heart of Pommard abounds with treasure. You have a direct view on the laboratory where chocolates come from. Here, freshness is guaranteed : the chocolates stays only a few days on the stalls, and the creations matched to the seasons. The choice is wide, it is available in all its forms (tablets, disç, rectangular, in pearls, barrels and even vine tendrils) and caters for every taste ! The flavours are fruity (vine peach, blackcurrant or cherry for example), pralines (brown, black, milk or rock) or syrupy (mirabelle plum, cherries and raspberry). You will fall for the chocolate 92% pure cocoa from Madagascar and for the spreads... Pure delights ! Also think of Appellation Chocolat at snack time : the ice-creams, sorbets and macaroons are exquisite in summer. The hot chocolate in winter is perfect ! Note that Appellation Chocolat participates in many chocolate shows in the region, in Beaune, Nuits-Saint-Georges, Santenay, Talant up to Paris.

General view of Pommard.

In the surroundings

■ **DOMAINE PASCAL MURE**
2, Grande Rue
VOLNAY ✆ +33 (0)3 80 21 61 15
www.domaine-mure.com
contact@domaine-mure.com

Sale and tastings by appointment. Network "Welcomme to the farm" and "Of vineyards in cellars". Bottles from €7.30 to €25.10 with removal with the property.

Domaine Pascal Mure is a family estate where Pascal and Violette Mure assisted by their son Fabien maintain a sense of reception and sharing of unique vineyard passion. They cordially welcome us in their house of Volnay where we can admire the oak barrels in which a traditional vinification takes place. It is not rare to see them at one of the regional shows, at the gourmet fair of Dijon in particular, at the « Bienvenue à La Ferme » stand, network of which they are very active members. Domaine Mure extends on nearly 9 hectares between Beaune, Pommard, Volnay and Monthelie. The production is primarily red in Villages and Premiers Crus. The wines are sold at reasonable prices. You can, according to your desires, consume them immediately or keep them in cellar. Ask for advice at the time of tasting. The labels with contemporary design reflect the dynamism of the house well. Since 2013, Pascal Mure proposes also his vintage of Crémant. An estate to discover absolutely, if it is not already done, for the beauty of its wines and the extreme kindness of its owners.

PONT DE PANY & SOMBERNON – BETWEEN THE OUCHE VALLEY AND MOUNTAIN

Located in the middle of Côte-d'Or, Vallée de l'Ouche lures visitors thanks to its privileged natural environment and its cultural heritage that brings you naturally to the doors of Auxois at Sombernon. Since 1 January 2014, the Communautés de Commune of Vallée de l'Ouche and that of Sombernon have merged, implementing an overall tourist logistics of the territory Ouche and Montagne. We like strolling on the edges of Ouche or the canal of Burgundy, going on a tour of these beautiful landscapes in any season, exploring all these attaching villages of the edges of Ouche, but also those that are nestled in the surrounding reliefs. Whether on foot, by bike, on boat or on kayak, come to admire the environment of the valley of Ouche and to enjoy the activities in relation to green tourism. The generous nature promises beautiful walks or more sporting hikings. The wealth of the Vallée de l'Ouche is also due to its historic heritage. The old churches, laundrettes, bridges... are as many reason for a getaway to discover the villages ! Without forgetting the famous places such as the sites of Mâlain and its castle, Barbirey and its gardens, Velars and Notre-Dame-d'Etang.

Sightseeing

■ **HIKING TRAILS IN OUCHE ET MONTAGNE**
✆ +33 (0)3 80 33 33 59 – www.ouche-montagne.fr

Several hiking trails are suggested, including the Roches d'Orgères to Fleurey-sur-Ouche trail and the Mâlain path departing from the village church. Each hiking trail has an explanatory map available either at the Velars-sur-Ouche, at the Tourist Office of Sombernon or online on www.ouche-montagne.fr. The first trail has comment panels to accompany what you will discover along

Appointement at Sombernon to join the Office de Tourisme Ouche et Montagne

Low season : open Monday to Friday from 9 am to 12 pm and from 1 pm to 5 pm. High season : Monday to Friday from 9 : 30 am to 12 : 30 pm and from 1 : 30 pm to 5 : 30 pm. High season in July and August. Low season closing during certain weeks, consult the website of the city.

Since 1st January 2014, the Communities of the municipalities of Sombernonnais and of la Vallée de l'Ouche merged : there are now 32 towns and 10,500 people who got married. Discover unique and charming villages and enjoy a rejuvenating stay via a range of restaurant and quality hotel. Let yourself be charmed by its rocky and suitable sites in the green outdoor suitable for open air activities (swimming, hiking, climbing, fishing, etc.). Located in the center of Sombernon, the tourist office will help you organize your stay and find the informations you need on Sombernon and its region : activities, lodging, excursions. Enjoy exhibitions of local artists (painting and photography) at the tourist office.To discover this exceptional territory, paths of discovery are available for all tastes : the Voie Romaine Sombernon- Alésia on 34 km, The Boucle of Trois Châteaux of 22 km along the tank Panthier and enable to discover the castles of Loiserolle, Chateauneuf and Commarin as well as the 1 km walk to Baulme-la-Roche. The nature lovers and sports activities will certainly find their happiness.

■ **OFFICE DE TOURISME OUCHE ET MONTAGNE**
Parc Spuller
SOMBERNON ✆ +33 (0)3 80 33 33 59

the way. Go on the second trail by renting a « magical gathering » trail bag at the Tourist Office in Sombernon. This backpack allows you to discover the heritage of the Mâlain village with friends or family. An extraordinary hike ! A third path offers a majestic view point over the village Baulme-la-Roche. This 500 m path is also accessible to disabled people.

■ COMMUNAUTE DE COMMUNES OUCHE ET MONTAGNE- CCOM
5, place de la Poste ✆ +33 (0)3 80 49 77 43
www.ouche-montagne.fr
office.tourisme@ouche-montagne.fr
The Tourism office is located in Sombernon.
Communautés de Communes du Sombernonnais and the Vallée de l'Ouche have merged under the name « Ouche et Montagne » since 1st January 2014. There are now 32 towns and more than 10,500 inhabitants who joined their destiny. Communauté de Communes develops a touristic logistics at the service of visitors in connection with *Conseil Départemental*. There are already 5 picnic areas available to tourists along the Burgundy canal and the road bike. Two pedestrian trails are registered at the PDIPR : the Roches d'Orgères in Fleurey-sur-Ouche and the Mâlain trail departing from the village church. Others are under preparation around Pasques, Lantenay, Barbirey and Saint-Victor-sur-Ouche. An area of car-pooling and a service area for camping-cars are created close to the A38 and shops of Velars-sur-Ouche. The CCOM is striving to develop its reception capacities (cottages, guesthouse...) and to enhance its major tourist sites. It then continues, in connection with the owners of the Gallo-Roman Mâlain excavations of (the State and the archaeological Group of Mesmontois), the development of the Mediolanum site for an opening to the public. This site forms with the museum and the castle, which hosts cultural events, a tryptic that deserves a visit.

In the surroundings

Barbirey-sur-Ouche

■ LES JARDINS DU CHÂTEAU DE BARBIREY ★
2, rue du Chateau ✆ +33 (0)3 80 49 08 81
www.barbirey.com – jardins@barbirey.com
From May 1st to May 31st and from September 1st to November 1st : open at weekends and holidays of 14 : 00 to 18 : 00. From June 1st to August 31st, Tuesday to Sunday of 14 : 00 to 19 : 00. Opened all the year for the groups on go (minimum 10 people). Free for under 2-year-olds. Adult : €6. Child (from 3 to 12 years old) : €3. Group (10 people) : €5 (guided tour €7). Chambres d'Hôte. Children welcome. Jardin remarquable label.
It is a meeting with art and nature in the Château de Barbirey's gardens. Around an old eighteenth-century manor farm, this 8-hectare landscaped park highlights different regional natural environments where everyone stroll at their own pace and discover over the boardwalk a place of life, poetry and meetings. Recreated and remodelled thanks to the motivation of three associations, these gardens cleverly combine the most worked and the wilder areas. The varied atmospheres create surprise and charm at any moment, gardens and orchard blend wild banks, undergrowth, the pond without forgetting works by artists who punctuate the plant course-promenade. Classified as 'remarkable gardens » in 2004, they were classified on the French Supplementary Historic Monument the following year. There are living areas which regularly host exhibitions, shows, concerts and events for plant collectors, mature and amateurs, weddings and other seminars. Throughout the season, do not miss the visit of the gardens or rent one of the cottages to enjoy more of the place.

La Bussière-sur-Ouche

■ ABBAYE DE LA BUSSIÈRE-RESTAURANT LE 1131
RD 33 ✆ +33 (0)3 80 49 02 29
www.abbayedelabussiere.com
info@abbayedelabussiere.fr
♿
Relay & Castles. Closed January in the mid-February. High season : open Monday to Saturday for lunch; Monday and Tuesday for dinner. Closed Mondays and Tuesday between November and March. Brunch Sunday for lunch 2 times a month starting from March 20th, 2016. Booking advised. Children's menu : €19. Wine by the glass. Gourmet Menus du Restaurant the 1331 : 3 main courses : 80€, 6 main courses : 98€, 8 main courses : 114€. American Express. Groups welcome (by reservation). Garden. Terrace. A Michelin star.

If you are to make only one gourmet getaway in the proximity of Dijon, go to the restaurant the 1131. Its name refers to the date of foundation of the Cistercian abbey. Its thousand-year-old walls shelter a gastronomic restaurant but also the Le Bistro des Moines, a more classical restaurant that offers a refined cuisine elaborated with market produces. On its side, the 1131 are one of the best tables of the region. Like us, you will undoubtedly fall in love with the green and flowered park, the old stones, the antique furniture, silky fabrics, the tasty and creative cuisine. At the end of 2015, the excellent chef Emmanuel Hébrard went for new adventures. He left the cuisine to Guillaume Royer who is from Vandenesse-en-Auxois, a few kilometers from the Abbey. Guillaume Royer has worked with great establishments Relais & Châteaux and the spangled restaurants. In 2015, he obtained the title Meilleur Ouvrier de France in the « Gastronomy » category. His dishes will convince you. As he pass in the Abbey, you can thus taste fresh and smoked eel of lake cooked with fennel, citrus fruits and spices vinaigrette or kale braised with raw Morvan bacon and cooked with the truffle flavor. As for dessert, the soufflé with lemon of Menton served with an ice-cream and marinated citrus fruits with Mâlain saffron. A word summarizes the setting, the cuisine and the reception : sublime ! Le 1131 is one of our favorite tables that we highly recommend you to discover.

■ LE BISTROT DES MOINES / ABBAYE DE LA BUSSIÈRE

RD 33
✆ +33 (0)3 80 49 02 29
www.abbayedelabussiere.fr
info@abbaye-de-la-bussiere.com

From May to September : Monday to Saturday for the lunch. Monday and Tuesday for dinner for the dinner. Opening from October to April : Wednesday to Saturday for the lunch. Booking advised. Menu from €30 to €38 (for dinner). Menu at €28 : starter and main course or main course and dessert. Menu at €32 : starter and main course + cheese or dessert. Menu at €36 : starter and main course + cheese + dessert. Burgundian menu : €35. Groups welcome. Terrace.

The chef Guillaume Royer prepares the menu of Le Bistrot des Moines. As Meilleur Ouvrier de France 2015, he offers a tasty market cuisine for a rural and gourmet getaway. It evolves according to the seasonal products and allows you to discover the Abbaye de la Bussière at a reasonable price. The menu is renewed every month. You will find : Landes's duck foie gras mid-cooked with its candied pear and its orchards chutney, Iberian pork marinated in a pearled juice and accompanied by mashed potatoes, or fish fillet cooked with butter, meunière sauce and its cabbage variation. For an end with sweet touch, you have the choice between caramel custard and its ice-cream with cinnamon, a fondant with the chocolate and its pear sorbet or the dessert of the day. Fresh ingredients, dishes presented carefully and impeccably served : Le Bistrot des Moines offers you a tasty lunch in a sublime setting. If you happen to be passing in the region, do not hesitate to come back to Le Bistrot des Moines to discover Burgundian flavours. Soon during the fine days, benefit from the hotel's terrace and the beautiful view it offers on the park. You will only have one wish while leaving : to come back as quickly as possible in this sumptuous place, property of the charming Cummings family. A simple fine and creative cuisine.

Fleurey-sur-Ouche

■ Ô P'TIT REPÈRE DU GOÛT

8, rue des Vieilles-Carrières
✆ +33 (0)3 55 40 31 85
www.optitreperedugout.fr

Closed Sunday for dinner and Wednesday for dinner, Monday all day. À la carte : Around €22. Lunch menu : €13.90 (starter + main course + dessert. €11.90 : Starter and main course or Main course and dessert). Covered terrace.

Located in a bucolic setting, on the banks of the Burgundy Canal, in the valley of Ouche, P'tit Repère is an ideal gourmet stopover ! It remains constant in quality. The room is very pleasant : contemporary decor with exposed stone walls as background. On sunny days, a covered terrace overlooks a small japanese-style garden. Michael Felmann, former chef in the prefecture of Dijon, prepares dishes that change with the seasons. He uses high quality products : Montbéliard beef, farm duck breast and whole fish arrives to be cut as fillets or saddle... Low temperature cooking beautifully preserved the ingredients' flavours. You can enjoy very Burgundian dishes, including the snails' turnover with garlic cream, or more southern with fried fresh anchovies. Le hake fillet with gingerbread breadcrumbs with Martinique vanilla sauce is a success ! The desserts are also a great success. Praline flaky crisp and milky mousse or simple Irish Coffee, you are going to feast ! A charming welcome and refined dishes for an address that is a safe bet and whose access from Dijon is easy with the Lino.

■ REINE DE DIJON

1, Rue des Combets
✆ +33 (0)3 80 76 05 10
www.reinededijon.fr
contact@reinededijon.fr

No on-site sales. Products available in delicatessen and large surfaces.

Reine de Dijon, which has been producing mustard since 1840, is one of the first French manufacturers of the famous condiment. If the brand's logo is a bright lily flower on a royal blue background of the most beautiful effect, in 2015, a new style but in a limited serie will become the product line for delicatessen. The design of the label takes over the historical code of the brand, which gives it a little vintage look rather high standard that will attract lovers of delicatessen. This range is relatively prepared with certified products like the cream of cassis and mainly elaborated with grain of mustard seeds cultivated in Burgundy. Set in Fleurey-sur-Ouche since 1996, the factory produces more than 80 tons of this condiment daily ! Reine de Dijon develops and offers a comprehensive range of mustard, from the most classic to the most elaborate based on herbs and always more surprising spices. There are about twenty different recipes added regularly by creative and seducing novelties. These are answers to new desires of curious gourmets, like us. Packagings are offered in pots of 25, 100 or 200 g, glass, tube or sandstone with elegant and easily identifiable presentation. You will find these mustards in fine deli, hypermarket and very often in restaurants serving traditional mustard that they buy under the Dijona brand. The factory Fleurey has modern production equipment allowing to manage these multiple variations. Reine de Dijon responds the demand of the most discerning by preparing the mustards certified organic as well as the delicious Moutarde de Bourgogne, IGP, produced with mustard seeds and AOP white wine of Burgundy.

Gissey-sur-Ouche

■ LA CAVE À PIZZA ET PAS QUE ÇA

80, rue Moulin-Thibel
✆ +33 (0)3 80 40 07 52
www.lacaveapizzaetpasqueca.fr
contact@lacaveapizzaetpasqueca.fr

Opened the every day midday; Friday and saturdays the evening. Booking advised. Children's menu : €7.80 (drink included). Lunch menu : €10.80 (starter and main course or main course and dessert). €12.80 (starter + main course + dessert of the day with 1/4 of wine or a half. Every midday except the samedis and dimanches). Pizzas between €8.50 and €13. Pizza child with 6€. Groups welcome (on booking. To be appropriate of the menu with the chef). Terrace.

The pizzas of François Pirès were already known by many amateurs when he realised his dream by opening his restaurant. The room is nicely decorated : pristine white walls, Scottish red tablecloths and large slate on the fireplace. A large terrace is available in the inner courtyard in summer. From there, you can see some farm animals including chickens... Children love ! The delicious pizzas and the dishes are all homemade. They change with the seasons and the mood of Christophe Chartenay, the former chef of *Théâtre des Sens* of Dijon who runs the kitchen. For starter, you can beging with a Burgundian speciality like the snails, the stewed rabbit with tarragonand mustard cream. As main course, do not hesitate to choose the casserole of veal kidneys with truffle oil... A delight ! The lamb shank with peppered mint cooked during 7 hours is also very appetizing. As for wine, a beautiful list of Burgundian wines awaits you, sold by the bottle or by the glass. And after this good meal, strolling along the Ouche is a real pleasure ! A family address where a pleasant atmosphere prevails.

Malain

■ SITE DU CHÂTEAU DE MÂLAIN

Rue du Four
✆ +33 (0)3 80 23 66 08
www.gam.malain.fr
malaingam@laposte.net

Closed from November 1st to March 31st. Low season : open at weekends from 2pm to 6pm. High season : every day from 2pm to 7pm. High season in July and August. Free for under 10-year-olds. Adult : €3. Child (from 10 to 16 years old) : €1. Group : €5. For groups : guided tour all year of the castle, the museum and the Gallo-Roman site by reservation. Activities.

Chateau de Mâlain overlooks the village of its imposing ruins and offers stunning views of the valley of Ouche. If a large part of the walls and some rooms like the dungeon and chapel are remains of the 12th and 13th centuries, most of the remains date from the late 15th century. The castle had a significant power issue, during the Religious Wars. It has undergone extensive renovation conducted by volunteers of Groupe Archéologique du Mesmontois (GAM), which aim is to revive the site. In the course of the work, the building regained shape and no less than eight rooms (eleven eventually) are now open to the public. Throughout the year, several theatrical performances and concerts take place within the premises of the castle. If you are visiting Mâlain, enjoy also visiting the other two sites managed by the GAM : archaeological and ethnographic museum and the excavation of the Gallo-Roman site of Mediolanum.

The Burgundy Canal.

GOLF DE LA CHASSAGNE
Restaurant Côté Green
Chemin de La Chassagne
✆ +33 (0)3 80 40 78 57 / +33 (0)6 19 33 25 11 / 06 12 60 57 98
www.golflachassagne.com
accueil@golflachassagne.com
Open all year. Closed days of snow. Low season : every day from 9am to 7pm. High season : every day from 9am to 7.30pm. Pro-shop. Price subscription : from €130 to €790 depending on the age. Rates Green Fairies : from €21 to €31 per day. Handing-over depending on subscriptions. For the possibility groups of apéritive initiation. Restaurant open of semi March to November 1 by reservation. Soon : seminar room.
Dear friend golfers, if you do not know yet the golf of Mâlain, named Golf de La Chassagne, it means that you lack a nice experience. This golf, created in 2011 by Philippe and Sébastien Rance, is their 3rd course after that of Précy-sous-Thil (9 holes) and that of Tanlay in Yonne (9 holes). Equipped with 9 holes for the moment (with 5 in the process of being created), it extends on a space from 20 ha within a property of more than 100 ha. And if you realize that it is located in the Coomb of the relief of Mâlain, in nature, you've got it ! It is crossed by Douix and is decorated with cliffs. Splendid at every season. This course is at the same time technical and sporting. The fairways are hilly, the greens spectacular : panoramic views on Château de Mâlain or other coombs, but also in heights and with obstacles that are sometimes vertiginous. Note that the place is also a forest park open to the public for walks on the marked trails that respect the space of the golfers. Our advice, come to eat in the Club House that continues to grow with more comfort, a more large pro shop and new services. Since its creation, the golf safeguards the environment by optimizing its water management whose reserve is made up during winter. With a water jet if it pleases you. The site of the Golf of Mâlain is exceptional !

Lantenay

GALERIE VERRTIGE
16, rue des Martyrs-de-la-Résistance
✆ +33 (0)3 80 48 23 53 / +33 (0)6 80 36 59 70
www.verrtige.com
contact.verrtige@yahoo.fr
Open every day from 10am to 7pm. Except absence for exhibitions. Not to hesitate to take appointment. Member of the Workshops of Art of France, first professional body of the crafts.
The galerie Verrtige of Lantenay, is definitely worth the detour, is next to the workshop of Florian Rosier, where you can admire, buy and even order works of this glass-maker craftsman. Passionate about the glass material, Florian became became a journeyman glassmaker after a diploma from the CERFAV and several experiences with stained glass artists before creating his own gallery in 2003. Florian Rozier uses the techniques of molten glass and molded crystal and fusing- thermoforming for flat grassland that he models in 3D. All his works are simple : decorative objects, basins, vases, dishes, lamps sculptures. All translucent and sometimes decorated heartily with pigmented forms. These works are striking, the themes are often philosophical and carry a message… Their prices start from less than €100 and ca reach up to thousands of euros; you can order a specific topic. You can also bring an piece of glass to restore, the glass Master will put his love and his talent to repair the cracks of your molten glass.

Saint-Victor-sur-Ouche

ECLUSE DE LA CHARME N°28 NEW
Chemin de la Charme
✆ +33 (0)3 80 51 08 75
www.ouche-montagne.fr
office-tourisme@ouche-montagne.fr
Open from July 2nd to August 27th, 2016 Tuesday to Friday and the weekend for activities. Closed on Monday.
Located at Saint-Victor-sur-Ouche, Ecluse de la Charme offered for more than 20 years of concerts, open-air cafés, exhibitions, conferences, workshops and meetings around tasting of local products. The activity ceased a few years ago but the Communauté de Commune of Ouche and Montagne decided to reopen the place to the public from 2 July to 27 August 2016. The Association Départementale De Développement et d'Animation du Milieu Rural (ADDAMIR 21) also takes part in the project. From Tuesday to Friday, you will find there a lot of tourist information thanks to an antenna of the Tourist Office of Ouche and Montagne. You can also benefit from a shop selling local produces. At the weekend, the address will become the place for concerts, exhibitions and various entertainments. A catering space will then be offered to the holiday-makers. Ecluse de la Charme has the sense of the reception, tourism and sharing !

Velars-sur-Ouche

CHAPELLE DE NOTRE-DAME-D'ÉTANG
45, Notre-Dame- d'Étang road
✆ +33 (0)3 80 33 33 59
www.notre-dame-detang.fr
asso@notre-dame-detang.fr
The voluntary ones accommodate you the weekend in high season. Information at the Tourist Office. Visit of group by appointment (starting from 6 people).
Built in the late 19th century, on top of a 545 metres high hill, the chapel Notre-Dame d'Etang is visible from afar particularly from the railway, the canal and the motorway from and towards Paris.
Since the discovery of a statue at the top of the « mountain » by a herdsman in 1435, the Montagne d'Etang became a place of hiking and pilgrimage.
The monument, ranked as a Historical Monument, is still being restored. The monumental cast-iron statue, 8 metres high and weighing 10 tons which was completely renovated regained its place in March 2015. It shines henceforth the glares of its restored gilding.

L'AUBERGE GOURMANDE
17, allée de la Cude ✆ +33 (0)3 80 33 62 51
www.auberge-velars.com
christophe.faivre@club-internet.fr
Closed the 1st fortnight of January. Open from Thursday to

© CCVO

The Combe d'Arvaux.

Monday and on public holidays for lunch; from Thursday to Saturday for dinner. Menus from €31 to €58 (menu of the market at €22.50 for lunch and dinner on weekdays except public holidays). À la carte : around €45. Children's menu : €11. Groups welcome. Garden. Terrace. Catering service.
Whether you come to L'Auberge Gourmande with your friends, family and even for a business lunch, you will spend a very pleasant moment with the gastronomic food and efficient service of the address in a serene and peaceful atmosphere. The very trendy decor immediately seduced with its dark hardwood flooring, curtains and carmine window's frames contrasting with the white tablecloths and the walls. Chic and refinement prevail... just like the cuisine ! Christophe Faivre, reinvents the Burgundy traditions by working the products with a perfect know-how. The dishes are as stylish as tasty. Its menu changes about every three months according to the seasons. We are accustomed to enjoy subtle flavours' combinations of the chef. And that's what we are looking for. As starter, snail are served with cream of cottage cheese with breaded pig's trotter and eggs' quenelle. The wild boar mixes with dry ham with dates and red beetroots' chantilly. Your dishes are enhanced with several flavours. And the dishes on offer will delight everyone. The intensity of the pleasures lasts till the dessert and even till the coffee that is always accompanied by small delicacies. This is undoubtedly a gourmet address. The service is impeccable. Delphine Faivre maintains a family atmosphere that goes well with the hotel.

SOMBERNON

On its promontory, near Auxois, Sombernon dominates both the Ouche Valley and Dijon Mountain. A privileged site that invites vacationers using the motorway link below, to branch off, when having a breath of fresh air and some pictures. The view is worth the detour.
Sombernon is a charming village overlooking the valleys. The writer and poet Henri Bourguignon Vincenot presented Sombernon as the « roof of the western world. » Surrounded by forests, water and greenery, this town has much to offer and each year attracts many travellers.

■ OFFICE DE TOURISME OUCHE ET MONTAGNE

Parc Spuller
✆ +33 50°3 80 33 33 59
www.ouche-montagne.fr
office.tourisme@ouche-montagne.fr
Low season (from November to February) : open on Wednesday and Friday from 9.30am to 12pm and from 2pm to 5pm. Mid-season (March, April, May, September and October) : open Tuesday to Friday from 9.30am to 12pm and from 2pm to 5pm. High season (from June to August) : open Tuesday to Sunday. Shop. Exhibitions.
Located in the centre of Sombernon, the tourist office will help you organise your stay and find the information you need on the territory of the Communauté de Communes of Ouche and Montagne. Hiking, visits, activities, accommodation, catering service... There are no shortage of activities and the Tourist Office detains all the information for all your trips. The team of the Tourist Office of Ouche et Montagne will be happy to welcome you in its buildings to present the assets of the territory. In the heart of the Burgundy Franche-Comté region, at the crossroads of Auxois, Côte-d'or vineyards and Dijon urban area, the Ouche territory and Montagne offer multiple landscapes throughout the canal or on the mountains that introduce Auxois. By bicycle, car, boat or on foot, there are plenty of way to discover these beautiful landscapes.

Sightseeing

Via Romana Sombernon Alésia

Inaugurated in 2010, the 34 km long Roman road links Sombernon to Alise-Sainte-Reine. It revives the road laid out for the went along armies under Augustus. Caesar that road go and defeat Vercingetorix. The road starts at the wash house of Villotte in Sombernon and continues between Oze and Ozerain, passes near the vineyard of Flavigny and ends up to the excavation site of Alésia. For several years now, the Trial court-nature Sombernon-Alésia is organised early April on this road. It is a training race to the championship appreciated by the licensees, a race on the hills where the numerous participants and public enjoy an exceptional site. The statue of Vercingetorix is the finish line.

Knife & Fork

LE SPULLER

42, rue Ferdinand-Mercusot
✆ +33 (0)3 80 53 71 27
www.lespuller.fr – lespuller@orange.fr

♿

Open from Tuesday to Saturday for dinner; from Tuesday to Sunday for lunch. Booking advised. Menus from €20 to €32. À la carte : around €12. Children's menu : €9 (up to 10 years old). Lunch formula : €13.50 (starter, main course, dessert). Express formula : €10.50 (starter and main course or main course and dessert). Panoramic view. Seminars up to 30 people. Weddings. Bar. Hotel of 8 rooms (for 1-5 people). Holiday vouchers, Chèque Restaurant. Groups welcome (up to 100 people. Quotation on request). Terrace. Take-away.

As a professional of hotel business and catering service, Remy Sauvage tastefully renovated and decorated his establishment, making it warm and comfortable. For the cuisine, with the warm salad of époisses on gingerbread roasted with small bacon, the deer fillet or roasted half-lobster, you find something to delight your tastebuds ! In Le Spuller, there are a wide choice a wide choice of starters, grilled meats and fish. The chef also prepares very good homemade burgers, one of them is with foie gras. In addition to the desserts, we've noted a beautiful range of ice-creams with many rare flavors such as pear Williams, banana, mirabelle plum, morello cherry, creme brulee, milk jam, speculoos or nougat. The little bonus of this restaurant : the adaptable menus according your appetite that you can add or remove cheese or dessert as you wish. What remains to add is that there is a catering sevice at your disposal for wedding, baptisms or family meals. The two rooms of the restaurant can be rented. Friendly thematic evenings are organized four to five times during the year : sea sauerkraut, country music concert... The themes are varied and suit to the desires of the clientele ! A smart advice : book (well in advance) a table beside the bay window : the view is a splendid there.

In the surroundings

Grosbois-en-Montagne

RÉSERVOIR DE GROSBOIS

Route départementale 905

Open all year. Supervised swimming and snack in July-August. The reservoir of Grosbois located about twenty minutes away from Dijon, between Aubigny-lès-Sombernon and Grosbois-en-Montagne, is an inviting place for swimming. Created by a dam that borders it, this artificial lake offers a beautiful sandy beach that is well maintained and where you just need to throw your towel and enjoy the sun. On the right, a dike of rocks on which runs a grassy path, leads you to an excursion in nature to discover seven balconies of fauna and flora observation. Facing the beach and on the other shores, it is possible to abandon yourself to fishing. Do you want a cool drink or ice-cream ? Chalet de la Plage is pleased to serve you these few refreshments in July and August.

Blaisy-Bas

L'ORÉE DES CHARMES

56, rue d'Avau ✆ +33 (0)3 80 33 03 03
www.oreedescharmes.fr
oree.des.charmes@orange.fr

Logis (2 cocottes). Open for lunch and dinner Monday to Saturday. Closed during Christmas holidays. Booking advised. Menu from €28 to €55. Children's menu : €15. Lunch menu : €14 (starter, main course, dessert, coffee and ¼ of wine). Wine by the glass. Hôtel Logis 2 cheminées. Bar. Seminars. Holiday voucher, Chèque Restaurant. Groups welcome (up to 40 people, by reservation). Terrace. Air conditioning. Point reloads for scooters, motorbikes, electric cars and bicycles with electric assistance VAE.

It's been more than a year since Didier Pougeoise, experienced chef, has taken over Orée des Charmes. The restaurant changed register, now it offers a traditional cuisine, full of creativity and changes in the course of the season The dishes are prepared with fresh ingredients to get a result full of finesse. On the menu : black pudding and avocado scum with its balks of apple, foie gras cooked with cloth served with a small waffle and a chutney of kumquat or turbo with sausage with one buttered cabbage and a juice with the Pinot Noir of Burgundy. The desserts also reserve beautiful surprises. We appreciate this 100% homemade cuisine that privileges quality ingredients. Stones, exposed beams and contemporary decor blends perfectly whether in the restaurant room, the bar, the lobby of the hotel or in the rooms. The lunch menu remains economic and allows you to taste authentic and tasty meals.

PONTAILLER-SUR-SAÔNE ★

The Saone, the Albane, the Bèze, the Vingeanne, the Ognon, the canal between Champagne and Burgundy... Several waterways cross Pontailler which, as a frontier city experienced many tumultuous periods. It thus was plundered and many times crossed by the troops of the Langres and Champagne's lords. It is now a true little paradise for its 1,300 inhabitants, the fishermen and the lovers of the water activities : rental of the boats at the arranged beach, marina and supervised swimming in July and August. More generally, lovers of nature are charmed, since Pontailler is the departing point of many stroll on foot or by bike, in particular on the Voie Bleue. The small town, classified station verte, is thus conducive to relaxation. You will find in the center, built on a peninsula surrounded by the Saône and the Vieille Saône (the river changed bed at the beginning of the 20th century), the Saint-Maurice church of the 18th century and the laundrettes on variable level. Do not fail to join the statue of Notre-Dame of Mont-Ardoux. You will have a panoramic view on the plain of the Saône and the mounts of the Jura. The market day is held every Saturday morning.

■ OFFICE DE TOURISME DU CANTON DE PONTAILLER-SUR-SAÔNE

3, rue du 8 Mai 1945
✆ +33 (0)3 80 47 84 42
www.pontailler-tourisme.fr
info@pontailler-tourisme.fr
♿

Low season : open Tuesday to Friday from 10am to 1pm and from 2pm to 6pm; Saturday from 10am to 1pm. High season : Tuesday to Friday from 9am to 1pm and from 2pm to 6pm; Saturday from 9am to 1pm. Closed from November to March. Low season : April and October. Also open Monday (2pm-6pm) and Sunday (10am-1pm) in July and August. Label « Vélo » reception; . Bike rental adults and children in high season. Wifi.

There are all the necessary informations here, helpful leaflets and cards for your stay in Pontailler, Burgundy and nearby Franche-Compté. The Tourist Office provides information about the historical heritage to discover, (Talmay castle, chapels and local churches, many laundries), on all the activities you can practice and in the surrounding area (fishing, canoeing, water skiing, swimming) and provides you with many ideas for walks (circuit locks, circuit charming wood, etc.), including a discovery tour that has been specially designed for children, along the Saône. It allows them to discover the environment in a fun way and with a path that takes them from the Tourist Office up to Heuilley-sur-Saône. The discovery booklet costs €1 and the Tourist Office lends the necessary observation equipment (magnifying glass, forceps, herbarium sheets, scoop...). It is also possible to rent bicycles. (Roaming ensured with Auxonne OT, Mirebeau and the Vélorail of Vingeanne in Champagne-sur-Vingeanne). Finally art objects, local art and handicrafts items has been sold on the site in recent years. As bonus, a charming and efficient welcome !

Sightseeing

■ PARCOURS ECOPAGAYEUR DE PONTAILLER-SUR-SAÔNE

Tourist Office
3, rue du 8 Mai 1945 ✆ +33 (0)3 80 47 84 42
www.pontailler-tourisme.fr
saonerandeaukayak@hotmail.fr

Closed from October 1st to April 30th. Departure of Maison de l'Eau in Heuilley-sur-Saône. Open Tuesday to Sunday. By reservation. Adult : €16 (the half-day. €24 per day). Child (up to 12 years) : €12 (the half-day. €15 per day). Group (10 people) : €12 (the half-day. €15 per day for the adults. €10 per half-day. €12 per day for the children). Audio guide available directly on your smartphone via the application Stroll in Burgundy.

Parcours EcoPagayeur enables you to discover in an original way the flora and fauna aboard a canoe. On Saône Côte-d'Orienne, there are several possible starting points. The canoe clubs offer tours of two hours, half day or more on board a canoe for 2 to 3 people (2 adults and a child, for example). From Heuilley-sur-Saone, you sail on the Saône and Ognon. The rivers await you and ready to reveal their secrets ! Equipped with all necessary safety equipment, a guidebook and an audio guide, you are off on an adventure. You paddle at your own pace to explore the local heritage. An appropriate signage guides you and informs you of potential hazards, landing areas and portage. The guiding tools provided from the start help you discover the treasures and local attractions... from the history of agriculture through the aquatic fauna and the wealth of the biotope. The audio guide explains everything... It is your ideal companion. From 2016, you have the hikings and a great deal of information of the application *« Balades en Bourgogne »*. A pretty way to discover Pontailler-sur-Saône's surroundings.

■ VOIE BLEUE, PISTES CYCLABLES ET PARCOURS VTT

✆ +33 (0)3 80 47 84 42
www.pontailler-tourisme.fr

Plans of the tours available to the Tourist Office of Pontailler and on your smartphone via the application Stroll in Burgundy.

You can go along the Saone or join Dijon by bicycle. La Voie Bleue is a cycle track following the Saône, from Haute-Saône to Lyon. One of the tours starts from Talmay, passes through Pontailler and Lamarche to make you reach Auxonne. You can also stroll by bicycle from Vaux-sur-Crône to Lamarche-sur-Saône (1h30/15 km). The crossing of the forest estate of Longchamp and bathings in edge of the Saone are on the programme. 2 mountain bike paths of 6.5 and 8.8 km were signposted since spring 2016.

Knife & Fork

HOSTELLERIE DES MARRONNIERS
3, rue Saint-Eloi
✆ +33 (0)3 80 36 12 76
hostelleriedesmarronniers@orange.fr

Low season : open from Tuesday till Sunday at noon; Friday and Saturday in the evening. High season : from Tuesday to Saturday in the evening; from Tuesday till Sunday at noon. High season from the April 1st till November 30th. During low season upon reservation on Tuesday, Wednesday and Thursday in the evening for mini 6 people. Menus from 25 € to 39, 50 €. Children's menu : 10 €. Noon formula : 14 € (3 dishes, 12 € 2 dishes, 9.50 € today's special). Terrace. Brasserie-type bar – pizzas.

Hostellerie des Marronniers in Pontailler-sur-Saône became a small institution of good cuisine and convivial place. It's been 9 years now that Catherine Futelin maintains this capital that she built through requirements in her establishment and respect of clientele. The result is there, constant quality and the guests who are increasingly faithful. Set up within walking distance of the Saône and the port under large chestnut trees and having a fabulous terrace with the huge Bordeaux parasols, you cannot miss this restaurant. A team of 3 people prepares the traditional cuisine that is always concocted with the finest ingredients, meats and delivered fresh fish almost on a daily basis. The fish dishes on offer are beautiful, cod loin with a crust of gingerbread sprinkled with an orange butter, roast pike perch or quite simply fryed troutlet. As for meat, beef tatar, peking chicken, fillet of beef with morels, seared foie gras on duck aglets... the gourmets are delighted. The house also makes pizzas to enjoy on the spot in or to take away. The set menu at midday always proposes two choices per main course that consist always of one fish. The menus with the reasonable prices are well built, poached eggs, fried food, frogs' leg and fish or meats on the à la carte menu. All is homemade and the reception and the service are always irreproachable.

Sleeping

CAMPING DE LA CHANOIE
46, rue de la Chanoie
✆ +33 (0)3 80 67 21 98
camping.municipal1@orange.fr

Bathing; label reception bicycle. Open from April 15th to October 15th. Ground of 6 ha. 153 campsites (rental of chalets). Exposure : shaded/mid--shaded. Relief : dish. Campsite up to €4. Vehicle up to €2. 2 people up to €8. Chalets up to 6 people from €350 to €470 per week. Games for children. Pets allowed. Wifi. Catering facilities.

Camping de Pontailler-sur-Saône is a further testimony of the strength of tourism in Val de Saône. The residents of these few 153 locations (touristic and leisure) go back there year after year because they simply feel good. Family, friendly, it hosts tents, caravans and chalets on rental. Games for children allow families to spend a pleasant stay during holidays, between outdoor games and water games, the Saône is located a few metres away and a beach was built... Almost all the guests like the equipment, setting and entertainment.

In the surroundings

Heuilley-sur-Saône

MAISON DE L'EAU, DE LA PÊCHE ET DE LA NATURE
4, rue de Condé
✆ +33 (0)3 80 47 81 37 / +33 (0)3 80 47 48 29
www.cc-pontailler-sur-saone.fr
mepn@orange.fr

Closed from May 15th to September 15th. Low season : open on Tuesday and Thursday to Saturday from 3pm to 6pm. High season : Tuesday to Sunday from 3pm to 6pm. High season : July and August. Low season : May, June and September. Free for under 6-year-olds. Adult : €2. Child (from 6 to 18 years old) : €1. Children welcome (reception of the pupils and vacation centres).

Maison de l'Eau, de la Pêche et de la Nature allows you to know the environment of the Saône Valley much better. With its four museographic showrooms, you will discover local nature and fishing, with modern amenities, audiovisual techniques, aquariums and various educational spaces. The teaching room has various documentary resources and equipment observation and experimental available to the public. It is also a tourist information relay. The house welcomes children (from 6 years old) for discovery day in group. It is also a starting point for stages, fishing and EcoPagayeur routes that enable you to discover in an original way the fauna and flora on board of a canoe.

Lamarche-sur-Saône

LE BISTROT DE JULIE
Hôtel-restaurant Le Saint-Antoine
32, rue de Franche-Comté
✆ +33 (0)3 80 47 11 33
www.le-saint-antoine.fr
lesaintantoine@wanadoo.fr

Open Monday to Friday for lunch. À la carte of Saint-Antoine. Chef's suggestions. Boards pork-butcheries and cheeses at any hour. Lunch menu : €15 (2 dishes, €20 3 dishes + à la carte). Wine by the glass. Groups welcome. Garden. Terrace. Seminars – Hotel 3 stars with swimming pool and spa.

Le Bistrot de Julie is set up in the middle of Saint-Antoine, a 3-star hotel and restaurant with remarkable quality on the reception level as much as on its refined cuisine. At Le Bistrot de Julie at lunchtime on weekdays, its low price formulas, concocted by the team of Saint-Antoine, is highly prized and we should say that the dishes are delicious. The daily special is often that of the market, even of the mood of the Chef. The homemade pâté en croute followed by a cod loin and its cooked minute spinaches delighted us ! We dream of coming back in front of the suggestions : homemade foie gras, fricassée of snails with mushrooms, perfect eggs in wine sauce, homemade pike quenelles, flambéed calf's kidneys... Jean-Pierre Jagla, Julie his daughter and the team in the kitchen offers a 100% homemade cuisine, very evolutive and even creative. The Geranium sorbet proves that ! Since the restaurant of Julie is open, the establishment has undergone big renovation works, a real rejuvenation. Le Bistrot receives a contemporary deco, its covered terrace of modern furnishing is an invitation to a stopover. In summer, we prefer the terrace that is open to the gardens that Jean-Pierre Jagla is continuously rearranging. An advice : ask to see the statues of the local sculptor artist, Gauvain. They are rather astonishing, the *Coq*, last arrived, is monumental. If you like the place, stay there for a night, there are a pool and a spa !

■ **LE SAINT ANTOINE*****
32, rue de Franche-Comté
✆ +33 (0)3 80 47 11 33
www.le-saint-antoine.com
lesaintantoine@wanadoo.fr

Logis (3 cheminées). 10 rooms (including 2 suites). Double room €88; suite €130. Half-board (stop-over with special rates from €88 to €125). Breakfast : €9. Pets allowed (€7). Seminars. Wifi. Catering facilities (Bistrot de Julie at midday menu from €15 to €20 - Saint Antoine evening and Sunday lunchtime menu from €28 to €38). Hammam, sauna. Cabin of hydromassage with musicothérapie and luminothérapie €25 20 min.

Le Saint Antoine in Lamarche-sur-Saône continues to surprise us. Located near the banks of the Saône, it offers the opportunity for a comfortable stay. We could even put comfort in plural ! All the rooms were renovated in 2014. Thick carpets with contemporary designs, cozy duvets on the 160 cm or 2 X 90 beds, renovated bathrooms, beautiful curtains and fabrics and finally, air-conditioning in all rooms. Two restaurants are available, Bistrot de Julie at lunchtime with a beautiful terrace and the restaurant of Saint Antoine with gourmet menu at dinnertime. The large swimming pool is heated all year round. Since 2014, the hotel became a Spa because you have at your disposal a jacuzzi, sauna and hammam where you can decompress. Art lovers will be sensitive to some works exhibited in the hotel. The sculptures of Gauvain are remarkable and original, such as the giant cockerel. Le Saint Antoine experiences a renewal of youth in its decoration, which is sometimes original. But foremost enjoy the cuisine of Jean Pierre Jagla, the restaurant of Le Saint-Antoine is really fine, 100% homemade and respecting the seasons. You will love the family atmosphere of this establishment.

POUILLY-EN-AUXOIS ★

The small village of Pouilly-en-Auxois, located along the Burgundy Canal, has several tourist attractions : rich heritage (dovecotes, castles, fortified villages in the surroundings...), nature walks on bicycle or boat, on the towpaths, gastronomic discoveries... Many tourists come here at the beginning of summer. The main attraction is undoubtedly the marina of Pouilly-en-Auxois, where the Burgundy Canal passes. Cruises of 2 hours (or more) are carried out on board of the Billebaude, which passes under an underground vault of 3.3 km : very impressive ! Do not miss the « Hall de Toueur » fully glazed, built by the famous Japanese architect Shigeru Ban and which shelters a former electrical toueur that was used to tow boats. Built in 1893, it was used until 1987.

■ **OFFICE DE TOURISME**
DE POUILLY-EN-AUXOIS ET DE SON CANTON
La Capitainerie – 1 rue de la Coopérative
Port de plaisance
✆ +33 (0)3 80 90 77 36
www.pouilly-auxois.com
capitainerie@cap-canal.fr

Open all year. From November to March : Monday to Saturday from 9am to 12.30pm and from 2pm to 5pm. From April to October : Monday to Saturday from 9am to 12.30pm and from 2pm to 6pm and from June 15th to September 15th : Sunday from 10am to 12.30pm. In July and August : Monday to Saturday from 9am to 12.30pm and from 2pm to 6.30pm, Sunday from 10am to 12.30pm and from 2pm to 5pm.

Located on the marina, Capitainerie hosts the Tourist Office of Pouilly-en-Auxois. It is open all year and centralizes much information about the Township of Pouilly, the Auxois land and the neighboring countries like Morvan. In addition to the essential addresses, you can get books on the region for yourself, brochures and fact sheets on hikes and guidebooks. Do not hesitate to rent mountain bikes or VTC to take the cycle route, this towpath constructed and marked along the Burgundy Canal, which takes you to Dijon on one side and Tonnerre to the other... with muscular power ! If you prefer to view the nature of water, ask about the boat trip. There is also a circuit combining a boat trip with a train ride, followed by a tasting. In summer, the tourist office organizes thematic guided tours on reservation.

Bike hire

The tourist office of Pouilly en Auxois is a Burgundy Veli partner that offers racing bike rentals for ½ day to 5 days of VTC. These bikes can be returned in the station Montbard, Dijon in particular.

■ CAP CANAL – LE BATEAU PROMENADE LA BILLEBAUDE
Office de Tourisme La Capitainerie – La Capitainerie – 1 rue de la Coopérative Marina
✆ +33 (0)3 80 90 77 36 – www.cap-canal.fr
capitainerie@cap-canal.fr
Cruise of the Vault (2am)/individual : €13 by adult – €8 by child (3-12 years)/groups : €11 by adult – €7 by child (3-12 years). Cruise of the locks (day)/individual : €26 by adult – €16.50 by child (3-12 years)/groups : €24.50 by adult – €15.50 by child (3-12 years). Animated cruises : from €17.50 to €44 by adult – from €10 to €38 by child (3-12 years). Holiday voucher. Booking required. Free for under 3-year-olds. Navigation from April to October.
Experience unusual cruises at the top of the Burgundy Canal on board of La Billebaude, an electric boat with a capacity of 50 passengers. The promenade consists of the crossing of the famous Vault of Pouilly (underground illuminated of 3,333 m in which the canal is engulfed under the city) and the passage of lock(s). Animated cruises punctuate the season : snack cruise, meal cruise, gourmet cruise, musical cruise or DUO boat + mini train in July and August. You can embark up to 8 bicycles on board to pass the underground and to carry on your way roaming along the bike path of the Burgundy Canal. The reservation is imperative and the boarding is at the port of Pouilly-en-Auxois.

Knife & Fork

■ HÔTEL RESTAURANT DE LA POSTE
Place de la Libération ✆ +33 (0)3 80 90 86 44
www.hoteldelaposte-pouilly.fr
hoteldelapostepouilly@orange.fr
Closed 2 weeks in November and 1 week in March. Opened Tuesday to Saturday the evening; Tuesday to Sunday midday. Menu from €21 to €42 (+ à la carte). Children's menu : €9 (up to 12 years). Lunch menu : €14.50 (main course, dessert, café in week). Hotel. Chèque Restaurant. Catering. Banquets, combinations and groups.
Built as a coaching inn under Napoléon, this building, made of white stones, is an excellent gourmet relay. It is also family-run address which has been transmitted from generations to generations. The decoration, in a cosy and trendy style, is pleasant and the room is very bright with its large bay windows that looks out into place de la Libération. The chef, Anthony Bonnardot, gets his inspiration from local recipes to offers you an inventive and tasty cuisine. He prepares his dishes with local produces, fresh vegetables and obviously seasonal. The fish depends on the daily arrival. The à la carte formulas and menus, display very reasonable prices given the quality of the dishes. Anthony reserves a nice tribute to the terroir with a dedicated menu which presents in particular a roasted Charolais spare rib, a hare in chartreuse cabbage with foie gras with Burgundian sauce or a steam cooked pike perch chunk with Crémant de Bourgogne. It is quite simple, this menu celebrates the region and its treasures. As for the menu *saveur*, it sets the standard of delicacy much higher. And for once, children are not forgotten, they have a feast with a grilled meat or a homemade smoked salmon. A fashionable restaurant with a refined cuisine and a constant quality.

Sleeping

■ CAMPING VERT AUXOIS
15, Voute du Canal de Bourgogne
www.camping-vert-auxois.fr
contact@camping-vert-auxois.fr
Closed from the 1st of November to the 1st of April. 70 campsites (including 3 mobile home). Exhibition : mid--shaded. Floor : grassy. Relief : dish. Project of pool. 3 mobile home for 4-7 people from €270 to €450 per week. Tent Canada Trecks : from €192 to €228 per week. Package duo : from €15.50 to €18. Package comfort : from €17.50 to €22. Package hikers : from €11 to €14. Area for camper van. Catering facilities (snack and small terrace).
The campsite Pouilly deserves its 3 stars. Since Françoise and Hervé Fuchs have taken over it in 2013, it showed real and nice changes. Its brandnew toilet block, beautiful and well designed, offers all the comfort of a good campsite. As for the service, the creperie refreshment bar allows you to have a gourmet break. Françoise Fuchs profits from winter closure to maintain the trees and the rose plantation, and we must say that the campsite is well-maintained ! You have good camping pitches within a green setting and in the quiet for your tent and your camper van along the canal and a few steps from the city centre. For the less equipped, you can choose one of the 3 mobile homes or more atypical shelter. It's possible because the novelties are the Tent Canada Trecks (only one at the moment) of 12 m^2 with a bed with duvet, bedside tables and covered terrace of $5m^2$. The result is beautiful and natural setting that recalls the North America. A good option and an excellent price/pleasure ratio of the campsite ! And you have the convenience of ordering your breakfast.

Shopping

LA MAISON DE PAYS DE L'AUXOIS-SUD
Le Seuil
Rond-Point (sortie A6, direction Créancey)
✆ +33 (0)3 80 90 75 86
www.maison-auxois.com
info@maison-auxois.com
Open from Monday to Saturday from 10am to 6pm; on Sunday and public holidays from 3pm to 6pm. Closed at 6.30pm in July-August. La Maison de Pays is closed every Sunday and Saturday morning in January. Closed on December 25th and on January 1st. Tasting for groups between €5.50 and €10 per person. Information Point of the Tourist Office of Pouilly-en-Auxois and its Canton.
There are more than 115 craftsmen represented, more than 3,500 products including about half in food products and more than 40,000 visitors each year. Welcome to

Maison du Pays de l'Auxois it is sure that you will find what you want ! Truffles, cheese, sausages, about fifty wines, beers, spirits, jams, juices, mustards Fallot and Reine de Dijon, honey, gingerbreads, biscuits, anises, snails, foie gras... La Maison de Pays de l'Auxois can prepare food baskets on request. The best of Burgundy is represented here and where all gourmets find their happiness. The others can also have fun with wooden toys, jewellery, clothes and even beauty products. Since February 2015, this beautiful shop window of Auxois's region was completely renovated : 270 m² decorated in more trendy way, the newly arranged shop windows and the opening of a tasting center for groups. Few steps from the highway, the entrance of Pouilly-en-Auxois and the Canal de Bourgogne, don't miss it ! Our last favourite ? A nice board made from a bottle of wine by the glassblower Sébastien Dugué de Vieux Château.

In the surrounding

CHÂTEAU DE CHAILLY – HÔTEL – GOLF – RESTAURANTS
Rue Dessous
CHAILLY-SUR-ARMANÇON
✆ +33 (0)3 80 90 30 30 – www.chailly.com
reservation@chailly.com

Open all year. 45 rooms. Double room from €199 to €289; suite from €429 to €529. Buffet breakfast or in room (buffet €20, in room €25). Extra bed : €35 (for children from 12 to 16 years old). credit card and checks are not accepted. American Express. Pets allowed (€13 per night). Seminars. Receptions and weddings. Free Wifi. Catering facilities (two restaurants. Le Rubillon, at lunchtime. L'Armançon, in the evening). Hammam, whirlpool. Golf, tennis, bike rental, billiards, tasting cellar of wines.

This fortress built with the 15th century and converted in a hotel resort in 1990 is an exceptional place, classified Historical Monuments. Entirely renovated, the castle hosts now 45 rooms, an outdoor pool, a tennis court, a relaxation area and a golf course. Surrounded by a splendid green area, it offers you the best in the middle of Burgundy. Among the rooms at your disposal, some are more luxurious than others to make your stay still more unforgettable; in particular the suites of 90 square meters ! They are in the main building with view of the golf. The decoration is made with a great attention to detail : folding screen, sculptures, art déco bathtub, ceilings in wood beams... All the rooms are tastefully decorated because all of them were renovated in 2014, some in contemporary. Great paintings, news fitteds carpet and wall linings, coloured curtains, armchairs, compass tables of the Seventies... The hotel also accommodates you for your seminars with six lounges suitable for business meetings. For the relaxation, the Castle has a golf as well as two restaurants, the pool, the hammam, tennis, billiards as well as the massages on appointment. Moreover, the establishment sets up out-of-the-ordinary activities on request : treasure hunt, wine tasting in the vault by the former sommelier of Palais de l'Elysée, cooking classes, tasting of truffles, air balloon rides, thematic evenings. Here, it's no possible to get bored ! A simply perfect place.

CÔTE-D'OR

PULIGNY-MONTRACHET

Puligny and Chassagne... both towns share the name of Montrachet and the climate attached to it. A distribution that allows them to enjoy rents from the only wines to hold the prestigious grand cru appellation for Côte de Beaune. On these lands, the Chardonnay grape has its roots deep in a soil that is very advantageous due to limestone. The result : an exceptional wine which illuminates the eye with its green hues that characterize it and its almond aromas. Of the approximately 214 ha of the town, half is classified as Premier Cru appellation. The very name of Puligny would be due to the name of a Gallo-Roman vineyard owner, reflecting the presence of vineyards in this country for at least two thousand years.

Knife & Fork

LE MONTRACHET
10, place des Marronniers
✆ +33 (0)3 80 21 30 06
www.le-montrachet.com
info@le-montrachet.com

Closed from end of November to beginning of January. Open daily for lunch and dinner. Booking advised. Restaurant : lunch menu : €32; for lunch and dinner : 62 and €94. Wine by the glass. Hôtel Quatre stars and 1 Michelin star. American Express, Holiday voucher. Lift for the access to the restaurant. Groups welcome (on request). Terrace. Shop.

In this gastronomic restaurant, discover the cuisine without pretention of the Michelin star chef Luc Filoé. What is important for him is fist of all highlighting the products that he prepares, to emphasize flavours of the ingredients to find perfect balance. The setting itself is splendid with its exposed stones and its beams. In winter, you come here to taste a fillet of venison with foie gras, black truffle and potato soufflée. You'll find it difficult to choose between fish and meat for a while. We are called by the langoustines with curry, pineapple, coconut, new potatoes and by the fillet of Charolais beef and duck foie gras. How can you resist such sweet pleasures ? To accompany it all, enjoy a selection of excellent bottles offered by the sommeliers of the place. But what you must absolutely taste is obviously the montrachet. The cellar of the House has more than 1,000 references including 200 grand crus ! Very nice address with refined cuisine and elegant setting, with Thierry Gazagnes who manages everything !

Sleeping

LE MONTRACHET
10, place des Marronniers
✆ +33 (0)3 80 21 30 06 – www.le-montrachet.com
info@le-montrachet.com

Annual closing between the end of November and the beginning of January. Booking advised. 31 rooms (9 suites). From €150 to €290. Breakfast : €18. Extra bed : €20. Parking. Restaurant : Lunch menu €32, for lunch and dinner €62 and €94. Free Wifi. Provision of rewashing machine on request.

In an inn built in the 19th century within a wine-growing village, Le Montrachet offers you various rooms with evocative names : *1er cru*, *village* and *Grand cru*. The 1er cru rooms, spacious for entry levels (25 m^2) are all equipped with a telephone, a wi-fi access and an office corner. Since 2013, you can also choose to stay at Villa Christine, a bourgeois house with a garden and which is also located on place des Marronniers. The largest rooms in the hotel are the Grands crus, from 30 to 45 m^2, they offer all the comfort you can dream of. You are also welcome at the gourmet restaurant of the house that is located nearby. Enjoy your stay ! The cellar of the hotel gives you the opportunity to extend your pleasure by buying a good bottle (or many) that perhaps you have tasted beforehand during your meals.

In the surroundings

Chassagne-Montrachet

RESTAURANT ED.EM
4, impasse des Chenevottes
✆ +33 (0)3 80 21 94 94
restaurant-edem.com
contact@restaurant-edem.com

Open from Wednesday to Sunday for lunch and dinner. Booking advised. Menus from €35 to €100 (the market menu at €35 is served at lunchtime except on Sunday). 1 Michelin star.

When you have talent, you quickly draw attention. This is the case for Edouard Mignot and Emilie Rey who have settled in Chassagne since 2013. After experiences enriched alongside starred chefs, the last one in Lameloise, each of them brings his own expertise to the quality of their services. Edouard on the main courses and Emilia on the desserts. ED.EM offers an aesthetic and delicious gourmet cuisine, prepared with fresh ingredients that make us travel throughout France. Foie gras from Landes or Vendée, John Dorry fish from the Côte Bretonne, Bresse poultry. Roasted, stewed, reduced into juice or cold or mounted in soufflés, the products are left to the creativity of our young chefs. Above all, do not deprive yourself of the dessert as Emilie, a pastry chef, will amaze you. ED.EM restaurant immediately rose to the rank of gourmet restaurant. The wine list showcases the fields of Chassagne-Montrachet but also copiously offers the Côte Chalonnaise to remain reasonable in prices. It is in a quiet room with simple decoration that you will appreciate this restaurant whose destiny is confirmed as promising.

ESTATE OF PICARD'S FAMILY
Château de Chassagne
5, chemin du Château
✆ +33 (0)3 80 21 98 57
www.chateaudechassagnemontrachet.com
contact@domainefamillepicard.com

Open Monday to Saturday from 10am to 6pm. High season : Sunday from 10am to 6pm. High season : from April at All Saints. Possible delivery (60 names with the shop). Visit + tasting 5 wines 45 ' 17€. By reservation, tastings with Mâchon 40€/nobody and Table 65€/nobody.

The Domaine Famille Picard owns 135 hectares of vineyards (including about one hundred in Côte Chalonnaise). It produces about sixty appellations : Chassagne-Montrachet 1er Cru, Corton Grand Cru « Clos des Fiètres » and, of course, Chassagne-Montrachet Clos du Château. In Côte de Beaune, the family has a 35 hectares of vineyards that is biodynamically cultivated by Francine Picard and her master winemaker, Fabrice Lesne. The succesful experience of biodynamic farming in Côte de Beaune will extend to the Côte Chalonnaise where about twenty hectares of 1er Crus Mercurey are going to be treated. Note also its policy of only working with new barrels so as to preserve the mineral side of the terroir. This estate is a crucial stopover for lovers of wine, art and gastronomy. After the visit of the beautiful cellars of 11th and 14th centuries, the tasting of the best vintages is a must in a shop that combines history and modernity. The minerality of the wine is explained with the observation of the soil's sample in tubes and confirmed by our palates after. You should admire the huge triptych marquetry representing the castle and the Picard family. A unique work, made with 40 different species of wood that required 8 years work... To extend the pleasure, sit down around a Burgundian menu accompanied by wines from the estate (on reservation). You can also stay in one of the elegant guest rooms of the castle where contemporary decor blends perfectly with monthly art exhibitions.

Corpeau

L'AUBERGE DU VIEUX VIGNERON
Route de Beaune ✆ +33 (0)3 80 21 39 00
www.aubergeduvieuxvigneron.com
aubergevieuxvigneron@free.fr
« Maître Restaurateur » label. Closed two weeks in August and February. Open from Wednesday to Sunday for lunch and dinner. Booking advised. Menus from €20 to €29. Children's menu : €10 (with drinks). Lunch formula : €14 (starter, main course, dessert, a glass of wine). Groups welcome (a specific room can accommodate up to 55 people). Terrace. Activities. Caterer service. Wine estate.
L'Auberge du Vieux Vigneron in Corpeau is a place as we like it to be : a rustic atmosphere, beams, a fireplace, laughters and good mood at all tables. The hostel in all its splendor ! The chef Sylvain Férré puts all his talent at the service of tasty regional cuisine. You can opt for one of the regional specialties such as *escarbœuf* (a melting beef cheek confit with snails, a surprising and delicious blend) or for grilled meat from the fireplace, the sirloin flank steak accopanied with a Berthaut Epoisses sauce. You can also have a real gourmet pleasure with the Gratin of crayfish tail with Marc de Bourgogne ! And finish with a hot soufflé with sloe or a coupe vigneronne (cassis sorbet, cream of cassis and Marc de Bourgogne). In addition to these delights, there is an extremely well-refered wine list with 150 winegrowers and 300 appellations... People come from afar to L'Auberge an for good reason : Jean-Charles Fagot, your host, is also a winemaker. The terrace is very pleasant in fine weather. And groups are welcomed (on reservation) thanks to a new room that can accomodate 55 seats.

RECEY-SUR-OURCE

In the surroundings

Bure-les-Templiers

COMMANDERIE DE BURE-LES-TEMPLIERS
1, rue de l'Eglise
✆ +33 (0)3 80 81 31 67 / +33 (0)7 89 06 54 12
www.commanderie-bure-les-templiers.com
Open all year. Visit all year by appointment. Adult : €9. Group rate : €7.
In the 12th century, the lord of Bures, Payen became templar and donated all his goods on the newly founded order of Hugues de Payns and his companions. This Temple House is certainly one of the first that the Order owned. Weapons rooms, workshops, store rooms, gardens and dovecot. As the others farm of the monk- soldiers, it had a fortress look with a thick wall dominated by several towers. It is said that one hundred people could live there. With the disappearance of the Templars, Commanderie passes to the knights of St. John of Jerusalem then, sold to the Revolution and used as agricultural building. The owners did not care about. Stonework disappeared and... in 1953, a part was even cut down with explosive ! Since 2009, an association was created to restore it... Works are now in progress and you can visit it by appointment. You will notice its former splendour ! Do not miss the Guillaume de Fougerolles's tombstone, bays with benches of the watchmen and the monumental fireplaces. To help preserving these beautiful stones, do not hesitate to order terrines, books, postcards, notebooks or a online seal reproduction on the association's website. You can even join this for the modest sum of €20 per year.

LE SABOT DE VÉNUS
13, Grande Rue ✆ +33 (0)3 80 81 00 28
www.le-sabotdevenus.fr
lesabotdevenus050@orange.fr
Open all year round. From Monday to Saturday for lunch; on Saturday for dinner. On Friday night for group reservation only. Booking advised. Menus from €25 to €37(+ slate's suggestion). Lunch formula : €13.50 (starter, main course, dessert. €15 for starter, main course, cheese and dessert). Wine by the glass. Terrace. Sabot de Venus remains one of our favorite restaurants for this year 2016. We like the simplicity and quality of the reception of Sabrina and Arole Dupaty who gave to their restaurant the name of the largest mainland orchid blooming in our region. The restaurant is decidedly gourmet even the lunch menu. Every day, Arole, the chef delights us with beautiful dishes, scrupulously cooked according to the seasons, favouring local products, of quality, such as the farm Epoisses, the trout from Veuxhaulles-sur-Aube or Burgundy truffles that he will find himself. Arole recipes are prepared with simplicity, respecting the product but always with great skill. Cannellonis of trout and smoked salmon, Trout fillet with spices, Chicken supreme with Epoisses cheeses. Do not miss the roasted pear, it is famous. The food is authentic, the flavors are crisp, each dish is tasted with pleasure. And at the risk of repeating it, it all takes place in an almost familiar simplicity, which is very significant. Remember to book your outing on Saturday because it will be very quickly full. In summer, the terrace is very pleasant to enjoy the calm offered by this small village. And if you wish to stay a few days here, the owners opened a cottage in a typical farmhouse of Châtillonnais, a few steps from the restaurant.

Leuglay

■ MAISON DE LA FORÊT

1, ruelle de la Ferme
✆ +33 (0)3 80 81 86 11 / +33 (0)7 52 03 37 19
www.maison-foret.com
leuglay@maison-foret.com

Open from April 1st to September 7th and during All Saints holidays. Closing periods : possible visits on appointment. Open Tuesday to Friday from 9am to 12pm and from 2pm to 6pm; the weekend from 2pm to 6pm. Adult : €5. Child : €3. Detailed calendar of the outings and events on the website.

The nature opens its door to Maison de la Forêt. This place of exchange and discovery is located at the edge of Ource in Leuglay, in the heart of the future National Park « Des Forêts de Champagne et Bourgogne ». The purpose of the association is to make people discover and promote the forest heritage of Châtillonnais while sensitising a broad public about the environment and the woodwork. The house offers many activities around these themes. In the interpretation centre, you can explore the forest through tactile, olfactory and hearing experiences and complete the visit by the temporary exhibitions. Maison de la Forêt organizes numerous open air activities like walks, orchid outings or tree climbing. You can also go for discovery of mushrooms or of wild berries and why not familiarize yourself with the animal tracks, the call of the deer. For the more adventurous Maison de la Forêt offers games of track. The mission consists in finding clues by using a GPS. A sporting and recreational activity in a beautiful setting ! Established in the end of 2014, the arboretum develops and is visited freely just opposite the parking. With Maison de la Forêt, look at the forest from a different perspective and learn to listen to nature.

SAINT-JEAN-DE-LOSNE AND SEURRE ON THE SAÔNE RIVER ★★

Located at the confluence of the Saône, the Burgundy canal and the Rhin-Rhône canal, the city is a major inland waterways transport centre until the early 20th century but the road transportation development causes the decline of the marine economy. Fortunately for Saint-Jean-de-Losne, the river tourism has a very dynamic activity. Its port is frequented by more than 5,000 boats every year thanks to the Voie Bleue, there are more and more and more cyclists in the city. It is also an important centre of water sports. The Boat Show in April and the festival of « *Pardon des Mariniers* » in June and the Saint-Nicolas in December attract a huge public, without forgetting the *Vendredis des Quais* in July-August and the Salon Photo Nature du Val de Saône that takes place in March. The history of the city has been full of events since the Middle Ages :

- **Located in a privileged place**, with a bridge over the Saône, the city was a neutral ground between the Empire and the Kingdom of France, the city of Saint-Jean-de-Losne hosted a meeting between Louis VII and the Emperor Frédéric Barberousse in 1162.

- **Later on, this bridge over the Saône** became a strategic point of passage and a toll was set up there. Originally it was dependent on the Duke of Burgundy, the city was attached to the royal domain under Louis XI with the death of Charles The Bold, in 1477. The Saône became a border and remained so until the reign of Louis XIV, in 1678.

- **In 1636, during the Thirty Years' War, the Austrian troops**, run by Gallas, entered the kingdom of France by the cities of Gray and Dole. After having completely destroyed villages and towns of the right bank of the Saône (including Pontailler, Mirebeau, Talmay), Gallas decided to take over Saint-Jean-de-Losne and its passage on the Saône. After three attacks, the city withstood and the besieged inhabitants categorically refused to surrender : the Austrian troops then removed the camp and retreated towards the County. King Louis XIII awarded the heroic resistance of the inhabitants by removing the tax. Two flags taken from the Austrians during the attacks are still preserved in the Saint-Jean-Baptiste church.

- **With the French Revolution**, Saint-Jean-de-Losne was the first city in France to abandon its privileges. Under the Empire, it was, with Chalon and Tournus, the first town to receive the Legion of Honour.

Two poles of transshipment for the river transport remain intensive at the crossing of 3 railway lines and 3 canals :

- **Saint-Usage for the cereal production of the region.**

- **The Techno-port de Pagny-le-Château for the transport of wood**, building materials, salt or NOZ destocking products.

■ TOURIST OFFICE OF RIVES DE SAÔNE – BRANCH OF SAINT-JEAN-DE-LOSNE

2, rue de la Liberté
✆ +33 (0)3 80 37 15 70
www.saone-tourisme.fr
stjeandelosne@saone-tourisme.fr
Next to the Town hall.

Low season : open Tuesday to Friday from 9.30am to 12pm and from 2pm to 5.30pm; Saturday from 9.30am to 1pm. High season : Monday to Saturday from 9am to 12.30pm and from 2pm to 6pm. High season from 1st of April to 30th of September. English reception. Rental of adult and children's bike. SNCF ticket office.

The Tourist Office Rives de Saône in Saint-Jean-de-Losne has been set next to the town hall. You will find all necessary information on the city of Saint-Jean-de-Losne and its surroundings there to make your stay more pleasant. The office offers several types of guided tours upon reservation. A one-hour guided tour takes you on a tour of this city full of riches and retraces the history of the city. You will discover the town hall and its original 18th-century wallpaper, the church, with its listed

organ, Maison des Mariniers with a permanent exhibition on sea-faring, the marina, the water station, etc.). For the most gourmets, this visit can be accompanied by a tasting of local produces. Practical, the Tourist Office also provides SNCF Ticket. Since 2015, Balade de Marinier has become a must to visit the water station and its port or the historic heritage of the city. The 2016 novelties is the rental of bikes. This allows you to better enjoy the riches of Saint-Jean-de-Losne.

■ BALADE DES MARINIERS

Gare d'eau ✆ +33 (0)3 80 37 15 70
www.saone-tourisme.fr
contact@saone-tourisme.fr
Free access.
This touristic and cultural course, open since April 2015 with the initiative of the community of Rives de Saône communes and the financial assistance of the State, the Pays Beaunois and Europe, honours the life of the sailors and the activity of the professionals of river in Saint-Jean-de-Losne and Saint-Usage. Visitors and residents can discover or rediscover the wealth of the city of inland water, its history and evolution, in an original and fun way. The tour offers several options : the discovery of the life of the sailors, the technical tour that highlights the know-how of the companies, the grand tour of the water station and the heritage tour of the city centre of Saint-Jean-de-Losne. Various panels with comments and flash code are installed and that you can discover freely. You can download a guide on *smartphone* or tablet (can be borrowed at the Tourist Office). For a total immersion into the world of inland waterway transport, men and women who made its history.

■ BATEAU VAGABONDO

Quai National ✆ +33 (0)6 07 42 75 54
www.bateauvagabondo.com
bateau.vagabondo@orange.fr
In July-August, cruise with accompanying notes of 1h30 (13 km) for the individual ones, with operation of lock. In July-August : departure at 3.30pm every day except Monday and Tuesday. Adult : €12.50. Child (from 6 to 12 years old) : €10. Cruise-meal Sunday : €50.40. €37 for the children. For groups : all year by reservation.
Saint-Jean-de-Losne is the first fluvial marina in France. Surrounded by water and several large channels, it is a den of all boatmen ! This is especially the playground of Johny Mino, an atypical captain of the cruise Vagabondo. All aboard the National Platform to share a relaxing time aboard this boat that is comfortable for a cruise and where culture, history and gastronomy mixes. With no less than 120 cruise seats and 80 cruise meals, Vagabondo and its panoramic terrace take you on a ride with stunning views of nature and the city. Johny, like a gruff Indian makes you taste the charming banks of the Saône, the wonder of observing the wildlife and the pleasures of the table... like in the restaurant ! In summer, the cruise trip starts on Wednesday and Sunday from 15 : 30. The cruise meals for individuals take place of Sundays from July to August from 11h30 14h30. For groups, it is all along the year. Get more information : everything is possible, even renting the boat for seminars, family meals or a wedding party !

Sightseeing

■ LA MAISON DES MARINIERS – MUSEE DE LA BATELLERIE ★

3-5, rue de la Liberté
✆ +33 (0)3 80 72 32 62 / +33 (0)6 41 75 25 13
museestj@gmail.com
Open of Easter at the end of October. Open every day and public holidays from 10am to 12pm and from 2.30pm to 6.30pm. By appointment the rest of the year for groups. Free. Guided tour : €3.
La Maison des Mariniers is one of the oldest houses in the city. It dates from the 5th century and was built in mud, brick, terracotta and oak ceilings, according the tradition of the Saône's plain. The Burgundian Virgin, carved on a beam, is admirable. In addition to this advantageous setting, visitors can immersed themselves in the lives of sailors and skippers with a permanent exhibition on the old navigation. Photographs, models and objects reflect their daily lives : mechanical, lock, loading, net and a complete clothes of diver that you'd think it has come straight out of a Tintin adventure. Temporary exhibitions still add to the interest of the place. The association AQUA works throughout the year for the safeguard of the river heritage. Its members also offers you a visit of the renovation work site of the last wooden barge of France. The barge Aster goes back to 1950 and was in the beginning tractor drawn by horses. Today, it expects the visitors on the wearing of Saint-Jean-de-Losne. For more information, please contact La Maison des Mariniers.

■ SENTIER DES 5 VILLAGES
2, rue de la Liberté
✆ +33 (0)03 80 37 15 70
www.saone-tourisme.fr
contact@saone-tourisme.fr
The community of municipalities continues the creation of marked trails on its territory with « the path of the 5 villages » that starts at a distance of 18 km in the north of Saint-Jean-de-Losne. Along the way, walkers discover the docks of Saint-Jean-de-Losne, the towpath of the Burgundy canal, a washhouse recently renovated by the city of Montot, the banks of Ouche and various small villages. This tour is marked in yellow. Departure at the corner of rue Monge and the alley of Bastion des Charmilles where a totem will soon be installed. You can find the plans and description of all tours on the website of the Banks of Saône Tourist Office : www.saone-tourisme.fr

Knife & Fork

■ AUBERGE DE LA MARINE
Quai de la Hutte
✆ +33 (0)3 80 27 03 27
www.auberge-delamarine.com
aubergedelamarine@wanadoo.fr
Logis. Closed in January. Open Tuesday to Sunday for lunch and dinner. Menu from €15 to €33 (+ à la carte). Children's menu : €9.50. Lunch menu : €13 (starter, main course, dessert). Hotel of 15 rooms, from €70 per night. Groups welcome. Terrace.
Here is a table that has managed to maintain its course : i.e. offering a traditional, family and quality classic cuisine. The indoor rooms are perfect with their white and the floors to ceiling windows. The tables are spaced for a meal in all privacy. In summer, you can enjoy your meal on the pleasant terrace of the hotel. The reception is very professional and friendly. As fo the menu, there are numerous formulas and suits each season : grilled meat, vegetarian, dietetics or the daily special. You can taste there fish fryings, eggs in meurette, many other regional classics and calf's head that will respond to your need ! A fresh and homemade cuisine. Do not miss the frog's season. Here, they are fresh and prepared in a delicious way.

Sleeping

■ LES CHARMILLES
15, rue Monge
✆ +33 (0)9 84 19 19 55
www.lescharmillesbandb.jimdo.com
beatricecollenot@gmail.com
3 rooms. Single room €55; double room €63. Breakfast included. Extra bed : €30. Catering facilities (table d'hôte on reservation €25 all inclusive, €12 for child of less than 13 years. Barbecue and small cusine). Near to the port and the docks. Bike storage room and motorbikes. Parking nearby.
We do not imagine that, behind this simple façade, there is a little safe haven with the particular charm of banks of Saône. The guest house dating back to 1746 has kept its architectural typical features, quit inner courtyard, half floors, wood panelling, old terracotta floor tiles... The 3 rooms have a pleasant style, those upstairs overlook the garden and terrace, bathroom in the background, it is cosy with a little british style and even boat-like, but on land. Béatrice Collenot who welcomes you is very caring, from breakfast to table d'hôtes dinner. She prepares a real little burgundy feast, gougère and wine. Life at Charmilles happens inside a quiet house with an inner courtyard with flowers and trees where calm and serenity reign. When you enter there, you are at the city centre, on the left at 200m from the port, on the right at 200m from the Banks of Saône.

Leisure

■ PARCOURS ECOPAGAYEUR DE SAINT-JEAN-DE-LOSNE
Base Canoë-Kayak du Pays Losnais
Chemin de la Plage
✆ +33 (0)3 80 77 92 78 / +33 (0)3 80 39 17 99 / +33 (0)6 61 17 15 47
www.pagaies-des-bords-de-saone.fr
ecopagayeurstjean@orange.fr
Open from April to end of September. By reservation safe in July-August : open every day from 10am to 6pm. €13 per person for 2 a.m. (€11 for under 14-year-olds). Itinerant course : from €18 to €30 per person.
A unique concept in France set up at the initiative of the Regional Committee of Canoeing in Burgundy and managed in St. John by the Pagaies des Bords de Saône. The EcoPagayeur trip is intended to anyone who can swim. Go to the canoe- kayak, which is newly renovated, volunteer of the base will call you to give the necessary equipment (boat or car tandem very easy to maneuver, lifejackets, paddles, etc.) and then you can choose the option that best suits you ! You can choose between small EcoPagayeur, a loop circuit discovery of 2 to 3 hours intended to family wishing to explore the flora and fauna of the region or a hiking tour that can bring you to Seurre. It is very well organized : a volunteer at the base picks you up and takes you back to St. John. You go with a guidebook that leads you from tag to tag. A questionnaire in the form of treasure hunt, given at the start of the course, teaches you in a fun way all you need to know about the heritage, flora, fauna... A great way to discover the biodiversity of the river in fun way !

Boat

■ H2O – LES SPÉCIALISTES DU FLUVIAL
Port de plaisance
✆ +33 (0)3 80 39 08 08 / +33 (0)3 80 39 23 00
www.h2o-bateau.fr
h2o@h2ofrance.com
Open Monday to Friday from 9am to 12pm and from 1.30pm to 5.30pm; Saturday from 9am to 12pm. Schedule shop of upperworks.

H2O is a company specialised into the creation and the management of the river port, the repair, the maintenance, the arrangement, the upkeep and the sale of the new and used boat since 1987. H2O is also a harbourmaster of Saint-Jean-de-Losne, a second river port of France with nearly 500 boats at anchor and 130 boats in dry dock. H2O accomodates itself 500 boats. Nestled in the heart of the small town of Saint-Jean-de-Losne, it offers boaters fully equipped pontoon, electrical outlets, water points, wi-fi connection and a webcam to monitor your boat from a distance. In 2015, new arrangements are made for storing 50 to 80 boats in a closed building, and nearly 200 boats in dry docks, enough to secure and protect the draining. H2O has a permanent sale of a selection of over 100 new and used boats (the largest site in France), fluvial speedboat, sea speedboat, Dutch speedboat, including those of Linssen site, as well as equipped-boats. The hardware store, expanded in 2015 is one of the best supplied of the waterways, it offers customers an XXL choice of materials adapted to the equipment and boat maintenance. H2O, which employs 40 people, is also installed at Port Royal in Auxonne, a 150 rings port that will have a capacity of 300 places.

In the surroundings

Brasey-en-Plaine

■ **CHEZ FANNY**
15, route de Dijon
✆ +33 (0)3 80 57 35 54
www.pizzafanny.fr
pizzafannhie@aol.fr
Open daily for lunch and dinner. Snack menu, pizzas and traditional dishes. Children's menu : €6. Lunch menu : €12 (cold and hot buffet – starter, main course, cheese, dessert). Beginning of the evening service at 5.30pm. Covered terrace – Catering – Takeouts, possible deliveries at 10 km around the restaurant.

Chez Fanny is a lovely restaurant located in the middle of Brazey on a plain, on the main roads, you can find it at the foot of chestnut trees and cedars. Chez Fanny, born in 2011 (already 5 years ago) with take-away Pizza, evolves each year. Stéphanie and Mathieu Hierholzer are very enterprising, they invest regularly and surround themselves with talented people. In 2016, the team managed by Michael Bajotet, who has already worked at some restaurants at Côte d'Orienne. Chez Fanny has also its pastry chef who regularly follows a training on the techniques of the profession. As for the pizzaiolo, he participates in regional competitions in order to confront himself with his counterparts. The kitchen is beautifully equipped which enables good cooking and the a good elaboration of the « homemade ». The restaurant is settled in a new building, where the atmosphere is resolutely family and friendly. At lunchtime, those who do not choose a nice pizza will choose the daily specials, good price and maximum choice since the cold and warm buffet offers a choice between 3 or 4 alternatives with the 3 main courses. If you desire more classical main courses, the choice is up to you with the Sole meunière, Coq au vin (with yellow wine) or Steak or Andouillette. As for spring, the menu will be added with more gastronomic dishes. By the way, the room will have been renovated with new contemporary furnishings. It is the fifth birthday gift of the address to the guests !

SEURRE

45 km from Dijon, 25 km from Beaune and 30 km from Dole, Seurre, city of history and relaxation, stretches along the Saône.

In summer, the hometown of Bossuet family offers the pleasures of river tourism, fishing and water sports : canoeing, fishing, water skiing, Water Park with slides and Olympic pool. So join the banks of the Saône and go meet the fishermen to tickle carp, catfish and perch... Do not hesitate to taste the local specialties : fried, pochouse (assembly of four fish cooked in white wine) history lovers will gladly go along the streets of the city, discovering typical local materials : brick and wood. Go further, to the marina, after the lock where a hiking trail begins.

CÔTE-D'OR

The Jacquemart

12 panels displaying the main buildings and remarkable places were installed in the city. Discover the Hotel-Dieu, the English Garden, St Martin's Church, the oldest bridge of Seurre, home of the salt tax officer, Bossuet house, wooden house, the town hall, the wheat Market, the Jacquemart, the Ursuline Convent and the banks of the Saône. 2 starting totems located Place des Marronniers and Place des Quinconces recall the history of Seurre in its lines and have a map of location of the panels. Note that part of the text was translated into English and that children can pleasantly enjoy the visit since the small Jacquemart addresses on each sign a question, an enigma. Two small brochures are on sale at the tourism Office : one for adults, the other for children.

■ OFFICE DE TOURISME RIVES DE SAÔNE-ANTENNE DE SEURRE

13, rue Bossuet
✆ +33 (0)9 61 38 56 11
www.saone-tourisme.fr
seurre@saone-tourisme.fr

Open from April to September Monday to Saturday from 9am to 12pm and from 2pm to 6.30pm. Open from October to March Tuesday, Thursday and Friday from 9am to 12pm and from 2pm to 5.30pm and Saturday from 9am to 1pm. Open on Sunday (in July and August : Sundays even mornings. Closed public holidays). Guided tours for groups by reservation.

The tourist office is located in one of the most prestigious houses of the town, opposite the town hall : the Bossuet house. You will find many information about Seurre, Burgundy, Saône-et-Loire and Jura. The tourist office offers two tours of the city. The first includes a guided tour of Musée de la Saône and people from Saône. The second one allows you to explore the city, its historic centre, the houses of brick and half-timbered, the church, the old houses, etc. On request, you can also visit the lock and observe how it works. These tours are only possible for groups of more than 10 people and upon reservation.

■ VISITES COMMENTÉES

Office de Tourisme Rives de Saône – Antenne de Seurre
13, rue Bossuet
✆ +33 (0)9 61 38 56 11
www.saone-tourisme.fr
contact@saone-tourisme.fr

In summer season. By reservation. €3 guided tour/ €7 guided tour with tasting of regional produce.

In summer, the branch of the Tourism Office of Banks of Saône in Seurre invites you to discover the historical heritage of the city in about 1h30. The visit is marked by interesting stories of a commentator from Seurre. Gourmets can taste local produce. A good way to discover Seurre's heritage, historical and culinary delights !

Sightseeing

■ L'ÉTANG ROUGE – OPEN-AIR MUSEUM

✆ +33 (0)3 80 20 48 54
(Communauté de Communes « Rives de Saône »)

Free admission Mondays, Tuesday, Thursday and Friday of 9am with 17 h30. Guided tours by reservation Tel : 09 61 38 56 11. Adult : €3. Group (10 people) : €2.50.

At the exit of Seurre, at a stone's throw from Jallanges, a typical Burgundian village was reconstructed from old houses surrounding the municipalities; disassembled, repaired and transported to the site, they have been re-erected. We can now admire a half-timbered house of the 17th century, with an oven room, pig teaks, a barn, a dovecot, a farm laborer, presses of the 18th century, a school room and cadole... It is an opportunity to discover the ancient techniques and materials. An exhibition of old tools and equipment is installed in one of the buildings and descriptive panels of the site adorn the walk. And children from 8 years old can participate in a treasure hunt, « the mystery of the red pond ». They make an independent visit for €5 equipped with full kit (compass, flashlight, pencil, etc.) that allows them to solve enigmas. Success is guaranteed !

■ L'HÔTEL-DIEU ★

Hôpital Ernest Noël
14, Grande rue du Faubourg Saint-Georges
✆ +33 (0)3 80 20 39 19 – www.ch-seurre.net
hopitalseurre@wanadoo.fr

Open all year. Booking compulsory. Special rate groups. Free for under 12-year-olds. Adult : €6. Guided tour (duration 1.30am).

Like Beaune, Seurre has also a magnificent and very famous Hôtel-Dieu hospital. It was built during the 17th and 18th centuries, then the north wing was built in the second half of the 19th century. The establishment and its sick ward were managed by the hospitable nuns who offered various services : health care for patients, the elderly who are in need, surgeries, childbirth... You can visit the chapel, the Salle des Pôvres and its 18 beds, the pharmacy with a hundred of earthenware pots, as well as the bishop. As many splendid testimonies of the hospital life under the Old Regime.

Knife & Fork

■ LE GRILLARDIN

5, grande rue du faubourg Saint-Georges
✆ +33 (0)3 80 21 17 62 – www.legrillardinseurre.fr

Open Tuesday to Saturday for lunch and dinner. Set menu at €26.60. Children's menu : €8.15. Lunch menu : €14.90 (main dish and dessert. €19.90 starter main course). Wine by the glass. Terrace.

Grillardin is definitely a good address in Seurre. It is in a contemporary setting, that Stéphanie and Yves Marchal welcome you. The slate wall acts as the menu; the menus vary according market produces, the seasons and the chef's inspiration too. In the dishes, Grillardin shows its efficiency with a touch of originality in the presentation. Big butcher's dish à la plancha, Trio of fish à la plancha, but also crispy foie gras, Sweetbreads with ratafia essence. Otherwise, opt for the wide choice of pizza. In summer, the terrace can serve 110 tables in a beautiful bright ambience in the evening... and the Saône is not far for a digestive ride.

Leisure

■ CLUB D'AVIRON

Camping Municipal de la Plage
Route de Dijon ✆ +33 (0)6 27 02 23 29
avironseurre@gmail.com

Open all the Sunday morning for the initiates from 9.45am to 12pm all year (depending on weather conditions and believed...). Open on Saturday afternoon from 3pm to 5pm for the beginners. Rates : initiation €3. Licence minor : €60. Licence adult : €70.

Do you want to discover this new water sports that is very complete physically speaking ? You are welcome, from 11 years-old, if you know how to swim ! You don't need much strength, but you must apply and coordinate yourself well with your partners in order to have a balance in the water and then to propel yourself. Find the agenda of the club on the site : www.cda21.org/les-clubs-daviron/seurre/132-agenda-aviron-seurre.html

■ VOIE BLEUE SEURRE – SAINT-JEAN-DE-LOSNE – EUROVELO 6

✆ +33 (0)3 80 21 09 11 / +33 (0)3 80 29 05 48

EuroVelo 6 that connects Nantes to Budapest passes through Seurre and Saint-Jean-de-Losne. This is the Côte-d'Or General Council in the framework of its cycling policy created cycle routes and greenways. The 25 kilometres between Seurre and Saint-Jean-de-Losne have been completed two years ago. This easily accessible course combines greenways and passageways on roads and paths offering many sections along the Saône and many places to visit in the two towns.

Boat

■ CAPITAINERIE DU PORT DE SEURRE

Rue de la Raie Mignot ✆ +33 (0)3 80 20 31 05
capitainerie.seurre@rivesdesaone.fr

Flexible schedule dependings on the season. Information by telephone or e-mail.

The port and the river stop of Seurre allow the sailors to find water and electricity. The harbour, open all year round, has the following services : toilets, shower, washing machine and tumble dryer, Wifi. Tenants or owners of boats, remember this address ! It will help you on your next visit in this charming city crossed by the Saône.

Shopping

■ FAUBOURG DES SAVEURS

69, rue de la République ✆ +33 (0)3 80 20 71 70
www.faubourg-des-saveurs.com
contact@faubourg-des-saveurs.om

Open Tuesday to Saturday from 9am to 12pm and from 3pm to 7pm. Open on Sunday from 9am to 12pm in high season. By reservation fixed rate formulas tasting of the cheese-making heritage – from 4 to 12 people – €10 to €12 per person.

Faubourg des Saveurs is both a delicatessen and dairy but also a selection of regional specialties. Stéphane Vésin, your advisor, took over the address after a career of a chef then many stages of food trade with fish as main specialties. Now the AOC cheeses of France have no more secret for him, they tasted them all so who could be better to be your guide. The dairy section has a hundred varieties, from Corsica, Aquitaine, Auvergne, Franche-Comté or Normandy. The wine shop corner of thirty references allows you to choose the vintage that will best suit your cheese preferences. The delicatessen section allows you to discover chocolates, gingerbreads, fruit juices and jams with references like Manière, Mulot Petit Jean, Daniel Cachot, Fruirouge or Moutarderie Fallot... Without forgetting the teas, herbal teas or coffees coming straight from the Jura. Stéphane organises tastings for groups with a range of 5 cheeses accompanied by a glass of Haute Côte de Beaune or a Chablis, with crusty bread naturally !

In the surroundings

Chamblanc

■ SITE ANNE-MARIE JAVOUHEY – ROUTE DES ABOLITIONS DE L'ESCLAVAGE

High school Anne-Marie Javouhey
20, rue Anne-Marie-Javouhey
Association Sur la route des libertés de Chamblanc à Mana
✆ +33 (0)3 80 20 30 90
✆ +33 (0)3 80 21 11 60
www.abolitions.org
mairie.chamblanc@wanadoo.fr

Anne -Marie Javouhey born at Jallanges in 1779 founded in May 1807 the Congregation of Saint Joseph of Cluny. In 1819, the minister at the time requested her for Senegal which had just been linked to France. She discovered misery and heinous slave trade. She quickly realizes she only has recourse to the purchase of the black slaves to release them. In 1838, she found herself in Mana in Guyana where she released on May 13, 185 slaves and these ten years before the enactment of the Act of 1848. With the integration of the municipality of Chamblanc, Jallanges and Seurre on the way to the abolition of slavery, Anne-Marie Javouey is rank alongside Toussaint Louverture, Victor Schoelcher, Abbé Grégoire and the inhabitants of Champagney who, on March 19th, 1789, launched the first call of the people against the slave trade and slavery. To commemorate this action, on May 14th, 2011, 147 trees were planted in the presence of existing and identified descendants. The family home of Anne-Marie Javouhey, located in the school premises Anne-Marie Javouhey high school at Chamblanc, is to be visited. Also : the hiking trail that traces the milestones of the life of the missionary is to be visited.

Franxault

LAC DE CHOUR

✆ +33 (0)6 26 74 64 57
✆ +33 (0)6 22 68 06 72
www.lacdechour.fr
infoslacdechour@gmail.com

Closed of October at February 14th. February, March, April and May : open at weekends from 10am to 6pm. June, July and August : open every day from 10am to 8pm. September : open on Monday, Wednesday and the weekend from 10am to 6pm. Free for children under 5 years old. Camper van sites. Catering facilities with terrace at the edge of water. Catering facilities. Supervised swimming, petanque, pedal boats, inflatable structures for the small ones, fishing, beach, facilities, parking.

Le lac de Chour has a total area of 58 hectares, including 38 hectares of water.

This place has a lush vegetation which makes it beautiful so it's perfect for holidays in the wilderness. Valérie Million and Norbert Campioni succeeded and managed to create a link between respect of the nature and warm welcoming of many visitors. A part of the lake is reserved for bathing pleasure and idleness. The adventurers and the sportsmen will choose to travel by pedal boats or the tour of the lake on foot or by bicycle. The fishermen also have a space and various options to discover the beautiful freshwater fish livestock. The fishing lovers can even park their camper vans on one of the spots reserved for that purpose in direct access to the water. After those tiring activity, you can relax in the open air or visiting and tasting the delicious dishes of the restaurant at the chalet and in the terrace of 80 seats nearby the water. They offer simple dishes but the quality is on the top : meal salads, mussels or grilled meats especially the homemade ice-creams. Carp fishing, lachée de truite, dancing parties at night, stamina races of horses, triathlon, concerts... There are lots of entertainments and the pleasure is guaranteed ! Added by the quality of the magnificient water, the playground of bowls and the parking are convenient, Le lac de Chour will charm kidsl and parents for an outing by the water it will remain in your memory !

SAINT-SEINE-L'ABBAYE

OFFICE DE TOURISME DU PAYS DE SAINT-SEINE

Place de l'Eglise
✆ +33 (0)3 80 35 00 44
www.cc-forets-seine-suzon.fr
tourisme@cc-forets-seine-suzon.fr

Variable opening days depending on the seasons. Exhibitions. Guided tours for groups by reservation : €2 per person.

The Tourist Office of Pays de Saint-Seine is located at the foot of the abbey. Charming staff welcomes you with warmth and professionalism. You'll find all the practical information on lodging, meals and visits to the surrounding areas. You can buy local produce, books and some products from handicraft. Admire the model of the abbey, the facsimile terminal of the 13th century delimiting the former territory of the abbey (leased by the Archaeological Museum of Dijon) and copies of the statue of the goddess Sequana and the ex-votos found during archaeological excavations of the Seine sources. Panels give you indications about this Gallo-Roman sanctuary. In 2016, several exhibitions followed one another like that of the music instruments and harmony in summer... The hiking club « Sur les pas de Saint-Seine » organises two trips per month around the town. The trails are also accessible by mountain bike. In summer, there are night markets and guided tours that are offered by the tourist office. Upon reservation, discover the whole history of the abbey or the wind farm.

direct access to the beach	visually impaired disability	take away
bar	mental handicap	room service
laundry	motor disability	fitness room
air conditioning	garden or park	playroom / tv
nightclub	games	modern sanitary
cash machine	washing machine / laundry	water sports
drinking water	bicycle rental	tennis
horse riding	grocery store	archery
smoking area	airport shuttle	waterslide
non-smoking	fishing	fan
fitness	indoor swimming pool	toilet drain
miniature golf	outdoor heated pool	sailing
hard of hearing disability	outdoor pool	

Sightseeing

ABBATIALE DE SAINT-SEINE-L'ABBAYE ★

✆ +33 (0)3 80 35 00 44
www.cc-paysdesaintseine.fr

Open all year. Every day from 9am to 4pm. Free. Free tour. Guided tour all year for groups on request (€2). Information at the Tourist Office.

The abbey of Saint-Seine founded in the 6th century by Sigo, a monk from Moutiers-Saint-Jean hosted at the 8th a very famous resident : St. Benedict of Aniane, the reformer of the Benedictine order. This is where he took his vows. The community elects the abbot, but then he moved to Aniane near Montpellier. In the Middle Ages, the Abbey was one of the largest in Burgundy. The abbey was built in the early 13th century. Only the choir and transept have withstood time, the rest of the building burned in 1255. Work was resumed at the turn of the 14th and 15th centuries. The porch, is decorated with branches of vines. Watch them well : a snail is hiding in one of them ! Carved stalls of the 18th century are the work of the craftsman William Theiss Luxembourg. To see also : the frescoes of the 16th century. Please note : the abbey of Saint-Seine is a parish church since 1803. Every Sunday in summer, a Mass is still celebrated. Concerts are organised there. The address has an exceptional acoustic.

SAINTE-SABINE

Sainte-Sabine is a charming municipality with 200 inhabitants located a few minutes away from Pouilly-en-Auxois, 30 km from Beaune and 50 km from Dijon. History tells that, in the 12th century, a monk from the Abbaye de la Buissière went to Rome to bring back relic fragments (it was a current practice at that time to legitimize the building of a new religious establishment). He, then, came back from the Eternal City with a part of Saint Sabine's crane, a Christian martyr of the 2nd century. He died on his way back, in Lassey where Saint Martin established clergymen. The monks of Buissière came to pick the relic and their brother's dead body up. But a supernatural power kept them from moving forward. They left the Saint's relics in this place to which they give the name of Sainte-Sabine. In the 17th century, the De Messey family built there a splendid castle leaning over the valley. This castle is now a luxury hotel. Do not miss out this bucolic town, its 16th century church, the reliquary of Saint Sabine which is one of the most beautiful silverware of the 14th century, and the magnificent view on the Châteauneuf-en-Auxois. West of Sainte-Sabine, the Chazilly reservoir, favourite fishing place of the amateurs, is one of the five reservoirs which feed the Burgundy canal.

CHÂTEAU SAINTE-SABINE – RESTAURANT LE LASSEY

RD 970
✆ +33 (0)3 80 49 22 01
www.saintesabine.com
info@saintesabine.com

From April to October : closed on Wednesday with the lunch. From November to March : closed on Monday and Tuesday. Booking advised. Menu from €42 to €75. À la carte : Around €40. Lunch menu (Monday to Saturday) : from €26. Groups welcome (5 reception halls). Garden. Terrace.

Le Lassey, the restaurant of the Château Sainte-Sabine, offers a revisited cuisine that highlights the products of the region. The menu of the chef Sébastien Henry changes according to the season. Each midday, the restaurant offers a bistro-style menu with the rather exceptional price-quality ratio. In the evening, make your choice among the three elaborate menus. The menu « *dégustation* » is composed of 4 dishes chosen according to the arrivals of the market, cheeses and a sweet touch. Do not hesitate to try the adventure, you will not be disappointed ! The main courses are of a remarkable quality. The gourmet menu varies between land and sea, between snackéed oysters and duck foie gras, roasted scallops and fillet of Charolais beef among others. Lastly, the menu *gourmet* will make you want more, between the wild boar fillet with the juice of candied chestnuts and the pike quenelle with its periwinkles with parsley... The dish is suits perfectly the gourmet people. An exceptional table which, in our opinion, will soon be rewarded... During your lunch, dinner, one night or one week, Château Sainte-Sabine offers a magic... and unforgettable stopover !

CHÂTEAU SAINTE-SABINE – RESTAURANT LE LASSEY

RD 970
✆ +33 (0)3 80 49 22 01
www.saintesabine.com
info@saintesabine.com

Castles & Hôtels Collection. 22 rooms (two apartments being able to accommodate up to 5 people). Breakfast : €14. Room rates : between €110 and €220. Possibility of having rooms which communicate, on request. Pets allowed (€15). Free Wifi. Catering facilities (gourmet restaurant. Possibility of half-board).

Chateau Sainte-Sabine is among the most romantic places in Burgundy. Located between Dijon and Beaune, this splendid castle of the 17th century, built on a former monastery, is nested in the middle of a park of 8 hectares. It benefits from an ideal view on the medieval village of Châteauneuf-en-Auxois and the valley. It was taken over and since then beautifully renovated by Susanne and Jean-Louis Bottigliero, who have already been at the helm of Hostellerie de Levernois (five stars) and Hôtel du Parc (two stars), in Beaune. They transformed the castle into a charming hotel and restaurant that consists of 22 bright rooms, including two duplex apartments.

We were amazed by the taste and the modernity with which the rooms were decorated. Between traditional furniture, borderline vintage and bright and cordial colours... the rooms are very welcoming. Each room owns its equipped bathroom, a shower and a bathtub. Many visits, stroll and tastings are possible in the surrounding area. But there is no doubt that you will prefer to profit from the pool or the huge park where it is not rare to see deer, ducks or hares crossing there. Five function rooms can accommodate up to 70 people. The hotel offers various formulas : Golf (a tour is in the vicinity), Heritage, Truffle. Our very favourite ? The romantic getaway package that consists of a night at the castle, two breakfasts, two candlelit diners, two glass of champagne in an intimate place and a souvenir of Burgundy in the form of furnished basket. A gourmet and bucolic stay ! Unforgettable !

SANTENAY

« The Nice of Côte d'Or ». Such was the name given to Santenay by the Canon Kir. It should be said that this small Burgundian town displays an exhibition about the south. Sun and beautiful luminosity are well present ! It is known for its wines and its water. These are known as the ones that contain the most quantity of lithia in Europe and are recognized since the Antiquity period for their benefits : to cure diseases of the digestive system, diabetes, obesity, osteoarthritis but also the stress, thanks to their strong lithium content. At the late 19th century, four main sites were counted : the Salted fountain, the Santana source, the Carnot source and the Lithium source. Since 2010, an prefectoral order authorizes again the city to exploit its natural mineral water for therapeutic purposes. In other words, in 2017, Santenay will become again a true spa town. And we are glad of that ! And who says thermal spa also says... casino ! Santenay accommodates one of them since 1885. The one that exists today is very famous locally for its dynamism and its multiple entertainments.

But Santenay is also a city of wine. Its vineyard stretches over nearly 390 hectares, including 140 hectares in premier crus. Do not hesitate to push the door of the producers of the town who welcome you with open arms and make you discover the wine work and their passion for trade. A commune where it is good to live with its large area with water jets, its white stone houses, its Romanesque church of the 13th century, its slopes, superbly restored windmill, its multiple walks in the countryside...

OFFICE DE TOURISME BEAUNE & PAYS BEAUNOIS – ANTENNE DE SANTENAY
Place de la Gare ✆ +33 (0)3 80 20 63 15
www.beaune-tourisme.fr
tourisme@ville-de-santenay.fr

From January to March and in November and December : Tuesday, Thursday and Saturday from 2pm to 6pm. April, May and October : Tuesday to Saturday from 9.30am to 12.30pm and from 2pm to 6pm. From June to September : every day (and public holidays) from 9.30am to 12.30pm and from 2pm to 6.30pm. Open on Sunday (from May to September only). Closed from December 19th, 2016 to January 02nd, 2017. Free Wifi. Visited guided church and moulin by appointment : €3 per person, €2 from 10.

Located in the former railway station of Santenay, the tourist office is easily accessible thanks to its car park. You can get valuable information on Santenay, its surroundings and the region as a whole. The friendly and dynamic team offers you a visit of the mill and the church of the village all year long on request. Do not hesitate to ask for more information. Do you feel like enjoying a bike getaway ? It is possible to rent bikes here to have access to long-distance cycling route and the green lane. There are 10 bikes are at your disposal, including 3 for children and 4 electrical ones. The tourist office lends you for free accessories for your stroll, child seats and baskets. There is no excuse not to go to an adventure ! Recently, Antenne de Santenay has had a new look and has been completely renovated in a contemporary and welcoming atmosphere. On the programme : interactive touch screen at guest's use and a digital slide show of the local events.

Sleeping

CAMPING DES SOURCES
Avenue des Sources ✆ +33 (0)3 80 20 66 55
camping-de-santenay@orange.fr
Du Nord : Suivre A6, sortie 24.1 et quitter A6/E15. Prendre D1074, D974 et D974BIS en direction de Santenay.

Open from March 25th to October 31st, 2016. Ground of 3 ha. 150 campsites. Exposure : mid--shaded. Ground : grassy. Relief : dish. Campsite + vehicle + 2 people (with 10 A) from €18.20 to €21.50. Campsite + vehicle + 2 people from €14.70 to €18. Mobile home for 4-6 people from €320 to €549 per week. Package Cyclo-Rando Stop 1 person; without electricity : from €5 to €7 per night. Holiday voucher. Games for children. Pets allowed (€1.50 per day). Area for camper van. Wifi. Excursions (hikings).

In the heart of the vineyards of Burgundy, the Camping des Sources, which is wooded and shaded, gets its name from the many natural mineral springs that surround it. The Route des Grands Crus is the real avenue of Champs-Elysées of Burgundy. Many prestigious and sometimes unusual places will reveal you the secrets of viticulture. Halfway between Beaune and Chalon, the campsite is ideally located for cycling tours. The Eurovélo 6 is a journey to Burgundy by following the Loire, the canal du centre and then the Saône. This cycling course takes many greenways and passes by Santenay, less than 500 metres from the campsite. Located in the heart of the vineyards, this campsite has 150 spacious locations bordered on a 3-hectare field. You can stay in traditional campsites or in latest generation mobile homes. Take the many cycling paths to discover the secrets of viticulture.

Going Out

■ JOA CASINO DE SANTENAY

9, avenue des Sources
✆ +33 (0)3 80 26 22 44
www.joa-casino.com
contact-santenay@joa.fr

Open all year. Sunday to Thursday and public holidays from 10am to 2am; Friday and Saturday from 10am to 4am. Opening until 4am public holiday days before. Formal dress required. Catering facilities. Shop. Entertainment. Seminars. Receptions.

A building that looks like a rich mansion that would almost remind of Deauville : two square towers surrounding a majestic balcony, white walls and cozy interior combining class, sophistication and luxury... English roulette, black jack, poker tables, 150 slot machines... The casino de Santenay offers all possible games ! A discovery space is dedicated to beginners trained by a staff member for their first steps. It also receives dinner shows and houses a restaurant overlooking the vineyards. Ready to take down the jackpot ?

Shopping

■ CLOS BELLEFOND – DOMAINE LOUIS NIE

2, route de Chassagne
✆ +33 (0)3 80 20 60 29
www.closbellefond.com
clos-bellefond@wanadoo.fr

Open every day. Preferably by appointment. Tasting offered if purchase. On reservation for group : from €5 per person. Wine and cheeses tasting from €10. Groups up to 50 people. English speaking reception. Possible delivery (new website of online purchase).

It's impossible to miss because it is located in the centre of Santenay, Clos Bellefond is a family estate with a 120 years long history. Bernard Chapelle, owner and president of the travel agency of Santenay has a strong sense of hospitality for its visitors with whom he willingly shares his passion. Now, the estate can accommodate large groups. Here's an advice for our friendly foreign tourists, Laurence his wife has a perfect command of English. The vineyards of the estate stretch over 9 hectares, and produce Village et Premier Cru appellation on Santenay, Chassagne-Montrachet, Volnay and Pommard. No less than 80 references, all of them are vintage confounded with 10 names of the house. The range is completed by small batches on wholesale trade, white in particular, which represent only 10% of the volume. Harvesting is done by hand, the sorting is rigorous, and the wines are aged in oak during 18 to 20 months. The reception is available every day, on the estate on weekdays and rather in the family home of the neigbouring Large Streets at the weekend. The jewel of the house is Santenay Clos Bellefond Village, typical wines of the Côte de Beaune. This monopoly extends over 1.5 hectares of vineyards in the heart of the property. Bernard Chapelle can prepare a wine-cheeses tasting on reservation. One of his suggestions can be the pairing of cheese of Cîteaux with Chassagne-Montrachet Premier Crus Morgeot... A successful pairing ! Though Bernard Chapelle feels pleased to see his loyal customers again, he now offers a new service, that of buying wines online.

DOMAINE FLEUROT LAROSE – RENÉ FLEUROT ET FILS

Château du Passe-Temps
7, route de Chassagne
✆ +33 (0)3 80 20 61 15
fleurot.larose@wanadoo.fr

Open Monday to Friday from 8am to 12pm and from 1.30pm to 5.30pm. Visit and tasting the weekend by appointment. Spoken languages : French, English and Japanese.

A family-run enterprise founded in 1872, the Domaine René Fleurot-Fleurot Larose et Fils is located in Santenay, in Château du Passe-Temps. These specialists of the great wine of Burgundy transmit knowledge each other from generation to generation. Nowadays, Nicola is at the helm of an activity which has managed to keep its traditions while innovating at the same time. At Domaine Fleurot Larose, the modern methods of winemaking are combined with ancient Santenay practice to make sense and experience rhyme with technical progress. The prestigious cellars stretch over 1,400 m² at a depth of ten metres, where the nectars cultivate all their flavours. You will be warmly welcomed and carefully advised on the millesimes you are interested in.

Each has its own specialty and you will undoubtedly appreciate, the offered choice whose names already make you dream : Santenay Village, Montrachet-Chassagne Abbaye de Morgeot 1er cru Monopole, Santenay Clos du Passe-temps 1er cru, Bâtard-Montrachet Grand Cru, Monopole Chassagne-Montrachet Clos de la Rocquemaure 1er cru and the Fine et le Marc of Burgundy... You can also buy ratafia and wine jam made from Chassagne-Montrachet Clos de la Rocquemaure... A true delight with the foie gras ! Taste and you will be convinced ! An excellent address to keep and regularly frequent. Located on an exceptional terroir, Domaine Fleurot Larose also offers you the possiblility to visit the cellar and enjoy a tasting session.

MESTRE PÈRE ET FILS

12, place du Jet-d'Eau ✆ +33 (0)3 80 20 60 11
www.mestre-pere-et-fils.fr
gilbert.mestre@wanadoo.fr

Low season : open Monday to Saturday from 10am to 6pm. High season : every day from 10am to 6pm. High season from April 6th to December 7th. Tastings, visit of the cellars and reception of groups on appointment. Label "Vineyards and Discovered" and member with the charter "Of Vineyards in Cellars".

The least we can say is that the Gilbert Mestre estate has the sense of hospitality. Between the open house day, which takes place every first weekend of December (since at least 25 years !), and the shop set on the Place du Jet d'Eau, everything is made to encourage you to discover this estate. And if you do not come to them, they will come to you by taking part in many shows in Burgundy, Rhône-Alpes, Champagne and Franche Comté. After several generations of winemakers, it is the three brothers, Gerard, Michel and Gilbert, who share the tasks of the house with each other. The grounds extend over 17 acres of vineyards spread over five villages of Côte De Beaune for appellations in Santenay, Aloxe-Corton, Ladoix, Maranges and Chassagne-Montrachet, in red and in white, with many premier crus and two grand crus : red Corton, Les Languettes and the famous Corton Charlemagne. The estate remains faithful to its principles : respect for the natural balance of the soils, manual harvest, sorting of grapes in fermenting room, traditional vinification and refining in oak barrels during 18 to 20 months in cellars that you can visit. Lovers, do not hesitate to enquire about the pretty collection of old vintages...

PROSPER MAUFOUX – MAISON DES GRANDS CRUS

1, place du Jet-d'Eau ✆ +33 (0)3 80 20 68 71
www.maufoux-chambre-beaune.com
contact@prosper-maufoux.com

Low season : open Monday to Saturday from 10am to 1pm and from 2pm to 6pm. High season : every day and public holidays from 10am to 1pm and from 2pm to 7pm. High-season : from May to September. Closed on Sunday and Monday from November to March. April and October : closed only Sunday. Stroll in the vineyards and mâchon : €59 per person.

Maison des Grands Crus has two superimposed sublime vaulted cellars that date back to the 15th century. It is in this splendid setting that you can taste and buy the wines of Prosper Maufoux. There is a wide choice of appellations : Santenay, Chassagne-Montrachet, Puligny-Montrachet, Meursault, Volnay, Pommard, Charmes-Chambertin, Corton-Charlemagne, Nuits Saint Georges... The finest vintages are represented ! Another asset of this attractive restaurant ? They offer old vintage as the Batard-Montrachet Grand Cru 1997. On the online sale, you can find also the Santenay 1er Cru « Les Gravières » of 2011, Clos-Vougeot Grand Cru 2011 or the Mercurey 2012. A good place to refuel with beautiful bottles.

SAULIEU ★

Today Saulieu, located in the regional natural Park du Morvan and bordering Auxois, is the capital of the Christmas tree. The famous Route Nationale 6, long time ago Franciliens was connected to le soleil du Midi and was quite useful since many years until the construction of the autoroute du Soleil which attracted vehicles from the city. A significant loss for the local economy at that period of time ! However, the city managed to implement plans and develop many advantages. Le Relais and Châteaux Bernard Loiseau became, as popular as the basilica Saint-Andoche or the sculptor François Pompon, international ambassador, making Saulieu an interesting stop in Bourgone. It is one of the gourmet stops amongst the most famous in the world ! The restaurant has been run by two of the popular names in French gastronomy, Alexandre Dumaine, at the beginning of the 20th century, and Bernard Loiseau who bought the property in 1982. Today, Patrick Bertron successfully managed to continue the work of those famous Head Chef while Bernard Loiseau team has settled in Paris, Dijon and Beaune. This city is attracting, blooming and full of history. The roads leading to this property have many magnificent views. You should pay a visit to the two statues of Pompon : le Grand Taureau et l'Ours located in the northern and southern entrances of Saulieu.

OFFICE DE TOURISME DE SAULIEU

24, rue d'Argentine ✆ +33 (0)3 80 64 00 21
www.saulieu-morvan.fr
ot@saulieu-morvan.fr

Low and mid-season after the Heritage Days : open from 10am to 12pm and 2pm at 5pm. Closed Sunday and Monday. High season as from May : open from 9.30am to 1pm and from 2pm to 6.30pm and Sunday from 10am to 1pm and from 2pm to 5pm. Tourism label & Disability.

The pretty town of Saulieu, labeled « *Villes et Villages fleuris* », is mainly famous for its Musée François Pompon, its Saint-Andoche basilica and its gastronomy. Indeed, it is in this city that the famous Relais Bernard Loiseau settled and which keeps on innovating and diversifying its activity. But Saulieu is also the ideal station for your sports and nature leisures desire. Whether you are amateurs or enthusiasts of strong feelings, there must be a suggestion which suits you in the regional nature park of Morvan ! The lovers of sculpture and art will be surprised by the many treasures of Saulieu, of the Musée Pompon to the advertising frescoes of the Nationale 6. Did you know finally that Saulieu is the capital of the Christmas tree ? The Tourist Office proposes you to discover the wealth of a city full of history, with the dynamic local production and the tough legends. Whether you wish to ride a bike or to walk around the megaliths, dolmens and others atypical rocks, know that in Saulieu, there is something for everyone ! Welcome to the gates of Morvan where you are welcomed with professionalism and sympathy !

Sightseeing

■ LA BASILIQUE SAINT-ANDOCHE ★

Place Docteur-Roclore ✆ +33 (0)3 80 64 07 03

Guided tours organized by the Pastoral one of tourism.

This Basilica, typical of the Cluny style, was built in the twelfth century by the Bishop of Saulieu on the probable site of the martyrdom of saints evangelists Andoche and Thyrse. Romanesque capitals are intact. Three types can be distinguished : decorative (acanthus foliage, ferns), symbolic (the wyverns, owls, bees), historic (passages of the Bible). Note that the largest organ of the basilica is one of the most beautiful instruments of Burgundy at both visually and sound level. Charlemagne donated his Gospel book to the parish during his visit in Saulieu. The one you can discover here is a (good) copy of the original which is in the Louvre.

■ MUSÉE FRANCOIS POMPON ★★★★

Place du Docteur Roclore

✆ +33 (0)3 80 64 19 51 – www.saulieu.fr

museefrancoispompon@wanadoo.fr

♿

Closed in January and frévrier as well as on May 1st and on December 25th. Open on Monday from 10am to 12.30pm; Wednesday to Saturday from 10am to 12.30pm and from 2pm to 6pm; Sunday and public holidays from 10.30am to 12pm and from 2.30pm to 5pm. Closed at 5.30pm of October in March. Free for under 18-year-olds. Adult : €3. Group (10 people) : €2 (per person). Children welcome. Guided tour (approximately 45 minutes). Label Musée de France.

This museum is located beside the Saint-Andoche basilica. It is the only one to bear the name of the sculptor of Saulieu. Born in Saulieu in 1855, François Pompon comes to settle in Dijon in 1870. As a stonemason at the cemetery of Péjoces the day, he attended the classes of the Ecole des Beaux-Arts at night. A few years later, he went to Paris to hone his talent. The sculptor Aimé Millet was among his professors but also Auguste Rodin, the owner of the workshop where he worked. Today, François Pompon is known for his unfussy animal sculptures, white or black, with simplified and polished forms. Among them, the Polar bear whose reproduction can be seen at the entrance of the Darcy garden in Dijon. As for the Pompom de Saulieu museum, it exhibits more than twenty works of the artist, made of bronze or plaster. If the sculptor is honoured, specialized rooms have other themes connected to the history of the region. Thus, you can discover collections dealing with the culture of Morvan, the sacred art or popular traditions. A room is also dedicated to French gastronomy that highlights grand chefs such as Alexandre Dumaine or Bernard Loiseau who succeeded one another at the head of La Côte d'Or hotel and restaurant in Saulieu. You should also visit : the granite Gallo-Roman steles of Morvan coming from the ancient necropolis Sidolocum (Saulieu). Musée François Pompon regularly organizes temporary exhibitions, conferences and workshops of cultural mediation. At the end of your visit, do not hesitate to pass by the shop. Who knows ? Perhaps you will go home with a pretty reproduction of a work of the famous Burgundian sculptor.

© ERIC VOILLEQUIN

The entrance of Saulieu with Ours Pompon.

Knife & Fork

RELAIS BERNARD LOISEAU
2, rue d'Argentine
✆ +33 (0)3 80 90 53 53
www.bernard-loiseau.com
contact@bernard-loiseau.com

3 stars Michelin restaurant. Annual closing : from mid-January to mid-February. Open from Thursday to Monday from noon to 1.30pm and from 7pm to 9.30pm. Closed on Tuesdays and Wednesdays. Reservations recommended. Menus from €155 to €225. Children's menu : €19 (with drink. Special à la carte for children up to 12 years-old). Lunch formula : €70 (Nationale 6 menu : starter, fish, meat, dessert. Every day of the week, except on the day of festivities and the day before festivities). Wine by the glass. « Les classiques de Bernard Loiseau » menu : €180. Gift boxes available. American Express. Groups welcome. Garden. Shop. 5-stars hotel. Spa.

This house which became mythical is the ideal place for a quality getaway in Burgundy. Located on the Nationale 6, Saulieu always had a role of city-stopover. Today, you stop there for the pleasure of enjoying the subtle cuisine of Patrick Bertron. He who worked during 20 years with Bernard Loiseau maintains his image brilliantly. It preserved certain classics of the Master like the jambonnettes of frogs with mashed garlic and parsley juice, the free range poultry and pan-fried duck foie gras with truffled mashed potatoes or the famous chocolate cornflake treats and its candied orange coulis... But Patrick Bertron also shows unbounded demanding and creativity to wake up your senses and to surprise your palate. Black cardamom, grated white truffle, Jerusalem artichoke and citrus fruits... flavours are worked with passion, just like the materials and the presentation. To accompany these divine dishes, the restaurant has one of the most beautiful wine cellars with Burgundy wines (15,000 bottles) as well as a wine bar which contains more than 40 references offered by the glass. The « Loiseau » spirit is really there, in the dishes and the atmosphere of this restaurant which does not cease innovating while respecting the tradition. A big bravo !

Sleeping

HOSTELLERIE DE LA TOUR D'AUXOIS
Square Alexandre-Dumaine
✆ +33 (0)3 80 64 36 19
www.tourdauxois.com
info@tourdauxois.com

Closed from December 20th to February 11th. Closed of the hotel Mondays from October to March included. Restaurant closed Monday lunchtime and evening, Tuesday and Saturday lunchtime. 29 rooms (including 6 suites). Double room from €85 to €119; suite from €134 to €149. Breakfast : €13 (in high season and €10 in low season). Closed parking (by reservation). Offers packs stays. Lift. Seminars. Receptions and weddings. Free Wifi. Catering facilities (menu at €27 and €39 + Card. Lunch menus from €16.90 to €19.90). Satellite TV. Swimming pool heated from June to September. Terraces and park. Beauty treatments, massages.

La Tour of Auxois is a magnificent hotel. Built on ramparts of the 14th century, the superb building dates back to the 17th century and was renovated while preserving the charm of the place. Chic, friendly, welcoming, comfortable, appropriate qualifiers abound to describe the services offered to visitors. For several years, Aneline and Vincent Fournier could be proud to have managed brilliantly the reception and the services offered to their passing guests. La Tour d'Auxois managed to perfect its offer to better serve its clientele. The rooms, including 6 duplex suites, reveal the authenticity of the hotel, with exposed beams, tiles on the floor, classic furniture and very neat decor. All the comfort you would expect from a hotel of such standing is there. And even more... You will appreciate the typical views that the rooms offer on the city, and in season, the heated swimming pool with a beautiful terrace is the ideal place for an exquisite relaxation ! Note that the restaurant will delight the most demanding tastebuds with its dishes with Burgundian touches.

RELAIS BERNARD LOISEAU
2, rue d'Argentine
✆ +33 (0)3 80 90 53 53
www.bernard-loiseau.com
contact@bernard-loiseau.com

Relais & Châteaux. Closed from mid-January to mid-February. Closed weekly on Tuesday and Wednesday. 19 rooms (and 13 suites). Double room from €165 to €395; studio/apartment from €605 to €705; suite from €435 to €535. Breakfast from €28. Relais & Châteaux. Spa, pool for swimming, treatment rooms. Offers of « all inclusive » stays. 2 rooms with special bathrooms. Babysitting. Pets allowed (free). Free wi-fi. Catering facilities (3 stars Michelin restaurant from €70 the menu). Sale point (Bernard Loiseau branched products).

Drinking a tea in the lounge-library, enjoying the flowery garden, resting in an elegant decor, having a moment of relaxation in the Spa, enjoying a gourmet subtle cuisine... Le Relais Bernard Loiseau offers you an infinity of pleasures in a splendid building that we do not need to present anymore. Become mythical thanks to its catering facilities, Le Relais Bernard Loiseau also shelters a 5-star luxury hotel with remarkable comforts and services. The 32 rooms, including suites and apartment, are regularly renovated and redesigned for a stunning result. The authenticity of the place is preserved with its exposed stones of Burgundy, its terracotta floor tiles and its old wood panelling. Among the top-of-the-range services offered by the hotel, let us quote the fitness room located in the old and authentic cellar of the restaurant, the spa with its hammam and its treatment rooms or the external heated pool accessible as of the arrival of the fine days. For the children, a game room is available with a baby-sitter on request. What better way to begin your day than to have your breakfast in the Alexandre Dumaine dining room. The portrait of this great chef stands in the middle of an authentic decor of the beginning of the 20th century. The room was classified as Historical monuments in 2010. In Saulieu, the dream thus is not only in your dishes, it can be prolonged in relaxation, rest and to the shop. Le Relais Bernard Loiseau maintains its image of excellence to offer you a luxury stay in the middle of Burgundy ! Several fixed rate formulas are proposed combining relaxation, oenology or cooking classes. In 2015, Dominique Loiseau was crowned Femme en Or in the « Entreprise » category. Restaurateur of talent, she knows how to mobilize her team and to highlight the tradition spirit while diversifying the activities of her establishment.

Shopping

CADEAU GOURMAND
Nouvelle adresse
4, rue Sallier
✆ +33 (0)3 80 64 31 79
cadeausaulieu@orange.fr
Open on Tuesday from 10.30am to 12.30pm and from 2.30pm to 7pm; Wednesday to Saturday from 9am to 12.30pm and from 2.30pm to 7pm; Sunday from 10am to 12.30pm.
Located in the middle of the commercial side streets of Saulieu, Cadeau Gourmand is the shop you should not miss to bring a gourmet souvenir of the region. François Dubois who created this shop 10 years ago already has just arranged this latter on rue du Sallier. A revival that sweetly smells the quality and local ingredients and that enlarge its wine trade with Cave de la Basilique. You naturally find the great names of mustard, like Fallot or Reine de Dijon, Anis de Flavigny, the liqueurs and alcohols Edmond Briottet, nectars and syrups Emmanuelle Baillard. Many articles are produced in Morvan, like honey of gingerbreads and beer. By the way, the Beer section is interesting, because it makes us discover several local productions. Le Cadeau Gourmand regularly renews its selections with the season of the seasons and the innovations. The ray preserves and terrines enable you to prepare a complete and very qualitative meal but above all gourmet. If your choices are intended to be offered, do not hesitate to make up a gift basket that you can exactly calculated but that will surely make effect ! The red Bordeaux façade with the most beautiful effect is an invitation to push the door.

In the surroundings

La Roche-en-Brénil

BCA 4X4
Le Crossaint
✆ +33 (0)3 80 64 78 00
www.bca4x4.com
bca4x4@wanadoo.fr
Stroll in 4x4 through the landscapes of Morvan. Fixed rate formulas à la carte and adapted to the seasons.
BCA 4x4, specialist in the 4-wheel drives of the brand Toyota offers to discover Morvan on board its fleet of all-terraing vehicles, 7 Land Cruiser ready to climb on the forest roads. La Roche-en-Brenil is the ideal departure point to visit the region in a different way, outside the roads, on a well-trodden course trail blending discovery of new landscapes and driving exercises. The strolls are always accompanied, Michel opens the road and Hélène his wife follows the crew. With 4 to 5 passengers per car, 7 Toyotas run quietly in convoy, sometimes crossing exceptional pathway. The adventure is convivial with Michel who skillfully animates the team. The course can be extended on 40 to 110 km, with stopover in restaurant even in cottage. Discover superb lakes, forests that makes you experience a change of scenery, seizing views and always in harmony with nature. The adventure can be done in any season, except when there is too much snow. On the other hand, some snow does not stop your 4-wheel drives ! Possibility of tailored course according to your desires.

François Pompon museum, in Saulieu.

Saint-Martin-de-la-Mer

■ DOMAINE DE LA PIERRE RONDE

Lac de Chamboux
✆ +33 (0)3 80 84 13 07
www.domainedelapierreronde.com
domainedelapierreronde@gmail.com

Open all year round. Inuit, Tipis, Trapper tents, Yurts, House of Hobbits. Exposure : shaded. Ground : grassy. Beach. Inuit tent : €50. Yurts from €120 to €170 (for 10 people). House of hobbit (2 to 5 people) : €170 for a weekend. €150 per week. Seminars. Catering facilities (by reservation : breakfast €6. Caterer meal). Excursions (box for horses. Donkey or horse rides).

This is one of our real favourite addresses. Gaëlle Lajuge and Yannick Boisfard created Domaine de la Pierre Ronde on the site of a former camping. This is a « magic and timeless » place located on the border of the Lake Chamboux. You are in the nature, in the quiet and away from technological waves, but only 5 km from Saulieu. This site allows you to be close to stars and taste the sensuousness of the place. There are yurts, tipis, tents of trapper, Inuit tents and even a hobbit house on the 10 hectares parkland ! In total, ten fixed locations with a capacity of 60 people in total in summer time and 40 in winter. As for the comfort, the choice is wide : simple Inuit tent without equipment as yurts with comfortable beds, a wood-burning stove and even a bathtub. Domaine de la Pierre Ronde is the ideal place for those who want to get close to nature while having a stay in unusual facilities. Those who seek to get close to nature by staying in unusual facilities. The facility of the hobbit's village (Yes, as in the movie) should be finished for the summer 2017. The village will then be composed of 3 houses under the ground, a elf house and and tchatched cottage of witch. It will be also decorated with garden, small house, vegetable ways and a medicinal communal garden. Wherever you sleep, know that you will leave Pierre Ronde a little transformed after a return to the healthy sources.

SEMUR-EN-AUXOIS ★★

Nestled in the hollow of a bend in Armançon, the spur on which Semur is built is a real natural defense against external dangers. The site favoured the human settlement and the construction of a fortress in the Middle Ages. But the town heritage listed as « town of art and history » is not limited to the majestic towers, the fortified gates and the remains of the ramparts. The protected sector of Semur has beautiful mansions, three urban walk, ancient wine growers' houses and a superb collegiate church. In the course of the walk, take a good look of the façades of the houses : you can find various inscriptions, quotes from another era like this « enduring and crying » engraved at rue Buffon. The motto of the city is inscribed under one of the gates of the city : « The Semur inhabitants are very pleased to meet foreigners. » Welcome to one of the most beautiful stopover in Côte-d'Or where guests are welcomed with gentleness and friendliness.

■ MAIRIE DE SEMUR-EN-AUXOIS

7 bis, place de l'Ancienne Comédie
✆ +33 (0)3 80 97 01 11
www.ville-semur-en-auxois.fr
accueil@ville-semur-en-auxois.fr

Open Monday to Friday from 9am to 12pm and from 1.30pm to 5.30pm. The service of the passports and indentity cards of the town hall by appointment accommodates you Monday to Friday from 9am to 11.30am and from 1.30pm to 5pm as well as Saturday from 9am to 11.30am.

■ OFFICE DE TOURISME DE SEMUR-EN-AUXOIS

2, place Gaveau ✆ +33 (0)3 80 97 05 96
www.tourisme-semur.fr
info@tourisme-semur.fr

Open Monday to Saturday from 9.30am to 12.15pm and from 2pm to 6pm. High season : Sunday from 10am to 12.30pm and from 2pm to 6pm. High-season : from June to end of September.

Located in the heart of the medieval city, the Tourist Office of Semur-en-Auxois is a very nice place where kind and professional welcome is awaiting for you. There are many brochures offering a thousand original activities and especially (what a smart idea !) menus of local restaurants. Practical and nice to decide where to make a gourmet break ! There is also a corner shop where you can unearth souvenirs as the Paris coin with the colors of the medieval town of Semur-en-Auxois. Discovery tours invite you to tour the city. During the summer season, guided tours of the medieval city are organized. Every Tuesday afternoon at 3pm, lady Sandrine (in period costume) makes you discover the places. Some Friday evening, she is even accompanied by beggars of the Middle Age... so feel free to find out more on the scheduled date. Booklets specifically designed for children are available. A warm, dynamic and professional welcome.

■ LE PETIT TRAIN TOURISTIQUE DE SEMUR

Rue de l'Ancienne Comédie
✆ +33 (0)3 80 97 05 96

Every day Tuesday to Saturday over the period from July 1st to August 31st. Departures with 2.30pm – 4pm – 5.30pm, in front of the Tourist Office. Night Saturday at 9.30pm. Adult : €5. Child (from 4 to 16 years old) : €2.50. Duration : 1am. Further information to the Tourist Office.

The small train offers a pleasant discovery of Semur to all. It allows you to explore the city without getting tired, by admiring at leisure the most picturesque and most remarkable squares. The tour is accompanied by comments presenting the main attractions as well as the history of the city. Lovers of photographs will be delighted after a stop at the belvedere. The nocturne of Saturday is particularly recommanded to enjoy the illuminations. The departure is from the tourism office which does not skimp on the ways to satisfy visitors !

Semur-en-Auxois.

Knife & Fork

LE COMMERCE

19, rue de la Liberté
✆ +33 (0)3 80 96 64 40
hotelducommerce21@orange.fr

Open Monday to Thursday from 6am to midnight; Friday and Saturday from 6am to 2am; Sunday from 9am to midnight. Restaurant – Tapas bar – Wine bar – Cocktails – Bar of atmosphere weekends. On weekdays, end of the service from noon to 3pm and at 11pm for dinner. Booking advised. À la carte : Around €15. Children's menu : €9. Lunch menu : €12.90 (starter, main course, dessert). Wine by the glass. Holiday voucher, Chèque Restaurant. Groups welcome (by reservation). Baby chairs. Terrace. Activities.

Since November 2015, Julien Brossard and Romain Malegue has been in charge of Le Commerce. This hotel restaurant operates also as a tapas bar, wine bar-ambiance of cocktails and bar at the weekend. Julien and Romain wish to make this fully renovated establishment a must-go address in Semur-en-Auxois. More contemporary, the decoration is cordial and highlights the exposed stones of the room. Wooden barrels bring a little touch of authenticity to the space and come to point out the wealths of our terroir. It is the chef Alix Pechon who officiates at the catering service. His specialties are : scrambled eggs with truffle, fillet of rossini beef and of dessert a delicious brioche in grandma's way ! With family or between friends, you can also share Swiss main courses such as a fondue or a toasted cheese... Conviviality is guarranted ! The plus : the wine bar allows you to enjoy a vintage of the region or to eat tapas if you are a little bit hungry. Le Commerce is an establishment where it is good to have a meal, a drink or for an evening. Recommended.

Sleeping

HÔTEL DE LA CÔTE-D'OR

1, rue de la Liberté ✆ +33 (0)3 80 97 24 54
www.auxois.fr – info@auxois.fr

Logis (3 cheminées). Open all year. Reception Monday to Friday from 7am to 9pm and Saturday and Sunday from 8am to 12pm and from 4pm to 8pm. 17 rooms. Double room from €95 to €115; triple room from €115 to €133; suite from €135 to €150. Full-board. Half-board. Breakfast in the room and in buffet : €12 (continental Breakfast : €7). Extra bed : €18. Open parking included (lift since parking). Stop-over with special rates €96. Holiday voucher. Pets allowed (€7). Seminars. Free Wifi. Catering facilities (wine bar). Satellite TV.

At the 17th century, at the time as of stagecoach, this old station relay accommodated already travellers ! Now, Hôtel de la Côte-d'Or, fully renovated, displays a beautiful ochre facade. Inside, exposed stones, fireplaces and wooden beams provides a character to the spacious and comfortable rooms. Between tradition and modernity, the hotel of Côte-d'Or will surprise you by its arrangement and its mix of materials. Véronique Jobic, the owner of the places, is creative and effective. She carries a constant treatment to her guests and not short of new ideas to improve the reception of the guests. The 17 rooms of its establishment are tastully decorated : warm colors, modern materials and duly chosen decoration items. Comfort is essential in this haven of relaxation : king-size bed, shower or balneo bath, reversible air conditioning, flat-screen TV set, reading light and kettle. The services are also up to the reputation of the establishment : welcome tray, lift, room service, W-Fi access and free car park. Sound-proofing is given a particular attention, the streets are paved in the beautiful medieval town of Semur-en-Auxois. For a drink in the evening, you just nee to go to the ground floor. Fun wine, « Z », displays a lounge and cosy atmosphere. At the

The old town of Semur-en-Auxois.

breakfast, taste one of the many flavors of artisanal jams manufactured in Semur. The hotel of Côte-d'Or guarantees you a comfortable stay in an original and neat setting.

Leisure

FRANCE MONTGOLFIÈRES

4, bis rue du Saussis ✆ +33 (0)3 80 97 38 61
www.francemontgolfieres.com
reservation@francemontgolfieres.com

From April to October. Adult : of 178€ until 249€. Children (6-12 years) : 158€. No the possibility of flight for the pregnant women and the children of less than 6 years. Flights with the rising or the sunset.

Based in Semur-en-Auxois, the company France Montgolfières organizes flights on ball almost throughout France : Val de Loire Fontainebleau, Provence, Pyrenees, Rhône-Alpes, Auvergne, Champagne, Périgord... For Burgundy, the departures are from Vézelay, Beaune or Avallon. Plan approximately 3-4 hours including 1 hr for the flight. The travel by balloon is true historic journey that enable you to reconnect with nature and to be aware of all the beauty of the environment and the landscapes... seen from above ! This enables you to take the high ground and experience another outlook of the castles, the manor houses and the abbeys you fly over. The landing is gently made and is followed by the famous « Toast des Aérostiers » during which you receive your « Certificate of ascension ». For the groups, there is nacelles with a capacity of 16 people. The organization offers packages combining a flight with nights in charming hotel or castle... which gives an opportunity to live an unforgettable experience !

Shopping

L''ÉPICERIE DE SEMUR

12, rue de la Liberté ✆ +33 (0)3 80 92 25 82
vins.sur.vins@wanadoo.fr

Open from 8am to 12.30pm and from 2pm to 7.15pm. Open every day mid-April with septembe. Closed on Monday from October to mid-April. Open on Sunday (and public holidays from 8.30am to 12.30pm, all year).

L'Epicerie de Semur, as straight out from a postcard picture, is almost the ideal delicatessen ! Here, the shelves are filled with quality local and regional ingredients. From here and elsewhere... Wine of Burgundy, Italy, Portugal, crémants and champagne... Trust the advice of Christophe Caironi and Linda to make your choice. In the beautiful shelf of Italian products, you'll find finely sliced meats, fresh pasta, antipastis and cheeses to complete your basket. Take profit from the booming ray of cheese. L'Epicerie de Semur is not very big, however, its shelf space, full of products, is impressive. But that's not all ! L'Epicerie de Semur is adapted in the course of the seasons : fruit and vegetables of the moment, fair of wine, Beaujolais nouveau... Christophe Caironi expands his wine ray, count on his advice to satisfy your needs. The attentive service of Christopher and the charming one of Linda, with delicious Italian accent will also delight you.

In the surroundings

Epoisses ★

CHÂTEAU D'ÉPOISSES ★

✆ +33 (0)3 80 96 40 56 / +33 (0)1 42 27 73 11
www.chateaudepoisses.com
visites@chateaudepoisses.com

Interior of the castle open with the visit (guided 45 minutes) in July-August only from 10am to 12pm and from 3pm to 6pm. Closed on Tuesday. From April 1st to October 31st, interior open with groups (minimum 12 people) by reservation with possibility of making a tasting of Époisses. (€8). Free for under 12-year-olds. Adult : €8. Child (from 12 to 18 years old) : €4. The park is open all year from 9am to 7pm (€2 per person. Free for under 18-year-olds).

Époisses is a small fortified village protected by a double wall with a church, beautiful stone houses and a sixteenth century dovecot. The castle was founded in the 6th century. It was the residence of the kings of Burgundy and has sheltered Queen Brunehaut. The Grand Condé, Chateaubriand, and Queen Elizabeth II of England have lodged there. Madame de Sevigné, who was also received in these places, wrote about it : « This house has an amazing size and beauty. » By the way, the castle library contains several of her letters. Inside, you can find her room, as well as rich and varied furniture (paintings, tapestries) in the large living room or Italian gallery. It is the same family that owns the place since the second half of the 17th century. The mere walk in park and in the garden is worth the visit, its dovecot with 3,000 nests is impressive.

© ERIC VOILLEQUIN

Château d'Epoisses.

AUBERGE DU CHÂTEAU

21, rue des Eperons
✆ +33 (0)3 80 89 30 13
www.aubergeduchateau-restaurant.com
dom.simonneau@orange.fr

Open all year. Daily for lunch; Friday and Saturday for dinner. Menu from €18.50 to €23.50. Children's menu : €10. Lunch menu : €12 (starter, main course, dessert). Groups welcome. Terrace.

L'Auberge du Château located opposite the famous watch tower of Château d'Epoisses is an address that seduces at any season, in winter for the warmth of its room with exposed stones and contemporary furnishing and in summer for its friendly small terrace. Dominique and Sandrine Simonneau concoct us a traditional cuisine of quality, containing regional produces, in particular local cheese, Epoisses Berthaut ! Indeed, we find it on many dishes, it is legitimate whereas nobody has enough of it. Rochers d'Epoisses with gingerbread as starter, mousseline of Epoisses gratin with cream, pork tenderloin with Epoisses sauce, ham with the bone with Epoisses sauce ! Lovers of the famous cheese, you will be delighted ! The desserts are for the pleasures of all, frozen nougat, chocolate entremet, île flottante, ultra gourmet classic.

DÉLICES DU TERROIR

5, place du jeu de Paume
✆ +33 (0)9 82 40 12 97
✆ +33 (0)6 86 65 13 07
delicesduterroir21@gmail.com

Open from Friday to Wednesday and on public holidays. Open on Sunday (possibility to taste the products on site). Credit card not accepted.

The shop of Agnès Guillaume located in the heart of Époisses, just opposite the castle is an endearing shop dedicated to discovery of regional produce of Burgundy and Jura also. Agnès, is one of those passionate and generous people that you rarely meet. Native of Franche-Comté, she has long sold local produce in the markets, then she chose Époisses to open this very welcoming shop with rustic and refined decor (wood panelling, nice furniture, many decorative objects...). Here everything sweetly smells authenticity and the taste of beautiful things. Delicatessen meats, fruits and vegetables, cheese, wines, liqueurs, vinegars, gingerbread, mustard... Regional products are particularly well enhanced and the choice is important ! The wine shelf is very well stocked. Délices du Terroir is in constant evolution. The trends of the moment are the 2 small terraces or the tables installed inside where you can enjoy a mâchon at any time of the day and where, some nights, concerts are organised. Agnès can also prepare you cheeseboards and charcuteries for your private evenings. She succeeded in imposing her style, that of the good mood and conviviality which rhyme with quality and delicacy.

FROMAGERIE BERTHAUT

Magasin l'Echauguette
Place du Champ-de-Foire
✆ +33 (0)3 80 96 44 44
www.fromagerie-berthaut.com
contact@fromagerie-berthaut.com

Open Tuesday to Saturday from 9.30am to 12.15pm and from 2pm to 6pm.

At Berthaut's, cheese, and the époisses in particular, is a passion that is passed down over 50 years. A passion for a cheese with a unique flavor : a soft texture and beautiful orange by weeks of ripening in which it is rubbed with a solution, increasingly rich in marc de Bourgogne. Berthaut Cheese, leader of the AOP, ships on all continents, and is known as the flavors of époisses beyond our borders. In the range of Berthaut cheeses, époisses is accompanied by other cheeses like : the affidélice refined with chalabis, the soumaintrain, and the trou-du–cru whose name makes one ready to smile. At the store, you will also find comté, chaource, Morbier, or cream cheese as well as wine, terrines, jams, honey and other sweets. Each month, a cheese from another region is on the spotlight to discover the wealth of other flavors !

Pont-et-Massène

■ LE PARI DES GOURMETS

10, rue du Lac
✆ +33 (0)3 80 97 11 11
www.leparidesgourmets.fr
leparidesgourmets@orange.fr

Open all year round. Except during the Christmas holidays. From November to mid-February : open for lunch and dinner on weekdays, by reservation on weekends (for groups). In high season from mid-February to October : closed on Sunday evening. Menus from €24.50 to €38.50. Lunch formula : €12.90 (3 main courses). Ardoise fixed rate formula at €16.50 for 2 main courses. €19.50 for 3 main courses. Hotel with 16 rooms. Terrace.

Le Pari de Gourmets, it is that of Yannick and Laurent Savioz. A won bet. We like the worked, original and always well-presented cuisine of the new owners of Hôtel du Lac de Pont. After several years spent in the beautiful establishments's kitchen throughout France, they chose Semur in Auxois to express their talents. Le Pari des Gourmets is characterized by an aesthetic cuisine, drawn and coloured with perfect cooking and flavours. The à la carte is even brilliantly organized, it is adapted to the times of the week. The offer of the day at lunchtime at the bar or on the terrace cannot disappoint, that of the slates with 2 or 3 dishes changes every week. For the gourmets, from Friday evening to Sunday at lunchtime, the house offers menus even more gourmet where the chef is astonishing in his variations : Crusty cigarette of pike accompanied by caramelized potatoes. Mignonnette of Pork and raviolis of pear with two wines. We salivate in advance. We remain on one of our very favorite, which is the egg soufflé in red wine sauce, a classic that is brilliantly revisited. First-class honour for the desserts and even the children's menu. And the cherry on top, the price is reasonable ! In summer, think of booking a table under the pergola of the terrace. The Restaurant is right beside Lac de Pont whose renovation is completed.

VENAREY-LÈS-LAUMES

Green valleys, hills and mountains... You are in Auxois, the one which has seen the unfolding of a turning point in the history of our country, where, in 52 BC. AD a decisive battle ends the fierce insight of the « irreducible » Gauls. The Gauls and the Romans supposedly clashed on the heights of Alise-Sainte-Reine. The Muséoparc Interpretation centre of Alesia must absolutely be visited ! A short distance away, stand other witnesses of a rich past : Semur-en-Auxois and its majestic walls, the medieval village of Flavigny-sur-Ozerain and its anises, the Castle of Bussy Vitteaux, Salmaise and its halls of the thirteenth century, the sources of the Seine, the medieval town of Marigny-le-Cahouët...

■ OFFICE DE TOURISME PAYS D'ALÉSIA ET DE LA SEINE

1, Avenue de la Gare
✆ +33 (0)3 80 96 89 13
www.alesia-tourisme.net
alesia-tourisme@wanadoo.fr

Open from April 1st to September 30th Monday to Saturday from 9.30am to 12.30pm and from 2pm to 7pm. In July and August the office is also open Sunday from 10am to 12pm. From October 1st to March 31st : open Monday to Saturday from 10am to 12pm and from 3pm to 5pm.

The Tourist Office in Pays d'Alésia is a crossing point during your visit in the region. Located in the heart of the new art and congress center, it is easily accessible and nearby a large car park. You are welcome with a smile by Delphine and Gael and you will also find all information and services to arrange your stay. Particularly the access ticket to neighbouring Museopark. You can receive all advice to enjoy Pays d'Alésia, its heritage, its events, its landscapes, its gourmet produces and sports activities. The country d'Alésia is a canton of 24 communes including Bussy-Rabutin with its splendid renaissance castle, Flavigny-sur-Ozerain classified as most beautiful village in France or Salmaise, with its Medieval halls. Picturesque villages full of history are worth a visit ! A guided tour is available for groups on reservation.

Knife & Fork

■ LE P'TIT CHEZ SOI

29, rue Marcelin Berthelot
✆ +33 (0)3 80 89 29 51
le-petit-chez-soi@orange.fr

Open Monday to Friday for lunch; Thursday to Tuesday for dinner. Suggestions on the board. Lunch menu : €13 (starter, main course, cheese, dessert). Wine by the glass. Wine bar - Sale of wines – Aperitifs Concerts – Concerts – Theater. Terrace.

Raphaël Redondo created Le P'tit Chez Soi in 2010, a traditional Bistro whose daytime menu sometimes has Spanish accents, just like that of Raphaël for our greatest pleasure. You come at lunchtime for the dayly specials or for a salad improvised with pretty spice-flavoured products. The Slate includes inspirations of the moment : salads or steak with époisses. You can also choose a pizza, Catalan, Oriental or the classic ham-cheese. Like everything else, prices are also very reasonable there. Raphaël often prepares his Tapas, rolled pancakes sliced into gourmet medallions, salty or sweet, they are delicious. But Le P'tit Chez Soi will also please with its wine list, more than 300 references, from France but also the World, Spain, Portugal, South Africa, Chile, Australia... Some are served by the glass, others as takeaway. The interior decoration is warm, picturesque until the billiard room where a fresco of Raphaël has pride of place, painter in his free time ! To crown the presentation, know that the address Le P'tit Chez Soi looks like a small village, an area of the unknown Venarey, paved sidewalks, shaded terraces... like in Spain.

RESTAURANT L'ESPRIT

6, avenue de la Gare ✆ +33 (0)3 80 89 88 67
www.restaurantlesprit.fr
lesprit@restaurantlesprit.fr

Low season : open from Tuesday to Sunday for lunch; from Tuesday to Saturday for dinner. High season : from Monday to Saturday for dinner; every day for lunch. Menus from €18 to €25 (+ à la carte). Lunch formula : €13.50 (starter, main course, dessert, 1/4 of wine). Terrace.

At the beginning of the 20th century, the hotel of the Vénarey train station run by the Lesprit family was a highly renowned restaurant. After being closed for 18 years, the building was completely renovated to house apartments as well as a new restaurant named L'Esprit. Welcome to the 21st century. If the architecture has kept the charm of the era, everything is renovated. Dark frames, white walls decorated with shimmering original works, contemporary furniture, chairs in bright colours, it is joyful and welcoming. In summer, a beautiful terrace keeps you outside and when it rains, everyone goes in the spacious interior. A young team is at your service while the experienced chef prepares a homemade cuisine with Burgundian accents. Snails, poached eggs, frogs' legs, beef fillet… At lunchtime on weekdays, you will willingly be seduced by the daily menu, three main courses with their ¼ of wine at very reasonable prices. It is the same case for the good wine list but with some grand crus at €100 to really enjoy yourself. You are already charmed by the look of the restaurant. Easy to find, it is opposite the new Tourist Office and the train station.

LE TRIANON D'ALÉSIA – RESTAURANT ET HÔTEL

19, avenue Jean-Jaurès ✆ +33 (0)3 80 97 16 68
www.letrianondalesia.fr
letrianondalesia@gmail.com

Open all year. Daily for lunch and dinner. Set menu at €30. À la carte : Around €20. Children's menu : €9 (starter, main course and dessert up to 12 years). Lunch menu : €14 (appetizers buffet, main course, buffet of cheeses and desserts). Wine by the glass. Hotel of 9 rooms open 7 days a week. Holiday voucher, Chèque Restaurant. Groups welcome. Terrace.

Le Trianon d'Alésia has just changed its chef and the dining-room has been air-conditioned since the summer 2015. This establishment is simple and nicely decorated. The exposed stones, the contemporary furnishing and the comfortable seats make it a pleasant and warm place. We are allured by the large convertible terrace that can be covered or uncovered according to the season. Built like a canopy, green plants still enhanced this space and give us the impression to eat on the veranda of a garden. As for the dish, the new chef Francis is a former pizzaiolo who likes traditional cuisine. What about his specialties ? The beef tongue, the sirloin… and pizzas of course ! He offers a wide choice to enjoy on the spot or as take-away. At Le Trianon d'Alésia, the lunch menus are very gravitational and hearty. As for the service, it is attentive and cordial, just as we like it. If you stay in the hotel of Trianon, completely new, know that the breakfasts are consequent and nicely presented.

Sleeping

LE TRIANON D'ALÉSIA – RESTAURANT ET HÔTEL

19, avenue Jean-Jaurès ✆ +33 (0)3 80 97 16 68
www.letrianondalesia.fr
letrianondalesia@gmail.com

♿

Opened all year round. Reception from 7am to 3pm and from 6pm to 10pm. 9 rooms. Single room €60; double room €70. Full-board : €100. Half-board (one-night stopover €75). Breakfast : €7.50. Extra bed : €20. Parking nearby. Travel cots on request. Holiday vouchers. Free wi-fi. Catering facilities (menus : €14 at lunchtime or 30€ – Terrace). Entertainments.

Hôtel du Trianon d'Alésia is a brand new establishment, which is completely renovated by Maria Durand and Philippe Pican. Just above their restaurant, the 9 rooms available are modern, comfortable and functional. Each one of them is revived by a single colourful wall, which adds joy without creating a feeling of being closed. The bathrooms have a correct size, equipped with a shower or a bathtub. The rooms enjoy every current comfort, TV, telephone and sound insulation. Whether you go to Trianon d'Alésia for a night stay or for a meal, the prices are reasonable and the welcome is warm. The important things for Maria and Philippe is to receive all their guests with the same conviviality. The establishment has also a room for the disabled or with a disability. As large as pleasant, Trianon d'Alésia has its own restaurant, air-conditioned with a covered terrace. It is thus the ideal place for a stay if you want to visit the historical site of Alésia, to enjoy the canal of Burgundy or to go and see the lions of the park of Auxois, but also to stroll on Côte d'Or.

VITTEAUX

OFFICE DE TOURISME DU CANTON DE VITTEAUX

16, rue Hubert-Languet ✆ +33 (0)3 80 33 90 14
www.vitteaux-tourisme.com
ot.vitteaux@wanadoo.fr

Low season : open Tuesday to Saturday from 9.30am to 12.30pm and from 2pm to 6pm. High season : Tuesday to Friday from 9am to 12.30pm and from 2pm to 7pm; Saturday from 9.30am to 12.30pm and from 2pm to 6pm. High season : from June to September. Low season : from November to May. Attention, the OT is closed on Saturday afternoon between November and February. Open on Sunday (from 10am to 12.30pm in July and August only).

The Tourist Office of the community of the communes in the canton of Vitteaux is located in an old timber-framed building of the 14th century. With a small inner courtyard typical of medieval houses, with external staircase housed in a turret and gallery passage, the office is located in a privileged place. It hosts art exhibitions from April to September. In addition to a great deal of information, you can find the blond Vitteaux plums ! These are brought from the East during the Crusades by the lord of Saffres and are back into production now. It is impossible to come to Vitteaux without tasting these famous fruits ! The books available on the spot inform you more about the city, the region, the surrounding municipalities, the historic buildings and even about traditional recipes. Some are even reserved for children. It is also an opportunity to discover all the possibility of hiking paths. Auxois is a dynamic country. Many events are held there throughout the year as the many horse races in July and August.

Going Out

■ **PÔLE HIPPIQUE DE L'AUXOIS**
Marcilly-Dracy
© +33 (0)3 80 33 95 00 / +33 (0)3 80 49 60 16
www.hippodromes-centre-est.com
fede.centreest@fncf.asso.fr
Chase 2016 : Sunday, July 3 and Sunday, August 7. Concessions : €2.50. Normal rate : €5. Free for under 12s.
Each year, two large equestrian events are held on the racetrack, each attracting between 1,000 and 1,500 visitors trying their luck at the counters of the PMU installed on site ! Each time, there are nine trotting or galloping races on the prepared runways of about 1,200 m and bringing together locals and racegoers in the region. The rest of the year, it is on this site that horse competitions organized by Vitteaux Jumping take place. Note that this is the only racecourse in the Côte d'Or and it is a major equestrian centers in Burgundy.

In the surroundings

Arnay-sous-Vitteaux

■ **PARC DE L'AUXOIS** ★
RD 905 © +33 (0)3 80 49 64 01
www.parc-auxois.fr - contact@parc-auxois.com
Park open every day on Sunday and public holidays included from February 13th, 2016 (if weather permits) to November 11st, 2016 included. Low season : open every day from 10am to 6pm. From April to September : open every day from 10am to 7pm. Cafeteria open from March 26th, 2016. Free for under 3-year-olds (on presentation of proof). Adult : €15. Children (from 3 to 12 years old) : €10.50. Season Pass (Adult : €38. Children : €26). Holiday vouchers.
If the Parc de l'Auxois has attracted 75,000 visitors in 2015, it is thanks to its surface of 40 hectares exclusively dedicated to the discovery of animals from the whole world. It has 500 animals from all over the world. In addition to the zoological gardens, you can enjoy the water space and leisure area. It provides something to do for adults and children for a whole day ! In order to make the trail a pedagogical one, the animals sheltered there are classified by continent.

Therefore, each animal evolves in the heart of appropriate vegetation, with stream, trees and small huts. The mini-farm is full of ferrets and dwarf goats that you can stroke. Baribal bears, wolves and raccoons await you in the North America part while you see llamas and alpacas in South America space. Do not miss the lemurs of Madagascar that you can approach very closely in the contact spaces. In 2015, the lions came to complete the space dedicated to Africa, for the greatest happiness of the visitors. The park has also its own attraction. The « Jungle aventure » space allows children to have lots of fun with games and entertainments. In the Antilles space, the pool and the water park delight families in July and in August. Other activities are available : mini-golf, little train, merry-go-round for children, maze with exotic birds. For lunch break, cafeteria and appropriate picnic areas are also available for visitors. Finally, the shop allows everyone to have a little souvenir. New surprises will mark the season 2016 : the arrival of the Arctic wolves, predator of the far north, the creation of new spaces of contact where the visitors will mix with the deer and the wallabys, without forgetting « Zebr'Adventure », the new merry-go-round for the whole family ! Recently, you can also please your close relation by giving them the opportunity of becoming animal caretaker just for one day : an intense experience.

Thorey-sous-Charny

■ **DOMAINE AURÉLIEN FEBVRE**
21, rue Avau
✆ +33 (0)03 80 64 65 12 / +33 (0)06 73 26 90 12
www.domaine-aurelien-febvre.fr
contact@domaine-aurelien-febvre.fr

Reception by appointment. Telephone before coming. Classes of tasting, classes of size and half-day discovered of the vineyard (by reservation).

This is the third and last estate producing the IGP coteaux de l'Auxois. Aurélien Febvre, a qualified oenologist, has undertaken to revive the family estate for several years with skill and passion. The 10,000 bottles produced each year are certified organic. Aurelian offers two Chardonnay vintages : Le Thorey, quite mineral, and En Aparté, a vintage from the oldest vineyards of Auxois since they are nearly 70 years old ! Since then, it has offered a red wine, blend of Pinot Noir and... a gamaret, grape variety of Switzerland. Enjoy another novelty of the year : the vinification is done in... clay amphorae ! Here, you do not fear innovation and it is a real success. As bonus, tasting courses, half-days and discovery of the vineyard are available. Many reasons to pass through Thorey-sous-Charny !

VOSNE-ROMANÉE ★

It is said that during the Revolution, the wine from Vosne-Romanée was officially proclaimed « the most excellent wine of the French Republic ». Both castles are not to be visited, but the town has other mansions, that should absolutely be visited : the detached house of Goyotte (hunting lodge of the seventeenth century acquired by the Prince of Conti), the priory of Saint-Vivant... The vine yards has six remarkable Grands Crus : Romanée-Conti, Romanée, Romanée-Saint-Vivant, La Tache, Richebourg and Grande Rue. These wines are remarkably fine and deserve to be among the best. There are also 14 premiers crus (Aux Malconsorts, Aux Reignots, Le Clos-des-reas, etc..), high quality wines as well.

Knife & Fork

■ **LE RICHEBOURG BAR RESTAURANT**
Ruelle du Pont ✆ +33 (0)03 80 61 59 59
www.hotel-lerichebourg.com
hotel@lerichebourg.com

♿

Open all year round. From Tuesday to Saturday, from 12am to 13 : 30am for lunch and from 19 : 30pm to 21 : 30pm for dinner. Reservation recommended. Menus from €35 to €45. Average price : around €20. Lunch fixed rate formula 19 € for 2 main courses or €20 for 3 main courses. Wine available by the glass. Afterwork fixed rate formula with massage and access to meals and Spa : €75 to €95. Wine bar and 4 star Spa Hôtel. American Express accepted. Holiday vouchers and meal vouchers accepted. Groups welcome upon reservation. Garden. Terrace.

Le Richebourg, a wonderful 4-star hotel in Vosne-Romanée, hosts a restaurant that you will appreciate for its refined greeting and the quality of the gastronomy it offers. In a modern stylish setting, you can savour culinary creations releasing the scent of local ingredients. Jules Viard, the new chef, works with fresh and seasonal products. What he loves the most : reinterpreting classic dishes and combining flavours. His cooking uses the typical products of the rich Burgundian gastronomy, although he likes to add exotic twists for an even better result. An example : the Burgundy snails are decorated with eggplant pulp, mushrooms and garlic cream. A treat for lovers of snail. The lamb shank is accompanied with chervil mousse. During the week days, you can have the menu of the market. The tasting menu changes according to the choices of the chef and to seasonal products. Constantly renovating its gastronomic offer, Vin-T-age is a restaurant we recommend for its charming and classy service ! The large terrasse is a real enjoyment, the prices of the lunch menu are more than attractive, and note that the wine menu is a wonder. Why not enjoy to the fullest by offering yourself one of the afterwork formulas, including meal and wine tasting and access to the spa ?

Sleeping

■ **LE RICHEBOURG SPA & HÔTEL**
Ruelle du Pont ✆ +33 (0)03 80 61 59 59
www.hotel-lerichebourg.com
hotel@lerichebourg.com

Reception 24 hours a day. 26 rooms (including 6 suites). Double room from €189 to €249; suite €299. Breakfast buffet or in room : €19. Extra bed : €41. Garage :

€10. Individual stop-over with special rates at €159. American Express, Holiday voucher. Hotels & preference – Spas de France. Pets allowed (€15). Seminars. Internet access. Wifi. Catering facilities (Le Vin-T-Age restaurant). Sales (gifts, regional products...). Hammam, spa bath, sauna.

Spacious, contemporary, designer : Le Richebourg has everything for your need ! Set up in the heart of Côte de Nuits in the prestigious village of Vosne-Romanée, Le Richebourg is a charming 4-star hotel that promises you a prestigious stay of 100 % relaxation. It owns 26 bright and coloured rooms that subtly combine contemporary style and traditional style. Whether you travel alone, in couple or with your family, you will appreciate the elegant materials and the relaxing atmosphere of the place. Thick carpet or parquet flooring, comfortable bedding, bathroom with shower and bathtub, safe, satellite television, minibar and especially Spa ! A Pass'Détente is offered to each guest of the host, then slip on your bathrobe and enjoy the hammam or the sauna. The Spécial Cocoon rooms are as for them provided with their own infrared sauna : a true bonus for romantic weekends ! Two spacious apartments are also available for the families. Wherever you sleep, you can admire a very charming view, whether it overlooks the vineyard, the garden or the narrow streets of the village. As for the restaurant, a new chef has just arrived. Go to Vin-T-Age to discover its modern and gourmet cuisine. We appreciate this upscale establishment for the services offered and the quality of its reception where luxury rhymes with relaxation and discovery of fine wines. The hotel organizes for instance visits and tastings in partnership with Domaine Mongeard Mugneret, a wine grower of Vosne-Romanée.

Shopping

DOMAINE FRANCOIS LAMARCHE

9, rue des Communes
✆ +33 (0)03 80 61 07 94
www.domaine-lamarche.com
vins@domaine-lamarche.fr

Open Monday to Thursday from 8am to 12pm and from 2pm to 5pm; Friday from 8am to 12pm. Visit and tasting preferably by appointment.

Settled on prestigious lands, the Domaine François Lamarche has been passed on from generation to generation, just as the love of well done work. Since 1797, the wines of the region offer all the riches of their juicy bunches to grape-pickers. Today, it is Nicole Lamarche who runs the estate with talent and rigour. Since 2006, she handles alone the vinification process for a result that meets our expectations. Only superb wines are produced here, especially the exceptional « La Grande Rue », a monopoly grand cru, right next to the plot of Romanée-Conti... Concerned about the planet, the estate, which stretches on 11.50 hectares, goes from a reasoned farming to a 100%organic farming. Within this family company, the appelations of premiers and grands crus make us dream : from Grands-Echezeaux to Clos-de-Vougeot via the Vosne-Romanée Les Chaumes... A visit upon appointment is indispensable to meet this enthusiast family. They will all be happy to transmit their know-how and make you discover the treasures of their cellars. Wines known for their elegance, extraordinary balance and delicate bouquet by the biggest critics of French and international guides. An entire programme for connoisseurs or lovers ! A rare address which is ideal to discover the wonders of our terroir.

General view of Vosne-Romanée.

In the surroundings

RESTAURANT SIMON
12, place de l'Eglise
FLAGEY-ECHÉZEAUX
✆ +33 (0)03 80 62 88 10
www.restaurant-simon.fr
contact-restaurant-simon.fr

Open all year. Monday to Saturday for lunch and dinner. Booking advised. Menu from €40 to €85 (menu discovered : 5 main courses €65, 6 main courses €75,7 main courses €85). Lunch menu : €19.50 (starter, main course, cheeses or dessert). Wine by the glass. Gift voucher for 2 people, €130 and €160. American Express, Holiday voucher, Chèque Restaurant. Groups welcome (by reservation). Terrace. Take-away. Reception, banquets. Private room for 15 peoples. Possibility of privatizing the restaurant for reception.

Christian Quenel is the new owner of the establishment. The chef is well-known by Dijon residents as he was at the helm of Fredline, his former restaurant located in the heart of the city of the dukes. After a passage to Le Richebourg hotel and restaurant, Christian Quenel settles in the village of Flagey-Echézeaux, between Vougeot and Vosne-Romanée. A discrete but charming campsite for a chef who mixes tradition and modernity skilfully. The room is as comfortable as accessible with its warm colours and its a huge fireplace. In February 2016, embellishment works will be undertaken will relate in particular to the hotel's terrace. Another innovation : a free wi-fi access for the guests. The regional specialty of the restaurant offers a bistronomic evolutionary cuisine with revisited seasonal ingredients. The presentation is particularly neat and the dishes become the original setting of coloured creations. The address simply offers an excellent quality/ price ratio with a gourmet cuisine at reasonable price. To realize it, you just have to indulge yourself with the formula at lunchtime. You can for example taste poached eggs with Crémant de Bourgogne. If you choose the menu at €40, choose the excellent sweetbread accompanied by a sauce with Porto and its mushroom fricassée. It's difficult to resist ? The à la carte also reserves very nice surprises. Creativity and conviviality will undoubtedly make the fame of this restaurant.

VOUGEOT

About fifty hectares of vineyards surrounded by high walls, a castle, a famous gate... Chateau du Clos de Vougeot, proudly settled in the heart of the vineyard, is undoubtedly one of the most famous images of Burgundy. The castle has been the ownership of the Company of friends of the Chateau du Clos de Vougeot since 1940 and it is managed by the Confrérie des Chevaliers du Tastevin and the vineyards that surround it is divided between more than 80 owners. A little important precision : the expression « Clos de Vougeot » refers to the castle and with a *clos* that surrounds it. The term « Clos-Vougeot », meanwhile, is reserved for name grand cru. But there are other wines that the grand cru with Vougeot : many names « village » and premier cru... clear ? Now there's not any misunderstanding, welcome to Vougeot, in the heart of Burgundy, land of vineyards, prestigious wines and beautiful stones.

Castle Of Clos De Vougeot

Château du Clos de Vougeot, classified as a Historical Monument since 1949, can be visited every day of the year (except for January 1st and December 24th, 25th and 31st), 9 pm to 6 : 30 pm from April to September and 9 pm to 11 : 30 am and 2 pm to 5 : 30 pm from October to March (closing at 17 : 00 on Saturday). The last departure of the guided tour, in French, German or English on request, takes one hour before closing.The tour lasts 45 minutes, with a projection images of the activities of the Confrérie des Chevaliers du Tastevin.
Unlimited Pass is available for frequent visitors, at €15 for a year.

Sightseeing

LE CHÂTEAU DU CLOS DE VOUGEOT ★★★
Rue de la Montagne
✆ +33 (0)03 80 62 86 09
See page 9.

Sleeping

HOTEL DE VOUGEOT
18, rue du Vieux-Château
✆ +33 (0)3 80 62 01 15 – www.hotel-vougeot.com
contact@hotel-vougeot.com

Annual closure from the end of December to the end of January. Label Vineyards and Discoveries. 16 rooms. Double room from 69 € to 133 €. Breakfast : 12 € (child : 8 €). Additional bed : 19 €. Parking included. Holiday voucher. Animals accepted (additional 8 €). Seminars. Free wi-fi. Restoration (upon reservation, tray meal mâchon-type served in room or on the terrace : 22 €). Sale (wines).

Hôtel de Vougeot is a hotel set up opposite the vineyards and with the castle of Clos de Vougeot. Scattered in several buildings with character, it offers a remarkable view of the vineyards or the village. As for the interior style, it is typical of Burgundy and the regular renovations of the 16 rooms bring a decoration that mixes historic architecture and contemporary touches, the stone and the beautiful floors blend now with elegant curtains with noble red and gilded patterns whereas the bathrooms are modernized too. The TV sets are all in big screen version, up to 110 cm. It is sober and very comfortable. You will love the proximity of the vineyards on which the beautiful terrace looks out into and where the guests of the hotel enjoys a wine tasting accompanied by a mâchon.

Horse working on the Clos de Vougeot vineyard.

Clos de Vougeot castle.

Brotherhood Of The knights Of The Tastevin

It started on 16 November 1934 in the nuiton Caveau in Nuits-Saint-Georges. In the context of the economic crisis of the years 1930, Burgundy, despite a very good vintage, is sold with difficulty. Some Burgundians met and solemnly undertook to fight « in favour of the wines from France in general and those of Burgundy in particular ». Since the cellars are desperately full, for lack of buyers, they had to revive the old Bacchic brotherhoods of the seventeenth and eighteenth centuries, fallen into oblivion to empty the cellars amongst friends in joy and good humor and thus promote great Burgundies. After the war, the Brotherhood acquired the prestigious Château du Clos de Vougeot, which allows it to have control over the vineyards, and it is this prestigious setting, in the heart of vinous Burgundy, which now houses the cheerful meetings. In our time, be inducted Knight of Tastevin is exceptional !

CONFRÉRIE DES CHEVALIERS DU TASTEVIN
✆ +33 (0)3 80 62 86 09
www.tastevin-bourgogne.com
info@tastevin-bourgogne.com

For the lovers of beautiful stones, the vault of the hotel shelters a superb well decorated with a curbstone. You can also taste and buy the wines of about twenty estates of Côte-de-Nuits or Côte-de-Beaune there. The breakfast, served in the form of a generous buffet in an authentic room of the hotel, makes you discover local delicacies. Several restaurants are immediately accessible on foot. Alain Senterre, the owner, accommodate his guests with great attention. Even Raoul, a mixed-breed dog of labrador and cocker spaniels is very nice. He assists perfectly his Master.

In the surroundings

Gilly-lès-Cîteaux

CHÂTEAU DE GILLY
✆ +33 (0)3 80 62 89 98 – www.chateau-gilly.com
gilly@grandesetapes.fr

Open all year. Sunday for lunch. Low season : Tuesday to Saturday from 12pm to 2pm and from 7pm to 9pm. High season : Tuesday to Saturday from 12pm to 2pm and from 7.30pm to 9.30pm. Booking advised. Menu from €28 to €72. À la carte : Around €50. Lunch menu : €32 (starter, main course, dessert). Wine by the glass. American Express. Groups welcome. Baby chairs. Garden. Terrace.

The gourmet restaurant Le clos Prieur is an exceptional place located in the heart of the castle Château de Gilly. You will be fascinated by the majestic fireplaces, the vaulted rooms with intersecting ribs, the tapestries, the paintings, the warm atmosphere, etc. Here, everything is about history, heritage and Art. A perfect, smiling, friendly and attentive welcome awaits you on your arrival. The service will kindly accompany you to your table and will detail the menu to you with sound advice or suggestions as bonus. The chef has changed recently. Now, it is Franck Paget who runs the kitchen. He is known for his training alongside Joël Robuchon and Antoine Westermann. We enjoyed the new suggestion of the lunch menu and we were not disappointed. We began with a Hake rolled and stuffed with snails, its gratin of crozets with eyngii mushrooms and its emulsion of cremants. A real delight. We continued with a local dishes : the bourguignon beef and potato gnocchi. There's no need to say that everything is homemade ! As for dessert, beautiful chocolate entremet to end with a sweet touch... You will appreciate the charm of the place as much as the gourmet menu of the restaurant !

CHÂTEAU DE GILLY
✆ +33 (0)3 80 62 89 98 – www.chateau-gilly.com
gilly@grandesetapes.fr

Open all year. 48 rooms; double room from €130; suite from €495. Half-board. Breakfast : €25. The children of less than 12 years profit gracefully from an extra bed in the parents' room. Breakfast offered. On their arrival, gift personalized for more the young people, afternoon snack of reception and surprised for largest. Belongs to the network « Great stop-overs françaises ». Babysitting. Games for children. Pets allowed (supplement €20). Receptions and weddings. Wifi. Clos Prieur, menu at €23 and €29 with the lunch, from €52 with the dinner. Billiards.

Château de Gilly is located in an exceptional setting. A few kilometers from Dijon and close to the famous Clos Vougeot, the former residence of the abbots of Citeaux offers the pleasures of a luxury hotel in a historic location. Authenticity is guaranteed with the moat, fireplaces, the period rooms, skillfully restored ancient rooms... A charm that extends to the 48 comfortable rooms where the decor is elegant and refined while enjoying pleasant modern comforts. You will discover a unique universe in each room from the classic room to the suite junior, via the the Deluxe room. They all offer a delightful view over the French gardens, the Vouge River or the village. The staff will make every effort to satisfy all your desire, whether you want a fruit basket, a bottle of champagne, a relaxing treatment, an helicopter ride, a cellar's visit, truffles. You can also enjoy the swimming pool, the terrace and the garden during fine weather. Feel also free for a stroll by mountain bike at your disposal. Don't also miss the numerous themed parties for all the festival on calendar. Your stay will be rythmed by musical rendezvous in autumn and in winter. Musical aperitive are held on the terrace in July and August as sculpture exhibition on the French garden. Château de Gilly is also a restaurant where you will undoubtedly enjoy the exceptional gourmet cuisine of chef Franck Paget. We strongly recommend this idyllic place !

■ L'ORÉE DES VIGNES
6, route d'Epernay
✆ +33 (0)03 80 62 49 77
www.oreedesvignes.com
info@oreedesvignes.com

Double room from €70 to €195. Breakfast : €12. Extra bed : €15. Closed parking included. Stop-over with special rates : €90. Caution : Fridays of February are regarded as high season. Two rooms are especially arranged for the disabled guests. Pets allowed (€5 by animal and per day). Seminars. Free Wifi. Canal+.

Halfway between Gevrey-Chambertin and Nuits-Saint-Georges, this charming hotel is in the middle of the territory that gathers the most prestigious wine appellations. With Agnès Billaut and Caroline Ciamos at the helm, Orée des Vignes accommodates you in one of its twenty-six rooms. The building, a nicely renovated former farmhouse of the 16th century, offers all the comfort expeted for a three-star address. Les Sarments, Le Cep, Le Millésime : the rooms with personalized decoration, are spacious and air-conditioned, each of them equipped with a TV, a safe and wi-fi... The hotel also accommodates you for your seminars in two splendid rooms with the exposed beams. With its sublime garden, the place is calm, green and offers a relaxing break and discoveries. In the vault, a pretty bar enables you to taste a selection of wines of the local wine growers. L'Orée des Vignes also offers a Gourmet Getaway stay with hotel night and gourmet dinner. You can even offer it to a friend ! A nice address in a resting environment.

NIÈVRE

Tower of the cathedral

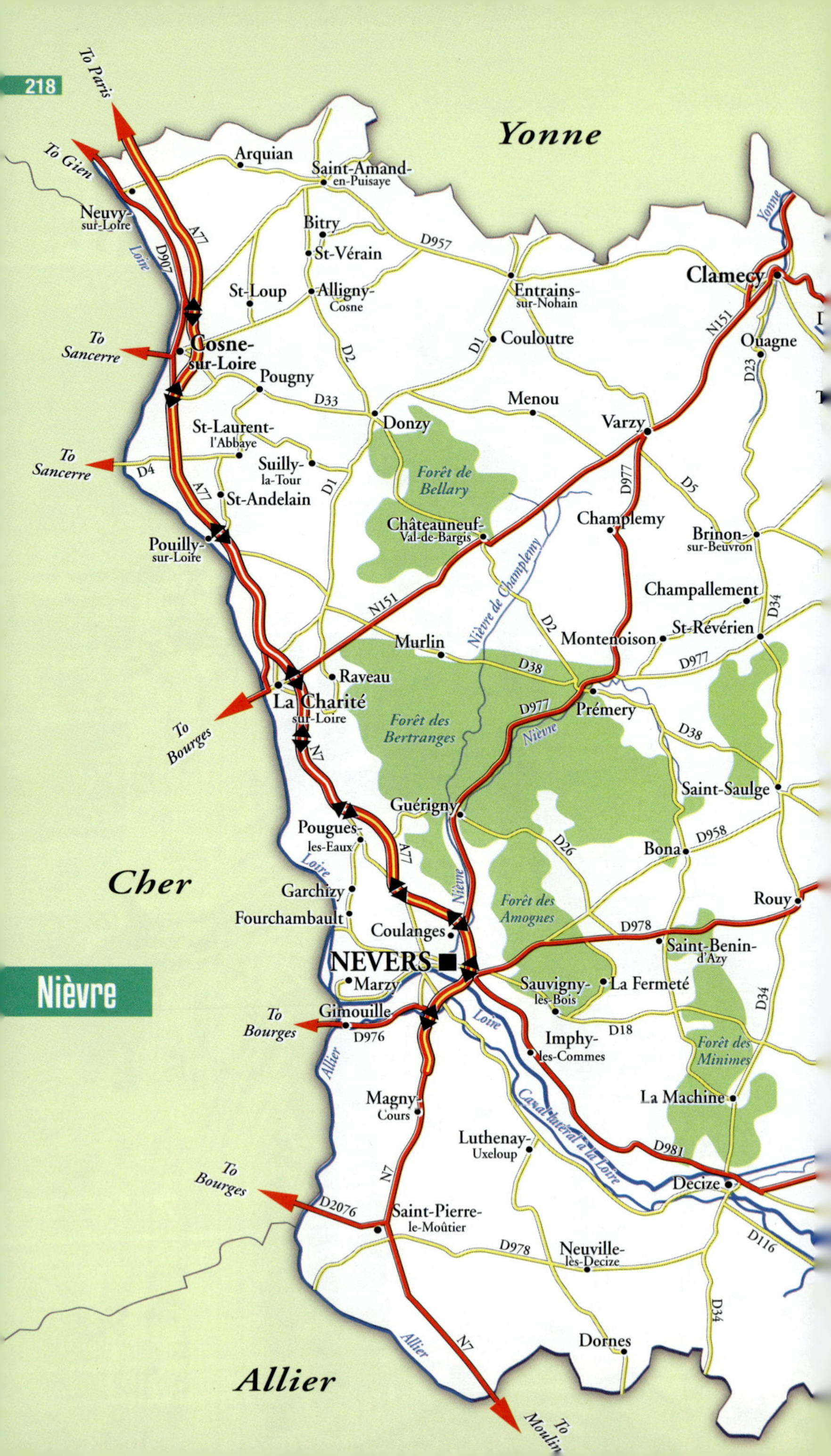
Yonne
Cher
Allier
To Paris
To Gien
To Sancerre
To Sancerre
To Bourges
To Bourges
To Bourges
To Moulins
Arquian
Saint-Amand-en-Puisaye
Neuvy-sur-Loire
Bitry
St-Vérain
St-Loup
Alligny-Cosne
Entrains-sur-Nohain
Clamecy
Cosne-sur-Loire
Couloutre
Ouagne
Pougny
Menou
Donzy
Varzy
St-Laurent-l'Abbaye
Suilly-la-Tour
St-Andelain
Forêt de Bellary
Châteauneuf-Val-de-Bargis
Champlemy
Brinon-sur-Beuvron
Pouilly-sur-Loire
Champallement
Murlin
Montenoison
St-Révérien
Raveau
La Charité-sur-Loire
Prémery
Forêt des Bertranges
Saint-Saulge
Guérigny
Pougues-les-Eaux
Bona
Garchizy
Fourchambault
Coulanges
Forêt des Amognes
Rouy
NEVERS
Saint-Benin-d'Azy
Marzy
Sauvigny-lès-Bois
La Fermeté
Gimouille
Imphy-les-Commes
Forêt des Minimes
Magny-Cours
La Machine
Luthenay-Uxeloup
Decize
Saint-Pierre-le-Moûtier
Neuville-lès-Decize
Dornes
Loire
Allier
Yonne
Nièvre
Nièvre de Champlemy
Canal latéral à la Loire
A77
N7
N151
D907
D957
D1
D2
D4
D5
D23
D26
D33
D34
D38
D116
D18
D958
D976
D977
D978
D981
D2076

Yonne
Côte-d'Or
Saône-et-Loire
Nièvre
Highway
Main road
Main road
Secondary road
Prefecture
Subprefecture
City, village
Highway Exit
Forest
To Vézelay
D951
Neuffontaines
Bazoches
St-Martin-du-Puy
St-Agnan
Parc Régional du Morvan
Canal du Nivernais
D985
D42
Anthien
Lormes
Dun-les-Places
St-Brisson
Gouloux
Corbigny
Brassy
Vauclaix
D971
Montsauche-les-Settons
Les Settons
Moux-en-Morvan
Ouroux-en-Morvan
Lac des Settons
Yonne
Montreuillon
Lac de Pannecière-Chaumard
D958
D945
D944
D37
Planchez-en-Morvan
Alnain
Aunay-en-Bazois
Tamnay-en-Bazois
St-Péreuse
Château-Chinon
D978
Châtillon-en-Bazois
Alluy
D978
Arleuf
To Autun
St-Léger-de-Fougeret
D18
Fâchin
Moulins-Engilbert
D27
Forêt de Vincence
Parc Régional du Morvan
D38
Vandenesse
D26
Saint-Honoré-les-Bains
Lac de Chèvre
Larochemillay
To Autun
Canal du Nivernais
Cercy-la-Tour
D985
D27
D981
Alène
Fours
D981
Luzy
D979
To Vichy
To Vichy
0
10 km

CHÂTEAU-CHINON ★

« Small town and famous name », was once said of Château-Chinon. This saying has taken all its meaning in 1981 with the election of François Mitterrand as President of the Republic. Mayor of Château-Chinon for 22 years (1959-1981), he was also General Counsel of the canton of Montsauche, President of the General Council and Member of Nièvre.

■ OFFICE DE TOURISME DE CHATEAU-CHINON ET SA REGION
6, boulevard de la République
✆ +33 (0)3 86 85 06 58
www.ot-chateauchinon.com
tourisme@ot-chateauchinon.com
Open Monday to Friday from 9am to 12.30pm and from 2pm to 6.30pm; Saturday from 10am to 12.30pm and from 2pm to 5.30pm; Sunday from 10am to 12.30pm.
All the necessary information to stay in the heart of Morvan : sports and cultural activities (museums, François Mitterrand tour...), accommodation, restaurants, outing good plans, discoveries... Many information brochures are available, the wi-fi is free. Local artists and craftsmen are honoured through regular exhibitions. A dynamic team that will be attentive to your desires ! Good plan on their website, the possibility to download one of the 29 topoguides « *Balade en Haut Movan* » for ideas for walks.

Knife & Fork

■ LE VIEUX MORVAN
8, place Gudin ✆ +33 (0)3 86 85 05 01
www.auvieuxmorvan.com
hotel.restaurant@auvieuxmorvan.com
Qualité Tourisme label. Logis (3 cocottes). Booking advised. Menu from €18.50 to €45.50. Lunch menu : €12.50 (only Wednesdays, Thursday and Friday). À la carte. Holiday voucher. Groups welcome. Terrace.
The Vieux Morvan welcomes you downtown. Spacious and bright, with a modern touch, it immerses you in a warm atmosphere that the cuisine of the chef Jean-Michel Réaux divinely joins. Burgundian and Morvandelle traditions subtly combine to offer you refined dishes. Let your mouth water with some appetizers, followed by a samossa of scallops and prawns, soya and sesame juice on a bed of salad that is followed by a breaded calf sweetbread, pesto of fresh tomatoes and basil, you will appreciate the fresh and semi-dry Morvan cow, to finish with the « Vieux Morvan » dish, pear with red wine and its cranberry espuma. Delicious. Labelled Logis de France, the address is also a hotel of 22 rooms.

Sleeping

■ HOTEL DU PARC – RESTAURANT LE RELAIS GOURMAND
Route de Nevers
✆ +33 (0)3 86 79 44 94
Closed in February. 25 rooms (including 16 air-conditioned). From €47 to €63. Full-board : €74. Half-board : €59. Open parking. Stop-over with special rates for reps : €60. Holiday voucher. Pets allowed. Seminars. Free Wifi. Satellite TV, Canal+.
Located at the entrance of Château-Chinon, this hotel is an intitution ! The hotel offers bright and spacious rooms with all modern comforts. We love this view of the green and wild Morvan mountains. You will enjoy both the friendliness and the warmth of the welcome, in a natural setting for a nice repairing night ! Note that the establishment has also a restaurant.

■ LE VIEUX MORVAN
8, place Gudin
✆ +33 (0)3 86 85 05 01
www.auvieuxmorvan.com
hotel.restaurant@auvieuxmorvan.com
Qualité Tourisme label. Logis (3 cheminées). Open every day, Sunday and Monday only by reservation. 24 rooms. From €63 to €85. Half-board (from €83 to €91 for 1 person, from €120 to €136 for 2 people, from €181 to €189 for 3 people). Buffet breakfast or in room (€8.50 and €9.50). Parking included. Stop-over with special rates for reps at €68. Pets allowed (with €5 extra). Free Wifi. Satellite TV, Canal+.
In the heart of the city, this massive mansion offers twenty bright, spacious and nicely furnished rooms, with country or city view, ideal for a traditional stay in the Morvan, starting point for an discovery getaway of the green countries of living waters. Good value for money, and elegant service for this address which is also a restaurant.

Canal Du Nivernais

Induced by the need of the City of Paris to be supplied in wood, the construction of the Canal du Nivernais was undertaken in 1784 and was not completed until 1843. Enabling the junction between the two pools of the Loire and the Seine, it consists of 110 locks. 180 km long, it began its course in Saint-Léger-des-Vignes, and completes it in Auxerre. To supply water canal, two ponds have been created in the late 18th century : the ponds of Baye and that of Vaux. Considered one of the most beautiful canals in Europe, the Canal du Nivernais is now entirely devoted to pleasure, and Baye and Vaux ponds are known for their extraordinary birdlife. You can therefore choose a cruise on the Canal du Nivernais, on board electric boats, where, the beauty of the landscapeis complemented by three tunnels will follow one another including the famous tunnel La Collancelle, 760 m long, then the beautiful work of the Scale of Sardy, passage of sixteen consecutive locks. Thanks to discovery trails through the educational terminals and observatories, you will discreetly discover the fauna and flora of the surrounding sites.Information : www.canal-du-nivernais.com

In the surroundings

Châtillon-en-Bazois ★

Moulins-Engilbert ★

■ **COMPTOIR GOURMAND**
1, place Boucaumont ✆ +33 (0)3 86 84 26 85
comptoirflorence@wanadoo.fr
Open Tuesday to Saturday from 9am to 12.30pm and from 3pm to 7pm. Open on Sunday (from 10.30am to 12.30pm).

Florence Bouchoux welcomes you in her charming shop full of gourmet products from Burgundy and Morvan. Whether for a special occasion, a company gift or just to indulge yourself, you will inevitably find your happiness among the diversity of the available products : homemade jams, honey of Morvan, beers, fruit creams, local wines from Tannay, craquants du Val de Loire... Do not hesitate to request a tailor-made composition, the owner will be happy to make it for you !

Saint-Honoré-les-Bains ★

NIÈVRE

CLAMECY ★

This picturesque town with its ancient city-centre classified as « protected area », its narrow and winding streets and beautiful old houses with tiled roofs, is the home of John II of Burgundy, Count of Nevers, called Jean Clamecy. There are also among the children of the city Claude Tillier, author of My Uncle Benjamin, Romain Rolland, Alain Colas and many more... It is in the sixteenth century that Clamecy enjoyed an era of prosperity and revealed its true character thanks to the invention of floating wood, which provisioned Paris with firewood. Four thousand people were living from this activity. During the Restoration, 500 floaters, with agile fists and republican fervour, laid claim to defend their rights, fighting against injustice. Rebellious and tumultuous the four centuries of float transformed Clemecy forever. A charming town whose history is reflected in every corner, dynamic shopping and galore activities, in brief it is a city that should absolutely be discovered !

Sightseeing

■ **MUSÉE D'ART ET D'HISTOIRE ROMAIN ROLLAND** ★
Avenue de la République
✆ +33 (0)3 86 27 17 99
www.musees-bourgogne.org
museedeclamecy@wanadoo.fr
♿

Closed from November 15th to March 15th. Open from 10am to 12pm and from 2pm to 6pm. Closed the Sunday morning and Tuesday from May 2nd to September 30th; closed the Sunday morning, Monday and Tuesday from October 1st to April 30th. Free for under 16-year-olds. Adult : €3. Group (10 people) : €1.50. Guided tour (by reservation. Possible also free on MP3, in French, German and English). Shop. Activities.

Established in the former hotel of Bellegarde since the 60s, the museum acquired the adjacent buildings that are the birthplace of Romain Rolland and Edme Courot, to exhibit donations that came to enrich the initial collections. The visitor begins the exploration with the basement of the hotel with archaeological collections of the Compierre, Brèves and Corvol l'Orgueilleux site. The visit continues with the fine arts room, sheltering paintings from the 16th to the 20th century. The 19th century is represented, among others, by works of Horace Vernet. *Le Mur au chien de Cueco* is one of the important paintings in the room of contemporary art. In the room devoted to Charles Loupot, objects and advertizing posters trace his career. The room of earthenware shows the evolution of the decor and the colours of this activity born in the 16th century. The Romain Rolland fund underlines the richness of the works presented, including rare illustrated editions of his novel Colas Breugnon. The visit ends with the spectacular room under the roof of the hotel de Bellegarde, devoted to wood floating which made the wealth of Clamecy for four centuries.

© LAËTITIA STEIMETZ

La rue du Canal in Clamecy.

Knife & Fork

L'ANGELUS
11, place Saint-Jean
✆ +33 (0)3 86 27 33 98
www.restaurantlangelus.fr
restaurantlangelus@orange.fr
Closed during the year's end celebrations. July-August : closed on Monday and Sunday for dinner. Low season : also closed Wednesday for dinner. Booking advised. Menu from €29 to €37. Children's menu : €11. Fixed rate formula : €22 (except Saturday for dinner and Sunday). Wine by the glass. À la carte. Holiday voucher. Groups welcome. Terrace. Pets allowed.
Collégiale Saint-Martin is the worthy neighbour of this half-timbered house of the sixteenth century.
The sign of the Angelus is characterised by its elegance, like a promising first impression of the charms that you will enjoy once you are seated inside or on terrace. Cyrille Girault, renowned Nivernais Toque, will offer you a seasonal cuisine, with creative touches that embellish with delight the local produce. It was on a very summer day that Futé sat down on the terrace of this restaurant opposite the Collegiate. The service is efficient and attentive. On the menu of this lunch, Futé enjoyed a fine pie with andouillette of Clamecy enhanced by a cream with mustard seed followed by a cake of pike perch with vegetable brunoise and its shellfish bisque with colombo. The chef perfectly controls his cooking. It is also an excellent chef that we have discovered. The desserts become simpler but moreover the creme brulee and its homemade shortbread biscuit did not bring us down again from our cloud. Inside, the colourful decoration and the small elegant touches of the owner add much charm. A very good address.

Sleeping

HOSTELLERIE DE LA POSTE
9, place Emile-Zola
✆ +33 (0)3 86 27 01 55
www.hostelleriedelaposte.fr
hotelposteclamecy@wanadoo.fr
Logis (3 cheminées). Open all year. 24 rooms (including a room for the disabled guests €92). Double room from €68 to €79; suite from €99 to €114. Half-board (€98, 1 person and €160 for two). Breakfast : €10. Stop-over with special rates for reps at €85. Holiday voucher. Pets allowed. Seminars. Catering facilities.
This former coaching inn of the 17th century will welcome you for a pleasant stay under the sign of friendliness and relaxation. Each of the 24 rooms have modern comfort and refined decoration. The breakfast room is bright and you may like to enjoy a snack in the morning there. A very good address in the heart of the city, which continues its renovations work and beautification and is now equipped with a lift. The establishment is renowned for its very good restaurant and Petit Futé confirms it !

In the surroundings

Champlémy

LE BISTRÔ À MALICES
2, Grande-Rue
✆ +33 (0)3 86 60 11 07
www.le-bistro-a-malices.com
contact@le-bistro-a-malices.com

Open on Friday from 7.30pm; the weekend from 12.30pm and from 7.30pm. Apart from this schedule, as of 6 people by reservation. Booking advised. Wine by the glass. Set menu : around €30. Free wi-fi. Parking nearby.
Located on the way to Saint Jacques-de-Compostelle, Bistro à Malices awaits you in the heart of the small village of Champlemy. Anne activates the café of her grandparents, for the greatest delight of the people who see one of their old brands waking up. The charm is intact : Anne has kept the friendly atmosphere of the café with its beautiful tableclothes, its linen napkins. For the cuisine, you can taste family treasures decorated with Anne's personal touch. A unique menu that changes every week : consisting of an appetizer, a starter, a main course, a round of cheeses and a dessert. These are rich simplicities that excite our tastebuds. Randomly taken from suggestions, a gazpacho of cucumber, salad of pink grapefruit, avocado and prawns, Breton monkfish poached in coconut milk, ginger and garlic with a cream of peas and a tiramisu with red fruits. Anne also offers food and wine carefully considered with her wine merchant. She speaks German and English for the happiness of foreigners. Beautiful discovery !

Entrains-sur-Nohain

■ MAISONS DES FOUILLES

8, rue des Promenades
✆ +33 (0)3 86 29 22 06
High season : open every day from 3pm to 7pm. Open holiday Saturday, Sunday and ovens in May, June and September, from 3pm to 7pm. Groups by appointment. Adult : €2. Child : €1.
La Maison des Fouilles exhibits part of the lost property brought to light in the region of Entrains, such as fibulas, tools, the limestone statues of the gods venerated in the ancient Gallo-Roman city. An interesting example of the distant past of the city and its surroundings : the richness of the objects shows at which extend the city was developed. A place to see. Please note, for groups, permanent access is possible on appointment.

Tannay

■ LES CAVES TANNAYSIENNES

11, rue d'Enfer
✆ +33 (0)3 86 29 31 59
www.caves-tannay.com
contact@caves-tannay.com
Open Tuesday to Saturday from 9am to 12pm and from 2pm to 6pm. Low season : Sunday and public holidays from 10am to 12pm and from 3pm to 6pm. High season : Sunday, Monday and public holidays from 10am to 12pm and from 3pm to 6pm. Apart from this schedule, visits possible by appointment. High season from May 1st to September 30th, low season from October 1st to April 1st. Bottle from €6.
The vineyard of Tannay is first of all a history of impassioned men who meet in 1995 with the will to make reappear an almost forgotten heritage. The cellar is located in the heart of the small town of Nevers and has a beautiful character. Its construction dates from 1568 and its facade still raises the remains of the old days. Before entering, do not hesitate to read the precepts that decorate the wall on the road side. Inside, the cellar master Cyrille Ponnelle welcomes you and makes you discover the wines of Tannay and their growing reputation. It is good to point out that here the grape harvest is exclusively manual, we harvest plot by plot in order to ensure the better quality and the selection of grapes during the harvest and before they arrive at the cellar. You will find the control of the classic vine in Burgundy way. You will find the following grape varieties : melon (old Burgundian grape variety) and white chardonnay, pinot noir and red gamay. Please note that the Cuvée des Flotteurs is characterized regularly by its great rewards. The Tannaysiennes cellars also produce their ratafia (liqueur wine). A good place, with the appreciable reception and the expert advice ! Do not hesitate to make a stop in these cellars, during opening hours, or by appointment. It should be noted that the language of Shakespeare is commonly spoken.

CORBIGNY

Nestled at the edge of Morvan and Nivernais, this small flowered city benefits from the meeting of several commercial, tourist and river channels. On the way to Saint-Jacques de Compostela and the « Route Buissonnière », Corbigny is 45 km south of Vézelay and its famous basilica. City gate of the regional park of Morvan, it abounds in majestic forests, the rivers are full of fish, and has a rich historical heritage with three massive towers of the fifteenth century, such as that of the Madeleine, recall the time when the city was fortified. Crossed by Anguisson and the stream of Tanner, Corbigny offers many flowered bridges in summer, which added to the charm of old houses, give the town a picturesque note that is very popular among walkers.

Sightseeing

■ L'ABÉÏCITÉ – ABBAYE DE CORBIGNY ★

Tourist Office
8, rue de l'Abbaye
✆ +33 (0)3 86 20 02 53
www.abeicite-corbigny.com
Open Monday to Saturday from 9am to 12pm and from 2pm to 6.30pm. Free. Rooms to be rented : from €50 per day depending on the selected room.
Jean Omelane, adviser of the duke of Orleans, began the renovation (using materials of the previous building) of the fifth, and the current abbey. The date (September 27th, 1754) and the name of the project manager (Dom Laudel) are engraved on a stone foundation of the abbey.

During the Revolution, the abbey of Corbigny became the property of the city and its buildings successively housed the municipality, the magistrate, the stud Cluny, military hospitals, and finally schools. Although it underwent many mutilations, inflicted by successive occupiers, the abbey of Corbigny is classified as a Historical Monument since November 1999. The discovery of the abbey can be done according to 2 formulas : a free tour with 17 explanatory panels, and an audio visit on digital tablet. The cellars tour of the fifteenth century at the rooftops is meanwhile punctuated by 33 explanatory panels.
Established in the heart of the city and in the Corbogeois heart, the abbey which houses the Abéïcité association, intends to be a place for creation and invention. Four troupes were housed there in a long-lasting way : the Compagnie Déviation(visual and musical performances), the TéATR' éPROUVèTe (« proximity theatre »), the Compagnie Les Alentours Rêveurs (contemporary dance), and the Compagnie Métalovoice(«industrial poetry, artistic experimentation and on the crossroads of various disciplines»).
Exhibitions are regularly organised and the artists of different backgrounds settled in residence for a time.

Leisure

LOCABOAT HOLIDAYS
THE PENICHETTE COMPANY
Port de la Vauvelle
La Chaise
✆ +33 (0)3 86 20 07 29 / +33 (0)3 86 91 72 72
www.locaboat.com
info@locaboat.com
From €896 per week. €30 for an animal.
Here, you are offered the rental of houseboats of five to twelve people, comfortably equipped. You can embark for amazing cruises to discover the most bucolic corners of the surrounding region, for one to two weeks of nonchalance in the rythm of calm waters of the canals. A very original way to spend a pleasant family holiday, at least very relaxing, far from the stress of large cities...

In the surroundings

Bazoches

CHATEAU DE BAZOCHES ★★
✆ +33 (0)3 86 22 10 22
www.chateau-bazoches.com
chateau.bazoches@wanadoo.fr
Open mid-March at November 11 included. See schedule on the website. Free for under 7-year-olds (and disabled). Adult : €8.50 (€6.50 for the adults holders of the many family card). Child (from 7 to 14 years old) : €4. Group (20 people) : €6.50. Student : €6.50. Guided tour (for groups on request). Shop.
Overlooking the village of Bazoches, the castle of Vauban is nestled in lush greenery, impressing visitors with its rigorous architecture, which reflects eight centuries of France and Morvan history. Built in the twelfth century by Jean de Bazoches, large local lord, the castle belonged to 40 successive owners from Chastellux and Vauban families, whose current owners are direct descendants. Rebuilt many times, it is to Vauban, who bought it in 1675 by gratification granted by Louis XIV, that it owes its transformation into a military garrison. Vauban liked to go in these places where he made a good number of plans of strongholds, and developed methods of attack and defence that made its reputation. Also, for its history, its architecture and its stunning views of the Morvan and the basilica of Vézelay in the distance, the castle Bazoches is one of the most beautiful jewels of Nievre ! Note that the following services exist in Bazoches : wedding in the gardens, lunch and dinner in the prestigious gallery, exceptional dinner in the dining room (information : amaury.desigalas @ wanadoo.fr).

Ride on the river in Chaumot.

Chaumot

■ RESTAURANT DU CAMPING DE L'ARDAN

Route de Germenay ✆ +33 (0)3 86 20 07 70
www.camping-bourgogne.com
campingdelardan@wanadoo.fr

Open from April 1st to October 1st. Open Wednesday to Monday. À la carte : Around €15. Credit card not accepted. Terrace. Activities.

Le camping de l'Ardan gained a good reputation after the broadcasting «Bienvenue au camping» broadcasted in January 2015 on TF1, he also owns a restaurant called Rappellons which is always open for outsiders of the camping. This restaurant is located on an Island in the middle of the river of Ardan and le canal du Nivernais. It has a relaxing, familiar and animated atmosphere. The dutch managers are fond of music. If you are lucky enough you may have the opportunity to listen to Cornelia singing Piaf or Brel... Each thursday evening in the summer, there are live concerts organised on the little stage, outside in front of the restaurant's terrace, the customers can enjoy the show there. 30 to 50 dishes are offered during those evenings, thus the best you can do is to book ! The card of the restaurant is focused on traditional french cookery merged with some Dutch delicacies : magret de canard à l'orange, pavé de charlais au champignon, camembert cuit à la confiture de framboise, papillotte de saumon, croquettes de viande, soirée hareng cru... the price is truly attractive. Le restaurant du camping de l'Ardan is quite friendly and the setting is totally magnificent !

Lormes

■ GORGES DE NARVAU

Listed as historic site, the Gorges of Narvau were excavated by Auxois in the granite edge of the western Morvan, southwest of Lormes. The mills area and successive waterfalls are worth visiting, especially during spring when the bluebells illuminates the undergrowth. Nature here is queen, steep slopes sheltering forestry groups of shady ravines. The gorges are also a paradise for those who love climbing. The arrowed pedestrian paths and a picnic area punctuate the site offering more attractiveness to this beautiful setting. A plan of the gorges is free at the tourist office.

■ MORVAN VACANCES

2, rue des Teureaux
✆ +33 (0)3 86 22 80 17
www.morvanvakanties.nl
morvanvacances@orange.fr

Open all year. Tipi, €70/night and €425/week – Yurt, €80/night and €475/week – Caravan, €175 the weekens and €525/week. Cottage from €375 per night. Mountain bike rental, 1/2 day, €12 for the children and €18 for the adults. Holiday voucher. Pets allowed. Outdoor lounge, sheets rental, washing machine, tumble dryer, dishwasher.

It is with happiness and kindness that this Dutch couple opens the doors of their various accommodations, for a stopover or a longer stay in the heart of Morvan. Be it the new Gîte Teureaux or the Gîte des Rôches, in a former school that can accommodate up to 30 people, you will find all the necessary comfort for a peaceful holiday. The Châlet Romanesque on the other hand can accommodate up to 4 people that can enjoy enclosed garden of 800 m². Finally, those who prefer unusual accommodation, choose the teepee, the yurt, or the caravan, fully equipped, that can accommodate up to 6 people, in the beautiful setting of the pond campsite. It should be noted that, another is cottage available to rent at Chaumeçon.

COSNE-COURS-SUR-LOIRE ★

At the confluence of the Loire and Nohain, Cosne-sur-Loire is actually called Cosne-Cours-sur-Loire, since these municipalities have associated their fate in 1973. Last city of Loire from the north of Nièvre, it offers mixed waters, but also changing landscapes : the Nivernais, Puisaye and the Berry meet here, at the crossroads of two regions, Burgundy and Berry, of four AOC, Sancerre, Pouilly Fumé, Pouilly-sur-Loire and Coteaux du Giennois and of 4 departments, Nièvre, Cher, Loiret and Yonne.

Sightseeing

■ MUSÉE MUNICIPAL DE LA LOIRE ★

Place de la Résistance ✆ +33 (0)3 86 26 71 02
www.mairie-cosnesurloire.fr
musee@mairie-cosnesurloire.fr

Reopening on March 1st, 2015. Low season : open on Monday and Wednesday to Friday from 10am to 12pm and from 2pm to 5.30pm; Saturday and public holidays from 2pm to 5.30pm. High season : Monday and Wednesday to Friday from 10am to 12pm and from 2pm to 6pm; the weekend and public holidays from 2pm to 6pm. Low season from November to December, high season from March to October. Free for under 18-year-olds. Adult : €3.50. Group (10 people) : €20 (+ entrance fee). Reduced rate €2. Children welcome (free booklet-game with the reception for children over 7 years old). Guided tour (€2.50 + entrance fee). Shop. Activities. Spoken English.

The ground floor of the museum is fully dedicated to the royal river. Evoked through the landscapes, painted by Eugène Messemin and Claude Rameau at the beginning of this century, the Loire is presented here in various aspects : old pictures, testimonies of disappeared or scarce activities like drawing sand, commercial fishing, or yet sea-faring. The upper floor is devoted to fine arts : collection of modern paintings, representative of the school of Montparnasse between 1910 and 1925. Tin collections and earthenware are presented in two adjacent rooms. Children from seven years can discover the collections in a fun way, through a booklet-game and explanations of the Green parrot that guide them along the Loire.

Knife & Fork

LE SQUARE
1, Square Gambon
✆ +33 (0)3 86 28 17 75
lesquare@free.fr

Closed 10 days at the end of February and 10 days end November October-beginning. Open Friday to Tuesday from 11am to midnight. À la carte : Around €10. Children's menu : €7.50. Lunch menu : €13 (except the weekends and public holidays). Wine by the glass. À la carte and slate of innovations. Plates of tapas : €6. Terrace.

A cozy atmosphere and brasserie spirit for this establishment, where conviviality rhymes with musicality and delicacies ! You will enjoy the beautiful terrace on summer evenings, (heated in winter), you will enjoy tasting in the menu of the day a pan-fried beef in Auvergne way (Roquefort and walnut) served with big homemade fries to end on a sweet note with a Forêt Noire for example, or if you prefer a sea version, choose the lacquered trout steak with maple syrup and ginger, followed by a large rum baba with strawberries and chantilly. The Indian, Berrichonne, Italian gourmet slices of bread are a success. In the evening and on weekend, a selection of dish on the slate comes and completes the menu. You will also treat yourself to subtle old aperitifs, and what could be nicer than a mini-tapas evening at the cocktail bar ? Le Square is a good address where to eat but also a very friendly address to have a drink in full afternoon or in the evening. Belgian beer lovers – Duvel, Maredsous, Vedett, Meteor... – will be charmed. Futé also appreciated the ultra-fresh fruit cocktails made with sorbets. A very pleasant Cosnois place.

Sleeping

LE PRIEURE SAINT-AGNAN
Place Saint-Agnan
✆ +33 (0)6 19 91 96 82
www.prieuresaintagnan.com
leprieuresaintagnan@gmail.com

Gîte de France (4 épis). Open all year. 5 rooms. Single room from €90; double room from €98; triple room from €120; suite from €110 to €150. Breakfast included. Extra bed : €20. Closed parking included (car, motorbike, bicycle). Free Wifi.

Véronique and Gilles Cegretin welcome you in this former Benedictine priory adjoining the bell tower of the Saint-Agnan church. Passionate about travelling, the couple has explored more than 35 countries of the world. Witnessed by the furniture, the paintings and the countless books that open with 1 001 histories. In the heart of the historic neighbourhood of Cosne, this 19th century house opens you the doors of its five rooms with discreet charm and absolute comfort. The beds have mattress overlays, some are 180x200 cm, others 160x200 cm, one thing is certain : you will sleep the sleep of the just. The art of hospitality starts here by a Sancerre bottle that is offered to you upon your arrival and continues throughout your stay by multiple information which is brought to you on the winegrowing estate and on the sites to visit in the surrounding areas. You will enjoy relaxing in the library lounge, strolling in the beautiful garden that overlooks Loire, offering a stunning view of the wild river, and from May to September, tasting the joy of being able to swim in the pleasant heated swimming pool. An ideal place for relaxation and discovery of the Loire region !

In the surroundings

Donzy

MOULIN DE MAUPERTUIS – ECOMUSEE DE LA MEUNERIE ★
Rue André-Audinet ✆ +33 (0)3 86 39 39 46
www.moulindemaupertuis.jimdo.com
moulin-maupertuis@wanadoo.fr

Closed from November 1st to April 30th. Low season : open every day from 2pm to 6pm. High season : every day from 2pm to 7pm. Free for under 6-year-olds. Adult : €4.80 (students and children at €2.50). Group (10 people) : €3.80 (school €2). Guided tour. Activities.

In the heart of Donzy, on the Nohain river, stands the Moulin de Maupertuis. This 900 m^2 former flour mill, spread over four floors, became in 1989 an eco-museum of mill thanks to the Donziais Cultural Association for the promotion of the Moulin de Maupertuis site and many other partners. It is listed in the Supplementary Historic Monument since 1991. Each year, volunteers improve the museum by bringing innovations, such as the installation, in 1992, of a water wheel built in the old style, dismantled in 1969. You must come to see these machines of yesteryear millers coming to life again, as well as the various themed exhibitions on bread and mill, without forgetting night and musical tours set up last year. A very recreational visit for pupils. Note that it is also possible to come to celebrate your birthday at the mill, for a festive atmosphere, inside as outside, far from the beaten tracks !

Pougny

LANGLOIS PERE & FILS
Le bourg
✆ +33 (0)3 86 28 06 52 / +33 (0)6 30 84 11 37
www.domaine-langlois.fr
catmi-langlois@orange.fr

Open Monday to Saturday from 9.30am to 12.30pm and from 2.30pm to 7pm. Open on Sunday (by appointment).

The Langlois family estate stretches over 17 ha, organized as follows : 1 ha of Pouilly-Fumé, 11 hectares of Coteaux-de-Giennois and 5 ha of Vin de pays. A range of wines and fruit cream which can be enjoyed in the privacy of the small reception room, or as a group in the spacious dining room, fully restored for your comfort. Quality wines, award-winning and renowned, but also the famous blackcurrant liqueur, considered for its unparalleled purity and flavor, just as the wild blackberry cream and bilberry liqueur.

Saint-Amand-en-Puisaye castle

Saint-Amand-en-Puisaye

■ LA PETITE MAISON AMANDINOISE

18, Grande-Rue
✆ +33 (0)3 86 39 63 21
✆ +33 (0)6 59 07 24 34
http ://lapetitemaisonamandinoise.fr
frederiqueserin@free.fr

Gîte de France (3 épis). Open all year. 3 rooms (an accessible room with the disabled guests). Single room from €60 to €70; double room from €65 to €80; triple room €95. Breakfast included. Extra bed : €15 (on request). Rate 4 people, €110 - 5 people, €125. For all the rooms, cheaper rates as of €2 the night. Holiday voucher. Free Wifi.

Nestled in the heart of the village, this écogîte, with three guesthouse offers, you the charm of an eighteenth-century architecture. Whether In the Côté Cour, Côté Jardin or Côté Ciel, here you are away from home. The atmosphere is cosy, tones underline the natural sweet life in these places. Outside, the magnolia will provide you with shade in the garden for a stay in serenity in the heart of the village of potters.

Suilly-la-Tour

■ CHÈVRERIE DE LA FILLOUSE

La Fillouse, 9, rue des Ecoles
✆ +33 (0)6 84 98 53 74 / +33 (0)3 86 26 37 83
chevreriedelafillouse@gmail.com

♿

Open Monday to Wednesday and Saturday from 9am to 12pm and from 5pm to 7pm; Thursday and Friday from 5pm to 7pm; Sunday from 9am to 12pm. Welcomme to the farm.

In the middle of the valley of Nohain, la chévrerie de la Fillouse is a beautiful stopover to discover the beauty of the delicious goats'cheese of the region. Here Raphaël Bourdon manages himself to produce milk of his goats, crottin, bûches, pyramids and other cheese products... those cheeses can be eaten as appetizers as well as in salads ! A good thing to know : crottin are certified by AOC, Chavignol goat cheese (crottin) and all the cheeses are produced starting from the milk of the 110 Alpine goats nourished with cereals manufactured in the farmhouse or in the local farmhouses. In summer, it is possible to come and visit La Chèvrerie de la Fillouse, you have an opportunity of tasting and purchasing cheeses froçm the region directly at the farmhouse. To conclude, La Chèvrerie de la Fillouse is a magnificient property made of wood, it's tidy and pleasant, friendly welcome, added by the beauty of their cheeses thus the visit will satisfy everyone whether kids or parents !

DECIZE ★

Enclosed between two arms of the Loire, firmly set within its walls, this small town is one of the major entertainment centres in the region, the real crossroads of waterways between the Canal of Nivernais and the Canal Lateral at Loire. We should not leave without following the magnificent promenade des Halles, which was planted in 1771 and is 985 meters long, is one of the oldest plantations of plane and linden in France as well as a unique place in Europe (site as classified at the Inventory of Historical Monuments in 1932). Similarly, the marina is now a must for the tourist life of Decize : balcony on the Loire with its large hosting capacity and its recent developments make it a more user-friendly place that should not to be missed.

Sightseeing

RUINES DE L'ANCIEN CHATEAU

Guided tours only by reservation. Credit card not accepted.
The oldest mention concerning the castle of the counts and dukes of Nevers dates back to the 11th century. Only the first elevation levels (except for the donjon, which contains a statue of the Virgin) various newly clear main buildings have been preserved.

Knife & Fork

LE CHAROLAIS

33 bis, route de Moulins ✆ +33 (0)3 86 25 22 27
franck.rapiau@wanadoo.fr
Open Wednesday to Saturday for lunch and dinner; Sunday for lunch. Booking advised. Menu from €30 to €51. Children's menu : €13.50. Fixed rate formula : €18.50. Wine by the glass. Toasted slice of bread rebukes from €10. À la carte. Cookery classes (Monday for dinner, Wednesday for dinner and Thursday for dinner). Terrace.
The chef Frank Rapiau offers a refined cuisine, combining creation and tradition by using a wide range of regional products evolving throughout the seasons. He tries very hard to make everything home untill bread and ice-creams. The meat is obviously under the Charolais label; the choice of fish is of extreme demands, without forgetting the desserts whose exquisite finesse delights the senses. On weekdays, at lunchtime, we opted for a cream of pumpkin and potatoes, smoked bacon, thick cream and toasted bread, then a Scottish salmon as a pot-au-feu «in my own way» to end on a caramelised apple-pear clafoutis and salted caramel sauce. The sandwiches are of a very good quality-price ratio but lacks seasoning (no sauce with the fish, no chutney with the foie gras...) Note that cooking classes are very regularly organised, as well as musical evenings. Vibe side, the colourful cutlery bring much gaiety. The covered terrace with its veils on the ceiling gives a very pleasant light and summer atmosphere.

RESTAURANT DU PORT

Bassin de la Jonction ✆ +33 (0)3 73 15 00 04
www.port-decize.fr
port-decize@ccsn.fr
♿
Open all year. Thursday to Tuesday from 11am to 2pm and from 6pm to 10.30pm. Booking advised. Menu from €15 to €37. Children's menu : €8 (for children under 12 years old). Daily special : €9 (daily menu at €12). À la carte. Chèque Restaurant. Groups welcome. Baby chairs. Garden. Terrace. Wifi.
Located on the Decize port, this restaurant that invites you to taste fish specialities, labelled meats of extreme tenderness, dishes made from regional produce, skillfully selected wines. The menu is mouthwatering, the setting is contemporary and the atmosphere is warm. To awaken your tastebuds, duck foie gras and its compotée of onion and mixed salad, then a skewer of prawns sauce with tarragon, a farm white cheese and very gourmet chocolate mousse ! Guests will also appreciate to eat on the waterside terrace. The establishment is also a hotel.

Sleeping

HOTEL-RESTAURANT DE L'AGRICULTURE

20, route de Moulins
✆ +33 (0)3 86 25 05 38
www.hotelagriculture.fr
hoteldelagriculture@wanadoo.fr
♿ ❄
Reception bicycle. Open 7 days a week. 15 rooms (including 7 air-conditioned and 1 for the disabled guests in ground floor). Double room from €64 to €72. Half-board : €65. Breakfast : €10 (4.50 for children under 10 years). Parking included. One-night stopover with special rates : €73 and €85 depending on the selected menu. Menus from €18 to €39.50. Free Wifi.
Agriculture works for the good reputation of the region. Marie-Claire and Olivier Ranvier welcome you in one of their fifteen rooms with a particularly neat comfort, just like the decoration, simple but stylish. A pleasant breakfast room, with a copious buffet. Indeed, pastries, bread, homemade jams, orange juices, eggs, cheese and possibility of adding ham for those who wish it wait for you upon awakening. The very attentive reception contributes to making the stay delicious. A good address in Decize. The establishment is also a restaurant.

Leisure

AQUATOON

Stade nautique
High season : open every day. Free.
This completely free attraction site completes activities, present at the Pointe des Halles nautical stadium. Made up of thirteen different games, Aquatoon is accessible from 1 year of age, according to three distinct areas : blue for children, yellow for adults and green for the whole family. As a real playground, kids have fun sliding on the big ladybug, passing under the water tunnel, watering themselves with water cannons, climbing on blue Hippo or yellow dragon... Colorful details and playful forms, there is enough to have fun free !

In the surroundings

La Machine

MUSÉE DE LA MINE ET PUITS DES GLENONS ★

1, avenue de la République
✆+33 (0)3 86 50 91 08
musee.lamachine@ccsn.fr
From March 1st to October 31st. Adult : €6 (€4 for only one site). Child (from 6 to 18 years old) : €3. Group (12 people) : €5 (for the school groups, €2 for groups of more than 12 people). Guided tour. Shop.
The visit of La Machine must go with that of the Mining museum, created on the initiative of a group of former miners who work at safeguarding a collective memory. The museum restores the daily life of this small city, both in terms of social life on the surface and the work at the

bottom of the mine. A palaeontology and mineralogy collection brings a scientific complement to the ethnological and historical background. With the mine-image (near the well of Glénons), topped with a helmet and equiped with a lamp, you will learn the different forms of coal mining, reconstituted in a remarkable manner, for a fun and sensitive approach of the mining trade ! Every year, a temporary exhibition enriches the museum's collections.

Rouy

■ PANIER BIO DE LA FERME DU VAL D'OSSEUX

Nadine et Jean-Paul-Loisy
Osseux ✆ +33 (0)3 86 60 20 63
www.levaldosseux.fr
jpnloisy@wanadoo.fr

Open on Monday, Tuesday and Thursday to Saturday from 9am to 12pm and from 3pm to 6pm; Wednesday from 9am to 12pm. Parking. Area Camper van.

The way leading to Ferme du Val d'Osseux is located on the D132, the panels will guide you until you reach the spot. In Easter 2014 La Ferme du Val d'Osseux has opened a shop reserved for local bio products. Here it is a whole philosophy encouraging the daily life of the farmhouse since the events of 2007 which initiate Nadine and Jean-Paul Loisy to start and run a bio farming business and then they obtained a certification in 2012, the 50th years of the cheese factory. Since then, the 80 milk cows are treated with homeopathy. They are nourished of dried hay in grange due to the solar energy gathered in the subceiling. For the manufacturing of the cereals they do not use pesticide, nor weedkiller. Thus the cows (Holstein and Jersiaise) produce good and healthy used to manufacture cheeses of farmhouse : le Nivernais au cœur coulant, la Tommette et la Val d'Osseux. In addition, the quality ingredients of the farmhouse of Val d'Osseux, you have the opportunity to run your own business with a basket full of bio products : jams, oils, apples juice, honey, herbal teas, eggs, lentils... This farmhouse is truly friendly and it's very active compared to other farmhouse and the welcoming is truly warm and pleasant ! Before leaving, you should check the system of the basin which allows to oxygenate and regenerate the water drawn from the soils before filling the feeding troughs of the cows. This address is perfect !

Saint-Léger-des-Vignes

■ MUSÉE DE LA MARINE FLUVIALE / TOUEUR

39, route Nationale
✆ +33 (0)3 86 50 91 08
musee.lamachine@ccsn.fr

Open every day and public holidays from 2pm to 6pm. Open from June 20th to August 31st. All year by appointment for groups. Free for under 6-year-olds. Adult : €2. Child (from 6 to 18 years old) : €1. Holiday voucher. Shop.

This centre of tourism and cultural interpretation is housed in the former metal corner-piece of the city, at the zero point of the Canal du Nivernais. Its mission is to relate the history of the Canal du Nivernais, that of inland shipping and the transport of coal through a scenography highlighting the Toueur Amp V tugboat. Dating back to 1933, the latter was used to tow barges traveling on the Canal du Nivernais to the Canal Latéral à la Loire, and this, over 2 km away. Movies, an interactive model of Saint-Leger and its region and photos and paintings complete the setting. Outside, a belvedere offers a breathtaking view of the Saint-Léger dam, the town of Decize and the junction of several rivers that are Canal du Nivernais, Aron, Vieille-Loire and the Canal Latéral à la Loire. Temporary exhibitions animate the buildings every year.

Vandenesse

■ L'AUBERGE DU BECASSIER

2, route de Moulins
✆ +33 (0)3 86 30 70 30

15 days annual closing, at the end of June, at the beginning of July. Open Monday to Saturday for lunch. Open Saturday for dinner and Sunday booking compulsory. Menu from €22 to €28. Lunch menu : €12.50. Changed à la carte every 3 months. Caterer.

The Chef of this delightful little country restaurant, Autun native, knows what tradition means : a respect for fresh ingredients, work of quality, for a local and generous cuisine which can flatter our tastebuds – Foie gras, chicken fricassee with mushrooms, chocolate mousse... Here simplicity knows how to be great ! A good address popular with locals, and visitors passing through. Very warm. To recommend without moderation.

NIÈVRE

© DELPHINE TABARY

Prieuré de la Charité and Pont de Loire.

LA CHARITÉ-SUR-LOIRE ★

Essential Burgundy step on the road to Saint Jacques de Compostela, the fortified city welcomed the pilgrims, who would stop and enjoy the hospitality and charity of the monks. This virtue was so well practiced that the city has kept the name. Listed as a Unesco World Heritage Site, and labelled since November 2011 City of Art and History, La Charité-sur-Loire amazes by its numerous historical evidences and invites walkers to stroll through the city but also and especially on the exceptional site of the Priory which after 10 years of work inaugurates the fully restored cloister and that is opened to the public. Also City of Book and Word, the life of the city is regularly punctuated by artistic events, concerts, exhibitions, market of old books. A dynamism which emphasizes an ambitious cultural project, that of the City of the Word, supported by the label of Centre Culturel de Rencontres that the city obtained in 2012 : combining a remarkable site, the priory, a predominant theme, the word and the creation that are attributed to it, with a good quality cultural program, these distinctions give the city a cultural brightness and a national notoriety !

OFFICE DE TOURISME

5, place Sainte-Croix
✆ +33 (0)3 86 70 15 06
www.lacharitesurloire-tourisme.com
contact@lacharitesurloire-tourisme.com

Low season : open Tuesday to Saturday from 10am to 12pm and from 2.30pm to 5.30pm. High season : every day from 9.30am to 12.30pm and from 2.30pm to 6.30pm. High season from May to September, low season from October to April. Closed of Christmas holidays at winter holidays. Internet access, €1.50 per half hour.

The Tourism Office offers individual guided tours in July and August and for groups all year round. Shops, postcards, books and exhibition rooms dedicated to local artists are at your disposal. A warm welcome, good advice and many outing ideas are offered. Electric bike rental and multimedia guides. Maps and discovery booklets are also sold.

© LAËTITIA STEIMETZ

The Priory of Notre-Dame de la Charité.

Sightseeing

LE CLOÎTRE

The cloister, which only wings north and east, displaying a neo-classical style of the late xviie, are visible today, was rebuilt in xviiie century. The complex is built on the Gothic cloister, which «archaeological windows» remain. The cloister served the chapter house, the Notre-Dame Church and the refectory. After 10 years of restoration, the cloister is today free for you to discover concerts and other events during the many festivals offered by charitoise city. Note now the presence of beautiful stained glass windows, designed by Christopher Wool, opened in fall 2012 (see box below). Opened October 20, 2012, these windows are the work of New York artist Christopher Wool, who was allowed to try to work the glass. Designed and made in the workshop of master glassmaker Burgundy Pierre-Alain Parot, stained glass animate the five bays of rooms and chapter Mérimée, without ostentation, but with a much greater depth and purity. This work allowed to combine contemporary black, gray and white with a touch of occasionally bright yellow opalescent reinterpretation of pictorial technique Christopher Wool. A plumb line undulates over the windows, awakens the entire work, and gives the whole harmony that blends Gothic architecture. For this work, the twenty-first century is part of the priory.

EGLISE PRIEURALE NOTRE-DAME-DE-LA-CHARITE ★★

5, place Sainte-Croix

Free tour.

Notre-Dame-de-la-Charité-sur-Loire is the largest Burgundian church after that of Cluny. With its 122 m long, 27 m high and 37 m wide, this church could receive 5,000 pilgrims. The chevet of the priory church, built between 1059 and 1135, is in itself a masterpiece : the decoration of the chancel has a particular beauty, with capitals decorated with animals and plants, as well as the corner pieces of the large arcades where a fabulous bestiary appears on rectangular medallions. For your information, in 1840, it was projected to cross the nave by the paris Nevers royal route, but Prosper Mérimée, then inspector of Historical Monuments, obtained from king louis-philippe that he should abandon the project, and made the building listed historical monument. It was the wrong move ! Last precision : the gothic doorway of the church was subject to restoration that were completed at the end of 2012. The actual position was saved and preserved of any extra damage. The Charitois had the joy of discovering the gate restored on December 15th 2013, during the christmas season, under a sublime pyrotechnical flashover !

The vineyards of the Côtes de La Charité

From the Middle Ages, the climate of the ligerienne valley and the exposition to the heights overlooking the Loire, allowed the property and the development of a large vineyard which was rapidly acquiring the Benedictine monks. In the 16th century, the vineyard had a substantial increase, receiving a warm welcome on Burgundy tables. But this reputation will be practically destroyed in the 19th century by the phylloxera. The revival of this vineyard will be done in the 1980s thanks to a handful of passionate winemakers who will strive to make it reappear. Today, the vineyard consists of small plots stretching over 54 hectares, mainly in the cities of Nannay, Chasnay and La Celle-sur-Nièvre. Ten winemakers cultivate these vineyards that have a protected geographical indication : Domaine Jean Pabion, La Charité – Le Vin, La Charité – Domaine du Puits de Compostelle, La Celle-sur-Nièvre – Domaine de la Religieuse, La Celle-sur-Nièvre – Domaine de la Petite Forge, Raveau – Domaine de Vernière, Chasnay – Domaine des Pénitents, Chasnay – Domaine de Poulanges, Parigny-les-Vaux – Domaine Serge Dagueneau et filles, Pouilly-sur-Loire.
Information : Tourist Office of La Charité on the Loire and www.cotes-de-la-charite.com

Sleeping

CHATEAU DE GERIGNY
Gérigny
✆ +33 (0)6 82 28 18 76
www.chateau-de-gerigny.fr
3.5 Km north of La Charité-sur-Loire.

Gîte de France (4 épis). 7 rooms. Double room €70. Breakfast included. Rental of the castle in its totality (20 people), weekend : 3 days and 2 nights, €1400. Week : 5 days and 4 nights, €2000. 8 days and 7 nights : from April 1st to October 31st, €2800; from November 1st to March 28th, €3000. Seminars. Receptions and weddings.

In this magnificent castle, whose oldest parts date back to 1491, Laurence and Pascal will reserve the warmest of welcomes. Curved moat, where carp and pikes cross, the castle can be rented in its entirety, and therefore accommodate up to fifteen people. The seven rooms, which can be rented as a guesthouses according to availability, can accommodate your nights in an enchanting setting. The lounges and spacious rooms will be the framework of convivial moments around a table beautifully set with crystal glasses, crockery, earthenware, candlesticks... The gourmet kitchen will be at your disposal, with the possibility to appeal a catering service. In short, a magical place to gather with family or friends. We love it !

Shopping

CONFISERIE DU PRIEURÉ
11, place des Pêcheurs
✆ +33 (0)86 70 01 81
lechocolat.charpentier@laposte.net

Open Tuesday to Sunday from 9.30am to 1pm and from 3pm to 7pm.

At the foot of the Priory and in a more than charming decor, you can enjoy the renowned Charitois, soft caramel with chocolate or coffee, coated with cooked sugar, taste the Pavé du Prieuré or the Arlequin; and delight yourself with a homemade hot chocolate... what a festival of treat ! In summer, enter the door close to the porch, and a charming small yard welcomes you to enjoy the homemade ice-creams. A well-established house in the Charitois city, which owes its reputation to the quality of its products and thoughtful service. Connoisseurs will tell you, it is a key stopover of Charité regarding local specialties.

LE VIN
7, place des Pêcheurs ✆ +33 (0)3 86 70 21 30

Open Tuesday to Saturday from 10am to 1pm and from 3pm to 7pm.

A must in the charité city located at the foot of the priory church : a wide range of wines, many wines from the terroir but also very good, French wines to complement its cellar or to offer beautiful and good present ! You will also find other types of alcohol, whisky and Armagnac. Quality and advice. A good address.

In the surroundings

Pouilly-sur-Loire

LE PAVILLON DU MILIEU DE LOIRE ★
17, quai Jules-Pabiot ✆ +33 (0)3 86 39 54 54
www.pavillon-pouilly.com

From April 1st to May 31st : open Wednesday to Saturday from 2pm to 6pm. From July 1st to August 30th : Wednesday to Sunday, from 2pm to 6pm. From October 1st to November 21st : Wednesday to Saturday, from 2pm to 6pm. Closed in June and September. Adult : €4 (reduced €2). Child (from 12 to 17 years old) : €2. Large families : €11. Credit card not accepted. Tourism label & Disability. Children welcome (workshop €6.50/ child, birthday, package €60). Guided tour. Shop.

In the heart of the Loire Valley, Le Pavillon du Milieu de Loire displays a unique environment. The longest river of France, halfway along the road that separates the source of the estuary, has shaped the landscape here, giving birth to natural habitats, which shelter a specific fauna and vegetation. Let us firstly explore « la Loire des îles ». This room exhibits, in a skillful staging, the sand banks with a mosaic of natural environments with their numerous inhabitants. The second room tells the fantastic adventure of the migration through the exhibition «à tire de plumes». Do not miss : descents of the Loire by Rabaska canoe (a large Canadian canoe with a capacity of 12 passengers), to the discovery of natural reserve and its inhabitants at sunset.

LE RELAIS DE POUILLY
Quai de Loire ✆ +33 (0)3 86 39 03 00
www.relaisdepouilly.com
info@relaisdepouilly.com

Logis (2 cocottes). Open all year. Menu from €23.90 to €29.90. Children's menu : €8. Buffet at €16.20. Rooms from €58 to €90, breakfast €10, extra bed €12. VRP, €84. Groups welcome. Garden. Terrace.

This restaurant proposes different menus and delicious dishes at several levels of gastronomy. We prefer Charolais Red Label in pavement, rib steak or flap, but fish also have their beautiful part. Delicious desserts are à la carte, such as the extremely simple, but excellent baked apple. As for us, we suggest you à la carte a salad of hot dung, followed by scallops' risotto in the fresh herbs, or even a browned of andouillettes in Pouilly-sur-Loire, to finish on an ice-cold nougat and its chocolate in pistachio nuts. The wine list proposes a good selection of local vineyards : Sancerre, Pouilly ... Very beautiful terrace overlooking the hotel's park, for a moment of relaxation dreamed in edge of the Loire. The establishment is also hotel.

CAVES DE POUILLY-SUR-LOIRE – LES MOULINS A VENT
39, avenue de la Tuilerie
✆+33 (0)3 86 39 10 99
www.cavespouillysurloire.com

Open Monday to Friday from 8am to 12pm and from 1.30pm to 6pm; the weekend and public holidays from 10am to 12pm and from 2.30pm to 6.30pm. Visit of the wine storehouses by reservation for groups. Cellar being able to accommodate up to 50 people.

Founded in 1948 by a handful of winemakers, the Caves of Pouilly offer a wide range of pouilly-fumé, Pouilly-sur-Loire and Coteaux-du-Giennois. 150 acres of clay soil where flint and marl are meeting, Caves of Pouilly produce sauvignon blanc, pinot black and Chasselas. Among the many wines presented, you will appreciate the Tuileries Coteaux-du-Giennois. But the star remains pouilly-fumé several of which several awards came to reward the quality of the homemade nectar.

© LAÉTITIA STEIMETZ

Belvédère of Saint-Andelain.

Prémery

MUSÉE DU GRES ANCIEN
3, Grande Rue
✆ +33 (0)3 86 68 10 32
www.grespuisaye.fr
contact@grespuisaye.fr

Open all year by appointment for groups of more than 10 people, and from July to September, every weekend, from 2.30pm to 6.30pm. Adult : €4.

After a passionate quest for more than 25 years, Annick and Thierry Leproust have put together a unique collection of ancient sandstone, more than 1,200 pieces are presented here. Three themes are discussed in this permanent exhibition : traditional sandstone from Puisaye, including the famous «blue» from Puisaye, traditional sandstones of Berry, among others with unusual works of the Talbot family, and finally, the sandstone from the school of Carriès (1888-1914), an artistic movement which had a considerable impact on the evolution of modern ceramics.

Saint-Andelain

LE BELVÉDÈRE
A 77, sortie N°25.

Open all year. Low season : every day from 9am to 6pm. High season : every day from 9am to 8pm. Low season from November to April; High season from May to October. 1 token €2, 3 tokens €5, 7 tokens €10. Payment only by credit card. Checks are not accepted.

The highest point of the city of Saint-Andelain, on the right bank of the Loire, this former water tower was subject to a beautiful renovation, thus equipping it with a glazed platform and amenities which facilitates its rise. At its top, you will, therefore, have a panorama stretching from the south of the Loiret to Nevers. Stunning on sunny days ! Note that a camcorder, located at its top, makes this view accessible by broadcasting images in real-time on a big screen on the ground floor of the building. It is therefore possible to observe the landscape without being at the top of the belvedere. The floors also have a beautiful scenography highlighting local history. And for the small history, Saint-Andelain was famous in the 19th century as the town where you could discover the 23 bell towers, hence the 23 festoons which still decorate the emblem of the city today.

LES ROULOTTES DE POUILLY-SANCERRE
La Moynerie
✆ +33 (0)3 86 39 14 72

Open all year. 3 caravans being able to accommodate up to 5 people. Breakfast : €8. Night at €80 (supplement for €5 anybody). Pets allowed (€5). Catering facilities (kotagrill (Finnish barbecue) in rental, possibility of reserving its meal).

Indulge in a atypical stay in the heart of the vineyards of Pouilly ! The caravans of Mr.Redde, fully equipped are located welcomes at the edge of the Moynerie vineyards, his vineyard, having views over the hills of Sancerre. For your enjoyment, you can explore the vineyards, visit the vault, and treat yourself with fruity flavours of the wine area !

■ **DOMAINE DE LA MOYNERIE**
La Moynerie
✆ +33 (0)3 86 39 14 72
www.michel-redde.com
thierry-redde@michel-redde.com
Visit of wine storehouses for groups by reservation.
For seven generations, the family farm is located on the area of La Moynerie in the heart of the Pouilly vineyards appellation area. From the forty acres of vineyards on the slopes overlooking the Loire and facing south, spread rich and harmonious wines, but the jewel of the vineyard is to be sought in the fifteen acres estate planted on the hill of Saint-Andelain, on a clay-flinty local which gives this typical minerality to the excellent Pouilly-Fumé.

Tracy-sur-Loire

■ **CHÂTEAU DE TRACY**
✆ +33 (0)3 86 26 15 12
www.chateau-de-tracy.com
Open Monday to Friday from 8am to 12pm and from 1.30pm to 5.30pm. Open on Saturday by appointment. Reception of the public and tasting Monday to Friday. Guided tour and tasting for groups of 4 to 40 people, on appointment only. Online sales.
The castle's history began in 15th century, on a former estate of more than 600 years, with a family in the beginnings and a knowledge that is passed from generation to generation, always with this spirit of quality and Scottish excellence that describes the wines from the estate of Tracy. This vineyard, planted exclusively in sauvignon, affirmed is through a sustainable culture and respect for the environment, therefore producing wines with the character and powerful character, found willingly on the best restaurants in the region.

LUZY

Knife & Fork

HÔTEL DU MORVAN NEW
26, rue de la République
✆ +33 (0)3 86 30 00 66
www.hotelrestaurantdumorvan.fr
hotel.morvan@orange.fr
Closed on Saturday at noon, on Sunday in the evening and on Monday. Reservation recommended. Menus from €35 to €93 (menu at €93 served to all the guests). Children's menu : €14 (for children under 12 years). Vegetarian menu at €35. American Express. Terrace. Take-away.
In this establishment recently redesigned, two kitchens are offered : a bistro cuisine at Bistrot du Morvan and a gourmet cuisine in La Table de Jerôme. The reception is friendly and the table is of a nice quality. A lunch at Table de Jérôme is the certainty of enjoying an ingenious cuisine of a passionate chef who never fails to surprise us each time we go there. The cosy and contemporary room get you on board of nice culinary journey with a view of the garden. The product is wisely sublimated to offer you the refined and creative dishes, in the manner of a rib steak in a wine sauce or this delicacy with lemon, finished like a diamond and that astonish you with its taste and its texture.

Shopping

■ **PÂTISSIER CHOCOLATIER JEAN-MARC BERNIGAUD**
18, rue de la République ✆ +33 (0)3 86 30 04 70
patisseriebernigaud@orange.fr
Open Tuesday to Saturday from 8am to 12.15pm and from 2.30pm to 6.30pm. Open on Sunday (from 8am to 12.15pm).
The storefront is already a beautiful invitation to gluttony : push the door, and here you are in the middle of all the delights ! Jean-Marc Bernigaud, master craftsman chocolatier-confiseur, prepares his best creations like the craft chocolate praline that you can enjoy its exquisite taste in the famous brioche with chocolate praline, and specialties such as «Carrés du Barron», the «Craquelins» or also the «3 Berdineries du Morvan»...... Pastries, ice-cream and the sweets are as many sweet caprices to satisfy. An excellent address.

In the surroundings

CABANES LACUSTRES
Ettevaux
HAIR
✆ +33 (0)3 86 30 16 41 / +33 (0)6 66 59 66 47
www.cabanes-lacustres.fr
ettevaux@orange.fr
Open all year. 3 rooms. Double room €80. Breakfast included. Night for 2 people on weekdays €125, the weekend for 2 people €135. Rental of activities by reservation from €70; rental of various kits nature from €25. Meal region €27.
If the paradise exists, it should be located somewhere in Poil ! Two charming small lake huts point their roof on two ponds. One rather oriented to fishing, and the other to a more poetic stay ! You can access the huts with arm's strength by a small boat... an expedition for the beginners ! A corner for relaxing with a tiny bench, a mezzanine rooms, a simplicity brimming with poetry, a terrace to chill out and take your breakfast, and play through the Robinsons, a solar shower and composting toilets. Eco-friendly accommodation in the heart of nature, with the frogs as neighbours, stars to dream, in short, a true moment of absolute relaxation ! And we heard that two huts will soonly stand in the estate. A great favourite !

© PHOVOIR

General view of Montsauche-les-Settons.

MONTSAUCHE-LES-SETTONS

Lake Settons is the major tourist attraction of Morvan. Straddling the towns of Montsauche and Moux, the site combines entertainment and scenery. Drafted in the eighteenth century, the project was taken over by the local leaders of the July Monarchy. It was decided to build a dam and a lake to improve the timber floating on the Cure and navigation in case of drought on the river and on the Yonne. Started in 1854, the work was completed in 1858. The end of the floating of wood would gradually change the vocation of Settons. At the end of the First World War, a regional tourism appeared around the lake, which they began to develop. Year after year, the tourist attraction of the site increases, and Parisians started to come. In 1971, a naval base is born : this is the beginning of a dynamic tourism for the region. Recent developments of the lake now allow to circumnavigate the latter while having the feet dry ! The 15 km gateway that completely merges in the landscape, allows everybody a ride close to nature. A curiosity : the bridge of 225 m in Chevigny allows to walk directly over the water.

■ **BATEAU LE MORVAN**
Rive gauche
✆ +33 (0)6 33 47 76 48
✆ +33 (0)3 85 52 52 17
www.settons-tourisme.com
bateau.morvan@orange.fr

Open of Easter at the end of September. Adult : €8. Child : €4. For groups, discovery day €32. Rental of pedal boats starting from 12 €/1am, electric boat rental : 35 €/1am. Credit card not accepted. Holiday voucher. Guided tour.

Another way to discover the hidden beauty of Lac des Settons is by crossing its waters on board the Morvan, a cruise boat with panoramic views : the captain will comment about the history of the lake, its wildlife and flora during the 40-minute ride. Exciting and relaxing, this guided tour is very informative and meant for a large public. The cruise is only possible in season. Daytrips can be realized by groups.

Knife & Fork

■ **LES GRILLONS DU MORVAN**
Lac des Settons – Rive droite
✆ +33 (0)3 86 84 51 43
www.lesgrillonsdumorvan.com
info@lesgrillonsdumorvan.com

Closed on Wednesday all day and Thursday for lunch. Booking advised. Menu from €17 to €27. From €6 to €15. Daily special : €13. Possible gluten-free menu. À la carte. Rooms from €54 to €70. Breakfast €8.50. Animals €4, horses €6. Groups welcome. Baby chairs. Shop.

The chef, Frédéric Gomez, offers a cuisine that varies according to the season and the market produces with a desire to be creative in his local culinary traditions approach. The menu offers you a warm salad of snail, then as main course a casserole of salmon with goat's cheese, it continues with a cottage cheese with fresh cream and honey, to complete your meal on a sweet touch with stewed apples and rhubarb with almond crumble. Also try the generous dishes à la carte and homemade ice cream, perfect for cooling off in summer afternoons. We appreciate the panoramic dining room where you can see the Cure flowing. A good address. The address is also a hotel.

Sleeping

■ **SETTONS COTTAGES**
Les Genièvres
Route Touristique
✆ +33 (0)3 86 76 04 99
✆ +33 (0)3 86 76 02 N39
www.settons-cottages.fr
information@settons-cottages.fr

Open of at the end of March at November 15th, 2016. Chalets : the week from €360 to €780, mobile home from €400 to €500 per week. Hut in the trees, €95 per night on weekdays and €115 per night the week Breakfast €7.50. Session spas 20 €/35 min. Treatments and massages by appointment from €30. Holiday voucher. Games for children. Pets allowed (€30 extra the week). Cleaning service. Catering facilities (Finnish grill). Sale (regional produce, ices and drinks with the reception). Outdoor lounge, sheets rental, tumble dryer. Whirlpool. Activities. Canoe rental €15/hour and 30 €/demi day; stand up 20€/demi day.

Stretching over two acres, the village consists of chalets and mobile homes located 50 m from the lake Settons (south bank). Well equipped and with great comfort, these accommodations are a guarantee of relaxing moments in a green setting. And for more change of scenery, make a night stay in the cottage perched at 7 m high : with a 14 m^2 terrace overlooking the forest, you will appreciate the comfort of this room of 2 persons offers (for children up to 12 years old). Do not hesitate to play volleyball and bocce ball, or enjoy the whirlpool and the Hawaiian or Swedish massages (by appointment) offered by the fitness chalet, while children play on the playground. Unless you prefer the tranquility of your private pitch of 500 m^2. Canoes, stand up and kayak rental is also offered. An ideal place for a stay in the *heart* of the Nivernais green lung !

Campsites

■ CAMPING PLAGE DES SETTONS

Rive Gauche
Lac des Settons
✆ +33 (0)3 86 84 51 99 / ✆ +33 (0)6 62 98 95 97
www.camping-chalets-settons.com

Ground of 2.30 ha. 68 campsites. Exposure : shaded. Ground : grassy. Relief : dish. Chalets for 5-7 people. Package from €9 to €15. Chalets for 5-7 people, from €55 to €95 per night. Holiday voucher. Games for children. Pets allowed. Area for camper van.

68 locations and chalets for five to seven people, located at the edge of the lake. A green setting, an omnipresent nature and especially very pleasant and well equipped family structures. The activities are numerous, whether within the camping or in the region. To complete the picture, a warm welcome from the owners is reserved for you. Everything is there to make you spend unforgettable moments of relaxation in the heart of the Regional Natural Park of Morvan.

Leisure

■ ECO-BASE DU LAC DES SETTONS

Base Activital
Les Branlasses
✆ +33 (0)3 86 84 51 98
www.activital.net
settons@activital.net

Closed from November 1st to March 31st. Activities framed from €23 for the adults. Equipment rental from €8. Possible accommodations on the premises in chalet, cottage and campsite.

Lac des Settons is truly turned to green tourism, in the programme : rowing, sailing, canoeing, stand-up paddling, Fun boat, water cycling, mountain biking, fishing... As for the banks, they are the place of numerous hiking courses, through small bridges and observatories set around the lake, offering the beauties of morvandelle nature to those who wish. A whole team of professionals who are aware of sustainable development is at your service to advise you and make you benefit from their knowledge. Activities for all tastes and all ages.

In the surroundings

Brassy

■ HÔTEL DU NORD

Le bourg
✆ +33 (0)3 86 22 28 94
www.morvan-hotel-du-nord.com
contact@morvan-hoteldunord.com

Closed from February 1st to February 15th. Closed Sunday for dinner. Menu from €19 to €39. Children's menu : €10 (for under 12-year-olds). Lunch menu : €12 (weekday lunchtime). Wine by the glass. À la carte. Rooms from €40 to €52, breakfast €6.50. Animals €2. Groups welcome. Terrace. Caterer. Coaching kitchen.

In the kitchen, the chef Philippe Briard blends market arrivals to his desire to offer a gourmet and traditional cuisine. On the menu, you will find regional dishes like Morvan saupiquet : fish is also highlighted for the delight of gourmets and gourmands are not left with the dessert menu which offers a variation of sweet flavours. On the menu for us, a saupiquet of Morvan, followed by an andouillette of Clamecy roasted with mustard, a small green salad with walnut, and finally a gingerbread roasted with orange fricassée. The establishment is also a hotel.

Dun-les-Places

■ OKHEANOS LOISIRS

Bornoux ✆ +33 (0)3 86 84 60 61
www.okheanos.com
infos@okheanos.com

Open all year. Hikings quad starting from €50/pers – rafting €45 descent – hydrospeed €48/pers – hot dog €45/pers – paintball €32/1.30am. Activities for individual and groups. Gift voucher. Possible reservation on line. Spoken English.

The leisure centre offers various activities, for an hour or for two days : rafting, hydrospeed, whitewater swimming in the turbulent waters of the Cure or Chalaux river, canoeing, hot-dog (inflatable canoe for two people), hiking with quad on rental or with your own quad, paintball, kart race, rally adventure... Organization of «turn-key» stays for groups and companies. Note the possibility to offer a gift voucher : a good idea for adventurers !

Ouroux-en-Morvan

MINI MUSÉE DU VIN ET DE LA TONNELLERIE

Cave Barbotte

✆ +33 (0)3 86 78 20 11 / +33 (0)3 86 78 24 01

Open all year. Monday, Tuesday, Thursday and Friday from 9am to 12pm and from 2pm to 5pm; Saturday from 9am to 12pm; Sunday from 9.30am to 12pm. Free.

The Barbotte family, in the wine trade for five generations, has, in their cooperage workshop, the history of wine and the production of the barrels through an exhibition of machines and tools relating to the work of the vineyard. Interesting testimony of the know-how of our forefathers. A small local museum as we like, well presented, with the rich and varied collections. To make known to younger generations.

Saint-Agnan

LA VIEILLE AUBERGE DU LAC

Le Bourg ✆ +33 (0)3 86 78 71 36

www.lavieilleaubergedulac.com

Open every day from 8am to 9pm. Booking advised. Menu from €19.50 to €22. Children's menu : €10 (for children under 12 years old) . 13, €50. 8 rooms from €60 to €85. Groups welcome. Terrace.

In the heart of the Morvan Regional Natural Park, Vieille Auberge du Lac is a quality gourmet stop. In a sober rustic setting, the dining room that can accommodate up to 70 people will be the cavern of all local flavours. As starter, you have the crayfish ravioli with a sauce with shallots, you can continue with a duck leg and its vegetables, a little freshness of the terroir with a white famrm cheese and finally a sweet coquetry with a chocolate fondant and its ice-cream with fir buds. A sympathetic address that is also a hotel.

DANDELION

Le Jarnois ✆ +33 (0)6 31 91 85 57

www.tisanedandelion.fr/

dandelion.cie@gmail.com

Dandelion is a farmhouse specialized in flavor and medicinal plants, created in 2013, managed by Chloé Fourcault, «a nature lover and a gardener» as she likes to be defined. It is here, in Saint-Agnan, in the middle of massif du Morvan, where many plants (about 20) are cultivated, gathered and dried (hawthorn, hysope, lemon-yellow thyme...), while other wild plants are planted in the nature. Working in the field of bio so no pesticide nor manufactured fertilizer used, they only use dung, ash of leafy trees and some homemade mixtures of plants are used for farming here. All the products are homemade. Three herbal tea collections to the sale : this is truly simpple, the Fleur of... and the Mid-season. Some delicate mixtures, tasty flavours of the products will please you but you have to book for this opportunity, or in the point of sell where you will find the list on the website.

Saint-Brisson

MUSÉE DE LA RESISTANCE EN MORVAN ★★

Maison du Parc naturel régional du Morvan

✆ +33 (0)3 86 78 72 99

www.museeresistancemorvan.fr

Closed from December to March. Open at weekends of Easter 2016 then from April 2nd to November 11th, 2016. Opening all year for groups, by reservation. From May to September from 10am to 1pm and from 2pm to 6pm. April, October and November from 10am to 1pm and from 2pm to 5pm. Closed on Tuesday all day and Saturday morning, except in July and August, open every day. Free for under 8-year-olds. Adult : €6.50. Group (10 people) : €3.50. Reduced rate (groups + 10 people, from 8 to 15 years old children, students, unemployed, family of + 4 people) : 4€. Audio-guided in French, Dutch and English. Tourism label & Disability. Lift. Children welcome. Guided tour (on request). Shop. Activities.

This recently renovated Musée de la Résistance, consists of three rooms each dealing with a specific theme, houses essentially collections from the region. The first room evokes the Occupation of the Morvan, the changes it imposed on daily life, the propaganda and the Nazi repression, the second evokes the Résistance in a moving way, and the last one is devoted to the Libération and memories. Also note that the hotel now looks ahead to the future by offering a digital gallery dedicated to the maquis of Morvan.

LE BISTROT DU PARC

Maison du Parc

✆ +33 (0)3 86 76 03 25

www.lebistrotduparc-morvan.fr

Open Saturday to Thursday from 10am to 6pm. High season : every day from 9.30am to 8.30pm. Set menu at €16.50. Fixed rate formula : €13.50 (starter and main course or main course and dessert). Shop. Activities.

In the new Space of Saint Brisson, you can spend a pleasant time at Bistrot du Parc. In a very bright atmosphere thanks to large windows opening onto the park, you can taste the true products of Morvan : local with their partner Morvan Terroirs or regional with the Morvan Bio grocery. In the brasserie, we have the choice between soups of the moment, generous gourmet dishes and, daily special prepared by Agnès, the hostess. During our visit, we opted for the «Au fil de l'eau" dish with trout fillet of Moulin de la Petite Verrière, potted trout from the fish farming of Morvan, soft white cheeses from Flo's with herbs, new potato salad from Ferme des Zamis and beet slices, toast of Fournil d'antigny. Don't hesitate to sip a fresh juice or a seasonal *smoothie* on the beautiful terrace... in short you can fully enjoy this friendly setting. We love it !

Find the index at the end of this guide book

Pont de Loire.

NEVERS ★★

The country of Nivernais feeds on the prestige of its worthy representative, Nevers. With its heritage and cultural influence, the august city listed among the Towns of Art and History, dominates this corner of the Nièvre. Highlighted, the church of Saint-Etienne, internationally known for the purity of its Romanesque architecture, became a case study for those who want to learn the shapes and lines that period. The cathedral, the belfry, the Ducal Palace, the City Hall, reflect the prestige of the capital. City of Commerce, it is also a city of art with the importance of its potters who bore the reputation of Nivernais in the kingdom, and a museum will soon highlight its story. This country is crossed by the Loire, where water has also imposed a character and legends, nourished by the habits, customs and legends of the caste of boatmen. Finally, the Nevers-Magny-Cours, which hosted for many years the Grand Prix Formula 1, still offers extensive media coverage during the Bol d'Or. Engine noise with the silence of the countrysides, there is only a step that nature lovers will certainly cross by walking along the trails to explore the wonders of Mother Nature...

■ **OFFICE DE TOURISME DE NEVERS ET SA RÉGION**
Palais Ducal – Rue Sabatier
✆ +33 (0)3 86 68 46 00
www.nevers-tourisme.com
contact@nevers-tourisme.com
Low season : open Monday to Saturday from 10am to 12.30pm and from 2pm to 6pm. High season : Monday to Saturday from 9.30am and until 6.30pm; Sunday from 10am to 1pm and from 2pm to 6pm. Spoken languages : English, German, Spanish and Dutch. Public holidays of May and April, 10am at 1pm and 2pm at 6pm. Closed on January 1st, 1st and November 11th and on December 25th. Online store.
Many brochures and documentations (in various languages, Braille and large prints). Aquarium with fish from the Loire. Exhibition rooms with faience from Nevers. Shops with local products, handicrafts, postcards of the region (also available online). Rent audio guides (available in English, French, German, Spanish and Italian), to discover the city through its stories and legends. Please note : the Tourism Office regularly offers the sales of tickets for shows and concerts, as well as the sale of seats for the House of Culture (Sundays from May to September, and Monday all year).

Sightseeing

Monuments

■ **CATHÉDRALE SAINT-CYR-SAINTE-JULITTE** ★★
✆ +33 (0)3 86 36 41 04
(Association Regards sur la Cathédrale)
www.membres.lycos.fr/cathedralenevers
cathedralenevers@caramail.com
Built at the highest point of Nevers, the Saint-Cyr-Sainte-Julitte cathedral has the distinction of having two chancels : the first romanesque, on the west, the other Gothic, on the east. Its history is complex : it was built on a baptistery of the 6th century, consisting of an ambulatory rotunda opening on eight cells. Successive fires led to its reconstructions in the 12th and 13th centuries. The Religious War has also deteriorated it; in the 14th century, the choir is reconstructed with ambulatory. The cathedral was particularly ravaged by the bombing of July 16th, 1944. At least, two bombs reached the building, causing the collapse of the choir's vaults and the destruction of many windows. Long and expensive restoration works were necessary. More recently, the modern stained glass windows emerged : four artists are at the origin of the works including, Claude Viallat, François Rouan, Jean-Michel Albérola and Gottfried Honegger. Their creations in curved lines, with the refined biblical scenes, and all abundant colours, bring a special light to the places from which emanate peace and calm. Let us stress that the colossal project of replacement of the stones of the tower, which began in 2011, was completed in 2015, now revealing a brilliant turn, highlighting the beauty of the sculptures that adorn it.

Door of Croux.

Nave of Saint-Cyr et Sainte-Julitte de Nevers cathedral.

Saint-Cyr et Sainte-Julitte de Nevers cathedral.

The Ducal Palace.

PALAIS DUCAL ★★

Rue Sabatier

Guided tour (every Sunday from April to October at 3pm).

The ducal palace was built in the second half of the fifteenth century, at the request of Jean de Clamecy, family member of the dukes. Clèves and Gonzague Families completed the building in the Renaissance style. Its façade is decorated with two octagonal turrets and a central tower, rich in bas-reliefs, rebuilt in the nineteenth century as the originals. These sculptures evoke especially the legend of St. Hubert and the swan knight, the famous ancestor of the house of Cleves. A plate reminds us that two nivernais princesses became queens of Poland : Louise-Marie de Gonzague and Marie of Grange d'Arquian. In front of the ducal palace the Place de la République, which reminds us of the Hunchback of Féval Paul and his kind and generous hero, a knight of Lagardère. Today, the ducal palace serves as an exhibition centre. It has an amazing aquarium of Loire fish, as well as the reception rooms of the city and the city council. The entrance hall, also houses the Tourist Office.

Museums

MUSÉE DE LA FAÏENCE ★

16, rue Saint-Genest ✆ +33 (0)3 86 68 44 60
www.musee-faience.nevers.fr

Low season : open Tuesday to Friday from 1pm to 5.30pm; the weekend from 10am to 12pm and from 2pm to 6pm. High season : Tuesday to Sunday from 10am to 6.30pm. High season, from May to September; Low season, from October to April. Free for under 18-year-olds. Adult : €6 (€3 half price). Group (10 people) : €5. Children welcome. Guided tour.

Located in a beautiful garden in the space of the former cloister of the abbey of Notre-Dame, behind the walls of the city, the museum offers an area four times larger for their exhibition than the former one to its collections. Spread over 1700m², they consist primarily of an exceptional collection of almost 400 pieces of Nevers earthenware from the late 16th century to the late 20th century. An entire room of the museum is dedicated to arts and little-known crafts : lacquered figurines also known as spun glass called «from Nevers». This unique set in Europe, both for its volume as its variety, 250 pieces, as well as the statuettes paintings on religious or secular subject, will be shown to the public. Visitors will also find a breakfast room with the sculpture of the 19th century, a gallery of paintings from the 19th century, extended by a space reserved for painting and the decorative arts of Montmartre period; a room of coins and medals from antiquity to the 20th century; a 17th and 18th century lounge and gathering furniture, paintings and works of art; cabinets of graphic art : prints, drawings and watercolours, as well as a background poster of the artist and newspaper illustrator, Albert Solon. There are educational spaces for young public and a resource center dedicated to pyrotechique is open to the public to read books on this field.

Knife & Fork

UNE NOTE DE VIN
60, rue de Nièvre
✆ +33 (0)3 86 37 79 90
www.unenotedevin.fr
contact@unenotedevin.fr

Open Wednesday to Saturday for lunch from 12pm to 2pm and for dinner from 6pm to 10.30pm. Possible privatization of the whole of the places. Terrace in summer. Booking advised. Wine by the glass. Chèque Restaurant. Groups welcome. Activities.

This wine shop and wine bar is located in the Saint-Arigle district for the delight of the fine wine lovers. In a warm and cosy atmosphere, local wines necessarily hold a place of honour. You can also travel to various national vineyards among the hundreds of wines on offer, or choose from a selection of wines on the slate, while enjoying the daily special and putting up perfectly with the crus of the wine list, artfully explained and advised by your host. To tantalize you : Charolais beef's cheek stew with organic vegetables and mustard, Label Rouge salmon of Scotland, beurre blanc and lemon comfit... Also do not hesitate to taste the boards of charcuterie of the Southwest or the exquisite burrata with bufflonne milk... We love it !

Sleeping

LE BEAUSEJOUR
5 bis, rue Saint-Gildard
✆ +33 (0)3 86 61 20 84
www.hotel-beausejour-nevers.com
info@hotel-beausejour-nevers.com

Double room from €38 to €53. Buffet breakfast : €7.50. Extra bed : €10. Garage. Stop-over with special rates for reps €68. Holiday voucher. Wifi. Satellite TV.

Just minutes from the train station, and facing Espace Bernadette Soubirous, this fully renovated hotel displays a simple surroundings. The reception is done in a guesthouse style, friendly and warm, and the rooms, with classic decor and soft, for a peaceful. The pleasant terrace will welcome you for a tasty breakfast buffet. A small hotel in all simplicity, all in all very pleasant, ideal for exploring the city and its surroundings and find a refreshing rest when you get back.

Shopping

AU NEGUS
96, rue François-Mitterrand
✆ +33 (0)3 86 61 06 85

Open on Monday from 2.30pm to 6.30pm; Tuesday to Saturday from 9am to 12pm and from 2pm to 7pm. Annual closing in January and February.

From the name of a gourmet specialty, is made of a crunchy cooked sugar layer containing, a real small delight, delicious soft caramel chocolate. This softness itself takes its name from the sovereign of Ethiopia, Négus Ménélik, visiting at the time of its creation, in 1902. This house, founded in 1893, has a reception with a remarkable character with its antique formwork, while the interior layout is oriental style. Other specialties will undoubtedly delight gourmands : the abyssin flavoured with coffee, the lolottes (fruit jellies soaked with caramel), and famous Skobellefs (praline chocolate ganache with butter, coated royal ice cream).

RAGUENEAU CHOCOLATIER
13-14, place Carnot
✆ +33 (0)3 86 59 47 45
www.ragueneau-chocolatier.com
ragueneau.chocolatier@hotmail.fr

Open Tuesday to Saturday from 9.30am to 12.30pm and from 2.30pm to 7.30pm; Sunday from 10.30am to 12.30pm.

It is just a few metres from the old shop that this talentuous and rigourous chocolate maker artisan moved. The new shop window has a direct view of the laboratory and invites you to enter a gourmet, magical and ingenious universe. The chocolates made the reputation of Christophe Ragueneau who was the official supplier of the Elysée a few years ago. Efficiently assisted by his wife Carole, he offers a range of fifty fine and very elegantly distinguished chocolates, bars, the luxurious coffrets and collections made in original homemade mould. Heel, handbag, rugby ball : you have the choice of the moulds. In addition to the delicious chocolate, with tonka bean, sesame, the Timut pepper that evokes the grapefruit or with foie gras, the house offers in summertime the Italian ice-cream with Madagascar's vanilla and sweet pancakes. The house is traditional, but matching today's taste, as witnessed by the code Flash associated with each chocolate that allows you to get practical informations on the ingredients on your phone. An address that continuously surprises us !

In the surroundings

Pougues-les-Eaux

CASINO
Avenue de Paris
✆ +33 (0)3 86 90 17 00
pougues.groupetranchant.com
infopou@groupetranchant.com

♿

Open all year. Every day and public holidays from 10am to 3am. Space of the Big games, open every day from 9pm to 3am (4am Friday, Saturday and eves of public holidays). Bar open from 10am to 3am. Free admission, presentation of the identity card required.

This establishment, in direct connection with A77, offers to «lovers» games like to others, an area of 4,460 m^2, surrounded by a wide stretch of water, all set in a beautiful park of 28,000 m^2. Judge by yourself the various facilities at your disposal, to make you spend pleasant moments : the stunning slot machines room with its 192 machines, distributed according to the stakes; the

Canal bridge of Guétin de Gimouille in Cuffy.

big games with 7 rooms, with a more intimate and cozy atmosphere, where English roulette is close roulette and finally the Poker room with 3 restaurants where tournament are regularly organised. You find the traditional games : the Texas Hold'em Poker, the Stud Poker, the Black Jack. Among the novelties : the roulette is not anymore reserved to the schedules of table game since there are now ten electronic roulette posts. The other entertainments are : ambiance bar «Le Privilège» where themed evenings are organized enables you to organise easily even and a performance hall, L'Eclipse with a capacity of 600 people, for special evening events and concerts as well (Irma in September, Daniel Guichard in November). It should be noted that a free shuttle bus was set up : every Thursday it will serve Marzy, Nevers, Varennes-Vauzelles, Fourchambault and Garchizy ! (online registration and subscription).

Sauvigny-les-Bois

■ LE MOULIN DE L'ETANG

64, route l'Etang
✆ +33 (0)3 86 37 10 17
www.moulin-de-letang.fr
restaurant@moulindeletang.fr
Annual closing : two weeks in February, two weeks in August. School holidays of the area B. Booking advised. Menu from €26 to €43. À la carte. Holiday voucher, Chèque Restaurant. Groups welcome. Baby chairs. Terrace. Take-away. Catering.
As its name suggests, this charming restaurant is located on the edge of the pond : the chef, François Martin, brilliantly combines the freshness of seasonal ingredients and flavours of the Nivernais local products. On the menu, the various fish dishes stand harmoniously alongside pieces of meat, and the game in hunting season. A la carte, we thus have a salad of prawns, a homemade duck breast, a stew of deer and its vegetables, an aïoli of cod loin... And for those who are keen on sweets, do not hesitate to choose the Délice de Pierre, a chocolate fondant with great delicacy... It's an excellent address in an enchanting setting. Good to know, the chef also offers takeaway, to postpone the gastronomic pleasure at home !

Urzy

■ LA FONTAINE CAVALIER

Domaine Jeunot
Urzy ✆ +33 (0)3 86 57 41 71
www.fontaine-cavalier.com
contact@fontaine-cavalier.com
En direction de Magny Cours sur l'autoroute
Open on Monday and Tuesday from 12pm to 2.30pm; Thursday to Sunday from 12pm to 2.30pm and from 7.30pm to 10pm. Menu from €29 to €39. Lunch menu : €15 (starter and main course/main course and dessert. 3 : €19). Wine by the glass. Groups welcome. Terrace.
Similar to other well-known restaurants, La Fontaine Cavalier is well hidden. It's short walk of 5 minutes of Nevers, first of all a bucolic setting will welcome you so you can have some fun. The restaurant is in the middle of a renewed former cowshed they succeeded to merge tradition and modernism. Whether for lunch or dinner, in summer on the terrace or in winter in the corner of fire, customers always appreciate this restaurant. Because a good cooking cannot be achieved without the right selection of quality ingredients, before starting to cook the chef begins to collect and purchase fresh products in the market essential for a perfect menu.

He will offer you an appetizer. It was carefully and well-prepared, and now the pavé de sandre rôti sur peau offered with risotto of lens and a brunoise de légumes. Delicious ! Besides, the cheese board offers opportunity to discover some local specialties. Sweetened flavours were all prepared with keenness and delicacy : macaroon and coconut moss, pears pie caramelized with some honey and rosemary, feuillantine pastry of roasted pineapple and chantilly of Bourbon vanilla. Because all is homemade, and it takes some time to prepare the dishes so you have to be patient. The terrace is truly wonderful because there is a beautiful view of the woods and the meadows. There is special place lounge where you can enjoy the taste of the appetizers or coffee thus you get a real pleasure there. In summer, they regularly organise some thematic and musical evenings in the restaurant. La Fontaine Cavalier is a magnificient restaurant and they offer tasty delicacies in Nevers.

LA FONTAINE CAVALIER
Domaine Jeunot
Urzy
✆ 03 86 57 41 71
www.fontaine-cavalier.com
contact@fontaine-cavalier.com

Open all year. 3 rooms. Double room from €70. Breakfast included. Free Wifi. Catering facilities (menu from €19 to €39).

It's not far from Nevers, but it's far from urban activity, the guest rooms of the Hotel La Fontaine Cavalier offer a wonderful setting for one night or more in the countryside of nivernaise before setting out and visit this part of Bourgogne. The decoration is magnificent, hearty, so you will quickly feel comfortable in. The new beddings are truly cozy and offers the best comfort. When you are within the rooms you can enjoy a magnificient view of the woods and the surrounding meadows. Not far from there, the paintball of the plain where you can enjoy lots of entertainments : laser game, mini-golf, inflatable structures and of course paintball. Before leaving do not forget to go to the restaurant, this is an excellent hotel so we recommend it to you, managed by a true Master the head chef Eric Nobécourt.

Varennes-Vauzelles

LE HUBLOT
Place Paul-Langevin
✆ 06 86 08 00 51

Open all year. Closed depending on the periods of draining known aquatic center. Monday to Saturday from 10am to 8pm. Dinner by reservation with minimum of 5 people. Le Hublot (daily special), €7. Menu at €13.50 with entrée+plat+dessert+café. Children's menu from €7. Breakfast from €2.20. Birthday, child and adult, €7/pers, offered for the person celebrating her birthday. Terrace. Pets allowed, air-conditioned room, groups welcome.

It's adjacent to the aquatic center, this tea room/restaurant is truly cozy and friendly ! Florie welcomes you with a big smile on her face, with the opening hours of the center, and the evenings on bookings. She offers a large diversity of friendly formulas for you, it's a great help if after taking your bath you happen to be hungry, or when you're sharing a breakfast with some friends. In the menu, homemade hearty dishes and delicious desserts, for a cooking that mixes flavours, original and creative. In the menu, for instance there are salmon samossa, chicken legs à la Basquaise and the red pepper foodstuff, a blanquette of turkey with grapefruit, a crumle apples and camembert... of salads, sandwiches (Hub'), and in the future, paninis. Added by the external terrace which is truly pleasant and the other one in the interior of the aquatic center, there you can take a little break and eat some delicacies ! To vote by plebiscite !

POIVRE ROUGE
NEW

Parc d'activité tertiaire du bengy
✆ 03 86 37 55 62
www.poivre-rouge.com
♿

Open all year. Every day. Booking advised. Children's menu : €5.95. Fixed rate formula : €8.10 (main course and dessert). Formule Bistrot, €9.90 and €14.90. Fixed rate formula Freedom, €12.50, €15.50 and €18.40. Appetizers buffet at €6.50 and €10.50 in single main course. Chèque Restaurant. Groups welcome. Terrace.

New chain that developed in the area, perfectly implemented near the A77 and in the proximity of Nevers. Poivre Rouge has a lounge atmosphere with warming tonalities and there is a large central space or on a lit de glacé pilée, where you can taste the freshness of the buffet appetizers : mixed salads, charcuterie, salmon and crustaceans, sauces... you have the choice to eat them as appetizer or in a single dish. There are many different formulas for all of the appetizers, grilled meat with fine pieces of meat prepared with kindness, burgers, big plates... concerning the desserts, it's classical, there are frosted and frozen ! Kids will appreciate the space reserved for them and the small gifts supplied with their special menu. The terrace is quite wide and there's a parking.

LA PLAINE ESPACE LOISIRS
Chemin des Sables
✆ 06 68 53 42 01
www.la-plaine-espace-loisirs.fr

Open Wednesday to Monday from 2pm to 6.30pm. Except school holidays : open only Wednesdays, Saturday and Sunday from 2pm to 6.30pm. Paintball : €25 the 200 balls (provided facility). Mini-golf : €3.50, Laser Tag : €6 20 min. Bouncy castle : €2 the 15 min or €7 per hour. Blowpipe : €8 30 min.

This area is full of leisure activities. The site allows you to practice paintball, laser tag, mini-golf, to shot by sarbacarne or enjoy the bouncy castle. La Plaine Espace Loisirs has a snack bar for refreshments (without alcohol).

SAÔNE-ET-LOIRE

Cluny Abbey.

© VENTDUSUD / SHUTTERSTOCK.COM

Highway
Main road
Secondary road
Prefecture
Subprefecture
City, village
Highway Exit
Forest
Nièvre
Saône-et-Loire
Allier
Loire
Chissey-en-Morvan
Anost
Lucenay-l'Evêque
Parc Régional du Morvan
Reclesne
D980
D981
Sully
D978
Curgy
Epinac
D973
Autun
Forêt des Battées
Bibracte
St-Léger
D981
Forêt de Planoise
D978
N80
Etang-s.-Arroux
Mesvres
Marmagne
St-Pierre-de-Varennes
La Chapelle-sous-Uchon
Arroux
D994
Uchon
Montcenis
Torcy
N80
Montchanin
La Boulaye
D985
Issy-l'Evêque
Cronat
Toulon-s.-Arroux
Montceau-les-Mines
Blanzy
N70
Sanvignes-les-Mines
St-Vallier
Gourdon
D973
Bourbon-Lancy
Marly-sur-Arroux
Perrecy-les-Forges
N70
Gueugnon
D60
D60
D60
Neuvy-Grandchamp
Génelard
St-Aubin-sur-Loire
Palinges
St-Vincent-Bragny
Rigny-sur-Arroux
D994
D985
D7
D979
Canal du Centre
St-Aubin-en-Charollais
Baron
Digoin
N79
N70
Forêt de Charolles
To Moulins
Paray-le-Monial
N79
Charolles
D982
D985
D79
Montceaux-l'Etoile
Varennes-l'Arconce
Anzy-le-Duc
Curbigny
Le Briant
La Clayette
Marcigny
St-Christophe-en-Brionnais
Varennes-sous-Dun
Semur-en-Brionnay
D987
Canal de Roanne à Digoin
Mussy-sous-Dun
Chauffailles

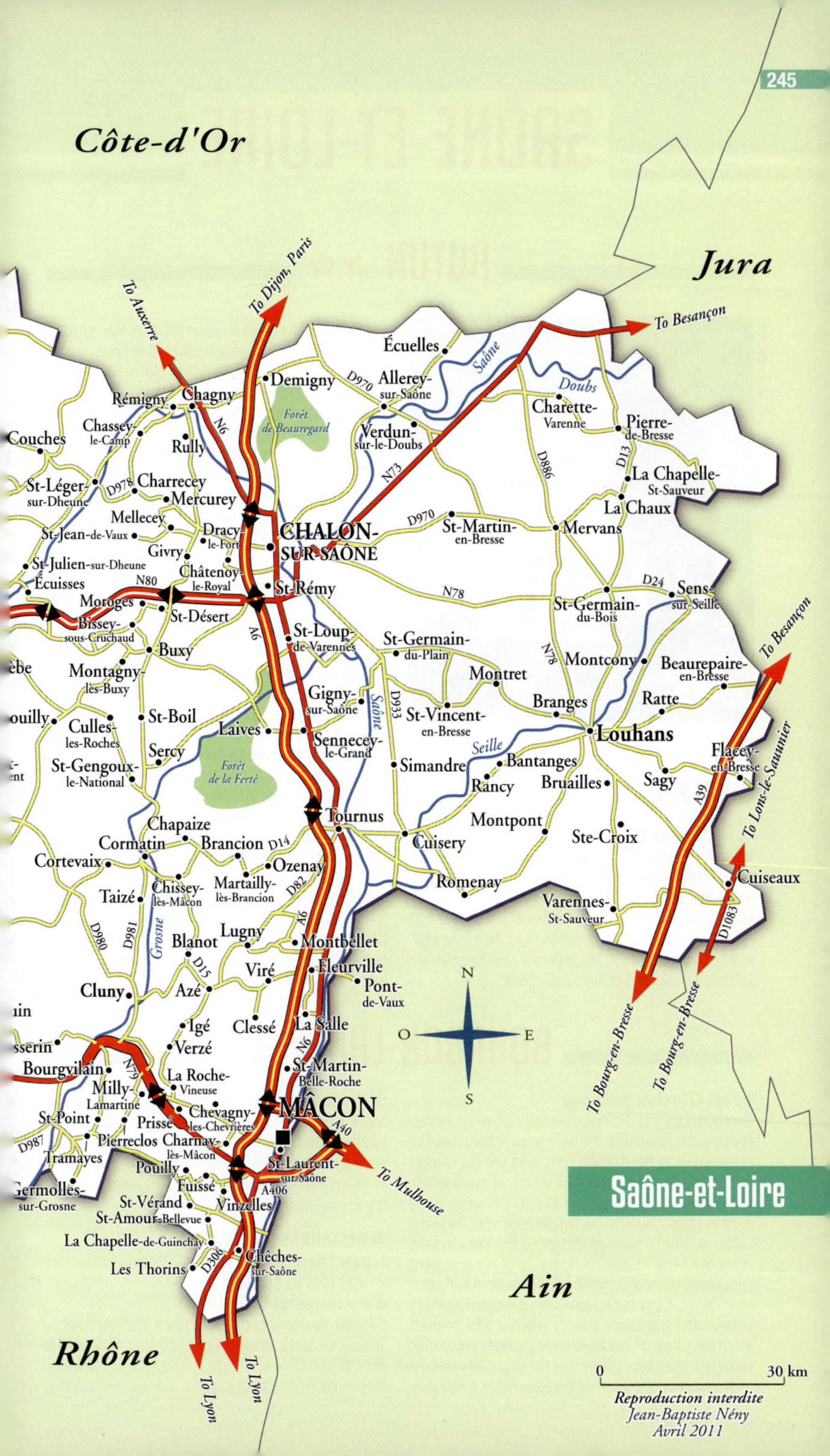

Saône-et-Loire

SAÔNE-ET-LOIRE

AUTUN ★★

Temple de Janus.

Sightseeing

■ **MUSÉE DES ENFANTS DE TROUPE** ★★
Quartier Gangloff - 3, rue des Enfants-de-Troupe
✆ +33 (0)3 85 86 55 37
museedesenfantsdetroupe.fr
Monday to Friday except public holidays of 2pm with 17 h30. Apart from these time slots, group tours are likely to be organized on request. Possible group tours with other schedule. Exceptional openings in July-August. Free.

Located near the Lycée Militaire d'Autun, this museum has centuries of history, connecting all the pupils to the schools, military middle school and high school. The old seminar built in the 17th century including a part of the high school as well as the museum has an outstanding architecture. The roof tiles are pure Burgundian tradition which makes the overall magnificient. Concerning the museum, it's linked to the wing of the old seminar on two levels. At the ground floor, the large room known as « la cuirasse » welcomes the visitor on his way visiting to the crypt located at the basement.

In the surroundings

■ **LA FOLINE**
Les Graillots
Route d'Autun
ANOST
✆ +33 (0)6 08 05 31 04
www.brasserie-la-foline.f
contact@brasserie-la-foline.fr
In 75 Cl, cardboard of 3 bottles €14, 6 bottles €27. In 33 Cl, only as a blonde, box of 6 bottles €13. Rental of printers and barrels of 20l on quotation.
On the heights of Morvan, in the small village of Anost, the Brasserie La Foline manufactures homemade bio beers. The manufactured beers are well-known for their flavours available in 4 colours : blonde, white, ginger and brown, that can be drunk in bottles or barrel during your family events for example. High fermentation beers but not pasteurized, manufactured in the rule of Art.

BOURBON-LANCY ★

Pays Charolais-Brionnais
Bourbon-Lancy is the only thermal station in Saône-et-Loire. It is located on the right bank of the Loire. The site belongs to the Aeduan Celts who see the sources as a divine manifestation and worth of celebration. The god of water and sources Borvo or Borno has the right to citizenship like his female colleague Damona. Later on, the Romans re-designed the area to fully enjoy the benefits and performance of these waters. We already know that they treat rheumatism and other annoyances. These baths were richly decorated and very popular and stays were already organised for courses, a diet can prove it ! The Revolution changes everything and it is in the 19th century that the popularity restarts with new developments like the New Water Hospital, in the former convent of the Visitation or a more modern basin. A bottling factory put in glass the soda water of Lymbe. At the end of the century, a hotel and a casino were constructed. The casino was destroyed by a fire in 1934 and a new building dedicated to games was built. It was permanently closed in 1986.

■ **RESTAURANT DU CLOÎTRE**
1, parc Thermal
✆ +33 (0)3 85 89 18 91
www.restaurantducloitre.fr
« Maître Restaurateur » label. Open Monday noon to Sunday for lunch. Booking advised. Menu from €20 to €39. Children's menu : €9.50. À la carte. Groups welcome. Terrace. Caterer. 3 cocottes Logis.

At the heart of the Thermal Park, on the floor of the Grand Hotel, in the former convent of the Visitandines built in the eighteenth century, and whose terrace on ground floor overlooks the arches of the old cloister : the stage is set ! In the nice and bright room, with a terrace, you will enjoy the chef's cuisine, « active supporter of the homemade », and promoted Maître Restaurateur. From fresh produce, mainly from local producers, your palates will enjoy skillfully prepared traditional flavours in order to highlight all its richness. In summer, we liked the small board for freshness, salad, duck breasts, homemade terrine, which were followed by a puff pastry of gariguettes, gazpacho with ginger, biscuit to eat with spoon and its beggar with mint.

BUXY

Buxy, land of the Counts of Chalon, still has vestiges of its enclosure walls (Round Tower and Tower of the King), probably erected by Count William I in the twelfth century. Three doors gave access to the Châtel, with a drawbridge for each. After the annexation of Burgundy by King Louis XI in 1477, the governors of the Dukes were replaced by judges and royal guards until the Revolution, when Buxy became the main town of the district. Buxy is also known to have been an important religious centre. A society of priests, named Mépart, was already there in 1253. In the sixteenth century, there was one priest for about 60 people ! This period was the most important for Mépart and the arrival of Protestantism marked its decline. The region of Buxy is also famous for another of its treasures : a brown and grey stone called « Buxy ». Coveted land, several castles were built and still stand in the landscape like the one belonging to Pontus Thiard who was the bishop of the fifteenth century in Bissey-sur-Fley or Messey-sur-Grosne.

In the surroundings

Montagny-lès-Buxy

The village of Montagny is famous for the label to which it gave its name. Buxy, Montagny, Jully and St. Vallerin are four towns that benefit from it. Montagny is the southernmost appellations of the Côte Chalonnaise. Its vineyard consists exclusively of Chardonnay plants. The characteristics of the soil and the ideal location of the vines enable to produce a white wine that some compare with the appellations of Côte-d'Or. The montagny from the cellar of Buxy regularly receives honours contests. We can also go there via the greenway loop five.

CHÂLON-SUR-SAÔNE ★

Nationally recognized for its annual festival of street art « Chalon in the street », organized in late July, Chalon-sur-Saône is a festive but also full of history city since prehistoric men were installed there and the Roman has made it a strategic centre. During the Revolution, during the introduction of new administrative districts, Chalon is superseded by Macon as head of the department and loses its status of bishopric (1790) The city will experience a boost with the construction of the Canal du Centre (eighteenth end early twentieth century) and that of the canals of Burgundy and the Rhone-Rhine who further develop regional trade through the river. It is at the same period that Nicéphore Niepce develops several revolutionary processes including photography. The first picture of the world was taken near here. During World War II, the city experiences an uncomfortable situation. From June 1940 to November 1942, the demarcation line passes through Saone, Chalon being in the occupied zone and the left bank as from Saint-Marcel was in the free zone. Today, the second largest city of Burgundy has become a city of images which focuses on the future and new technologies. But many vestiges of its medieval past are still attracting tourists...

The bridge of Burgundy, on the Saône.

OFFICE DE TOURISME
4, place du Port-Villiers
✆ +33 (0)3 85 48 37 97
www.achalon.com

Low season : open Monday to Saturday from 9.30am to 12.30pm and from 2pm to 5.30pm. High season : every day and public holidays from 9.30am to 12.30pm and from 2pm to 6pm. Wifi. Gift shop and bookstore. Tourism label & Disability.

A beautiful Tourist Office located in the heart of the city centre and within walking distance from Saône. The team is dynamic and the very vast Office offers you a large amount of documentation. The services offered on site are numerous : ticketing, bicycle renting, reservation of cruise meals...The Office also offers a multitude of additional services : sale of tickets, books about the history of the city, postcards, the touristic maps, the souvenirs and local food products. The Office also organises local activities during the summer.

Sightseeing

Monuments

CATHEDRALE SAINT-VINCENT ★
9, place Saint-Vincent

Open all year. Free. Tourism label & Disability.

Former headquarters of the diocese of Chalon-sur-Saône, the Saint-Vincent cathedral stands in the heart of the old town. Surrounded by shops and restaurants, those who visit the city must absolutely visit the cathedral. The Saint-Vincent cathedral is classified as a historical monument since 1903 and its two towers were listed in 1991. Built in the 5th century, on the site of a temple probably dedicated to Mars, rebuilt between the 11th century and the 16th century, the cathedral has two architectural periods : the Romanesque age and the Gothic age. Inside, you note the beauty of some marquees and the lateral chapels closed by stone railings (regional characteristic) in the south side. Other chapels shelter a vast tapestry of the Blessed Sacrament executed around 1510, a stone statue of the late 15th century, a painting on wood of the painter Richard Tassel dating back to 1608, representing Christ with angels and, in front of the sacristy, a stained-glass window of the 16th century evoking the Apocalypse. The beautiful cloister dates from the 14th century and has four wooden statues. The organ of tribune dates back to the 17th century. The buffet is classified as a historical monument in 1846. The building has, in addition, a model for the visually impaired, located at the entrance.

Museums

MUSÉE NICÉPHORE-NIEPCE ★★
28, quai des Messageries
✆ +33 (0)3 85 48 41 98
www.museeniepce.com
contact@museeniepce.com

Open all year. Low season : Wednesday to Monday from 9.30am to 11.45am and from 2pm to 5.45pm. High season : Wednesday to Monday from 10am to 6pm. In July and August, open from 10am to 6pm. Free. Guided tours for the individual ones : €3.55. Groups of 10 to 30 people : €54.50 - from 31 to 60 people : €88.80 - from 61 to 89 people : €61.89. Children welcome. Guided tour. Activities.

Chalon-sur-Saône is the cradle of photography, it is perfectly normal that its inventor, Nicéphore Niepce, is honoured here. This is the case in this museum, undoubtedly one of the oldest and one of the richest dedicated to photography. The oldest machines that are exhibited here were developed as from 1816. You will discover, moreover, the oldest photography in the world. Housed in the former hotel of the royal Transport since 1972, the museum has therefore these treasures, as well as an exceptional collection of other photographic items. The daguerreotype room, designed by Daguerre and first camera sold, as well as daguerreotype room marketed by Chevalier in 1840, make up a unique set in the world. Following this series, the collection consists of dozens of prestigious machines that allow you to follow the technical evolution, to the device used by the Apollo mission to photograph the moon. The museum also offers many temporary exhibitions to honour the history of the photo or the audacity of some photographers.

In the surroundings

Lux

HOTEL-RESTAURANT LES CHARMILLES
RN6
Rue de la Libération ✆ +33 (0)3 85 48 58 08
www.logislescharmilles.fr
hotel.les.charmilles@wanadoo.fr

Logis (2 cheminées). Front desk open from 6.30am to 11pm Monday to Saturday and from 7am to 9pm Sunday and public holidays. 33 rooms (four-people room : €78 to €104. Quintuple room : €88 to €112). Single room from €45 to €72; double room from €48 to €80; triple room from €66 to €94. Breakfast : €8.50 (all-you-can-eat buffet). Extra bed : €10. Parking included (individual garages : €8.50). Cot, changing mats, bottle-warmer free. Package evening-stop-over : €66. American Express, Holiday voucher. 3 handicap-accessible rooms including 2 with garden view and swimming pool. Games for children. Pets allowed (€8.50). Seminars. Free Wifi. Catering facilities (Restaurant des Grands raw. Menu business from €14.90 to €16.90, regional menu at €28, gourmet menu at €37. Children's menu : €9 (menu of the angels). Catering). Vinothèque. Grands Cru of Burgundy from €50. Satellite TV, Canal+.

Les Charmelles is a beautiful and great establishment of 33 rooms combining history and modernity. The rooms are bright and comfortable with the contemporary decor and it's suitable for couples, business trips as well as families with single rooms to the family rooms for 4 to 5 persons. Outside, the pool, the garden, the petanque field and the games for kids are essential for a pleasant stay. Enjoy the spacious dining room of the restaurant where you can eat a hearty breakfast focused on pastries, pancakes, fruits, cereals, charcuteries and milk products. And if you are not satisfied yet, you will come back to the restaurant to taste giant salads, fresh tagliatelle with carbonara or bolognaise sauce to eat on the inch or of the bruschettas of goat, pavé de bœuf and homemade desserts (chocolate moss, the dayly pie, lemon tiramisu) for those who are willing to spend their time and to taste the chef's specialities. Bonus : the restaurant has an exceptional wine bar including the 33 grand crus de Bourgone !

Saint-Rémy

■ LA GRENOUILLE GOURMANDE
58, route de Lyon ✆ +33 (0)3 85 48 18 57
www.la-grenouille-gourmande.com

Open every day from 11.45am to 1.30pm; Tuesday to Saturday from 7pm to 9pm. Menu from €13 to €24.50. Children's menu : €5.90 (steak+dessert. Children's menu at €8.50 : frogs +dessert). Lunch menu : €13.50. Menu sauerkraut royal : €13.50. Terrace. Take-away.

It truly fits its name, la Grenouille Gourmande is a restaurant expet of frog. Here, they feast on the frogs' legs with parsley or creamy since more than 10 years. M. Despignes and his wife offer traditional and regional cookery made with fresh ingredients in a warm and family atmosphere. The restaurant is located at the roundabout between Chalon and Saint-Remy, having 3 rooms of 90 seats and the terrace has the capacity of twenty seats. It's perfect for family meals, birthdays and other ceremonies, besides the prices are truly attractive and the dishes are ample. In addition this restaurant La Grenouille Gourmande offers soucrout as well as fried mussels. It's enough to satisfy your belly.

CHAROLLES ★

In this small town in southern Burgundy, the easiest and most common image is obviously that of the Charolais meet. The pleasures given by the meat should not overshadow those of the eyes. The landscapes of this water-city have given it the enviable and rewarding surname of « Little Charolais Venice. » The river of Arconce and Semence peacefully flow and along their intramural courses, there are 32 bridges and footbridges, some of which directly join villages. The ancient Celtic village has a long history. The county of Charolles created in the thirteenth century was the possession of the Dukes of Burgundy. Charles the Bold built a fortress of which remains today a famous tower. It was only during the second half of the eighteenth century that Charolles will definitely be attached to the kingdom of France. Finally, back to the palace, for the gourmet this time, after the beautiful things now the tasty ones. It celebrates red meat but also poultry and delicious goat cheeses which have been rewarded with an appellation of origin « Charollais », a cylinder 15 cm high and ten inches diameter. The art of the table will be complete if we add the fact that the local potteries are most famous.

■ OFFICE DE TOURISME
24, rue Baudinot, Couvent des Clarisses
✆ +33 (0)3 85 24 05 95 – www.ville-charolles.fr

Open Monday to Friday from 10am to 12pm and from 2pm to 5pm. Also open : Saturday and Sunday during the period of tourist frequentation. Guided tours for groups : €3/pers so more than 15 people, €4/pers so less than 15 people.

The Tourist Office of Charolles provides all documents to discover the Charolais-Brionnais. On sale, the guide of the Charolais-Brionnais, Country of Art and history which is a wealth of information to discover the architecture, the museums and landscapes of the region. Housed in a building dating from the 16th century, the Tourist Office is located in the former convent of Clarisses. An ideal setting that gives a foretaste of the rich heritage of the region. The Tourist Office organises guided tours of the town for groups. You can therefore discover the museum of Prieuré, the pottery of Charolles, the site of lime kilns, the banks of the Arconce river. The hotel also provides the calendar of the flea markets and the organised hikes.

Do not miss : the Maison du Charolais at the town exit. All information on the Charolais meat is available in this space which explains the characteristics of the charolais beef's breeding and also allows you to enjoy it on the spot !

direct access to the beach	visually impaired disability	take away
bar	mental handicap	room service
laundry	motor disability	fitness room
air conditioning	garden or park	playroom / tv
nightclub	games	modern sanitary
cash machine	washing machine / laundry	water sports
drinking water	bicycle rental	tennis
horse riding	grocery store	archery
smoking area	airport shuttle	waterslide
non-smoking	fishing	fan
fitness	indoor swimming pool	toilet drain
miniature golf	outdoor heated pool	sailing
hard of hearing disability	outdoor pool	

Sightseeing

LA MAISON DU CHAROLAIS

43, route de Mâcon
Sortie 12
✆ +33 (0)3 85 88 04 00
www.maison-charolais.com
maisonducharolais@orange.fr

Annual closing on November 1st and included from December 25th, 2016 to January 2nd, 2017. Open every day from 10am to 6pm. Free for under 6-year-olds. Adult : €7.50 (free tour with audioguide and tasting or €5.50 without tasting). Child (from 6 to 12 years old) : €3.50 (visit with audioguide or treasure hunt). Groups welcome, leisure centers, pupils by reservation to the 03 85 88 04 00. Average duration of the visit : 1.30am. Tourism label & Disability. Audiodescriptive visit for the visitors partially-sighted persons. Branchless label and Adventures Kids. Catering facilities (restaurant "La Table" open daily for lunch and Friday and Saturday evening (see heading « the couvert »)). Shop. Activities during school holidays. Free access for Nuit des Musées and the Heritage Days.

Welcome to Maison du Charolais ! Here, the Charolais is at home. It is logically in the heart of the birthplace of this exceptional and internationally recognised bovine race that Maison du Charolais is located. Visit its museographic space and discover all the secrets of the exceptional quality of the Charolais meat, from the characteristics of its territory to the particularity of its grass that explain its great tenderness. Not to be missed : the artistic temporary exhibition 2016 of the « Arts créatifs clunisois » which draws the Charolais portrait and its cousins !

This visit, fun and interactive, ideal for family, ends on the belvedere with a magnificent panoramic views on the landscapes of the region. At the end of the visit, enjoy a tasting session accompanied by a glass of good wine to learn some tips and advice for cooking the Charolais meat well.

Real cultural and gastronomy place, Maison du Charolais ensures the promotion of Charolais terroir through various events throughout the year *(full program of entertainment : www.maison-charolais.com)*.

During school holidays : dramatised visits, creative workshops, cooking classes, conferences, exhibitions... Supplement your knowledge on Charolais meat while taking part in the cooking workshops regularly organized to learn how to cook Charolais beef like a real Chef !

Before leaving, go for a little visit in the shop with its wide range of products of arts and crafts (culinary pottery) and its most appetising regional products : beef sausages, wines, liqueurs, jams and honey, fruit juice, AOC Charolais goat's cheese, oils and vinegars, gingerbread and cakes, terrines and cooked dishes « Charolais dans l'assiette » including the AOP Charolles Beef pot-au feu terrine, first food innovation of Burgundy in 2014 but also the Charolais beef cooked with cream, lentils and carrots, third innovation of Burgundy in 2015.

LA TABLE

Route Centre Europe Atlantique
43, route de Mâcon
Sortie 12
✆ +33 (0)3 85 24 00 46
www.maison-charolais.com

Open all year. Annual closing on November 1st and included from December 25th to January 1st. Every day and public holidays from 10am to 6pm. Free for under 6-year-olds. Adult : €7.50 (free tour with audioguide and tasting or €5.50 free tour with audioguide or tasting). Child (from 6 to 12 years old) : €3.50 (free tour with audioguide or booklet-games and tasting). Group (20 people) : €5 (guided tour : package €35 for more than 20 people). Reception of the pupils and the leisure centers quotation to the 03 85 88 04 00 - dramatized Visit : 7.90 €/adultes and €6.50/child from 6 to 12 years old - average duration of the visit : 1.30am. Tourism label & Disability. Audiodescriptive visit for the visitors partially-sighted persons. Activities adults and children throughout the year. Catering facilities. Shop. Discounts with the card large families, the cheque book Stroll in Burgundy of the South, card Harvest and Cezam like for the people in disabilities.

The Maison du Charolais, located in the heart of the cradle of this exceptional bovine breed, and its museum space invite you to discover how the « Charolais » transforms grass into quality meat. The three thematic levels of the museum, unique in France, detail everything that gives the meat its remarkable flavour : the passion of the breeders and virtues of the fields. This fun and interactive visit, ideal for family, ends on the belvedere, which allows you to enjoy the view. At the end of the visit, a facilitator will entrust the participants the secrets of cooking Charolais meat, during a tasting accompanied by a glass of good wine.

Varied entertainment around the « Charolais » are also scheduled throughout the year. The updated information are available on the site : www.maison-charolais.com. The Charolais is also : a shop of more than 700 references of products (craft of art, regional products...), restaurant « La Table », the path of the fields and lime kilns, (6 km walk with departure and arrival on the parking of the House of the Charolais), a playground for children...

Knife & Fork

LA TABLE

Route Centre Europe Atlantique
43, route de Mâcon
Sortie 12 ✆ +33 (0)3 85 24 00 46
www.maison-charolais.com

Open daily for lunch like Monday, Wednesday, Friday and Saturday evenings. Menu from €10 to €29. Children's menu : €12 (for children under 12 years old). Fixed rate formula : €15 (daily special + dessert). Wine by the glass. Groups welcome. Terrace.

As a logical extension of La Maison du Charolais, the restaurant « La Table » showcases the Charolais AOC meat

« Bœuf de Charolles » and « Charolais de Bourgogne ». Of course, you will find on Charolais meat on the menu ! It is the Chef, Frédéric Navez, who is at the controls of this beautiful, spacious and bright restaurant. As a master chef of France, he and his team strive to sublimate an already exceptional meat each day. On the plate, Charolais beef is eaten in tartare sauce, in cassolette or in burger. The flank steak and the rib steak cooked on a frying pan with a Bresse's butter and that you can enjoy with a light taste of hazelnut with Burgundy snails or fresh Charolais goat cheese sauce. Big eaters can even try the tasting-sized dishes of « « Charolais de Bourgogne » XXL or enjoy the 3 pieces (flank steak, aglet, shank, beef chuck and pear/whiting). Above all, La Table devotes to favour the local products : the Charolais AOC goat cheese of Saint-Vincent de Bragny, the AOC cream and butter of the Etrez's dairy, the saffron of Sainte-Foy or the beer of Pouilly-sous-Charlieu. There are only good and local products ! There is nothing to say apart from : let's go to La Table !

Sleeping

■ **CLOS DE L'ARGOLAY**
21, quai de la Poterne
✆ +33 (0)3 85 24 10 23 / +33 (0)6 75 25 03 47
www.closdelargolay.fr
closdelargolay@orange.fr

Closed in December and January. Reception from 4pm to 7pm; to warn the owners if you arrive after 19 : 3 rooms. Single room from €95 to €105; double room from €115 to €125. Bed of 180X200. Breakfast included. Possibility of garage : €10/night. Cot : €10/night. Credit card not accepted. Do not accept the animals. Internet access. Wifi.

Jean-Luc and Pascal welcome you in this charming 18th-century house, located in the centre of Charolles. The door opens onto an inner garden, ideal to laze on sunny days. This attractive guesthouse offers suites. In the main building, guests have the choice between Fragonard I and II and Chateaubriand I and II, in pastel shades, wooden period furniture mix with Louis XVI, Napoleon III and a 1930s touch. Guests are quiet with, on one side, a courtyard view and, further on, the village church, recently restored. On the ground floor, a large room with fireplace is available for breakfast as well as a large lounge, in red and cosy tones. A small adjoining room serves as a smoking room with, among others, the original armchairs, initially created to dress a boat. The other side of the courtyard, in an old printing house, the Diderot duplex, more contemporary, opens onto a wooden terrace. A perfect place for a honeymoon ! A lounge with summer also allows guests to be in the cool during the summer heat. Dolce vita in Charolles... Let us add that this guesthouse won the champions final of a programme (Bienvenue chez Nous) broadcasted on TF1. Suffice to say that this address is really among the most *futé*.

LA CLAYETTE

Knife & Fork

■ **HÔTEL-RESTAURANT DE BOURGOGNE**
9, route de Charolles
✆ +33 (0)3 85 28 90 50
www.hoteldebourgogne.fr
hoteldebourgogne0421@orange.fr

Establishment open in 7 days a week. Open from 12pm to 2pm and from 7.30pm to 9pm. Menu from €21 to €38. Children's menu : €10. Caterer. Takeout. 13 rooms, from €52.

This former relais de Poste is now a hotel restaurant offering a warm welcome. In the heart of the land brionnaises, the chef Clovis changes his regional cookery according to the seasons, the local flavors are simple and ample. In the Bourgogne menu, they offer you le feulleté de Saint-Jacques and la soupe de poisson crémée, and then le demi pigeon farci added by l'escalope de foie gras poélée and juice with Armagnac to conclude with a cannelé au chocolat, panacota and coulis de clémentine. Pay attention to the deadline and the quality within the hotel where the 13 rooms which are comfortables and contemporary will make your stay pleasant and peaceful.

Sleeping

■ **LES BRUYÈRES**
9, Route de Gibles ✆ +33 (0)3 85 28 09 15
www.campingbruyeres.com

Open du 1er April at November 1st, 2016. Booking is essential. 90 campsites. Exposure : mid--shaded/sunny. Ground : grassy. Relief : dish. Campsite + vehicle from €4.80 to €8. 10 chalets for 2-6 people from €340 to €500.50 per week; 4 bungalows up to 5 people from €210 to €350. Package for 2 people from €12.50 to €20.40. Animals accepted with extra charge, €2 and €2.50 depending on the period. Games for children. Bathroom for babies. Area for camper van. Free Wifi. Snack bar.

By the edge of the beautiful Lake of La Clayette, this campsite Les Bruyéres offers a pleasant setting with the nature as background. Equipped of 90 spots, the cottages have blue colour azur, and bungalow tents, it can also welcomes camping vans and get profits throughout the years by several services such as bike rental, mini golf, fishing card or pool with slide... The campsite is located not far from the city centre and the castle, and it is the perfect place for a peaceful stay.

In the surroundings

LE DOMAINE DE NOYER
SAINT-CHRISTOPHE-EN-BRIONNAIS
✆ +33 (0)3 85 25 10 10
www.domainedenoyer.fr
t.farjas@natura-meeting.fr

Open all year. For 31 people. From €1700 per week. Pets allowed. Seminars. Catering facilities.

It's located in the heart of the brionnaise countryside, Le Domaine de Noyer is truly an oasis of peace. Thérèse and Philippe Farjas skilfully restored this farmhouse the 21th century, succeeding to keep the lofty materials such as the wood and the stone, merging this authentic decor with a contemporary design it's a combination of furniture and today's colours. This house has the capacity to accommodate 12 customers, the cottage 14 people and the suite 5 people, allowing a large accommodation, perfect for seminars especially weddings , these are welcomed here. This guest house is truly charming !

CLUNY ★★★

City of Art and History, cultural and touristic site, active and dynamic, this is how we present the small town of Cluny. With an unusual heritage : abbey, medieval house, museum, Hotel-Dieu and beautiful National Stud, the Clunysois are proud to welcome more than 70,000 visitors each year. The city and its region are equipped with wide and varied welcoming structure, hotel, camping, self-catering cottages, there are several services all of exceptional qualities. There are also many restaurants serving Burgundian gastronomy. There are so many reasons to wander in the streets and to discover this fabulous place. A beautiful case where every summer the « Grandes Heures de Cluny » is celebrated, and where, after the theatrics of this festival of classical music, we rejoice with a glass of wine. There is also the Jazz Festival which celebrated its 25th years of existence. Another reputation of the city : its National Stud, which will delight all fans of riding.

© SYLVAIN SONNET

Saint-Pierre-et-Saint-Paul abbey.

OFFICE DE TOURISME DE CLUNY
6, rue Mercière
Tour des Fromages
✆ +33 (0)3 85 59 05 34 / +33 (0)3 85 59 06 95
www.cluny-tourisme.com
contact@cluny-tourisme.com

Low season : open from 9.30am to 12.30pm and from 2.30pm to 5pm. High season : every day from 9.30am to 6.30pm. Open in April, May, June and September, every day from 9.30am to 12.30pm and from 2.30pm to 6.30pm. The small town of Cluny as a rixh history and an exceptional heritage. Many elements including the Tourist Office promote through an important documentation. The sites to visit are numerous : the Benedictine abbey, the Hôtel-Dieu, the national stud farm, the Tour des Fromages wich offers a superb view of the city. Guided tours are organised in the medieval city. The city also organises night rounds lit by torches in the neighbourhoods without forgetting the unusual visits to discover the secrets of Cluny. The city also has many museums to discover : Palais Jean de Bourbon, the Maison de patrimoine, the Musée du Poilu... The Clunisois also offers a green and idyllic setting, ideal for a stroll along the Voie Verte, horse riding, donkey riding. To discover as well : the Roseraie and the Jardin médicinal des Simples inaugurated in 2010.

Sightseeing

ABBAYE DE CLUNY ★★★
Palais Gélase
Place du 11-Août-1944
✆ +33 (0)3 85 59 15 93
cluny.monuments-nationaux.fr
abbaye-de-cluny@monuments-nationaux.fr

Open every day April, May, June and September, from 9.30am to 6pm. July and August, from 9.30am to 7pm. From October to March, from 9.30am to 5pm. Closed on January 1st, May 1st, 1st and November 11th, December 25th. Free for under 25-year-olds. Adult : €9.50 (+ €4.50 for the audioguide). Reduced rate : €7.50. Audioguide for a couple €6 at an extra charge to the admission fee. Tourism label & Disability. Children welcome. Guided tour (guided tour to the 03 85 59 15 93, conference visit for groups by reservation to the 03 85 59 82 72). Shop.

It is no longer the famous abbey, home of the Cluniac Order, which affirmed its supremacy in the monastic world of medieval Europe. The order embodied in its illustrious abbots as Peter the Venerable, abbot of Cluny from 1122 to 1156, or Hugh of Semur, abbot from 1049 to 1109, which erected the third abbey church (Cluny III), consecrated in 1130 and the tallest building in Christendom – 187 meters long – before the building of St. Peter's in Rome. Today, little is remaining of the former power. The Revolution has been there : Cluny became a national asset, was used as a quarry, before being gradually dismantled until 1823. The place still however exudes the grandeur of Clunisian which despite their original vow of poverty and observance of the rule of St. Benedict, had gradually acquired a taste for opulence, until the decline of Cluny in the end of the middle Ages. We can now admire some of the south of the transept, which gives an idea of the gigantism of the abbey church, two abbey churches of the 15th century and also convent buildings built in the 18th century. In the Ochier museum are preserved relics and models of the old monastery and the medieval village. The 3D reconstructions and models that punctuate the visit help the imagination to get an idea of what the grandeur of the building was before. The abbey now bears the Patrimoine Européen label.

LA CITÉ MÉDIÉVALE

6, rue Mercière
✆ +33 (0)3 85 59 05 34
www.cluny-tourisme.com
contact@cluny-tourisme.com

Low season : open Monday to Saturday from 9.30am to 12.30pm and from 2.30pm to 5pm. High season : every day from 9.30am to 6.30pm. Discovered monastic borough. 3 tours. Rates : €2 only, €11 with the tickets of visit of the abbey. Tactile shelves : €9.

The tour begins with the lovely Place de l'Abbaye, bordered on one side by the stables of Saint-Hugues (recently restored) and the other one, by the Gothic facade of the thirteenth century called by Pope Gélase. By taking the rue du 11 Aout 1914, we arrive at Notre Dame and his court of the thirteenth century. By climbing la rue Municipale, you then enter through a small door in the cloister of the abbey and the convent buildings were rebuilt in the eighteenth century. There are few remains of this prestigious monastic complex dismantled after the Revolution. Today, we can see this heritage disappeared in part thanks to digital. However, from the tenth and eleventh centuries, it is around the abbey, the biggest of all Western Christianity before St. Pierre in Rome and whose radiance and influence extended throughout Europe, that the city prospers and grows. More than 150 houses still bear witness to the splendor of this era. This set of Romanesque civil architecture is well placed in second position just after Venice. We will not miss hotel des Monnaies and rue d'April.

HARAS NATIONAL DE CLUNY ★

2, rue de la Porte-des-Prés
✆ +33 (0)3 85 59 85 19 / +33 (0)6 22 94 52 69
www.haras-nationaux.fr
haras.cluny@haras-nationaux.fr

See programming on the website.

Haras de Cluny is one of the 23 regional centers « Haras national », whose headquarters is in Correze. Supervised by the Ministry of Agriculture, its jurisdiction extends from the production to the marketing and the use of horses, and the development of regional equestrian activity. It is part of the « French Institute of the Horse and Riding » (a public institution) gathering the Harras National (stud farms) and the Ecole Nationale d'Equitation (national horse riding school).

It is Colbert, under Louis XIV, who established the administration of studs in 1665 to meet the needs of war horses. During the Revolution, the first six royal stables were closed. And, in 1806, Napoleon restored the institution of stud by a decree deciding the creation of thirty standards deposits, which is that of Cluny. Stallions that were first installed in the stables of Saint-Hugues were then housed in the current building since 1811. The stud currently has fifty standards : Thoroughbred horses for producing saddle horses for racing, the saddle stallions of French and Arabic type for producing horses for sport or leisure and finally stallions of strokes (Percheron, comtois auxois). In the course of the year, studs offer the discovery of the stables, their residents, honored saddler and a collection of horse-drawn vehicles, during guided tours. The days and time of visits varies according to the season.

From April to October, fifty equestrian events take place. The most famous is the National Horse Show of Ascension. From July to August, on Cluny Thursdays, are also opportunities for a unique encounter with the world of horses, thanks to horse shows.

Today, in the heart of the abbey city there is the rhythm sounds of horses again and again every day. Over 200 years of equestrian history have forged identity in this landmark heritage.

MUSÉE D'ART ET D'ARCHÉOLOGIE ★

Palais Jean-de-Bourbon
✆ +33 (0)3 85 59 12 79 / +33 (0)3 85 59 89 99 / +33 (0)3 85 59 89 96
www.musees-bourgogne.org
musee@cluny.fr

Closed on May 1st, 1st and November 11th, on December 25th and on January 1st. From October to March from 9.30am to 5pm. From April to June and in September, from 9.30am to 6pm. In July-August, from 9.30am to 7pm. Free for under 18-year-olds (and for the 18-26 years of the 27 countries European and resident regular nonEuropean on the French territory). Adult : €9.50 (only one ticket for two sites : Palais Jean de Bourbon /Mus ée and the Abbey, validate 2 days). Group (20 people) : €7.50 (school complex free tour : €30). From 18 to 25 years old : €4.10.

The municipal museum celebrated its 150 years in 2014. Located in the sumptuous abbot's residence Jean de Bourbon, it houses important works of medieval sculpture of Cluny, from the village and the abbey. The exhibition, the museum allows you to admire the life-full size reconstruction of part of the large Portail de Cluny III, a genuine work of art of Romanesque sculpture. The museum includes also an old library that preserves uncommon printed inherited from the cluniac library and houses temporary exhibitions.

Knife & Fork

AUBERGE DU CHEVAL BLANC

1, rue Porte-de-Mâcon
✆ +33 (0)3 85 59 01 13
www.chevalblanc-auberge.com
chevalblanc.auberge@orange.fr

Open from Friday to Wednesday from 18h30 to 21h30; daily from 11h30 to 14h30. Menus from 19.90 € to 39.50 €. Carte : 15 €. Children's menu : 12 €. Dish of the day : 10 €. Wine by the glass. Lunch menu : 13.50 € (weekdays). Welcoming of groups. Baby chairs. Animals are accepted.

Located at the entrance of Cluny, just before getting into the heart of the city, L'Auberge du Cheval is a beautiful and large traditional house that has preserved its stone walls that also makes its charm. The wood panelling, the exposed beams and the wooden furniture provides this address all its authenticity, especially in the main dining room and the group rooms that welcomes seminars and family gatherings. The bar is modern with its decoration and more contemporary furnishing. L'Auberge du Cheval Blanc offers a family Burgundy cuisine, prepared with fresh local products. The house specialities are the duo of poached eggs in red wine sauce (a real treat that the Burgundian are crazy about !), the Burgundy snails with parsley butter, the bourguignon beef in « grandmother » way and Charolais steak. There are only good things to enjoy and discover the good local recipes. A nice traditional and authentic address with an excellent value for money.

AU BON POINT

1, place du Champ-de-Foire
✆ +33 (0)3 85 59 23 24

Closed on Sunday. Low season : open Monday to Thursday from 9am to 3.30pm; Friday from 9am to 3.30pm and from 6.30pm; Saturday from 10am to 3.30pm and from 6pm. High season : Monday to Saturday for lunch and dinner. In summer the restaurant is open, non stop from morning to evening. Menu from €13 to €15. Children's menu : €8. Fixed rate formula : €13.50. Wine by the glass. Plate "Good point" €13.50 + drink from €2.20 to €4.50. Hot toasted slices of bread : €12. Salads : €10. Terrace. Free parking.

The warm welcome of the Alexia is still there. The setting is just as pleasant. Works enabled to make the place brighter with in particular an open kitchen that makes all the particularity and the charm of the place. The fancy and warm decoration makes you want to settle there for a long time in room, at the bar or on the south facing terrace in summer. The dishes on the menu are simple and family. New dishes came to complete the menu. The house offers scallops accompanied by risotto with vegetables, French Charolais meat, sandwiches and salads according to the seasons and an original tomatoes and basil mille-feuille. As for desserts, Au bon point concocts tarte tatin with its scoop of vanilla ice-cream, pastries in grandmother's style (cakes, madeleines) or a gourmet coffee, it's a safe bet. You will have a treat. Au bon point remains a warm and smart address.

CAFÉ DU CENTRE

4, rue Municipale ✆ +33 (0)3 85 59 10 65
cafe.ducentre@live.fr

Open Tuesday to Friday from 7am; Saturday from 6.30am; Sunday from 8.30am to 2pm. Service of for lunch until 2.30pm and for dinner from 7pm and until 10.30pm Friday and Saturday for dinner. Closed weekly Sunday for dinner and Monday all day. Breakfast at €6.50. À la carte : Around €10. Children's menu : €7. Daily special : €8.50. Salmon duet : €6. Terrace. Wifi, bar.

Café du Centre is real institution in Cluny. Called « Chez Sissis », Lucienne and Alexis Tribollet have managed the address for a long time. Now, it is Laurence and Emmanuel who are at the helm of the establishment since 1 June 2013. It is still a family business because Laurence was in Café du Centre. Today, she runs the kitchens and she is the Chef. The à la carte menu remains traditional and family with daily specials which very change frequently. On the menu, traditional and family dishes : blanquette of veal, calf's head in sauce gribiche with its steamed potatoes, Burgundy beef accompanied by the wines of the regions. You should stay at the aperitif, the house offers strong cheese and sausage at midday and evening. A pleasant eating and especially a winning recipe.

RESTAURANT LA PETITE AUBERGE

18, place du Commerce
✆ +33 (0)3 85 59 02 96

Open on Monday and Tuesday from 12pm to 2pm; Thursday to Sunday for lunch from 12pm to 2pm and for dinner from 7pm to 10pm. Open Monday for dinner in summer. Daily menu : €12. Children's menu : €9.50. Daily special : €9. Pizzas from €7 to €9.80. Holiday voucher, Chèque Restaurant. Terrace. Take-away. Activities. Parking. The dogs are allowed.

Do you like pizza ? You will be served ! There's no need to go to Italy. Go to place du Commerce at Angelica and Florent, kings of the pizza within the Cluny fashion. At La Petite Auberge, pizzas can be enjoyed on the spot or to take away and you can do all sort of mixes. You will find the traditional ones : eastern, forest, four seasons, bolognaise and others more exotic like the Creole or the Andalusian. The pizza with snails is back to Burgundy and the gourmet people will try the tartiflette or the pizza of the chef. The vegetarian people are not left behind with the pizza without meat. The house offers also fresh pasta and specialties Charolais meat such as the chunk or the steak that completes a menu that is already generous. With its small terrace, its fair-sized room with simple decoration, La Petite Auberge is a pleasant address which offers a good value for money and a gourmet break and cordial amidst of Cluny.

RESTAURANT LE BISTROT

14, place du Commerce ✆ +33 (0)3 85 59 08 07
lebistrot.cluny@orange.fr

Closed on December 25th. Open on Monday from 8.30am to 7pm (last sitting at 7pm); Wednesday to Sunday from 8.30am. Closed Tuesday all day. Menu from €13 to €16. À la carte : Around €11. Daily special : €9 (daily menu : €12.50). Menu suggestion €16 Saturday and Sunday. Garden. Terrace. Activities. Patio at the bottom of the restaurant, admitted dog, wi-fi.

Welcome at Chez les garçons ! This colourful bistro with original decoration and that leaves room to imagination, accommodates concerts (but you have to squeeze a little), plays, organizes evenings and broadcasts matches... A true place of life located at Cluny where it is also possible to have a drink among friends or even to enjoy the dishes cooked by Jean-Marc. This passionate of cuisine offers grandma's style seasonal dishes and concocts mixed salads, raviolis, lasagnas of eggplants, *osso bucco* of turkey, fresh tagliatelle, covered with meringue lemon-yellow tart, Burgundian *tiramisu dessert*, chocolate fondant and a whole range of creme brulee. The à la carte menu is varied and the really friendly setting makes you want to spend time there between friends. A friendly and smart address.

CORMATIN ★★

Sightseeing

■ CHÂTEAU DE CORMATIN ★★

Le Bourg
✆ +33 (0)3 85 50 16 55
www.chateaudecormatin.com

Open every day, including Sundays and public holidays, from March 28th to November 11th, 2016. Free for under 7-year-olds. Adult : €10. Child (from 8 to 17 years old) : €5. Group (20 people) : €8 (school, €5). Students : €6.50. Free tour of the park, the rooms 1900, the cellars and the room of the models : €6 by adult, €3 by child (8-17 years), €3 (school). Guided tour (of the castle and access to the park; booking required for groups from March 15th to November 30th).

Built in the early seventeenth century, after the religious wars by Antoine du Blé of Huxelles the Governor of Chalon, this Renaissance castle attracted nearly 70,000 visitors each year and hosts many festivals. The sumptuous apartments, six golden halls, water put back in the ditches and recomposed gardens makes the Cormatin a Mâcon castle the most inspired of the Loire castles. There is a change of ownership but it's to Pierre-Henri de Lacretelle that the frequent visits of Lamartine is owed, visits which the man of letters qualifies as « a living attraction of art and delight » The current owners have really revived the castle, famous for its sumptuous intact decor of Louis XIII. The 12-hectare park is also worth a visit, with its large maze leading to the belvedere-aviary, its flowerbeds, vegetable old style garden and its extensive water features.

Sleeping

■ CAMPING LE HAMEAU DES CHAMPS

25, route de Chalon
✆ +33 (0)3 85 50 76 71
www.le-hameau-des-champs.com
camping.cormatin@wanadoo.fr

Campsite open from April 1st to September 30th. Rental of mobile home all year. Ground of 1.5 ha. 50 campsites (39 campsites with electricity and 10 chalets). Exposure : mid--shaded. Ground : grassy. Relief : dish. Campsite + vehicle + 2 people from €4.70 to €6.20. 4 chalets for 6 people from €445 to €510 per week; 5 chalets for 4 people from €360 to €415. 1 adult : from €3.70 to €4.20. 1 child : from €2.20 to €2.70. Electrical connection : €3.50. Tourist tax : €0.30/ night. Holiday voucher. A chalet accessible to 5 disabled guests. Pets allowed (€1). Free Wifi. Catering facilities (snack bar). Activities.

The campsite is aptly named. Its layout gives it looks of a small village. A quiet and spacious village where it is pleasant to pitch your tent or settle in a mobile home. Comfortable and modern, the Camping du Hameau des Champs is ideally located and allows you to visit many sites that are worth visiting : the caves of Blanot and Azé, the Cormatin castle, the tour of Romanesque churches, the site of Taizé. The greenway nearby offers the opportunity of beautiful walking or cycling in the Cluny countryside. The bonus : the staff of the campsite speak English, German, Spanish and Italian.

Shopping

■ CAVEAU DU FIGUIER

18, Rue Principale
✆ +33 (0)3 85 50 10 16
✆ +33 (0)6 03 74 13 61
www.caveaudufiguier.com
lefiguiercormatin@outlook.fr

Open every day from 10.30am to 1pm and from 3pm to 8pm. Open from April 1st to November 11th. Off-season, the vault is open on Friday and Saturday from 10.30am to 1pm and from 3pm to 7.30pm and Sunday from 10.30am to 1pm. Other days by appointment.

Located within walking distance of the castle of Cormatin, Caveau du figuier has offered for more than twenty years an extensive wine list (more than 300 references) and alcohols to taste with moderation among which whiskies from Scotland, Japan, Ireland, Cognac, fruit alcohols, Calvados, beers. Caveau also offers a wide range of regional produces to spice and aromatize your dishes. You will find there tapenades, organic jams, honey, aromatized vinegars, artisanal lemonades. And to avoid being caught unaware, the Vault offers several tools and accessories of the table : corkscrew, pump with wine, drinks, carafes, pourer, champagne stopper... A true cave of Ali-baba, an ideal place to leave with arms loaded with gourmet gifts and souvenirs. The house also offers gift vouchers to please your close relations in any opportunity.

In the surroundings

Chissey-lès-Mâcon

MUSEE DE LA NATATION
Prieuré du château de Lys W
✆ +33 (0)3 85 50 78 06

Open in July-August from 3pm to 6pm. The rest of the year by appointment. Free.

It's a museum unlike any other, settled for a few years at the priory of Château de Lys in the heart of the small town located on Chissey-les-Mâcon. Created by Richard Alix, former director of swimming pools, passionate about his job, the museum traces the history of swimming in the sea, river or pool and the evolution of sports of swimming. You will see there : photos of champions, posters of sporting events, medals, paintings, postcards, a bathing suit of woman dating back to 1860 and two exceptional models representing a bath dating back to the 19th century and the first French pool in Paris built in 1884. The collections grow richer each year thanks to the research make by Richard Alix and to gifts. At Lys, there is no big lake or access to the sea but the museum offers a beautiful opening to the sea in the heart of the Mâcon.

CHEVRERIE LA TRUFIERE
Lys
✆ +33 (0)3 85 50 15 26
www.chevrerielatrufiere.fr
chevrerielatrufiere@orange.fr

Open every day from 9am to 12pm. Open from mid-March to mid-November.

Meee ! Come and meet the 150 goats of Chèvrerie La Trufière which trott in the green pastures of the Mâcon. The chevrery was established in 2000, the cheese factory was built between 2000 and 2001 and the shop opened in 2005. He offers a range of 11 pure goat's cheeses of the terroir to enjoy half-dried, fresh or refined. Taste also the Cabrin, the Clochette or the Tome de Lys. During the summer, the cheese factory offers fresh cheeses coated with 4 flavors (garlic and herbs, shallot, curry, paprika). All the cheeses are produced directly on the spot and made from the alpine goats milk fed with the hay and with GM-free cereals and the farmhouse respects the ecological gestures.

POTERIE DE LYS
Hameau de Lys
✆ +33 (0)3 85 50 12 65

Open on Monday, Tuesday, Thursday and Friday from 10am to 12pm and from 2pm to 6pm; the weekend from 2.30pm to 6.30pm. Open from March to December. Reception of groups : Up to 12 people. Tourism label & Disability.

Claude Mouton called Léo set up his pottery workshop in the heart of the hamlet of Lys. Do not hesitate to visit this small hamlet of Chissey-the-Mason and make a short stopover in this workshop where Claude Mouton exhibits his decorated sandstone works, simple rooms, paintings and enamelled terracotta vases. He will explain how he works and he will invite you to try the experience of soil's polishing. A pleasant visit to make in the region for children and adults.

COUCHES

DOMAINE LA BONNEAU
La Bonneau
✆ +33 (0)3 85 49 59 33
✆ +33 (0)6 61 36 31 03
www.domaine-la-bonneau.com

Gîte de France (3 épis). Open all year. 3 rooms. Double room €63. Breakfast included. Table d'hôte on reservation, €25. Wifi.

On Route des Vins, a former wine farmhouse dating from 18th century, entirely and tastefully renovated, will be the setting of an authentic stay in Burgundy. The three rooms, Floral, Olivine and Amethyst, are spacious, offering a classic charm, and the calm that goes well with the countryside. You will appreciate the homemade breakfasts, the terrace during the fine days, and the flowered and wooded estate where you can enjoy a leisurely stroll.

DOMAINE LES BERTRANDS
6, route de Chalencey
✆ +33 (0)3 85 98 01 82
www.domainelesbertrands.com

Open all year. 5 rooms (1 studio and 1 cottage). Single room €70; double room €90; suite €150. Breakfast included. Closed parking included. Studio, €90 per night. Cottage €350 the weekend. Seminars. Free Wifi. Ping pong table.

Located on a green estate of 15 ha, on the edge of route des Grands crus and Voie Verte, this wine farmhouse of 17th century welcomes you for a charming stay. The 5 rooms are cosy, perfectly equipped with a king size bed, a walk-in shower (towels and bathrobes at guest's disposal), with a lounge area and a flat-screen TV. A quiet place where epicureanism prevails, you will enjoy the swimming pool, the terrace, the inner courtyard, in short all these little details that will make your stay a moment of pleasure. The gite L'Ecureuil can accommodate independantly up to 6 people. Note that it is possible to privatise the estate, and that groups, seminars are welcome, as the musical residences or cultural training.

LE CREUSOT ★

Sightseeing

■ **PAVILLON DE L'INDUSTRIE – CHÂTEAU DE LA VERRERIE** ★
Rue Jules-Guesde
✆ +33 (0)3 85 55 02 46
www.pavillon-industrie.fr
Castle of the Glassmaking : free access at outsides, the Tourist Office and the park. Musée de l'Homme et de l'Industrie. Closed in January and December, as well as on May 1st, 1st and November 11th. Low season : open Wednesday to Monday from 2pm to 5.30pm. High season : every day from 10am to 12.30pm and from 1.30pm to 6.30pm. School holidays of spring and autumn : every day from 10am to 12pm and from 1.30pm to 5.30pm, except Tuesday. The admission ticket gives access to the Musée de l'Homme et de l'Industrie and the guided tour of Petit Théâtre. Adult : €9.80. Reduced : €6.30 (from 10 to 18 years old young people, students). Family rate : €15.80 (2 adults and at least a child of more than 10 years). Free for under 10-year-olds (and for unemployed people, the students of the Community area, the holders of the guides Time Pass and those having the card « Tourism Pro » Pass;).Program of visits adapted to the pupils. Possible privatization of the places.
Located in the room of palm game of château de la Verrerie in Creusot, Pavillon de l'Industrie is dedicated to the great industrial adventure of Creusot. *Understanding the past to imagine the future* is the vocation of this place.
The visit of the address is thus fascinating. The rich collections is highlighted by new technologies like interactive tablet given to each visitor and included in the entrance fee. The movies and the entertainment of synthesis immerse visitors in the heart of industry from past to present. The know-how, the productions, men and women, politicians and social struggles, as the evolution of the site make visitors aware that industry has its place in the French economic landscape. They discover the long industrial adventure of Creusot, city of all energies that is resolutely oriented toward the future.

Knife & Fork

■ **LE CREUSOTIN**
36, rue Jean-Jaurès
✆ +33 (0)3 85 55 47 04
Open Monday to Friday from 11am to 2.30pm and from 6pm to 9.30pm; Saturday from 6pm to 10pm. Burgers €5.80. Burgers without bread from €4.60. Salad €9. Sandwiches €4. Paninis from €4.70. Bruschettas from €7.90. Americans from €6. Services for dinner aperitifs. Terrace.
Romain Luquet opens the doors of his pleasant restaurant to you, colourfull, in the atmosphere and in the dishes on offer as well ! A brasserie spirit with daily special simmered as the flank steak and its sauce with shallot served with tasty homemade chips that you can continue with a homemade dessert with for example a panacotta with blackberry, a more than gourmet break with homemade burgers, without bread, generous and tasty, like the Creusotin Burger and its potato pancake, or the paninis, a delight for that with the Raclette or salmon, sandwiches, the bruschettas, the Americans (homemade bread furnished with a steak, French fries, a sauce at choice with onion or with fried vegetables...). Every dish is homemade, and if you wish to organize a dinner aperitif, feel free to do it, the chef will satisfy you !

■ **HAMIDÉLICES CRÊPERIE**
40, rue Jean-Jaurès
✆ +33 (0)3 85 67 03 69
Open from 11.45am to 3pm and from 6.45pm to 9.30pm. Menu from €8 to €15. À la carte. Terrace. Take-away.
A colourful creperie, as much in the decoration, the reception as in the dishes on offer ! A concentrate of good mood that will cause happiness. Hamida offers Breton galette and galette of the world, cooked dishes as the famous royal couscous, wraps for more freshness, gourmet salads, and of course of the Oriental pastries to crunch without restraint ! A friendly restaurant that has also its tea room !

Shopping

■ **CAFÉS MONIKA**
325, rue des Bruyères
✆ +33 (0)3 85 56 06 17
www.cafesmonika.com
Open Tuesday to Friday from 8am to 12pm and from 2pm to 6pm.
It's been a little more than fifty years that Cafés Monika has worked with the legend of Burgundy roasts. Initially turned towards the professionals of the sector, the company opened shop of factory at the beginning of 2000. Organic coffee, compatible capsules with the house's brand, Delonghi espresso machines, etc. Online order and possible delivery !

CUISERY

This village overlooking the valley and the calm waters of the Seille is steeped in history; it offers few sights for walkers, but mostly calm and serenity to its inhabitants. Its creation dates back to the twelfth century, when the lords of Bâgé, powerful lords of Savoy, created a lordship, that is to say, a lordship in their addiction. It became in 1289, the property of the Duke of Burgundy and then Royal châtellenie from 1477 to the Revolution. Today Cuisery kept the appearance of a medieval village where flower stalls of booksellers and book craftsmen, as the village has officially become in July 1999 the fourth « Book Village in France ».
This initiative has literally breathed a new life to Cuisery. Now people will come to « snoop or antiquing » a book or an old 33 Tours in the High Street, during the book market held on the first Sunday of each month. Cuisery is also the Eden centre, the marina with two landing quays and a tree. It is true that there is not only one tree but there is only one cedar in Cuisery which had been planted in 1734 by Bernard de Jussieu when he brought two seeds back from Lebanon. The second tree is located in the Jardin des Plantes in Paris.

Sightseeing

CENTRE EDEN ★

126, rue de l'Eglise ✆ +33 (0)3 85 27 08 00
www.centre-eden71.fr – eden71@cg71.fr

Open from April 2nd to November 2nd. Open Tuesday to Sunday from 2pm to 6pm. In July and August, open 7 days a week from 10am to 6pm. Free for under 18-year-olds (unemployed and for all, each 1st Sunday of the month). Adult : €4. Group (10 people) : €3 (free tour). Natural planetarium/Getaways : €6 for the adults and €4.60 for the children, by reservation. Ludic visit of the museum with tactile shelf (rental : €5). Translation for the foreigners. Tourism label & Disability. Label Adventures Kids. Exemption from payment for the disabled person and her guide. Written texts. Children welcome. Guided tour (€5.50 by reservation). Shop. Activities.

Welcome in the house of biodiversity. Centre Eden is a museographic space that shows the diversity and the wealth of the Burgundian natural habitats. Various themed rooms (room of the ground, water, air, clues, weather) allows you to know everything about the soil, the insects, the birds, the aquatic fauna of the region and you will even learn the animals tracks. A planetarium installed in the park offers a educative trip to the space. A temporary exhibition completes the museographic visit. To discover until 2nd November, the fossils exhibition which offers an attractive travel in the past. Centre Eden is a place that is dedicated to families and invites you to discover all its corners and angles during the open door's days on 2nd and 3rd April. Many entertainments are organized all the year and in particular during summer. Workshops getaway are on the programme. In one day, half-day or in the evening, go with family in nature and discover on the spot the small water animals, the fossils. You will learn how to recognize the clues left by the animals or to constitute an herbarium. In October, dramatized visits entitled « sleeping Castle » will allow you to know more about the history of the building which shelters the Centre Eden which remains a ludic and educative site, ideal to discover for the whole family.

NOTRE-DAME CHURCH ★

Open. Groups : visit by appointment near the Tourist Office. In July-August : guided tour for all, organized by the Tourist Office every Thursday at 3pm.

The Notre-Dame church in Cuisery, in the Gothic style, was built between 1510 and 1520. It is a bull of the pope who was at the origin of the construction of the church. It was classified as a Historical Monument in 1996. You should not miss a magnificent triptych representing the Death of the Virgin, the Visitation and the Saints and a remarkable collection of paintings by Italian, Flemish and French schools made by patrons which is Denier of Caesar, the Adoration of the Magus. You must also see the stalls and remarkable wall paintings of the 16th century in the Caron Chapel. The work classified as historic monuments are gradually restored, with the aim of making the Notre-Dame church, one of the main centres of tourist interest in Cuisery with the Eden Centre and the Village du Livre.

Knife & Fork

HOSTELLERIE BRESSANE

56, route de Tournus ✆ +33 (0)3 85 32 30 66
www.hostellerie-bressane.fr
contact@hostelleriebressane.fr

« Maître Restaurateur » label. Closed from January 1st to January 31st. Open Tuesday for dinner; Wednesday to Sunday for lunch. Menu from €19 to €40. Lunch menu : €19 (only on weekdays). Regional menu : €30. Gourmet amusement : €40. Garden. Terrace.

Located in the heart of Cuisery, the restaurant « L'Hostellerie bressane » is one of the must-go gastronomic establishments in the region. With its beautiful terrace in the entrance and its pleasant garden hidden from public view at the back, L'Hostellerie bressane is an ideal place for a family meal every Sunday midday. The restaurant is spacious, stylish decor mingles with the more traditional aspects with other more modern ingredients. As for the cuisine, the pleasure of the eyes and the pleasure for the senses intertwine. Cyrille Jobert, his wife and his team offer a gastronomic and regional cuisine. You can enjoy wild Burgundy snails collected by hand as well as perch muslin or the pike quenelle. Burgundian Bresse establishment, you can not miss the poulard of Bresse with morels and yellow wine or the minute sautéed calf's kidney with mustard accompanied by fresh tagliatelle.

Sleeping

■ HOSTELLERIE BRESSANE
56, route de Tournus
✆ +33 (0)3 85 32 30 66
www.hostellerie-bressane.fr
contact@hostelleriebressane.fr

Logis (3 cheminées). Closed on Wednesday and Thursday. 15 rooms. Double room from €75 to €100; suite from €110 to €120. Buffet breakfast : €11. Garage : €10 (free secure private parking). Family room up to 5 people. A room for disabled guest. Pets allowed (€10 extra). Internet access. Free Wifi. Break-lunch : €19. Regional menu : €30. Gourmet amusement : €40. Satellite TV.

This Logis De France, between the Saône and Seille, is divided into two parts. The first building, charming hotel, houses seven bright, fully renovated spacious rooms, all of them very well-equipped with a capacity of four people. A second building called « *L'Annexe du jardin* », located in the back of Hostellerie Bressane, has six rooms, quiet and equally spacious and well-equipped, in a green setting that a small garden and a pleasant pool offer. On the first floor of the « *L'Annexe du jardin* », two junior suites attic Room called *Chambre bleue* and *Chambre verte* are awaiting you. The exposed beams give to the place, with its comfortable facilities, an undeniable charm. Enough to spend a pleasant stay in the heart of a burgundy Bresse.

Shopping

■ LA BISCUISERY
Rue du Moulin ✆ +33 (0)7 50 49 01 74
www.biscuisery.com

Open Wednesday to Sunday from 10am to 7.30pm. Open public holidays.

A real address of quality and a very human adventure. Biscuisery reopened its door 2 years ago at a few metres from the campsite and the Village du Livre and it is a real success. The success is all the more deserved since Jean-Baptiste Maret puts all his heart and his energy in it. At Biscuisery, everything is homemade and above all, everything is handmade ! Jean-Baptiste kneads his pasta in a wooden kneader. He uses organic and local ingredients. A sign of quality for biscuits made with corn flour and milk that everybody loves. The specialities of the house ? Shortbread made with spelt flour, meringues, Bresse wafers with cream, vanilla and raspberry and pancakes with caraway, Parmesan and ginger. A true delight since we know exactly what we eat. All products are sold in the reception area in the 1st floor where there is also a juice bar. A tea room of 50 seats also allows you to enjoy biscuits of the house while enjoying one of the 10 organic teas of your choice. At Biscuisery, you preserve time for yourself and for others. In his 100% craft shops, Jean-Baptiste Maret decided to highlight the human by organizing guided tours of Biscuisery for groups. Everyone can use their hand to knead the pasta and make their own biscuit. The visits are free.

In the surroundings

Romenay

LE LION D'OR
7, place Occidentale ✆ +33 (0)3 85 40 30 78
www.liondor.romenay.com
Closed 3 weeks in January. Open Monday to Saturday from 7am to 3pm; Wednesday to Sunday from 6pm to 10pm. Hotel with 8 rooms from €44 to €62. Menu from €15.50 to €27. Lunch menu : €13.50 (menu worker : €12.50. Fixed rate formulas : €14, €16 and €18). Menu of the amateur : €17, menu of the expert and menu of the pro : €20, menu of the expert : €27. American Express, Chèque Restaurant. Activities. Bar, retransmission of matches, activities with musical groups once a month.

In the heart of Romenay, Le Lion d'Or hotel and restaurant is located in an imposing and historical building. Eric and Mimi Mazzarese offer traditional and regional cuisine based on Burgundy snails, frogs or breast with chopped parsley and Bresse chicken with Forestiere sauce. As a family home, the restaurant offers formulas at low prices for the small budget like the menu for worker. The big appetites will also find their happiness thanks to the menus of the pro, of the expert and the connoisseur who offer pieces of the butcher, steak and 360g double Charolais beef tartare. The restaurant also organises musical evenings and rooms are available for family meals, banquets and seminars. Go also to the bar from 18 : 00 pm to 20 : 00 pm. It is *Happy Hour* time. Eric will be happy to make you discover his cocktails and beers. Le Lion d'Or is also a hotel and offers 8 charming rooms at low prices, well equipped, with free wi-fi, terrace and TV.

DIGOIN ★

BATEAU PROMENADE
La maison du Bateau
Port de plaisance
Rive droite ✆ +33 (0)3 85 53 76 78
www.croisiere.fr – laurence@croisiere.fr
Open from March to October. Adult : €7.80 (for 1 hour of cruise). Child (up to 16 years) : €4.70 (for 1 hour of crosière). Walk of 1h30, adult €9.80, child of less than 16 years, €5.50. Cruise with meal from €32.50. Children welcome (label Adventures Kids. Booklet for children under 10 years old). Guided tour.
Digoin has been a town of marine tradition since the roman era. It is crossed by three rivers : Loire, Arroux, and Bourbince and by three canals : Canal du Centre, Canal Latéral à la Loire and the Canal de Roanne. All the walks depart from the marina, the right bank, and include the crossing of Digoin, the passage of the tubular bridge and the first lock of the Canal Latéral à la Loire, the sailing in the large pool. All the cruises are commented by an entertainer who will answer all your questions, and you will thus discover the tubular bridge of Digoin, the lockage, the history of the canals and the river transportation, the fauna and the flora.

Knife & Fork

LES DILIGENCES
14, rue Nationale ✆ +33 (0)3 85 53 06 31
www.les-diligences.com
hotel-les-diligences@wanadoo.fr
Closed on Monday and Tuesday (except July-August). Menu from €20 to €39.50. Children's menu : €10. À la carte. Rates hotel : room from €60 to €80. Breakfast at €8 and €10. Half-board from €68 to €72. Stop-over with special rates for reps €70.
Les Diligences is an address with French ceilings, stone walls and a superb tiled stove, a traditional ambiance with a chic decor and refined dining room for an elegant rusticity. The cuisine is generous : fricassee of vine stock in the Bordeaux's way, piperade of snails with garlic, soup of red mullet with saffron, flat sausage of rabbit with peach and its 3 mashed potatoes, fillet of Charolais beef with 5 peppers, casserole of calf's kidney with Noilly Prat... As for the hotel, it is calm and the setting is pleasant. The rooms are neat and perfectly equipped. Some enjoy views of the Loire river and have a private balcony. The duplex room is equipped with a balneotherapy. A gourmet and resting stop with pleasant hosts.

L'AUBERGE DE VIGNY
Auberge de Vigny ✆ 03 85 81 10 13
www.aubergedevigny.fr
« Maître Restaurateur » label. Open Wednesday to Sunday from 12pm to 1.30pm and from 7pm to 9pm. Booking advised. Menu from €26 to €41. Children's menu : €7.50. Good gifts. Groups welcome. Terrace.
Located between Paray le Monial and Gueugnon, L'auberge de Vigny welcomes its guests in its room with fireplace or on the covered terrace overlooking the flowery park. The Chef Christophe Lagarde, recently promoted Maître Restaurateur, prepares its dishes wish fresh products, for an authentic and creative cuisine. On the menu, you will enjoy a stew of squid and small légules sauce poulette with lemongrass, your taste buds will appreciate the wrapped stuffed cabbage with snails, braising juice and red onion confit, a touch of freshness with a farm white cheese with cream, to complete this meal with a biscuit molten chocolate cake, creamy with banana and passion juices. An excellent address.

LE MERLE BLANC
36, route de Gugnon ✆ 03 85 53 17 13
www.lemerleblanc.com
lemerleblanc@wanadoo.fr
Closed the 24 and December 31st. Menu from €26.70 to €41.90. Menu at €21.90 except Sunday and public holidays. À la carte. Rates hotel : room from €67, breakfast at €9.50 in room and €11.50 in room. Supplement animals €7.

It is a very beautiful address that accommodates the travellers and the gourmets. Le Merle Blanc, under the aegis of Monsieur Regnault, is presented in the form of an enthusiastic defender of the French cuisine, skillfully worked and enriched. There's no mystery for that, a rigorous selection of seasonal ingredients and a consistent choice of menus, so that every palated finds its happiness. Everything is served in copious portion ! Among other suggestions, you have : the Charolais fresh goat with the beetroot coulis and its homemade smoked salmon, vinaigrette sauce with vodka, the eggs in red wine sauce, the Charolais steak with herb butter, Swedish potatoes and pan-fried mushrooms with garlic and parsley, red mullet fillets with herb crust, its basmati rice and tomato of Provence, the hot soufflé with chopped pistachio , prune mousse glazed with Armagnac... As many suggestions to make your tastebuds quiver. You leave the restaurant to find the privacy of the hotel with his twelve perfectly equipped and soundproofed rooms.

Leisure

■ **CANALOUS**
Port Campionnet
✆ 03 85 53 76 74
www.canalous-bourgogne.com/fr
resa@lescanalous.com
♿

From €745 to €4590 per week. From €90 to €180 1/2 day and the day. Tourism label & Disability.
Discover the river tourism by renting a houseboat licence free, with a fleet available for rent for 2 to 12 people. Travelling along de river, you will enjoy the sweetness of a trip on the canals (canal du Centre, canal de Roanne à Digoin, canal latéral à la Loire), the lock crossing, the countryside within reach. Rental available from 1/2 day to a week. A fleet labeled Tourisme et Handicap.

Digoin.

GUEUGNON

CAMPING MUNICIPAL DU VAL D'ARROUX**
TOULON-SUR-ARROUX
✆ +33 (0)3 85 79 51 22

Open from April to October. 68 campsites. Exposure : shaded. Ground : grassy. Relief : dish. €9.70 per night. Games for children. Area for camper van. Wifi.

A municipal campsite, located at the edge of Arroux, for holidays in the green. Near the city center and therefore to all the amenities, this campsite is a haven of peace : shaded areas, for tents and caravans, as well as an area reserved to motor homes. A games area for children, and the opportunity to freely get to the mini-golf for campers. Numerous activities in the vicinity make this campsite the perfect place for a family vacation.

LOUHANS ★

Nestled in the heart of a region with lush valleys, small lakes and calm rivers, Louhans deserves its ranking among the « most beautiful detours in France. » Remnants of its medieval past give the city an authentic and picturesque character, same as these arcades along the High Street. But Louhans is also a city of commerce, showcase its rich hinterland. Since the end of the Middle Ages, it imposed itself as a city of trade and crafts, due to its position on the Seille River and its location on the major trade routes linking Italy and Jura. The strength of its markets (do not miss the one held on Monday), added to the reputation of its poultry persist for centuries. Louhans was the birthplace of Ferdinand Berthier (dumb) in 1803. He is a professor at the National Institute for Deaf-Mutes in Paris and founder of the Universal Society of the Deaf-mutes.

Knife & Fork

LA TABLE DE GUILLAUME
5, place Saint-Jean
✆ +33 (0)3 85 75 48 52

Closed on Monday and Sunday for dinner. Open Wednesday to Monday for lunch. Menu from €19.50 to €22. Lunch menu : €14.50. Chèque Restaurant. Terrace. Pets allowed. Parking nearby.

Guillaume and his team have been welcoming guests since June 2012 in this establishment with strong colors. La Table de Guillaume is located in the city center, next to the Arcades, La Table de Guillaume has an indoor terrace covered with about a hundred seats and a dining room of sixty seats equipped with bar in wooden color, which gives the place a warm and friendly appearance. The cuisine is traditional and the à la carte menu, simple and not too loaded, changes four times a year with the seasons. As starter, we will try the spring rolls snail with creamy époisses soup followed by the frog legs with cream or the stuffed Bresse chicken before finishing with a small raspberry tart or a molten chocolate cake. Appetizing ! A bistro and welcoming atmosphere for this semi-gastronomic restaurant using local products. The must-eat of the Chef : Burgundy snails and Bresse Chicken.

Sleeping

HOSTELLERIE DU CHEVAL ROUGE
5, rue d'Alsace
✆ +33 (0)3 85 75 21 42
www.hotel-chevalrouge.com
hotel-chevalrouge@wanadoo.fr

Tables & Inns of France. Annual closing of Christmas at January 20th. Hotel closed on Monday evening. Reception from 7.30am to 11am and from 4pm to 10.30pm. 14 rooms. Double room from €57 to €65. Half-board (80 at €120). Breakfast : €8.50. Extra bed : €10. Garage : €9. Holiday voucher. A room for disabled person. Pets allowed (€9). Free Wifi. Restaurant open Monday, Friday, Saturday and Sunday lunchtime and evening, Wednesday and Thursday evening. Closed on Tuesday. Menus from €20 to €35, regional menu at €25 and children's menu at €10. Satellite TV.

Located in a former Relais de Poste, this Logis de France is characterized by its typical Burgundian Bresse architecture. The Hostellerie du Cheval Rouge is well located on the edge of the 157 arches that form the main street of Louhans and a few steps from the Tourist Office. It is in this lovely hotel, 2 star,

2 chimneys at the Logis De France and bearing the Qualité Tourisme label, with rustic setting that has embraced modernity, that Marie-Claire and Pierre Aubry welcome you. On the Hotel side, there are fourteen comfortable rooms with simple and brilliant colors. As for the restaurant : The great hall has a country-style aspect, ideal for family or groups meals, while a more contemporary terrace welcomes you in summer. The clucking of the unavoidable Bresse poultry adds charm and authenticity to the place. As for the cuisine, we appreciate the gourmet menus and local specialties that combine the necessary frogs' legs, snails, poultry terrines or fish, pike and carp and of course, the unmissable Bresse chicken. The wine list focuses on wines from Burgundy and Jura.

In the surroundings

Rancy

LA TAVERNE BRESSANE
807, route de Louhans
✆ +33 (0)3 85 74 62 39

Closed 3 weeks in January. Open Monday for lunch; Wednesday to Saturday for lunch and dinner. Open in continuous working day Sunday. Open 7 days a week from June 15th to September 15th. Menu from €20.50 to €29.50. Children's menu : €8.50. Traditional menu of the market of Louhans : €17.50. Holiday voucher, Chèque Restaurant. Groups welcome (up to 100 people). Baby chairs. Terrace. Parking + bar.

Located on the road that leads to Louhans, on the small town of Rancy, La Taverne Bressane is beautiful and large house with two rooms and a bar, a lovely terrace, and can accommodate a hundred guests. Outside, the decor recalls the Haute-Savoie, its native department of the two owners, Jacques and Marie-Françoise. Inside, traditional furniture, decor including chickens and casseroles is reminiscent of Bresse. By the way, the house offers both traditional Bresse menus and Savoyard specialties. In summer as in winter, you can enjoy tartiflette, fondue, small breaded Reblochon or flambéed scabbard fish with first quality beef skewers, Dauphin gratin and salad. The house also serves frogs with cream, Bresse poultry and favours combination of salad during the summer. As for the desserts, La Taverne Bressane offers crème brûlée, rum baba and molten chocolate cake.

The restaurant is also a privileged address with the guest houses who like to accommodate its customers into them. The restaurant opens its terrace in summer and welcomes groups for private events such as weddings and birthday parties.

Sornay

AUBERGE DE L'ÉCLUSE
1068, route de Branges

Open Thursday to Sunday for lunch and dinner. Open from April to mid-September. Booking is essential. À la carte : Around €35. Lunch menu : €17. Menu frying at €25 (entrée+friture+dessert). Garden. Terrace.

Located in a splendid rural and green setting along the Seille, the restaurant l'Ecluse is a pleasant nice address full of fine gravel and composed of a modern wooden furniture which brings much warmth and softness to the place. The owners, Jean-Michel Simerey and his partner Claire Kozlowski, have particularly taken care of the presentation. As Seille is in the vicinity, l'Ecluse offers a fresh cuisine based on frogs, frying and fillets of perch. The viande charolais meat and the Bresse chicken are also on the menu. The products are fresh, from local producers and all the dishes are homemade. Same requirement for the wine list which showcases the estates of Saône-et-Loire, Beaujolais and Côtes-du-Rhône. A very exotic and charming address to test as soon as possible !

direct access to the beach	visually impaired disability	take away
bar	mental handicap	room service
laundry	motor disability	fitness room
air conditioning	garden or park	playroom / tv
nightclub	games	modern sanitary
cash machine	washing machine / laundry	water sports
drinking water	bicycle rental	tennis
horse riding	grocery store	archery
smoking area	airport shuttle	waterslide
non-smoking	fishing	fan
fitness	indoor swimming pool	toilet drain
miniature golf	outdoor heated pool	sailing
hard of hearing disability	outdoor pool	

LUGNY

We are here in this part of Macon which is called the High Macon. Lugny is the chief town of a canton of 19 municipalities with a population of nearly 8,000 residents. It is located between vineyards and Saone. It is not surprising that this picturesque country is appreciated for the walks, in woods and valleys ! The geography has been generous with this section of Saône-et-Loire. Vines grew there and made the most of the sunshine. A land of tradition where there are Romanesque churches. The local vineyards consisted of 355 ha and are looked after by the members of the cooperative of Lugny.

Knife & Fork

AUBERGE DE LA PLACE
Place de la Mairie ✆ +33 (0)3 85 50 93 88
Open all year. Monday to Saturday from 8am to 3pm; Friday and Saturday for dinner from 6pm to 9.30pm. Set menu at €12 (starter and main course + cheese (or dessert) +café). Children's menu : €6. Lunch menu : €9 (main course + cheese (or dessert) + coffee). Takeouts : 9.8 or €7. Chèque Restaurant. Groups welcome (groups of up to 15 people). Terrace. Take-away.

Auberge de la Place is aptly named since it is located on the central square of Lugny. You cannot miss this pleasant establishment and the Agathe's smile. Sit on the terrace in summer and take the time to have breakfast in the morning (the address opens early in the morning) or eat an ice-cream in the afternoon. The place is quiet and offers stunning views of the village of Lugny. Inside, the restaurant can accommodate about thirty seats. The decoration is simple and without fuss. The cuisine is traditional and homemade. On the menu : the must-eat Charolais *steaks* and sausages, without forgetting the fried mussels which make you feel like in seaside holiday, even if Lugny is far from the ocean. The house specialties : the homemade steak burger, *cheddar*, tomatoes, onions and offers a full meal to lunchtime and allows Auberge de la Place reach young public. The takeaways are popular. As for wine, the restaurant favours local winemakers and independent winegrowers of Mâcon Lugny and of course of Chardonnay. A pleasant address, cheap and with a very friendly welcome.

Shopping

CAVE DE LUGNY
95, rue des Charmes
✆ +33 (0)3 85 33 22 85
www.cave-lugny.com
magasins@cave-lugny.com
Low season : open from Monday to Saturday from 8.30am to 12.30pm and from 1.30pm to 6pm. High season : from Monday to Saturday from 8.30am to 12.30pm and from 1.30pm to 7pm. Opening hours of the shop in Chardonnay from Tuesday to Saturday from 9am to noon and from 2pm to 6pm (7pm, from June to September). Open on Sunday and public holidays from 10am to 12.30pm and from 2.30pm to 6pm (7pm from April to September). Closed in January and February. Visit of the Crémant de Bourgogne Wine storehouse in Chardonnay with tasting in 3 formulas €3, €7 and €10.

Cave de Lugny is impossible to miss, it is one of the most important buildings of the village. It must be said that in Lugny, the Cellar is an institution. Founded in 1927, the winegrower's Cooperative of Lugny was the second cellar cooperative established in Mâconnais after that of Saint-Gengoux-de-Scissé. Wine growers who set up in the municipalities adhered to the cooperative very soon after. Cave de Lugny is the first producer of Bourgogne's wine (a third of volume) and the first Burgundy wine producer in volume (6% of the total production of the region with a production of almost 10 million litres of wine) in a vineyards area of 15 km^2 all around the Cellar. Cave de Lugny has two shops : the one in Lugny and the other in Chardonnay, without forgetting the sales outlet of Saint-Gengoux-de-Scissé, managed by an independent cellarman. The quality of wines of Cave de Lugny is widely acknowledge as well as its professionalism. To get the best of the vineyards, only the best potential plots are used for the vintages. The Cellar also committed itself to promote quality with a continuous production and the development of a strategy « winemakers in sustainable development » -it received by the way this label- to offer the best terroir. The address produces 16 different appellations of Burgundy and widens out its range thanks to the multiplication of the localities and the refinement of the knowledge of terroir. Among the highlighted white, you will find the famous Mason-Villages, Mâcon-Lugny and Mâcon-Chardonnay or Burgundy Chardonnay and Burgundy Aligoté. For the red, smooth and light based on Gamay for Macon and Pinot Noir for Burgundy ones, you can have a glass of Mâcon-Cruzille. Finally, Cave de Lugny offers an original range of Crémant De Bourgogne derived from the association of Chardonnay and Pinot Noir. Les Crémants de Bourgogne Brut, Blanc De Blancs, Vintage or Rosé have the wind in their sails and managed to find their niche on the nice restaurants. Note a new : Blanc De Noir (80% Pinot and 20% Gamay). Anyway, feel free to pay a visit. The doors are wide open and the staff will be happy to explain the production process. They will also give advice on the wines to purchase. There is an online purchase on the address website. Visits are only at Chai Crémant de Bourgogne in Chardonnay with tasting only for groups in 3 formulas : 1/ for groups of 20 pers. minimum duration 1h30 - 2/ for groups of 20 pers. minimum duration 2 hours (wine and cheese tastings and decorated glass to take away) – 3/ for groups between 10 and 20 pers. Possibility of purchase on the online store.

In the surroundings

Azé

GROTTES D'AZÉ-RIZEROLLES
Rizerolles ✆ 03 85 33 32 23
grottes.aze@cg71.fr
A 12 km de l'autoroute A6 (sortie 28 Mâcon nord)

Open from March 27th to October 2nd then from October 20th to October 31st. Open every day from 10am to 12pm and from 2pm to 7pm. Departure of the guided tours from 10.30am, 2.30pm and 4pm in low season and of 10.30am, 1pm, 2.30pm 4pm and 5.30pm in July and August with extra departures depending on the attendance. Booking is essential. Free for under 6-year-olds. Adult : €7. Child : €4. Group : €5 (€5 adults, €3 child-students). Family rate : €15 starting from 2 children. Guided tour. Catering facilities. Shop. Picnic tables, free parking. Visits dramatized with Sha-Manaze, the prehistoric man Thursdays in June August July by reservation.

Although Mâconnais is best known for its grapevines, it has other hidden treasures in its underground. The site of Les Grottes d'Azé is classified for its natural historic heritage. The visit begins with the underground river that presents many examples of layers, holes, fossils, the stalactiques and stalagmites. The prehistoric cave has been used as shelter by men since 300,000 years but it contains also exceptional remains of cavern bears and lions, the whole emphasized by a scenographic lighting. The archaeological museum also preserves an impressive collection of fossils, minerals, bones, tools, obtained as a result of archaeological excavations and the shop offers souvenirs on sale (cuddly toys, books, minerals...). A discovery that lasts approximately 1 hour and half to experience with family and that you can not afford to miss !

Viré

CAVE DE VIRE
2, place André Lagrange ✆ 03 85 33 10 57
www.cavedevire.fr

Low season : open Monday to Saturday from 9am to 12.30pm and from 2pm to 6pm; Sunday and public holidays from 10am to 12.30pm and from 2.30pm to 6pm. High season : Monday to Saturday from 9am to 12.30pm and from 2pm to 7pm; Sunday and public holidays from 10am to 12.30pm and from 2.30pm to 7pm. Closed the Sunday afternoon in January and February.

La Maison... Cave de Viré north of Mâcon is a long history that goes back to 1928. At the start, the cooperative winery is famous for the quality of its white wines. Its alliance with the cellar of Sennecé-lès-Mâcon strengthens its production. The appellation Viré-Clessé in 1998 and becomes the 5th communal name of Built. Today, Cave de Viré consists of 300 ha of vineyards attached to the cellar, 145 co-operators including 40 vine growers and many appellation : AOP Mason, AOP Viré Clessé, AOP Crémant de Bourgogne... Go to La Maison... Cave de Viré is open 7 days a week in 2000 at the foot of production buildings and discover the white wines, straw-yellow colour or crystalline color and crémant with fine bubbles. You can taste the product range for free and leave with gourmet baskets and gift boxes. A nice and tasty address and typical of Mâcon.

MÂCON ★★★

Mâcon is turned towards Lyn rather than Burgundy, but that doesn't make it charmless. Its conviviality and its round tiled roof give a little Mediterranean touch that will enchant visitors. A sweet life that is also expressed in the diversity and quality of its wines whose reputation is well established (National Wine Fair takes place every spring in Macon), as well as its gastronomy that should be discovered in one of the many restaurants.

Celtic port of Eduens and oppidum for the Romans who had already understood the strategic importance of the ancient Matisco. Crossroads of trade routes and crossed by Agrippa, the main artery of the Romanized Gaul, the city strengthens in the IVth century.

In the Middle Ages it became a county attached to the Duchy of Burgundy. Bordering town between France and Savoy, it will be, during the years of religious wars, an entrance for Switzerland or the German mercenaries. In 1790, the city became the capital of the department of Saône et Loire that has newly been created.

During the Second World War, Macon was the first city in the free zone between Paris and Lyon. And in 1974, the Council of Europe gave it the Prix de l'Europe.

Today, Macon has many architectural vestiges of its past, a heritage that can be discovered by strolling through the old town. On the docks, the statue of Lamartine recalls that this illustrious poet and politician, is a native of Macon. His memory is still present on the esplanade, recently renovated on the beachfront of Saone.

As for the economy, the city was a stopover for aircraft in the year 20 to 30 and saw the birth of a French motorcycle Monet-Goyon (MG), a brand founded on April 2, 1917 by Joseph Monet, engineer, and Adrien goyon, a rich heir. Today, this city of history and culture also demonstrates its dynamism in sports, rom golf to. . ., polo, windsurfing and boating. Indeed, Macon annually hosts the spectacular grand prix of powerboat !

OFFICE DE TOURISME DE MÂCON
1, place Saint-Pierre ✆ 03 85 21 07 07
www.macon-tourism.com

Low season : open Tuesday to Saturday from 9.30am to 12pm and from 2pm to 6pm. High season : every day and public holidays from 9am to 7pm. Open in April, May, September and October Monday to Saturday from 9.30am to 12.30pm and from 2pm to 6pm and public holidays from 10.30am to 12.30pm and from 2pm to 6pm. Open in June from 9am to 12.30pm and from 2pm to 6.30pm 7 days a week and public holidays from 10am to 12.30pm and from 2.30pm to 6pm.

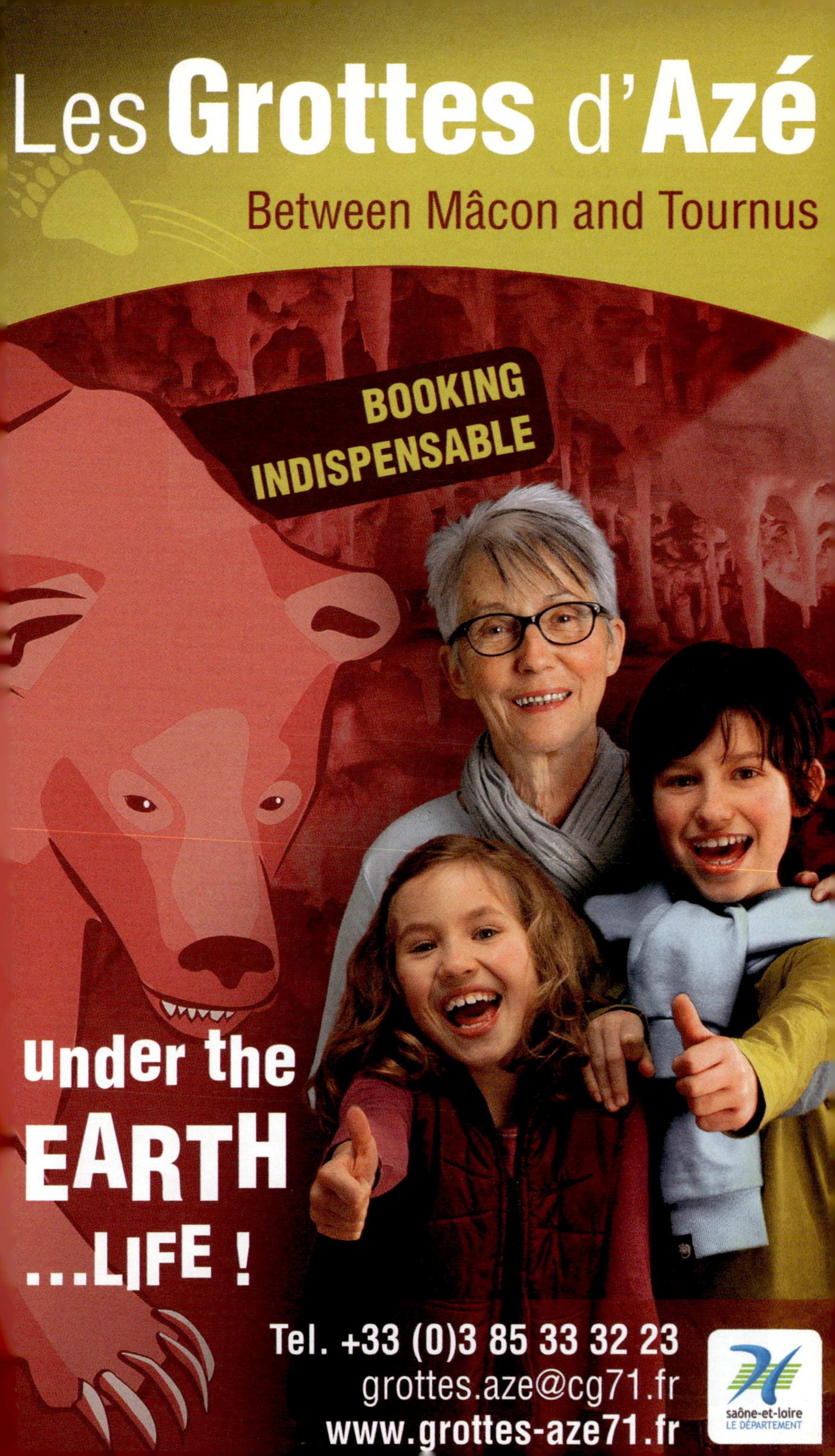

Les Grottes d'Azé
Between Mâcon and Tournus
BOOKING INDISPENSABLE
under the EARTH ...LIFE !
Tel. +33 (0)3 85 33 32 23
grottes.aze@cg71.fr
www.grottes-aze71.fr
saône-et-loire LE DÉPARTEMENT

A stone's throw from the town hall and Saint-Pierre church, the tourist office boasts of a large beautiful lounge, with armchairs and also a new multimedia space with a wide and interactive touch screen enabling you to find a large number of practical information. Those who are allergic to computers can be reassured, the Tourist Office is full of tourist brochures allowing you to prepare your stay and discover Mâcon and the Mâconnais, the Wine Road and the events' guide. For more information, do not hesitate to ask for advice to the agents. The property also sells ticket for shows, cruises on the Saône and the Seille, air balloon rides. Take profit from the shop to take home products around wine (drinks, bottles, corkscrews,...), mugs and gourmet products. In summer, the hotel organizes guided tours focused on the history of the city and its most unusual aspects.

CROISIERE SUR LA SAONE
375, rue Alain Colas ✆ +33 (0)3 85 21 07 01

Open every day from 3pm and from 5pm. From April 1st to October 31st. Minimum : 6 people Max : 12 people By reservation near the Tourist Office of Built. Adult : €15. From 3 to 12 years old child : €8. Child of less than 3 years : free.

Discover Mâconnais differently and embark on board the terrace boat « Fantaisie Evasion » for a stroll accross the water of 1 hour and a half. Departure from the marina of Mâcon and direction north to discover the Saint-Jean island. While returning through the diversion canal, you will see the bridge of Geneva, the river port of Darse, the Mitterrand bridge before going along the city to the edges of the Lamartine esplanade, under the Saint-Laurent bridge before returning to the port. You can bring your lunchbox on board.

Sightseeing

APOTHICAIRERIE DE L'HOTEL-DIEU
344, rue des Epinoches
✆ +33 (0)3 85 39 90 38
musees@ville-macon.fr

Open from June 1st to September 30th, every day (except Monday) from 2pm to 6pm. Closed on July 14th. The rest of the year, open by appointment. Free. Guided tour (duration : 30 min, by reservation near the museum of the Ursulines).

Located in the middle of the Hôtel-Dieu between 1761 and 1170 according to the plans of the architect Germain Soufflot, the pharmacy preserved its original decor. The vast room located at the ground floor of the Hôtel-Dieu thus offers a nice diving in the time and allows you to appreciate a set of Louis XV wood panelling in magnifying glass in ash and elm tree. The floor is also from the former period. In the imposing glazed furniture, you can admire an important collection of jars with pharmacy in rare earthenware and from a Mâcon's factory.

HÔTEL DE VILLE
quai Lamartine ✆ +33 (0)3 85 89 71 00

Open Monday to Friday from 8.30am to 6pm; Saturday from 9am to 12pm.

The Macon City Hall is found in the former Montrevel hotel, built between 1746 and 1751 by Abel-Michel Chesnard de Layé who passed it on to his son in 1753, who himself defeated it in 1767 in favour of Comte Melchior de Labaume de Montrevel. Rich owner in Bresse and in Macon, he then undertook major expansion. He built the great Comedie hall (now the Council Chambers), hosting a stall, an orchestra and a stage surrounded by two sets of boxes. There he played many parts that please the nobles and bourgeois of Macon. Comedie was destroyed by fire on the night of 8 to 9 February 1907. Before being guillotined during the French Revolution, the count of Montrevel sold his hotel to the city of Macon on March 8, 1793. You can admire the lavish woodwork in the marriage hall, a library housing the medallion portraits of ancient philosophers. In the entrance hall, you will find the stairs with its wrought iron railing as well as the large living room for weddings and the boardroom that are worth seeing.

MAISON DE BOIS
Place aux Herbes

Open every day from 7.30am to 1am. Daily special : €9.50. Main course and dessert : €13. Catering facilities. Terrace.

Built between 1490 and 1510, La Maison de Bois is undoubtedly the oldest house in Mâcon and also the most famous. Its façade entirely built in wood is decorated with a multitude of statuettes in grotesque appearances composed of fastasmatic characters with masks of men and monkeys, grinning, fidgetting, sitting, winged and sometimes naked. Moreover Maison de Bois would have been in the 16th century the headquarters of the bacchic brotherhood of Malgouverne, assembly of young people judged lawless and dissolved in 1625.

The Saône in Mâcon.

Maison de Bois is a real institution in Mâcon, a must-visit place because of its building materials. It is also a bar and a familiar catering area for the Mâcon's inhabitants who like to hang around there until late in the evening. Historical monument since 1920, Maison de Bois is owned by the municipality since 1992. In 2011, the hotel was completely renovated and is a little rejuvenated thanks to a new modern terrace that highlights more the historical heritage. A stopover for a drink in Maison de Bois is a must!

Knife & Fork

LE BISTROT GOURMAND

3, place Gardon ✆ +33 (0)3 85 38 15 83

Open all year. Monday, Tuesday, Friday and Saturday for dinner; Monday to Saturday for lunch. Booking advised. Menu from €18 to €24. À la carte : Around €11. Children's menu : €6. Daily special : €9. Wine by the glass. Menu bistro : €18. Gourmet menu : €24. Coffee uninterrupted the day. Terrace. Take-away.

With its characteristic red checkered tablecloths, the bistro table is traditional with regional menus and with a touch of modernity in a contemporary and dynamic decor. On your plate : pig trotters, andouillette and Lyonnaise sausage. All products are fresh and come from local producers. A selection of wines changes every month and showcases the Mâconnais white wines (Saint-Véran, Pouilly-Fuissé) without forgetting Burgundy and Côtes-du-Rhône among the other safe bets. The restaurant organises regularly entertainment and created an piano bar ambiance on Fridays. The welcome and the atmosphere are warm. Futé loves and strongly recommends.

ER BLEIMOR

12, rue Gambetta ✆ +33 (0)3 85 39 02 22

Closed Saturday for dinner, Sunday and Monday. Open Tuesday to Friday; Saturday for lunch. Booking advised. Children's menu : €8.80 (menu Ship's boy). Daily specials : €9.90 (pancakes from €3.20 to €10.80).

The facade of the restaurant, painted in blue and white, transports us already. Inside, the journey to Britain continues with : cream-colored walls, blue window paneling, reminiscent of the houses on the island of Sein, overlooking the sea at the end of the room, music ... everything is there. And the good smell of pancakes, nobody can resist it! La Crêperie « Er Bleimor », just had a facelift. Appointed in 2005 as « Crêperie Ambassador » by the Tourist Office of Rennes, for the quality of its services, it is part of the Breton Federation of Pancakes (crepes made by hand) since 2013. It Suffice to say that this is THE reference Brittany Macon.

For over 22 years now, Isabelle and Christian have been dedicating themselves to making their guests enjoy genuine Breton pancakes. And they succeed. Among the 80 crepes or pancakes proposed, the vegetarian made has many rivals, the celtic (Guéméné sausage, cheese, egg and onion compote) or hermione (Guéméné sausage, potatoes, cream) attract lovers of « pays des menhirs », « fleur de sel » (salted butter caramel) or « vallée d'Auge » (caramelized apple calvados) attract the attention of gourmands. For cocktails, Breton beer or bolet de cidre will accompany the tasting. You have to choose between the vintages of Bigouden country Rennes, Fouesnant or Rhuys Peninsula. As the regulars would say : the pancake is « the best in Macon ! ». A stopping place convenient for an escape and for gourmets. Word of Petit Futé, enjoy!

L'ÉTHYM'SEL

10, rue Gambetta ✆ +33 (0)3 85 39 48 84

Open on Monday and Thursday to Saturday for dinner; Wednesday to Monday for lunch. Closed on Sunday and Monday in July-August. Menu from €33 to €53. Children's menu : €11. Lunch menu : €19 (starter + main course + dessert). Menu weekend : €33. Menu flavour : 42 at €46. Amusement : €53 (weekend, public holidays and evenings). Chèque Restaurant.

With its contemporary setting, its simple and mild colours, take the time to relax a little by sitting at the table in the Ethym'Sel restaurant, located near place Genevès, a stone's throw from the Saône. But do not be fooled by this apparent softness. It is in the dish that you find the grain of salf of the restaurant. The dishes are concocted and beautifully prepared by the Chef, Patrick Chantemesse, maître-restaurateur. House specialities : gourmet salad with duck foie gras chips and warm terrine, duck breast smoked with beech wood and a piece of Charolais rumsteak with shallot sauce. As for desserts, the Chef goes to the sun and offers fruity flavours. Try the pineapple carpaccio with fresh mint, the traditional French toast with mango soup flavoured with vanilla or more classic, choose the gourmet coffee. An quality address which skilfully combines gastronomic cuisine and family cuisine, all at very affordable prices.

LE LAMARTINE

259, quai Lamartine
✆ +33 (0)3 85 35 16 63 / +33 (0)6 10 77 75 06
www.lelamartine.com

Closed on December 24th at the evening and on December 25 as well as on December 31st at the evening and on January 1st. Open 7 days a week for lunch and dinner. Menu from €13.80 to €39.50. Daily special : €9.80 (only at lunchtime). Wine by the glass. Menu the Lamartine : €20.70, tasting menu : €27.50, menu of the delights : €39.50. Dessert of the house day : €6.50. American Express, Holiday voucher, Chèque Restaurant. Groups welcome (possibility of composing your menus on request). Terrace.

Located on the docks of the Saône, Lamartine is registered in the Mâcon's gourmet landscape for long years. Indeed, the restaurant goes back to 1804. The decoration preserves this aspect of the 19th century and takes you several years back, in a chic and authentic setting, making the original and undeniable charm place. A portrait of the poet Alphone of Lamartine, Mâcon celebrity of the 19th century, stands in good place on the walls of the restaurant. A spirit « Bouchon of Lyon » prevails in the cuisine and every day the chefs revisit the traditional dishes in which they bring an original touch. You will taste the house specialities : sweetbread, fried mussels, frogs' leg and calf's head without forgetting the fish and a wide choice of made desserts, also homemade. Opened every day, the restaurant boasts of a pleasant terrace that immerses you in the middle of the Mâcon life rhythmed by the very close Saône river. A sure and pleasant address as Futé likes it to be.

LA MAISON MÂCONNAISE DES VINS
484, avenue du Maréchal-de-Lattre-de-Tassign
✆ +33 (0)3 85 22 91 11
www.maison-des-vins.com
contact@maison-des-vins.com

Open every day from 10am and until 10pm. Service uninterrupted 7 days a week. Cold service of 10 : 00 at 11.45am and from 2.15pm to 6.45pm. Shop open 7 days a week from 9am to 7pm. Menu from €13.50 to €24.50. Children's menu : €9.50. Wine by the glass. Groups welcome (to lunch of business, birthday, cocktails, buffets and evenings possible). Garden. Terrace. Shop. Large car park.

Founded in 1958 by professionals of the vineyard, Maison Mâconnaise des Vins is one of the crucial addresses of Mason. It's impossible to miss with this large building lined with ivies, surrounded by greenery and laying out in terrace of a stunning view on the Saône. We would be actually tempted to say that new visitor of the region should make a stopover at Maison Mâconnaise des Vins. This unique Burgundy stopover of the south promotes all the wine appellation of Saône-et-Loire. The shop is open every day and offers Mason, the wines of Givry, Pouilly-Fuissé, the Saint-Véran of the Mercurey 1er cru and many other wines, red or white from the local terroir. La Maison Mâconnaise des Vins is also a restaurant run by Florence Dupont and Martial Bonin. This latter has passed in many great addresses before moving to Mason. The cuisine is fast and neat. The Chef starting is inspired by the Burgundian traditional dishes. The menu is rich and varied. You will find the Burgundy snails as starter, the andouillette gratin, the paving stone of beef or the Charolais cow steak among others and as dessert, the lemon pie with apricots or apples competes with chocolate mousse with panacotta or with Mâcon wafer. Just a wide choice ! Highly prized by the inhabitants of Mâcon, La Maison Mâconnaise des Vins can accommodate families and groups thanks to its three rooms with a capacity of nearly 300 seats. The rates are very reasonable, the service is fast, effective and pleasant and non-stop every day. To discover absolutely !

RESTAURANT PIERRE
7-9, rue Dufour
✆ +33 (0)3 85 38 14 23
www.restaurant-pierre.com
info@restaurant-pierre.com

Closed 10 days in January and March. Open Tuesday to Saturday for dinner; Wednesday to Sunday for lunch. Menu from €26 to €88. Children's menu : €18 (menu young person gourmet). Lunch menu : €28 (only Wednesday, Thursday, Friday and Saturday). Wine by the glass. Amusement : €36. Gourmet menu : €51. Gourmet menu : 68 at €78. Menu discovered : €91. American Express. Shop.

Restaurant Pierre has become an institution in Mâcon. It has enjoyed a Michelin star since 1997. There is no doubt that the requirement of the Chef Christian Gaulin, passionate about his trade and the quality, plays a big part in that. His wife, Isabelle, accompanies him since the beginning of this adventure in 1991. She supervises the quality of the service. A clever combination that makes sparks on the plate. The menu, rightly filled, changes with the seasons. The regional produces are highlighted. The chef does not hesitate to make a tour of the France regions to fill his menus with duck foie gras of the Southwest via the Bresse poultry and the closer Charolais tournedos before leaving for Saint-Brieuc to offer us scallops accompanied by a saffron sauce of the Burgundy, enhanced and just the right amount. The desserts also vary according to the desires of the Chef who combines chocolate, lemon, pineapple, hot delights softened by a tablespoon of sorbet or vanilla frosted verrine. The charm of the stone, clear warm colours and the simplicity of the decor comes to complete the pleasure of the palate.

Leisure

CENTRE AQUATIQUE DU MÂCONNAIS VAL DE SAÔNE
Rue Pierre-de-Coubertin
✆ +33 (0)3 85 21 11 30 / +33 (0)3 85 38 46 74
centreaquatique@camval.com

Open all year. Low season : Monday, Thursday and Friday from 12pm to 7pm; Tuesday from 12pm to 10pm; Wednesday from 9am to 7pm; Saturday from 10am to 6pm; Sunday from 9am to 1pm and from 3pm to 6pm. High season : Wednesday to Monday from 10am to 10pm; Tuesday from 10am to 9pm; Sunday from 10am to 7pm. Admission : €4.70. Subscription : €42 (less than 18 years : €21.20). Child : €2.20. Less than 18 years or student : €2.85. Sports field, course teenager, spa.

This aquatic centre is perfect to enjoy water in summer as in winter. The summer, enjoy the Olympic pool, the ornamental pool and the sporting pool. The children will adore the early childhood pool and the paddling pool. The slide offers beautiful opportunities of sliding. In winter, a spa is open and offers good moments of relaxation in warm and at the waterfront. The aquatic centre of Mâconnais-Val de Saône attracts many holiday makers thanks to its seven pools and proposes numerous activities : aquabike, aquababy, aquagym, etc. Some 10,000 m^2 of lawn and 3000 m^2 of beaches outdoor and covered make it possible to play or enjoy the sun. A multi-sports field and a teenager course supplement this entire modern and functional amenity. Easily accessible, it puts at the disposal of swimmers a parking of 200 places.

Going Out

Bars & Pubs

LE VOLTAIRE
228, quai Lamartine
✆ +33 (0)3 85 39 11 70
www.levoltaire71.fr
angel.evenement71@orange.fr

Open Monday to Wednesday from 8am to 1am; Thursday to Saturday from 8am to 2am; Sunday from 9am to 9pm. Card of cocktails to the blender : €5.50 without alcohol and 6.50 and €7.50 with alcohol. Shooters : €30 the meter. From September to April, once a month one evening with DJ. Terrace. Catering facilities. Activities. Concerts.

It is one of the most fashionable addresses in Mâcon. Le Voltaire is a bar where you can come for a drink of course, sip a cocktail, inside in the large dining room or outside on the terrace in summer. The wine list is rich. But Le Voltaire is also one of the night addresses, one of the establishments where young people of Mâcon like to end the evening. As Le Voltaire is always busy, it has been renovated and has a new look. The decoration is new. The house opted for grey sober tones and chic with mirrors and cushions. The terrace was also rearranged, enlarged with the installation of new furniture. Le Voltaire focused also on a new menu with new cocktails and new hot and cold drinks to discover. The house keeps on organising themed parties once a month such as the girl parties, the special Halloween, speed-dating, etc. The bar makes every effort to enliven the event and create surprise. At night, Le Voltaire is empowered at 100,000 volts, at daytime it is a relaxing place where it is pleasant to hang around on the terrace with a view of the dock. In winter, enjoy the chalet. Le Voltaire offers crepes and waffles to warm you up. It's an address where you can stop and have fun thoughout in any season.

Shopping

Gourmet Basket

CHOCOLATERIE LES CYGNES
26, rue Philibert-Laguiche
✆ +33 (0)9 62 23 87 31 /+33 (0)7 78 63 65 02
www.chocolat-macon.fr
lescygnes.71@gmail.com

Open on Tuesday from 10am to 7pm; from Wednesday to Saturday from 9am to 7pm. Open in summer on Tuesday from 2pm to 7pm.

It is difficult to resist the temptation of chocolates, dragees, macaroons, gingerbreads, candies and other candied fruits. Enthusiast, Nicole Proust works with her favorite. The confectioneries change with the seasons. For Christmas, try the risotto or the small rum babas. The chocolates are manufactured by French and Belgian craftsman-chocolate makers who commit themselves to work only the products of high-quality, mainly resulting from the fair trade and guaranteed without GMO. Supporting the short tours and regional know-how, Chocolaterie des Cignes also selects a wide range of local produce, honey, dry macaroons and other jams carefully packed by Nicole Proust who rivals in imagination to make original box-gifts. Do not resist the temptation and mark a break in this chocolate shop, for coffee or tea and enjoy some of its delicious specialties. The chocolate shop is sometimes open to some craftsmen and thus mixes pleasure of the eyes and the tastebuds. Gourmet and Futé address.

L'ÉPICIER DES VINS DU MONDE
57, rue Gambetta ✆ +33 (0)3 85 20 84 86
contact@edvm.fr

Open Monday to Saturday from 10am to 7pm.

Eric Boirivent and his team offer a range of wines from the four corners of the world : Argentina, South Africa, Australia, New Zealand, Holland, Peru, Morocco... and of course, French wines and wines of the Mâconnais region. The store has no less than 148 references from 30 different country. An other section of the shop is mostly dedicated to champagnes with a prestigious selection of brands (Taittinger, Veuve Cliquot, Deutz...), or about 112 references. And to complete the gifts box that Epicier des Vins du Monde also offers to its guests, you will find a whole range of delicatessen including caviar, foie gras and salmon for the most elegant dishes but also spices, olive oils, mustard, jams, teas, herbal teas and other organic products.

Wines & Spirits

■ **L'ÉPICIER DES VINS DU MONDE**
57, rue Gambetta
✆ +33 (0)3 85 20 84 86
See page 271.

■ **LA PLACE AUX VINS**
56, place aux Herbes
✆ +33 (0)3 85 30 36 11
sarl.agnesmugnier@aol.com
Open on Tuesday and Wednesday from 2pm to 6pm; Thursday from 2pm to 7pm; Friday from 10am to 12pm and from 2pm to 6pm; Saturday from 9.30am to 12pm and from 2pm to 7pm.
The place is new. La Place aux vins settled down at the famous Place aux herbes, one of the historic and touristic places of the city centre of Mâcon, close to many shops and restaurants. Henri Mugnier and his wife, Agnès, open their shop in April 2014. Previously, they run Crémants Henri Mugnier in Charnay. A real institution specialised in the preparation of Crémant de Bourgogne. With their proven experience and address book of winemakers, the couple left the place for new adventures by opening this new shop. In this pleasant light and modern space, La Place aux vins offers a wide variety of Burgundy wines, crémants, champagnes, other liquors and spirits at reasonable prices but also plenty of local products : Julie's donkey milk soap, only producer of the region, located around Cluny, oil, salt, pepper, terrines of deer, honey and gingerbread provided by Mickael Rebaudet, breeder of deer and beekeeper at the Apicerf farm in Cluny, homemade jam... The warm welcome and the sympathy of the owners make the place more enjoyable. Enjoy their advice and their professionalism, they know what they are talking about. Do you need gift ideas ? La Place aux vins will provide you with the gourmet baskets which will please your friends.

In the surroundings

Arbigny

Le gîte

■ **LE MOULIN DE LA BREVETTE HOTEL**
404, chemin de la Brevette
✆ +33 (0)3 85 36 49 27
www.moulindelabrevette.com
contact@moulindelabrevette.com
Logis (2 cheminées). Qualité Tourisme label. 19 rooms. Double room from €50 to €68. Parking. Family rooms from €90 to €140. Breakfast : €9. Pets allowed (€10 per night). Free Wifi.
The favorite of the smart. A favorite that we could share with millions of televiewers, since Moulin de la Brevette won the TV programme « Bienvenue à l'Hôtel » broadcasted on TF1 ! It's normal when you know the beauty of the places and the quality of reception of Violet and Philippe Buchaillard. And even more normal when you could appreciate the nature of restoration works of this former mill of the 18th century. Lastly, all the installations are finished after 5 years work, a splendid work completed by the managers; but for each guest, it is just the beginning and a paradise opens at each stay. Far from the hustle and bustle and the noise of the world, Moulin de la Brevette is a haven of peace, a place for relaxing in the middle of a preserved nature. You will easily let yourself lulled by the noise the river, the song of the birds playing in the trees of the park. All the member of the family is very pleased, the children play on the playground and the parents can play petanque. There are no catering facilities on the spot, but a partnership with an excellent restaurant in the close vicinity for quality meals. The flowered terrace is an invitation to relaxation, reading, having a drink while discussing. And as the splendid exterior, the interior is also fully renovated ! Starting with the « new » rooms with soothing colours, with the touches evoking nature, and perfectly equipped : bathroom with shower and toilets, desk with telephone, flat-screen TV and wi-fi access. The breakfast, tasty and generous (bread, charcuterie, cheeses, brioche, cereals...), allows you to have a great start of the day. What could be more natural and more fantastic than coming to laze, to rest and to energize yourself in a mill ? One of the most smart addresses in this guide.

Chaintré

■ **LA TABLE DE CHAINTRÉ**
72, place Luminaire
✆ +33 (0)3 85 32 90 95
www.latabledechaintre.com
info@latabledechaintre.com
Closed Sunday for dinner, Monday and Tuesday. Open Wednesday to Saturday for dinner from 7pm to 9pm; Wednesday to Sunday for lunch from 12pm to 1.30pm. Set menu at €60.
Take a trip in the heart of Pouilly-Fuissé wine-growing region and make a stopover at Place de l'Eglise, in the old grocery shop of the village that became a famous restaurant whose decor has undergone a facelift. Floriane and Sébastien Grospellier are happy to offer their tasting menu that changes every Tuesday. The seasonal cuisine of La Table de Chaintré, awarded with one star, can serve more than 20-30 gourmets daily. The unique and a little unusual menu is prepared freely to exalt the best flavours of the local produces and from elsewhere. This spring, depending on the supplies, you could enjoy : The green asparagus of Domaine Saint-Vincent poached « right away », tepid egg yolks, a vinaigrette with the Parmesan of « *Vacche Rosse* » and with roasted hazelnuts, chips of pork belly of « *Cul Noir* » and young shoots from Annie Bertin; an Arctic Char of Cevennes poached slowly, served cold on a mashed potato « *Alliance* » and green onion from Annie Bertin, a vinaigrette with the sorrel and a sour cream with trout eggs; a piece of Pork

« Mangaliza/Nustrale », well-seasoned with parsley and cooked on a high-side frying pan, simmered baby carrots and small leeks from Annie Bertin, a simple juice of deglazing. The bread, made of wheat flour from organic farming, is also homemade for a cuisine full of flavours. Nice wine list. A particularly *smart* address.

■ CAVE ET CAVEAU DE CHAINTRE

Clos Reyssier
180, route de Juliénas
✆ +33 (0)3 85 35 61 61
✆ +33 (0)3 85 35 67 65
www.cavedechaintre.com
cavedechaintre@wanadoo.fr

The shop of sale is open from 9am to 12pm and from 2pm to 6pm Monday to Saturday. In summer, opening until 7pm. The vault is open every day, including public holidays, from 10am to 12.30pm and from 3pm to 7.30pm. On the Via Agrippa, the site of Chaintré is famous since ancient times and it is not surprising that the Cave de Chaintré is itself built on the site of a Gallo-Roman villa which was one of the largest wineries in the region. At Chaintré, it is not only the history and views that are exceptional, there is also a vineyard ideally exposed in the last ramparts of Macon, overlooking the plain of the Saone. The Cave Chaintré founded in 1928, is one of the oldest in France and, to our taste, one of the best. In respect of the Burgundian tradition, it offers outstanding white wines from Chardonnay, flourishing on clay-limestone soils. This cellar of human dimension, where one is always received for tasting with a smile, produces excellent Pouilly-Fuissé is regularly awarded medals, of which are a Cantrius, a Chevrieres or a Clos Reyssier. Among the other wines not miss to discover, in a large modern and bright shop, in shades of ocher and green apple are : Pouilly – vinzelles, the saint-véran, the Macon – Fuissé and Mâcon – chaintré for whites. The winery also offers a Moulin-à -vent, a saint-amour, a juliénas for red. The winery also produces a rosé wine and a delicious Crémant de Bourgogne. The shop also has some local products to complement its gourmet basket : marc de Bourgogne, creme de cassis, honey, jams ... there is a possibility of visiting the winery on booking, with commentary in French and in English.

Charnay-lès-Mâcon

■ T-BONE

103, Grande-Rue de la Coupée ✆ +33 (0)3 85 22 01 02
www.t-bone-charnay-macon.fr
hello@t-bone.fr

Open Monday to Saturday for lunch from 12pm and for dinner from 7pm. Children's menu : €8. Salads from €9 to €12, pizzas from €7.50 to €14, pasta from €6.70 to €12 and meats from €13.40 to €19. Groups welcome (reception of groups and sporting events). Terrace. Take-away. Buffets dinner with the request (on the premises or take-away) – 3 rooms – Parking.

The restaurant has expanded and there is still a lot of people of T-Bone, a guarantee of customer conquered. On site, the capacity is impressive as the quality of service. The team is fast and efficient with smiles and kind words. A Pizzeria of course, and the specialty is meat, hence its name ! Connoisseurs do not make mistakes, and often choose T-BoneVBF or Charolais steak. Others will enjoy the wide selection of pizzas (at low prices), salads, pasta or fishes. The restaurant offers, moreover, dishes and takeaway pizza. The desserts are simple but gourmet. As soon as the weather permits, the large terrace is requested. Parties are organized occasionally. A festive place, a simple and excellent value for money ! A Futé address to share.

■ BULLES DE VIE

226, rue des Petits-Champs
✆ +33 (0)3 85 38 05 51
www.bullesdevie-charnay.fr
bullesdevie.charnay@gmail.com

Open on Monday from 12pm to 8pm; Tuesday to Friday from 10am to 8pm; Saturday from 10am to 7pm. Facial : €35 (other facials from €65 to €95). Depilation : €10 (full depilation : €48). Aquasens pass of 2am for access to the aquabike, swimming pool, hammam, sauna : €25. Massages of the body : from €30 to €65. Take a break and offer yourself some oxygen bubbles. You just have to set foot at Bulles de Vie to feel already relaxed and regenerated. You will enjoy widely the fitness area which offers swimming pool, sauna and hammam and even a few kilometres on aquabike. Massage sessions of the whole body and face with various scents finish putting your body into perfect condition. The wide time slots allow the workers to have a break at noon or to get back into shape in the evening before dinner. A nice idea gift to be offered and a pleasant moment of relaxation for holidaymakers looking for comfortable spaces to get pampered or to recover vitality.

■ **ÉCLAT DE CHOCOLAT**
99 bis, Grande-Rue de la Coupée
✆ +33 (0)3 85 22 01 45
Low season : open Tuesday to Saturday from 9am to 12.30pm and from 2.30pm to 7pm. High season : Tuesday to Sunday from 9am to 12.30pm and from 2.30pm to 7pm. Low season : from November to March. High season from October to April. Intervene on order : macaroons and various verrines.
Talent, sympathy and flavours, these are the three ingredients that make up the recipe of the success of this shop run by Mickaël Martin and his wife. Talent because after having won three tablets in 2012, four in 2013, the young chocolate-maker won the silver tablet at "*Guide des croqueurs de chocolat*" in 2015. A nice consecration for this friendly couple that sculpts its chocolate delicacies with passion and showcasing the local produces. As for speciality, you will find the Rocher de Solutré consisting of a caramelized almond coated with chocolate, the Pavé de la Coupée that is a wink to Charnay, consisting of nougatine with salted butter and dried fruit and finally, the Coeur de Bourgogne composed of flakes of cassis and ganache of Madagascar. A true explosion of flavours and tasty journey for the taste buds. The Bresse's inhabitants can enjoy in their turn these delicacies, "*Eclat de Chocolat*" opens a second shop in Bourg-en-Bresse at 9 rue Pasteur. Let's get there !

Crèches-sur-Saône

■ **CHÂTEAU DE LA BARGE**
Relais du Silence
Route des Bergers
✆ +33 (0)3 85 23 93 23
www.chateaudelabarge.fr
info@chateaudelabarge.fr
Closed during the Christmas holidays. Open daily for lunch from noon to 1.30pm and for dinner from 7.30pm to 9pm. Menus from €49.50 to €93. Children's menu : €11.50. (Bistro menu). Bistrot Menu from €20 to €30 (served every day, for lunch and dinner). Four-star hotel. Rooms from €110 to €170. Breakfast : €15. Groups welcome. Garden. Terrace. Heated outdoor swimming pool.
It is a land of milk and honey located between the mountains of Mâcon and Beaujolais. Located in Southern Burgundy in a green setting that shelters, – a park of 4 hectares – a sumptuous residence and a castle of the 17th century. Open on the vines of Pouilly-Fuissé, happiness and all the team of the adorable Patrick Revoyre efficiently assisted by Juliette his daughter awaits you in all seasons. In summer, it is a pleasure to settle down on the terrace, enjoying the natural shade of the big old trees and the sweetness of life in the heated poolside. In winter, this beautiful home offers a majestic setting for your romantic dinners as well as your family meals. Chateau de la Barge is also a wonderful place to organise your wedding party, receptions, and also your seminars. The comfortable and spacious rooms offer all the tranquility and necessary comfort -largely deserved four star- to relax. It feels so good that we want to extend his stay at each visit and we enjoying his time in the lounge bar. A pleasure that undoubtedly reached its peak at the table

of Château de la Barge. Two chefs -Arnault Jarjat and Frantz Alexandre- demonstrate their talent to present fine cuisine, where tradition is combined with modernity, always for our greatest pleasure : the foie gras in all its form, snacked scallops in purses, next sweetbreads like nowhere else or a surprising sea bream and lobster that goes perfectly together or a splendid sole... Dishes that tell a story, until the dessert with a Big Bang with dark chocolate and pear pieces of sparkling brightness of sugar. The wine list is outstanding. Chateau de la Barge makes us sail towards happiness. A really Futé address. An exceptional address that was voted as best hotel in the TV programme « Bienvenue à l'hôtel » in TF1.

Dompierre-les-Ormes

■ LAB 71

2, chemin du Molard
✆ +33 (0)3 85 50 37 10
www.lab71.fr – lab71@cg71.fr

Closed on 1st of May and during Christmas holidays. Open Monday to Friday from 10am to 6pm. Free until the age of 18 (free for disabled people and accompanying them, job seekers and RSA beneficiaries). Adult : €4.50 (reduced : €4 (student)). Care for children. Guided tour (for groups : €6/person from 10 adults, €4/child). Activities.

Lab 71, a structure of the Department of Saône-et-Loire, is a place especially designed to learn while having fun on the theme of sustainable development. Scientific, educative and interactive workshops in connection with the school programs allow the young people and the families to explore the world of sciences, innovation and cultures. To be discovered on 800 m^2, exhibitions, interactive modules, workshops to better understand the evolution of the practices and the interest of a good food « between reason and excess ». Moreover, the weekends event will highlight a particular aspect of our food throughout the year. Appointment on 9th and 10th April, 4th and 5th June, 23rd and 24th July, 17th and 18th September and 8th and 9th October. Note that discovery workshops for the entire family are offered on Tuesdays, Wednesdays and Thursdays during school holidays.

Prissé

VIGNERONS DES TERRES SECRETES
Les Grandes Vignes

✆ +33 (0)3 85 37 64 89
✆ +33 (0)3 85 36 60 64
www.terres-secretes.com
contact@terres-secretes.fr

Low season : open Monday to Saturday from 9am to 12.30pm and from 1.30pm to 6.30pm; Sunday from 9am to 12.30pm and from 2pm to 6.30pm. High season : Monday to Saturday from 9am to 12.30pm and from 1.30pm to 7pm; Sunday from 9am to 12.30pm and from 2pm to 7pm. Caveau Lamartine in Sologny. Opening hours : Tuesday to Sunday from 9.30am to 12.30pm and from 3pm to 7pm. Manoir des Grandes Vignes 3 épis Gîte de France : 11 rooms in group cottage. Rate : €22.50 per night and per person. Car Park.

The unique cooperative cellar in the perimeter of the Grand Site Solutré-Pouilly-Vergisson is awaiting you, where you will discover the two shops located at Chai de Prissé and Caveau de Sologny ! To facilitate the access to this know-how, the vine growers of the secret grounds have carefully decorated with flower the external edges of the cellar. There is a large car park for bus transporting group. A caravan with five locations is available for a night stay. The wine-growers of the secret grounds bring together 120 professionals spread on nearly 950 ha including 650 in Chardonnay. Respectful of the territory, they are committed to a sustainable development approach that includes 37 commitments to preserve the environment, from the stages of the wine production to the local life. It is by the way the objective that Boutique de Prissé organises every third weekend of October for 20 years, the gourmet weekend with culinary demonstration, tasting and exposition of the art and food craft. You just raise your eyes towards Roche de Solutré and Vergisson and you will be aware of the importance of the remarkable sites that surround the vineyards of the Vignerons des Terres Secrètes whose wines are equally remarkable. The production includes a wide range of appellations from the most beautiful villages of the region called the « Lieux-dits » : Saint-Véran Croix de Monceau, Mâcon Milly-Lamartine, Mâcon La Roche-Vineuse for white wines, Mâcon Pierreclos for red ones. Another range features « les Sentinelles » from old vineyards with reduced efficiency but with prestigious wines : Pouilly-Fuissé, Mâcon-Villages, Mâcon-Rouge. You should not forget : Crémant de Bourgogne, light, which can be enjoyed natural as long as the art of the bubble is controlled. For your comfort and pleasure, Vignerons des Terres Secrètes offers you a stay in Manoir des Grandes Vignes (3 épis Gîte de France), cottage including 11 rooms (in weekdays starting from 10 people and the weekend starting from 25 people) if you come in group. Call ✆ 03 85 37 84 99.

Saint-Laurent-sur-Saône

AU FEU DE BOIS

121, rue de la Levée ✆ +33 (0)3 85 39 27 65
www.au-feu-de-bois.com
contact@au-feu-de-bois.com

Closed Saturday for lunch and Sunday all day. Menu from €13 to €22. À la carte : Around €14. Children's menu : €8.50. Lunch menu : €13 (starter + main course + dessert). Daily special : €9 - Main course and dessert : €11. Express menu : €16.20. Pizza from €9.70 to €11.80. Terrace. Take-away.

The pizzeria « Au feu de bois » has a large number of regulars among Mâconnais and Bressans. The house proposes nearly 35 different pizzas with the most varied toppings (calzone, snails, bacon, seafood, mozzarella...) but also the traditional cuisine (pasta, gnocchis, flank steak with shallot, tartiflette, beef carpaccio, homemade hamburger...) and the regional specialties (andouillettes, Bresse chickens, Charolais meat...). The stones and exposed beams without forgetting the tablecloths on the tables give a certain charm to the spacious dining room. The facade was renovated. Cooked in a wood-burning oven of more than 400 years, the pizzas are delicious, at the same time fine, crusty and odorous as desired ! Living space, the pizzeria also exhibits photographs of artists. A gourmet and authentic address, a very Futé address.

■ A LA TÊTE DE LARD
194, quai Bouchacourt
✆ +33 (0)3 85 38 74 38
www.alatetedelard.fr
Closed on Tuesday and Wednesday. Open Thursday to Monday for lunch and dinner. Closed only Tuesday in summer. Booking advised. Menu from €20 to €30 (stay-at-home out of pot : €18.50. Cassoulet of pigs feet out of pot : €17.50). Children's menu : €8. Daily special : €9 (starter + main course + dessert €13. Between + main course or main course and dessert €11). Air-conditioned room. Terrace.
Who does not know « La tête de lard » on the banks of Saint-Laurent island. The address is known for its spacious dining rooms and its huge terrace and especially for its red checked tablecloths typical of bouchons lyonnais. The decoration is authentic, wooded, in traditional bistro way and immediately gives an impression of warmth. The cuisine typical of the bouchons lyonnais is resolutely traditional. Here, the pork is king and in the pork, everything is delicious. Starting from the sauerkraut stuffed with grilled slice of bacon through the cold cuts platter or andouillette, « La tête de lard » keeps its promises. The house also cooks veal, beef and Saone obliges, some fish. The restaurant also offers ready-made meals, special aperitif with charcuterie or pots for the most gourmet like the beef stew in a pot or the cassoulet of pig's trotters in a pot too ! In the summer, it is better to book in advance. Despite its fifty places, the tables is often full. The rich and delicious cuisine, the beauty of the banks of Saone without forgetting the sympathy of the team are very valuable there.

Saint-Amour-Bellevue

■ CAVEAU DE SAINT-AMOUR
Plâtre-Durand
✆ +33 (0)3 85 37 15 98
tourisme@saint-amour-bellevue.fr
Opening hour : Tuesday to Saturday 10 : 00 at 12 : 00 and 15 : 00 at 19 : 00 Sunday the 10th H at 12 : 00 and 14 : 30 at 18 : 30 - closed Monday.
The cellar of Saint-Amour-Bellevue accommodates you in his lovely vaulted cellar and will make you discover the joys of the local wines. The territory producing the saint-amour is of a surface of 320 ha and produces one of rarest Beaujolais crus. From the granitic sub-soil, made up of clay and silica, the floor of the surrounding vineyards is only suitable for the black gamay with white juice, which most Beaujolais presented are resulting. Evoking fruit and flower, the Saint-Amour has a velvet dress, crimson red, a brightness of ruby, and a delicate flavor of red fruit raised of a floral touch of peony. Balanced, with the delicate roundnesses, it will appear after a maturing period of 2 or 3 years. The cellar offers a nice anthology of the wines from the locality, choice supplemented by a selection of wines of the neighbouring territories.

Solutré-Pouilly

■ GRAND SITE DE FRANCE
SOLUTRÉ POUILLY VERGISSON
Maison du Grand Site
✆ +33 (0)3 85 35 82 81
www.solutre.com
grandsite@cg71.fr
Closed on January 1st, on May 1st and the 24.25 and December 31st. Low season : open every day from 10am to 5pm. High season : every day from 10am to 6pm. Museum of prehistory : open every day from 10am to 6pm from April to September, from 10am to 12pm and from 2pm to 5pm from October to March. Free. Rates for the museum : adult : €3.50, groups : €2.50, students : €2. Free admission for under 18-year-olds and for all first Sunday of the month. Tourism label & Disability. In 2012, special mention of the jury « heritages for all, heritages for chacun ». Children welcome (entertainment for the pupils). Guided tour (with a guide of country). Catering facilities (open as of April and until September). Shop. Activities.
Real entrance to the site of Solutré-Pouilly-Vergisson, the Maison du Grand Site is a reception structure which offers to the public a large number of services (snack, shop, toilets, etc.). Its aim is to make known the heritage of the territory. The Maison du Grand Site is a way of developing the Grand Site of Solutré-Pouilly Vergisson, which has gained the Grand Site De France label in 2013. A beautiful recognition for this heritage which was also favoured the former president, François Mitterrand, who never missed his ascent of the rock of Solutré each year. The Maison du Grand Site is the gateway to the Musée départemental de la Préhistoire, and the botanical and archaeological park. It houses a permanent exhibition which is dedicated to the history of the landscape and its preservation, a shop to get the maximum number of books and souvenir objects, a catering place, terraces, a heated picnic room, three activities rooms and toilets. Continue the discovery of the Grand Site with the visit of the Musée de la Préhistoire de Solutré, located at the foot of the rock of Solutré, an ancient hunting site frequented for 50,000 years. Redesigned and revitalised in 2014, the museum offers a new museography, new collections, themed exhibitions and shows. The archaeological and botanical garden located on the site of excavations completes the museum. It also contains a large variety of plant species that are typical of the natural habitat and the significant results of archaeological research. The ways to discover the richness of the Grand Site's landscapes in all its forms are numerous : take the paths of green Walks or stroll on donkey back to discover the village of Vergisson. Paragliding flights are also organised : thrills guaranteed and breathtaking landscapes !

Vinzelles

LE RESTAURANT DU CAVEAU DE VINZELLES

100, Terres Neyme
✆ +33 (0)3 85 35 61 10
www.restaurant-caveau-vinzelles.com

Open daily for lunch. Open for dinner starting from 25 people. Children's menu : €7.50. Menu at €12 (except weekends and public holidays), €18 and €25. Baby chairs. Terrace. Parking.

The reason why you make a research in *Petit Futé* is to profit from beautiful region that includes both eating pleasures, pleasures of wine and the pleasure of being together. Don't look for any further, you found this address : the restaurant of Caveau de Vinzelles. More crucial as it is located nearby (1 km) a highway exit – fill your spare time and indulge yourself with pleasure ! – and that it is leaned on the famous Cave des Grands Crus Blancs and with a tasting cellar. An address that has the good taste to open daily for lunch and had a plan to open a pizzeria during our visit (at the level vault) to vary the pleasures (also open every day and on Friday and Saturday evening). Note that Jerôme, the owner, had run Italian restaurant for 10 years in Macon). The restaurant, meanwhile, continues to treat us with excellent traditional cuisine, prepared with quality ingredients : a salad of calf's foot to start, a Bobosse andouillette, calf's head with gribiche sauce, pot-au-feu scallops and prawns with pouilly fuissé – a little wonder –, a beautiful beef steak or Burgundy snails to continue. Finish with a real rum baba. Enough to really enjoy oneself. Is it necessary to talk about wine list ? Of course, it bears the colours of the nearby cellar, between the big Blanc de Bourgogne and Beaujolais vintage. Recommended excellent pieces of advice for a perfectly attuned with the best rates. A particularly *Futé* address.

CAVE DES GRANDS CRUS BLANCS

2367, route des Allemands
✆ +33 (0)3 85 27 05 70
✆ +33 (0)3 85 35 61 10
www.lesgrandscrusblancs.com

Open Monday to Saturday and public holidays from 9am to 12.30pm and from 1.30pm to 6.30pm. The restaurant opens Sundays and public holidays. Meal at midday, service dinner by reservation. Online sales.

Located in the heart of the vineyards of Mâconnais, Cave des Grands Crus Blancs is a beautiful space dedicated to wine. It is impossible to miss it from the road since the hotel operated a vast makeover by repainting its façade in bright red. The nearby flower bed was dressed with large giant glass and a decoration symbolising the universe of the cellars and wine. An original dressing that highlights all the wines produced by this large hotel. The white wines are obviously honoured and you can find the Pouilly-Vinzelles, Pouilly-Fuissé but also Mâcon Chaintré and Mâcon Loché among others. But the house does not only produce white wines. It produces also quality intense and deep red wines like Saint-Amour,

Juliénas, Chénas or Beaujolais in store without forgetting Crémant de Bourgogne (raw, half-dry, rosé), that you can enjoy in their natural state. In the shop, you can take the time to taste before making your choice and a space is even dedicated to children who can read and play on the spot. The restaurant, which adjoins the cellar, allows you to prolong the pleasure. There again, important works have been carried out. The room was recently renovated, the decor modernised til the menu that was remodelled by offering pizzas to enjoy on the spot or to take away in addition to traditional dishes. The restaurant also continues to offer sale of wine.

MESVRES

The peaceful Valley of Arroux lazily goes between the forests of the Morvanand and the Charolais groves, till the Loire. Nature is everywhere and there are many hiking trails, horseback riding and cycling. The guidebook with 12 thematic tours (forest, fishing...) in Beuvray in Val d'Arroux, long of 4 km to 16 km, could be obtained at the visitor's centre, the town hall or in cafes of the regions. But this green case is also a paradise for fishermen, three rivers (Arroux, the Mesvrin and Braconne) and five ponds for all types of fishing.

Mont Beuvray

Mount Beuvray is located in the south of the Morvan Regional Natural Park. At a height of 820 m, it dominates the valley of Arroux and is the starting point for many tours of natural sites and numerous hiking trails. It owes its fame to its Gallic history since it was once the capital of Eduens, the powerful Bibracte. High place of knowledge with a rich natural heritage, it is one of the most visited sites of Morvan.

BIBRACTE, MUSÉE DE LA CIVILISATION CELTIQUE ★★

Mont-Beuvray
✆ +33 (0)3 85 86 52 35
www.bibracte.fr
info@bibracte.fr

The museum is open from March 12th to November 13th, 2016, from 10am to 6pm and until 7pm in July and August. Exceptional opening until 10pm Wednesdays in July and August. Possibility of opening all year for groups, by reservation. Free for under 12-year-olds (and for €3 the child of a family). Adult : €7.50 (reduced rate : €5.50). Rate Passport (visit of the site, the museum and the temporary exhibition) : 12€ for an adult; 10€ in reduced rate. Rate Gallic Day (visit of the site, the museum and the temporary exhibition + meal to the Cauldron) 27€ for an adult; 12,50€ in reduced rate. Tourism label & Disability. For the reception of disabled people, please contact the following address e-mail : p.plaza@bibracte.fr. Children welcome (stroller three wheels any ground and baby carriers lent free to the museum). Guided tour. Catering facilities (Le Chaudron restaurant, baby chair). Shop. Activities.

Located in the heart of Burgundy, Bibracte is an extraordinary natural and archaeological site, labelled Grand Site de France since 2007. This label was renewed in 2013 for a further 6 years period. Nestled in the stunning setting of the regional natural park of the Morvan, the Bibracte archaeological site invites you to discover the riches of the Celtic civilisation of the 2nd and 1st century before Christ. In fact, the antique city of Bibracte was built on Mont Beuvray by the Gallic people of Eduens. It is also in Bibracte that Vercingétorix held the first general uprising of the Gallic tribe against the Romans in 52 BC. Stretching over 200 hectares, this magnificent site offers a large number of activities to visitors where the pleasure to discover a majestic nature mingles with scientific and historical knowledge.

The Bibrate site houses a rich museum on Gallic life, installed on the slopes of Mount Beuvray. The permanent exhibition allows you to discover the Celtic civilisation and to better understand the utility of the *oppida*, fortified towns that played the role of economic and political centres. These oppida are often coinsidered as the first towns of the north of the Alps. At Bibracte, you can find thrilling archeological pieces as well as replica and video. These cultural mediation processes allow visitors to place them into the history and to get themselves to the daily life of our ancestors. The site of the archeological excavation is visitble throughout the year. The nature is also worth a detour. Mont Beuvray is covered by a 1,000 ha forest of beech softwood. During the fine weather, you can even see the Mont Blanc. Bribracte is an exceptional natural and archeological site that offers you a historic stroll in an obiquitous and magnificent nature.

In the surroundings

Bibracte

LE CHAUDRON DE BIBRACTE
Mont Beuvray
✆ +33 (0)3 85 86 52 40
Every day in August July from 11am to 6pm, from 11am to 5pm apart from these two months (exact dates on the website of the museum). Booking is essential. Set menu at €18. Children's menu : €12 (for the child of less than 12 years). Picnic basket, €8 and €15. Snack at €8.
Be prepared to live an archaeological and gourmet experience ! Here, you will discover how the Gallic cooked, with ingredients and ustensils they used. You will awaken your palates with dry vegetables and cereals, aromatic plants, very used in the Gallic dishes. On the menu : « Dunno-uindos », cabbage macerated and lentils sauce cumin – « Laros-bostia », chicken with spinaches and crushed wheat sauce with mushrooms – « Becos », fresh cheese with honey – « CaloCatanos – Melissos », rolled of prunes with poppy. A Barley beer to accompany all this ! In order for you experience to be complete, you will taste your meal in tableware copied from the Celtic tableware, with wooden spoon and knife (but no fork !).

HÔTEL DU MORVAN*
Le Bourg ✆ +33 (0)3 85 82 51 06
www.hot
eldumorvan.com
contact@hoteldumorvan.com
7 rooms. Double room from €37 to €51. Half-board (from €50 to €114). Breakfast : €7.40. Menu from €15.50 to €28.10. Card. Free Wifi.
In the middle of the Morvan, this establishment is the perfect place to explore the local wealth. Overlooking the charming square, the hotel has a human scale since it has only 7 rooms. Comfortable and cozy, you will like them by their authentism and the welcome offered by your hosts is very friendly. As for the restaurant, you will be able to enjoy of a local cuisine, homemade, with some local specialties. Very pleasant !

La Boulaye

LE MOULIN RÉNOVÉ
Le Bois du Caveau ✆ +33 (0)3 85 79 58 43
www.chambres-hotes-la-boulaye.com
torrione.christian@wanadoo.fr
5 rooms. From €90 to €150. Breakfast included. Free Wifi. Sauna.
Le Moulin Rénové is aptly named ! Back in 1835 it was an oil mill, it is now a superbly restored building, discrete refuge of your romantic getaways in the land of Burgundy. 5 rooms are at your disposal : comfortable and all harmoniously decorated, they offer very beautiful volumes since some of them are on two floors. Antique furniture settles in the lounge and the desk which you will have the leisure to find in all the rooms. The spacious dining room will be pleasant for the breakfasts by the fireplace, and the garden will accommodate the table d'hôte in the early summer heat. A sauna and a pool sublimate this place which will charm you !

Etang-sur-Arroux

LES GOURMETS
45, rue Gabriel-Bouthière
✆ +33 (0)3 85 54 11 75
Daily menu €12. Terrace.
An establishment which is really aptly named ! Here, the gourmets and gourmands will be at ease, and their palate will be satisfied ! A cuisine with regional touches, fully realized with seasonal ingredients, to sublimate its bitronomic character. So, you will be able to enjoy a green and red tomato gazpacho, to continue with a quail stuffed with oyster mushrooms and roquefort and carrots fondant, unless you are tempted by the lobster navarin with seasonal vegetables, then you will fall for the Breton shortbread with strawberries and creamy with the vanilla of Madagascar. All with finesse and subtlety of flavours, we love it !

MONTCEAU-LES-MINES ★

JÉRÔME BROCHOT
7, place Beaubernard
✆ +33 (0)3 85 67 95 30
www.jeromebrochot.com
jb@jeromebrochot.com
Hotel closed Sunday for dinner and opening from 5pm Saturday. Open Tuesday to Sunday for lunch and dinner. Booking advised. Menu from €49 to €110. À la carte : Around €50. Children's menu : €18 (for children under 12 years old). Lunch menu : €29 (Tuesday to Friday, except weekend and public holidays). Cookery classes Saturday morning : €90 /pers, groups of 8 to 10 people Groups welcome. Baby chairs. Terrace. Pets allowed.
Jérôme Brochot welcomes you in his spacious and cozy restaurant which can accommodate couples and family meals. The decoration is contemporary, the warm colors and bright. In the kitchen, Jérôme Brochot, 1 Michelin star since more than 10 years now, works wonders and attracts celebrities scrolling in his establishment. It should be said that he made his ranges with the greatest : Loiseau, Blanc, Lameloise. Now, it is a cuisine close to the Burgundian local that he proposes all while

decorating it of new flavours. Thus, the eggs meurette with red Santenay are available with a fricassée of small onions, smoked bacon and mushrooms of the moment, the simmered poulard of Bresse is deglazed with crémant de Bourgogne and is accompanied by Carnaroli rice with chicken broth and young vegetables. As for the dessert, we advise you the fine pie with raspberries with bitter almond cream and its unstructured vacherin with Burgundy blackcurrant. An explosion of flavours, a colourful painting, a real delight ! Tuesday to Friday, at lunchtime, let yourself be guided by the chef and his inspiration, it is worth the detour. The curious ones will prolong the experience by following the chef cooking classes. An essential address to discover in Montceau.

PARAY-LE-MONIAL ★★

Knife & Fork

LE BOSSU

Z.A. du Champ-Bossu
✆ +33 (0)3 85 88 02 33 – www.lebossu.fr

Open all year. Monday to Saturday from 9.30am to 7.30pm; Sunday from 10.30am to 3pm. Dinner by reservation. Menu from €20 to €25. Children's menu : €7.50. (€11.50 and €13.50. Daily special €9). Groups welcome (180 seats. 3 rooms). Baby chairs. Terrace.

For a lunch break or a small snack with the family, Le Bossu welcomes you in a spacious setting, with warm colors and contemporary spirit. Fresh products, Charolais meat from local producers, creative ideas, here are some that we propose you to taste : salad of lemon-flavoured fennel and smoked coalfish, Charolais beef tartare with knife, tiramisu dessert with red fruits. A beautiful terrace completes the whole, and the opening 7 days a week is appreciated.

BRASSERIE DE LA POSTE

Cours Jean-Jaurès
✆ +33 (0)3 85 81 69 97 / +33 (0)6 98 92 00 30
www.brasseriedelaposte.net

Set menu at €21.80. Children's menu : €6.50. Daily special : €8. À la carte. Groups welcome (from 10 to 70 people). Terrace.

It is in the heart of the historical districts of the city, in the old covered market, that the chef Xavier Bonnot welcomes you. This brasserie with contemporary tones offers simple, tasty and generous cuisine, based mainly on local and seasonal products. On the menu, you will find the sausage of Marius, the flank and Charolais rib steak with Béarnaise sauce for example, duck breasts with candied red wine, roasted zander and its sorrel sauce, and as for sweet treats, tarte tatin, chocolate mousse and profiteroles are obviousl part of it !

LA TAVERNE

Route de l'Aérodrôme ✆ +33 (0)3 85 88 85 49
www.lataverne-paray.fr
lataverne.paraylemonial@gmail.com

Open all year. Wednesday to Sunday and public holidays from 11.30am to 3pm and from 5.30pm to 11pm. Menu from €15 to €27. Lunch menus, except Saturday and public holidays, from €8.50 to €13. À la carte. Groups welcome.

Do you want a warm, cozy, or very cocooning atmosphere ? So do not hesitate, come to La Taverne. In the room with fireplace or in the veranda flooded with light, you will appreciate the setting, and even more the cuisine offered here. It is generous, tasty, simple, and is renewed twice a year with a summer menu and a menu for the cold period. The dishes of the mountain are mixed with salted pancakes and swords of la Taverne, planchas and large fresh salads. Private parties are organized every Monday and Tuesday on booking.

Going Out

AU CAPPUCCIO'

Place de la Visitation
✆ +33 (0)3 85 81 06 80
au-cappuccio@hotmail.fr

Terrace. Take-away.

Au Cappuccio' is a small cozy tea room. The Italian music sets the tone from the entrance. The house speciality is of course the iced cappucino. The owner also offers a wide choice of pasta dishes generously decorated with Italian sauce (penne, fagottini, tagliatelle, carbonara, arrabbiata, pesto, bolognese...). And for dessert, the guest can enjoy the delicious ice granites crushed as well as milkshakes with a choice of 18 flavours (banana, cherries, kiwi, berries. . .), or one of the 12 hot chocolate flavours, without forgetting the organic green tea with lamenthe and fresh fruit juices. Very pleasant terrace in fine weather.

Shopping

LE MARIGNY

8, place Lamartine
✆ +33 (0)3 85 81 06 35

Open Monday to Saturday from 7am to 7pm; Sunday from 7am to 12.30pm. Online store.

Located at the foot of Tour Saint Nicolas since 1900, Le Marigny is a gift shop selling religious items, including icons made in Paray-Le-Monial, monastic products with in particular cosmetic products manufactured by the Benedictine nuns of Bouzy la Forêt and Chantelle abbey, but also Burgundy souvenirs items like snowballs, collection or mugs.

PÂTISSERIE CHOCOLATERIE CHARLES PUBILL
25, avenue Charles-de-Gaulle
✆ +33 (0)3 85 81 11 38
Open every day from 7.30am to 8pm.
Getting into the shop of Charles Pubill, it is a step in the delicacy ! This master chocolate maker has the donation to carry out sweets, pastry and chocolate, which will delight your taste buds. From the traditional Easter eggs, via the gingerbreads and fruit pasta for Christmas, chocolate box and figurine to be crunched, the tiles with amandesou still the marron glacé, entremets, and melting logs, everything here is source of culpability ! But what a delights ! We cordially recommend it that is not to say !

ROMANÈCHE-THORINS ★

Romanèche-Thorins, wine mecca, can be accessed via Fuissé, Saint-Veran, Saint-Amour and Julienas... Many evocative names for grands crus and vineyards landscape with changing colours depending on the seasons. Arrived in Macon by joining the N6.

MUSÉE DÉPARTEMENTAL DU COMPAGNONNAGE ★
Le Bourg
✆ +33 (0)3 85 35 22 02
www.musee-compagnonnage.cg71.fr
Next to the Town Hall
Open all year long. Low season : every day from 14h to 18h. High season : every day from 10h to 18h. Free until 18 years old. Adult : 4 €. Group : 3 €. Students and companions : 3 €. Audio-guide in French, English, German and Dutch. Notebook game for children. Shop. Entertainments.
The companion is etymologically someone with whom we share bread. But Compagnonnage, in the sense that it was registered in the Masterpieces of the Oral and Intangible Heritage of Humanity in 2010, is sharing more than the bread with its neighbour : it shares its knowledge. Everyone has heard about Compagnonnage, but few really know where it comes from and what it really is. This Musée Départemental du Compagnonnage succeed in the challenge of showing us the history of this vocational training institution, whose peculiarity was the long journey during which the young apprentices would « enrich » humanly and professionally by getting into contact with the more experienced, forming the most skilled labour. A real « masterpiece » as you can admire inside the museum through the collective works of the companion, who made their Tour De France. It is through the history of Pierre-François Guillon, who left Romanèche-Thorins in 1866 to follow his carpenter training, that we have an insight on the significance of this transmission of professional gestures, accompanied by morals and a genuine spirituality. This young Companion founded in 1871 the School of Trait, where he has taught the framework, the staircase, the joinery and the carved stone to students from all over the world for 52 years. This museum, built in 1928 by the General Council of Saône-et-Loire, does not only house incredible masterpieces, diagrams, indicating the way in which the materials were worked, models and the symbolic of the Companions. Renovated and expanded in 1994, the museum also hosts now regularly temporary exhibitions. From 2nd May to 2nd November 2016, the museum offers the exhibition *Labyrinthe,* by the collective of sculptors and engravers Towards-Places. Each of the 9 artists, with its specific techniques, ventures in the infinite possibility of the maze.

TOUROPARC ZOO ★★
La Maison Blanche
400, rue du Parc
✆ +33 (0)3 85 35 51 53
www.touroparc.com
information@touroparc.com
♿
The zoological gardens are opened all the year, except the 24.25, December 31st and January 1st. Opened the every day as from 9 : 00. Attractions function all the year. In July and August, the watery tobbogans are accessible from 13 : 30 to 17 : 30. Possible catering facilities on the spot and picnic tables at disposal. Free for under 3-year-olds. Adult : €18.90 (€21.90 July and August). Child (from 3 to 12 years old) : €15.90 (€18.90 July and August). Annual pass : €55 for the adults, €47 for the children. Visit privilege on booking. Holiday voucher. Children welcome. Catering facilities. Shop.
Surrounded by real nature enthusiasts, immerse yourself into the animal world by sharing a new vision at Touroparc.zoo. Touroparc.zoo is a formidable project undertaken by Doctor Franck Chaduc for the animal cause – in particular for the conservation of endangered species and the protection of nature – which takes life in a green environment, with animal welfare as priority. In the middle of Beaujolais, at 30 minutes from Lyon, Touroparc.zoo offers another vision, another approach of the animals. Within a natural setting of 12 hectares, where the original environments are reconstituted by passionates, more than 700 animals belonging to 140 different species bloom in all serenity. Discovering Touroparc.zoo, it means taking height like giraffes of the West which look at you in the eyes on the Sentinel, living a astonishing face to face with all the boarders and having a new vision on the animal world. Without forgetting the *rencontres-soigneurs*, which is a privileged moments during which the animalist will tell you about their dear animal and will answer all your questions. Touroparc.zoo shows new points of view and is a ludic day with the entertainments like the monorail, the tree climbing, the old bangers, the carrousel and the mini train. A refreshment center during the summer with water slides (in July and August), the paddling pool and plenty of discovery for kids and adults. A visit where all the family get educated and has fun in the same day : it is really *Futé* !

SENNECEY-LE-GRAND ★

LE SENNECEY

15, avenue du 4-Septembre-1944
✆ +33 (0)3 85 44 82 34
www.restaurant-le-sennecey.com

Open Thursday to Tuesday for lunch; Friday and Saturday for dinner. Open for dinner on weekdays on request for the group meals. Menu from €26.50 to €30.50. À la carte : Around €30. Lunch menu : €13. Desserts : €7. Chèque Restaurant. Groups welcome (by reservation). Terrace.

Le Sennecey is a magnificent little place located in the heart of Sennecey-le-Grand, along the main street. The restaurant, full of charm, with its elegant and simple décor, is run by Magali and Damien. The house offers traditional and simple cuisine with two main menus and a menu on weekdays at lunchtime. Among all the homemade dishes, Le Petit Futé recommend as starter the frogs with parsley or chicken liver terrine and its comptée with red onions. You will continue with chicken breast with morels served with fresh tagliatelle or charolais beef steak in Bordeaux way and its dauphinois gratin. You will finish the desserts with half-cooked chocolate or iced nougat or you can choose the cheese plate. The house offers a nice wine list with wines from Beaujolais, Bourgogne or Alsace. In summer, the terrace offers a nice setting for lunch even if the proximity of the road is not ideal. A pretty little unpretentious address which looks after its products and favours the 100% homemade.

TOURNUS ★★

Known since the sixth century due to shrine dedicated to Saint Valerian who came to preach here and died a martyr, the city became a religious centre in the ninth century, with monks from Noirmoutier who took the relics of their saint patron Philibert with them. Many know Tournus as a historic and gastronomic place. From the A6 motorway, we perceive both imposing and majestic towers of the abbey overlooking the proud medieval city. We discover while strolling downtown and along the picturesque alleys, shops or many mansions. Stretching along the Saône between the Bresse plain and the hills of southern Burgundy, Tournus is also a place of living and a popular place for holidays. Many activities are possible due to a local dynamism and an ecologically preserved environment. Hiking, cycling or horse trails and individual navigation, guided or on cruise, Tournus opens the doors of the South.

Tournus.

OFFICE DE TOURISME DE TOURNUS
2, place de l'Abbaye
✆ +33 (0)3 85 27 00 20
www.tournugeois.fr
Open Monday to Saturday from 9.30am to 1pm and from 2pm to 6.45pm; Sunday and public holidays from 10am to 1pm and from 2pm to 6.45pm. Firm at 6pm from March to June and in October and at 5pm in January, February, November and December.
The welcome is warm at the Tourist Office of Tournugeois right next to the abbey. You will find all the necessary documents and practical information to discover the town of Tournus and the surrounding villages there. Feel free to ask for advice to the agents who will make you known the little trick.
Award-winning of the 2015 competition EDEN 2015 on the theme « Gastronomie et tourisme local », the town of Tournus and the entire Tournugeois are rich gastronomic events such as the markets, gourmet walks in summer and in particular, the Franco-Gourmande festival which takes place in June. Explore also the natural pathways by using green walks winding through the local countryside without forgetting the Voie bleu that offers an exceptional discovery tour on foot, by bicycle or on horseback along the Saône. Finally, do not miss to make a break in the Tourist Office because the hotel is located in the heart of the tourist activities, between the must-visit abbey, craft shops which provide good gift ideas and the cafés that offer a beautiful gourmet break in a setting full of history and charm.

Sightseeing

ABBAYE SAINT-PHILIBERT ★★
12, Place des Arts
✆ +33 (0)3 85 51 03 76 / +33 (0)3 85 27 00 20
www.tournugeois.fr
In the city -centre of Tournus. Next to the tourism Office, a minutes walk from Tournus.
Open all year. Low season : every day and public holidays from 9am to 6pm. High season : every day and public holidays from 8am to 7pm. Mass Sunday at 10.30am. Audioguide : €5. Rental at the Tourist Office. Guided tour (for groups by reservation).
You can see the Saint-Philibert abbey, the only monastery of the 12th century preserved in Europe, when you arrive at Tournus. At night, its large illuminated towers that overlook the city are a feast for the eye. A Romanesque architecture jewel, the abbey was built by monks fleeing the Noirmoutiers to house the relics of their founder, St Philibert. Visit : the abbey church, the cloister, the chapter house, the refectory and the cellar. The crypt and the upper chapel also deserve a visit. A real living place, the abbey is not only a religious building, it shelters all year round many events and exhibitions, handicraft markets including *Salon des Antiquaires* which has hosted for over 40 years in the cellar of the monks without forgetting many concerts and recitals enhanced by the particular sound offered by the place.

MAIRIE DE TOURNUS
Place de l'Hôtel-de-Ville
✆ +33 (0)3 85 27 03 20
www.tournus.fr – mairie@tournus.fr
Open on Tuesday from 9am to 12pm and from 1.45pm to 5pm. On the premises, leaflets on the spot to visit in Tournugeois and of the practical information.
Small town of a little more than 5,000 inhabitants located halfway between Mason and Chalon-sur-Saône, Tournus called the « Porte du sud », won in 2015, the EDEN contest on the theme of gastronomy and local tourism This distinction rewards Tournus and its residents for its actions for the promotion of local gastronomy. In summer, the city attracts many visitors charmed by the historic aspect of the city, its many traboules, its docks of the Saône and of course, its good gourmet addresses. Numerous yachtmen make a stop along the Saône and stay a few days in the city to take profit from the big market day on Saturday. Not to miss : the visit of the Saint-Philibert abbey, jewel of 12th century ! Other crucial places : Hôtel-Dieu hosting the Greuze museum and the museum of the bicycle which recalls the history of the little queen. And of course, Tournus is not gourmet city for nothing. The city with not less than four starred chefs and excellent tables to taste without moderation !

Knife & Fork

LA BOHÈME
57, rue de la République
✆ +33 (0)3 85 32 97 03
Located in the centre of Tournus, in the pedestrian street, within walking distance of the cinema and the town hall.
♿
Open all year. Thursday to Tuesday for lunch from 12pm to 1.45pm; Thursday to Sunday for dinner from 7pm to 8.45pm. Closed Monday for dinner, Tuesday for dinner and Wednesday all day. Closed Sunday for dinner in low season. Menu from €15 to €21 (menu at €21 for dinner). Children's menu : €8. Lunch menu : €13 (daily special : €8). Holiday voucher, Chèque Restaurant. Groups welcome. Terrace.
The setting of this small restaurant of about thirty seats is really warm and friendly. The space is small but gives a cocooning side which is rather pleasant. Almost all the tables have a view of the central kitchen where you can see the chef working live. The menu is light and not very loaded because everything is homemade. On the menu : try the pike quenelles, the duck breast or the free-range chicken. As for dessert, try the Swiss tart with homemade apple sauce and raspberries or choose the gourmet coffee. The latter changes every day and faith of Petit Futé, it is really delicious and copious. Well, consider leaving room for dessert, you will not be disappointed.

BRASSERIE LE PARISIEN
12, quai Nord
✆ +33 (0)3 85 32 15 29
Located on the banks of the saône, close to shops and the city centre.
♿

In summer, open daily for lunch and dinner, except Thursday all day. The rest of the year, open daily for lunch and dinner, except Sunday for dinner, Wednesday for dinner and Thursday all day. À la carte : Around €20. Free Wifi. Holiday voucher, Chèque Restaurant. Groups welcome. Baby chairs. Terrace. Pets allowed. Bar.

With its view of the Saône, its terrace open in summer and its traditional menus at affordable prices, the brasserie Le Parisien is a good address recommended by Petit Futé for lunch. Tourists are not misled and at noon in summer, the terrace is often full. It must be said that the place looks like a small coastal restaurant. It's normal for a brasserie named after an old boat that was used to transport goods and travellers, three times a week, between Chalon and Lyon, at a time when the river transport was booming. To honour this time, the restaurant sets up the large model of a beautiful boat. As for the cuisine, traditional card and menus with Burgundy snails as starters, casserole sweetbreads, fresh ham, free-range chicken and steak in the dishes. The wine list offers a good selection of Burgundy wines. A sympathetic address and not expensive.

MEULIEN
1 bis, avenue des Alpes
✆ +33 (0)3 85 51 20 86 – www.meulien.com
vmeulien@wanadoo.fr

Open Wednesday to Saturday for lunch and dinner; Sunday for lunch. Booking is essential. Menu from €41 to €92. À la carte : Around €60. Children's menu : €25. Wine by the glass. Groups welcome. Large car park in the back of the restaurant.

The restaurant of Valéry and Véronique Meulien is always full. Especially in the evening, the address attracts a large number of guests. We must say it is owing to kindness and the warm welcome that the couple and the whole team managed to seduce many people. As the restaurant Meulien is now part of the Michelin-starred addresses and it joined the closed circle of the best restaurants in Tournus. It is evidenced by its recent participation in the festival Franco-Gourmandes. Slight rise of prices did not prevent guests from eating there, knowing they will find their happiness. The reason is that the restaurant has performed wonders for many years. On the plate, the pleasure of the eyes precedes the pleasure of the stomach. The table laying is impeccable, minimalist, products are higlighted. There is no question of hiding them with ornaments. Start with wild prawns accompanied by pepper or Bresse scallops with touch of horseradish. The cuisine of Valéry Meulien like travelling and does not hesitate to combine bold and distinctive flavours. Continue with Breton lobster roasted with tandoori or with French venison associated with blueberries and cranberries and risotto with yellow wine. The desserts are equally exotic. Try the Brazil macae chocolate in cigar hot and crispy or the guanaja Sphere and geranium, a combination of Burgundy cassis' heart and Brazil Kent mango covered with hot mango coulis and passion fruit. Simply delicious !

LE REMPART
2 et 4, avenue Gambetta
✆ +33 (0)3 85 51 10 56 - www.lerempart.com
reception@lerempart.com

« Maître Restaurateur » label. Annual closing from end of March to beginning of April and from end of November to beginning of December. Open Wednesday to Sunday for lunch and dinner. Menu from €41 to €91 (menu at €41, €61, €71 and €91). À la carte : €65 environ.19, €90. With the Bistro, menu from €19.90 to €29.90. Carte du Bistrot : €27. Tourism label & Disability. Groups welcome. Terrace.

Rempart is part of the very select club of Tournus with Michelin star. The chef Jérémy Degras and his team received the famous star in 2013 thanks to a creative cuisine despite the cannons of regional gastronomy. Take it easy in Quartier Gourmand and taste regional products revisited by the Chef, Charolais meat, Bresse poultry via snails and other local products. On the menu : grilled prawns, Bresse chicken, pike quenelles, scallops. By the way, the chef does not stay on Burgundy but travels to the four corners of France and revisits the Brittany and Provence's local produces. In addition to Quartier Gourmand, Rempart has another catering space : the Bistro. Brasserie of Rempart, Bistrot offers local cuisine. In summer, meals are served outside, in the elegant romanesque patio. Finally, enjoy the combination of the 4 star hotel and the gourmet restaurant by buying gift boxes or special offers which combine stay at the hotel and meal in the restaurant. You can enjoy Rempart from all angles !

AUX TERRASSES
18, avenue du 23-Janvier
✆ +33 (0)3 85 51 01 74
www.aux-terrasses.com
courrier@aux-terrasses.com
Located along the RN6, at the entrance of Tournus.

Annual closing in January and June during 2 weeks. Open Tuesday to Saturday for lunch and dinner. Booking advised. Menu from €36 to €85. Children's menu : €17 (less than 10 years). Lunch menu : €25 (Tuesday at Friday, except public holidays). American Express, Holiday voucher, Chèque Restaurant. Terrace. Shop.

Michelin starred chef, Jean-Michel Carrette, is part of the club of the 4 starred chefs of Tournus. Succeeding his father, Michel Carrette, Jean-Michel took up the torch with dignity and managed to reinvent cooking while maintaining the heritage. One of the menus pays tribute to the father's figure by offering, among others, Bresse chicken with morels and yellow wine. The tone is set. The menu gives room and space to the produce from the Burgundy region. Frog legs and saddle of lamb for the classic ones, fillet of hare à la plancha or pigeon breast for audacious ones. A fine wine list completes all of it. As for desserts, we recommend the poached Williams pear with tarragon. A pure delight ! Resolutely modern, welcoming and very pleasant, the chef does not hesitate to leave his cuisine and take part in the Frenc gourmet festival held in Tournus in June that combines music and cuisine. A new addition : the good gifts that allow you to offer kitchenware or a good restaurant to discover the skills of the chef and his delicious menus.

Sleeping

HÔTEL LE SAUVAGE
15, place du Champ-de-Mars
✆ +33 (0)3 85 51 14 45
hotel.le-sauvage@orange.fr

Single room €58; double room €68. Breakfast : €8. Garage : €9. Pets allowed (€6 extra). Seminars.

With its red lights and its imposing building, the hotel and restaurant Le Sauvage can be seen from afar. It's impossible to miss it. It overlooks place du Champ de Mars in the city centre where it is easy to park. Built in a former coaching inn dating back to the 18th century, recent works modernized the address with a beautiful modern wooden terrace with a beautiful access ramp for the disabled. On sunny afternoons, many people come for a coffee or a beer on the terrace. Inside, the hotel displays a more traditional decor, a little bourgeois but upmarket and resolutely elegant. In this three-star hotel, nearly thirty comfortable rooms, simple and with modern furnishings enable you to spend a pleasant stay. The rooms can accommodate one to five people. Some enjoy a view of the Abbey Saint-Philibert, others with a lounge area. You don't need to go far for a meal. Le Sauvage is also a restaurant open 7 days a week and serves regional cuisine in a traditional setting. The quality/price ratio is excellent. A three-star address affordable for all.

HOTEL-RESTAURANT GREUZE
5-6, Place de l'Abbaye
✆ +33 (0)3 85 51 77 77
✆ +33 (0)3 85 51 13 52
www.hotelgreuze.fr
contact@hotelgreuze.fr
Located along the RN6, 100m from the Tournus train station, 1 km from 27 of highway A6 exit to Macon. The Entrance and parking at the hotel, avenue Gambetta. Near the Saint Philibert abbey and Tourist Office.

Open all year. Extra bed : €30. Suite from €450. Apartments from €255. Rooms from €115 depending on the category. Breakfast : 6,12,16 or €26 depending on the composition. Free secured parking space. Pets allowed (€14 extra). Seminars. Free Internet access. Free Wifi. Catering facilities (closing weekly Tuesday and Wednesday. Service from 12pm to 1.30pm and from 7.15pm to 9.15pm Thursday to Monday. Menus from €40 to €98. Children's menu : €20. Advance booking advised). Satellite TV.

The hotel restaurant Greuze is a chic Tournus address. With suites at the foot of the Saint- Philibert, the hotel is named after the famous tournusien painter, offers 21 rooms, 2 apartments and 3 suites that combine elegance and ancient furniture. The hotel-restaurant Greuze is located in the city center, near the Greuze Museum and shops and it bathes in unspoilt nature which makes it a perfect romantic break. It's left for you to get a taste of fine homemade dshes of Yohann Chapuis, the chef of Greuze restaurant who was awarded a Michelin star. Yohann Chapuis is a true artist, native of the area and a lover of local products. Traditional dishes such as frog legs, parts of veal or foie gras tarts are identified and explode in the mouth thanks to delicious and original accompaniments like : quinoa, mushrooms, artichokes or egg yolks emulsion. A pure delight !

LE REMPART
2 et 4, avenue Gambetta
✆ +33 (0)3 85 51 10 56
www.lerempart.com
reception@lerempart.com

Family room at €169. Double room from €109 to €179; triple room €159; suite from €199 to €269. Breakfast : €12 (or €16). Garage. The 23 rooms and the 11 suites non-smoking, are soundproofed, air-conditioned, Flat screen tv, cable, minibar, safe. Parking. Disabled access. American Express. Seminars.

Rempart is a delicious 4-star and upmarket hotel, ideally located downtown within few steps from the Abbey Saint-Philibert and few metres from the banks of the Saône for a beautiful walks along the river. Historic house, Rempart is a former gamekeeper's house built in 15th century on the old city walls. 23 rooms and 11 very elegant suites are offered in a decor that combines historical context and modernity. In fact, the hotel was renovated and offers comfort and modern facilities. Upstairs, four soundproofed and air-conditioned meeting rooms accommodate seminars and conferences with a set of modern facilities with its screen, video projector via the microphones. As for meals, the hotel also has a michelin-starred restaurant that is worth the detour and will awaken your tastebuds. A complete high quality address.

AUX TERRASSES
18, avenue du 23-Janvier
✆ +33 (0)3 85 51 01 74
www.aux-terrasses.com
courrier@aux-terrasses.com
Located along the RN6, at the entrance of Tournus.

Logis. Annual closing in January and June during 2 weeks. Closed on Sunday evening, Monday, Tuesday lunchtime. Terrace and parking. 18 rooms. Single room €77; double room from €93 to €180; studio/apartment €210. Breakfast : €17. Extra bed : €15. Holiday voucher. Pets allowed (€10 extra). Seminars. Free Wifi. Catering facilities (lunch menu at €25. Menu from €34 to €80. Children's menu : €17). Sale (goods gifts). Satellite TV.

The Hôtel Aux Terrasses is one of the first addresses you see when you arrive in Tournus, from Mâcon. The hotel offers large rooms with contemporary and modern decoration. The layout and the colours are neat, the furniture comfortable and modern. The charm of these rooms most of which have a small private terrace lies in the mix of the materials. Stones, wood, metal, leather, all these elements are cleverly combined to offer spaces for relaxation and tranquillity. The rooms are also soundproofed so you do not get bothered by the traffic from the departemental road that passes nearby. The setting is warm, elegant and refined. A very beautiful place.

Shopping

LA BANQUE DES GRANDS CRUS
58, rue Docteur-Privey
✆ +33 (0)3 85 51 78 74
www.labanquedesgrandscrus.com
contact@labanquedesgrandscrus.com
Open every day from 9am to 7.30pm.
Follow the barrel ! Located right in front of the address, it sets the tone and it indicates the entrance of the Banque des Grand Crus. Here, no need to rob the owner, the New Zealander passionate of oenology, Benjamin Needham. He will be pleased to make you taste some of his best wines. In fact, the address has more than 800 wines from Burgundy, of course, from Bordeaux but also other regions of France and from abroad (Spain, New Zealand, South Africa...). In addition to the wines, the Banque des Grand Crus is also a paradise for rum and whisky lovers. The cellar has hundreds of references : whiskeys of Scotland and Ireland, the United States and even Japan, rums of the Antilles, Reunion, Colombia or Mexico. Journey for the tastebuds, Banque des Grand Crus dazzles you with all the flavours from elsewhere. Around wine, you will also find books to know more about them, the corkscrews to open them and the carafe to drink them. The cellar thus offers a wide range of accessories for the delight of lovers and provide good gifts ideas. One thing is certain, if you do not need to rob Banque des Grand Crus, you are likely to take it off of all of its treasures !

LES VIGNERONS DE MANCEY
RN6, en Velnoux
✆ +33 (0)3 85 51 71 62
www.lesvigneronsdemancey.fr
contact@cave-mancey.com
Le long de la RN6. Depuis la sortie 27, prendre direction Chalon-sur-Saône.
Open on Sunday and public holidays from 9.30am to 12.30pm and from 3pm to 6pm. High season : Monday to Saturday from 8.30am to 12.30pm and from 1.30pm to 7pm. From October to April, open from 9am to 12.30pm and from 2pm to 6.30pm Monday to Saturday. Sessions of tasting with accompanying notes : from €10 to €30.
Located along the RN6, with a large car park, the cellar of the wine growers of Mancey is a magnificent site that emphasizes the terroir of Burgundy and wine know-how. A scenographic space offers a travel in the middle of the vineyard and the wine. Discover the various Burgundian names (there are about hundred !), AOC, grape varieties but also the cycle of the vineyard and the work of the wine grower. You will be able to then practice your knowledge by going in space tasting. Recreational entertainments request the taste, the sense of smell and the touch and learn how to recognize the flavours and the characteristics of the wines of the region. A free tasting is of course organized at the end of this training. All that remains to do is to return to the sale space of more than 150 m^2 to finish your travel and leave with your arms filled with the wines from the about twenty available Burgundian estates. Several local produces (jams, chutney, etc) and table accessories are also on sale.
More than a simple shop, the cellar of Vignerons de Mancey is an initiation course around the vine and wine and also a cultural centre hosting temporary exhibitions and events. A beautiful space that combines pleasure and discovery !

In the surroundings

Brancion (Martailly-lès-Brancion)

LA CHAMBRE DES BUISSONNATS
✆ +33 (0)3 85 51 26 33
✆ +33 (0)6 78 41 55 24
Open all year. Single room €40; double room €50; triple room €65. Breakfast included. Parking. Cot. Reception bicycle and horses. Free Wifi.
Christine Talmey welcomes you in her pleasant family chambres d'hôte located at in the village of Martailly. The building is absolutely charming and looks like a small house of happiness with its large green garden, its small wooden bridge without forgetting the beauty of the surrounding countryside and the surrounding vineyards. La chambre des Buissonnats offers a room being able to accommodate from 2 to 4 people in an authentic and wooded setting. The place is ideal for a family vacation and for nature lovers who can benefit from the welcome bicycle and horses of the establishment.

Lacrost

LE MEIX DES FORT
1, route des Alpes
✆ +33 (0)3 85 51 79 88
✆ +33 (0)6 72 40 74 89
www.lemeixdesfort.com
lemeixdesfort@orange.fr
Gîte de France (3 épis). 5 rooms. Single room €65; double room €70. Breakfast included. Extra bed : €15. Closed parking. Free Wifi.
A real haven in the South a few kilometers from Tournus. Le Meix des Fort, they are five guest rooms (two double rooms and three family rooms) settled in an old farm of the 17th century fully restored and surrounded by a beautiful wooded park of 1 ha. The building is very beautiful, made of stone and absolutely charming. The five rooms are well equipped, spacious, bright with double beds, antique furniture renovated and a pastel colour decoration. Two rooms are on the first floor with independent access and the three other rooms have a separate entrance. Enjoy a pleasant stay in this place full of history and located at the crossroads of Bresse and Tournugeois to visit the variety of riches that these regions offer (historical sites, walks in Lacrost, cellars, restaurants...).

Ozenay

CHATEAU DE MESSEY

✆ +33 (0)3 85 51 33 83
www.chateaudemessey.com
chateau@demessey.com

5 rooms (4 rooms + 1 dormitory. (20 beddings on the whole)). 2 beds children. Weekly rental : €4800. Weekend : €800/night (3 nights minimum). Remain week : €700/night. Seminars. Receptions and weddings. Cleaning service. Catering facilities (partnership with Le Relais d'Ozenay). Whirlpool. Excursions (organization of visits in Domaine Belleville with Rully and Manoir Murisaltien with Meursault).

Marc and Vinciane Dumont, winegrowers, welcome you in the magnificent château de Messey, a wonderful building of the 9th century, long and made of stone, smelling good the summer and holidays, surrounded by 6 hectares of vineyards. With a capacity of 4 rooms and 1 dormitory with double beds and single beds, all renovated and modern and full of charm, the castle allows you to spend a pleasant stay in an idyllic setting and with high-quality services. Prices are high but with a large garden, a swimming pool, a spa and high-quality services, these prices are justified. It is also the ideal place to organise reception, weddings and seminars. Also enjoy your stay to discover the wine tradition of château de Messey that dates back to 10 centuries and taste the Mason-Cruzille and Mâcon-Chardonnay produced by the couple. You can visit the fermenting room and the breeding cellars, taste a selection of wines from the estate while enjoying the typically Burgundy cuisine prepared by the excellent gourmet addresses in the area.

CHATEAU D'OZENAY

Lieu-dit Bourg
✆ +33 (0)3 85 51 77 93 / +33 (0)6 16 82 32 93

Capacity of 7 people. Double room €120; suite €140. Breakfast included. Extra bed : €35.

Spend holidays in a Historical monument ! Château d'Ozenay dating from the 13th and 17th centuries has been owned by the Ozenay family since 1664. The setting of this imposing castle is just splendid. The building located in the middle of the village of Ozenay is surrounded by a French garden crossed by La Natouze river. The place is simply magical and really relaxing. Le château d'Ozenay welcomes you in its suite Empire located in the 1st floor, spacious room overlooking the garden and in the round room of the medieval tower, facing south with a view of le Colombier. Taking into account the beautiful surroundings and castle's history, the overnight fee is really affordable. The address is absolutely charming.

YONNE

The city-centre of Auxerre.
JOSIANE TAXEL

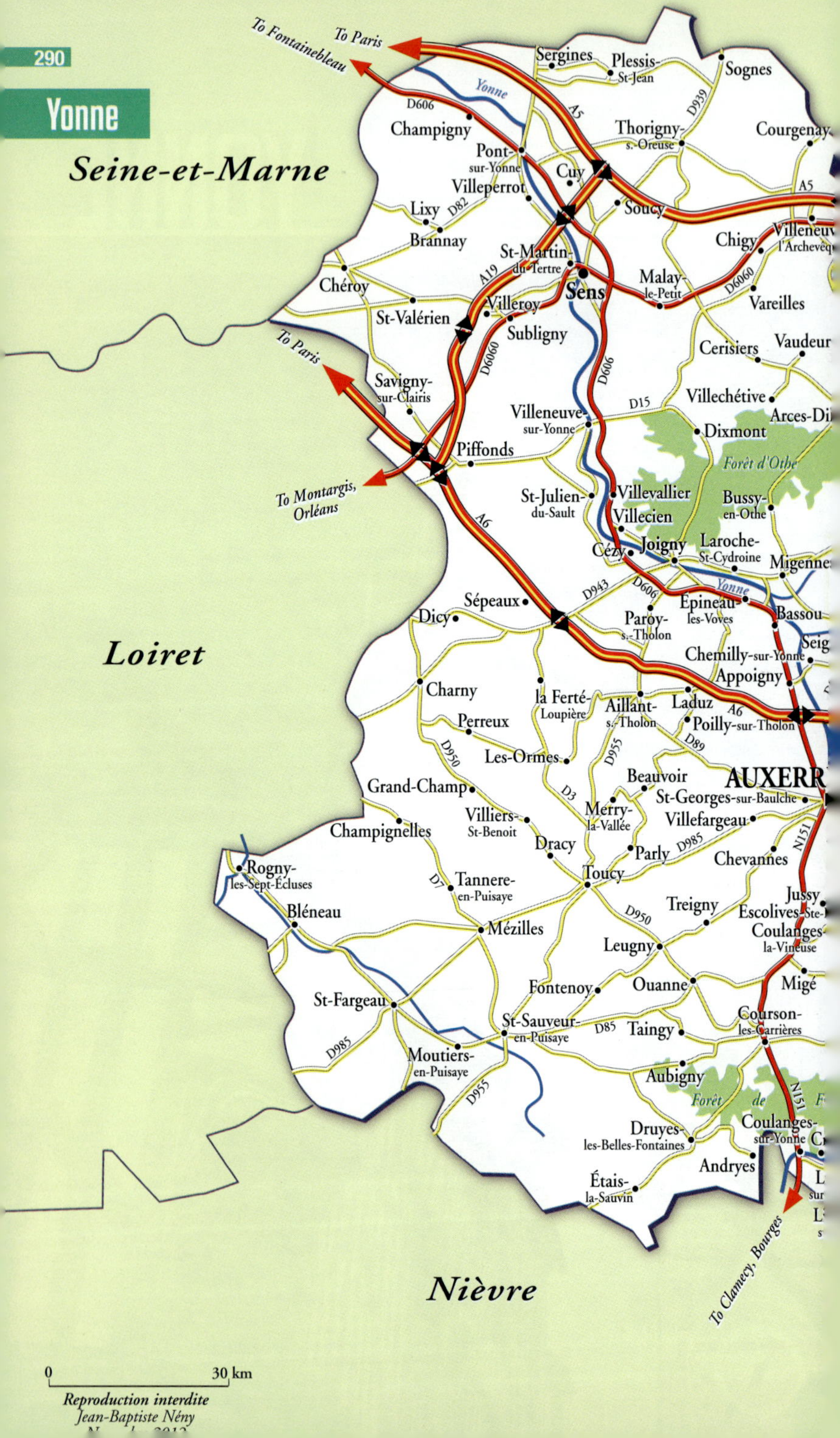
Seine-et-Marne
Loiret
Nièvre
To Fontainebleau
To Paris
To Paris
To Montargis, Orléans
To Clamecy, Bourges
Yonne
Yonne
D606
A5
D939
D82
A19
D6060
D6060
D606
D15
A6
D943
D606
A6
D89
D950
D955
D3
D985
D7
D950
D85
D985
D955
N151
N151
Sergines
Plessis-St-Jean
Sognes
Champigny
Thorigny-s.-Oreuse
Courgenay
Pont-sur-Yonne
Cuy
Villeperrot
Lixy
Soucy
Brannay
Chigy
St-Martin-du-Tertre
Malay-le-Petit
Chéroy
Sens
Vareilles
St-Valérien
Villeroy
Subligny
Cerisiers
Vaudeur
Savigny-sur-Clairis
Villechétive
Villeneuve-sur-Yonne
Dixmont
Piffonds
Forêt d'Othe
St-Julien-du-Sault
Villevallier
Bussy-en-Othe
Villecien
Cézy
Joigny
Laroche-St-Cydroine
Épineau-les-Voves
Sépeaux
Dicy
Paroy-s.-Tholon
Bassou
Chemilly-sur-Yonne
Appoigny
Charny
la Ferté-Loupière
Aillant-s.-Tholon
Laduz
Poilly-sur-Tholon
Perreux
Les-Ormes
Beauvoir
St-Georges-sur-Baulche
Grand-Champ
Merry-la-Vallée
Villefargeau
Villiers-St-Benoit
Champignelles
Dracy
Parly
Chevannes
Rogny-les-Sept-Écluses
Toucy
Tannere-en-Puisaye
Treigny
Escolives-
Bléneau
Mézilles
Leugny
Coulanges-la-Vineuse
Fontenoy
Ouanne
Migé
St-Fargeau
St-Sauveur-en-Puisaye
Taingy
Courson-les-Carrières
Moutiers-en-Puisaye
Aubigny
Forêt de
Druyes-les-Belles-Fontaines
Coulanges-sur-Yonne
Andryes
Étais-la-Sauvin
0
30 km
Reproduction interdite
Jean-Baptiste Nény

N
O
E
S
Highway
Main road
Secondary road
Preture
Subprefecture
City, village
Highway Exit
Forest
Yonne
To Troyes, Dijon
To Troyes
To Troyes
Aube
Côte-d'Or
To Dijon
To Chalon-sur-Saône
Chailley
Venizy
Neuvy-Sautour
St-Florentin
Brienon sous-Armançon
Flogny-la-Chapelle
Percey
Pontigny
Méré
Rouvray
Ligny-le-Châtel
Montigny-la-Resle
Lignorelles
La Chapelle-Vaupelteigne
Beine
Venoy
Chablis
Épineuil
Tanlay
Tonnerre
Bois de Rugny
Cruzy-le-Châtel
Gigny
Bois de la Ville
Ancy-le-Franc
Canal de Bourgogne
Armançon
Serin
Ravières
Nuits
St-Bris-le-Vineux
Vincelottes
Irancy
Cravant
Vermenton
Noyers-sur-Serein
Aisy-sur-Armançon
Nitry
Massangis
Accolay
Joux-la-Ville
Châtel-Gérard
Forêt de Saint-Jean
Serein
Cure
Mailly-le-Château
Arcy-sur-Cure
Coutarnoux
l'Isle-sur-Serein
Châtel-Censoir
St-Moré
Réserve Naturelle du Bois du Parc
Montréal
Sauvigny-le-Bois
Guillon
Givry
Vault-de-Lugny
Avallon
Asnières-sous-Bois
Asquins
Pontaubert
Vézelay
Island
Cussy-les-Forges
Ste-Magnance
Chamoux
St-Père
Pierre-Perthuis
St-Germain-des-Champs
St-Léger-Vauban
Chastellux-sur-Cure
Quarré-les-Tombes
N77
D905
D91
D965
D952
D944
D956
D606
D86
D957
D944
A6

AUXERRE ★★

Paved streets in a city-centre having a rich historical heritage. Auxerre has two charming museums, the Museum and the hotel Leblanc-Duvernoy. From the bridge Paul Bert, we understand that the city was under the influence of religion throughout history. The bells stand out : the Cathedral Saint Etienne, St. Peter's Church and the Abbey of Saint-Germain. The monumental heritage also includes St. Eusebius church, the clock tower or even the City Hall... Colourful shops in framed wood houses that have been very well renovated a few outdoor cafes where those addicted to stadiums discuss about football, and restaurants with gourmet menus. The city floors and goes down to the docks, newly rebuilt and which is now more conducive to walks. Getting lost in the neighbourhood of the Navy and see the boats go by, is real fun

But Auxerre is not only this. Beautiful exhibitions in small galleries have really flourished in the last decade. Although sometimes it is calm, Auxerre is also in full cultural development and the offer is real : concerts, theatre, festivals and events in every corners of the city, boost local life.

Strategically located between Paris and Lyon, Auxerre housed over the centuries many personalities, like St. Germain, bishop of the city who makes many pilgrims come to the town. Jeanne d'Arc bestowed the city of Auxerre by its presence in 1429. March 17, 1815 in front of the County, Marshal Ney threw himself into the arms of Napoleon (back from Elba) before walking with him in Paris. Finally, the one who gives its name to several places here is Paul Bert. Scientist and statesman of the Third Republic, he was born in Auxerre, like the poet Marie Noël (1883-1967), who received the Grand Prize of the French Academy as well as the film director Jean-Paul Rappeneau.

■ OFFICE DE TOURISME D'AUXERRE

Bureau principal
1-2, quai de la République
✆ +33 (0)3 86 52 06 19
www.ot-auxerre.fr
info@ot-auxerre.fr

Low season : open Monday to Friday from 9.30am to 12.30pm and from 2pm to 6pm; Saturday from 9.30am to 12.30pm and from 2pm to 6.30pm; Sunday from 10am to 1pm. High season : Monday to Saturday from 9am to 1pm and from 2pm to 7pm; Sunday and public holidays from 9.30am to 1pm and from 2.30pm to 6pm. Closed on December 25th and on January 1st.

Tourist information, sightseeing tours for individuals and groups. Vtc rental bikes with electric assistance, and electric boats. Exchange foreign currencies sundays and public holidays. Shop : maps, guides, books, posters, postcards, souvenirs (Cadet Roussel), programs festivals and exhibitions. Note that a second information point is city centre, next to the Tour de l'horloge.

■ LES BATEAUX DE L'AUXERROIS

105, rue des Mignottes
✆ +33 (0)6 30 37 66 17 / +33 (0)9 75 23 27 89
www.bateauxauxerrois.com
info@bateauxauxerrois.com

The abbey of Saint-Germain, reflections in the Yonne.

Saint-Étienne cathedral in Auxerre.

Opening on April 9th, 2016. Every day except Monday. Every day in July and August. Closed on May 1st and on July 14th. To invite to know the schedule. Free for under 4-year-olds. Cruise 1am, 1.30am and 2am. Ticket office on the dock, vis-a-vis the boat. Possible cruise for groups.
This is an original outing that will appeal to adults and children : a kind of Burgundy ferry On board Hirondelle 2, you can discover Auxerre from another angle and enjoy the peace of water. You can rest and relax during a one hour cruise or a three hours lunch-cruise. Cameras are highly recommended You will have a very enjoyable moment especially on sunny days.

Sightseeing

Monuments

■ CATHEDRALE SAINT-ETIENNE ★★

Rue Fourier
✆ +33 (0)3 86 52 23 29
www.cathedrale-auxerre.com
contact@cathedrale-auxerre.com
Open all year. Low season : from 7.30am to 5pm. High season : every day from 7.30am to 6pm. No the visit during the offices. Visit of the treasure and the crypt : high season from 9am to 6pm, closed on Sunday morning; low season from 10am to 5pm, closed on Sunday. Free for under 12-year-olds. Group (20 people) : €4 (free for the pupils). Crypt : €3; treasure : €1.90; crypt and treasure : €4.90. Free for under 12-year-olds. 20% of discount on the entrance of the crypt with Pass' Yonne.
Around 400, the bishop Saint Amâtre founded a small shrine, which was enlarged and embellished over the centuries, the building got burnt and was rebuilt several times, until the construction of a Romanesque cathedral from 1023. In the early 13th century, Bishop Guillaume of Seignelay decided to rebuild it for the fifth time. The choir was demolished and renovation works continued until the 16th century. With 68 m high, the north tower dominates the town. The south tower remained uncompleted. Its new façade is richly decorated with sculptures that were mutilated by the Huguenots in the 16th century. A choir and an ambulatory from the early 13th century, a splendid example of Gothic architecture, are elegantly refined.
A magnificent series of stained glass from the 13th century surround it, a 16th century stained glass adorns the large rosette. The 11th century crypt is the only Romanic vestige of the building : it has several paintings, including one very rare of Christ, on a white horse, escorted by four jumper angels on the barrel vault of the axial chapel. Inspired by a vision of Apocalypse, it is the only representation of this kind in France. The treasure brings together pieces of gold, enamelled 13th century reliquaries and illuminated manuscripts.

■ CHAPELLE DES VISITANDINES – FONDATION FRANCOIS BROCHET

100, rue de Paris ✆ +33 (0)3 86 18 05 50
Open from July 1st to September 30th. Open Wednesday to Sunday from 2pm to 6pm. Free.
Along the streets, impossible not to cross the impassive Marie Noël Restif de la Bretonne, Cadet Roussel and Jean Moreau – Auxerre former mayor and inventor of the famous chocolate cake – sculpted by François Brochet. The chapel of the Visitandines includes the major work of the sculptor, engraver, painter and writer from auxerre (1925-2003), the massacre of the innocents. 95 long polychrome statues of uncluttered oak or lime present the reflection of the artist on the ravages of the wars, initiated in 1956 after his return from indochine. The soldiers had monuments, the innocent victims never. The murderers did not appear : only martyrs interested sculptor. Visitors can enter 17th-century chapel, a few steps from the house of Dr. Petiot terrible. Looking at the statues there is a bit like humanizing them; there is something lively in their expression. A short visit that is worth the detour.

Auxerre

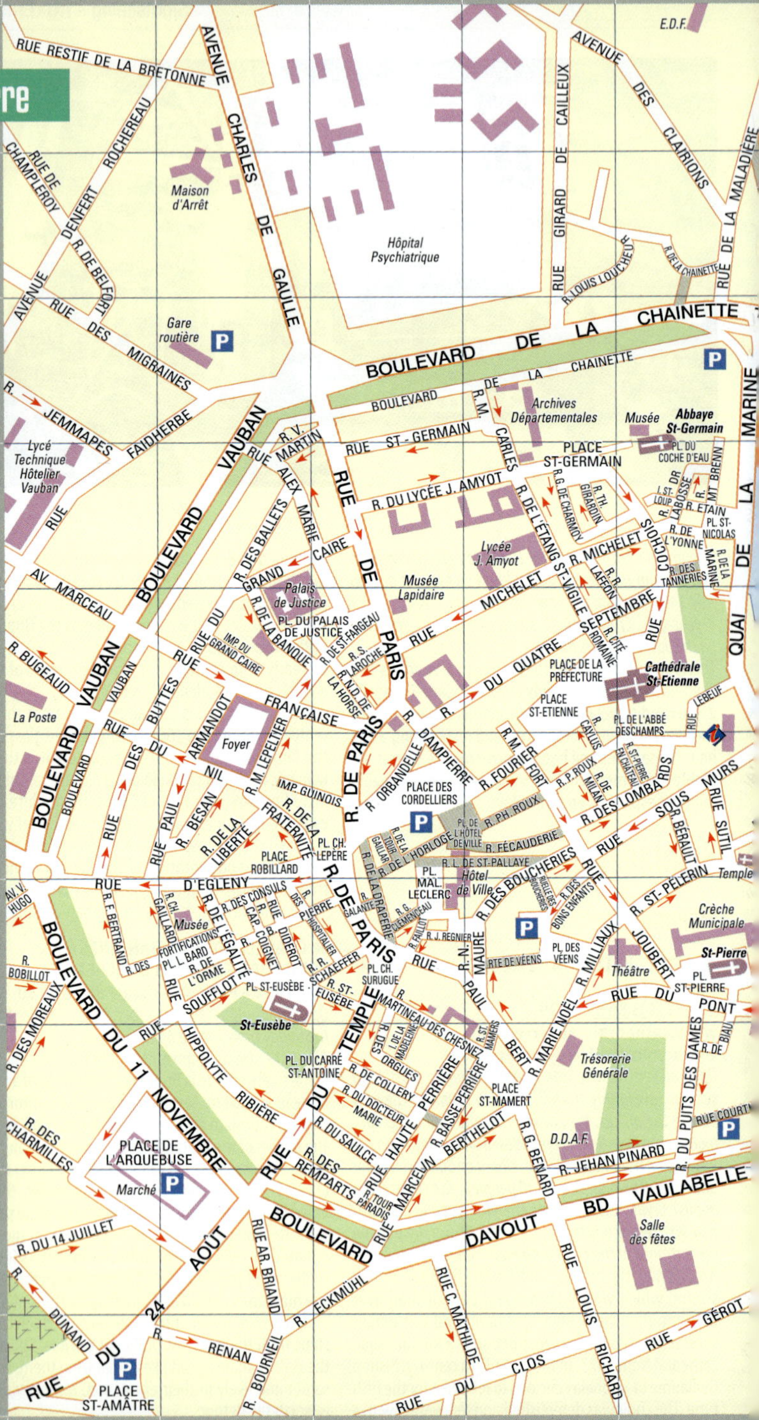

A
B
C
D
E
2
3
4
5
6
7
8
9
10
RUE RESTIF DE LA BRETONNE
AVENUE CHARLES DE GAULLE
E.D.F.
AVENUE DES CLAIRIONS
RUE DE LA MALADIÈRE
RUE GIRARD DE CAILLEUX
R. LOUIS LOUCHEUR
R. DE LA CHAINETTE
RUE DE CHAMPLEROY
RUE ROCHEREAU
DENFERT
R. DE BELFORT
Maison d'Arrêt
Hôpital Psychiatrique
AVENUE
RUE DES MIGRAINES
Gare routière
BOULEVARD DE LA CHAINETTE
BOULEVARD DE LA CHAINETTE
R. JEMMAPES
FAIDHERBE
Lycé Technique Hôtelier Vauban
RUE
BOULEVARD VAUBAN
R. V. MARTIN
RUE ALEX MARIE
RUE ST - GERMAIN
R. M. CARLES
Archives Départementales
Musée
Abbaye St-Germain
PLACE ST-GERMAIN
PL. DU COCHE D'EAU
R. DU LYCÉE J. AMYOT
R. G. DE CHARMOY
R. TH. GIRARDIN
R. DE L'ÉTANG ST-VIGILE
I. ST-LOUP
R. DR LABOSSE
R. MT BRENN
R. ETAIN
PL. ST-NICOLAS
R. DE L'YONNE
R. DES TANNERIES
R. DE LA MARINE
QUAI DE LA MARINE
RUE DE PARIS
CAIRE
GRAND
R. DES BALLETS
AV. MARCEAU
Palais de Justice
PL. DU PALAIS DE JUSTICE
R. DE LA BANQUE
IMP. DU GRAND CAIRE
R. DE ST-FARGEAU
R. S. LAROCHE
R. N. D. DE LA HORSE
Musée Lapidaire
Lycée J. Amyot
R. MICHELET
MICHELET
R. R. LAFFON
RUE COCHOIS
RUE DU QUATRE SEPTEMBRE
R. ROMAINE
R. CITÉ
PLACE DE LA PRÉFECTURE
Cathédrale St-Etienne
PLACE ST-ETIENNE
R. CAYLUS
PL. DE L'ABBÉ DESCHAMPS
RUE LEBEUF
R. BUGEAUD
La Poste
VAUBAN
RUE DU
BUTTES
RUE FRANÇAISE
ARMANDOT
Foyer
R. M. LEPELTIER
R. DE PARIS
R. ORBANDELLE
R. DAMPIERRE
R. M. FOURIER
FORT
R. P. ROUX
R. DE MILAN
R. ST-PIERRE EN CHATEAU
R. DES LOMBARDS
RUE SOUS MURS
RUE SUTIL
BOULEVARD VAUBAN
RUE DES NIL
RUE PAUL
R. BESAN
R. DE LA LIBERTÉ
R. DE LA FRATERNITÉ
IMP. GUINOIS
PLACE DES CORDELLIERS
PL. DE L'HÔTEL DE VILLE
R. PH. ROUX
R. FÉCAUDERIE
PLACE ROBILLARD
PL. CH. LEPÈRE
R. DE L'HORLOGE
R. DE LA TOUR GAILLARD
R. L. DE ST-PALLAYE
PL. MAL. LECLERC
Hôtel de Ville
R. DES BOUCHERIES
R. BERAULT
RUE
Temple
AV. V. HUGO
RUE D'EGLENY
R. F. BERTRAND
R. CH. GAILLARD
R. DES CONSULS
R. DE L'ÉGALITÉ
R. CAP. COIGNET
RUE DIDEROT
R. PIERRE
DES HOSPITALIER
R. GALANTE
R. DE LA DRAPERIE
R. G. CLEMENCEAU
R. FAILLOT
R. J. REGNIER
R. N. MAURE
R. DES BONS ENFANTS
R. ST-PÉLERIN
Crèche Municipale
Musée
FORTIFICATIONS
PL. L. BARD
R. DE L'ORME
SOUFFLOT
R. SCHAEFFER
R. ST-EUSÈBE
PL. CH. SURUGUE
RUE PAUL BERT
RTE DE VÉENS
PL. DES VÉENS
R. MILLIAUX
Théâtre
JOUBERT
St-Pierre
PL. ST-PIERRE
RUE DU PONT
R. BOBILLOT
R. DES MOREAUX
BOULEVARD DU 11 NOVEMBRE
RUE
PL. ST-EUSÈBE
St-Eusèbe
HIPPOLYTE RIBIÈRE
RUE DU TEMPLE
R. MARTINEAU DES CHESNEZ
R. DES ORGUES
I. DE LA MADELEINE
R. ST-MAMERS
R. MARIE NOËL
Trésorerie Générale
R. DE BIAU
RUE DU PUITS DES DAMES
PL. DU CARRÉ ST-ANTOINE
R. DE COLLERY
R. DU DOCTEUR MARIE
PERRIÈRE
R. BASSE PERRIÈRE
PLACE ST-MAMERT
R. DES CHARMILLES
PLACE DE L'ARQUEBUSE
Marché
R. DU SAULCE
RUE HAUTE
R. DES REMPARTS
RUE MARCELIN BERTHELOT
R. G. BENARD
D.D.A.F.
R. JEHAN PINARD
RUE COURTOIS
R. TOUR PARADIS
BOULEVARD DAVOUT
BD VAULABELLE
Salle des fêtes
R. DU 14 JUILLET
RUE DU 24 AOÛT
RUE AR. BRIAND
R. ECKMÜHL
RUE C. MATHILDE
RUE LOUIS RICHARD
RUE GÉROT
R. DUNAND
R. RENAN
R. BOURNEIL
RUE DU CLOS
PLACE ST-AMÂTRE
RUE

F
G
H
I
J
1
2
3
4
5
6
7
8
9
10
RUE DES CHAMPOULAINS
RUE DE L'ORCERIE
RUE DU MOULIN DU PRÉSIDENT
RUE THOMAS ANCEL
RUE BRICHOUX
R. L. CROCHOT
AVENUE JEAN JAURÈS
l'Yonne
VOIE PRIVÉE
RUE BOURBOTTE
RUE HÉRIC
RUE BERCIER
PONT DE LA TOURNELLE
PONT MOREAU
PLACE LAMARTINE
AVENUE
RUE DE BRAZZA
RUE CHARLES PÉGUY
AVENUE DE LA TOURNELLE
RUE SAINT MARTIN LES SAINT-MARIENS
RUE JULES GUIGNIER
RUE ETIENNE DOLET
RUE DE LABORDE
R. DU PORT GERBAULT
ALLÉE DE BRÉCHOL
R. SIMON CHENARD
COULONS
RUE DE BRAZZA
RUE KRÜGER
RUE CAMILLE DESMOULINS
PRÉS
RUE DE L'AVENIR
QUAI DE L'ANCIENNE ABBAYE
Port de Plaisance
Chambre de Commerce et d'Industrie
GARE ST-GERVAIS
RUE DES MIGNOTTES
RUE DES PRÉS
RUE DE SPARRE
RUE PAUL DOUMER
RUE JULES FERRY
BOURGEOIS
R.L.
R.G. BROTTIER
AV. DE LA RÉSISTANCE
QUAI DE LA RÉPUBLIQUE
R. DES TANNEURS
RUE C. ROUSSEL
PL. J. JAURÈS
AVENUE GAMBETTA
PONT P. BERT
Ecole National de Musique
R. THIERS
RUE DE L'ILE AUX PLAISIRS
AV. DU MARÉCHAL JUIN
R. SAINT-GERVAIS
RUE ST-PÉLERIN
R. GIRARD
IMP. DES COLLINETS
PONT
PIERRE
DU
QUAI DU BATARDEAU
R. A. CHALLES
A. DES 3 MAN...
P. PITON
VERT
R. CAMPAN
R. DE JOIE
Bibliothèque
R. D'ARDILLERE
R. DU PUITS GUÉRIN
VAULABELLE
R. MAX QUANTIN
Police
PLACE ACHILLE RIBAIN
BOULEVARD
RUE DE PREUILLY
R. MAX BLONDAT
RUE GÉROT
N
O
E
S
ALLÉE DE L'ARBRE SEC
Stade Auxerrois
0
100 m
SÉNONS
Reproduction interdite
Jean-Baptiste Nény
Mars 2012

Street index of Auxerre

A

B

C

D

E-F

G

H

I-J

© PHOVOIR

The abbey of Saint-Germain-Auxerre.

© CLAUDE NISSENS – FOTOLIA

Auxerre's Clock Tower.

© JOSIANE MAXEL

Auxerre city centre and Clock Tower.

© JEAN-JACQUES CORDIER – FOTOLIA

The abbey of Saint-Germain d'Auxerre.

ÉGLISE SAINT-EUSEBE ★

Place Saint-Eusèbe ✆ +33 (0)3 86 52 06 19

Free.

A transitional nave between Romanesque and Gothic style of the 12th and 13th centuries, a 15th-century Romanesque bell tower with arrow, 16th-century chapels, one of which contains the relics of Saint Germain of Auxerre, elegant Renaissance choir with beautiful stained glass windows of the 16th, etc. The interior is in sparkling white. Completely restored after a fire which destroyed it in November 1996, Saint Eusebius has regained its beauty. As a monastery originally founded in 637 and a priory in the 12th century, its apse collapsed in 1523. The religious wars disrupted the end of its reconstruction. Converted into a prison in 1793 and then a centre of Theo philanthropic worship in 1798, it is only under the Concordat that it regained its parish function. According to a legend, the invocation of St. Tetrice, whose relics are preserved in the altar cured toothache. Note the amazing and mysterious small head carved above a large arch of the nave. Its choir, regretted by its ardent supporters, makes sometimes appearance that is always appreciated. The church also hosts concerts at Christmas.

L'ABBAYE SAINT-GERMAIN ★★

2, place Saint-Germain ✆ +33 (0)3 86 18 02 90
www.auxerre.culture.gouv.fr
poleartsetpatrimoine.maire@auxerre.com

Visit every day except Tuesday. From May 1st to September 30th, from 9.45am to 6.45pm. From October 1st to April 30th, from 10am to 12pm and from 2pm to 5pm. Attention the site and the exhibitions are not at the same time open, it is more careful ask for information. Free for under 16-year-olds (students less than 26 years). €6 price of the guided tour of the crypt. Reduced rate and groups starting from 20 people €4. Holiday voucher. Children welcome (teaching visits). Guided tour. Shop.

The remains of the bishop St. Germain died in Ravenna at the court of Galla Placidia in 448, were returned to his diocese of Auxerre. The legend says that on his path, nature awoke and everything blossomed again. Queen Clotilde, the wife of Clovis, built a basilica in the sixth century of the oratory where the saint was buried. The former Carolingian Romanesque abbey Enlarged in the ninth century, was partly rebuilt in the thirteenth to the fifteenth century. After the demolition in 1811 Romanesque bays that connected the bell tower to the choir, the beautiful spire of the twelfth century became isolated, planted like a candle pointing the sky before the rest of the buildings. The crypt is not to be missed on any pretext. if there is one thing to see in Auxerre, it is certainly the jewel heritage : when you look, listen, feel, you enter in connection with the origins of the city. This underground church built from 841, has the tomb of St. Germain in a vault. It houses the oldest Carolingian murals in France.

TOUR DE L'HORLOGE ★

Rue de l'Horloge

The high tower of the 15th century which overlooks the half-timbered houses from the city center was built on the foundations of a building of the former Gallo-Roman castrum. Used as a prison, it was transformed into a clock and belfry as from 1483. The two dials, from the 17th century, has the particularity to indicate solar and lunar hours. The Bailiff Roussel (1743-1807) who inspired the famous song « Cadet Roussel » lived in the premises and his statue by François Brochet adorns a fountain on the Place Charles Surugue. The tower was destroyed by a fire in 1825 extensively rebuilt in the late 19th. Immediately to the left side of the City Hall, by turning your back to the tower, a nameplate indicates the house where the future libertine author Restif de la Bretonne, born in Sacy in Yonne in 1734 who was apprentice to the printer Master Baker from 1751 to 1755. The tower is not open to the public.

Museums

MUSEE LEBLANC-DUVERNOIS ★

9 bis, rue d'Egleny ✆ +33 (0)3 86 18 05 50

Open Wednesday to Monday from 2pm to 6pm. Free admission for all. Children welcome (workshops ask for information). Activities.

Housed in a beautiful mansion of the eighteenth century, this fascinating little museum with rich collections is devoted to ceramics, tapestries and the eighteenth century. It has beautiful collections of national and regional pottery, Auxerre was an important center of production. The revolutionary period is particularly rich. You can also admire beautiful utilitarian sandstone from Puisaye and very rare tapestries from Beauvais of eighteenth tracing the history of the Chinese emperor Kang Xi. Temporary exhibitions occupy the ground floor regularly. Little known by many auxerrois, yet it is a place that exudes a special and romantic emotion. On the occasion of the Museum Night at the beginning of spring the music room returns to its roots with beautiful concerts.

MUSEUM D'HISTOIRE NATURELLE ★

5, boulevard Vauban ✆ +33 (0)3 86 72 96 40
www.auxerre.com
museum.mairie@auxerre.com

Reopening on January 4th, 2016. Open from January to December, Monday to Friday from 1.30pm to 5.30pm, Sunday of 14 : 00 at 5.30pm, closed Saturday and public holidays and included from December 24th to January 1st. Group all year by reservation. Free. Free reception of groups of children and adults (Monday to Friday from 9am to 12pm and from 1.30pm to 5.30pm). Guided tour (on request for groups on the annual exhibitions).

Here is a bourgeois house of the nineteenth century with a pleasant French garden, with beautiful species like ginko biloba. Walking there is a real pleasure and help to be cut off from the hustle and bustle of the town. On two floors, the collections of the Natural History Museum are related to nature and date back to the eighteenth century for the oldest. Two to three annual exhibitions generally invade the ground floor : each time, very different themes, as the one recently proposed : « A garden of plaster ». Far from the stereotype of the old museum where dust accumulates on the windows, this place is alive, bright and always seduces children The exhibitions are suitable for young people, who learn there while having fun. One room is dedicated to the more auxerrois of scientists : the famous Paul Bert, former statesman. See also, the paleontology parts and geology with impressive skeleton of cave bear and two fossils of ichtyosauruses : impressive.

Knife & Fork

LA FOLIE
6, avenue du Maréchal Juin
✆ +33 (0)3 86 33 76 79 / +33 (0)6 82 30 62 35
www.restaurantlafolie.fr

Open every day from 11.30am to 2.30pm and from 7pm to 10.30pm. Booking advised. Menu from €58 to €85. Lunch menu : €18 (main course + coffee and preciousnesses). Fixed rate formula Business €25, starter and main course or main course and dessert €35. À la carte : starter at €18, main course at €28, dessert at €16. Groups welcome. Garden. Terrace.

Emilie Depierre and Julien Martinat had a real heart for this unusual place of the baroque architecture of the late nineteenth century, nestled in a beautiful park overlooking the Yonne. La Folie Yver – it is the name given to this building – welcomes about twenty seats on the two floors, and offers seats on the terrace from which you have an incomparable view of the river and the île aux Plaisirs... And pleasures, you'll have them by coming to enjoy the chef's cuisine : you will first of all admire the culinary poetry that the carte reveals and you will admire the fineness of the dishes, and finally, our taste buds can vibrate with pleasure. Judge for yourself : cream of cauliflower with mint and fine slices of morteau, epigram of lamb from the Clavisy farm, wood-moss juice and tempura of mushrooms and berries, tart with beetroot sugar and ice cream with hay. Also note that a small cellar awaits you to enjoy a glass of wine that you will choose yourself to accompany your meal. An exquisite address.

LE JARDIN GOURMAND
56, boulevard Vauban
✆ +33 (0)3 86 51 53 52
www.lejardingourmand.com
contact@lejardingourmand.com

« Maître Restaurateur » label. Open Wednesday to Sunday 12 : 00 at 1.45pm and from 7.30pm to 9.15pm. Booking advised. Menu from €49 to €125 (tasting menu at €125 been used for the unit of the guests). Children's menu : €27. À la carte. Groups welcome. Terrace.

Nestled in an old bourgeois house, Le Jardin Gourmand invites you to follow a whole Epicurean partition as you lunch or dine in the dining room or on the new terrace. Pierre Boussereau, former pastry chef of Dodin-Bouffant and Olivier Laplaine are at the helm of this extraordinary garden. All his products, the cooking, the presentation of his dishes that he matches with the paintings, this passionate is still attached to his roots, the Burgundy, with farm meat of Morvan, fish that are not bred, regional cheeses and of course, with fine Burgundy wines. Here is an extract of the menu : duck foie gras with bread with nut chutney and lemon orange fig and green tomatoes, farm Avallonais veal fillet, strips of bacon of Colonnala and Lomo de Pala Negra, puree of split peas and celery sticks fondue, refined platter of cheese of Pascal Leroux and Marie Christine Basseporte, a series of 3 sorbets and 3 desserts. He invites us to discover a permanent blending of flavours, combining each New Year's Day vegetables, aromatic herbs and edible flowers in his garden on the altar of the cuisine. One of the best restaurants of Yonne.

PAUSE GOURMANDE
1, rue Fourier ✆ +33 (0)3 86 33 98 87
www.lapausegourmande-89.com

Open Tuesday to Saturday from 9am to 5.30pm. Menu from €24 to €30. À la carte. Chèque Restaurant. Groups welcome (up to 25 while reserving in advance). Take-away. Shop. Caterer.

You think it looks like a beautiful bakery ? Behind this gourmet front, you will find a restaurant that is very successful in the city centre. Salads, prepared light meals and works of art to crunch are available. Here, the flavours and colours take shape and are harmonious. Guests have an eye on the chef thanks to the open kitchen The monthly menu is full of surprises and changes every month, as its name suggests, allowing our taste buds of experts to delight in this feast – you can judge for yourself : the duck foie gras in nougat's way, hazelnuts, soft apricots, almonds, marmalade of shallots and raspberries, accompanied by toasts. Let us continue with wild and cubic roast salmon shrimps and their zucchinis risotto and mushrooms of the forest. You still have delicacies in the dessert, a homemade creme brulee with vanilla, biscuit with orange and cocoa nibs. Make also a break in the afternoon with a small homemade cake, of course. Modern, welcoming and friendly, it is an address that is very appreciated by the team of Petit Futé. It also offers catering service.

LE PETIT MONDE D'EDITH
13, rue Fourier ✆ +33 (0)3 86 51 49 69

Open Tuesday to Saturday from 12pm to 2pm. Tea room open from 2.30pm to 5.30pm. Closed certain public holidays. Booking advised. Wine by the glass. With slate, from €10.50. Credit card not accepted. Groups welcome.

Prevails here an atmosphere of family home : patina and waxed old objects and toys of yesteryear, old pictures and frames, a paradise for bargain hunters Edith welcomes her guests with warmth and smiles. We like to chat with her, and we soon become a regular, absolutely addicted to this place as frozen in time Its pies, its vegetable mixtures and dishes are a real treat to be enjoyed without moderation A place full of delight for both the eyes and the taste buds. It is best to book as the place is very popular

LE P'TIT MARMITON
26, avenue du 24-Août ✆ +33 (0)3 86 51 50 29
www.leptitmarmitonauxerre.fr

Open every day from 12pm to 1.30pm and from 7pm to 9.30pm. Booking advised. Menu from €29 to €37. Children's menu : €15. Fixed rate formula : €18 (except weekends and public holidays). À la carte. Holiday voucher, Chèque Restaurant. Groups welcome (up to 20 people). Baby chairs. Terrace. Take-away.

A warm welcome for a revisited Burgundian cuisine, creative and faithful to seasonal ingredients. A menu that changes every two to three months. On the menu, we choose a tempura of Burgundy snails and parsley cream and pan-fried foie gras, then scallops accompanied leek fondue with its foie gras sauce... delicious. Let us continue with fried bouchons de comté and their saladine with nut oil, to finish in an exquisite way with a joconde cake, mango and vanilla cream. Some classics are all the same, such as the calf's head, poached eggs in wine sauce and the charolais beef piece. This restaurant is highly appreciated

■ **LA TOUR D'ORBANDELLE**
34, place des Cordeliers ✆ +33 (0)3 86 52 31 46
www.latourdorbandelle.com
contact@latourdorbandelle.fr
♿

Open all year. Every day from 11.30am to 11pm. Suggestion of the day : €14.50 (every day). Tour fixed rate formulas from €10. Possible online order for takeaways, 20% discount. Diners Club, Holiday vouchers. Groups welcome (by reservation). Terrace. Take-away. Air conditioning. Veranda. wi-fi. Pets allowed.

One of the best plans to eat at any time in Auxerre and a nice success for this young boss with a promising future The restaurant offers a studied menu and fresh products cooked by a chef and a second one who are faithful to the place for some time You can be served here every day from 11 : 30am to 11pm, quickly and with a smile... More than a pizza, we strongly advise you to choose a burger on the menu like the pepper burger Tour, the blue burger Tour or the Chavignol burger Tour, and then for example ice-cream – you will certainly treat yourself. There is also a wide range for grilled meat, mixed salads and gourmet desserts. A smart address for all tastes and all appetites, run by a boss and staff who are on great form This restaurant uses only high quality products and you can also order online, modern... Pleasant terrace and veranda. Another important point, the large public parking located in front of the hotel.

Sleeping

■ **HOTEL IBIS AUXERRE CENTRE**
1, avenue Jean-Jaurès
✆ +33 (0)3 86 48 30 55 – www.ibishotel.com
h1361@accor.com
♿ ❄ 🍸

Qualité Tourisme label. Open all year. Reception 24/24. 50 rooms (including 3 for disabled guests). from €70.55. Breakfast : €9.90. Garage : €10. American Express, Diners Club, Holiday voucher. Pets allowed (€5). Free Wifi. Satellite TV, Canal+.

Within walking distance from the city centre, the hotel has the advantage to offer comfortable rooms, especially with the new beddings « « Sweet Bed by Ibis », and spacious, with simple and contemporary lines. It offers a magnificent view, the most played image of Auxerre : opposite you, the view of its churches and the prefecture takes shape, overlooking Yonne and the port. This heritage is lit with elegance in the evening. In the morning, start the day with a hearty breakfast served by a very welcoming and friendly staff, who show a discretion and a remarkable efficiency. A beautiful and very pleasant hotel for a stop in the city of Paul Bert. The small advantages that we enjoy : rooms with balconies overlooking the most beautiful view of the city, and free car parks at the foot of the hotel.

■ INTER HOTEL NORMANDIE
41, boulevard Vauban
✆ +33 (0)3 86 52 57 80
www.hotelnormandie.fr
reception@hotelnormandie.fr

Open all year. Reception 24/24. 47 rooms (1 apartment from 1 to 5 people). Double room from €82 to €115; triple room from €91 to €125; studio/apartment from €135 to €150. Buffet breakfast : €9.80 (child of less than 12 years : €5). Garage : €7. Family room 1 to 4 people, from €115 to €135. Evening business from €88 to €105. Sauna : €6. American Express, Diners Club, Holiday voucher. Pets allowed. Seminars. Free Wifi. Satellite TV, Canal+. Sauna.

Classicism and elegance are the keywords of this hotel located on the boulevards, on the site of the old ramparts. The modern rooms do not sacrifice comfort in this beautiful house of the nineteenth century : all the doors meet the standards of 2011, soundproofing and insulation, new TV screens of 28 or 32 inches with new channels, recreation room, billiards, sauna. Terrace, garden, a pleasant reception. A pleasant breakfast room to enjoy A place for any form of rest, at walking distance to the city center and the cinema. Do not hesitate to go regularly on their website, where special deals are regularly offered : special weekend, family offer, palate-pleasure discovery...

■ LE PARC DES MARÉCHAUX
6, avenue Foch
✆ +33 (0)3 86 51 43 77
www.hotel-parcmarechaux.com

Open all year. 25 rooms. Single room from €91 to €156; double room from €121 to €156; triple room €162. Buffet breakfast or in room : €13. Shows for seminars from €85. American Express, Diners Club, Holiday voucher. Pets allowed (€11). Seminars. Free Wifi. Satellite TV, Canal+.

It was in 1854 that the Napoleon III style mansion was born. A family of magistrates in Paris are the proud owners. The characteristic building traversed decades and eras until 1980 when it became the Park Marshals. The charm of this period is intact, the comfort of the 21th century and more. The twenty-five rooms, furnished with care and air-conditioned are each named after one of the marshals of France, with a special preference for those of the Empire. The comfort of the rooms and three rooms are at your disposal, the friendliness and charm of the bar, beauty of the park with old trees, not to mention the relaxation time by the pool : everything comes together for a charming stay near the historic center.

Cottages

■ MAISON DES RANDONNEURS
5, rue Germain-Benard
✆ 03 86 41 43 22
maison.rando@gmail.com

La Maison is open all year. From March to October : booking required for groups. Reception of individual on the premises every day from 4pm to 7pm from April to October. From November to March, booking compulsory. €18 per night, breakfast : €5.60. Outdoor lounge, sheets rental, washing machine, tumble dryer.

In the city center, located in the beautiful Paul Bert park, Maison des randonneurs offers a simple stopover accommodation with a meeting lounge, large dining room and equipped kitchen. This beautiful rehabilated bourgeoise house haults valiant pilgrims of Compostela, mostly in summer, during the low season and also welcomes groups, students or workers. Cooking in this stopover house, is a like playing the scientists Those who will cook evening pasta in the kitchen will be in the first laboratory of Paul Bert, who lived in this building. On the practical : a closed bike garage, sales of IGN card and car luggage service until the next step.

Leisure

■ LES BATEAUX ELECTRIQUES
✆ +33 (0)3 86 52 06 19 /
+33 (0)6 25 04 43 88
www.ot-auxerre.fr
contact@ot-auxerre.fr

Open from mid-April to end of September, Wednesday to Sunday as well as public holidays. From €13 per half hour at €85 the day (ID and guarantee required from €200 with the reservation).

That can take up to five people, these license, quiet and fun electric boats, have an autonomy of 7 : 00. Ideal to discover the beauties of the auxerrois along the Yonne and the canal du nivernais in an ecological way You can go from the locks and going to Champs-sur-Yonne. Binoculars can be provided and you can moor on a bank for a picnic shaded with family, friends or lovers. Absolute anti-stress with the current. The boat rental is labelled « Famil'Yonne » and « Vineyards and discovery ».

Going Out

■ LE PULLMANN BAR
20, rue d'Egleny
✆ +33 (0)3 86 52 09 32

Annual closing 3 weeks from end of August to beginning of September. Open Monday to Friday from 5pm to 1am; Saturday until 2am.

Is it brown, blonde or amber ? He knows it and can also advise the amateur to find him one that will please him. Some 120 types of beers and fifty cocktails with and without alcohol. The carte also comprises of high-quality liquor, including cognacs, Armagnac, several whiskeys and rums. The owner, sometimes a bit grumpy, talks nevertheless with passion and erudition of its multitude of products. Essential and sublime Trappist, very distant or near by beers, a culinary journey in a warm atmosphere where great music does not prevent conversations at a brisk pace on the comfortable benches. A must for Auxerre evenings.

Shopping

Gourmet Basket

■ ARÔMES ET DOUCEURS

rue de l'Horloge
✆ +33 (0)3 86 33 01 95
Open Tuesday to Saturday from 10am to 12.30pm and from 2.30pm to 7pm.
A grocery mingling smells of teas and chocolates, jams and other delicacies... of all shapes and colors that are sure to apeal to you Our taste buds salivating already for these delicacies.... It is tempting. Long series of coffees : mocha, Kenya, Maragogype. The Dijon heritage is also being honored with the divine gingerbread of the house of the Mulot Petit Jean and the best mustard in the world (without any chauvinism)from Edmont Fallot.

■ LA BOURGOGNE EN TOUTE SIMPLICITE

12, rue Fourrier
✆ +33 (0)3 86 51 23 56
www.bourgogne-en-toute-simplicite.fr
Open on Monday and Wednesday from 9.30am to 5.30pm; Tuesday, Thursday and Friday from 9.30am to 6.30pm; Saturday from 10am to 7pm; Sunday from 10am to 12pm. Purchase order downloadable on line.
A pretty little shop a few steps from Saint-Etienne Cathedral in a medieval house. A pleasant reception and especially good advice on Home wines (no less than 65 different wines of Burgundy), but not only local produce Some local crémants and champagnes from a neighboring region, sweets of icaunaises and other specialties such as Fayot mustard. Gourmet gifts ideas guaranteed

CHOCOLATERIE OLIVIER VIDAL

3, place Charles-Surugue
✆ +33 (0)3 86 52 04 25
www.oliviervidal.fr/
contact@oliviervidal.fr
Open on Monday from 3pm to 7pm; Tuesday to Friday from 9am to 7pm; Saturday from 9am to 1pm and from 2pm to 7pm. Black chocolate 7.70 €/100gr. Rough-hew for 6 people €28. Macaroons : 25/30 €, pyramid from 24 to 112 macaroons from €36.20. Good of online order.
Olivier Vidal, Meilleur Ouvrier de France as a chocolate-maker, confectioner, offers us the very essence of his creations. You can enjoy chocolates, with orange or lemon peels, black or milk; you will appreciate the almond/hazelnut biscuits; you will damn yourself for the caramel coulis and the spread, and you will happily bend to the tasting of the cakes whose subtle fineness in the mouth brightens our taste buds. Note that (only) every Saturday, you can enjoy nature or almond croissants, as well as classic chocolate bread or also enhanced with almonds. And for the New Year celebrations, emanations of ginger, orange, spéculos come to caress your senses, carrying you out for the discovery pyramids of macaroons or Yule logs with names as soft as their flavours. A big favourite of Petit Futé. An address to jealously keep.

■ GREGORY FERET

88, rue de Paris
✆ +33 (0)3 86 52 11 64
Open Tuesday to Saturday from 9am to 7pm; Sunday from 10am to 1pm.
Since the launching of Soissons Auxerrre, the fame of this chocolaterie-pastry-confectionery has been established. A dark chocolate ganache and caramelised hazelnuts coated with white chocolate has revived the taste of the bean grown in the fifteenth century. As for Guy Balls, a delicious wordgame, is a confectionery designed for fans, sold in a sock in the colors of the AJA. Another pun (play of words) ? The winds of angels, a luscious dark chocolate caramel harboring a wine and alcohol of the cru. Innovations and taste surprises next season, as zozios, biscuits to nibble all day. A dozen flavors : licorice, rosemary, lemon... We also gladly let ourselves be tempted by the macaroons, and the filled cocoa pods. A warm welcome.

Wines & Spirits

LES AGAPES

13, rue de Preuilly
✆ +33 (0)3 86 52 15 22
www.les-agapes-caviste.fr
ragaine.marc@wanadoo.fr
Open Tuesday to Saturday from 9am to 12.30pm and from 2pm to 7pm. Possible delivery (under certain conditions. Deposit-sale). Classes of tasting : 50 €/h, wines and travel (except Auxerre) with the load of the guest (from 7pm every day except Sunday).
For 20 years, this small family business offers a wide range of French and foreign wines. Marc Ragaine was elected the best independent wine merchant in the world, sommelier of the Tour d'Argent in Paris, 3rd best young sommelier of France and best young sommelier in Paris : what else can we say ? He will advise you on what suits you best among its 700 references. A judicious choice of subtle nectars, glassware and many gift ideas. Your host also offers tasting courses at home, from 1 to 8 people in Auxerre and its surroundings.

■ BACCHUS ET GAMBRINUS

32, avenue Jean-Mermoz
✆ +33 (0)3 86 41 74 21
Open Monday to Thursday from 10am to 8pm; Friday and Saturday from 10am to 9pm. Carte Club. Card gifts from €20.
The specialist in beers and spirits on Auxerre. With no less than 480 references to the purchase and 250 references available for tasting, you will inevitably find the beer that will excite your taste buds. Major brands of reputation, others less well-known but equally tasty, foreign beers, craft beers... A space tasting that it is possible to hire, gift boxes, and the advice offered by a friendly and dynamic team.

In the surroundings

Accolay

HOSTELLERIE DE LA FONTAINE
16, rue de Reigny
✆ +33 (0)3 86 81 54 02
www.hostelleriedelafontaine.fr
hostellerie.fontaine@gmail.com
Open Wednesday to Saturday from 12pm to 2pm and from 7.15pm to 8.15pm; Sunday. Booking advised. Menu from €32 to €51. À la carte. American Express, Holiday voucher. Groups welcome. Garden. Terrace.
On the road to Avallon, Accolay has hidden within its walls a valuable restaurant skillfully managed for over 20 years by the chef Alain Pohu. Gourmet and refined, the cuisine of the place, with hints of the terroir, is punctuated with light creative touches. Some ideas of the dishes to water your mouth : snails casserole in crust Chablis way, trout fillet with red lentils, Chaource cream, crusty sweetbread with honey and carrots, beef steak with époisses sauce... The fresh and market produce are in the spotlight and are worked with dexterity by a passionate maestro. Our favorite is the dining room, which is an old cellar of the 17th century that retains all the charm of white stones The garden and the shaded terrace also hide their little treasure...

Appoigny

KYRIAD – RESTAURANT LE MARAIS
RN6
7, route des Bries
✆ +33 (0)3 86 53 25 34
www.kyriad-auxerre-appoigny.fr
appoigny@kyriad.fr
Open all year. Reception 24/24. 110 rooms. €72. Buffet breakfast : €8.50. Parking included. Menu from €13. Holiday voucher. Seminars. Internet access. Free Wifi. Catering facilities (menu from €16 to €36). Satellite TV, Canal+.
The hotel, whose facades have been recently refurbished, offers a hundred rooms, all benefiting from air conditioning and modern comfort with Internet connection in the entire property. The team is friendly and dynamic, and will satisfy your needs. The setting is nice, not far from the city, but quiet The hotel also has a restaurant, Le Marais which is classified as « Restaurant de Tourisme » and « Restaurateur de France », and offers specialties from the region to discover on the terrace in fine weather.

Bazarnes

AUX CROISSANTS GOURMANDS
21, rue de Vézelay
✆ +33 (0)3 86 32 29 19
Two gourmet addresses as desired We have a soft spot for their desserts, such as the Marie-Antoinette, blackcurrant cheesecake and brown whipped cream blackcurrant, the Absolue, vanilla ganache and streusel pistachio-hazelnut, but also for their candy apple macaroons, chocolate-banana, salted caramel butter, speculoos raspberries... Delicacies in terms of looks and taste The lemon tarts, raspberry or chocolate also attract our eyes, and in salty version, you can easily let yourself be tamed by the goat fougasses, bleu and bacon with fresh cream. Trust them for your birthday cakes, your wedding cakes or your Yule logs. You are advised by our tastebuds

Chemilly-sur-Yonne

LE BORVO
Route de Beaumont
✆ +33 (0)3 86 47 82 44
www.leborvo.fr – contact@leborvo.fr
Shop open Monday to Saturday from 9am to 6.30pm all year. Special opening some Sunday in December (ask for information). Courses discovered from January to November guided tour for individual Saturday at 3pm by reservation all year. Online store. For an order placed before 9am, assured delivery out of relay parcel in 48h maximum. Course discovered for groups of 20 to 40 people by reservation. Possible rental for the family seminars and events. American Express.
Salmon from Scotland or Norway from direct and processed locally, that's smoked salmon Borvo : simply excellent, one of the best ever. The house offers other dishes such as : foie gras, a wide range of dishes, a nice deli catering and a few glass pots containing coq au vin, brandade of salmon and other dishes cooked on site. unmissable also is : beef bourguignon. Colorful and in all beauty, sweets and fantasy alcoholic bottles alongside wines and spirits of the region. A reference house outside the borders of the department, Borvo is created in 1980 by Daniel Raymond, a former Michelin starred chef cook. The visitors should open the eye, more than 800 products are available. In addition to the store on a plain, contemporary architecture is inspired by the Royal Saltworks of Arc-et-Senans, the back of the stage is to be discovered. Exciting

Chevannes

CHÂTEAU DE RIBOURDIN
✆ +33 (0)3 86 41 23 16
www.chateauderibourdin.com
chateau.de.ribourdin@wanadoo.fr
Gîte de France (4 épis). Open all year. 5 rooms (including one for the disabled guests). Single room from €65 to €90; double room from €80 to €90; triple room €120. Breakfast included. Room for 4 people : €150. Good gifts. Credit card not accepted. Pets allowed (€10 in addition). Free Wifi. Cleaning service. Sale (Burgundy wines). No TV. Activities. Excursions (proposals of stroll).
In the outbuildings of a sixteenth-century castle, surrounded by a lovely flowered with bower hedges, trees and lawn, this is the ideal place to regenerate youself

in the open air. Make the most of the ambient charm in one of the five comfortable rooms all highlighted with a certain romanticism. Personalised with delicacy, they all offer a beautiful view of the countryside. A fine place with a very pleasant charm of yesteryears.

Cravant

■ OFFICE DE TOURISME ENTRE CURE ET YONNE
Halte Nautique
✆ +33 (0)3 86 81 54 26
www.coeurdelyonne.com
informations@coeurdelyonne.com
High season : open Monday to Saturday from 9.30am to 1pm and from 2pm to 6.30pm; Sunday from 1pm to 5pm. From April to October, Monday to Saturday, 9.30am-1pm/2pm-5.30pm. -. Bike rental : 1/2 day €10, 1 day €19.
The Chalet de l'Office de Tourisme is located on the nautical stopover of Bazarnes, at the edge of the Canal du Nivernais. Here, you will find a plethora of information about the heritage of the Vallée de la Cure, holiday ideas, outings and walks, especially along the Green lane and the Canal du Nivernais, and also good places where you can eat, and also a space dedicated to handmade products from local producers. Bike rental is also possible in summer. Also note that it is now possible, in real time, to become aware of the information provided by the tourist office via your smartphone (www.yonne-tourisme.mobi).

Escolives-Sainte-Camille

■ SITE ARCHEOLOGIQUE ★
9, rue Raymond-Kapps
✆ +33 (0)3 86 53 39 09
www.yonne-89.net/Escolives.htm
archeo.escolives@wanadoo.fr
Open all year. Closed on January 1st, May 1st, November 1st and December 25th. From January to March, in November and December, open on weekdays and €2 and €4 weekends of each month; from April to October, open every day. Free. Credit card not accepted. Children welcome (educational workshops, visits). Guided tour (10h-11h-14h-15h-16h-17h. Duration visits 1am. To prevent for a visit other than in French). Shop.
Situated along the old Roman road of Agrippa, the site takes its origins near the source of Creusot, which attracted man since the Neolothic age. The periods that have succeeded on the site are evidenced by the ruins of a villa, those of Gallo-Roman baths and a Merovingian cemetery. Guided tours are very significant, especially for students, and takes us through the ages in the afternoon. Very entertaining

Merry-la-Vallée

■ LE GALOPIN
6, place Henri-Chamvres
✆ +33 (0)3 86 73 22 46 / +33 (0)6 08 82 77 53
www.le-galopin-gastronome.fr
legalopintraiteur@wanadoo.fr

Dovecot.

Open Tuesday to Sunday. Booking is essential. Menu from €32 to €48. Fixed rate formula Bistro : starter and main course or main course and dessert, €19, starter + main course + dessert, €26. Terrace. Catering on all France.
Nested in the small village of Merry-la-Vallée, the chance seldom led there... It is thus by its quality that this small place of delicacies has established a solid reputation. This former presbytery, emphasized by a painter decorator, is one of the famous addresses of the department where gourmets go with pleasure. How to resist to the charm of the vaulted dining rooms ? As for the à la carte, the chef honours the gourmet heritage with a tip of creativity and much personality. The senses are perfectly happy In Bistro version, you find for example a terrine of homemade andouillettes and its onion jam, smoked duck confit with rosemary and a furnished faisselle. The establishment also proposes a conference room perfectly equipped, and a cottage for 15 people.

Parly

■ AUX QUATRE VENTS DE L'ART – CENTRE D'ART GRAPHIQUE
La Métairie Bruyère
✆ +33 (0)3 86 74 30 72
lametairieb@gmail.com
Open every day from June to September. From October to May, schedule depending on exhibitions, ask for information, or by appointment. Two galleries to be visited from June to September. Off-season by appointment. Major inspection the morning at 10am (workshops to envisage minimum 2 : 00). Visit of the showrooms only : €3, from 6 to 15 years old children : €1.50. Guided tours of the workshops, adult €5, child of less than 15 years €2.50, studying €3. Courses possible. credit card and checks are not accepted. Children welcome (child workshops and pupils, package from €155). Activities.

The buildings of this unique place in Europe dedicated to graphic arts is set near the town of Parly; it was also owned by the singer Julien Clerc at the beginning of his career. A guided tour presents the various workshops, their techniques and functions. Various activities : lithography, typography with wood and lead in the old and a fifteenth century Gutenberg style, engraving and amateur engraving are organised in the centre throughout the year. Artists come to mark their prints. It is particularly appreciated and we liked it.

Rouvray

■ LE STYLISS

Route d'Héry
✆ +33 (0)3 86 47 85 76
www.styliss.fr
contact@styliss.fr

Open all year. Monday from 2.30pm; Friday from 10.30pm to 5am; from 10.30pm to 6am. Same schedule for the eves of public holidays. €2 Fridays and €4 Saturday and eves of public holidays. 1 bought bottle = 5 entrances offered. 1/2 bought bottle : 3 entrances offered. Checks are not accepted. Activities.

A Friendly staff for the largest nightclub in the Yonne. And people come from afar to dance RnB, rock, to techno or the accordion on Mondays afternoon, the jukebox is complete. Here the music is good The music sounds and above all it does not cheat The leisure center at flux in at night, with some rooms opening on the programmes of the 90's. The atmosphere will remind you sometimes some good dances that we know in the campsites at the seashores. A real friendly popular mix of all ages. That music with major chords : so there is no track without a dancer If the drummer explodes, the shock is left to you Be careful because you might get carried away into the end of the night...

© JOSIANE MAXEL

The Roman church of Prégilbert.

Saint-Georges-sur-Baulche

■ FRANCE A VELO

74, Grand-Rue ✆ +33 (0)3 86 42 35 96
www.franceavelo.com
info@franceavelo.com

Tours bicycles, fixed rate formula freedom, bike rental. Bike rental : from €10 to €79, one half-day at 7 days. in option, bicycles for child and trailers for children.

This tour operator specializes in discovery tours by bicycle. Whether you are accompanied by professional guides or not, you will certainly find a circuit adapted for you. From the Auxerrois vineyards to a discovery of the treasures of Yonne, everything has been designed to complement your tour. People who do not have a bicycle can also use this tour operator who also rents some.

Venoy

■ LE MOULIN DE LA COUDRE

8, rue des Gravottes ✆ +33 (0)3 86 42 50 47
www.moulindelacoudre.com
moulin@moulindelacoudre.fr

Restaurateurs de France. « Maître Restaurateur » label. Open from 12.15pm to 1.30pm and from 7.15pm to 8.30pm. Booking advised. Menu from €25 to €51. €13 and €17. À la carte. Rooms from €79 to €159, breakfast €12. Animals €10. Holiday voucher. Tourism label & Disability. Groups welcome.

Welcome to Moulin de la Coudre. You can have lunch and have dinner, spend one or many nights, and also have family meeting in this renovated and neatly decorated building. In the kitchen, the Chef Jean-Pierre Vaury offers a creative cuisine that draws its inspiration from the land and Burgundian know-how and just to get you started, we've chosen on the à la carte menu : a fried and breaded foie gras, bread-crumb of gingerbread and kumquat marmalade, it already leaves our palate in turmoil... let us continue with a spinal column of wild boar à la plancha and long pepper, and if you prefer fish we recommend you the fillet of scorpion fish and its cream in the green crab. Finish with finesse with a perfect ice-cream flavoured with red Ratafia and the heart of quince. Near the fireplace in winter, or on the shaded terrace in summer, the moment promise to be delicious one. An air of countryside to enjoy as much as you like

Vermenton

■ ABBAYE DE REIGNY ★

✆ +33 (0)3 86 81 59 30
www.abbayedereigny.com
abbayedereigny@orange.fr
Car : 2 km south of Vermenton since the RN6.
TER Burgundy at Vermenton.

No visits during the concerts and other events of the abbey. To check the programming. From May to September : Sunday afternoon (departures at 3pm, 4pm and 5pm). July and August : every day except Sunday morning and

Monday (departures at 10.15am, 11.15am, 3pm, 4pm and 5pm). Free for under 11-year-olds. Adult : €8. Child (from 12 to 18 years old) : €4. Group (15 people) : €7. Family rate (2 adults and 2 children and more) : €20. Visit in supplemented spoken language (LPC). Children welcome (visits with themes, activities and guides specialized). Activities. Possible English visit.

Fifth daughter of Clairvaux, on the right bank of the Cure, the ancient abbey founded in 1128 retains an exceptional dining room with paintings of the early fourteenth century, a centre for cultural events. You can still see a dovecot of the seventeenth century and the foundations of demolished buildings, including the second abbey rebuilt in the eighteenth century by Claude-Nicolas Ledoux, a visionary architect born in Yonne, famous for his Salines in Arc-et-Senans. Reigny received up to 300 monks and lay brothers. Between the Hundred Years' War, the Huguenots and the French Revolution, it suffered a lot and was much damaged. It lost its power and splendor. It retains many vestiges of its past grandeur. The ancient scriptorium was converted in the eighteenth century into apartments, some of which were frequented by Coco Chanel. Also made into a cottage and guesthouse.

■ SAVEURS DU TERROIR

13, rue du Général-de-Gaulle
✆ +33 (0)3 86 81 59 48 / +33 (0)6 08 17 55 69
saveursduterroir@yahoo.fr

Accommodate groups for tasting, by reservation.

Saveurs du Terroir shop perfectly bears its name François Kwiatkowski welcomes you in its warm and friendly shop where he has the best local wines and from the region. The large cabinet is full of excellent delicacies, showcasing the wealth of the region. You will have fun by personalizing a small basket of local : fine wines and liquors, meat of Morvan, sweets and other delicacies will capsize your tastebuds to remember the Burgundian flavours Also note that François opened a very pleasant tea room, just next to its charming shop : teas, Italian hot chocolate, coffees tastefully selected and sweet delicacies will delight you for a gourmet moment of relaxation. Exhibitions are regularly organised, as well as theme evenings. Nice place to be visited without moderation

AVALLON ★

Avallon has long been a strategic point overlooking the valley of Cousin. A large section of the walls is still visible. The terraced gardens which rise below, surrounded by dry stone walls, are worth a visit.

The lower part of the city reminds a little about the spirit of the village; it is already the countryside. A fine introduction to the discovery of Morvan. The historical centre goes, from the big bustling street to the old collegiate Saint-Lazare; there are several places and curiosities in this sub-prefecture of 8,250 inhabitants. Beautiful tower houses of the fifteenth and the sixteenth and seventeenth houses can be seen along the streets. Vauban, genius architect, supremely reigns here, as he was born a few kilometres away. Avallon is also the beautiful valley of the Cousin which offers splendid walks.

The City Hall.

© JULIA VALENTIN

Stroll in the heart of the historic city of Avallon.

■ **OFFICE DE TOURISME D'AVALLON**
6, rue Bocquillot
✆ +33 (0)3 86 34 14 19
www.avallon-morvan.com
From September to June, Monday to Saturday from 9.30am to 12.30pm and from 2pm to 6pm. In July and August, Monday to Saturday from 9.30am to 12.30pm and from 1.30pm to 6.30pm, Sunday from 10am to 12pm and from 2pm to 4pm. Rental of vtc Sunday and Monday only (check rates).
The tourist office now offers guided tours retracing the history, heritage and architecture of Avallon. Accompanied by Amelie, a national interpreter, you will discover this charming town at the gates of Morvan and visit places that are not accessible in normal times like; La Tour de l'Horloge, l'Orgue de Saint-Lazare and La Maison des Syr Domecy. Beautiful walks in perspective Do not miss the application for free on the App Store allowing you to discover the city with the family by involving children in challenges throughout your walk.

Sightseeing

■ **MUSÉE DU COSTUME** ★
6, rue Belgrand
✆ +33 (0)3 86 34 19 95
Guided tours from April 15th to November 1st every day from 10.30am to 12.30pm and from 1.30pm to 5.30pm .30. Adult : €5. Child (up to 18 years) : €3. Group (10 people) : €3.
Far from vintage and from makeover, here is a visit with a good smell of clothes and wax. It highlights the fashion over time, staged in a reconstituted atmosphere. A hundred suites and thousands of accessories... The dream of many girls. Each year, a new collection : the 2016 exhibition shows the place of the flower in the 18th century fashion till nowadays. The sewing is an art that has survived throughout the centuries, and that you can find in the twelve rooms of this beautiful mansion of the 17th and 18th centuries, former property of the Condé family. A place ready to visit, where we do not balance the anecdotes.

■ **TOUR DE L'HORLOGE**
Grande-Rue
Dominated by a tower of the fifteenth century of 49 meters high and topped by a slate bell tower, that majestic door, marks the entrance to the ancient Roman castrum, the remnants of this era are visible at the Museum of Avallonais. To join the university of Saint-Lazare, you must pass under the monument, coming from the shopping street. A very beautiful testimony of the historical past of Avallon open to the public as part of the guided tours from now on.

Knife & Fork

■ **L'HORLOGE**
63, Grande-Rue ✆ +33 (0)3 86 46 75 24
Booking advised. Menu from €13.90 to €16.90. Children's menu : €8. À la carte. Groups welcome. Terrace.
This restaurant has found its brands at the foot of the Clock of Avallon In a warm atmosphere that combines the red and black, exposed beams and the benches, Alexandre and his team offer an original cuisine : fresh seasonal products are the base of his dishes, providing quality and generosity in flavours : smoked salmon chive sauce, marbled parsley of the region, veal medallion, burger of l'Horloge, pana cotta with seasonal fruit, gourmet coffee of l'Horloge... A beautiful terrace, very pleasant in summer, in particular, the dinner aperitifs concerts. An address to be kept in your tablet and a nice location in the city

■ **IBIS AVALLON – RESTAURANT LA TUILERIE**
33, rue de la Bergerie ✆ +33 (0)3 86 33 01 33
www.hotelavallon.fr
H1740@accor.com

Open all year. Every day. Menu from €10.90 to €18.90. Franck and Pascal Boisselier are in charge of the Ibis hotel, and also have the pleasure to independently run the « La Tuilerie » restaurant. Their chef, Thibault, cultivates a 100%-homemade cuisine which makes local flavours a wealth for your taste buds. On the menu of this semi gourmet restaurant, the traditional oeufs meurette, the tails of crawfish and their risotto, and for the sweet flavours, the homemade large profiterole will not leave you unmoved The welcome is warm and the atmosphere friendly, with a wonderful view of the green park where the establishment is located. Very good value for money.

■ **LE VAUDESIR**
84, rue de Lyon
✆ +33 (0)3 86 34 14 60
levaudesir.avallon@orange.fr
Open all year. Closed from March 1st to March 8th. Closed on Monday all day and Wednesday for dinner and Sunday for dinner. Menu from €17 to €38. Wine by the glass. À la carte. Holiday voucher, Chèque Restaurant. Garden. Possible service with the Garden.
After having made his classes at Robuchon as well as in Hôtellerie des Clos, Cécile Riotte Jeanne has been settled in the former Café des Minimes to open this charming restaurant. A bistro decor with warm atmosphere reinforced by the presence of the fireplace that crackles, a delicate and gourmet cuisine, revisited by the culinary inventions of Cecile. On a pretty table set with topping and elegant and neat tableware, let yourself be surprised by the subtle alliances of seasonal flavours, by the mixture of spices, by the color and texture play... Some examples to whet your appetite : salmi of chicken and chutney of coriander potatoes, cod blanquette, Tartar of crab and its tabbouleh, tomatos and vinaigrette, Crimean tomato burger and pineapple with carrot salad and rips of pork sparerib with honey... an excellence that you can find in the desserts with in particular the Mount Blanc mousse coconut chocoou and the gingerbread with chocolate and its spice ice-cream. Taste, generosity, an excellent value for money, in short, a restaurant with the cuisine 100% homemade, to be discovered urgently Certainly among the 3 top of the best addresses in the city A real favorite

Sleeping

■ **LES CAPUCINS**
6, avenue Président-Doumer
✆ +33 (0)3 86 34 06 52
www.avallonlescapucins.com
hotellescapucins@wanadoo.fr
Logis (2 cheminées). Open all year. 23 rooms. From €54 to €90. Buffet breakfast : €8.50 (€4 for children under 10 years old). Extra bed : €10. Closed parking included. Free Wifi. Satellite TV.
A pleasant stay in the heart of Avallon. This address offers the tranquillity of a charming middle-class residence and the proximity of the centre. Its 23 rooms offer a bright and colourful setting and perfectly equipped with all modern comfort (LCD TV, luxury Italian showers...). With its newly-created garden, the building offers rooms on the ground floor, in the quiet. A quality welcome in this establishment whose restaurant serves fine cuisine highlighting regional specialties at very reasonable rates.

■ **HOSTELLERIE DU MOULIN DES RUATS**
Vallée du Cousin
23, rue des Iles-Labaume
✆ +33 (0)3 86 34 97 00
www.moulindesruats.com
contact@moulindesruats.com
Open from February 26th to November 13th, 2016. 25 rooms (including a suite). From €93 to €145; suite €165. Half-board (from €191 to €263 for 2 people). Breakfast : €15. Extra bed : €20 (cot offered). Closed parking included. Pets allowed (€12). Seminars. Free Wifi. Satellite TV.
This former flour mill of the 18th century is now a beautiful residence with the classic charm. In this idyllic setting, Jocelyne Rossi welcomes you amidst of tradition and modernity, in a refined atmosphere where your stay will be like a serene and saving stop in the heart of Burgundy. 25 rooms with particularly refined decor, and equipped with all modern comfort (Wi-Fi, television with satellite channels, direct dial telephone...), with view of the garden or river, and some with a private terrace. You will love to relax in the lounge with its library, enjoy a drink in the bar or browse the garden where the Cousin flows. The address also has a restaurant, offering a quality of the very pleasant services Very beautiful place where it is possible to enjoy various stay formula to enjoy the place as well as possible.

■ **IBIS AVALLON – RESTAURANT LA TUILERIE**
33, rue de la Bergerie
✆ +33 (0)3 86 33 01 33
www.hotelavallon.fr
H1740@accor.com
Open all year. 42 rooms (including two reserved to the disabled guests). Double room from €69. Breakfast : €9.50. Open parking included. Pets allowed. Free Wifi.
The Boisselier brothers, Franck and Pascal, already own the Kyriad hotels of longvic, Ibis in Perrigny-les-Dijon and Jacquemart hotel, are also in charge of the Ibis of Avallon. It is in an absolute quiet, in the heart of a green setting, just a stone's throw from Parc Naturel Régional du Morvan, that the doors of this red ibis hotel open, completely renovated. The 42 rooms are spacious, with zen atmosphere, perfectly equipped with wi-fi and TV, and has stylish bathroom. The bedding « *Sweet Bed by Ibis* » will offer you just a cosy comfort. The restaurant has a terrace with a nice view of the surrounding nature. A chef works on site at the « La Tuilerie » restaurant and offers a semi- gourmet cuisine, with fresh products, for gourmet dishes such as the homemade Burger with 2poisses... A complete place for a relaxing stay or a working seminar.

■ **LE RELAIS FLEURI**
La Cerce
✆ +33 (0)3 86 34 02 85
www.hotel-relais-fleuri.com
Contact@hotel-relais-fleuri.com

Logis (3 cheminées). Qualité Tourisme label. Open all year. Fixed rate formula 19.5 with the lunch Monday to Friday. 48 rooms. Breakfast : €14. Rooms from €93. Stop-over with special rates for reps from €93 to €99.50. Pets allowed (€7.10). Seminars. Receptions and weddings. Satellite TV.

This hotel offers comfortable, elegant and well decorated rooms, arranged around the main building. They are organised as individual bungalows, on the ground floor, on the park of 5 hectares with flowers and trees. A very nice swimming pool awaits you with its deckchairs and its bar, as well as the tennis courts, petanque and ping-pong that will make you have a pleasant stay. The establishment also has a restaurant with gourmet menus and rich in Burgundian flavours.

In the surroundings

Montréal

■ **MAISON CRÈME ANGLAISE**
22, Grande Rue
✆ +33 (0)3 86 32 07 73 / +33 (0)6 88 71 83 75
www.maisoncremeanglaise.com
bonjour@maisoncremeanglaise.com

Open all year. Double room €90. Breakfast included. 2 Cottages from €500 to €1,300 per week. Pets allowed (€5 in addition). Free Wifi. Sauna.

Unearthed just for you, a gourmet address coiled in the middle of a charming medieval village of Montreal : 3 chambres d'hôte and 2 cottages with So British flavour. Christine and Graham invite you to push the door of their nice stone house, with the authenticity marked by the beautiful furniture and warm tones which make the atmosphere even more friendly. The cottages are just like the house, perfectly equipped and with stylized decoration. You will like to have your breakfast on the terrace which overlooks the swimming pool and beyond, the garden opening onto the countryside. A real haven of peace.

Vault-de-Lugny

CHÂTEAU DE VAULT DE LUGNY
11, rue du Château
✆ +33 (0)3 86 34 07 86
www.lugny.fr
hotel@lugny.fr

Open from March 18th to November 1st, 2016. Open every day from 12pm to 1.30pm and from 6.30pm to 9pm. Booking is essential. Menu Gourmand at €65, tasting menu « special 30 Ans » at €150 with a glass of champagne Vegetarian menu as from May. Menu Drives out in season. Children's menu. Lunch menu : €30 (with the lunch Monday to Friday except public holidays, and €39 the evenings and weekends). Boxes gifts from €40/ pers – Package relaxation sublimates with the meal and the access to the swimming pool area from €69 per person. American Express. Groups welcome. Baby chairs. Garden. Terrace.

For several years now we have voted by plebiscite this address, and for good reason In an enchanting setting, the restaurant of Château de Vault de Lugny is one of the most prestigious restaurants of Burgundy and certainly the one that has the best value for money of the region. In the kitchen, a team carried out by Free Bowanee, chef from Mauritius and Karina Laval, pastry chef. In the dining room, you are proposed to enjoy the multiple flavours offered by the local, punctuated with exotic notes, worked with delight and knowledge, to offer a remarkable gastronomy to you. On the autumn menu, we chose, pan-fried escalope duck foie gras with verjuice « Monsieur Paul Bocuse », followed by a supreme and pheasant legs with violet cream and trimming in « Matignon » way, to finish in subtlety and exoticism with an iced square with white chocolate, zests of combava on a shortbread with spices, mango and passion creamy. Delight sublimated by a food and wine pairing of the most subtle. Exquisite moments, and especially a sumptuous address which celebrates, in this year 2016, its 30 years of existence : on this occasion, you will have the privilege to taste the menu « 30 ans », but also every month, a different theme to treat your taste buds with excellence. An unique place that will incense you.

CHÂTEAU DE VAULT DE LUGNY
11, rue du Château
✆ +33 (0)3 86 34 07 86
www.lugny.fr – hotel@lugny.fr

Open from March 18th to November 1st, 2016. Room available at 3pm. – 20% in March and October. 14 rooms (2 suites). Breakfast : €18. Extra bed : €40. Garage included. Cot : €18. Rooms and suites from €195 to €536 on weekdays and from €295 to €710 weekends and public holidays. 1/2 bottle of champagne €45, red rose bunch €65. Package « Escapade » from €310 and up to €595. Babysitting. Pets allowed (€18 for the dogs of less 15kg, and €25 for the dogs of more than 15kg). Seminars, receptions and weddings limited to 35 people. Swimming pool area and jacuzzi. Gourmet cookery classes and vegetarian. Tasting cellar and many activities around truffle in season.

Exceptional... everything has been said But let us be more loquacious to describe you the prestigious setting of the château de Vault de Lugny. Dating back to the 13th and 18th centuries, the rooms and the suites reflect the beauty of the decors of yesteryear : French ceilings, floor and wood panelling of oak tree, marble fireplace, taffeta and silk canopy beds, mural fabrics in Jouy canvas... Elegant, spacious, bright, romantic as desired, the rooms and the suites offer the French luxury to you. The discrete service is perfect, and your stay in this prestigious setting will leave you an imperishable souvenir. Let the charm act

The bridge of Guillon.

again by benefitting from the heated indoor swimming pool, located in the old vaulted cellars of the castle, and recognized as one of most beautiful swimming pools in France. Stroll in the park to discover the century-old trees, or listen to the lapping of the river, you will spend a very pleasant moment. The gourmets will be happy to settle in the elegant dining room of the restaurant to taste there a gourmet, refined and creative cuisine. A pure wonder... Enjoy these moments, you are in a privileged place in the middle of Burgundy.

CHABLIS ★

The small town of 2600 inhabitants is internationally renowned for its white wine. Surrounded by approximately 4,200 acres of vineyards, the city has existed for several generations. The first writings about this town date back to the year 510. In 867, Charles le Chauve donated this land to the monks of Tours fleeing the Norman attacks. They brought with them the relics of Saint Martin, which were kept for ten years in the city. It was the religious who planted vines and, due to the port of Auxerre and the proximity of Paris, made this wine be known by the kings of France and even beyond the borders of the kingdom. Looted and burned by the Huguenots in 1568, Chablis was reconstructed though. But phylloxera fiercely struck its prosperity in the late nineteenth and attacked almost all the vineyards. Through transplantation of American plants, production could restart. In 1940, a German bombing heavily damaged the heritage. Today, Chablis has won back its cheerful appearance. These Vineyards offer one of the most beautiful scenery in the area, with changing colours depending on the time of day and the seasons. And its wine is still an exceptional ambrosia. A real pleasure to be enjoyed in one of the many caves surrounded by the monuments tracing the history of this small town which bears a great name. On Sunday morning, the village is animated by a very nice market.

■ OFFICE DE TOURISME DU PAYS CHABLISIEN
1, rue Maréchal-De-Lattre-de-Tassigny
✆ +33 (0)3 86 42 80 80
www.chablis.net – ot-chablis@chablis.net

Low season : opened Monday to Saturday of 10 : 00 to 12 : 30 and 13 : 30 to 18 : 00. High season : the every day of 10 : 00 to 12 : 30 and 13 : 30 to 18 : 00. Of mid-June at mid-September, closing at 19 : 00. Visit of the city, €5/pers. Bike rental, all the year on booking.

A dynamic and friendly team offers you many ideas of outings, accommodation, good places to eat, and relevant information on les domaines de Chablisien. A tour of about 1 : 30 to discover the city and its riches. The tour des Eglises (148 km), and the tour of Lavoirs (147 km) in Pays Chablisien. A comprehensive guidebook on hiking trails in the territory is on sale. Memories and local specialties.

Sightseeing

■ COLLÉGIALE SAINT-MARTIN ★
Place du 19-Août
Adult : €3. Guided tour.

The former collegiate canons of Saint-Martin of Tours, a small replica of the Cathedral of Sens, fleeing the Norman invasions, settled in Chablis for a while and has an interesting historical particularity : the leaves of the lateral portal. Very many horseshoes are nailed there. The Pilgrims on the road to Saint-Jacques-de-Compostela, perched on the door the iron of their lame or injured horse to ask Saint-Martin for healing. Jeanne d'Arc would have nailed an iron o her war-horse in 1429. The bell tower dates from the mid nineteenth century.

© AM STOCK NATURE

View of Chablis.

Knife & Fork

LA CUISINE AU VIN
16, rue Auxerroise
✆ +33 (0)3 86 18 98 52
www.lacuisineauvin.fr
info@lacuisineauvin.fr

Maître Restaurateur. Restaurateurs de France. Qualité Tourisme label. Opened of Easter to All Saints. Opened Thursday to Sunday of 19 : 00 to 21 : 00. Booking advised. Set menu at €35. Children's menu : €10 (for under 10-year-olds). (Tuesday to Friday). Wine by the glass. À la carte. American Express. Tourism label & Disability. Groups welcome.

Here, the stone matches the design. Take a seat in the basement in the vaulted cellars, modern and transparent furniture in Phillipe Starck trend. This is class, trendy and refined : we just love it. The tasteful decor prevails both in the culinary arts that offers the menu. Daniel-Étienne Defaix has surrounded himself with talented professionals to provide subtle flavor and creativity, all added by the expertise of the oenologist. A menu according to the seasons, which favors Yonne local products and also some neighbouring regions. You will also enjoy vegetables from the restaurant's garden, located in the castle's vegetable garden. Here are what the place particularly holds for you : a shallot tatin and its pan-fried foie gras cutlet, a sirloin and its Soumaintrain sauce, a cottage cheese with pepper-salt and fine herbs, a hot soup of grapes... an excellent restaurant.

LA FEUILLETTE 132
8, rue des Moulins
✆ +33 (0)3 86 18 91 67
www.chablis.net/lafeuillette132/
lafeuillette132@chablis.net

Closed 2 weeks in December. Open On monday and from Wednesday to Saturday lunch and dinner; Tuesday and Sunday noon. Menu at € 25. Wine by the glass. Menu. Chèque Restaurant. Groups welcome. Banquets, weddings, Home catering up to 800 people.

A beautiful restaurant with a beautiful room of the 13th century, and a nice restaurant that knows how to accommodate traditional Burgundian cuisine with subtlety. A la carte at the time of our passage, we chose dishes cooked with wine : Persillé de Bourgogne with Chablis, sea trout fillet with Crémant de Bourgogne, strawberry with Chablis, infusion of long pepper and Williams pear sorbet. A wine list, rich with 140 references, which are that blend delicately with the gourmet dishes offered in the à la carte. In short, an institution that is worth a visit and that we have to make known.

AU FIL DU ZINC
18, rue des Moulins
✆ +33 (0)3 86 33 96 39
www.restaurant-chablis.fr
aufilduzinc@orange.fr

Open Thursday to Monday from 12pm to 2pm and from 7.30pm to 10pm. Booking advised. Set menu at €52. Starter and main course or main course and dessert, €25. Starter + main course + dessert, €30. Groups welcome.

When a Japanese duo with beautiful Parisian references partners with Fabien Espana, young owner with an already established Icaunaise experience, (former owner of Soufflot in Irancy), that gives an explosive result In an open space with neo-bistro atmosphere, with exposed beams and stonework, displays of metal and beautiful zinc bar, the chef Ryo Nagahama and the pastry chef Vanessa Lang, offer you a fine gourmet cuisine with fresh seasonal produce. Three simple formulas, regularly renewed, and a Tasting menu which offers six successive dishes inspired by the desires of the chef. You enjoy a starter which consists of foie gras, pear and brioche, you savour a cod loin accompanied by potato and chanterelles, finally, you succumb to the sweet pleasures with a Dulce de Leche with wild fruits. An establishment we appreciate and that we let you discover with envy.

Sleeping

HOSTELLERIE DES CLOS
18, rue Jules-Rathier
✆ +33 (0)3 86 42 10 63
www.hostellerie-des-clos.fr
contact@hostellerie-des-clos.fr
Open seven days a week. 36 rooms. Half-board. Buffet breakfast. Garage (closed). Rooms from € 67. Stay from € 270. Animal accepteds (€ 7). Seminars. Banquets and weddings. Free wi-fi.
A very nice hotel in the heart of Chablis where rooms give way to an elegant, minimalist decor. The spacious lounges offer a relaxing environment to enjoy an aperitif. The Places are charming, the staff is discreet but present if you need them, and we let ourselves go easily to wellness & do nothing but be pampered The address is also one of the best Coulon-sur-Yonne restaurants.

Shopping

CAVEAU LAROCHE
10, rue Auxerroise
✆ +33 (0)3 86 42 89 28
www.larochewines.com
info@larochewines.com
Opened Monday to Friday of 9 : 00 to 12 : 30 and 14 : 00 to 18 : 00; saturdays until 19 : 00. Opened Sunday (of 10 : 00 to 13 : 00 and 14 : 00 to 18 : 00; closed the Sunday after Christmas at Easter). Bottle from €13.50. Guided tours on booking (by telephone or e-mail), of the cellars of the monasteries, with tasting of 3 wines. Services for the groups of 7 to 12 people from €35/pers.
A nice vaulted cellar in a building of the eighteenth century. You will find the production of the Laroche estate, Petit Chablis, Chablis, six Chablis premier cru wines, four Chablis grand cru, grand cru Blanchots and Laroche productions from around the world, as well from Languedoc and Chile or South Africa, the wine countries in full winery development. A lovely visit to these caves is concluded by the tasting of 3 of these Chablis nectars. Beautiful ideas also to be discovered for groups.

LA CHABLISIENNE
8, boulevard Pasteur
✆ +33 (0)3 86 42 89 98
www.chablisienne.com
Caveau@chablisienne.fr
High season : open every day from 9am to 7pm. From January to March, from 9am to 12.30pm and from 2pm to 6pm, from April to June and from September to December, from 9am to 12.30pm and from 2pm to 7pm. Open all year except December 25th and January 1st.
The cooperative now has some 300 members including 200 wine growers and 1,300 hectares, or 25% of the vineyard. Founded in 1923 it has accumulated numerous awards over the years. Six Grand Cru Chablis and the Château Grenouille Tête de Cuvée, fifteen Chablis Premiers Crus, not to mention the Chablis and Petit Chablis. An excellent quality/price ratio for those who wish to learn about the wines of the region. Very warm welcome.

CHÂTEAU LONG DEPAQUIT
45, rue Auxerroise
✆ +33 (0)3 86 42 11 13
Open Monday to Friday from 9am to 12.30pm and from 1.30pm to 6pm. Open all year Monday to Saturday. From November to March closed on Saturday.
This very beautiful estate, (65 hectares), with its castle and park in the heart of the city is the only one to offer the grand cru classified by La Moutonne : enjoying a monopoly on this small plot, the estate has more than one exhibition for the quality of its wines, in the midst of Vaudésir and Preuses wines. The reception is perfect here with thirteen other chablis references to discover including six First Growths, like Vaillon, Vaucoupin, Montée de Tonnerre, among others. Only appellations talk to connoisseurs, what an attractive address.

The Porte Noël in Chablis.

DOMAINE DU CHARDONNAY
Moulin du Pâtis
✆ +33 (0)3 86 42 48 03
www.domaine-du-chardonnay.fr
info@domaine-du-chardonnay.fr
Open Monday to Friday from 9 : 00 to 12 : 00 and 13 : 30 to 17 : 00. Online shopping. Bottle from € 10.50.
Etienne Boileau, William Nahan and Christian Simon, manage the 37 hectares of their planted Chablis A.O.C vineyards. Producers of great white wines, their operation promotes quality work, the results of which are among the many medals obtained at national competitions. The vault opens its doors for tastings. New buildings installed in the courtyard favours the reception that is already very pleasant, like the know-how.

DOMAINE POMMIER
31, rue de Poinchy
Poinchy
✆ +33 (0)3 86 42 83 04
www.denis-pommier.com
contact@denis-pommier.com
Open every day on only go. Closed on weekends.
Set in 1990, Isabelle and Denis Pommier took over 2-hectare family land to develop it and now they have 16 hectares of vineyards. On the menu are several Chablis and Burgundy appellations. A long duration job that is the result of the passion of these winemakers. An ethic : a reasoned culture, then since two years, an agriculture that clearly moves to the organic one. As result, it got many awards and was recognised as one of the best local table.

In the surroundings

Beine

MUSEE DE LA VIGNE ET DU TIRE-BOUCHON
4, rue de l'Equerre ✆ +33 (0)3 86 42 43 76
www.chablis-geoffroy.com
info@chablis-geoffroy.com
Open all year. Monday to Friday from 8am to 12pm and from 2pm to 5pm. Saturdays by appointment. Paying free tour. Tourism label & Disability. Guided tour.
Installed in the cellars of Alain Geoffroy area, this museum represents years of collection directed by Alain Geoffroy in person. Passionate about his job and an inveterate collector, he has amassed over 1,500 corkscrews, each more original than the other, from France and also Italy, Germany or the United States. Zigzag and Thomason mix corkscrew in knots and many others. Added to this is a large collection of old tools series depicting the daily work of the winemaker. Finally, very good silver wine taster completes this very interesting museum.

DOMAINE ALAIN GEOFFROY
4, rue de l'Equerre ✆ +33 (0)3 86 42 43 76
www.chablis-geoffroy.com
info@chablis-geoffroy.com
Open Monday to Friday from 8am to 12pm and from 2pm to 5pm. Saturdays by appointment. Groups by reservation (even schedule but closing at 4pm Friday).

© PHOVOIR

General view of Beine.

The Alain Geoffroy estate is a family business that has existed for several generations over 45 hectares of vineyards producing Chablis wines, fresh and fruity wines with fine minerality. Tasting of these wines is available at the vault : retail selling and free tasting for individuals and groups, visit of the cellars and installation of wine making process followed by a commented tasting of Chablisians wines. The estate organises seminars and ceremonies at the Baudon priory, with panoramic views of the Chablis vineyard, for a 250m² equipped and air-conditioned place that can accommodate 150 people sitting and 250 standing.

Chitry-le-Fort

DOMAINE DU CHATEAU DU VAL DE MERCY – CUVERIE CAVES ET CAVEAU DE DEGUSTATION
Place de l'église ✆ +33 (0)3 86 41 48 00
www.valdemercy.com
Tasting by appointment.
We like reception of this house, friendly, passionate and the professionalism of their winemaker engineer Bertrand Thibault. The vineyard of Château du Val de Mercy extends over 30 hectares and is divided between the Chablisien and Auxerrois. Rigor and tradition combines to offer us great quoted and award-winning wines. A beauregard 2003 in Chablis premier cru in a nice floral expression. Also a generous white burgundy Chitry 2005. A great place in a village of character.

Montigny-la-Resle

LE SOLEIL D'OR
3, RN 77
✆ +33 (0)3 86 41 81 21
www.lesoleil-dor.com
le-soleil-dor@wanadoo.fr
Logis (3 cocottes). The restaurateurs de France. Maître Restaurateur. Closed from January to February. Reservations recommended. Menus from € 30 to € 56. € 12 and € 15 (for children under 12 years old). Lunch menu : £ 18 (except On sundays and bank holidays). Menu. Vegetarian dish, 20 €.tarifs of the rooms : from € 69 to € 95, breakfast at € 12. Stopover at special rates for reps : € 83. Groups welcome.
The elegance and charm in this authentic setting would be obvious to you. A creative cuisine on the menu, without derogating from traditional recipes of the region. As long as you are conscious of the contents of your plate, be aware that this restaurant offers an organic menu every lunch time, which you compose yourself. For our part, we liked the poached scallops, safron sace of Yonne that we continue with the fabulous sea discovery, served with its parnsip and its fennel in the way of a tatin and for a smooth end a cream marbled brown. An ideal place which offers similar benefits in terms of accommodation

Préhy

COULANGES-LA-VINEUSE ★

Knife & Fork

J'MCA RESTAURANT
12, rue André-Vildieu
✆ +33 (0)3 86 34 33 41
www.jmca-restaurant.fr
Open Tuesday to Sunday from 12pm to 1.30pm; Thursday to Saturday from 7.30pm to 9pm. Booking advised. Menu from €24 to €38. Children's menu : €10. At lunchtime : starter and main course/main course and dessert €15, starter and main course + cheese or dessert €18, starter and main course + cheese + dessert €21. À la carte (only for dinner and the weekend). Groups welcome.
From the church square, the fully glazed facade of this establishment is intriguing… Once you walk out the door, the elegant atmosphere of wood with white and gray tones reinforced by the crimson of the hangings is obvious to you : this restaurant will enliven your senses And that is confirmed by reading the menu where Aline and Charles want to highlight the local flavours, for a very fine cuisine, highlighting the gourmet traditions of the region. We enjoy the tasting game with as a starter, a half- cooked foie gras with ratafia of Burgundy served with an apricot chutney and its brioche, continue with white fish of Lake Geneva and its coulis of grilled peppers, and conclude carefully with a fishing poached with syrup accompanied by its raspberry sorbet and its gilded tile. In bistro version at lunchtime, it is also appreciable Nice place to be voted by plebiscite.

In the surroundings

Migé

LE MIGÉEN
26, Grande-Rue ✆ +33 (0)9 53 98 05 48
www.lemigeen.fr
Open Tuesday to Friday from 12pm to 1.30pm; Friday and Saturday from 7pm to 9pm. Booking advised. Set menu at €19. Children's menu : €12. Daily special : €7.90 (express formula €12.90). Chèque Restaurant. Groups welcome. Shop. Coffee and general store.
Nice small restaurant with home cooking, simple and tasty. A beautiful discovery in the middle of Migé On the menu, it offers a fresh salad and his beetroot mousse, followed by a duck breast with époisses sauce and its trimmings, to finish with a creme brulee with pistachio. You will also appreciate the hearty paella dishes or fried mussels. Good to know that the establishment is diversified by making restaurant but originally it is a pleasant grocery very largely provided fruit and vegetables, charcuteries and cheeses and other products that we always need to have on hand. Place to vote by plebiscite.

Saint-Bris-le-Vineux

CAVES BAILLY-LAPIERRE
Quai de l'Yonne
Hameau de Bailly ✆ +33 (0)3 86 53 77 77
www.bailly-lapierre.fr

Open every day of the year. In July and August from 10am to 6.30pm nonstop. Visits for groups from 20 people, all year by appointment. €4.50 per adult (visit, tasting and flute souvenir). Provide warm clothing. Visits for individuals on weekdays (every day from April 18th to September 30th, 2015). In July and August, every day from 2.30pm to 5.30pm. €5.

Only 10 minutes from the A6, halfway between Beaune and Paris, and housing 7.5 million bottles on 4 ha, these cellars located in an underground limestone quarry are among the largest in France. Overlooking the beautiful valley of Yonne, the site is a true feast for the eyes and also for the taste buds because Crémant de Bourgogne is produced here, made with among others the Pinot Noir grape and other more original assemblies. For lovers of sculptures, some works are carved in stone and visible in the cellars. First the site was a mushroom bed then inhabited by the cooperative cellars from 1972. They are now 430 winemakers, suppliers of grapes who guarantee the success of this cooperative The Bailly Lapierre cellars, which still won 9 medals in 2015 at the Concours Agricole de Paris, produce in the pure tradition the Crémant de Bourgogne including the famous cuvée « Vive La Joie ». You will also find Irancy and Saint-Bris for those who love it. Note that you will have the opportunity to visit the cellars (more than 15,000 visitors per year) and buy on site some good bottles at the shop area. The place is gorgeous in the summer. Excellent reception, smart address.

JOIGNY ★★

Located on a hillside, and overhung by vines producing among others AOC Côte Saint-Jacques, Joigny becomes in the tenth century, the seat of a county under that of Champagne. On a spur of the plateau of the Forest of Othe, the city occupies a strategic position. Beautiful houses with carved facades dating from the fifteenth and sixteenth centuries, adorn the streets. Partially damaged by bombing during the Second World War, it also managed to restore its heritage. The author Marcel Aymé, who refused the Legion of Honour, was born there. The writer became famous with his Tales of the perched cat, the wall pass, Uranus and many other tasty novels and short stories. Joigny, City of Art and History, where the art of living is combined with its gourmet restaurants, walks along the Yonne and its covered market. Join it.

Sightseeing

MUSÉE DE LA RÉSISTANCE – GROUPE JOVINIEN BAYARD ★★
✆ +33 (0)1 75 43 04 28
http ://museedelaresistanceenligne.org
musee@aeri-resistance.com

Open from April 1st to April 30th and of October 8th at the beginning of November Wednesday and Saturday from 2.30pm to 5.30pm. From May 1st to October 5th Wednesday, Saturday and Sunday from 2.30pm to 5.30pm. Free. Guided tour (for groups made up by reservation near the Tourist Office of Joigny Tel. 03 86 62 11 05).

This museum was founded in 1946 in Joigny – a small town with an important strategic location : road network, railways and canals – where a group of resistance took the name of « Bayard » in 1941 headed by the commander Paul Herbin nicknamed « Hubert ». This organisation was linked to both Libération-Nord and to the section of SOE (*Special Operations Executive*, the British Secret Services). Acting in Jovinien, this network is particularly illustrated by actions of sabotage on the line Paris-Lyon-Mediterranean between Brienon-sur-Armançon and Villeneuve-sur-Yonne for the rail yard of Laroche-Migennes. It has also participated in the escape network « Bordeaux-Loupiac ». Once Yonne released, a part of the group joined with the regiment of Volontaires de l'Yonne the troops of General de Lattre and participated in the liberation of Alsace then occupy the region of Baden in the southwest of Germany. Through original documents and objects, the museum also presents the jovinien group of Bayard as well as the events of the Second World War from its beginning until the Liberation.

Remarkable facades

In the streets of the old Joigny , do not forget to admire the remarkable facades of some of the oldest houses in the city. A tour to be done on foot or bike and that will make you to discover the birthplace of Marcel Aymé like Sainte Sophie Barat, do not miss the Baillie house dated sixteenth century, which now houses the Animation Heritage Service. Continue by passing in front of the house of the Tree of Jesse, also of the sixteenth century where you can admire the beautiful carved wood decoration tracing the family tree of Christ. The house of the Pillory will also attract your attention : this renaissance residence offers passers-by a very refined decor of scales of wood and engoulants, finally complete your walk by the house of Ave Maria which develops on its façade, or more precisely on pillars, the theme of the Annunciation. An architectural and decorative expansion which makes the richness of the heritage of Joigny.

Knife & Fork

■ LE CANOTIER
1, promenade du Chapeau
✆ +33 (0)3 86 62 16 71
www.lecanotier-joigny.fr

Open Monday to Friday for lunch. Set menu at €18.50. Fixed rate formula from €12.50. Groups welcome. Terrace.
On the banks of the Yonne, Le Canotier is a friendly place to stop for tasting a generous and family cuisine. Catherine and René Louvel open the doors of their establishment with a very modern atmosphere, in shades of reddish grey and black. Everything is homemade here, with seasonal ingredients, to enjoy local flavours. You can have a buffet at will for a reasonable price The starters are full of fresh salads and regional charcuterie, the main courses are hearty, as on the slate during our visit, calf's head with gribiche sauce, or salt pork with lentils and as for dessert, homemade chocolate mousse was our favorite one, but we could also have chosen for fine tart with caramelized apples. Two terraces for summer meals, and convenient, free car park next to the restaurant. An address to be quickly discovered.

■ LE PARIS-NICE
Rond-point de la Résistance
✆ +33 (0)3 86 62 06 72
www.leparisnice.fr
parisnice@wanadoo.fr

Logis (3 cocottes). Open Tuesday to Saturday for lunch and dinner; Sunday for lunch. Menu from €30 to €43. Burgers house, pizzas, toasted slices of bread giant, salads from €12. Paris-Nice menu at €22 Tuesday to Friday evening. Le Bistrot de Joigny menu from €18, Tuesday to Friday evening, except public holidays. Holiday voucher. Garden. Terrace. Caterer.
Paris-Nice is one of the best tables of Yonne, the reason is that the house grows the perfect reception where conviviality in room and harmony of flavours in cuisine mix. The chef, David Le Corre, combines art and bistronomy in a significant control of flavours, colours and textures. On the menu of the Terroir, you will likely to choose the small fondue with Burgundian cheeses and its potatoes skewer with dry ham, followed by a muslin of coalfish, salmon and scallops and its mussel cream with Aligoté, then end with the molten chocolate cake and its marshmallow teddy. We appreciated the formula « Bistrot de Joigny » where you can compose your own menu with the buffet of starters and the gourmet ideas of Claire and David. And we cannot finish without talking about the small names spotted on the à la carte menu of the Bistro : « *La Bien de Chez Nous* », for the giant toasted slice of bread with époisses, « *C'est Moi la Plus Belle* » for one of the largest salads, « *Profite demain on dîne chez ta mère* » for the pizza with Chaource, or « *Gros Charolais* » for one of the homemade burgers And if you wish to meet the chef, get registered at the cooking classes, it is suggested for adults as for the children This restaurant is really a gold nugget The establishment is also a hotel, of course.

Sleeping

■ LE PARIS-NICE
Rond-point de la Résistance
✆ +33 (0)3 86 62 06 72 www.leparisnice.fr
parisnice@wanadoo.fr

Logis (2 cheminées). Qualité Tourisme label. Closed from August 19th to September 2nd. Closed on Sunday evening and Monday. Reception to 23. 10 rooms. Breakfast : €8. Parking. Rooms from €48. Holiday voucher. Pets allowed (with €4 extra). Receptions and weddings. Free Internet access. Free Wifi. Gourmet restaurant. Satellite TV.
Like the restaurant, the ten rooms will bring you peace and warmth. They are real small cocoons where it is pleasant to bask gently. The comfort is queen, just like home. To satisfy you, Claire and David are very caring. A few steps from the passage of the bridge of the city is enough for adventurers to discover the small steep streets of the medieval city. The hotel also has a restaurant and also a store full of gift ideas. A good address.

Guesthouses

■ LE MONTANT AU PALAIS
49, rue Montant-au-Palais
✆ +33 (0)9 84 54 88 00
✆ +33 (0)6 67 35 53 05
www.lemontantaupalais.com
coudyser.pierre@neuf.fr
Open all year. 3 rooms. Single room from €55 to €75; double room from €70 to €95; triple room €120. Breakfast included. Wifi. Hammam.
In the heart of the historic area of Joigny, Pierre and Yolaine Coudyser open the doors of their charming mansion of the 17th century to you. A haven of peace awaits you here : the 3 rooms; Pierlaine, Régina and Karen, as well as the suite « Audrey » display great comfort : electric beds, private lounge, or bathrooms with hydro-massage shower and Turkish bath with aromatherapy. The patio will be very pleasant for breakfast on sunny days, and you can walk in the old town from this place of character.

In the surroundings

Charny

■ CAMPING LES PLATANES***
41, route de la Mothe
✆ +33 (0)3 86 91 83 60
www.campinglesplatanes.fr
info@campinglesplatanes.fr

Qualité Tourisme label. Open from April 1st to October 31st, 2016. Booking is essential. Exposure : shaded/ sunny. Ground : grassy. Relief : dish. Bungalows for 4-5 people from €210 per week; mobile home for 4-6 people from €210. Campsite : Package from €6.50 for 1 people, and from €11.50 for 2 people. Activities.
The welcome of Géraldine and Marc is warm in this three-star campsite. For your accommodation, you can choose not only between the traditional campsite with suitable packages, but also the Canvas bungalow fully equipped for your comfort, or the 2016 innovation, spacious mobile homes with terrace. The animation of the team is dynamic so that you will be probably pleased : sports and evening entertainment in July and August, and there is always the possibility to have a sun-basking on the pool deck.

Migennes

■ LE BOAT
52, rue Pierre-et-Marie-Curie
✆ +33 (0)3 86 80 08 60 –www.leboat.fr
migennes@connoisseur.fr
Low season : open every day from 9am to 12.30pm and from 2pm to 5.30pm. Off-season closed on Sunday. Provided life jackets.
Very beautiful boats with two to twelve people are available to surf at the beginning of Migennes either the Burgundy canal, or on the Yonne in the direction of Auxerre or Management. The boats are without a license, and it is not necessary to have experience in sailing. On the canal, it takes about 20 to 40 minutes per lock : take time to admire the beautiful landscape that unfold, punctuated reflection of the churches and hills in the water.

direct access to the beach	visually impaired disability	take away
bar	mental handicap	room service
laundry	motor disability	fitness room
air conditioning	garden or park	playroom / tv
nightclub	games	modern sanitary
cash machine	washing machine / laundry	water sports
drinking water	bicycle rental	tennis
horse riding	grocery store	archery
smoking area	airport shuttle	waterslide
non-smoking	fishing	fan
fitness	indoor swimming pool	toilet drain
miniature golf	outdoor heated pool	sailing
hard of hearing disability	outdoor pool	

© JOSIANE MAXEL

The castle of Dracy.

NOYERS ★★

Knife & Fork

■ **LA VIEILLE TOUR**
1, rue de la Porte-Peinte ✆ +33 (0)3 86 82 87 36
Open Monday to Wednesday and Saturday from 12pm to 2pm and from 7pm to 8.45pm; Friday for dinner. Booking advised. Menu from €18 to €25. Terrace.
No wonder that this restaurant nestled in the heart of the medieval city of Noyers. The chef Laurens Kluyver cultivates the taste of good A simple and original cuisine, with spicy flavours or garden herbs; judge for yourself : soup of forgotten vegetables, beef bourguignon, banana cheese cake or the must of desserts, tart with candied ginger, unbeatable speciality of the chef always present on the menu. A very friendly service, which is much appreciated in summer, on the shaded terrace in the pretty courtyard of the establishment. A very nice place

In the surroundings

Nitry

■ **LA BEURSAUDIERE**
9, chemin de Ronde ✆ +33 (0)3 86 33 69 69
www.beursaudiere.com
message@beursaudiere.com
♿
Closed in January. Open daily for lunch from 12pm to 1.30pm and for dinner from 7.30pm to 10pm. Booking advised. Menu from €25.90 to €56.60. Children's menu : €12. Wine by the glass. American Express, Diners Club, Holiday voucher. Groups welcome. Terrace.
A local restaurant, in a beautifully restored place (3 large dining rooms to accommodate guests and a sheltered terrace), with exposed beams, a rustic setting that is not overrated : the wood-burning oven of the restaurant serves as a grill, the menu changes seasonally, the cuisine is creative while getting close to traditions. On the menu in three dishes, we suggest you take the lukewarm pork pie with andouillette of Chablis, warm wine jelly, Dijon mustard juice, then to continue in the second with royal bream and its flake of bread, puree of cauliflower, risotto and iced fennel, and to end with a souffléed tart with confit pumpkin and cinnamon that we advise to accompany with a glass of soft Gaillac... A treat both for the eyes and the taste buds. As for accommodation, the inn is located in a former priory of the 11th century with two dovecotes. The rooms bear the names of ancient trade and are decorated accordingly. Beams, stones, charm... It's simply magnificent.

■ **LA GRANGE DE MARIE**
1, voie des Préaux © +33 (0)3 86 33 60 92
www.lagrangedemarie.com/fr
contact@lagrangedemarie.com

Sainte-Vertu

■ **AUBERGE DU MOULIN**
1, rue du Moulin © +33 (0)3 86 75 95 33
www.moulinsaintevertu.fr
Open on Wednesday and Sunday for lunch; Thursday to Saturday for lunch and dinner. Booking advised. Set menu at €26. À la carte. 6 rooms from €75 to €95, free for children under 4 years old. Groups welcome. Terrace.
Auberge du Moulin is a real institution in Sainte-Vertu, and its change of ownership with Véronique Teysseire and Pascal Moreau enchanted a good number of regulars of the place. As much as they strive to follow some dishes initiated by Louisette Brazilier, , symbolic figure of Moulin, in the kitchen. Thus you will enjoy a refined cuisine in this beautiful home nestled at the edge of the Serein, with much femininity and showcasing local produce with rich and tasty dishes. For us, we delightfully savoured duo of poached eggs in red and white, followed by revisited parmentier of Chaource andouillette, a touch of freshness with cottage cheese and its red fruit coulis and a laudine with apples to conclude. A real moment of pleasure Note that the restaurant offers hotel services. What a nice restaurant.

SAINT-FARGEAU ★★

Saint-Fargeau, stands on the bank of the Loing among beautiful wooded landscapes in Puisaye. Joan of Arc came here before going to the coronation of Charles VII in 1429. The Fief belongs to Jacques Coeur in the fifteenth century then housed the Grande Mademoiselle, cousin of Louis XIV, exiled there after the Fronde. The castle, which served as the backdrop to the television series « *Au plaisir de Dieu* » reborn every summer in a great light and sound. Playful volunteers help for years to revive the great moments of the history of this monument. Saint-Fargeau also stands near the water 3 km away is Lake Bourdon, ideal place to rest, or for a picnic. Today it is a shaded beach for the Poyaudins, but this lake was originally created to supply the Briare Canal in 1901.

Knife & Fork

■ **LE MONTECRISTO**
14, rue des Lions © +33 (0)3 86 74 17 33
Annual closing from December 24th, 2016 to January 3rd, 2017. Closed weekly : from January 3rd to March 22nd, Sunday for dinner and Tuesday for dinner and Monday all day; from March 23rd to June 30th and from September 1st to November 5th, Monday all day. Open Sunday to Thursday from 12pm to 1.30pm and from 7pm to 9pm; Friday and Saturday from 12pm to 1.30pm and from 7pm to 9.30pm. Open 7 days a week in August July and during school holidays. Booking advised. Menu from €19.90 to €22.90. Children's menu : €8.90. (€11.90 and €14.90). À la carte. Pizzas from €7.90. Holiday voucher, Chèque Restaurant. Groups welcome. Terrace.
Le Montecristo, a few steps from the Château, welcomes you in a friendly and relaxed atmosphere. The modern tones of the room reflects a menu punctuated of the local culinary traditions, such as the fricassée of frog legs with parsley, the egg casserole with Soumaintrain, the roasted ham in Chablisienne way or the calf's head Gribiche sauce. The lovers of Mediterranean flavours will not be left behind, and will appreciate the pastas, the Italian salad with mozza di bufala, but also the pizzas that the chef prepares in different ways, making us travel from Val d'Aoste to the poyaudines territories. The terrace overlooking the Bourdon adds character to this address that we recommend you without restraint.

Shopping

■ **LA BALADE GOURMANDE** NEW
11, rue Max-Pautrat
© +33 (0)3 86 45 74 97
© +33 (0)6 36 02 58 86
Open Tuesday to Saturday from 9am to 7.30pm; Sunday from 9am to 1pm. Possible delivery (deliverable gourmet baskets in a radius of 12 km around Saint-Fargeau).
David Géneau invites you to La Balade Gourmande, a new brand in the picturesque street of Saint-Fargeau near the Castle A delicatessen which clearly desires to make you discovering Burgundy through its crunch and drinking gourmet wealths, David selected very rigorously many regional products... The wood furniture abounds in salted softnesses (mustards, oils, tapenades...) and sweetened (gingerbreads and Maison Toussaint biscuits for example...), and the racks offer a beautiful range of wines of Yonne. You can come to taste the products on the spot this summer, the place will be full of charm, there is small shaded terrace... Gourmet boxes and baskets suggest you ideas of gifts. Gourmet pleasures to bring as memories, and specialties to reclaim for the residents The friendliest welcome, so it is good to go and visit quickly It will be also possible to sleep on the spot for the luckiest, David indeed currently restores the very comfortable apartments at very good value for money...

■ **PÂTISSERIE FLECHAIS**
1, rue des Lions
© +33 (0)3 86 74 06 71
www.patisserie-flechais.com
patis.flechais89@orange.fr
Open Thursday to Tuesday from 8.30am to 1pm and from 2.30pm to 7pm. Open every day in August July, from 8am to 7.30pm and until 10pm on performance night with the castle. Closed in February and 15 days in October.

This is a required address for the greedy ones, with many house specialties : The famous macarons de La Puisaye, les feuillantine pastries, 4 kinds of tender croquets : with the grapes dry-hazelnuts or chocolate-almond, orange-almond, with nuts) or the chocolates house.

There is a pleasant open-aired terrace face up the castle, a good place for a drink or a small tea. Patrick and Lucette can also welcome you with their fast formula lunch, the small quiches house...

There are more than twenty kind of ice creams houses in the summer, le Jacques-Cœur or la Maryline, moult délices etc. For the small hollows, it is a greedy pleasure We like. The view is splendid, the place is full of charm.

In the surroundings

Mézilles

LE MOULIN DE CORNEIL
3, place Lucien-Gaubert
✆ +33 (0)7 83 43 27 45
(€13 and €15). À la carte. Fixed rate formula "Prime rib" for 2 people, €50 and €52.

Located in this former mill, this restaurant is warm and friendly. You will appreciate its setting with countryside spirit simply highlighted by hexagonal floor tiles, exposed stonewalls and brown beams. As for the cuisine, it is simple, it makes you feel like home Fresh and seasonal products are widely used, prepared simply enough to raise their flavours.

The lunch menu awakens with fish rillette with herbs, then continue with lamb shoulder roasted with olive pesto and for the end a delicious nutella and pineapple crème brûlée. A sympathetic address.

Toucy ★

LE DÉLICE DES GALETS
7, place de la République ✆ +33 (0)3 86 44 83 67
www.ledelicedesgalets.fr/
Menu from €24 to €36. Chef's suggestion, €14 in 2 main courses and €18 in 3 main courses, only for lunch Wednesday to Saturday.

Eric Gallet and Camille Picon invite you to discover their inventive cuisine. Based on fresh seasonal products and resulting primarily from local products, the menu offers this touch of modernity that awakes our tastebuds and our taste desires. On the menu Pierre Larousse, we invite you to start with pan-fried foie gras, apples, vanilla, chutney onions and mangoes, then continue with a lamb shank, juice with thyme, muslin with white cocos. A plate of refined cheese, mixed green salad with hazelnut oil will lead you to the sweet delicacies with a carpaccio of pineapple, banana and lime. Exquisite feast A fine wine list completes the whole. An address that has many lovers.

Villiers-Saint-Benoît

CYCLORAIL
Usages ✆ +33 (0)3 86 45 70 05
Open all year. By reservation From €27 to €59 for the individual ones. Special rates for groups.

Machines in four places, including two for bicyclists : the physical effort is divided No yellow jersey, nor with peas, here we pedal relaxed; a 7 year old child leaves himself very well. The fifteen vélorails circulate on the way one-way, of Villiers-Saint-Benoît to Saint-Martin-sur-Ouanne and Charny. Nearly 30 mi ticket. If one arrives cyclorail opposite, do not panic An ingenious system allows you to return vehicles. And hop : bicycles are exchanged Each continues its journey in sense. Pauses discovered, restaurant or picnic brings a more charm to this very nice initiative To arrive 1/4 of time before leaving for the recommendations.

SAINT-SAUVEUR-EN-PUISAYE

It is the birthplace of the writer Colette. Perched on a hill, from the ancient walls, there only remains the big Saracen tower of the twelfth century. The castle, where there is a Colette museum, the church and the landscape of Puisaye, all these give to this place rural flavours. The village is also marked by the culture of ceramic with a very fine pottery market in July.

In the surroundings

Treigny

LE CHANTIER MEDIEVAL DE GUEDELON
RD955
✆ +33 (0)3 86 45 66 66 – www.guedelon.fr
Open from March 14th to November 1st, 2016. Open from 10am. See calendar of the opening days on the website. Free for under 5-year-olds. Adult : €16. Child (from 5 to 17 years old) : €11. Group (20 people) : €10. Card Pass Wall (unlimited access all year) : adult €26 and child €20. Guided tour (in addition to the admission ticket). Catering facilities. Shop. Activities.

Michel Guyot, owner and restorer of the castle of Saint-Fargeau, launched a one day challenge to build a castle using the methods of the thirteenth century, with Marilyne Martin at his side. The idea was born in 1997 : it went for 25 years of work In summer, costumed workers work every day : quarrymen, stonemasons, woodcutters or carters, just to name a few, will share their passion for this recognized adventurous educational interest. The site, which needs no introduction, has been the subject of numerous TV reporters; no surprise whatsoever the most visited paying tourist point paying of the Yonne, and the second of Burgundy after the Hospices de Beaunes ... A pleasant walk in the heart of Puisaye, with a visit to this particular site, the first rooms castle entertained by the friendly village artisans and their pets. The ideal family visit Note that you can now feast yourself in the 3 areas : Taverne, Encas and Epicerie.

SENS ★★

This Icaunaise sub-prefecture of nearly 27,000 inhabitants today works much according to the time in Paris as several people are working in Paris. But the city has kept its provincial charm and acquires its own identity. Gallo-Roman village and then a great religious centre as the bishopric of Paris depended on the Archbishopric of Sens, this archiepiscopal city gave birth to the first Gothic cathedrals. Wide tree-lined boulevards drawing the outline of the ancient walls, centre with right angled streets, covered market, it is a pleasure to stroll there.

■ OFFICE DE TOURISME DE SENS ET DU SENONAIS

Place Jean-Jaurès
✆ +33 (0)3 86 65 19 49
www.office-de-tourisme-sens.com
otsi.sens@wanadoo.fr

High season : open Monday to Saturday from 9.30am to 1pm and from 2pm to 6.30pm. High season, August July. From September to June, Monday to Saturday, 9.30am-12.30pm/2pm-6pm. From May to October, Sunday and public holidays, 10.30am-1pm/2pm-4.30pm. €6 the guided tour.

Two other tourist information points are open in summer: one is found at Cathedral Square and the other at the Moulin à Tan Park. At your disposal are many brochures on tourism, guides of the city and surrounding areas. Guided tours will be organised in the city of Senon, and audio-guided tour of Saint-Etienne cathedral (sound recordings available on www.ZeVisit.com). Do not hesitate to inquire about participation or see the city's attractions program.

© JULIA VALENTIN

La Maison d'Abraham.

Sightseeing

■ CATHEDRALE SAINT-ETIENNE ★★★

148, rue des Déportés-et-de-la-Résistance
✆ +33 (0)3 86 65 06 57

Open every day from 8am to 6pm. Free. Guided tour (audio-guide, €6/pers – brochure of visit on sale at the Tourist Office 0.50 €.Visite with a guide and access at the top of the Tower South, by reservation from June to August).

Its construction began in 1130. Using an innovative concept, the vault with intersection of ribs, in fact the prototype of the great Gothic cathedrals. It inspires many religious buildings. But many times are superimposed. Improved in the 14th century, construction continued from the 15th to the 18th century and testifies of various builders techniques. The north tower was never completed. The south tower collapsed in 1268 and was rebuilt in late 13th century; its upper part dates from the 16th century. Many outdoor statues were destroyed or badly damaged by the revolutionaries during the Terror in 1793. The gorgeous nave, the transept added in the 15th century and the beautiful stained glass of the late 12th to the 17th centuries with some contemplation. The chapels are full of historical anecdotes and receives the St. Louis altar, in memory of his marriage in 1234, and the tomb of first son of Louis XV and his wife.

■ PALAIS SYNODAL – MUSEES DE SENS ★

135, rue des Déportés-et-de-la-Résistance
✆ +33 (0)3 86 64 46 22
www.musees-bourgogne.org
contact@cerep-musees-sens.net

Open all year. Low season : Monday, Thursday and Friday from 2pm to 6pm; Wednesday, Saturday and Sunday from 10am to 12pm and from 2pm to 6pm. High season : Wednesday to Monday from 10am to 6pm. Free for under 18-year-olds. Adult : €6 (reduced : €3.50). Exhibition Orangery €2 - Ticket twinned €7. Guided tour.

The orangery of 1684, with its small garden, has been fitted out into an exhibition hall. Adjoining the cathedral, the synodal palace buildings (13th century, restored by Viollet-le-Duc) the former archbishop's palace (16th and 18th centuries) house three museums. The treasure is both artistically and historically invaluable and is one of the most beautiful in France. Precious liturgical vestments, the 8th century Saint Ebbon chasuble and Saint Thomas Beckett's 12th century priestly vestments can be found here along with woven silk goods, tapestries, enamels, ivory, beautiful objects, etc. The silverware like the holy Reliquary of the 12th century shines brilliantly. The synodal palace with its dungeons with walls covered with ancient graffiti and especially its magnificent synods room vaulted with warheads is worth visiting. Prehistoric, proto-historic and Gallo-Roman creations, sculptures and paintings from the 15th to the 20th century are complemented by the Marrey collection. You can also find works by Brueghel, Boudin, Watteau de Lille, Rodin and a unique set of furniture and ceramics by Raymond Sube Jean Mayodon.

Moulin park of Tan, tropical greenhouses.

YONNE

PARC DU MOULIN À TAN – SERRES TROPICALES

28, chemin de Babie
✆ +33 (0)3 86 95 38 72
espacesverts@mairie-sens.fr

Remarkable garden. Open all year. Tropical greenhouses, on weekdays from 1.30pm to 5pm, the weekend, from April to September, from 2pm to 5.30pm, and from October to May, from 2pm to 5pm. Park open every day : from April to September, 8am-8.30pm, in March and October, 8am-6.30pm, from November to February, 8am-5.30pm. Free. Distinction « 4 fleurs » and label « cities and villages fleuris ».

You can find in this park around an old tannery fitness trail and farm animals that make children smile. Playgrounds and trails stretch, refreshed by the rustling of the river and offer a sumptuous place to breathe and relax with family. Do not miss : the municipal greenhouses open to the public where six hundred square metres restore three types of climates. Cactus, warm greenhouses, epiphyte plants, change of scenery guaranteed. Many panels provide information to visitors. Located in the Moulin de Tan Park, the tropical greenhouses offer us a real change of scenery : 600 m^2 of exoticism, over 1,500 plants, orchids, cacti, bromeliads, carnivorous plants, and especially, the jewel of this winter garden, the amazing Victoria Cruziana, the splendid giant Amazonian water lily whose leaves can reach 3 metres in diametre. The time of a visit in the heart of the tropics is a total escape.

Knife & Fork

LA CUISINE DE LOLIE

75, Grande-Rue
✆ +33 (0)3 86 88 43 51
lacuisinedelolie.fr
lacuisinedelolie@gmail.com

Menu from €26 to €38. Children's menu : €10. (€15 and €18.50 Monday to Saturday). Gourmet workshop for children, €18, €36 for the adults, booking compulsory.

A creative cuisine in the heart of the city and in the quiet : we love it On the menu, everything are in finesse and blend flavours from elsewhere, we start with fresh salad of wild prawns, then we continue with a tajine of Challans duckling thigh, enhanced by the finesse of some soft spices, and we end this lunch with shortbread tart with Dosnon honey and walnuts. Happiness for our senses We will especially appreciate the terrace in a private courtyard of the city, possibility of customized services for private events, as well as numerous themed parties throughout the year. Attend also the very trendy cooking classes for kids as for the adults.

LA MADELEINE

1, rue d'Alsace-Lorraine
✆ +33 (0)3 86 65 09 31
www.restaurant-lamadeleine.fr
lamadeleine3@orange.fr

Open all year. Closed fifteen days in June and August. Open Tuesday soir to Saturday. Booking is essential. Menu from €67 to €116. Fast lunch menus at €49.50, Wednesday to Friday for lunch, except days before and public holidays. American Express.

One of excellent restaurants in the department that we owe to the talented Patrick Gauthier. An inventive and refined tasty cuisine with great attention to detail. Judge by yourself with an extract of « Menu dans la Saison » : asparagus of Saint-Vincent, the organic and Comté egg, suckling lamb, chistera, spiced fingerling potatoes and bacon, cheese of milk of cow, goats and sheeps, the apple and the quince accompanied by the almond milk and the humour or the chef that can surprise you... A charming place for a moment of intense gastronomic delight. Take the time to savour, to taste with pleasure. A great address which your delicate palates will remember.

LE MAD'HER

84, Grande Rue

✆ +33 (0)3 86 64 56 10 / +33 (0)6 19 22 01 80

Open Tuesday to Saturday from 12pm to 2.30pm and from 7pm to 9.30pm. Menu from €15 to €19. Daily special : €12.50. Groups welcome. Baby chairs. Terrace.

A restaurant with a family atmosphere, with simplicity in the decoration, the warm welcome and in the generosity of the dishes. A refined cuisine underlining the local and season product. You will appreciate in particular the homemade foie gras, the frogs' leg, the veal cutlet and its fingerling potatoes of Touquet, the Tartar of bar granny smith and mangos, les nems au gianduja or la poire pochée au Jet 27. It's delicious, the service is effective and the value for money is reasonable .

Sleeping

LES 5 SENS

33, rue du Général-de-Gaulle

✆ +33 (0)6 10 12 57 65

www.lescinqsens.eu - resa@lescinqsens.eu

Reception between 6pm and 8pm. €70. Breakfast included. Free Wifi.

A few steps from the magnificent cathedral, the 5 Sens offers a haven of peace in the heart of the city. Peace and tranquility reigns here. In this house, each room is decorated with care and elegance. The five bedrooms are real cozy nests which are decorated in relaxing colors. Last night it was in the dining-room with a rustic charm that guests take their breakfast. The winter garden and lounge are perfect to immerse yourself into a book or simply enjoy a moment of rest. The hostess also offers gourmet cuisine that delights all the senses...

In the surroundings

Maillot

CAFÉ THÉ SENS

ZA du Saule Fendu 5, rue de l'Europe

✆ +33 (0)9 83 08 86 75

www.cafethesens.com/accueil.html

contact@cafethesens.com

Open Monday to Saturday from 7am to 7pm. Coffee €1.80 - Tea, €2.40 - Chocolate, €2.50 - fruit juice Drink, €2.25.

Morgane Peuziat, a coffee roaster, invites you to a sensory trip of a short distance She roast the selected coffee that she has chosen carefully by hand, for their subtle flavours and their qualities. The ingenious mixture will amaze you You will also appreciate the finesse of the teas « Tea Forté », 100% Organic , proposed with tasting and also with the sale in bulk and in pyramids. To fill the offer, Morgane proposes chocolates and delicacies of creators as well as objects and utensils related to these hot drinks. For companies or groups, it is possible for you to attend discovery conferences and breakfasts of work as well.

Pont-sur-Yonne

AUX TROIS ROIS

6, avenue de la Résistance

✆ +33 (0)3 86 96 32 39

www.auxtroisrois-89.com

auxtroisrois89@wanadoo.fr

Open on Tuesday and Sunday for lunch and for dinner. Menu from €16 to €26.50. Fixed rate formula bistro :

Tonnerre.

€12 for lunch and €13 for dinner. À la carte. Groups welcome (reception hall : 120 people). Garden. Terrace.
Located on the banks of Yonne, Aux Trois Rois restaurant provides quality services in a pleasant and friendly setting. In one of the two dining rooms or on the terrace, you can enjoy the traditional cuisine served in these places. Thus, we invite you to enjoy the Burgundy snails with chablis, fricassee of frogs' legs in Provence way, beef tartare, a set of crayfish with prawns or escalope of salmon with sorrel cream. The desserts are also homemade. The establishment is also a hotel and has a beautiful garden with swimming pool.

Soucy

PUB DE LA FONDERIE
Chemin des Patouillats ✆ +33 (0)6 83 55 45 16
Open from 6pm to 1am. New space with a lounge spirit , Le Pub de La Fonderie welcome the night owls in a festive atmosphere. The wide circular bar imposes its central location and encourage exchanges Evenings aperitif/ burgers in collaboration with La Remorque are regularly organized, and the evening entertainments by local DJ as well. Diffusion of sporting events and billiards (one is a circular) at disposal.

TONNERRE

LE MOULIN D'ARNAUD
12, avenue du Chevalier-d'Eon
✆ +33 (0)3 86 55 19 35
Open Tuesday to Saturday from 6.30am to 7.30pm; Sunday from 7am to 1pm.
Arnaud and Severine have opened here the fame and the attempting Le Moulin d'Arnaud bakery three years ago. Offering kneaded and cooked breads on the spot for a whole day, you will enjoy seeing the diversity of the breads proposed on sale : bread with garlic, figs, barley and sesame, but also le Pain du Mineur au froment et chicon,le Pavé d'Eon nature ou au chorizo, without forgetting the pastries such as oreillettes aux abricots or the mini donuts lined with strawberry or with the chocolate/hazelnut. The greedy cannot neglet it.

VÉZELAY ★★★★

A site listed as Unesco World Heritage since 1979 (second rank for the beauty of its site) and admired every year by a million of visitors. On the « eternal hill » stands Vézelay. Founded in the ninth century, a monastery developed there and received in 1050 the relics of St. Mary Magdalene, the « repentant sinner. » Pilgrims massively come there, the city grows. It became a famous starting point for the pilgrimage in Compostela. Saint Bernard of Clairvaux preached the Second Crusade in 1146, in the presence of King Louis VII. The sovereigns Philippe Auguste and Richard Coeur de Lion met there in 1190 to begin the third crusade. And in 1248, St. Louis went there several times on pilgrimage. It is also here that the Franciscans founded their first convent in France in the early thirteenth century. But in that same century, a disaster happened New « true » relics of Mary Magdalene were discovered in Provence, in Saint-Maximin. Quickly, the icaunais pilgrimage declined. The abbey was sacked by the Huguenots and secularised during the Revolution. A fire ravaged it in the early nineteenth century. It was not until 1840 that Viollet-le-Duc saved it from ruin. Today, the basilica has regained its splendour. Tourists and pilgrims still climb the long steep street leading to the esplanade. Land rooted in the history of Catholicism, Vézelay nevertheless saw the birth in 1519 of Theodore Beze, who participated in the Reformation with Calvin. The author Romain Rolland lived there at the end of his life, just like another writer, Jules Roy. The beauty of the site and the charm of the narrow streets make this village a must where it is pleasant to eat in one of the many good Vézelay addresses.

OFFICE DE TOURISME DE VEZELAY
12, Rue Saint-Etienne
✆ +33 (0)3 86 33 23 69
www.vezelaytourisme.com
vezelay.otsi@wanadoo.fr
Open every day from 10am to 1pm and from 2pm to 6pm. High season : Monday to Saturday from 10am to 7pm; Sunday from 10am to 1pm and from 2pm to 6pm. Closed on Thursday from October to May; Sunday of All Saints at Easter. Pass discovered "Vézelay and Vézelien".
The tourism office offers all the necessary information for the visit of the beautiful old Vezelay town. You will also find a shop where touristic guides and dedicated works are sold in Vezelay and Saint-Jacques-de-Compostelle. A internet terminal, ticketing show and a fishing point are also available on the site.

LA MAISON DU VISITEUR
Place Guillon
✆ +33 (0)3 86 32 35 65
www.vezelay-visiteur.com
maisonduvisiteur@vezelay-visiteur.com
Open of Easter to All Saints. Open all year by appointment for groups, except from January 15th to February 15th. Low season : open Friday to Monday. High season : Wednesday to Monday. Free for under 6-year-olds. Adult : €8. Child (from 7 to 12 years old) : €3.50. Group (20 people) : €160 (extra person : €7; school groups : €3.50 and €5.50). Young people of more than 12 years and students : €6. Guided tour.

On the uphill slope that leads visitors to the Sainte-Madeleine Basilica, this house is a stopover required for those who want to explore the monument, and even an entire universe, to which we do not have the reading keys. A warm welcome that places us from the start in front of a mysterious door on which nails form a spiral; the spiral is one of the symbols you will find in the Basilica. Once you get to the threshold, a beautiful photomontage fills us with the atmosphere of Vezelay. « Live » songs, music, images and comments; everything immerses us in the history of this exceptional setting. In the basement of the house, you will discover how the builders of the Middle Ages positioned the building according to the movement of the sun (the bedside always pointed towards the East) and made the Basilica according to perfect proportions. Finally, some reproductions of magnificent capitals of the Basilica offer us a reading of these stone books. Exciting explanations and, in our view, it is essential to see the Basilica in a different light. For individuals, workshops and guided tours are also organised.

Sightseeing

BASILIQUE SAINTE-MARIE-MADELEINE ★★★★

✆ +33 (0)3 86 33 39 50
www.basiliquedevezelay.org
retraites@vezelay.cef.fr
Open every day from 7am to 8pm. No the visit during the offices. Guided tour (see the website).
Originally, a convent was founded in the 9th century in the neighbouring district of Saint-Père-sous-Vézelay by Girard de Roussillon. Monks replaced the nuns later but the monastery was destroyed during the Norman invasions. On the hill of Vézelay, less vulnerable location, a new abbey was dedicated at the end of 9th century. On 31st May 1146, Saint Bernard de Clairvaux preached the second crusade in the presence of King Louis VII there. For the third crusade in 1190, the king of France Philippe Auguste and the king of England Richard Cœur de Lion met in Vézelay before departure. In the 13th century, Saint Francis of Assisi decided to create the first mission of his Minorites in the French province here. Saint Louis went on a pilgrimage four times. It was in the 11th century that the abbey became known as Saint Magdalene, the repentant sinner. Indeed, the monastery has preserved its relics. Attracting more and more pilgrims and a stopover city on the road to Saint-Jacques-de-Compostelle, the Carolingian church had to be extended. But a fire destroyed the entire nave, which was rebuilt. The new chancel and the transept, both of Gothic style, were completed in early 13th century. At that time, Saint Maximin in Provence marked the discovery of the real relics of Saint Madeleine and gradually, Vézelay lost its prestige. Plundered and ravaged by the Protestants in 1569, the abbey did not escape the fury of the Revolution and was partly demolished at the end of the 18th century. It was at Mérimée, inspector of historic monuments, that the building on the brink of collapse was revived. In 1840, the young Viollet-le-Duc undertook the restoration and rebuilt, amongst others, the façade. Today, the basilica has preserved its beautiful Romanesque narthex of the early 12th century with its richly sculpted tympanum. A magnificent Christ, surrounded by a mandorla, seems about to rise. To see in the old monks' dormitory is the museum that houses the works of Viollet-le-Duc. Jubilee year of the Mercy is hold til 20 November 2016.

MAISON JULES ROY ★

Le Clos du Couvent
Rue de l'École
✆ +33 (0)3 86 33 35 01
mjroy@cg89.fr
Open from March 15th to November 15th. Open on Monday from 2pm to 5pm; Wednesday to Sunday from 2pm to 6pm. Groups : all year by reservation. Free. Activities.
In an elegant mansion at the foot of the Saint Mary Magdalene bascilica in Vézelay, you can see the desktop of the writer (« Les Chevaux du soleil ») as it was on June 15, 2000, the day he died. The living room and dining room are used for exhibitions related to literature, literary evenings etc. Beautiful cultural seasons in general A nice park with stepped terraces offers beautiful views of the horizon.

MUSÉE ZERVOS – MAISON ROMAIN-ROLLAND ★

Rue Saint-Etienne ✆ +33 (0)3 86 32 39 26
www.musee-zervos.fr
Open from March 15th to November 15th. Open Wednesday to Monday from 10am to 6pm (last visit at 17 : 20). Every day in July and August. Free for under 18-year-olds. Adult : €3. Reduced rate : €2. Guided tour. Shop. Activities.
Set in 2006 in the old house where lived from 1938 until his death in 1944, Romain Rolland, man of letters, born in Clamecy and Nobel Prize for Literature, the Museum of Modern Art comes from the Zervos legacy. In 1970, the Zervos spouses bequeathed to the town 800 works of art and prestigious documents. Among them is the famous collection of « Cahiers d'Art » published in Saint-Germain-des-Prés by Christian Zervos. This beautiful magazine published between 1926 and 1960 covers nearly half a century Parisian artistic activity. The collection includes works by Matisse, Picasso, Miro, Giacometti, Léger, Ernst, Kandinsky, Helion, Brauner, Calder mobiles... The museum has the finest pieces (renewed annually) and temporary exhibitions. Do not miss.

Knife & Fork

AUBERGE DE LA COQUILLE – RESTAURANT AND CREPERIE

81, rue Saint-Pierre
✆ +33 (0)3 86 33 35 57
www.aubergelacoquille.fr
Open from 11.45am to 2.30pm and from 6.45pm to 9.15pm. Menu from €15.80 to €23. À la carte. Groups welcome (reservation for events). Terrace. 3 reception halls : dining room with fireplace, medieval vaulted room, parlor 18th. Private terrace.
The Burgundian local cookery agrees here with the Breton culinary tradition for a true tasting journey. Visit this attractive restaurant of Vézelay belonging to Antoine and Béatrice Binet, to feel that you are in a dining room of

18th century, with fireplace. However, you can also take your meal on the terrace. For the groups, they will find the vaulted dining room of the 12th century A real untypical setting The menu offers you a fresh cookery, homemade, prepared with the products resulting from the agriculture of our region (charolais meat, wines of Yonne, beer of Vézelay...), and you will like also these ones : la terrine de campagne and its onion jam, l'andouillette à la sauce vézelienne au vin blanc and mustard, l'époisses Berthaut affiné au Marc de Bourgogne and finally, la poire vigneronne and its ball blackcurrant. . . Beautiful suggestions which will remind you your presence in one of the most beautiful sites of the Burgundy region. In spite of the name, You will be warmly welcomed for a true moment of pleasure even if you do not have the shell of the pilgrim around your neck. Do not forget also the exceptional lodges, for 2 people or groups, 100 meters from the Basilica. It is an excellent address.

■ **LE CHEVAL BLANC**
Place Champ-de-Foire
6✆ +33 (0)3 86 33 22 12
www.lechevalblancvezelay.fr
Closed Wednesday for dinner and off-season Thursday. High season : open every day from 12pm to 2.30pm and from 7.30pm to 10pm. Booking advised. Menu from €22 to €30. Children's menu : €14. Wine by the glass. À la carte. Groups welcome (maximum 40 people in the same room or 60 people out of two rooms). Baby chairs. Terrace.
This old stone house welcomes you in a charming decor, for a tour of flavours where creativity blends with traditions for a characterful cuisine that highlights local produces. The presentation of the dishes is an real feast for the eyes, refined and worked to the smallest detail. Our tastebuds subtly appreciated the many crayfish tails and crab and its citrus fruit vinaigrette, duck breast, puree of celery and chutney of apple and mango, and we ended with caramelized tile with almonds and strawberry enhanced with passion cream. A delight The establishment also offers rooms in the heart of Vézelay. A reliable address and a very neat cuisine.

■ **LA DENT CREUSE**
Place de la Foire
Rue Saint-Etienne and Place de la Foire
✆ +33 (0)3 86 33 36 33
www.restaurant-vezelay.fr
♿
Qualité Tourisme label. Open continuously every day from 11.30am to 6.30pm, from mid-February to mid-November. Continuously on Sunday and public holidays. Booking advised. Menus from €20.90 to €29.90. Children's menu : €7.50 (for children under 10 years old). Lunch formula : €14.90 (on weekdays). Pizzas from €8.90. P'tit Creux formula, €9.90. À la carte. Holiday vouchers. Groups welcome (up to 150 people). Terrace. Take-away.
This restaurant, located in an old building, has two accesses and a beautiful terrace with panoramic view of the surrounding countryside. It is very pleasant to have your meals there, in the shaded area outside as well as in rooms, recently modernized.

The external tympan of Sainte-Madeline Vézelay basilica.

Sainte-Marie-Madeleine de Vézelay basilica.

The « marcheurs de Dieu » a long time ago flowed the remains of « pêcheresse repentie ».

A menu rich in local flavours and must-eat specialities, but also some very pleasant creative note that the chef Yannick Vaillant has the secret. For the delight of your tastebuds with the typically local variation, let yourself be tempted by the homemade foie gras, fig chutney, jelly with Ratafia of Burgundy, then continue with the beef cut of the butcher and its Chaource sauce accompanied by fries and green vegetables. After that choose the fresh white cheese of of the countryside with fine herbs and shallots and end with relish with the pear with Burgundy wine and its blackcurrant ice-cream. You can find generous and tasty pizzas are on the à la carte menu that is possible to order as a take-away, following the example of the Charolais burger that we warmly recommend you. Finally groups will be warmly welcomed in the pretty vaulted room. It's an excellent address.

■ HÔTEL-RESTAURANT DE LA POSTE ET DU LION D'OR

Place du Champ-de-Foire
✆ +33 (0)3 86 33 21 23
www.hoteldelaposte-vezelay.com

Closed from January to February. Booking advised. Menu from €29 to €38. Lunch menu : €16 (and menu at €20). American Express. Garden. Terrace. Take-away. Shop.

Mr and Ms Leclerc, also owners of two good addresses in Auxerre (Les Maréchaux and Le Maxime), has managed, in a cosy setting, to perpetuate the so dear culinary tradition in Burgundy. It is the chef Romain Telle who runs the kitchen, deploying generosity and personal touches to deliver an authentic cuisine, full of flavours and sublime creative touches. You will enjoy a fusilier with vegetables and its herb sauce, or a medallion of veal with sage and its mashed truffle parsnips and other heirloom vegetables, and for a sweet touch, how about trying the cheesecake and malabar ? In bistro version at lunchtime and in the gourmet restaurant in the evening, you will love the quality of the service, the charm of the place and in fine weather, the pleasant terrace. The property is also a hotel offering excellent services.

Sleeping

■ AUBERGE DE JEUNESSE

Route de l'Etang ✆ +33 (0)3 86 33 24 18
www.camping-auberge-vezelay.com
auberge.jeunesse.vezelay@orange.fr

Open all year. Reception from 5pm to 8pm. 38 places. A departure after 10am involves the one day extra payment. Prohibited sleeping bag. €16 per night, €14 per night for the members of the Youth hostels. Heating : €3/pers. Seminars. Kitchen at disposal for the individual ones.

A good inexpensive place to stay and have friendly meetings. Because despite the appellation, there is no age to sleep in a youth hostel. The only condition is to be able to climb a bunk bed. 500 metres from the village, close to all amenities but in a quiet spot, surrounded by nature, the house invites guests to relax, wander in the quiet discovery. All in all, the hostel can accomodate 38 people. A relaxed and friendly reception. Each studio is equipped with a bathroom, toilet and a kitchenette (maintenance is charged to users, like the furnished collective kitchen and the dining hall). A good quality price ratio.

■ LE COMPOSTELLE

Place du Champ-de-Foire
✆ +33 (0)3 86 33 28 63 / +33 (0)6 60 74 54 71
www.lecompostellevezelay.com
le.compostelle@wanadoo.fr

Closed the first 3 weeks of December. 18 rooms. From €58 to €89. Breakfast : €9.50. Extra bed : €11. Free Wifi.

This renovated old home preserved much charm, enhanced by its private garden, its breakfast room with panoramic views and its flowered terrace overlooking the streets of the city. Simple, nice and comfortably equipped rooms will make your happiness for serene nights. The name reminds that Vézelay is located on one of the ways leading the pilgrims to Saint-Jacques-de-Compostelle. For small budgets, Le Compostelle offers attic rooms on the second floor, a little cheaper. A pleasant welcome for all visitors.

Cottages

■ GÎTE DE L'HORLOGE

81, rue Saint Pierre
✆ +33 (0)3 86 51 83 22

Open all year. From €280 to €300 per week depending on season. Weekend €90, night €45. Wifi. Sheets rental.

Located on the heights of Vézelay, 100 metres from the Basilica, Gîte de l'Horloge offers two accommodations. The first is in an independent house, with a kitchen on the ground floor, a living/dining room and a bathroom, the bedroom is upstairs. The second one is on the first floor of a house with independent access. This accommodation offers two rooms. Perfectly located, these cottages are a peaceful haven where you can lounge after having crisscrossed the beautiful countryside.

Guesthouses

■ CABALUS

Rue Saint-Pierre ✆ +33 (0)3 86 33 20 66
www.cabalus.com
contact@cabalus.com

4 rooms. From €46 to €62. Breakfast : €9.80. Tea room and simple catering facilities.

This house of the twelfth century, old hotel infirmary of the Abbey of Vezelay, has managed to retain its authenticity : by entering the tea room, you are in a good time and history. This magnificent vaulted room with its impressive fireplace exudes character and heat, what you also feel in the rooms made available by your hosts. The house is also intended to be a place where contemporary art mixes shamelessly with its ancient places : the Ap'Art shop displays unique objects of stone, wood and earth, and is also a place of exchange and sharing for artists, craftsmen, place of seminars and internships.

Shopping

MAGASIN DU DOMAINE MARIA CUNY

34, rue Saint-Etienne
© +33 (0)3 86 32 38 50 / +33 (0)3 86 33 27 95
www.domaine-mariacuny.com
maria@domaine-mariacuny.com

Open every day from 10am to 7pm. Open all year safe during the grape harvest and work in the vineyards by appointment.

This friendly shop offers wines produced in the area, based in Saint-Père-sous-Vezelay. Bourgogne vézelay Bourgogne rouge pinot noir et Bourgogne rouge gamay, the two old vines, wines worked with a passion as great as the quality and requirement of the product. The reception is nice, it is a house of trust, with in the Guide Hachette star. Tasting and wine sales throughout the year at the store. To be noted in your shelves, wine tourism holidays to discover the vineyard and the 4 seasons of the work in the vineyard. You have to choose a step of two days or a tour for the day (5 tours to choose) to share the daily life of the winemaker, visit the winery and the cellar, and discover the excellence of the wines combined with the Burgundian gastronomy. A beautiful experience.

MAISON DE L'ICÔNE

Place de la Basilique
© +33 (0)6 70 87 02 27
bonhomme4@wanadoo.fr

Open every day from 10am to 1pm and from 2pm to 6.30pm.

When you are facing the Basilica Sainte-Madeleine, right on the left in a small courtyard stands the Anne-Marie Bonhomme workshop. This iconographer, in addition to being sacred personality, is also an exciting artist who does not hesitate to explain her works, mark of spirituality which she paints in front of you, and the techniques she employs. Her icons are on sale in the shop. You should see it

L'OR DES ÉTOILES – L'ÂME ENCHANTÉE

11, rue Saint-Etienne
© +33 (0)3 86 32 38 38
© +33 (0)3 86 33 30 06
www.ordesetoiles.fr
librairie@ordesetoiles.fr

Online store.

Francette welcomes you with enthusiasm in the library of delighted Soul : facing the beautiful letters, illumination and calligraphy, the library offers youall the necessary equipment you would need to practice this art, and you can participate in one of many calligraphy courses organized by the library. You will find a sharp recorded musical selection of the world, as well as works of Romain Rolland, author particularly highlighted in this city where he lived until 1944. A library where you can go in search of the work which will make us escape.

In the surroundings

Asquins

ÉGLISE SAINT-JACQUES-DE-COMPOSTELLE

If the Basilique Sainte-Marie-Madeleine can be considered the starting point of the pilgrimage to Compostelle, then the Saint-Jacques Church in Asquins is more than a first stopover on the way. In fact, besides the fact that it houses a magnificent polychrome-wood reliquary of Jacques le Majeur, it would have as a chaplain a certain Aymery Picaud, a famous author of The Pilgrim's Guide, of which each pilgrim comes and honours memory. The Romanesque church, built in the twelfth century, was largely rebuilt in the course of the following centuries, the current bell tower dates back to the eighteenth century. Listed in Unesco World Heritage as a starting point of the pilgrimage, it remains an unmissable crossing point for pilgrims. The square offers a panoramic view of the surrounding countryside.

Mailly-le-Château

RÉSERVE LE BOIS DU PARC

© +33 (0)3 86 81 54 26
www.sitesnaturelsbourgogne.asso.fr

Guided tour (organized by the Inter-commune Tourist information centre Between Cure and Yonne).

The castle can not be visited, but there is a beautiful view of the valley of the Yonne. An old hot sea stretched at the foot of the limestone cliff on which is perched the high village. A surprising nature reserve, the only one in the department, welcomes you. The limestone comes from a gigantic fossilized coral reef, dating from the Jurassic, distant time when the warm waters covered the site ... Its uniqueness ? Besides the fossil corals beneath, by climbing the stairs leading to the top of the cliff, you can discover along an educational path a dry lawn and its sub-Mediterranean flora, which is one of the most persistent in north France. Amazing.

accès direct à la plage	espace fumeurs	jardin ou parc
bar	établissement non-fumeurs	jeux
blanchisserie	fitness	lave-linge / laverie
climatisation	golf miniature	location de vélos
discothèque	handicap malentendant	magasin d'alimentation
distributeur d'argent	handicap malvoyant	navette aéroport
eau potable	handicap mental	pêche
équitation	handicap moteur	piscine intérieure

■ **LE CASTEL**
2, place Saint-Adrien
✆ +33 (0)3 86 81 43 06
www.lecastelmailly.com
lecastelmailly@orange.fr
Open Monday to Saturday; Friday to Tuesday. Booking advised. Menu from €20 to €29. Children's menu : €9.50. À la carte. Hotel open 7 days a week. Single room or double from €69. Garden. Shop.
You'd enjoy living in the 18th century period in this beautiful home in the pretty little village of Mailly-le-Château. The Calm, charm and courtesy, these are the three qualities that best represents this property. From the small fortified town of the medieval city, you will overlook the Canal du Nivernais and Vézelay will be offered to you as a painting. Welcomed graciously, you will be invited to seat at table near the fireplace or under the arbor of limes on sunny days. As for the cuisine, the dishes, prepared with fresh produces, are inventive and tasty, judge by yourself : hot-air balloon of beef with foie gras, quenelles of pike with shellfish sauce, gratin souffléed with lemon and raspberries.

Pierre-Perthuis

■ **RESTAURANT DES DEUX PONTS**
Route de Seigland
✆ +33 (0)3 86 32 31 31
lesdeuxponts.free.fr
lesdeuxponts@gmail.com
Open from March to November. Booking advised. Menu from €23.50. À la carte. Groups welcome. Garden. Terrace. Receptions and seminars.
The worship of fresh ingredients, magnified by the cuisine of Philippe Bariteau A perfect blend between gastronomy and creativity, originality and terroir. The menu is generous, our preference went to the Charolais meat with mushroom duxelle and its wine sauce. Our appetite was fully satisfied with the lemon macaroon with an acidulous espuma and its orange sauce. Deux-Ponts also consists of 7 very charming rooms that will satisfy all your desire for serenity. A very good adress that we are not going to be fed up with.

■ **DOMAINE ELISE VILLIERS**
Précy-le-Moult (hameau)
✆ +33 (0)3 86 33 27 62
www.domaine.elisevilliers.com
contact@elisevilliers.com
Open every day from 9am to 7pm. Groups by appointment.
This estate of four hectares, a product of Vézelay chardonnay and pinot noir burgundy. Like the Vézelay vineyard the production is about 80% of Chardonnay. A home that combines expertise and quality to give you only the best of their vines, with the objective of moving towards organic labels. Numerous awards and medals for these wines of character. The vault opens to the public all year-round for tastings and sales of wine. Good to know : two cottages can accommodate you on the estate.

Saint-Père-sous-Vézelay

■ **AB LOISIRS**
Rue Gravier ✆ +33 (0)3 86 33 38 38
www.abloisirs.com
contact@abloisirs.com
Open all year. From 9am to 7pm. Activities from €15 (adults). Holiday voucher. Registration in possible line.
An outdoor leisure base set at the banks of Cure, for nature lovers Discover the Yonne differently, with direct contact with water, trees or rock. A team of professionals, all State graduates, are there to guide you. Mountain biking, horseback riding, rafting, caving and climbing, you will palpate Morvan with your fingertips Other activities that are even more sensational are available : Segway mobilboard, ultralight aviation and hot-air balloon. It is perfect for children, teenagers and families. The welcome is very friendly.

■ **BRASSERIE DE VÉZELAY**
Rue des Graviers ✆ +33 (0)3 86 34 98 38
www.brasseriedevezelay.com
contact@brasseriedevezelay.com
Low season : open Tuesday to Friday from 11am to 7pm; Saturday from 2pm to 7pm. High season : every day from 11am to 9pm. Visits for groups starting from 10 people. Spot wifi.
A brasserie nestled in the heart of the Morvan, along the Cure, which promotes traditional manufacturing methods, such as the water-malt-hop, respecting the purity law enacted in Bavaria in 1516. The organic beers, rich in taste : Light Blonde, the Brune, refined and la Blanch in all simplicity. You will find these beers at various retailers of Burgundy, was also available in 20 and 30 liters, as well as on menus of the best restaurants in the region. Note that, in the summer, you can dine at the brasserie : sandwiches, organic snacks and picnic boxes.

■ **CAVE HENRY DE VEZELAY**
4, route de Nanchèvres
✆ +33 (0)3 86 33 29 62
www.henrydevezelay.com
henrydevezelay@wanadoo.fr
Open Monday to Friday from 9am to 12pm and from 2pm to 6pm; the weekend and public holidays from 10am to 12.30pm and from 2.30pm to 6pm. Closed the Christmas Day and the New Year's Day. Flexible schedule dependings on the season.
The Henry de Vézelay winery cooperative groups 11 operators who represent about a third of the Vézelay vineyard, or some 34 hectares. If the melon, old grape of the region, is still produced to keep the tradition, it is mainly Vézelay burgundy that is to say a white chardonnay, who stars today in more than 80%. An excellent wine to enjoy contemplating the eternal hill, in honor of Mary-Magdalene... The Henry de Vézelay cellar also offers the red burgundy and pink burgundy and also the ratafia. By its name, this winery is a tribute to a monk called Henry, born in Vézelay in the thirteenth century and was elected bishop of Auxerre in 1278. Tasting is possible, and the reception is friendly.

INDEX

D

E

M

N

O

P

Q-R-S

T-V-Y